The October Testament

NMB
New Matthew Bible

Baruch House Publishing, British Columbia, Canada

We remember that which we first received,
and strengthen the things that are ready to die.
(Revelation 3:2,3)

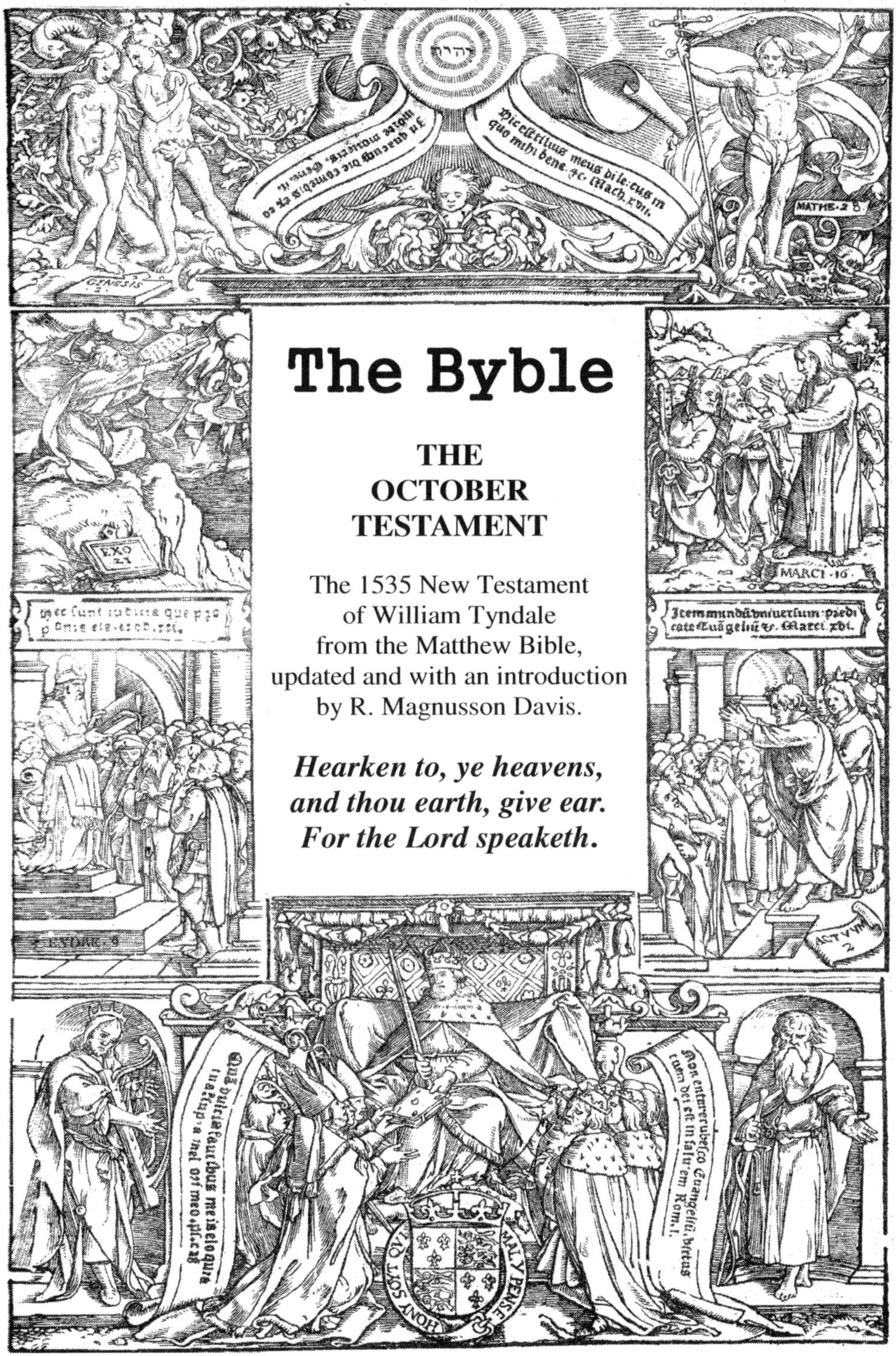

The Byble

THE OCTOBER TESTAMENT

The 1535 New Testament
of William Tyndale
from the Matthew Bible,
updated and with an introduction
by R. Magnusson Davis.

Hearken to, ye heavens,
and thou earth, give ear.
For the Lord speaketh.

The October Testament, New Matthew Bible (NMB)

First published 2016.

Hardcover bound edition printed in Canada:
First printing March 2016.
Second printing September 2016 with minor revisions.

Paperback (print on demand), CreateSpace store: www.createspace.com/5931370:
First printing April 2016. Revised periodically to October 3, 2017.

PDF edition available at www.octobertestament.com

Editing of early modern English text, introductory and supplementary material, and interior layout by Ruth Magnusson Davis.
Cover design by Iryna Spica.

Title page graphics (woodcuts) are from the editor's Matthew Bible. In the hardcover only, the coloured end papers replicate the marbled paper used when it was rebound in 1887.

Library and Archives Canada Cataloguing in Publication

Bible. English. Matthew's version
The Byble : the October Testament : the 1535 New Testament of William Tyndale from the Matthew Bible / updated and with an introduction by R. Magnusson Davis.

"Hearken to, ye heavens, and thou earth, give ear. For the Lord speaketh."
ISBN 978-0-9949227-0-0 (bound).--ISBN 978-0-9949227-1-7 (paperback)

I. Tyndale, William, d. 1536, translator II. Magnusson Davis, Ruth, writer of added commentary III. Title.

BS2050 2015 225.5'201 C2015-907934-9

Publisher: Baruch House Publishing, British Columbia, Canada
www.newmatthewbible.org
www.octobertestament.com

The October Testament is the New Testament of William Tyndale as it was contained in the 1549 Matthew Bible, now gently updated by Ruth Magnusson Davis, and retaining all the truth and beauty of the original.

The Matthew Bible is a little known Reformation bible. It formed the basis of all major English bibles, including the KJV, though unacknowledged.

The Matthew Bible is the only English Bible attested with martyrs' blood, symbolized by the rich colour of our cover.

William Tyndale, bible translator and martyr, was strangled and burned at the stake in Vilvoord, Belgium, in the year 1536, when he was about forty-two years old. He had lived many years in exile from his native England, working under cover in order to avoid capture by enemies who wished to stop his pen. His first New Testament was published in 1526, and his final revision, which is here, in 1535.

John Rogers, martyr and friend of William Tyndale, collated and first published the Matthew Bible in 1537, using the scripture translations of William Tyndale and Miles Coverdale. His bible was licensed by King Henry VIII, but was always unpopular with conservatives. In 1555, after Queen Mary ascended the throne, Rogers became her first burning victim, dying bravely in Smithfield and leaving a wife with ten children.

Table of Contents

The Importance of the Matthew Bible

THE Matthew Bible contains the English scriptures inspired by God, who worked through his chosen vessels, men he raised up and called to this work, during the critical period of the Reformation in the early 16th century. It was in this time that our Lord opened up his Word to the world again, after centuries of progressive darkening, so that its light could shine forth in the darkness.

The scriptures of the Matthew Bible are good and faithful – yea, very good and very faithful. Gifted scholarship, genuine love of God's word, inspiration, and a sincere desire for plainness, gave us a bible that is true, clear, and readable – more readable than many later versions, and truer.

The Matthew Bible shows spiritual insight, insight that only the Holy Spirit can give. It makes sense of the faith; by it, the Holy Spirit can teach deep things, precious things. If you are looking for spiritual understanding, here it is. An example is 1 Thessalonians 5:7. After Paul exhorts us not to sleep as others do, but to watch and be sober, the Matthew Bible tells us:

> For they that sleep, sleep in the night, and they that are drunk, are drunk in the night. But let us who are of the day be sober, armed with the breast plate of faith and love... (minimally updated)

Paul is drawing here upon rich and varied prophetic imagery. There is drunkenness that does not arise from strong drink, of which the Old Testament prophets speak. This is spiritual drunkenness, and causes spiritual falling. There is also a spiritual 'day' and 'night,' of which Jesus speaks in John 11, explaining that if a man walks in the night, he stumbles, because there is no light in him. However if he walks in the day, he does not stumble, because he sees the light of this world. Here 'day' is the light of the faith of Christ, by whom we see clearly, and 'night' is the darkness of unbelief or error. When we see by the light, we are walking in the day and are spiritually sober. But if we walk in error, we are "drunk in the night," a spiritual state. Likewise sleeping describes a spiritual state. (See John Rogers' note on Matthew 13:25 and Tyndale's on John 9:4.)

But modern versions have translated 1 Thessalonians 5:7 so that it is no longer a matter of being drunk in the night, but of *getting* drunk *at* night. For example:

> For those who sleep, sleep at night, and those who get drunk, get drunk at night. (New International Version,1973)

The NIV rendering suggests not a state of being, a spiritual thing, but night time revelry with strong drink, utterly a worldly thing. The spiritual meaning, readily accessible in Matthew, is darkened by a poor translation. There are many examples of darkening and lost understanding in modern versions – error that has nothing whatsoever to do with the underlying manuscript, but everything to do with the translators.

Another claim we can make for the Matthew Bible is that it is a truly separated and uncompromised work. We say this because the translators, William Tyndale and Miles Coverdale, were bound to no ruler or authority, no denomination, no requirement for consensus or compromise, but God only. Compromise was not a temptation, whether to curry favour or to promote the work, because the English authorities were at that early stage of the Reformation absolutely opposed to it. And no doubt this ensured purity and integrity; the Lord brought His word forth through men separated unto him at a time and in circumstances when He would stand alone in their concerns and affections, conscience and the Holy Spirit alone constraining them as they sought accurate expression.

We claim also that the Matthew Bible was written in the inspired language of the faith, words full of the Holy Spirit:

> I am the vine, and ye are the branches. He that abideth in me, and I in him, the same bringeth forth much fruit.
>
> Neither is that thing circumcision which is outward in the flesh, but he is a Jew which is hid within.
>
> Be not drunk with wine, wherein is excess, but be fulfilled with the Spirit, speaking unto yourselves in psalms and hymns and spiritual songs, singing and making melody to the Lord in your hearts.
>
> To give knowledge of salvation to his people for the remission of sins, through the tender mercy of our God, whereby the Dayspring from on high hath visited us.

Every discipline or area of study has its own language, which students and disciples must learn until they become well versed in it. It is no different with the language of our faith. And as we read and study God's word, the Spirit teaches us, so it is a joyous, ever fruitful study.

It is important to understand how well and fully the beautiful Matthew scriptures have served us since we first received them. They were largely adopted by the Geneva and King James bibles, and a body of rich theological and devotional works has developed over the centuries using much of their language and turns of phrase. Good books, hymns, and other valuable resources including the traditional English Prayer Book (which adopted and has retained Matthew's Psalter) are lost to us when too much is changed – especially when the bible becomes slang, or with 'paraphrases,' which are really no such thing when they change the meaning. In the New World Translation, the bible of the Jehovah Witnesses, the language is so altered that Jesus is no longer crucified, but "impaled," and that not on a cross, which has been a symbol of the faith for over twenty centuries, but on a torture stake. What is it to take up one's stake and follow the Lord? To be impaled to the world, and the world to us? And yet there are other modern bibles that follow this trend, all of which has contributed to darkening God's word again.

The *October Testament* turns back to that which we first received, but which is ready to die if we do not strengthen it (Revelation 3:2,3). We are confident that readers will find the language of the Matthew scriptures, here gently updated, to be the real and most pleasing language of the faith, expressing the real and heavenly doctrine. Here is the comfort of a sound translation, fully Trinitarian and agreeing with the general articles of the faith.

The *October Testament* will be of historical interest, coming as it does from an era of great religious tribulation when the word of God had been sorely put down, and revealing the Reformers' understanding of the times and the scripture. It will also be of literary interest. But its main value is devotional. Bought with blood and the toil of humble individuals, ever God's marks of authenticity, it reveals the Divine Hand, and yields up rich treasures to the earnest seeker. Here is the best Reformation bible, strengthened for today. Here is wholesome food for the soul.

R. M. D.

A Brief History of the Matthew Bible

THE STORY of the Matthew Bible, first published in the year 1537, is a story of faith and courage in the face of great opposition.

In England in the early 1500s there were laws prohibiting both the translation of the bible and the possession or reading of English scriptures. To defy these laws could mean imprisonment, inquisition, torture, or death by burning alive at a public stake. During the previous century, in the year 1401, King Henry IV passed a statute called *De Haeretico Comburendo,* or *On the Burning of Heretics.* This was in response to the teaching and English bible translations of John Wycliffe in the late 1300s. Many people welcomed them, and Wycliffe has been called the Morning Star of the Reformation. But religious leaders condemned Wycliffe and his translations. Any person who possessed a copy of his scriptures, which were then laboriously written out by hand, was to deliver it up. Failure to do so was punishable by burning alive, and the first dreadful burning occurred that same year. Then in 1408 came the *Constitutions of Oxford,* which among other things prohibited any person "by his own authority" from translating any text of scripture. It also prohibited the reading of future unauthorized translations.

These statutes were still in force in 1506 when the young William Tyndale, future unauthorized bible translator, and then about twelve years of age, began studies at Magdalen School in Oxford. In that same year, the bishop of Buckinghamshire tried eighty persons and sent two to be burned. Tyndale knew the times he lived in.

But the English people had gained an understanding, or at least a hope, of what it might mean if they could read the scriptures. Wycliffe had left his mark, and new influences were arising that would heighten conflict with the religious authorities. The new art of printing enabled the diffusion of learning, the pursuit of truth, and perhaps also a skeptical spirit. John Colet had lectured at Oxford on the epistles of Saint Paul before Tyndale went there, drawing many listeners, and increasing interest in the scriptures. There was a new scholarly interest in biblical languages: studies in Hebrew had begun, and in 1506 Johannes Reuchlin published a Hebrew grammar and dictionary that became a basic tool of the brave men who worked as bible translators during the Reformation. In 1510 the Dutch humanist Desiderius Erasmus, a scholar of ancient Greek and a proponent of vernacular scriptures, began to teach Greek at Cambridge in England, giving students the tools they needed to read and study the New Testament in its original language. The stage was set for the Reformation, a time that would see God's word emerge into light, albeit with continuing bloodshed and tribulation.

In 1516 Erasmus published the first edition of his Greek New Testament, known as the Received Text, which bible translators in many countries would turn to. About this time Tyndale, having earned his Master of Arts at Oxford, moved to Cambridge. Then, in 1517, Martin Luther, incensed over the hawking of indulgences by Rome, could keep still no longer, and nailed his ninety-five theses to the Church door in Wittenberg, Germany – an event credited with sparking the Reformation. He began to write, and his books and essays poured off the presses. An international tempest arose around him. In Cologne, the authorities staged public burnings of his writings. In England in 1521, Cardinal Wolsey presided over a burning of Lutheran books at St. Paul's Cross in London – books that were bringing Luther's hated 'new learning' into England.

These years also find a significant group of young Christian men gathered at Cambridge, a group that includes William Tyndale, Miles Coverdale, Thomas Cranmer (who later, as

Archbishop of Canterbury, gave England her Prayer Book), and Hugh Latimer (who became a noted preacher). All except Coverdale would later be burned at the stake by religious authorities. Legend has it that many of these young men were accustomed to meet with others at a local pub, the White Horse Inn, to discuss the 'new learning' and ponder current events.

Of the Cambridge saints, Cranmer, Tyndale, and Coverdale are all important in the history of English scriptures. The latter two, together with one John Rogers, defied the laws that prohibited translation and gave us the Matthew Bible, a seminal work that historians recognize as the real primary version of our English bible. This great work was thus born amidst all the blood, angst, persecution, and heroism of the Reformation.

This editor plans to shortly publish an illustrated history of the Matthew Bible under the title, *The Story of the Matthew Bible.* Meanwhile, what follows is a brief introduction.

The Men Who Gave us the Matthew Bible

William Tyndale (c.1494-1536): The name of William Tyndale will be well known to most who take in hand this *October Testament.* John Foxe described the young Tyndale as singularly devoted to the scriptures, who, when a student at Magdalen School in Oxford, read and expounded God's word privately with other students. Unless he had Wycliffe's forbidden manuscripts, which seems unlikely (he later wrote that he had no English translation to follow), he must have had the Latin Vulgate. Besides the Latin that all good schoolboys learned, and his native English, Tyndale was fluent in five languages, including German, French, and classical Greek. It was said of him that he was so gifted that he spoke them all like a native, and his Greek was unusually good. Later he became proficient in biblical Hebrew, which he learned on the Continent.

Tyndale believed God had called and prepared him to give England the scriptures in her own tongue. To this end he lived in exile on the Continent, hiding from enemies who wished to stop his pen. He succeeded in giving us three editions of the New Testament translated from the Greek, in 1526, 1534, and 1535 – which were, however, criticized by hostile religious leaders, and banned by King Henry VIII. In 1530 he published the Pentateuch, a pioneering work of translation from the Hebrew text. He also completed Jonah and the historical books of the Old Testament, but before he could publish them was betrayed, captured, and imprisoned for many months in Vilvoorde, now part of Belgium, but then under Spanish rule. In 1536 he was condemned for heresy and publicly executed. His famous last words expressed his abiding desire for the King to allow the scriptures in England: "Lord, open the King of England's eyes!"

Many have called Tyndale the father of modern English because his scripture translations, which went into the Matthew Bible and were then largely taken up in the King James Version of 1611, have been with us ever since, and have shaped our language.

Miles Coverdale (c.1487-1569): Of the three contributors to the Matthew Bible, only Coverdale survived the persecutions of the Reformation years, fleeing to the continent first during the reign of Henry VIII, when Tyndale was there, and again later to escape Queen Mary. Many years in Germany made him a master of that language. Some historians believe that Coverdale and Tyndale worked together from time to time, especially on the Pentateuch in 1529-1530.

Coverdale worked on several bible versions over the years, but his first and most independent work, a full bible that he published in 1535, has been called his best. He was not fluent enough in the biblical languages to translate directly from them, and therefore referred to other translations. He wrote in the prologue to his 1535 bible that,

"To help me herein, I have had sundry translations, not only in Latin, but also of the Dutch interpreters, whom, because of their singular gifts and special diligence in the bible, I have been the more glad to follow for the most part." By "Dutch interpreters" is meant the German translator Martin Luther and the Swiss divines who collaborated on the Zurich Version. That Coverdale also had Tyndale's English translations at hand is evident.

Coverdale's 1535 bible had the honour of being the first complete printed bible in English. His prophetic books are remarkably clear and lucid. Some of Coverdale's work was incorporated in the Matthew Bible, and in 1549 his Psalms were taken into Thomas Cranmer's Book of Common Prayer.

John Rogers (c.1500-1555): John Rogers and William Tyndale became friends in Antwerp, where Rogers was serving as chaplain to the English Merchant Adventurers. After Tyndale's martyrdom, Rogers was not prepared to let his legacy die with him. With Tyndale's revised New Testament of 1535 in hand, together with what he had been able to complete of the Old Testament, Rogers set out to publish a full bible. To supply what Tyndale had not been able to finish, he used Coverdale's Old Testament scriptures, including his Psalms, Proverbs, and Prophets, and his Apocryphal translations. Rogers is believed to have himself translated the prayer of Manasses.

Rogers also incorporated study aids into his bible. A lengthy 'Table of Principal Matters' is a summary of major doctrines of the bible that he translated from the 1535 bible of the French Reformer Pierre Olivetan. This compendious reference work expounds biblical themes organized alphabetically: Abomination, Abuses... Adultery, Advocate, Affliction, Angels, Antichrist... Baptism, Blasphemy... Beatitude... Free Choice or Free Will... and so on until the last entry, Zeal.

Rogers performed only minimal editing to the scriptures, confining his labour mainly to compiling and overseeing publication. He added chapter summaries to every book of the bible. He brought in Tyndale's prologue to Romans and many of his expository notes from the 1534 New Testament. He also added other commentaries – some his own and some from Martin Luther and other continental Reformers, which also include many references to the teaching of Church Fathers. The notes are altogether a potpourri of items of theological, historical, devotional, and philological interest. For the greater part they are not polemical, but elucidating. (A more thorough analysis of the notes will be contained in *The Story of the Matthew Bible.*)

Rogers also incorporated in his voluminous work an account of world history, "A brief rehersall of the yeares passed sence the begynnynge of the worlde, unto this yeare of oure Lorde M.ccccc.xxxvii." The history holds to a young earth.

The assembling and completion of the Matthew Bible, and its publication in so short a time after Tyndale's death, was quite a feat. In 1537 the complete work was printed, probably in Antwerp, which was then a lively centre of printing and publishing. 1,500 copies are believed to have been issued. The title page proclaims "The Byble/ which is all the holy Scriptures: in whych are contayned the Olde and Newe Testament truly and purely translated into Englysh by Thomas Matthew." It adds the moving words that we have also incorporated in our title page: "Hearken to, ye heavens, and thou earth give ear. For the Lord speaketh."

With all its study aids, the Matthew Bible was truly the first ever English study bible. Woodcut illustrations throughout the text bring to life the stories of Adam and Eve, incidents in David's life, and events and prophecies of the book of Revelation, including horsemen and a many-headed dragon.

Rogers' work contained a dedication to King Henry VIII that was signed by "Your graces faythfull and true subject, Thomas Matthew," and therefore quickly became known as the Matthew Bible, or Matthew's Version, after the mysterious translator.

John Rogers died in 1555. After being charged with heresy, and after a long period of imprisonment and inquisition in Newgate, he was burned at the stake, the first such victim of Queen Mary. John Foxe, in his *Acts and Monuments,* depicts him in the flames saying, "Lord, receive my spirit!"

The Matthew Bible is therefore attested with martyrs' blood, and is the only English bible so to be.

Who was "Thomas Matthew"?

When charged with heresy, Rogers was identified as using "the alias Matthew." He did indeed use that name in the publication of the Matthew Bible, however this was probably not to conceal his, but rather Tyndale's involvement in the work, since Rogers did not translate, nor even edit in any notable way. In the 1537 'Matthew,' the large ornate letters "WT" the end of Malachi are the only hint of Tyndale's presence.

Tyndale was unfortunately ill-regarded by many English authorities. In 1526, after his first New Testament had made its way into England, Henry VIII, on the advice of certain counselors, ordered them to be burned. Tyndale's books had also been banned by royal proclamation. But the King's approval was necessary if the Matthew Bible was to be authorized in England, and therefore Tyndale's involvement was disguised.

How or why Rogers chose 'Thomas Matthew' is unknown, but the biblical link, the names of two of Jesus' disciples, is obvious. Also, given the number of contributors to the Matthew Bible, it is a name that favours none. Considered in this light, 'Thomas Matthew' stands for Tyndale, Coverdale, and Rogers all together.

The Licensing of the Matthew Bible in 1537

The year 1535 saw the execution of Sir Thomas More, a man who had been one of Tyndale's most determined opponents, and one who had greatly influenced the King against him. After his fall from grace and death, men favourable to reform began to have more sway with the King, opening the way for an English bible. When copies of "Matthew's" version arrived in England in 1537, Thomas Cranmer, now Archbishop of Canterbury, declared that he liked it better than any translation he had ever read. By a letter dated August 4, 1537, he petitioned Thomas Cromwell, chief minister to Henry VIII and also favourable to reform, to have the Matthew Bible approved for sale in the realm, so that it could be read by every person without danger of prosecution or trouble, until such time as the bishops should set forth a better translation – which he thought would not be "till a day after doomsday."

It was God's blessing upon England that Thomas Cromwell was successful in obtaining the King's permission for the Matthew Bible to be read and purchased in the realm. And thus it was that in the year 1537, and despite Tyndale's involvement, Rogers' bible was licensed for use. Shortly after that, the King by a series of injunctions required English bibles to be set up in the Churches, thus assisting the advancement of the Matthew Bible, at least for the time being.

The 1549 Matthew Bible

After the death of Henry VIII in 1547, his young son Edward VI ascended the throne. With him came a fresh reforming influence, and his short reign saw the publication of many English bibles.

In 1549 Rogers published a second edition of 'Matthew,' printed in London. Woodcuts are confined to title pages; there are none within the text. All the study aids are present, though fewer glosses. The cover leaf again states that it was translated into English by Thomas Matthew, but Tyndale's presence is more evident. His prologues to the five books of the Pentateuch are now included, with credit to him. Rogers made a few edits to the scriptures, and there were some unfortunate printing errors. Below are some of the edits and errors to be found in the 1549 New Testament:

Bible verse	1537 Matthew Bible	1549 Matthew Bible
Romans 1:5	to bring all manner heathen people unto the obedience *of the faith*	the obedience *of faith*
Romans 5:11	our Lord Jesus Christ, by whom we have received *the atonement.*	By whom we have received *reconciliation.*
1 Corinthians 5:1	and such fornication as is not once named among the Gentiles: that one *should have* his father's wife	that one *should love* his father's wife
1 Corinthians 14:6	What shall I profit you, except I speak to you, other by revelation or knowledge, *or prophesying*, or doctrine.	"*or prophesying*" is omitted.
1 Corinthians 15:20	Christ...is become the first fruits of them that *slept.*	that *sleep*
2 Corinthians 9:8	that ye may be rich unto *all manner good works.*	*all good works.*
1 Timothy 6:9	They that will be rich fall into temptation and snares, and into many foolish and *noisome* lusts	and *innocent* lusts
Hebrews 5:4	No man taketh honour unto himself, but he that is called of God, as was *Aaron.*	as was *Adam*
1 Peter 4:19	Let them that suffer according to the will of God, commit their souls to him with well doing, as unto a faithful *creator.*	as unto a faithful *creature.*
1 John 2:28	And now babes, abide in him, that when he *shall appear*, we may be bold...	that when he *shall here appear...*

Rogers' great work ends with a table of readings "where in ye shal finde the Epistles and the Gosples after the use of Salysbury" for such traditional holy days as Advent, Christmas, Lent, Easter, saints' days, the Feast of Sweetbread, All Souls day, Ascension day, The Conception of our Lady, and many more in the Christian calendar. This is the calendar that was adopted also for use by Thomas Cranmer in the English Prayer Book. It might surprise many moderns to realize how much Tyndale and the English Reformers valued the round of the Christian year; Tyndale had incorporated at the end of his 1534

New Testament his own translations of many Old Testament passages for reading on various days.

At last, in closing, the 1549 colophon tells us we have reached:

**The ende of the new testa-
ment and the whole
Byble.**

**TO THE honoure and prayse of GOD
was this BYBLE prynted and
fynisshed, in the yeare
of OURE LORDE GOD**

MDXXXVII

**And nowe agayne accordingly imprented, and finy
shed the laste daye of Octobre. In the yeare
of our Lord God M.D.XL.IX.
at London.
By Wylliam Hyll, and Tho-
mas Reynaldes Ty-
pographers.
God save the kynge.**

The Matthew Bible was reprinted once more in 1551. According to bible historian and cataloguer A. S. Herbert, it agreed closely with the 1549 edition.

It is the 1549 edition of the Matthew Bible that we have used for the *October Testament,* and will use for the complete *New Matthew Bible,* God willing. In part we may thereby reap the benefits of Rogers' matured understanding.

It will perhaps be helpful to note that in 1549 a man named Edmund Becke published his own 'Matthew Bible,' but an altered edition. He significantly revised the notes, and used Tyndale's 1534 New Testament, not his 1535 revision. He added copious glosses upon the book of Revelation, while those in the real Matthew Bible were scarce. There are in circulation at the time of publication facsimile and on-line versions of Becke's edition which are misrepresented as the 1549 Matthew Bible, or as "The Tyndale Bible, Thomas Matthew." It is a matter of regret that, because of this, people will gain the wrong impression of the real thing. Becke's edition can be identified by its odious note upon 1 Peter 3:7, to the effect that if a wife won't do her duty, her husband should "beat the fear of God into her head." The tone of Becke's commentaries is often strident and unpleasant.

From the Matthew Bible to the King James Version

In 1538, King Henry had issued a royal injunction to set up a bible in every parish Church. There were then two complete English bibles in circulation: the Matthew Bible, and Coverdale's of 1535. However, there were not enough copies to meet demand. Furthermore, Coverdale's was criticized because it was not translated from the original languages, and the Matthew Bible offended in some of its notes. Therefore Cromwell, with Cranmer's approval, planned a new bible, and Coverdale was providentially appointed as chief editor.

Coverdale went to work immediately on a new English version; but this was not a new translation, only a revision. Significantly, Coverdale was required to use the Matthew Bible as his base. In this way, 'Matthew' was accepted into and entered the stream of English bibles. In 1539 Coverdale's first revision, known as the Great Bible, was issued. A second edition came out in 1540, to which Archbishop Cranmer wrote a preface, thus earning it the name 'Cranmer's Version.'

Further revisions of Matthew followed, from the Great Bible through to the King James Version. A fuller account will be given in *The Story of the Matthew Bible*, however we do know, as Professor David Daniell wrote in an oft-quoted passage from his biography, that almost seventy-five years later a great deal of Tyndale's work went directly into the KJV:

> New Testament scholars Jon Nielson and Royal Skousen, by a statistically accurate and appropriate method of sampling based on eighteen portions of the bible, have concluded that for the New Testament Tyndale's contribution is about 83% of the text, and in the Old Testament books that he translated, about 76%. It has also been estimated that in the Revised Version of 1818, about 80% of the New Testament is from Tyndale.

Tyndale's contribution to the KJV remains a little known fact in Christendom. How much of Coverdale's 1535 scriptures was brought into it is more difficult to estimate, but we can say confidently that, through the stream of English bibles from the Reformation to the publication of the KJV, the voices of both Tyndale and Coverdale have continued to reach English speaking people. However there have been changes, of course, including some that 'Matthew' might regret. Also, all the study aids, notes, and commentaries that Rogers gave us have been lost. Furthermore, the English language has seen developments that make this great work difficult, and indeed sometimes impossible, for us to understand today.

Here, therefore, we seek to give the world Tyndale's New Testament again, as contained and annotated in Rogers' 1549 Matthew Bible, and diligently emended for the twenty-first century with all the care that we could give. We pray that the Lord will bless and use this, our *October Testament,* and commend it to the judgment of sincere and believing readers.

R. M. D.

Preface: The Making of the New Matthew Bible

R. M. D. UNTO THE READER

Ruth Magnusson Davis

"HERE thou hast (most dear reader) the new testament or covenant made with us of God in Christ's blood." With these words, William Tyndale introduced his New Testament in 1534. Now, almost five centuries later, you have in hand, dear reader, his testament again, which I have updated as truly as I could in order to bring to light its full meaning, long obscured by the dusts of linguistic change.

When Tyndale introduced his New Testament, he included personal observations, and he also explained how he approached his work. I must do the same here, not because I claim any sort of equality with him, but so that readers may understand who I am, why I have undertaken this work, and how I have approached it. However, I would ask that people judge this work not by me, but by the fruit itself – the scriptures. For our Lord has told us to test the fruit.

Many people have asked if I would have undertaken the New Matthew Bible Project if I had known how much would be involved. The answer is 'yes.' Though admittedly I did not fully appreciate what it would require, and was apprehensive, I couldn't not do it; woe it is to me if I cannot work on the New Matthew Bible! This *October Testament*, the first fruits of ten years of labour – over six years full time – is therefore reaped with joy.

Why *October Testament?* It is, of course, a name reminiscent of Martin Luther's *September Testament*, and follows after. October is a time of harvest. It is also a month of milestones: in October the 1549 Matthew Bible was published; my copy is dated "the last day of October." It also happened to be the last day of October when I completed my work with the Matthew scriptures. It was October 31, 1517, when Luther nailed his ninety-five theses to the church door in Wittenberg, the event that sparked the Reformation. It was in October that Miles Coverdale published his 1535 bible, which John Rogers and I have both drawn upon. More personally, it was October 5 that I experienced the new birth, and it was October 6 that Tyndale is believed to have died – a synchronicity that reflects the calling I have felt to take up his legacy. I have also considered that October is a month which marks the approach of the end of the year, and the state of the world now leads me to wonder if this Testament marks the approach of the end of the age.

I am a simple, bible believing, born again Christian. I was granted faith as an adult, passing from death to life in the power of the Holy Spirit through the preaching of the gospel. After many years of seeking, I found life in the Lord Jesus and received divine love and forgiveness – though I little understood at the time what it all meant. This babe knew only that Jesus was the answer to her long search. How precious did that grace appear, the hour I first believed! Then after more seeking, now in the various branches of Christendom, I discovered the Reformation liturgy of Thomas Cranmer, and have been confirmed in the traditional Anglican Church. I find in Cranmer's Communion service (still used in traditional congregations, but also about ready to die if we do not strengthen it) that which is biblical, needful, and beautiful for corporate worship. Without any doubt, good liturgy offers protection from the devices and imaginations of men.

I practised law for 28 years before I retired to work full time on the New Matthew Bible Project. Though one ought not to place too much emphasis upon it, nonetheless it is true that legal studies and practice hone one's analytical and research skills. Before law school, I obtained an undergraduate degree in French and German, and through this learned that I love language and grammar. But in the end, it is the strong calling I have felt to do this work, my love of God's word and his people, and his amazing provision, which have set me on this path. After many years of reading different bible versions, I remained dissatisfied – something was missing, something was not right – until I found, first Tyndale, thanks to David Daniell's modern spelling editions of his translations, and then Coverdale's Old Testament in the Matthew Bible, by which time I had taught myself to read early modern English. I realized then that the world needed to have their translations again.

My guiding principle in the updating of the Matthew scriptures has been, not to make a modern bible from an old one, but to keep as much of the old as possible while making the language understandable for today. I explain in "The Importance of the Matthew Bible" that not only is divine truth here richly to be found, but also inspired language, the language of the faith, which the Holy Spirit can and does use. But eccentric spelling, together with syntax and grammar that obscure the meaning, must be updated. Obsolete words and expressions (advoutry, assoil, mete, sith, leasing, arede, be aknown of, by times) must be replaced. Words that have changed or narrowed in meaning (conceits, measure, tyrant, nephew, worm, meat, riot, multitude, despise, tempt, know, rejoice, improve, increase, declare, show, open, utter, fret, bid, go, remove, divide, creep, study, obey, nurture, natural, honest, comely, lewd, ghostly, single, expedient, and so on) need to be replaced where they confuse or mislead.

But where no real modern equivalent was available or seemed fitting, I kept certain words that with regular reading we may come to understand more fully in their biblical sense, such as 'edify' (support, build up, strengthen, inform), and also 'doctrine,' 'minister,' 'reward,' 'earnest' (in "the earnest of the Spirit" – 'deposit' seemed crass), 'tongue' (for language), and the phrase 'respect of persons.' In places I have explained the early modern and biblical use in marginal notes. Then again, rather whimsically and inconsistently, in a few passages I kept Tyndale's nomenclature, as in 'Zache' for Zacharius, and 'son Timotheus' for Timothy; also occasionally 'ye' and 'thou.' In this I was moved by a love for the old English that I am confident my readers will share.

I also selectively kept archaic constructions, such as "be not" for "do not be," constrained both by custom and by the euphony of rhythm (Be not afraid; also, let not your hearts be troubled). I kept "You shall call his name John," and similar manners of speech which, though not idiomatic English, are biblical and understandable. In certain contexts, however, I emended words that have pejorated, such as 'fool' and 'filthy,' which carry an offense that was uncharacteristic when Tyndale used them.

Readers will notice that I selectively retained the preposition 'unto.' This word is within the passive competence of most, if not all, native English speakers, and expresses some concepts in a way that no modern preposition can. It is now almost exclusively within the province of Christian parlance, and there it shall remain in the New Matthew Bible. I have also kept 'beseech,' 'brethren,' 'heathen,' 'the flesh,' and 'Abraham's seed.'

I have retained some of Tyndale's own translations that were not taken up in the KJV, such as 'congregation' to translate the Greek *ecclesia* (concerning which, please see the Supplement at the back of the *October Testament*). I have kept 'similitude' for 'parable,' and also 'sweet bread,' a rendering of peculiar beauty and expressiveness taken from

Luther, where others generally have 'unleavened bread.' Tyndale saw leaven as souring the dough (1 Corinthians 5), and therefore speaks of how believers should be: "the sweet bread of pureness and truth."

Of course, I consulted other translations as I went. My favourites are Wycliffe of 1380 and 'Matthew's' contemporaries, Coverdale of 1535 and the Great Bible. In not a few places I updated from Coverdale. He translated more freely than Tyndale, often to good effect, and sometimes used more contemporary language. For example, at 2 Corinthians 12:10, where Tyndale had, "Therefore have I *delectation* in infirmities," I went with Coverdale and put "Therefore I am *content* in infirmities." I also sometimes updated from Wycliffe's 1380 translation. An example is at Hebrews 9:27, where Tyndale had that "it is appointed unto men that they *shall once die.*" I followed Wycliff (as others also did) with "it is appointed unto men *once to die.*" It is a joy to remember the great men of God in this way. I also followed Wycliffe at 1 Corinthians 2:2, making Paul to say here that he knew nothing amongst the Corinthians "except Jesus Christ *and him crucified.*" The KJV followed Wycliffe also, and this wording, which expresses necessary truth succinctly and powerfully, has become proverbial. I believe Tyndale would approve of this emendment.

I have studied early modern English grammar and language as well as modern grammar. I have consumed early modern English texts, tracking word usages and patterns. I have read and re-read everything I could get my hands on from Tyndale and Coverdale, which has not only enabled me to learn their English, but also their theology, confirming that we are fundamentally in accord, which is how it must be.

With the online Oxford English Dictionary ("OED") as my chief resource, but with reference also to Cawdrey's little 16th century dictionary, Johnson, the Crystals' glossary of Shakespearean words, and my own notes, I have developed over 2,000 individual word studies. In these I separate and record the definitions for each questionable word in three categories. The first is meanings that were current in the early 16th century, but are now obsolete. These must be updated. The second category is meanings that arose later, and so could not have been intended by the authors of the Matthew Bible; these I must be careful not to read into their writing. The third category is meanings current then and now; these I can of course keep where appropriate. Thus I have developed my own form of Early Modern English Dictionary, customized for this work, which comprises about eight feet of binders behind my desk. My 'dictionary' also incorporates reference to the Greek; I used Strong's Concordance, Jay Green's Greek text with interlinear English, and certain other resources, to identify and record all Greek words or combinations of words that were translated by the English words or phrases under study. As time went on I looked for patterns, and often went back to revisit earlier decisions. When I get to the Old Testament, God willing, I will do the same with the Hebrew.

The OED, though an amazing resource, is not entirely exhaustive, nor could I expect it to be. Sometimes it misses earlier word usages, showing a later date than is accurate for the use or appearance of a word in English, or for a *seme* of that word (that is, one meaning or use of it as distinguished from others). Sometimes it misattributes Tyndale's or Coverdale's uses. Also, many entries have not been updated since the late 1800s, and are now out of date, showing as current certain words or *semes* that are now obsolete or obsolescent. I have tracked these items, in part with a view to submitting them to the OED, and have noted up my own word studies accordingly.

A significant feature of early modern English is the *polysemy* of words; that is, words had multiple meanings (*poly-* many; *semes-* meanings) – much more so than today. When a word has many *semes* or meanings, we say that it 'shows polysemy.' The early modern

English vocabulary was much smaller than ours today, and words typically showed great polysemy, so that one word was used to express thoughts for which we now use more and narrower words. An example is the noun 'mansion,' which once not only meant a large or stately house, but could refer to almost anything that served as a dwelling, including a tent, and was also used to refer to stopping places in a journey. Clearly 'mansion' said to our ancestors something quite different than it now says to us at John 14:2: "In my Father's house are many mansions." We are familiar with this verse because the KJV followed Tyndale here. But the KJV preferred 'house' at 2 Corinthians 5:1-2, where Tyndale again had 'mansion' in an obsolete *seme*:

> We know surely if our earthy *mansion* wherein we now dwell were destroyed, that we have a building ordained of God, an habitation not made with hands, but eternal in heaven. And herefore sigh we, desiring to be clothed with our *mansion* which is from heaven...

As I progressed with my work, I realized that often the words of early modern English and of biblical Greek showed similar polysemy. The two languages were a 'fit,' inasmuch as their vocabularies were roughly the same size and their words tended to multiple *semes* – sometimes sharing the same *semes,* as with the Greek verb *skandalizo* and the English verb 'offend.' Was therefore the 16th century English mind, naturally *polysemic*, as it were, better equipped to understand biblical Greek than is the modern mind, which is accustomed to markedly greater precision of linguistic thought? Might our modern approach to words and word use handicap a right understanding of ancient Greek? Perhaps we see here God's timing in choosing the early 1600s to open his word to the world in English, and also the value of mining the translations of Tyndale and Coverdale for their treasures.

With word polysemy comes a range of possibility, nuance, and intensity that is unfamiliar to moderns. 'Despise' to Tyndale might mean neglect, hate, or anything or everything in between. Therefore it is necessary now either to find the narrower word that is right in the context, or a way to convey the polysemy of the early word, for example by using two words, if that is right. But some loss in understanding is inevitable, because we just don't use words the same way any more.

I have also developed grammar studies. One absorbing review was of the English auxiliary verbs 'should' and 'might' in that-clauses of purpose and result. I almost always updated these. For example at John 16:4 Jesus said to his disciples, "These things I have told you, *that* when that hour is come, ye *might* remember." I updated to: "I have told you these things *so that* when that hour comes, you *may* remember them."

Readers may notice my pronomic emendation. For example, I sometimes name the subjects of verbs where Tyndale had the pronouns 'he,' 'she,' or 'they.' I did this if the antecedent was not immediately apparent. At Luke 9:53 I put "But *the Samaritans* would not receive him" for "*they* would not." Greek verbs are inflected to show person and number, and the subject is often omitted, being silently understood. Naming the subject rather than using a pronoun as Tyndale did does not add to or change the meaning, but only clarifies. It is another way to render the text colloquially, and twenty centuries later we sometimes need the extra clarity.

Also concerning pronouns, where it seemed important I sought unobtrusive ways to indicate number in the 2nd person, since English has lost that distinction with the loss of 'thee' and 'thou.' An example is Jesus' conversation with Nicodemus, where he switches from the singular 'thou' at John 3:10 to the plural 'ye' at verses 11 and 12. It seemed only right not to implicate Nicodemus, or at least not him alone, as one who did not receive Jesus' witness of heavenly things. 'Beloved' also becomes 'beloveds' in the *October Testament* when Paul is addressing a group, since our 2nd person pronouns do not provide contextual clues to number.

I followed the Matthew scriptures in omitting quotation marks, which were not then in use. If I thought the lack might affect comprehension, I found a way to compensate. As in Matthew, capitalization is minimal. Numbers, especially large ones, are usually but not always rendered in numerals; in Matthew, they were usually but not always in Roman numerals. Sometimes for formatting reasons I used the sign '&' instead of 'and,' which the printers of the Matthew Bible also did. Readers may discover minor inconsistencies here and there, which is as it was in Matthew, and ought to be considered part of the character of the work, especially considering that it is largely the labour of one person.

Terms and measures peculiar to 16th century British English have where appropriate been emended by the use of the original words translated or transliterated, such as 'denarius' or 'talent' where Tyndale might have used 'pence' or 'farthing' (and I have added a few glosses to explain their monetary value). Where Tyndale used 'Easter' and 'Whitsuntide,' I have used 'Passover' and 'Pentecost,' now universally appreciated for the Jewish feasts that they were, being types and shadows of the Christian feasts to come.

There are two opposite and equal risks in a work such as this. One is to update too much. The other is to miss a 'faux friend'; that is, a word or phrase we know today, but which is used in an obsolete *seme;* as seen above, there are many of these in the Matthew Bible. For example, the verb 'will,' usually used now as an auxiliary verb to indicate future tense, then often meant 'want' or 'desire.' At Luke 13:31 Tyndale had, "Depart hence, for Herod will kill thee," meaning "wants to kill you." Paul called Timothy his "natural son," not at all meaning it as we might understand it; we know from Acts 16:1 that Timothy was the natural son of a Greek man. The noun 'tradition' once had stronger force, meaning not so much something that is customary, but rather required by precept. I felt this needed to be updated, being often misunderstood today. And 'acquaintance' once meant a close friend, but now it means more nearly the opposite: someone who, though known to us, could not really be called a friend. The phrase 'once for all' did not mean to Tyndale 'once for everybody,' as it might appear in Hebrews where we learn about Jesus offering himself 'once for all.' It meant 'on one occasion only,' a *seme* we now express with the phrase 'once *and* for all' – which modern phrase, according to the OED, did not begin to supplant the old one until early in the 19th century.

I of course have needed also to look at punctuation, syntax, negations, conjunctions, conditional sentences, articles, and so on – including one of my favourite studies, ellipsis with the pronoun 'that' (as in "I am that I am", which I have written about elsewhere). But I risk becoming tedious.

I have done my best, with constant prayers for guidance, but cannot have succeeded perfectly in avoiding all error, especially working alone as I have done for the most part – not only in my studies and work with the scriptures, which have been all consuming, but also innumerable reviews and checking, and then page layout and the other tasks associated with self-publishing, not to mention maintaining the website, creating an order page, etc. It has been more than full time work. Yet I do not complain, but only explain, and also rejoice. And so I close with a promise like Tyndale's own of many years ago: if I perceive or learn that anything has escaped me, or could be better done, I will cause it to be amended as soon as I can.

I do wish to express my gratitude to the two people who have been my main supports. My volunteer Ruth Soffos, who counts herself a possible descendant of John Rogers, came on early in the project. She versified most of the New Testament, and performed accurate preliminary editing that saved me much time. My dear mother, Joan Davis, has read through the New Testament aloud more than once as we compared text, and was always eager to help and support. Mum, it has meant so much to have you alongside.

My brother Jesse helped with office and computer set up, and showed me how to use formatting tools. Michael Hendrix helped with proof-reading. Many of my subscribers, too many to name, a growing band of people from all around the world, encouraged and assisted me along the way. Several gave me helpful comments on papers I have written for various journals, including Pattie, Mary, Jan, Pete, Tom, Victor, and Sue. My sister Lynne, and friends Michael, Margot, and others, have helped in their ways. Robert Taylor kept me posted on matters of interest. And though I have never met him, I am thankful to David Daniell for his work advancing the knowledge and reputation of William Tyndale, and for his modern spelling editions of Tyndale's Old and New Testaments.

And last but not least, I think of my dear blue-eyed cat Koshka, who curled up on her cushion at the corner of my desk every day for over five years, my companion as I worked and studied hour after hour in my office. I miss you, little Koshka.

I thank God our heavenly Father for the indescribable blessing that this work has been.

May the God of truth bless his truth to our souls.

Ruth Magnusson Davis (October 2015)

In the Matthew Bible, the books of the New
Testament were closed in this
style, which is also
copied here.
Amen.

How to Read the Notes and Commentaries

WHEN we take in hand the Holy Scriptures, we want to be sure of what we have. In the Reformation of the 16th century, the men who risked their lives to bring God's word to us were diligent to explain and interpret the scriptures for the people. To this end, they often included commentaries, called 'glosses,' in their bibles. In the *October Testament*, the authors of the notes or glosses can be identified as follows:

(1) Except square-bracketed items, marginal glosses are from William Tyndale.

(2) The chapter end notes ("The Notes") are John Rogers' from a variety of sources.

(3) All square-bracketed items are this editor's wherever they occur.

In the 1537 Matthew Bible all the glosses were squeezed into the margins. Then in 1549 Rogers re-distributed them between the margins and chapter end notes called 'The Notes.' In the New Testament, he took the marginal glosses mainly from Tyndale's 1534 New Testament, but 'The Notes' were his own comments along with some from Erasmus, Church fathers, Martin Luther, other Reformers, and also more from Tyndale. I followed Rogers' format, but moved many of Tyndale's notes back to the margins, which was a better use of space and identifies his authorship. I also brought in some of Tyndale's 1534 notes that Rogers omitted. Occasionally Rogers put his notes in the margin; these I tried to catch and move to chapter ends in order to be consistent.

This format is unique to the *October Testament.* It is anticipated that in the full New Matthew Bible, glosses will be confined to end notes, eliminating at least one margin. Further, for the most part the full NMB will not contain my glosses. This *Testament* is therefore intended to serve as an introduction to the full work (which, God willing, will appear in due course) and as a sharing of useful things I learned along the way: historical, general, or philological information (when were the epistles written? what is a fuller? a sycamine tree? what does 'concupiscence' mean?), information about Rogers' references (who was Pliny? Vegetius?), sources of updates or emendments (Wycliffe, Coverdale? Cranmer?), information about bible times, notes where Tyndale differed from others, and expository glosses. The latter may contain the views of Martin Luther, St Augustine, or others, as well as my own as far forth as I believe the Lord has taught me, or may be taken from the extra-biblical writings of Tyndale or Coverdale themselves. Usually the work I quote from is identified. (See 'Abbreviations of Source References' at page 27). If omitted, the reason is usually that the gloss was an early one, taken before I began citing sources. An example of an added expository gloss is at 1 Corinthians 11, where Paul teaches about Holy Communion. The symbol ">" indicates that what follows is the view of the person named:

> [Coverdale>He that would sit now at the table of the High King, let him diligently consider what he receives in his soul through faith, namely, the body and blood of Jesus Christ, which feeds and nourishes him to eternal life (*Fruitful*)]

This added gloss (English updated) is from Coverdale's essay *Fruitful Lessons,* at page 207 of the Parker Society's collection of that and other of Coverdale's works. However, I do not give page numbers, etc., partly because it is not in the nature of this work so to do. Rogers did not include such details.

A few added glosses touch on modern issues, such as the rise again of chiliasm, which Rogers likely did not foresee, and for which I drew upon Augustine at Revelation 20.

It is perhaps not necessary to say that a quotation from someone does not indicate my agreement with everything they ever said or wrote, nor could it, even if I were able to read and judge everything, which I am not. Nor do I agree with all the glosses of the Matthew Bible, or perhaps with the way they are worded. What's more, the men quoted by Rogers or me frequently disagreed among themselves. Therefore the notes and commentaries herein are altogether a joint offering from many sincere minds, to be rightly weighed against the scriptures.

In his 1534 New Testament, Tyndale had marginal notes that simply pointed to a text so that the reader could quickly find his or her place. Rogers omitted most of these 'pointing glosses.' Formatting has permitted us to bring many back. Sometimes I expanded them: at 26:1 of Matthew's gospel, Tyndale had a pointing gloss saying "The passion." I expanded to "The passion foretold." In places I have added my own pointing glosses, none of which are square bracketed because the text is more attractive without them and it is not important to know the source.

The Matthew Bible notes are a treasure trove of doctrine and history, of love and faith, of insight and sound argument. However, I omitted or abbreviated a handful of them, partly for space reasons, and for the sake of peace. For example, at 1 Corinthians 7, I omitted a fairly long gloss concerning the relative virtues of chastity and marriage – the chapter speaks for itself. Great and sincere minds have disagreed concerning some things about which it is not necessary to be dogmatic. Moreover, the Matthew Bible spoke to a people largely illiterate and uninformed, in a time when enquiry apart from prevailing doctrine was dangerous. The *October Testament* speaks to a different world: a doctrinally more sophisticated, but also divided and skeptical Christendom, and a literate society where issues are openly argued and may (at least for now in some places) be freely explored. Therefore I was guided by an irenic spirit in the rare instances that I exercised such editorial license.

For those who wish to see or compare the original glosses to the New Testament, facsimiles of the 1537 edition are available. The 1537 notes are identical with those of 1549 except that some were omitted in the second printing. However, to the best of my knowledge, no facsimile of the genuine 1549 Matthew Bible is available at this time (see my discussion in 'History of the Matthew Bible').

'Matthew' contained a sprinkling of parallel scripture references, and there were more in Tyndale's 1534 New Testament. These were cited in Roman numerals, without verse numbers, but with letters indicating approximate location, as in "Esay.xl.b." Often they were misprinted, and sometimes illegible. It was painstaking to track them down, but I persevered single-handedly, and even added more myself. References to Old Testament passages might occasionally seem mysterious, where the Matthew Bible differs from other bibles.

White space in the margins may serve for the reader's own notes.

R. M. D.

Abbreviations of Source References in Annotations

1st Book or . . . . . *2nd Book*	Books One or Two of *The Laws of Ecclesiastical Polity* by Elizabethan divine Richard Hooker. First published in 1593.
Ag. Latomus	*Against Latomus,* Martin Luther's essay of 1521.
Answer	*An Answer to Sir Thomas More's Dialogue* by William Tyndale. First published in 1531.
City	*City of God* by Augustine of Hippo. Probably completed in the year 426. Books are identified by Roman Numerals, as in the original. For example at Rev 20, note (a), Bk XX means Book 20.
De Spiritu Sancto. .	*De Spiritu Sancto,* or 'On the Holy Spirit,' written by St. Ambrose about 381.
Doctrinal	*Doctrinal Treatises and Introductions to Different Portions of the Holy Scriptures,* being a selection of the works of William Tyndale published by the Parker Society.
E.H.	*Eusebius' Ecclesiastical History* by Eusebius Pamphilus, written in the early 4th century. Book and chapter are indicated.
Enchiridion	*The Enchiridion on Faith, Hope, and Charity* by Augustine of Hippo, written shortly after the death of St. Jerome in 420.
Exp 1Jo	*Exposition of the first Epistle of St John* by William Tyndale. Published in Parker Society volume.
Fruitful	*Fruitful Lessons upon the Passion, Burial, Resurrection, Ascension, and Sending of the Holy Ghost,* by Miles Coverdale. First printed about 1540. Published in Parker Society volume.
Heid. Disp.	*Heidelberg Disputation*, Martin Luther's essay of 1518.
Hom/ John or *Gal.* . or *2Tim, etc.*	*Homilies* of John Chrysostom on John's gospel and the epistles of the New Testament, as indicated. From the series, *A Select Library of the Nicene and Post-Nicene Fathers of the Christian Church* in 1886.
Obedience	*The Obedience of a Christian Man* by William Tyndale. First published in 1528.
Parable	*The Parable of Wicked Mammon* by William Tyndale. First published 1528.
Pearl	*A Spiritual and Most Precious Pearl,* 1550 translation by Miles Coverdale of the work of Otho Wermullerus (or Vuerdmullerus), a Zurich divine. Published in Parker Society volume.
Practice	*The Practice of Prelates* by William Tyndale. First published in 1530.
Prologue to . . . . . . *Numbers*	William Tyndale's prologue to the Old Testament book of Numbers.
Sundry	*Expositions and Notes on Sundry Portions of the Holy Scriptures,* Parker Society. Expositions of the scriptures by William Tyndale.

Abbreviations of the Names of the Books of the Bible

Old Testament

Ge	=Genesis
Ex	=Exodus
Lev	=Leviticus
Nu	=Numbers
De	=Deuteronomy
Jos	=Joshua
J'g	=Judges
Ru	=Ruth
1Sa	=1 Samuel
2Sa	=2 Samuel
1Ki	=1 Kings
2Ki	=2 Kings
1Ch	=1 Chronicles
2Ch	=2 Chronicles
Ezr	=Ezra
Ne	=Nehemiah
Es	=Esther
Job	=Job
Ps	=Psalms
Pr	=Proverbs
Ec	=Ecclesiastes
Song	=Song of Solomon
Isa	=Isaiah
Jer	=Jeremiah
La	=Lamentations
Eze	=Ezekiel
Dan	=Daniel
Ho	=Hosea
Joe	=Joel
Am	=Amos
Ob	=Obadiah
Jon	=Jonah
Mic	=Micah
Na	=Nahum
Hab	=Habakkuk
Zep	=Zephaniah
Hag	=Haggai
Zec	=Zechariah
Mal	=Malachi

New Testament

M't	=Matthew
Mk	=Mark
Lu	=Luke
Joh	=John
Ac	=Acts
Ro	=Romans
1Co	=1Corinthians
2Co	=2 Corinthians
Ga	=Galatians
Eph	=Ephesians
Ph'p	=Philippians
Col	=Colossians
1Th	=1 Thessalonians
2Th	=2 Thessalonians
1Ti	=1 Timothy
2Ti	=2Timothy
Tit	=Titus
Ph'm	=Philemon
Heb	=Hebrews
Jas	=James
1Pe	=1 Peter
2Pe	=2 Peter
1Jo	=1 John
2Jo	=2 John
3Jo	=3 John
Jude	=Jude
Rev	=Revelation

Apocryphal Books

Tob	=Tobit
Wis	=Wisdom of Solomon
Ec'us	= Ecclesiasticus
1Macc	=1 Maccabees
2Macc	=2 Maccabees

A Prologue Upon the Gospel of Matthew

Concerning the evangelists, you see in the New Testament clearly who they were. Matthew (as you read in M't 9, Mk 2, Lu 5) was one of Christ's apostles. He was with Christ all the time of his preaching, and saw and heard his own self almost all that he wrote. *W.T. (1534)* [Ed: Matthew is also called Levi in the other gospels. He wrote his account before the temple in Jerusalem was destroyed, perhaps as early as 50 A.D.]

Gospel means glad tidings.

The Gospel of St. Matthew

Chapter 1

The genealogy of Christ and marriage of his mother Mary.
The angel satisfies Joseph's mind.

David and Abraham are mentioned first because Christ was especially promised to them, to be of their seed. [*Son,* after the Hebrew, may include lineal descendants of any degree]

THIS IS the account of the genealogy of Jesus Christ,[a] the son of David,
the son also of Abraham:
2 Abraham begat Isaac;
Isaac begat Jacob;
Jacob begat Judah and his brethren.
3 Judah begat Perez and Zerah by Tamar;
Perez begat Hezron; Ge cc21,25, 29. 1Ch cc2,3 2Sa 12:24,25 Ru c4
Hezron begat Ram.
4 Ram begat Amminadab;
Amminadab begat Nashon;
Nashon begat Salmon.
5 Salmon begat Boaz by Rahab;
Boaz begat Obed by Ruth;
Obed begat Jesse.
6 Jesse begat David the king;
David the king begat Solomon, by her who was the wife of Uriah.
7 Solomon begat Rehoboam;
Rehoboam begat Abijah;
Abijah begat Asa.
8 Asa begat Jehoshaphat;
Jehoshaphat begat Joram;
Joram begat Uzziah.
9 Uzziah begat Jotham;
Jotham begat Ahaz;
Ahaz begat Hezekiah.
10 Hezekiah begat Manasseh;
Manasseh begat Amon;
Amon begat Josiah.
11 Josiah begat Jeconiah and his brethren about the time they were
carried away to Babylon.[b]
12 And after they were brought to Babylon, Jeconiah begat Shealtiel; 2Ch c36
Shealtiel begat Zerubbabel.

[13]Zerubbabel begat Abiud;
Abiud begat Eliakim;
Eliakim begat Azor.
[14]Azor begat Zadok;
Zadok begat Achim;
Achim begat Eliud.
[15]Eliud begat Eleazar;
Eleazar begat Matthan;
Matthan begat Jacob.
[16]Jacob begat Joseph the husband of Mary, of whom was born that
Jesus that is called Christ.[c]

[17]All the generations from Abraham to David are 14 generations. And from David to the captivity of Babylon are 14 generations. And from the captivity of Babylon to Christ are also 14 generations.

[18]The birth of Jesus Christ was this way: When his mother Mary was
betrothed to Joseph, before they came to dwell together, she was found
with child by the Holy Spirit. [19]Then Joseph her husband, being an
upright man, and loathe to make an example of her,* was minded to put Lu c1
her away quietly. [20]While he thought on these things, behold, the angel*
of the Lord appeared to him in a dream, saying, Joseph son of David, fear
not to take unto you Mary your wife. For that which is conceived in her
is of the Holy Spirit. [21]She will bring forth a son, and you shall call his
name Jesus. For he will save his people from their sins.

Example: that is to say, bring her out for punishment as an example to others.
Angel: that is, messenger.

[22]All this was done to fulfil that which was spoken about the Lord by
the prophet, saying, [23]Behold, a maiden shall be with child, and shall
bring forth a son, and they shall call his name Immanuel,[d] which is by Isa 7:14
interpretation, God with us.

[24]And Joseph, as soon as he awoke out of sleep, did as the angel of
the Lord had bid him, and took his wife unto him, [25]and knew her not till
she had brought forth her first son,[e] and called his name Jesus.

The Notes

Jesus (1:1) a) *Jesus*, or as in Hebrew *Jesua*, means 'saviour'.

Josiah (1:11) b) Here is left out in the books of our time that Josiah begat Jehoiakim, who begat Jeconiah (1Chronicles 3:14-17).

Christ (1:16) c) *Christ,* in Hebrew *Messiah,* signifies anointed. Jesus Christ is then the earnest and pledge of God's promise, by whom the grace and favour of God is promised to us, with the Holy Spirit who illumines, lights, and renews our hearts to fulfil the law.

Immanuel (1:23) d) Christ is called Immanuel, or 'God with us', in that he took the flesh of man and joined and knit himself to us, and became our brother (Hebrews 2:9-18).

First son (1:25) e) Her first son: not because she had any after, but because she had none before.

Chapter 2

The time and place of Christ's birth. The wise men offer their presents. Christ flees into Egypt. The young children are slain. Christ turns in to Galilee.

When Jesus was born at Bethlehem in Judea, in the time of Herod the
king, behold, there came wise men from the east to Jerusalem,[a] 2saying,
Where is he that is born king of the Jews? We have seen his star in the
east and have come to worship him.
3When Herod the king heard this, he was troubled, and all Jerusalem
with him. 4And he gathered all the chief priests and scribes of the people
and asked of them where the Christ was to be born. 5And they said to
him, At Bethlehem in Judea. For thus it is written by the prophet: 6And
[**Bethlehem** was also called Ephrath or Ephrathah in the Old Testament (see Ge 35:19)]
thou Bethlehem,[b] in the land of Judea, are not the least among the princes Isa c11
of Judah, for out of you shall come the leader who will govern[c] my Mic 5:2 Joh 7:42
people Israel.
7Then Herod privately called the wise men and carefully enquired of
them when the star had appeared, 8and sent them to Bethlehem, saying,
Go and search diligently for the child. And when you have found him,
bring me word so that I may come and worship him also.
9When they had heard the king, they departed. And lo, the star which
they saw in the east went before them, till it came and stood over the
place where the child was. 10When they saw the star, they were mar-
vellously glad, 11and went into the house and found the child with Mary
his mother, and kneeled down and worshipped him,[d] and opened their
treasures and offered to him gifts: gold, frankincense, and myrrh. 12And
after they were warned by God in a dream that they should not go again
to Herod, they returned into their own country another way.
13When they had departed, behold, the angel of the Lord appeared to
Joseph in a dream, saying, Arise, and take the child and his mother, and
Flee into Eygpt.
flee into Egypt, and remain there till I bring you word. For Herod will
seek the child to kill him.
14Then he arose, and took the child and his mother by night, and
departed into Egypt, 15and was there until the death of Herod, to fulfil
that which was spoken of the Lord by the prophet, which says, Out of Ho 11:1
Egypt have I called my Son.
16Then Herod, perceiving that the wise men had gotten around him,
was exceedingly angry, and sent forth and slew all the children that were
in Bethlehem and in all its vicinity – as many as were two years old and
under, according to the time that he had ascertained from the wise men.[e]
17Then was fulfilled that which was spoken by the prophet Jeremiah,
saying, 18On the hills a voice was heard, mourning, weeping, and great Jer 31:15
lamentation: Rachel weeping for her children. And she would not be
comforted, because they were no more.
19When Herod was dead, behold, an angel of the Lord appeared in a
dream to Joseph in Egypt, 20saying, Arise, and take the child and his
mother, and go into the land of Israel. For they are dead who sought the
child's life.
21Then he arose up, and took the child and his mother, and came into
the land of Israel. 22But when he heard that Archelaus was reigning in
Judea in place of his father Herod, he was afraid to go there. After he was

warned by God in a dream, he turned aside into the region of Galilee,
23and went and dwelt in a village called Nazareth, to fulfil that which was J'g 13:5
spoken by the prophets: He shall be called a Nazarite.

The Notes

The wise men (2:1) a) These were neither kings nor princes. Strabo [a Greek geographer and historian], who was in their time, says they were wise men among the Persians, like Moses was among the Hebrews. He says also that they were the priests of the Persians.

Bethlehem prophecy (2:5,6) b) Understand that because Christ was born there, Bethlehem betokens the Christianity which in the eyes of the world is little and contemptible, but in the eyes of God is great and precious.

Govern my people (2:6) c) To govern is to order and rule the people by teaching and example.

Worshipped him (2:11) d) The Hebrews often use this word *worship* for doing reverence with inclination and bowing of the body, as at Genesis 33:6 & 7.

Herod's slaughter of the infants (2:16) e) Macrobius [a Latin grammarian and philosopher about 400 A.D.] made mention in the second book and fourth chapter of his *Saturnalia* of how Augustus Caesar, hearing that Herod had likewise killed his own son, said, It is better to be Herod's swine than his son. [Herod, being a Jew, would not eat pork.]

Chapter 3

The baptism, preaching, and office of John the Baptist, and how Christ was baptized by him in the Jordan.

In those days John the Baptist came and preached in the wilderness of
Judea, 2saying, Repent: the kingdom of heaven is at hand! 3This is he of
whom it is spoken by the prophet Isaiah, who says, The voice of a crier in Isa 40:3
wilderness: Prepare the Lord's way, and make his paths straight.
4This John had his garment of camel's hair, and a girdle of skin about Mk 1:1-17 Lu 3:1-22
his loins. His food was locusts and wild honey.[a] 5At that time Jerusalem Joh 1:15-34;
and all Judea, and all the region round about the Jordan, went out to him, 3:22-36.
6and were baptized by him in the Jordan, confessing their sins.
7When he saw many of the Pharisees and of the Sadducees come to
his baptism, he said to them, O offspring of vipers, who has taught you to
flee from the vengeance to come? 8Bring forth therefore the fruits be-
longing to repentance. 9And see that you ones do not think to say in
yourselves, We have Abraham as our father. For I say to you that God is
able from these stones to raise up children to Abraham. 10Even now is the
axe put to the root of the trees, so that every tree which does not bring
forth good fruit is hewn down and cast into the fire. 11I baptize you in
water in token of repentance, but he who comes after me is mightier than
I, whose shoes I am not worthy to bear. He will baptize you with the
Holy Spirit and with fire. 12He has also his fan in his hand, and will purge
his floor, and gather the wheat into his garner, and will burn the chaff
with unquenchable fire.[b]
13Then Jesus came from Galilee to the Jordan, to John, to be baptized
by him. 14But John stopped him, saying, I ought to be baptized by you,
and do you come to me? 15Jesus answered and said to him, Let it be so

now, for thus it behoves us, to fulfil all righteousness.
Then John let him. 16And Jesus, as soon as he was baptized, came
straight out of the water. And lo, heaven was open over him, and John Mk 1:11 Lu 3:22
saw the Spirit of God descend like a dove and light upon him. 17And lo, Joh 1:32
there came a voice from heaven, saying, This is he: my beloved Son, in 2Pe 1:16-18
whom is my delight.

The Notes

Locusts (3:4) a) According to Pliny [Roman savant and author of *Natural History* in the first century], locusts are certain creatures that people of Parthia and Ethiopia used to eat. But some say the tops or buds of trees or fruits are meant. [Tyndale>John the Baptist came not to impress with his diet and strait living, which outward things pertain only to the taming of the flesh, but he came to preach, as the voice of a crier.]

Wheat and chaff (3:12) b) By the wheat and the chaff are understood the good and the evil. Luke 3:17.

Chapter 4

Christ fasts and is proved. He calls Peter, Andrew, James, and John, and heals all the sick.

Then Jesus was led away by the Spirit into wilderness, to be tried by the
devil. 2And when he had fasted forty days and forty nights, he was
afterwards hungered. 3Then the tempter came to him and said, If you are Mk 1:12,13
the Son of God, command that these stones be made bread. 4He answered Lu 4:1-13 De 8:3
and said, It is written: Man shall not live by bread alone, but by every
word that proceeds out of the mouth of God.
5Then the devil took him up into the holy city and set him on a
pinnacle of the temple, 6and said to him, If you are the Son of God, cast
yourself down. For it is written: He will give his angels charge over you,
and with their hands they will hold you up so that you do not dash your Ps 91:11,12 De 6:16
foot against a stone. 7And Jesus said to him, It is written also: You shall
not tempt the Lord your God.
8The devil took him up again, and led him to an exceedingly high
mountain, and showed him all the kingdoms of the world and all the
glory of them, 9and said to him, All these I will give you, if you will fall
down and worship me. 10Then Jesus said to him, Away, Satan! For it is
written: You shall worship the Lord your God, and him only shall you De 6:13; 10:12-21.
serve.
11Then the devil left him, and behold, the angels came and ministered
to him.
[**Taken**: cast into prison by Herod the tetrarch, see 14:3]
12Now when Jesus had heard that John was taken,* he departed into
Galilee. 13And leaving Nazareth, he went and dwelt in Capernaum, which
[**The sea**: Lake Galilee, also called the Sea of Galilee. In scripture, a 'sea' may be of fresh or salt water]
is a city upon the sea* in the coasts of Zebulun and Naphtali, 14to fulfil Lu cc 4,5
that which was spoken by Isaiah the prophet, saying, 15The land of Mk 1:14-45 Isa 9:1,2
Zebulun and Naphtali, by the way of the sea, beyond the Jordan, Galilee
of the Gentiles: 16the people who sat in darkness saw great light, and to
those who sat in the region and shadow of death, light has begun to shine.
17From that time Jesus began to preach and to say, Repent, for the

kingdom of heaven is at hand![a]
18As Jesus walked by the Sea of Galilee, he saw two brethren, Simon
who was called Peter, and Andrew his brother, casting a net into the sea,
for they were fishermen. 19And he said to them, Follow me, and I will
make you fishers of men. 20And they straightaway left their nets and
followed him.

21And he went onwards from there and saw two other brethren, James
the son of Zebedee and John his brother, in the boat with Zebedee their
father, mending their nets. And he called them. 22And they without delay
left the boat and their father, and followed him.

23And Jesus went about all Galilee, teaching in their synagogues and
preaching the gospel of the kingdom.[b] And he healed all manner of
sickness and all kinds of diseases among the people. 24And his fame
spread abroad throughout all Syria. And they brought to him all the sick
people who were taken with divers diseases and torments, and those who
were possessed with devils, and those who were mentally ill, and those
who were paralyzed; and he healed them. 25And there followed him a
great number of people from Galilee and the Ten Cities, and from
Jerusalem and Judea, and from the regions that lie beyond the Jordan.

The Notes

To repent (4:17) a) To repent is to think again, and to leave and change their evil life for the love of virtue and hate of sin, as at Mark 1:15 and Acts 3:19.

The gospel (4:23) b) The gospel is an open showing and preaching of the grace and redemption obtained and given through Christ.

Chapter 5

In this chapter and the two next following is contained the most excellent and loving sermon of Christ in the Mount, which sermon is the very key that opens the understanding into the law. In this fifth chapter especially, he preaches of the 8 beatitudes, or blessings; of manslaughter, wrath, and anger; of adultery, of swearing, of suffering wrong; and of love, even toward a person's enemies.

When Jesus saw the crowds of people, he went up into a mountain. And
when he was seated, his disciples came to him. 2And he opened his
mouth and taught them, saying:

3Blessed are the poor in spirit, for theirs is the kingdom of heaven.[a]
4Blessed are those who mourn, for they shall be comforted. Lu 6:20-49
5Blessed are the meek, for they shall inherit the earth.
Covenants 6Blessed are those who hunger and thirst for righteousness, for they
shall be filled.[b]
7Blessed are the merciful, for they shall obtain mercy.
8Blessed are the pure in heart, for they shall see God.
9Blessed are the peacemakers, for they shall be called the children of
God.[c]

[10]Blessed are those who suffer persecution for righteousness' sake,
for theirs is the kingdom of heaven.
[11]Blessed are you when men revile you, and persecute you, and
falsely say all manner of evil things against you for my sake. [12]Re-
joice, and be glad, for great is your reward in heaven.[d] For in the 1Pe 3:14-17
same way they persecuted the prophets that were before your days.

[13]You are the salt of the earth. But if the salt has lost her saltness,
Salt what can be salted with it? It is thereafter good for nothing but to be cast Mk 9:49,50.
out and to be trodden underfoot by men. Lu 14:34-35.
[14]You are the light of the world. A city that is set on a hill cannot be Mk 4:21-24
Light hid. [15]Neither do men light a candle and put it under a bushel, but on a Lu 8:16-18;
candlestick, and it gives light to all who are in the house. [16]Let your light 11:33-36.
so shine before men that they may see your good works and glorify your
Father who is in heaven.
[17]Do not think that I have come to destroy the law or the prophets.
No, I have not come to destroy them, but to fulfil them. [18]For truly I say
[**Jot**: smallest Hebrew letter. **Tittle**: a dot] to you, till heaven and earth perish, not one jot or one tittle* of the law
shall escape, till all be fulfilled. [19]Whosoever breaks one of the least of Lu 16:14-18 Jas 2:8
these commandments, and teaches men so, he will be called the least in
the kingdom of heaven.[e] But whosoever observes and teaches them, the
same will be called great in the kingdom of heaven.[f] [20]For I say to you,
unless your righteousness exceeds the righteousness of the scribes and
Pharisees, you cannot enter into the kingdom of heaven.
[21]You have heard how it was said to the people of the old time, You
shall not kill. For whosoever kills will be liable to judgment. [22]But I say
to you, whosoever is angry with his brother will be liable to judgment. Ex 20:13 De 5:17
Whosoever says to his brother, Racha! will be liable to a council. But
whosoever says, You fool! will be liable to hell fire.[g]
[23]Therefore when you are offering your gift at the altar, and there
remember that your brother has anything against you, [24]leave your offer-
ing there before the altar, and go your way first and be reconciled to your
brother; and then come and offer your gift.
[25]Reconcile with your adversary quickly while you are in the way
with him, lest the adversary commit you to the judge, and the judge
commit you to the officer, and then you be cast into prison. [26]Truly I say
to you, you will not come out of there till you have paid the last penny.[h] Lu 12:57-59
[27]You have heard how it was said to the people of the old time, You
shall not commit adultery. [28]But I say to you that whosoever looks on a
wife, lusting after her, has committed adultery with her already in his Ex 20:14 De 5:18
heart. [29]Therefore if your right eye causes you to offend, tear it out and Mk 9:43-48 M't 18:8,9.
cast it from you.[i] It is better for you that one of your members perish than
that your whole body should be cast into hell. [30]Also, if your right hand
causes you to offend, cut it off and cast it from you. Better it is that one
of your members perish, than that all your body should be cast into hell.
[31]It is said, Whosoever puts away his wife, let him give her a testi-
monial also of the divorce. [32]But I say to you, whosoever puts away his

wife (unless it be for fornication), causes her to break matrimony. And — De 24:1
whoever marries her who is divorced, breaks wedlock. — Mal 2:14,15; Mk 10:2-12
[33]Again, you have heard how it was said to the people of old time, Do — 1Co 7:4
[To **forswear yourself** is to break your oath to God, or to swear falsely, perjure yourself] — not forswear yourself,* but perform your oath to God. [34]But I say to you, — M't 19:3-9
do not swear at all – neither by heaven, for it is God's seat, [35]nor yet by
the earth, for it his footstool, nor by Jerusalem, for it is the city of that
great king. [36]Neither should you swear by your head, because you cannot
Let your yes be yes and your no, no. — make one hair white or black. [37]But let your communication be yes, yes,
and no, no. For whatever is more than that, comes of evil.
[38]You have heard how it is said, An eye for an eye, a tooth for a
tooth. [39]But I say to you, do not resist wrong. But whosoever gives you a
Right cheek — blow on your right cheek, turn to him the other. [40]And if any man would
sue you at law and take away your coat, let him have your cloak also. — Ex 21:24
[41]And whoever would compel you to go a mile, go with him two. [42]Give — Lev 24:20
to him who asks, and from him who would borrow, turn not away. — De 19:21
[43]You have heard how it is said, You shall love your neighbour and
hate your enemy.[j] [44]But I say to you, love your enemies. Bless those who
curse you. Do good to those who hate you. Pray for those who do you — Lev 19:18
wrong and persecute you, [45]so that you may be the children of your — Lu 6:27-36
Father that is in heaven. For he makes his sun to arise on the evil and on
the good, and sends his rain on the just and the unjust. [46]For if you love
Publicans [These were men, often Gentiles, appointed by the Romans to collect rents, taxes, customs, and tribute] — those who love you, what reward should you have? Do not the publicans
do the same? [47]And if you are friendly to your brethren only, what
singular thing are you doing? Do not the publicans do likewise? [48]You
must therefore be perfect, even as your Father who is in heaven is
perfect.

The Notes

Poor in spirit (5:3) — a) Of the poor in spirit is spoken at note (a) on Luke 6.

Hunger and Thirst (5:6) — b) To hunger and thirst for righteousness is to desire pure and true innocency, on account of which desire those who know their sins are grievously troubled and sore perplexed, of whom it is spoken at Luke 1:53.

Who are the children of God (5:9) — c) The children of God are those to whom the Lord by his promise has granted his divine blessings more abundantly than to others, as in De 14:2 and John 1:12,13.

Reward (5:10-12) — d) Reward is given to people for their work, but is not due for their work, as is said later in M't 20:1-16 by the parable of the vineyard workers.

Commandments (5:19) — e) To break commandments: this is what people are doing who say that Christ's commandments in these chapters 5, 6, and 7 are no more than wise counsels, inasmuch as he himself calls them commandments here.

To observe the law (5:19) — f) To observe the law is to do what the law bids with a free and generous heart; that is, it is to gladly live for God, and to do well – yea, even if we had no law (John 7:18; Ro 13:8-10; Ga 5:14).

Racha, fool (5:22) — g) According to Chrysostom, *racha* is a word of Syrian speech by which is shown that the mind is moved to anger. But under the word *fool,* Chrysostom and Augustine understand all manner of injury or offence of defamatory, taunting, or spiteful words.

The last penny (5:26) — h) 'Till you have paid the last penny' does not prove that the debtor will come out afterwards, any more than 'till she had brought forth her first son' (M't 1:25) proves she had one after, or, at Genesis 8, that another raven would come. See the places.

To tear out the eye (5:29) i) To tear out the eye is to mortify the carnal desires of the heart that proceed by means of the eye, and likewise regarding the cutting off of hands and feet.

Hate your enemy (5:43) j) The Pharisees added this to the commandment themselves because of that which is written about having no familiarity or friendship with the nations (Ex 34:11-13; De 7:2-5; Jos 23:12,13).

Chapter 6

Of alms, prayer, and fasting. Jesus forbids the care of seeking the things of this life.

Alms [charitable gifts and deeds of mercy]

Take heed to your alms, that you do not give in the sight of men with the
intent to be seen by them, or you will receive no reward from your Father
who is in heaven. [2]Whenever therefore you give your alms, do not make
a trumpet to be blown before you, as the hypocrites do in the synagogues
and in the streets in order to be praised by men. Truly I say to you, they
have their reward. [3]But when you give, let not your left hand know what
your right hand does,[a] [4]so that your giving may be secret. And your
Father who sees in secret will reward you openly.

[5]And when you pray, do not be as the hypocrites are. For they love to
Prayer stand and pray in the synagogues and in the corners of the streets,
because they want to be seen by men. Truly I say to you, they have their
reward. [6]But when you pray, enter into your chamber and shut the door
to, and pray to your Father who is in secret.[b] And your Father who sees in
secret will reward you openly.

[7]And when you pray, do not use vain repetitions like the heathen do.
For they think that they will be heard for their many words. [8]Be not like
them therefore. For your Father knows what you need before you ask of
him. [9]Pray therefore in this manner:

O our Father who art in heaven,
Hallowed be thy name. Lu 11:1-4
[10]Thy kingdom come.[c]
Thy will be done on earth as it is in heaven.
[11]Give us this day our daily bread.
[12]And forgive us our trespasses, as we forgive them that trespass against us.
[13]And lead us not into temptation, but deliver us from evil.
For thine is the kingdom and the power and the glory forever.
Amen.

[14]For if you forgive others their trespasses, your heavenly Father will Mk 11:25,26
Covenants also forgive you. [15]But if you will not forgive others their trespasses,
neither will your Father forgive you your trespasses.

[16]Moreover, when you fast, do not be sad like the hypocrites are. For
they disfigure their faces so they may be seen by men, how they fast.[d]
Fasting Truly I say to you, they have their reward. [17]But you, when you fast,
anoint your head and wash your face, [18]so that it does not appear to men
that you are fasting, but to your Father who is in secret. And your Father

who sees in secret will reward you openly.
[19]See that you do not gather for yourselves treasure upon the earth,
where rust and moths destroy, and where thieves break in and steal. [20]But Lu 12:15-21
gather treasures together in heaven, where neither rust nor moths destroy,
and where thieves do not break in or steal. [21]For wherever your treasure
is, there will your hearts be also.

A single eye, light.

[22]The light of the body is your eye. Therefore if your eye is single, all
your body will be full of light.[e] [23]But if your eye is bad, then all your Lu 11:33-36
body will be full of darkness. Therefore if the light that is in you is dark-
ness, how great is that darkness!

[**Mammon**: an Aramaic word, which Tyndale understood to signify riches and temporal honours, covetousness, and ambition (*Practice*)]

[24]No one can serve two masters. For either he will hate the one and
love the other, or else he will lean to the one and neglect the other. You
cannot serve both God and mammon.[*] [25]Therefore I say to you, do not be Lu 12:22-34
anxious about your life, what you will eat or what you will drink, nor yet
for your body, what you will put on. Is not life more than food, and the
body more than clothing? [26]Behold the birds of the air. They do not sow
or reap or gather into barns, and yet your heavenly Father feeds them.
Are you not of much more value than they?

[**Cubit**: an ancient measure of length, being the distance from the elbow to the tip of the middle finger. Since this varies among people, a standard cubit was used in building]

[27]Which of you, though he took thought for it, could add one cubit[*] to
his stature? [28]Why worry then about clothing? Consider the lilies of the
field, how they grow. They do not labour or spin. [29]And yet for all that, I
say to you that even Solomon in all his royalty was not arrayed like one
of these. [30]Therefore if God so clothes the grass, which is today in the
field and tomorrow will be cast into the furnace, will he not much more
do the same for you, O ye of little faith?

[31]Therefore do not be anxious, saying, What will we eat? or, What
will we drink? or, How will we be clothed? [32]After all these things the
Gentiles seek. For your heavenly Father knows that you have need of all
these things.[33]But rather seek ye first the kingdom of heaven and its
righteousness, and all these things will be ministered unto you.

[34]Care not then for the morrow, but let the morrow care for itself. For
the present day has ever enough of its own trouble.

The Notes

Give in secret (6:3)

a) By this our Saviour Christ shows that he does not wish us to be esteemed or honoured by men for our giving, but it should suffice that we are praised by God.

Enter into your chamber (6:6)

b) *Chamber* here signifies a private place, separate from all the noise of this world, such as is referred to in the last verses of Isa 26. Such a chamber you may make of your own heart, and there pray.

Thy kingdom come (6:10)

c) That is, may we who before have served the world hereafter come under the dominion and kingdom of Christ as he promises (M't 25:34).

Fasting (6:16)

d) By this it appears that the true fast is to put away altogether all wanton desires and lusts, etc., and to govern the body with suitable discipline and mortifying of the flesh, as it is said at Ps 34:13-14 and Isa 58:3-7.

The light of the body is the eye (6:22)

e) Here the body signifies the life with its works and deeds, and the eye signifies the thought and intent. [Ed: An eye that is single is pure in sincerity and simplicity, sound in the light of God's word and truth, and wholly dedicated to purity and truth.]

Chapter 7

Jesus forbids foolish and presumptuous judgment, reproves hypocrisy, exhorts to prayer, warns us to beware of false prophets, and so concludes his sermon.

Judge not, that you be not judged. 2For as you judge, so shall you be
judged, and the measure you use will be measured back to you. 3Why do
you see a speck in your brother's eye, and not perceive the beam that is Lu 6:37 Ro 2:1 &
in your own eye? 4Or why do you say to your brother, Let me take the note (a).
speck out of your eye, and behold, there is a beam in your own eye?
5Hypocrite, first cast the beam out of your own eye, and then you will see
clearly to pluck the speck out of your brother's eye.

6Do not give that which is holy to dogs, nor cast your pearls before
swine, lest they tread them under their feet and then turn and tear you to
shreds.[a]

7Ask, and it will be given you. Seek, and you will find. Knock, and it Ja 1:5
will be opened to you. 8For whosoever asks, receives; and he who seeks,
finds; and to him who knocks, it will be opened. 9Is there anyone among
Covenants you who, if his son asked for bread, would offer him a stone? 10Or if he
asked for fish, would give him a serpent? 11If then you who are evil know
how to give good gifts to your children, how much more will your Father Lu 11:9-13
who is in heaven give good things to those who ask him?

Do unto others as you would have them do unto you. 12Therefore whatever you would have others do unto you, so do unto
them. This is the law and the prophets. Lu 6:31

13Enter in at the strait gate. For wide is the gate and broad is the way
that leads to destruction, and many there are who go in at it. 14But strait is
the gate and narrow is the way that leads to life, and few there are who
find it. 15Beware of false prophets, who come to you in sheep's clothing,
but inwardly they are ravening wolves.[b] 16You may know them by their
fruits. Do men gather grapes from thorns, or figs from thistles? 17Like-
wise every good tree brings forth good fruit, but a corrupt tree brings
forth bad fruit. 18A good tree cannot bring forth bad fruit, nor yet can a
bad tree bring forth good fruit. 19Every tree that does not bring forth good Lu 6:43-49
fruit shall be hewn down and cast into the fire. 20Therefore by their fruits
you may know them.

21Not all who say to me, Lord, Lord, will enter into the kingdom of
Not all who say, Lord, Lord heaven, but he who does the will of my Father who is in heaven. 22Many
will say to me in that day, Lord, Lord, have we not prophesied in your
name, and in your name have cast out devils, and in your name done
many miracles? 23And then I will declare to them that I never knew them. Lu 13:23-30 2Th c 2
Depart from me, ye workers of iniquity! Ps 6:8

24Whosoever hears these sayings of mine and does them, I will liken
him to a wise man who built his house on a rock.[c] 25And much rain
To build on rock or sand descended, and the floods came, and the winds blew and beat upon that Lu 6:46-49
same house; and it did not fall, because it was grounded on the rock.
26And whosoever hears these sayings of mine and does them not shall be
likened to a foolish man who built his house upon the sand. 27And much

rain descended, and the floods came, and the winds blew and beat upon
that house, and it fell. And great was the fall of it.
[28]And it came to pass that when Jesus had ended these sayings, the
people were astonished at his instruction. [29]For he taught them as one Mk 1:22
having power, and not as the scribes. Lu 4:32

The Notes

Of holy things, dogs, swine (7:6) a) This holy thing is the word of God. Dogs are those who persecute the word. By swine, understand those who wallow in the dirt, or fleshly lusts, and who do not regard the word. Philippians 3:2.

False prophets, ravening wolves (7:15) b) False prophets are preachers who pervert and twist the word of God. Acts 20:30. Sheep skins signify the appearance of outward holiness. Ravening wolves are tyrants who delight in persecution and in shedding innocent blood. Acts 20:29.

Building on rock (7:24) c) This similitude of building denotes the rearing up and instruction of people's consciences by the word of the law and the gospel.

Chapter 8

Christ cleanses the leper, heals the centurion's servant, heals many other diseases, helps Peter's mother-in-law, stills the sea and the wind, and drives the devils out of the possessed man into the swine.

When Jesus came down from the mountain, crowds of people followed
him. [2]And lo, a leper came and worshipped him, saying, Master, if you Mk 1:40-45
are willing, you can make me clean. [3]And Jesus put forth his hand and Lu 5:12-16
Miracles touched him, saying, I will; be clean! And immediately his leprosy was
cleansed. [4]And Jesus said to him, See that you tell no one, but go and
show yourself to the priest, and offer the gift that Moses commanded, in Lev 14:2
witness to them.
[5]When Jesus had entered into Capernaum, there came to him a certain Lu 7:2-10
Centurion: captain of a 'century', or a hundred men. centurion,* who besought him, [6]saying, Master, my servant lies sick at
home, paralyzed, and is grievously pained. [7]And Jesus said to him, I will
come and heal him. [8]The centurion answered and said, Sir, I am not
worthy that you should come under my roof. But speak the word only,
and my servant shall be healed. [9]For I also myself am a man subject to
the authority of another, and have soldiers under me. And I say to one,
Go! and he goes, and to another, Come! and he comes, and to my servant, Do this! and he does it.
[10]When Jesus heard that, he marvelled, and said to the people who
followed him, Truly I say to you, I have not found such great faith, no,
not in Israel. [11]I say therefore to you that many will come from the east
and west, and will rest with Abraham, Isaac, and Jacob in the kingdom of
heaven, [12]but the children of the kingdom shall be cast out into outer
Outer darkness. darkness; there will be weeping and gnashing of teeth.
[13]Then Jesus said to the centurion, Go your way, and as you believe,
so be it unto you. And his servant was healed that very same hour.
[14]And then Jesus went to Peter's house, and saw his wife's mother

lying sick of a fever, [15]and touched her hand, and the fever left her. And
she arose and ministered to them.
[16]When the evening was come, people brought to him many who
were possessed with devils. And he cast out the spirits with a word, and Mk 1:29-34 Lu 4:38-41
healed all who were sick, [17]to fulfil that which was spoken by Isaiah the Isa 53:4
prophet, saying, He took on him our infirmities, and bore our sicknesses.
[18]When Jesus saw crowds of people around him, he directed to go
over the water. [19]And a scribe came and said to him, Teacher, I will
follow you wherever you go. [20]And Jesus said to him, The foxes have
holes, and the birds of the air have nests, but the Son of man has nowhere Lu 9:57-62
to rest his head.[a] [21]Another, who was one of his disciples, said to him,
Master, first allow me to go and bury my father. [22]But Jesus said to him,
Follow me, and let the dead bury their own dead.
[23]And he entered into a boat, and his disciples followed him. [24]And
behold, there arose a great tempest in the sea, insomuch that the vessel
was swamped with waves. And he was asleep. [25]And his disciples came
Jesus sleeps in the boat — to him and awoke him, saying, Master, save us! We perish! [26]And he said Mk 4:35-41 Lu 8:22-25
to them, Why are you fearful, O ye of little faith? Then he arose and
rebuked the winds and the sea, and there followed a great calm. [27]And the
men marvelled and said, What man is this, that both winds and sea obey
him?
[28]When Jesus had come to the other side, into the country of the
[**The Gergesenes** (or Gadarenes, as in Mk 5 and Luke 8) lived on the south eastern side of Lake Galilee]
Gergesenes,[*] two men possessed by devils met him, coming out from
among the graves. They were out of measure fierce, so that no one could Mk 5:1-20 Lu 8:26-39
pass by that way. [29]And behold, they cried out, saying, O Jesus, Son of
God, what have we to do with you? Have you come here to torment us
before the time be come?
[30]And a good way off from them there was a great herd of swine
feeding. [31]Then the devils besought him, saying, If you cast us out, let us
go our way into the herd of swine. [32]And he said to them, Go your ways.
Then they went out and dispersed into the herd of swine. And behold, the
whole herd of swine was carried with violence headlong into the sea, and
perished in the water.
[33]Then the herdsmen fled, and went their ways into the town and told
everything, and what had happened to the men possessed by the devils.
[34]And all the town came out and met Jesus. And when they saw him, they
besought him to depart from their shores.

The Notes

Son of man (8:20) — a) Christ calls himself the Son of man; that is, very natural man [having taken human flesh], showing in this his humility and goodness, having humbled himself so low for our salvation.

Chapter 9

Jesus heals the paralytic, calls Matthew from receipt of custom, answers for his disciples, heals the woman with the issue of blood, helps Jairas' daughter, gives two blind men their sight, and by driving out a devil makes a dumb man to speak.

[**Own city**: He returned to Capernaum, which was a centre of trade and government business on the north-western side of Lake Galilee]

Mk 2:1-12
Lu 5:17-26

Then Jesus entered into a boat, and passed over and went into his own city.* [2]And lo, they brought to him a paralyzed man lying in his bed. And when Jesus saw their faith he said to the paralytic, Son, be of good cheer; your sins are forgiven you. [3]And certain of the scribes said in themselves, This man blasphemes.

*This miracle shall be a sign to you that I have power to forgive sins

[4]When Jesus saw their thoughts, he said, Why do you think evil in your hearts? [5]Which is easier to say: Your sins are forgiven you, or to say, Arise and walk? [6]But so that you may know that the Son of man has power to forgive sins in earth*–

Then he said to the paralytic, Arise, take up your bed, and go home to your house. [7]And the man arose and departed to his own house. [8]And when the people saw it, they marvelled, and glorified God who had given such power to men.

Matthew [**Custom**: a toll or tax levied on commodities on their way to market, nowadays levied only on imported goods]

[9]And as Jesus passed onwards from there, he saw a man named Matthew sitting at receipt of custom,* and said to him, Follow me. And he arose and followed him.

Publicans eat with Jesus.

[10]And it came to pass, as he sat at food in Matthew's house, that many publicans and sinners came and sat down also with Jesus and his disciples. [11]When the Pharisees saw this, they said to his disciples, Why does your teacher eat with publicans and sinners?

Mercy and not sacrifice.

Mk 2:17
Lu 5:31
Ps 40:6
Ho 6:6
Mic 6:6-8

[12]When Jesus heard this, he said to them, The whole do not need the physician, but they that are sick. [13]Go and learn what this means: I have pleasure in mercy, and not in offering. For I have not come to call the righteous, but sinners, to repentance.

New and old do not agree.
[**New cloth**, etc: See explanations at Mark 2:21,22]

[14]Then John's disciples came to him, asking, Why do we and the Pharisees fast often, but your disciples do not fast? [15]And Jesus said to them, Can the wedding children mourn as long as the bridegroom is with them? The time will come when the bridegroom shall be taken from them, and then they will fast. [16]No one patches an old garment with a piece of new cloth. For then the new piece pulls away from the garment,* and the tear is made greater. [17]Neither do men put new wine into old wineskins, for then the skins burst, the wine runs out, and the vessels are destroyed. But they pour new wine into new wineskins, and so both are preserved together.

Mk c5
Lu 8:40-56

[18]While he was thus speaking to them, a certain leader came and did reverence to him, saying, My daughter is even now deceased. But come and lay your hand on her, and she will live. [19]And Jesus arose and followed him with his disciples.

[20]And behold, a woman who had been diseased for 12 years with an issue of blood came up behind him and touched the hem of his vesture. [21]For she said in herself, If I may touch but even his vesture only, I will be healed. [22]Then Jesus, turning about and seeing her, said, Daughter, be of good comfort; your faith has made you whole.[a] And she was healed

even that same hour.
[23]And when Jesus came into the leader's house and saw the minstrels
and the people making a noise [24]he said to them, All of you, go away, for
the girl is not dead, but sleeping. And they laughed him to scorn. [25]But as
soon as the people were put outside, he went in and took her by the hand,
and the girl arose. [26]And news of this spread throughout all that land.
[27]And as Jesus departed from there, two blind men followed him,
crying out and saying, O Son of David, have mercy on us! [28]And when
he had gone indoors, the blind men came to him. And Jesus said to them,
Do you believe that I am able to do this? And they said to him, Yes,
Two blind men are cured. Lord. [29]Then he touched their eyes, saying, According to your faith, be it
unto you. [30]And their eyes were opened. And Jesus charged them, saying,
See that no one knows of this. [31]But they, as soon as they had left, spread
abroad his name throughout all the land.
[32]As they went out, behold, people brought to him a dumb man, Mk 7:31-37
The dumb man is delivered. possessed by a devil. [33]And as soon as the devil was cast out, the mute Lu 11:14-23
spoke. And the people marvelled, saying, Never have such things been
Jesus is accused seen in Israel! [34]But the Pharisees said, He casts out devils by the power M't 12:24
of the chief devil.
[35]And Jesus went about all the towns and villages, teaching in their
synagogues and preaching the glad tidings of the kingdom, and healing
all manner of sickness and disease among the people.
[36]But when he saw the people, he had compassion on them, because Zec 10:2
they were worn and weak and scattered abroad, even as sheep having no
shepherd. [37]Then he said to his disciples, The harvest is great, but the
labourers are few.[b] [38]Therefore pray the Lord of the harvest to send forth
labourers into his harvest.

The Notes

Your faith has made you whole (9:22)

a) Faith is the righteousness of a Christian, which sets the conscience at peace and receives the everlasting inheritance (Galatians 4:4-7).

The harvest (9:37-38)

b) The harvest is the hearts of men prepared to hear the word, as it appears of the Samaritans (John 4:1-42).

Chapter 10

Christ sends out his twelve apostles to preach among the Jews, gives them charge, teaches them, and strengthens them against persecution and trouble.

And Jesus called his 12 disciples to him, and gave them power over Mk 3:13-19; 6:7-13. Lu 6:12-16
The apostles are sent unclean spirits, to cast them out, and to heal all manner of sicknesses and
all manner of diseases.
[2]The names of the 12 apostles are these: the first Simon, called also
Peter, and Andrew his brother; James the son of Zebedee, and John his
brother; [3]Philip and Bartholomew; Thomas, and Matthew the publican;
James the son of Alphaeus, and Lebbaeus otherwise called Thaddaeus;
[4]Simon the Canaanite; and Judas Iscariot, who also betrayed him.

[5]These twelve Jesus sent out and charged, saying, Go not into the roads that lead to the Gentiles, and do not enter into the towns of the Samaritans. [6]But go rather to the lost sheep of the house of Israel. [7]Go and preach, saying, The kingdom of heaven is at hand! [8]Heal the sick, cleanse the lepers, raise the dead, cast out the devils. Freely you have received; freely give again.*

Lu 9:1-6

[**Freely**: without payment]

*__Brass__: that is, money of brass.

[9]Do not possess gold or silver, nor brass* in your belts, [10]nor yet a bag for your journey; neither two coats, nor shoes, nor yet a staff. For the workman is worthy to have his keep. [11]In whatever city or town you enter, enquire who is worthy in it, and there remain till you leave. [12]And when you come into a household, wish it well. [13]And if the house is worthy, your peace will come upon it. But if it is not worthy, your peace will return to you again.

[14]And whoever will not receive you, nor will hear your preaching, when you depart out of that house or that town, shake off the dust from your feet. [15]Truly I say to you, it will be easier for the land of Sodom and Gomorrah in the day of judgment than for that place.

Ge 18:16-33; 19:1-28.

Sheep among wolves.

Wise as serpents and innocent as doves.

[16]Behold, I send you forth as sheep among wolves. Be therefore wise as serpents and innocent as doves. [17]Beware of men, for they will deliver you up to the councils, and will scourge you in their synagogues. [18]And you will be brought to the head governors and kings for my sake, in witness to them and to the Gentiles.

The Spirit speaks in us.

[19]But when they deliver you up, do not be anxious about how or what you will speak, for it will be given you even in that same hour what you should say. [20]For it is not you who speak, but the Spirit of your Father who speaks in you.

[21]Brother will betray brother to death, and the father the son. And children will arise against their fathers and mothers, and will put them to death. [22]And you will be hated by all men for my name. But he who endures to the end shall be saved. [23]When they persecute you in one place, flee into another. I tell you for a truth, you will not finish all the cities of Israel before the Son of man comes.

M't 9:34; 12:24.

Lu 12:1-7

[**Opened**: revealed, brought to light. The Gk *apokalupto* (601) means to take off the cover]

[24]The disciple is not above his teacher, nor yet the servant above his lord. [25]It is enough for the disciple to be as his teacher is, and that the servant be as his lord is. If they have called the Lord of the house Beelzebub, how much more will they call those of his household so?[a] [26]Fear them not therefore. There is nothing so closed that it will not be opened,* and nothing so hid that it will not be known.

[27]What I tell you in darkness, that speak in light. And what you hear in the ear, that preach on the house tops. [28]And fear not those who kill the body, and are not able to kill the soul. But rather fear him who is able to destroy both soul and body into hell. [29]Are not two sparrows sold for a copper coin? And yet none of them lights on the ground without your Father. [30]And now all the hairs of your heads are numbered. [31]Fear not therefore: you are of more value than many sparrows.

Confess

[32]Whosoever therefore acknowledges me before men, him will I

acknowledge also before my Father who is in heaven. [33]But whosoever
denies me before men, him will I also deny before my Father who is in
heaven.

[34]Think not that I have come to send peace into the earth. I came not
Not peace, but a sword — to send peace, but a sword. [35]For I have come to set a man at variance
against his father, and the daughter against her mother, and the daughter-
in-law against her mother-in-law. [36]And a man's enemies will be those of — Mic 7:6
his own household.

[37]He who loves his father or mother more than me, is not meet for
me. And he who loves his son or daughter more than me, is not meet for
me. [38]And he who does not take up his cross and follow me, is not meet — Lu 17:33 Joh 12:25
for me. [39]He who finds his life will lose it,[b] and he who loses his life for
my sake, will find it.

[40]He who receives you receives me, and he who receives me, receives
him who sent me. [41]He who receives a prophet in the name of a prophet — Mk 9:41
will receive a prophet's reward. And he who receives a righteous man in
the name of a righteous man, will receive the reward of a righteous man.
[42]And whosoever gives one of these little ones to drink a cup of cold
water only in the name of a disciple, I tell you of a truth, he shall not lose
his reward.

The Notes

Beelzebub (10:25) — a) *Beelzebub*, after the idol Bel, or Baal, is a name by which the Jews called Satan. It means master, or lord, of a fly [or, of the flies. Some say the name is due to the multitude of flies that swarmed to the wine and blood shed in sacrifices to Baal.]

Who finds his life (10:39) — b) To find his life is to satisfy the desire of his heart.

Chapter 11

John the Baptist sends his disciples to Christ, who gives them their answer. He rebukes the unthankful cities, and lovingly exhorts people to take his yoke upon them.

[**Their towns**: that is, in the region of Galilee]

And when Jesus had made an end of instructing his twelve disciples, he
went on from there to teach and to preach in their towns.[*]

[2]When John, being in prison, heard about the works of Christ, he sent
two of his disciples [3]and asked him, Are you he that was to come, or
should we look for another? [4]Jesus answered and said to them, Go and — Lu 7:18-23
tell John what you have heard and seen: [5]the blind see, the lame walk, the
lepers are cleansed, the deaf hear, the dead rise up again, and the glad
tidings are preached to the poor. [6]And blessed is the person who is not — Isa c60
offended by me.[*]

[**Offended by me**: see note (a) to Luke c7]

[7]And as they departed, Jesus began to speak to the people about John:
What did you go out into the wilderness to see? Did you go to see a reed
shaken with the wind?[a] [8]Or what did you go out to see? A man clothed in
soft raiment? Behold, they that wear soft clothing are in king's houses.
[9]But what did you go out to see? A prophet? Yes, I say to you, and more
than a prophet. [10]For this is he of whom it is written: Behold, I send my — Isa 40:3

messenger before your face, who shall prepare your way before you. Mal 3:1; 4:5. Mk 1:1-9 Lu 7:24-28
11Truly I say to you, among the children of women none greater than
John the Baptist has arisen. Notwithstanding, he who is less in the king-
dom of heaven, is greater than he.*

*Christ, who humbled himself to the cross, was less.

12From the time of John the Baptist to now, the kingdom of heaven is
sorely pressed, and those who go to it with effort seize it for themselves. Lu 16:16
13For all the prophets and the law prophesied with a view to the time of
John. 14And also, if you will receive it, this is Elijah who was to come.
15He who has ears to hear, let him hear.

16But to what can I liken this generation? It is like children who sit in
the market and call to their fellows, 17and say, We have piped to you, and
you have not danced; we have mourned to you, and you have not
sorrowed.[b] 18For John came neither eating nor drinking, and they say he Lu 7:29-35
has the devil. 19The Son of man came eating and drinking, and they say,
Here is a glutton and drinker of wine, and a friend of publicans and
sinners! Nevertheless, wisdom is justified by her children.[c]

Wisdom is justified by her children.

20Then Jesus began to upbraid the places in which most of his mir-
acles had been done, because they did not turn: 21Woe to you, Chorazin!
Woe to you, Bethsaida! For if the miracles that were shown in you had
been done in Tyre and Sidon, they would have repented long ago in Lu 10:13-16
sackcloth and ashes. 22But I say to you, it will be easier for Tyre and
Sidon at the day of judgment than for you. 23And you Capernaum, who
are lifted up to heaven, shall be brought down to hell. For if the miracles
which have been done in you had been shown in Sodom, it would have
remained to this day. 24But I say to you, it will be easier for the land of
Sodom in the day of judgment than for you.

25At that time Jesus concluded and said, I praise you, O Father, Lord
of heaven and earth, because you have hid these things from the wise and Lu 10:21-24
learned, and have revealed them to babes; 26Even so, Father, for so it
pleased you.

The wise knew not. Babes knew.

27All things are given to me by my Father. And no one knows the Son
but the Father; nor does anyone know the Father except the Son, and the
person to whom the Son will reveal him.

28Come unto me, all ye that labour and are heavy-laden,[d] and I will
give you rest. 29Take my yoke upon you, and learn from me, for I am
gentle and lowly in heart, and you will find rest for your souls. 30For my
yoke is easy, and my burden is light.

Gentle yoke

The Notes

A shaken reed (11:7) a) This is a figure of the doctrine that is not of God, which waves with every wind.

Piped to you (11:17) b) Here is a saying like that given at Isaiah 26:1-6, meaning, in different ways we have gone about to stir you to thanksgiving, but you have by no means been moved thereto. [The Isaiah reference is to 'Esa xxvi.a' in the 1549 MB. Ed]

Wisdom is justified by her children (11:19) c) That is, those who are the children of God receive his doctrine and his word as truth and wisdom, although the contrary part do not so receive it.

You who labour (11:28) d) Those who acknowledge their sins and are poor in spirit are here considered as labouring and heavy-laden.

Chapter 12

The disciples pluck the ears of grain. He defends them, heals the withered hand, helps the possessed man who was blind and dumb, rebukes the unfaithful who insist on having signs, and shows who are his brother, sister, and mother.

At that time Jesus went through the grain on the Sabbath days. And his
disciples were hungry, and began to pluck the ears of grain and to eat.
2When the Pharisees saw that, they said to him, Look, your disciples are Mk 2:23-28 Lu 6:1-5
doing that which is not lawful to do on the Sabbath day. 3He said to them,
Have you not read what David did when he was hungry, and those also
who were with him? 4How he entered into the house of God and ate the
hallowed loaves,* which were not lawful for him to eat, neither for those 1Sam 21:1-6
who were with him, but only for the priests? 5Or have you not read in the
law how the priests in the temple break the Sabbath day, and yet are
blameless? 6But I say to you that there is one here greater than the
temple. 7 So then if you had known what this means: I require mercy, and
not sacrifice – you would never have condemned the innocent. 8For the
Son of man is Lord even of the Sabbath day. Ho 6:6

[**Hallowed loaves**: consecrated holy bread under Mosaic law. Others have here showbread, bread of the presence, consecrated loaves, or loaves of presentation]

Mercy and not sacrifice.

9And he departed from there and went into their synagogue. 10And
behold, there was a man there who had a withered hand. And they asked Mk 3:1-6
him, saying, Is it lawful to heal on the Sabbath days? in order that they Lu 6:6-11
might accuse him. 11And he said to them, Which of you would it be, if he
had a sheep fallen into a pit on the Sabbath day, that would not take it
and lift it out? 12And of how much more value is a man than a sheep?
Therefore it is lawful to do a good deed on the Sabbath days.

Sabbath deeds

13Then he said to the man, Stretch forth your hand. And he stretched
it forth. And it was made whole again like the other.

14Then the Pharisees went out and held a council against him, how
they might destroy him. 15When Jesus knew that, he departed from there.
And crowds of people followed him. And he healed them all, 16and
charged them not to make him known, 17to fulfil that which was spoken
by Isaiah the prophet, who says: 18Behold my child, whom I have chosen,
my beloved in whom my soul delights. I will put my Spirit on him, and Isa 42:1-4
he shall show judgment to the Gentiles. 19He will not strive;* he will not
cry out; neither will anyone hear his voice in the streets. 20A bruised reed
he will not break, and a flax that begins to burn he will not quench, till he
sends forth judgment unto victory. 21And in his name shall the Gentiles
trust.

[**Strive**: the Gk *erizo* (2051) means to wrangle, to engage in argument]

22Then was brought to him one who was possessed with a devil, who
was both blind and dumb. And Jesus healed him, so that he who had been
blind and dumb both spoke and saw. 23And all the people were amazed Lu 11:14-23
and said, Is not this the Son of David? 24But when the Pharisees heard
that, they said, This fellow drives the devils out no other way but by the
help of Beelzebub, the chief of the devils.

Blind and dumb

25But Jesus knew their thoughts and said to them, Every kingdom
divided within itself will be brought to nothing. Neither can any city or

household divided against itself continue. 26So if Satan casts out Satan, then he is divided against himself. How then shall his kingdom endure? 27Also, if I by the help of Beelzebub cast out devils, by whose help do your children cast them out? Therefore they will be your judges. 28But if I cast out the devils by the Spirit of God, then the kingdom of God has come upon you.

Mk 3:22-30 Lu 11:14-19; 12:8-10.

29Or again, how can a man enter into a strong man's house and forcibly take away his goods, unless he first binds the strong man? And then he plunders his house. 30He who is not with me, is against me, and he who does not gather with me, scatters abroad.

Blasphemy unforgivable

31So I say to you, all manner of sin and blasphemy may be forgiven men, but the blasphemy of the Spirit will not be forgiven men.[a] 32And whosoever speaks a word against the Son of man, it may be forgiven him, but whosoever speaks against the Holy Spirit, it may not be forgiven him – no, neither in this world, nor in the world to come.[b] 33Either judge the tree good, and its fruit correspondingly good, or else judge the tree evil, and its fruit evil also. For the tree is known by its fruit.

See Heb 10:26 & note (a) thereon.

Offspring of vipers.

34O offspring of vipers, how can you speak good things when you yourselves are evil? For out of the abundance of the heart, the mouth speaks. 35A good man, out of the good treasure of his heart, brings forth good things. And an evil man, out of his evil treasure, brings forth evil things. 36But I say to you that for every idle word that men speak, they will give account at the day of judgment. 37For by your words you will be justified, and by your words you will be condemned.

Lu 6:43-45

Idle words

38Then certain of the scribes and Pharisees answered, saying, Teacher, we would like to see a sign from you. 39He answered and said to them, The evil and adulterous generation[c] seeks a sign, but there shall be no sign given to them except the sign of the prophet Jonah. 40For as Jonah was three days and three nights in the whale's belly, so shall the Son of man be three days and three nights in the heart of the earth. 41The people of Nineveh will rise at the day of judgment with this nation and condemn it, for they reformed at the preaching of Jonah, and behold, one greater than Jonah is here. 42The queen of the south will rise at the day of judgment with this generation and will condemn them, for she came from the furthermost parts of the world to hear the wisdom of Solomon, and behold, one greater than Solomon is here.

An adulterous generation seeks miracles and wonders.

Jon 1:17; 3:5-10. 1Ki 10:1-13 2Ch 9:1-12 Lu 11:29-32

43But when the unclean spirit has gone out of a man, he walks throughout dry places, seeking rest, and finds none. 44Then he says, I will return again into my house, the one I came out of. And when he comes back, he finds the house empty and swept and set in order. 45Then he goes his way and gets seven other spirits worse than himself, and so they enter in and dwell there. And the end of that man is worse than the beginning. That is how it will be with this evil nation.

Lu 11:24-26

46When Jesus was still speaking to the people, his mother and his brethren stood outside, desiring to speak with him. 47Then someone said to him, Look, your mother and your brethren are standing outside, and

Lu 8:19-21

want to speak with you. [48]He answered and said to the one that had told
him, Who is my mother? or who are my brethren? [49]And he stretched
Jesus' family forth his hand over his disciples and said, Behold my mother and my
brethren. [50]For whosoever does the will of my Father who is in heaven,
the same is my brother, sister, and mother.

The Notes

Blasphemy against the Spirit (12:31) a) This blasphemy is when people see and know the open and manifest truth of God and his word, their consciences being fully persuaded, and yet denounce it and persecute it, even to the utmost of their power, and say it is of the devil and not God.

Not in this or the next (12:32) b) Not in this world or the next: that is, never, as Saint Mark does well expound it at Mark 3:28-30.

An evil generation (12:39) c) An evil and adulterous generation is all those that do not believe in God and in his Son Jesus Christ (Mark 9:19; Luke 9:41).

Chapter 13

The parables of the seed, of the tares, of the mustard seed, of the leaven, of the treasure hid in the field, of the pearls, and of the net.

The same day, Jesus went out of the house and sat by the sea side. [2]And
crowds of people gathered to him, so greatly that he went and sat in a Mk 4:1 Lu 5:1-5
boat, and all the people stood on the shore. [3]And he spoke many things to
The parable of the sower. them in similitudes, saying, Behold, the sower went forth to sow. [4]And as
he sowed, some seed fell by the wayside, and the birds came and
devoured it up. [5]Some fell on stony ground where it had not much earth,
and it sprang up quickly, because it had no depth of earth; [6]and when the
sun was up, it caught heat, and for lack of rooting withered away. [7]Some Mk 4:2-20
fell among thorns, and the thorns sprang up and choked it. [8]But part fell Lu 8:4-15
in good ground, and brought forth good fruit: some a hundredfold, some
sixtyfold, some thirtyfold. [9]Whosoever has ears to hear, let him hear!

[10]And the disciples came and asked him, Why do you speak to them
in parables? [11]He answered and said to them, It is given to you to know Mk 4:21-25 Lu 8:16-18
the secrets of the kingdom of heaven, but to them it is not given. [12]For
whosoever has, to him will be given, and he will have abundance. But
Covenants whosoever has not, from him shall be taken away even what he has.[a]
[13]Therefore I speak to them in similitudes. For though they see, they see
not. And hearing, they hear not, neither understand. [14]And in them is
fulfilled the prophecy of Isaiah, which prophecy says: With the ears you Isa 6:8-10 Mk 4:11,12
will hear, but will not understand, and with the eyes you will see, and Lu 8:10
will not perceive. [15]For the hearts of this people have grown dull, and Joh 12:37-41 Ac 28:15-27
their ears are hard of hearing, and their eyes they have closed, lest they Ro 11:7-10
should see with their eyes and hear with their ears and understand with
their hearts, and should turn, so that I might heal them.

[16]But blessed are your eyes, for they see, and your ears, for they hear.
[17]Truly I say to you that many prophets and righteous men have desired Lu 10:23,24
to see those things that you see, and have not seen them, and to hear

those things that you hear, and have not heard them.
18 Hear therefore the similitude of the sower. 19 Whosoever hears the
The parable of the sower explained.
word of the kingdom and does not understand it,[b] there comes the evil
one, and catches away that which was sown in his heart; and this is he
who received the seed by the wayside. 20 But he who received the seed in
the stony ground is the person who hears the word of God, and at once
receives it with joy. 21 Yet he has no roots in himself, and therefore
endures but a season, for as soon as tribulation or persecution arises
because of the word, at once he falls. 22 He who received the seed among
thorns is the person who hears the word of God, but the care of this world
and the deceitfulness of riches choke the word, and so he is made
unfruitful. 23 But he who receives the seed in good ground is the person
who hears the word and understands it; who also bears fruit and brings
forth, some a hundredfold, some sixtyfold, and some thirtyfold.

Wheat and tares [**Tares**: probably meaning the poisonous seeds of darnel, a weed that looks like wheat in its early stages]

24 Another similitude he put forth to them, saying, The kingdom of
heaven is like a man who sowed good seed in his field. 25 But while
people were sleeping,[c] his enemy came and sowed tares[*] among the
wheat, and went his way. 26 When the blade had sprung up and had
brought forth fruit, then the tares appeared also. 27 Then the servants went
to the householder and said to him, Sir, did you not sow good seed in
your field? Where then did the tares come from? 28 He said to them, The
envious man has done this. Then the servants said to him, Do you want
us then to go and weed them out? 29 But he said, Nay, lest while you go
about to weed out the tares, you pluck up also with them the wheat by the
roots. 30 Let both grow together till harvest comes. And in the time of
harvest I will say to the reapers, Gather the tares first, and bind them in
sheaves to be burned; but gather the wheat into my barn.
31 Another parable he put forth to them, saying, The kingdom of
heaven is like a grain of mustard seed that a man takes and sows in his Mk 4:30-32 Lu 13:18,19
field, 32 which is the least of all seeds. But when it is grown, it is the
greatest among shrubs; and it is a tree, so that the birds of the air come
and build in its branches.
33 He told them another similitude: The kingdom of heaven is like Lu 13:20,21
leaven that a woman takes and hides in three measures of meal, till all is
leavened.
34 All these things Jesus spoke to the people by similitudes. And he
spoke nothing to them without similitudes, 35 to fulfil that which was Mk 4:33,34 Ps 78:2 Eph 3:9
spoken by the prophet, saying, I will open my mouth in similitudes, and
will speak forth things which have been kept secret from the beginning of
the world.
36 Then Jesus sent the people away and went indoors. And his dis-
ciples came to him, saying, Explain to us the similitude of the tares of the
The parable of the tares explained.
field. 37 Then he answered and said to them, He who sows the good seed
is the Son of man. 38 And the field is the world. And the children of the
kingdom, they are the good seed. And the tares are the children of the
wicked one: 39 the enemy who sows them is the devil. The harvest is the

end of the world, and the reapers are the angels. [40]For even as the tares Rev 14:15
are gathered and burned in the fire, so shall it be in the end of this world.
[41]The Son of man will send forth his angels, and they will gather out of
his kingdom all injurious things, and those who do iniquity, [42]and will
cast them into a furnace of fire. There shall be wailing and gnashing of
teeth. [43]Then shall the just shine as bright as the sun in the kingdom of
their Father. Whoever has ears to hear, let him hear!

[44]Again, the kingdom of heaven is like treasure hid in a field, which a Ps 119:162
person finds and hides, and for the joy of it goes and sells all that he has
and buys that field.

[45]Again, the kingdom of heaven is like a merchant who seeks good
pearls, [46]who, when he found one precious pearl, went and sold all that
he had and bought it.

[47]Again, the kingdom of heaven is like a net cast into the sea, which
Net cast into the sea. gathers in all kinds of fishes. [48]When it is full, men draw it to land, and
sit and gather the good into vessels, and cast the bad away. [49]So shall it
be at the end of the world: the angels will come out and separate the bad
from the good, [50]and will cast them into a furnace of fire. There will be
wailing and gnashing of teeth.

[51]Jesus asked them, Do you understand all these things? They said,
Yes, Lord. [52]Then he said to them, Therefore every scribe[d] who is in-
structed in the kingdom of heaven is like a householder who brings forth
out of his treasure things both new and old.

[53]And it came to pass, when Jesus had finished these similitudes, that
[**Own country**: Nazareth and its vicinity] he departed from there, [54]and went into his own country.* And he taught Mk 6:1-6 Lu 4:16-30 Joh 4:43,44
the people in their synagogues, insomuch that they were astonished and
said, Whence comes all this wisdom and power to him? [55]Is this not the
carpenter's son? Is his mother not called Mary? and his brethren James,
Joses, Simon, and Judas? [56]Are his sisters not all here with us? Where
does he have all these things from? [57]And they were offended by him.

A prophet is without honour among his own. Then Jesus said to them, A prophet is not without honour, save in his
own country and among his own kin.

[58]And he did not do many miracles there, because of their unbelief.

The Notes

More will be given (13:12) a) That is, to him that has a good heart toward God's word, to fulfil it, more grace will be given. And from him who does not have such a heart will be taken away even what knowledge he has, and his heart so hardened that he will not repent. [Tyndale> Here is a covenant to those who love the word of God, to further it so that they progress in it, and another to those who do not love it, that they will lose it and grow blind.]

The word of the kingdom (13:19) b) *Kingdom* signifies here the gospel, by which God reigns in the hearts of the faithful; and the same signifies Christ, who is our king and our kingdom reigning in us, and in whom we reign as we pray (Mathew 6:9-13).

People sleeping (13:25) c) This sleep signifies the negligence toward God and ignorance of him that people have, which come through concern for riches and the pleasures of this world.

Scribes (13:52) d) According to Erasmus in his annotations, a scribe was responsible to interpret the sayings of the prophets, as it appears in chapter 2 where Herod made enquiries of them.

Chapter 14

John is taken and beheaded. Christ feeds 5,000 men with five loaves and two fishes, and appears to his disciples by night upon the lake.

At that time Herod the tetrarch[a] heard of the fame of Jesus 2and said to
his servants, This is John the Baptist; he is risen again from death, and
therefore are such miracles wrought by him! 3For Herod had seized John,
John the Baptist is imprisoned
and bound him and put him in prison for the sake of Herodias, his brother
Philip's wife. 4For John said to him, It is not lawful for you to have her. Mk 6:14-29
5But when Herod would have put him to death, he feared the people, Lu 3:19,20; 9:7-9.
because they counted John as a prophet.

6But when Herod's birthday came, the daughter of Herodias danced
before them, and pleased Herod, 7whereupon he promised with an oath
that he would give her whatever she would ask. 8And she, being first
instructed by her mother, said, Give me here the head of John the Baptist
on a platter.

9And the king sorrowed. Nevertheless, because of his oath, and be-
cause of the people who were sitting also at the table, he commanded it to
John the Baptist is beheaded
be given her. 10And he sent and beheaded John in the prison. 11And his
head was brought on a platter and given to the girl, and she brought it to
her mother. 12And his disciples came and took up his body and buried it,
and went and told Jesus.

13When Jesus heard about this, he withdrew from there by boat into
an isolated place out of the way. But when the people heard of it, they Mk 6:30-44 Lu 9:10-17
followed him by foot out of their towns. 14And Jesus went forth and saw Joh 6:1-14
crowds of people, and his heart did melt upon them. And he healed
among them those that were sick.

15When evening was come, his disciples went to him, saying, This is
an isolated place, and the day is spent. Let the people depart so that they
can go into the towns and buy themselves some food. 16But Jesus said to
them, They have no need to go away; you give them to eat. 17Then they
5 loaves and 2 fishes
said to him, We have here only five loaves and two fishes. 18And he said,
Bring them here.

19And he directed the people to sit down on the grass, took the five
loaves and the two fishes, and looked up to heaven, and blessed, and
broke and gave the loaves to his disciples, and the disciples gave them to
the people. 20And they did all eat, and were satisfied. And of the pieces
that remained, they gathered twelve baskets full. 21And the men that had
eaten were in number about 5,000, as well as women and children.

22Directly after, Jesus got his disciples to get into a boat, and to go
over before him while he sent the people away. 23And as soon as he had
sent the people away, he went up into a mountain alone to pray. And
when night was come, he was there himself alone. 24And the boat was Mk 6:45-52
now in the middle of the sea, and was tossed with waves, for it was a Joh 6:16-21
contrary wind.

25In the fourth watch of the night[b] Jesus went out to them, walking on

the sea. [26]And when his disciples saw him walking on the water, they
Jesus walks on water — were troubled, saying, It is some spirit! And they cried out for fear. [27]And
straightaway Jesus spoke to them, saying, Be of good cheer, it is I. Be not
afraid. [28]Peter answered him and said, Master, if it is you, get me to come
to you on the water. [29]And he said, Come!

And when Peter had gone down out of the boat, he walked on the
water to go to Jesus. [30]But when he saw a mighty wind, he was afraid.
And as he began to sink he cried out, saying, Master, save me! [31]And
immediately Jesus stretched forth his hand and caught him, and said to
him, O you of little faith, why did you doubt? [32]And as soon as they were
in the boat, the wind ceased. [33]Then the men in the boat came and wor-
shipped him, saying, Of a truth, you are the Son of God.

[34]And when they had crossed over, they went into the land of
Gennesaret. [35]When the men of that place learned of him, they sent out
into all the area round about, and brought to him all that were sick, [36]and
asked him if they might touch the hem of his vesture only. And as many
as touched it were made well.

The Notes

Herod the tetrarch (14:1)

a) *Tetrarch* means lord of a fourth part; here, of the land of Judah, which was divided into four parts, as says Eusebius in Book 2, chapter 10. [Ed: The tetrarch Herod was known as Herod Antipas, and was a son of King Herod the Great (M't 2). During Jesus' adult ministry, Herod Antipas was tetrarch of Galilee, and also of Perea, an area which lay across the Jordan. He had inherited rule over these lands from his late father the king. But John the Baptist had said publicly that it was wrong for the tetrarch to have taken Herodias as a wife. She was not only the daughter of his half-brother Aristobulus, but was the wife of his half-brother Philip, who was still alive. Therefore when Herod married Herodias, he added taking a brother's wife (Lev 18:16) and incest (Lev 18:14) to the sin of adultery.]

Fourth watch (14:25)

b) The Hebrews divided the night in four parts called the four watches. The 4th watch was next to the morning and was called the morning watch, as at 1Sa 11:11.

Chapter 15

Christ defends his disciples, and rebukes the scribes and Pharisees for transgressing God's commandments through their own precepts. What goes into the mouth does not defile a man. He delivers the Canaanite woman's daughter, heals the multitude, and with seven loaves and a few little fishes feeds 4,000 men, as well as women and children.

Then scribes and Pharisees from Jerusalem came to Jesus, saying, [2]Why
do your disciples transgress the precepts of the elders? For they do not
wash their hands when they eat bread. [3]He answered and said to them,
And why do you transgress the commandment of God through your
precepts? [4]For God commanded, saying, Honour your father and mother, — Mk 7:1-13
and, He who curses father or mother shall suffer death. [5]But you say — Ex 20:12; 21:17.
every man should tell his father or mother, That which you desire of me, — De 5:16
to help you with, is given for God – [6]and so he should not honour his — Lev 20:9 Pr 20:20
father or mother. And thus you have made the commandment of God to — Eph 6:1-3

be without effect, through your precepts. 7 Hypocrites, well did Isaiah
prophesy of you, saying, 8 This people draws near to me with their Isa 29:13
mouths, and honours me with their lips, but their hearts are far from me.
9 And in vain they worship me, teaching doctrines which are nothing but
men's precepts.

10 And he called the people to him and said to them, Hear and under- Mk 7:14-23
What defiles a person stand: 11 that which goes into the mouth does not defile a man, but that Lu 6:45
which comes out of the mouth defiles a man.

12 Then his disciples came and said to him, Do you perceive how the
Pharisees are offended in hearing this saying? 13 He answered and said,
All plants that my heavenly Father has not planted[a] shall be plucked up
Blind leaders by the roots. 14 Let them alone. They are the blind leaders of the blind. If
the blind lead the blind, both will fall into the ditch.

15 Then Peter answered and said to him, Explain the parable to us.
16 Jesus said, Are you still without understanding? 17 Do you not see that
whatever goes in at the mouth descends down into the stomach, and is
cast out into the drain? 18 But those things which proceed out of the mouth
come from the heart, and they defile the person. 19 For out of the heart
come evil thoughts, murder, breaking of wedlock, whoredom, theft,
[**Blasphemy**, in early modern English, could mean both the vilification of God and people] bearing of false witness, blasphemy.[*] 20 These are the things that defile a
person. But to eat with unwashed hands does not defile a person.

21 And Jesus went from there, and withdrew to the coasts of Tyre and Mk 7:24-30
Sidon. 22 And a woman who was a Canaanite came out of the same region
and cried out to him, saying, Have mercy on me, Lord Son of David! My
daughter is piteously vexed with a devil. 23 But he gave her never a word
in answer. Then his disciples came to him and urged him, saying, Send
her away; she is following us, crying. 24 He answered and said, I am not
sent but to the lost sheep of the house of Israel.

25 Then she came and worshipped him, saying, Master, help me! 26 He
answered and said, It is not good to take the children's bread and to cast
it to dogs.[b] 27 She answered and said, True, Lord; nevertheless, the dogs
eat of the crumbs that fall from their master's table. 28 Then Jesus an-
swered and said to her, O woman, great is your faith! Let it be unto you
even as you desire.

And her daughter was made whole even at that same hour.

29 Then Jesus went away from there, and came near to the Sea of
Galilee, 30 and went up on a mountain and sat down there. And crowds of
people came to him, having with them people who were lame, blind,
dumb, maimed, and many others, and put them down at Jesus' feet.
31 And he healed them, and the people were in wonderment to see the
dumb speak, the maimed whole, the lame walking, and the blind seeing.
And they glorified the God of Israel.

32 Then Jesus called his disciples to him and said, I have compassion
on the people, because they have continued with me now for three days,
and have nothing to eat. I do not want to let them go away without eating, Mk 8:1-10
lest they faint along the road. 33 And his disciples said to him, Where

could we get enough bread in this remote place to feed such a great num-
ber of people? 34And Jesus said to them, How many loaves do you have?
And they said, Seven, and a few little fishes.

35And he directed the people to sit down on the ground, 36and took
Seven loaves — the seven loaves and the fishes, and gave thanks, and broke them, and
gave them to his disciples; and the disciples gave them to the people.
37And they did all eat, and were satisfied. And of the pieces left over they
took up seven baskets full – 38and yet those who ate were 4,000 men, as
well as women and children.

39And Jesus sent the people away, boarded the boat, and went to the
region of Magdala.

The Notes

Plants not planted by the Father (15:13) — a) Origen [c185-254 AD] and Chrysostom [c347-407 AD] understand this of the Pharisees, because of their evil opinions. Hilarius and Erasmus understand it of men's precepts. [Ed: Hilarius wrote in the early 4th century. Erasmus was a renowned 16th century scholar; it was he who compiled the Greek Received Text, God's choice and provision to his servants for translating the New Testament into vernacular languages. However, Erasmus was at odds with William Tyndale and Martin Luther regarding certain fundamentals of the faith.]

Cast bread to dogs (15:26) — b) The Jews call the heathen and Gentiles 'dogs' because of their idolatry.

Chapter 16

The Pharisees seek a sign. Jesus warns his disciples of the Pharisees' doctrine. Peter's confession. The keys of heaven. The faithful must bear their cross after Christ.

Then the Pharisees and Sadducees came and tempted Jesus, asking him
to show them some sign from heaven. 2He answered and said to them, At
evening you say the weather will be fair, and that because the sky is red;
3and in the morning you say it will be bad weather today, and that — Mk 8:11,12
because the sky is cloudy and red. O ye hypocrites, you can discern the — Lu 12:54-56
aspect of the sky, and can you not discern the signs of the times? 4The
froward and adulterous nation seeks a sign, but no other sign shall be
The sign of Jonah — given to them than the sign of the prophet Jonah.

So he left them, and departed.

5And when his disciples had come to the other side of the water, they
had forgotten to take bread with them. 6Then Jesus said to them, Take — Mk 8:13-21
heed, and beware of the leaven of the Pharisees and of the Sadducees.[a] — Lu 12:1-3
7And they thought in themselves, saying, It is because we have brought
no bread with us.

8When Jesus understood this, he said to them, O ye of little faith, why
are your minds cumbered because you have brought no bread? 9Do you
not yet perceive? Nor remember those five loaves when there were 5,000
men, and how many baskets you took up? 10Nor the seven loaves when
there were 4,000, and how many baskets you took up? 11Why do you not
perceive then that I was not speaking to you about bread when I said to
beware of the leaven of the Pharisees and of the Sadducees?

12 Then they understood that he was not telling them to beware of the
leaven of bread, but of the doctrine of the Pharisees and of the Sad-
ducees.

13 When Jesus arrived in the vicinity of the city which is called
Caesarea Phillippi, he asked his disciples, saying, Who do men say that I,
the Son of man, am? 14 They said, Some say you are John the Baptist,
some Elijah, some Jeremiah, or one of the prophets. 15 He said to them,
But who do you say that I am? 16 Simon Peter answered and said, You are
Christ, the Son of the living God.

17 And Jesus answered and said to him, Blessed are you, Simon son of — Mk 8:27-30; Lu 9:18-22
Jonah, for flesh and blood has not revealed that to you, but my Father
who is in heaven. 18 And I say also to you that you are Peter, and upon
this rock[b] I will build my congregation. And the gates of hell shall not
The keys. — prevail against it.[c] 19 And I will give to you the keys of the kingdom of
heaven:[d] whatever you bind upon earth shall be bound in heaven, and
whatever you loose on earth shall be loosed in heaven.

20 Then he charged his disciples to tell no one that he was Jesus the
Christ.

21 From that time on, Jesus began to explain to his disciples how he
must go to Jerusalem and suffer many things from the elders, and from
When anything is said or done that might move to pride, Jesus dashes them in the teeth with his death and passion. — the high priests and from the scribes, and must be killed, and rise up — Mk 8:31-33
again the third day. 22 But Peter took him aside and began to rebuke him,
saying, Master, spare yourself! This should not happen to you. 23 Then
Peter is Satan [Ed: see note at Mk 8:33] — Jesus turned about and said to Peter, Get behind me, Satan! You offend
me, because you savour not the things of God, but things of the world.

24 Jesus then said to his disciples, If any person would follow me, let
To take up the cross — him deny himself, and take up his cross and follow me.[e] 25 For whosoever — Joh 12:25,26; Mk 8:34-38; Lu 9:23-27; 17:33.
would save his life, will lose it. And whosoever loses his life for my sake,
will find it. 26 What will it profit a man, though he should win all the
whole world, if he loses his own soul? Or, what can a man give to
redeem his soul? 27 For the Son of man will come in the glory of his
Judgment upon deeds — Father with his angels, and then shall he reward every person according
to his deeds.

28 Truly I say to you, some there are among them that stand here who
shall not taste of death till they have seen the Son of man come in his
kingdom.

The Notes

Leaven (16:6) — a) In the scripture, leaven is sometimes taken in a bad sense, as here, and sometimes in a good sense, as above at 13:33.

Upon this rock (16:18) — b) Upon this rock, etc., means, as says St. Augustine: upon this confession that you have made, acknowledging me to be Christ, the Son of the living God, I build my congregation or church.

The gates of hell (16:18) — c) By the gates of hell are signified death, hell, desperation, sin, violent and tyrannical treatment, persecution, etc.

I will give you the keys of the kingdom, etc. (16:19) — d) Origen, in his first homily upon Matthew, affirms that these words were spoken as much to the rest of the apostles as to Peter. He proves it by John 20:22 & 23, where the keys were given. There Christ says to them all, Receive the Holy Spirit; he whose sins you remit are remitted, etc., or not remitted. Of the same opinion are Tertullian, Cyprian, Augustine, Jerome, and divers other old ancient doctors.

Let him forsake himself (16:24)

e) To forsake oneself is to do utterly against the will of the flesh, mortifying the affections of one's mind, and working the glory of God and the benefit of our neighbour, as is said at Romans 6 and Philippians 2.

Chapter 17

[Ancient tradition holds this as the place, but some disagree]

The transfiguration of Christ upon the Mount of Tabor.* He heals the frenzied boy, and pays the tribute levy to Rome.

Transfiguration

And after six days Jesus took Peter, James, and James' brother John, and
brought them up into a high mountain out of the way. [2]And he was
transfigured before them. And his face did shine like the sun, and his
clothes were as white as the light. [3]And behold, there appeared to them Mk 9:2-10 Lu 9:28-36 2Pe 1:16-18
Moses and Elijah, talking with him.

[4]Then Peter spoke and said to Jesus, Master, it is good for us to be
here. If you will, let us make here three tabernacles: one for you, and one
for Moses, and one for Elijah.

[5]While he was yet speaking, behold, a bright cloud covered them.
And behold, there came a voice out of the cloud, saying, This is my dear
Son, in whom I delight. Hear him!

[6]When the disciples heard this, they fell on their faces and were sore
afraid. [7]And Jesus came and touched them and said, Arise, and do not be
afraid. [8]And when they looked up, they saw no one but Jesus only.

After the high vision, Jesus puts them in mind of his death.

[**Restore all things**: Tyndale> that is, restore the scripture to the right sense again, thereby bringing men to the knowledge of their sins and to repentance, which is the only way to Christ (*Answer*)]

[9]And as they came down from the mountain, Jesus charged them,
saying, See that you tell no one about the vision until the Son of man is
risen up again from death. [10]And his disciples asked of him, saying, Why
then do the scribes say that Elijah must come first? [11]Jesus answered and
said to them, Elijah does come first, and restore all things.* [12]And I say to Mal 4:5,6
you that Elijah has come already, and they did not know him, but have
done to him whatever they pleased. In like manner will the Son of man
also suffer at their hands. [13]Then the disciples perceived that he was
speaking to them of John the Baptist.

[14]And when they had come to the people, a certain man came to Jesus
and kneeled down to him and said, [15]Master, have mercy on my son, for
he is delirious, and is sorely vexed. And often he falls into the fire, and Mk 9:14-29
often into the water. [16]And I brought him to your disciples, but they could Lu 9:37-43
not heal him. [17]Jesus answered and said, O generation faithless and per-
verse, how long shall I be with you? How long shall I suffer you? Bring
him here to me.

[18]And Jesus rebuked the devil, and he came out of him. And the child
was healed even at that same hour.

[19]Then the disciples came to Jesus privately and asked, Why could
we not cast him out? [20]Jesus said to them, Because of your unbelief. For I
say truly to you, if you had faith like a grain of mustard seed, you could Lu 17:5,6
say to this mountain, Move over there, and it would move; neither should

anything be impossible for you to do. 21 However, this kind does not go
out but by prayer and fasting.
22 As they passed the time in Galilee, Jesus said to them, The Son of Mk 9:31
man will be betrayed into the hands of men, 23 and they will kill him; and Lu 9:22
the third day he will rise again. And they sorrowed greatly.

[**Tribute**: payment to a foreign power, in acknowledgement of submission or as the price for protection. In Israel, taxes were collected to pay tribute to the Roman emperor]

24 And when they had come to Capernaum, men that collected the poll
money came to Peter and asked, Does your teacher pay tribute?* 25 He
said, Yes. And when he had come into the house, Jesus spoke first to
him, saying, What do you think, Simon: from whom do the kings of the
earth take tribute or poll money? From their children, or from others?
26 Peter answered, From others. And Jesus said to him, Then the children
are free. 27 Nevertheless, lest we offend them, go to the sea and cast in
your hook, and take the fish that first comes up. And when you have
opened its mouth, you will find a coin. Take it, and pay for me and you.

Chapter 18

He teaches his disciples to be humble and harmless, to avoid occasions of inducement to sin, and to forgive one another their offences.

Greatest in heaven

At that time the disciples came to Jesus, saying, Who is the greatest in
the kingdom of heaven? 2 Jesus called a child to him, and set him in the
midst of them, 3 and said, Truly I say to you, unless you turn and become Mk 9:33-37
as children, you cannot enter into the kingdom of heaven. 4 Whoever Lu 9:46-48; 17:1-4;
therefore humbles himself like this child, the same is the greatest in the 18:16; 22:26.
kingdom of heaven. 5 And whoever receives such a child in my name,
receives me. 6 But whoever hurts one of these little ones who believe in
me, it would be better for him if a millstone* were hung about his neck
and that he were drowned in the depth of the sea. 7 Woe be to the world
because of offences. However, it cannot be avoided but that offences will
come. Nevertheless, woe be to the man by whom the offence comes.

[**Millstone**: used in milling. Grains were spread on a flat lower stone and ground by an upper stone. Large millstones were powered by animals]

8 And so if your hand or your foot causes you to offend, cut it off and
cast it from you. It is better for you to enter into life lame or maimed than
for you, having two hands or two feet, to be cast into everlasting fire. Mk 9:42-48
9 And if also your eye causes you to offend, tear it out and cast it from
you. It is better for you to enter into life with one eye than, having two
eyes, to be cast into hell fire.
10 See that you do not despise one of these little ones. For I say to you
that in heaven their angels always behold the face of my Father who is in
heaven. 11 Yea, and the Son of man has come to save that which is lost.
12 What do you think: if a man has a hundred sheep and one of them has
gone astray, does he not leave the ninety-nine in the mountains and go Lu 15:1-7
and seek that one which has gone astray? 13 If it happens that he finds it,
truly I say to you, he rejoices more over that sheep than over the ninety-
nine that did not go astray. 14 In the same way, it is not the will of your
Father in heaven that one of these little ones should perish.
15 Moreover, if your brother trespasses against you, go and tell him his

[**Won**: this English verb once included the sense of redeeming, winning for the kingdom of heaven]

fault between him and you alone. If he hears you, you have won* your
brother. [16]But if he does not hear you, then take along with you one or Jas 5:16,19, 20.
two others, so that in the mouth of two or three witnesses every matter Lev 19:17
may be established. [17]If he does not hear them, tell it to the congregation. 2Co 13:1 Joh 8:17
If he does not hear the congregation, take him as a heathen man and as a
publican. [18]Truly I say to you, whatever you bind on earth shall be bound
in heaven, and whatever you loose on earth shall be loosed in heaven.[a]

[19]Again I say to you, if two of you agree in earth about any manner of
thing, whatsoever they desire, it shall be given them by my Father who is
in heaven. [20]For where two or three are gathered together in my name,
there am I in the midst of them.

[21]Then Peter came to him and said, Master, how often should I
forgive my brother if he sins against me? Seven times?

Forgiveness: 70 x 7 times

[22]Jesus said to him, I say to you, not seven times, but seventy times
seven times. [23]Therefore the kingdom of heaven is likened to a certain Joh 20:23
king who wished to take accounts from his servants. [24]And when he had Lu 17:4
begun the reckoning, one was brought to him who owed him 10,000
talents.* [25]Because he had nothing to pay with, his master ordered him to
be sold, and his wife and his children and all that he had, and payment to
be made. [26]The servant fell down and besought him, saying, Sir, give me
respite, and I will pay it every whit. [27]Then the lord had pity on that
servant, and released him, and forgave him the debt.

[**10,000 talents**: A talent was the largest denomination of currency. 10,000 signified a great or infinite number. Literally it amounted to several millions of today's dollars]

[28]And that same servant went out and found one of his fellows who
owed him 100 denarii,* and laid hands on him and took him by the throat,
saying, Pay me what you owe! [29]And his fellow servant fell down and
besought him, saying, Have patience with me, and I will pay you every-
thing. [30]But he would not, and went and cast him into prison till he
should pay the debt.

[**100 denarii**: then about 3 months' wages]

[31]When the other servants saw what had been done, they were very
grieved, and went and told their lord all that had happened. [32]Then his
lord called the man and said to him, O evil servant! I forgave you all that
debt because you begged me. [33]Was it not right also that you should have
had compassion on your fellow, just as I had pity on you? [34]And his lord
was angry, and delivered him to the jailers till he should pay all that was
due to him. [35]So likewise shall my heavenly Father do with you, unless
you forgive with your hearts each one his brother's trespasses.

The Notes

Whatever you bind or loose (18:18)

a) That is, whatever you condemn by my word in the earth, the same is condemned in heaven, and that which you remit by my word in earth, is remitted in heaven.

Chapter 19

Christ gives answer concerning marriage, accepts the young children, and teaches not to be full of cares, nor to love worldly riches.

And it came to pass, when Jesus had finished those sayings, he left

Mk 10:1-12 Ge 1:27; 2:24; 5:2. Eph 5:22-33 1Co 6:16

On divorce

Galilee, and went into the region of Judea, beyond the Jordan. 2And crowds of people followed him, and he healed them there. 3Then the Pharisees came to him, testing him and saying to him, Is it lawful for a man to put away his wife for any reason at all? 4He answered and said to them, Have you not read how it was that he who made man at the beginning made them man and woman, 5and said, For this thing shall a man leave father and mother and cleave unto his wife, and the two shall be one flesh? 6So then, now they are not two, but one flesh. Let not man therefore put apart that which God has joined together.

Lu 16:18 1Co 7:39 M't 5:31,32

7Then they said to him, Why did Moses direct to give a testimonial of divorce and to put her away? 8He said to them, Moses, because of the hardness of your hearts, suffered you to put away your wives. But from the beginning it was not so. 9I say therefore to you, whoever puts away his wife (unless it be for fornication) and marries another, breaks wedlock. And whoever marries her who is divorced, commits adultery.

On chastity

10Then Jesus' disciples said to him, If this is the case between man and wife, then it is not good to marry. 11He said to them, Not everyone can receive this saying, but only those to whom it is given. 12Some are chaste who were so born from their mother's womb. And others are chaste who were made so by men. And others are chaste who have made themselves chaste for the kingdom of heaven's sake. He who can receive it, let him receive it.

Mk 10:13-16 Lu 18:15-17

13Then young children were brought to him so that he could put his hands on them and pray. And the disciples rebuked the people. 14But Jesus said, Allow the children, and do not forbid them to come to me, for of such is the kingdom of heaven. 15And when he had put his hands on them, he departed from there.

Mk 10:17-27 Lu 18:18-27 Ex 20:12-17 De 5:16-21 Lev 19:18

The commandments.

16And a man came and said to Jesus, Good Teacher, what good thing should I do so that I may have eternal life? 17He said to him, Why do you call me good? There is none good but one, and that is God. But if you would enter into life, keep the commandments. 18The other asked him, Which? And Jesus said, Break no wedlock. Do not kill. Do not steal. Do not bear false witness. 19Honour father and mother. And love your neighbour as yourself.

Note a, Mk 10:21.

20The young man said to him, I have observed all these things from my youth. What do I yet lack? 21And Jesus said to him, If you would be perfect, go and sell what you have, and give it to the poor, and you will have treasure in heaven; and come, and follow me.

22When the young man heard these words, he went away grieved, for he had great wealth.

23Then Jesus said to his disciples, Truly I say to you, it is hard for a rich man to enter into the kingdom of heaven. 24And moreover I say to you, it is easier for a camel to go through the eye of a needle than for a rich man to enter into the kingdom of God.[a,b]

25When his disciples heard that, they were exceedingly amazed, saying, Who then can be saved? 26Jesus regarded them and said to them,

With men it is not possible, but with God all things are possible.
27Then Peter answered and said to him, Behold, we have left every- Mk 10:28-31
thing and followed you. What will we have? Lu 18:28-30
28Jesus said to them, Truly I say to you, when the Son of man sits in
the seat of his majesty, you who have followed me in the new birth* shall
sit also upon twelve seats, and judge the twelve tribes of Israel. 29And
whosoever gives up houses, or brethren, or sisters, or father, or mother,
or wife, or children, or lands for my name's sake, the same shall receive a
hundredfold, and shall inherit everlasting life. 30Many that are first shall
be last, and the last shall be first.

[**New birth**: v28 is updated from Coverdale's 1535 New Testament. Tyndale had 'second generation,' probably meaning 'second birth']

The Notes

A camel (19:24) a) Theophilactus reads 'a cable'. The Greek signifies both 'camel' and 'cable'.

A rich man (19:24) b) Here he is called rich meaning that he puts his confidence in his goods, a thing people do when they have all their delight and joy therein, as in Luke 12:34.

Chapter 20

Christ teaches by a similitude that God is debtor to no man, and how he is always calling people to his work. He teaches his disciples to be lowly, and gives two blind men their sight.

Vineyard labourers hired

For the kingdom of heaven may be likened to a householder who went
out early in the morning to hire labourers into his vineyard. 2And he
agreed with the labourers for a denarius* a day, and sent them into his Lu 13:23-30
vineyard. 3And he went out about the third hour* and saw others standing
idle in the market place, 4and said to them, Go ye also into my vineyard,
and whatever is right, I will give you. And they went their way.
5Again he went out about the sixth and ninth hour, and did likewise.
6And he went out about the eleventh hour and found others standing idle,
and said to them, Why do you stand here idle all the day? 7They said to
him, Because no one has hired us. He said to them, Go ye also into my
vineyard, and whatever is right, that you will receive.
8When evening was come, the lord of the vineyard said to his steward,
Call the labourers and give them their wages, beginning at the last till you
come to the first.
9And those who were hired about the eleventh hour came and re-
ceived every man a denarius. 10Then came the first, supposing that they
would receive more, but they likewise received every man a denarius.
11And when they had received it, they murmured against the master of the
house, 12saying, These last have worked only one hour, and you have
made them equal to us who have borne the burden and heat of the day.
13He answered to one of them, saying, Friend, I do you no wrong. Did
you not agree with me for a denarius? 14Take that which is your due, and
go your way. I want to give to the last one as much as to you. 15Is it not
lawful for me to do as I please with what belongs to me? Is your eye evil
because I am good?

[**A denarius**: a Roman silver coin. A day's wage for a Roman soldier, and fair pay]
***Third hour**: The Jews count one when the sun has been up for one hour, and so on.

Last may be first. 16 In like manner the last may be first, and the first last. For many are
Many called, few chosen. called, but few are chosen.
17 And Jesus went up to Jerusalem, and took the twelve disciples apart
along the way and said to them, 18 Behold, we are going up to Jerusalem.
And the Son of man will be betrayed to the chief priests and to the Mk 10:32-34
Passion foretold. scribes, and they will condemn him to death, 19 and will deliver him to the Lu 13:33
Gentiles to be mocked, to be scourged, and to be crucified; and the third
day he will rise again.
20 Then the mother of Zebedee's children came to him with her sons,
doing reverence to him and desiring a certain thing of him. 21 He said to Mk 10:35-45
her, What would you like? She answered him, Grant that these my two
sons may sit, the one on your right hand and the other on your left hand,
in your kingdom.
22 Jesus answered and said, You know not what you ask. Are you able
to drink of the cup that I must drink of, and to be baptized with the
baptism that I must be baptized with?
They answered to him, That we are.
23 And he said to them, You shall drink of my cup, and shall be
baptized with the baptism that I will be baptized with. But to sit on my
right hand and on my left hand is not mine to give, but is for those for
whom it is prepared by my Father.
24 And when the ten heard about this, they were indignant at the two Lu 22:24-26
brethren. 25 But Jesus called them to him and said, You know that the
lords of the Gentiles have dominion over them, and those who are great
exercise power over them. 26 It shall not be this way among you, but who-
soever would be great among you, let him minister to you, 27 and whoever
Greatness in servanthood. would be chief, let him be your servant – 28 even as the Son of man came
not to be served, but to serve, and to give his life for the redemption of
many.
29 And as they departed from Jericho, crowds of people followed
Jesus. 30 And two blind men sitting by the wayside, when they heard Jesus
pass by, cried out, saying, Lord Son of David, have mercy on us! 31 And Mk 10:46-52
the people admonished them to hold their peace. But they cried out all the Lu 18:35-43
more, saying, Have mercy on us, Lord Son of David!
32 Then Jesus stood still and called them, and said, What do you want
me to do for you? 33 They said to him, Lord, that our eyes may be opened!
34 Jesus had compassion on them and touched their eyes, and immediately
their eyes received sight. And they followed him.

Chapter 21

He rides into Jerusalem, drives the merchants out of the temple, curses the fig tree, and rebukes the Pharisees with the similitudes of the two sons and of the husbandmen who slew such as were sent to them.

When they drew near to Jerusalem and had come to Bethphage, to the
Mount of Olives, Jesus sent two of his disciples, 2 saying to them, Go into

A donkey and her colt

the town that lies in front of you, and immediately you will find a donkey
tied, and her colt with her. Untie them and bring them to me. 3And if
anyone says anything to you, say that the Lord has need of them, and
straightaway he will let them go.

Mk 11:1-10
Lu 19:28-38
Joh 12:12-19

4All this was done to fulfil that which was spoken by the prophet,
saying: 5Tell ye the daughter of Zion: Behold, your king comes to you,
humble and sitting upon a donkey and a colt, the foal of a donkey bred to
the yoke.

Isa 62:11
Zec 9:9

6The disciples went and did as Jesus told them, 7and brought the
donkey and the colt, and put on them their clothes, and set him thereon.
8And many of the people spread their garments in the road. Others cut
down branches from the trees and strew them in the road. 9Moreover, the
people who went ahead, and also those who came after, cried out, saying,
Hosanna to the Son of David! Blessed is he who comes in the name of the
Lord. Hosanna in the highest![a]

Hosanna to the Son of David

Ps 118: 26

10And when he came to Jerusalem, all the city was moved, saying,
Who is this? 11And the people said, This is Jesus, the prophet of Nazareth,
a town of Galilee.

12And Jesus went into the temple of God and cast out all the people
who sold and bought in the temple, and overturned the tables of the
money changers and the seats of the people who sold doves, 13and said to
them, It is written: My house shall be called the house of prayer. But you
have made it a den of thieves.

Buyers and sellers in the temple

Isa 56:7
Jer 7:11
Mk 11:15-17
Joh 2:13-17

14And the blind and the lame came to him in the temple, and he
healed them.

15When the chief priests and scribes saw the marvels that he did, and
the children calling out in the temple and saying, Hosanna to the Son of
David, they were indignant 16and said to him, Do you hear what they say?
Jesus said to them, Yea, have you never read: From the mouth of babes
and sucklings, you have ordained praise?

Psalm 8:2

17And he left them, and went out of the city to Bethany, and had his
lodging there.

18In the morning, as he returned into the city again, he hungered,
19and saw a fig tree by the road, and went to it, and found nothing on it
but leaves only, and said to it, Let fruit never grow on you from this time
forward.[b] And at once the fig tree withered away. 20And when his dis-
ciples saw that, they marvelled, saying, How has the fig tree withered
away so suddenly? 21Jesus answered and said to them, Truly I say to you,
if you have faith and do not doubt, you will not only do what I have done
to the fig tree, but also if you say to this mountain, Take yourself away
and cast yourself into the sea, it will be done. 22And whatever you ask in
prayer (if you believe), you will receive it.

Fig tree

Mk 11:12-14; 20-24.
Jas 1:5-8

23And when he had come into the temple, the chief priests and the
elders of the people came to him as he was teaching and said, By what
authority are you doing these things? And who gave you this authority?
24Jesus answered and said to them, I also will ask of you a certain

The authority of Jesus, where from?

Mk 11:27-33
Lu 20:1-8

question, which, if you answer me, I likewise will tell you by what
The baptism of John, where from?
authority I do these things. [25]The baptism of John: whence was it? from
heaven, or of men?[c]

Then they reasoned among themselves, saying, If we say from
heaven, he will say to us, why did you not then believe him? [26]But if we
say it was of men, then we fear the people. (For everyone held John to be
a prophet.)

[27]And they answered Jesus and said, We don't know.

And he likewise said to them, Neither will I tell you by what authority
I do these things. [28]What do you say to this: A certain man had two sons,
Two sons
and went to the elder and said, Son, go and work today in my vineyard.
[29]He answered and said, I will not, but afterward he repented and went.
[30]Then the father went to the second son and said likewise. And he an-
swered and said, I will, Sir. Yet he did not go. [31]Which of the two did the
will of the father?

And they said to him, The first.

Jesus said to them, Truly I say to you that the publicans and the
harlots shall come into the kingdom of God before you. [32]For John came
to you in the way of righteousness, and you did not believe him. But the
Publicans and harlots believe.
publicans and the harlots believed him. And yet you, though you saw it,
were still not moved with repentance, so that you might afterward have
believed him.

[33]Hear another similitude: There was a certain householder, who
planted a vineyard. He hedged it round about, and made a winepress in it, Mk 12:1-12
A vineyard let out to hire. [**Husbandmen**: the Gk *georgos* (1092) means a tiller of the soil, one who works the land.]
and built a tower, and let it out to husbandmen,[*] and went into a far Lu 20:9-19
country. [34]And when the time of the fruit drew near, he sent his servants Isa 5:1-7
to the husbandmen, to receive the fruits of it. [35]And the husbandmen
caught his servants, and beat one, killed another, and stoned another.
[36]Again he sent other servants, more than at the first, and they treated
them likewise. [37]Then last of all he sent to them his own son, saying,
They will respect my son. [38]But when the husbandmen saw the son, they
said among themselves, This is the heir; come, let us kill him, and let us
take his inheritance for ourselves. [39]And they caught him and thrust him
out of the vineyard, and slew him. [40]Now when the lord of the vineyard
comes, what will he do with those husbandmen?

[41]They said to him, He will miserably destroy those evil persons, and
will let out his vineyard to other husbandmen, who will render to him the
fruit in their seasons.

[42]Jesus said to them, Did you never read in the scriptures: The stone
which the builders refused, the same is set in the principal part of the Ps 118:22, 23.
corner; this was the Lord's doing, and it is marvellous in our eyes? Isa 28:16
[43]Therefore I say to you, the kingdom of God will be taken from you and Ac 4:10-12
will be given to the Gentiles, who will bring forth the fruits of it. [44]And Ro 9:33
whosoever falls on this stone, he shall be broken; but whomever it falls 1Pe 2:6,8.
upon, it will grind him to powder.

[45]When the chief priests and Pharisees heard these similitudes, they

perceived that he was speaking of them. [46]And went about to lay hands on
him, but they feared the people, because they took him as a prophet.

The Notes

Hosanna (21:9) a) *Hosanna,* in Hebrew *Hosiahna,* means, I pray thee, give salvation!

The fig tree (21:19) b) By this fig tree Christ effectively shows that the Jews, although they had an appearance of holiness by their outward observances, nevertheless did not have the fruit of charity. By which thing he signified that they would shortly be deprived and put from this false appearance by the destruction of Jerusalem.

From heaven or of men? (21:25) c) In scripture, a thing is considered to be of men when it is imagined or invented by men, and of heaven when it is of God.

Chapter 22

The marriage of the king's son. Tribute should be given to the emperor. Christ confutes the opinion of the Sadducees concerning the resurrection, and answers the question posed by the scribe.

Marriage of the son

And Jesus spoke to them again in similitudes, saying, [2]The kingdom of
heaven is like a certain king who arranged a marriage for his son, [3]and
sent forth his servants to call those who were bid to the wedding, and they
would not come. [4]Again he sent forth other servants, saying, Tell those Lu 14:16-24
who are bidden, Behold, I have prepared my dinner; my oxen and my Rev 19:6-9
fatted calves are killed, and all things are ready. Come to the marriage.

[5]But they made light of it and went their ways, one to his farmstead,
another about his wares. [6]The rest took his servants and shamefully abused them, and slew them.

[7]When the king heard about this, he was furious, and sent forth his
warriors, and destroyed those murderers, and burnt up their city. [8]Then
said the king to his servants, The wedding was prepared, but those who
were bidden were not worthy. [9]Go therefore out into the highways, and as
many as you find, bid them to the marriage.

[10]The servants went out into the highways and gathered together as
many as they could find, both good and bad, and the wedding was furnished with guests. [11]Then the king came in to visit the guests, and
spotted there a man who did not have on a wedding garment,[a] [12]and said
to him, Friend, how did it happen that you came in here and do not have
on a wedding garment? And the man was quite speechless. [13]Then said 2Co 5:3 Rev 16:15
the king to his servants, Take and bind him hand and foot, and cast him
into outer darkness; there shall be weeping and gnashing of teeth. [14]For
many are called, but few are chosen.

Many are called, few chosen.

[15]Then the Pharisees went and took counsel, how they might tangle
him in his words. [16]And they sent to him their disciples with Herod's Mk 12:13-17
servants, saying, Master, we know that you are true, and teach the way of Lu 20:20-26 Ro 13:6,7
God truly, neither mind any person, for you do not consider men's estate.
[17]Tell us therefore what you think: is it lawful to remit tribute to Caesar,
or not?

Tribute payments to Caesar [Israel had formerly taken tribute from others, as at 2Sa 8:2. To pay tribute offended those who interpreted the covenant promises carnally]

18 Jesus perceived their wickedness and said, Why do you bait me, you
hypocrites? 19 Let me see the tribute coin. So they brought him a denarius.
20 And he said to them, Whose image and superscription is this? 21 They
said to him, Caesar's. Then he said to them, Give therefore to Caesar that
which is Caesar's, and give to God that which is God's.

22 When they heard that, they marvelled, and left him and went their
way.

[**Sadducees**: a Jewish party of the intertestamental period, consisting of a traditional ruling class of priests who rejected important doctrines, including retribution in a future life and the existence of angels]

23 The same day the Sadducees, who say there is no resurrection, came Mk 12:18-27
to him and asked him, 24 saying, Teacher, Moses said that if a man dies Lu 20:27-40
having no children, the brother should marry the widow and raise up seed De 25:5-10
for his brother. 25 There were with us seven brethren. The first married and
died without issue, and left his wife to his brother. 26 Likewise the second
and the third, down to the seventh. 27 Last of all the woman died also.
28 Now in the resurrection, whose wife will she be of the seven? For they
all had her.

29 Jesus answered and said to them, You are deceived, and do not
understand the scriptures, nor yet the power of God. 30 For in the res-
urrection people neither marry nor are married, but are as the angels in
heaven. 31 As for the resurrection of the dead, have you not read what is
spoken to you by God, who says, 32 I am Abraham's God, and Isaac's
God, and the God of Jacob? God is not the God of the dead, but of the
living.

33 And when the people heard that, they were astonished at his teach-
ing.

[**Pharisees**: a small but influential Jewish lay sect of the intertestamental period, believed to have emerged from a back-to-the-scripture movement during the Babylonian captivity]

34 When the Pharisees heard how he had put the Sadducees to silence,
they drew together. 35 One of them, who was a doctor of the law, asked
him a question, testing him and saying, 36 Teacher, which is the chief
commandment in the law? 37 Jesus said to him, Love the Lord your God Mk 12:28-34
with all your heart, with all your soul, and with all your mind; 38 this is the Lu 10:25-37 De 6:5
first and the chief commandment. 39 And there is another like this: Love Lev 19:18
your neighbour as yourself. 40 On these two commandments hang all the
law and the prophets.

41 While the Pharisees were gathered together, Jesus asked them, Mk 12:35-37
42 saying, What do you think about the Christ? Whose son is he? They said Lu 20:41-44
to him, The son of David. 43 He said to them, How then does David in the Ps 110:1
Spirit call him Lord, saying, 44 The Lord said to my Lord, Sit on my right
hand, till I make your enemies your footstool?[b] 45 If David calls him Lord,
how is he then his son?

46 And no one could answer him a word. Neither did anyone from that
day forth dare ask him any more questions.

The Notes

Wedding garment (22:11)

a) This wedding garment is spoken of at Isaiah 61:10.

Until I make your enemies your footstool (22:44)

b) This is not to say that when the enemies of Christ are subdued, then Christ will no more sit on the right hand of God. Rather, it signifies that there shall be no end of that time, as it often does according to the manner of the Hebrews, as in M't 1:25 & 5:26. So 'until' is taken for a time without end, or Christ would have an end of sitting with his Father in heaven.

Chapter 23

Christ cries woe over the Pharisees, scribes, and hypocrites,
and prophesies the destruction of Jerusalem.

Then Jesus spoke to the people and to his disciples, 2saying, The scribes
and the Pharisees sit in Moses' seat.[a] 3All therefore that they bid you to
observe, that observe and do. But do not follow their works. For they say,
but do not do. 4Yea and they bind up heavy burdens, grievous to be borne,
and lay them on men's shoulders, but they themselves will not heave at
them with one of their fingers.

5All their works they do to be seen by men. They enlarge their
Phylacteries [generally considered to be boxes containing scripture verses, worn on arm or forehead] phylacteries, and make large borders on their garments. 6They love to sit Mk 12:38-40 Lu 11:37-52
uppermost at feasts, and to have the chief seats in the synagogues, 7and
greetings in the markets, and to be called Rabbi by men.

8But you shall not suffer yourselves to be called Rabbi. For one is
your Master – that is, Christ – and you are all brethren. 9And call no man
upon the earth your father, for there is but one your Father, and he is in
heaven. 10Do not be called teachers, for there is but one your Teacher, and
he is Christ. 11He who is greatest among you will be your servant. 12But
whosoever exalts himself, shall be brought low. And he who humbles
himself, shall be exalted.

13Woe is to you, scribes and Pharisees, hypocrites! For you shut up
The kingdom is shut the kingdom of heaven before men. You yourselves go not in, neither do
you suffer those who come to enter in.

14Woe to you, scribes and Pharisees, hypocrites! You devour widows'
houses, and that under a colour of praying long prayers, for which you
shall receive the greater damnation.

15Woe to you, scribes and Pharisees, hypocrites, who compass land
and sea to bring one person into your belief. And when he is brought in,
you make him twofold more the child of hell than you yourselves are.

16Woe to you, blind guides, who say that if someone swears by the
temple, it is nothing, but whosoever swears by the gold of the temple, he
offends. 17O fools, and blind! Which is greater: the gold, or the temple
that sanctifies the gold? 18And whosoever swears by the altar, it is
nothing, but whoever swears by the offering that lies on the altar, offends
– 19Ye fools, and blind! Which is greater: the offering, or the altar that
sanctifies the offering? 20Whoever therefore swears by the altar, swears
by it and by all that is on it. 21And whoever swears by the temple, swears
by it and by him who dwells therein. 22And he who swears by heaven,
swears by the seat of God and by him who sits upon it.

23Woe to you, scribes and Pharisees, hypocrites, who tithe mint, anise,
and cummin, and leave the weightier matters of the law undone: judg-
ment, mercy, and faith. These you ought to have done, and not to have
Blind guides left the others undone. 24Blind guides, who strain out a gnat and swallow
a camel!

25Woe to you, scribes and Pharisees, hypocrites, who make clean the
outside of the cup and of the platter, but within they are full of greed and

Inside of the cup excess. [26]You blind Pharisee: cleanse first the inside of the cup and plat-
ter, so that the outside of them may be clean also.
[27]Woe to you, scribes and Pharisees, hypocrites! For you are like
Whitewashed tombs whitewashed tombs, which appear beautiful outwardly, but within are full
of dead bones and of all uncleanness. [28]This is how you are, because
outwardly you appear righteous to men, when within you are full of hy-
pocrisy and iniquity.
[29]Woe to you, scribes and Pharisees, hypocrites! You build the tombs
of the prophets, and adorn the sepulchres of the righteous, [30]and say, If we
had been in the days of our fathers, we would not have been partners with
them in the blood of the prophets. [31]So then, you are witnesses against
yourselves, that you are the children of those who killed the prophets!
[32]Fill up then likewise the cup of your fathers. [33]Serpents and offspring of
vipers, how can you escape the judgment of hell? Vipers: M't 3:7.
[34]And so behold: I send to you prophets, wise men, and scribes. Some
of them you will kill and crucify, and some of them you will scourge in
your synagogues and persecute from city to city, [35]so that upon you may
Innocent blood come all the righteous blood that was shed upon the earth, from the blood
of righteous Abel to the blood of Zechariah, the son of Berechiah, whom 2Ch 24:20,21
you slew between the temple and the altar. [36]Truly I say to you, all these Lu 13:33-35
things will come upon this generation.
[37]O Jerusalem, Jerusalem, who kills prophets, and stones those who
are sent to you! How often would I have gathered your children together,
as the hen gathers her chicks under her wings.[b] But you would not. [38]Be-
hold, your habitation shall be left to you desolate. [39]For I say to you, you
will not see me henceforth until you say, Blessed is he who comes in the Ps 118:26
name of the Lord.

The Notes

In Moses' seat (23:1)

a) The scribes and Pharisees sit in Moses' seat, etc: Erasmus in his annotations notes that there are those who wrest this text to the purpose that we should obey all things the bishops command, or rulers (though they be wicked), for the sake of the office they are in. However Christ (says he) speaks of those that do truly teach the law of Moses, and not of such as wrap themselves in the decrees and ordinances of men. And even now, we must hear the bishop who does truly teach the gospel, though he hardly lives gospel-like. But who can suffer them to, against Christ's doctrine, make and unmake laws for their own profit, exercising upon the people plain tyranny, and weighing all things for their own advantage and authority? Those who, with precepts conceived for their own gain and despotic power, bind the people, do not sit in the chair of the gospel, but in the chair of Simon Magus and of Caiaphas. These are the very words of Erasmus on this verse. [Tyndale> Moses' seat is Moses' doctrine, as Christ's seat is Christ's doctrine.]

Under her wings (23:37)

b) We are hid under the wings of Christ when fully with all our heart we put our trust in his merit and mercy. Psalm 17.

Chapter 24

Christ reveals to his disciples the destruction of the temple, the end of the world, and the signs of the latter days. He warns them to awake, for the world will suddenly perish.

And Jesus went out and departed from the temple, and his disciples came
to him to show him the buildings of the temple. 2Jesus said to them, Do
you not see all these things? Truly I say to you, there shall not be left here
one stone upon another that will not be cast down.

Destruction of the temple foretold

Mk c13

3And as he sat on the Mount of Olives, his disciples came to him
privately, saying, Tell us when these things will be, and what sign will be
of your coming, and of the end of the world.

Lu 19:41-44; 21:5-19.

4And Jesus answered and said to them, Take heed that no one de-
ceives you. 5For many will come in my name saying, I am Christ! and
will deceive many. 6You will hear of wars and of the infamy of wars. But
see that you be not troubled. For all these things must come to pass, but
the end is not yet. 7For nation will rise against nation, and realm against
realm. And there will be pestilence, hunger, and earthquakes in all quar-
ters. 8All these are the beginning of sorrows.

Antichrist

Eph 5:6
Col 2:8

9Then they will put you to tribulation, and will kill you, and you will
be hated by all nations for my name's sake. 10And then shall many fall
into offence, and will betray one another, and will hate one another.
11And many false prophets will arise, and will deceive many. 12And be-
cause iniquity will have the upper hand, the love of many will abate.

Joh 15:18-27; 16:1-4.

13But he who endures to the end, the same will be saved. 14And this
glad tidings of the kingdom shall be preached in all the world, for a wit-
ness to all nations; and then shall the end come.

15When you therefore see the abomination that betokens desolation
spoken of by Daniel the prophet stand in the holy place, let him who
reads it, understand it. 16Then let those who are in Judea flee into the
mountains. 17And let him who is on the housetop not come down to fetch
anything out of his house. 18Neither let him who is in the field return back
to fetch his clothes. 19Woe shall be in those days to women that are with
child, and to those who give suck. 20But pray that your flight be not in the
winter, neither on the Sabbath day.[a] 21For then will be great tribulation,
such as was not from the beginning of the world to this time, nor will be.
22Yea and unless those days were shortened, no flesh would be saved.[b]
But for the sake of the chosen, those days will be shortened.

Da 9:27; 11:31.
Mk 13:14-20
Lu 21:20-24; 19:43,44.

23Then if any one says to you, See, here is Christ! or there is Christ! –
believe it not. 24For false christs* and false prophets will arise, and will do
great miracles and wonders, insomuch that if it were possible, the very
elect should be deceived. 25Take heed, I have told you beforehand. 26So if
they say to you, Behold, he is in the desert! go not forth; or, Behold, he is
in the secret places! believe it not. 27For as the lightning comes out of the
east and shines to the west, so will the coming of the Son of man be. 28For
wherever the dead body is, there will the eagles resort.[c]

[Tyndale did not limit **false christs** to the time before the desolation of Jerusalem. He said (in *Obedience*) that he put 'false christs' to keep close to the Greek *pseudo-christi*, but it means 'false anointed': anyone working deceptive miracles. See also Mk 13:6 & 13:21,22; 2Th 2:9]

Lu 17:22-24; 21:8.
Mk 13:21-23

29Immediately after the tribulations of those days, the sun will be
darkened, and the moon will not give her light, and the stars will fall from
heaven, and the powers of heaven shall move. 30And then will appear the
sign of the Son of man in heaven. And then shall all the kindreds of the

Lu 21:25-28
Mk 13:24,25
Eze 32:7,8
Isa c13
Joe 2:1-11

earth mourn, and they shall see the Son of man come in the clouds of
heaven with power and great glory. [31]And he will send his angels with the
great voice of a trumpet, and they will gather together his chosen from the
four winds, and from the one end of the world to the other.
[32]Learn from a similitude of the fig tree: when its branches are yet
tender and its leaves sprung, you know that summer is near. [33]So likewise
you, when you see all these things, may be sure that it is near, even at the
doors. [34]Truly I say to you that this generation shall not pass till all these
things be fulfilled.
[35]Heaven and earth shall perish, but my words will abide. [36]But of that
Heaven and earth shall perish. — day and hour no man knows – no, not the angels of heaven, but my Father
only. [37]As the time of Noah was, so likewise will the coming of the Son
of man be. [38]For as in the days before the flood they were eating and
As in Noah's time — drinking, marrying and were married, right up to the day that Noah Ge cc 6,7
entered into the ship, [39]and knew of nothing till the flood came and took
them all away, so also will the coming of the Son of man be. [40]Then two
will be in the fields; the one will be received, and the other will be Lu 17:34,35
refused. [41]Two will be grinding at the mill; the one will be received, and
the other will be refused.
[42]Watch therefore, because you do not know what hour your master
Awake and watch — will come. [43]Of this be sure: if the householder knew what hour the thief
would come, he would surely watch, and not allow his house to be broken
into. [44]Therefore you also be ready, because in the hour you think he
would not, the Son of man will come.
[45]If there be any servant faithful and wise, whom his master has ap-
pointed over his household, to give them food in due season, [46]happy is
that servant whom his master (when he comes) finds so doing. [47]Truly I
say to you, he will appoint him over all his goods. [48]But if the evil servant
says in his heart, My master will defer his coming, [49]and begins to smite
his fellow servants, yea and to eat and to drink with the drunken, [50]the
servant's master will come in a day when he is not expecting him, and in
an hour that he is not aware of, [51]and will separate him, and give him his
reward with the hypocrites. And there shall be weeping and gnashing of
teeth.

The Notes

That flight not be in the winter, nor on the Sabbath (24:20)

a) Not in the winter, because it was hard travelling, nor on the Sabbath, because they were commanded to go no further than a mile that day. Strabo (xvi book) records that Pompey actually took them on the Sabbath day [in 63 B.C.]. And so did Titus and Vespasian also, of whom Froutinus writes. [Titus and Vespasian sacked Jerusalem in 70 A.D., when the city was crowded for the Passover; the historian Tacitus numbered the people at over 600,000. Both the city and the temple were destroyed, in fulfilment of Jesus' prophecies. Many thousands were crucified by the Romans (M't 27:25). Ed.]

No flesh (24:22)

b) *No flesh* for no people.

Wherever the dead body is, there will the eagles resort (24:28)

c) [Point of interest: Following Chrysostom and other church fathers, Thomas Cranmer and some English Reformers taught this parable (in Matthew) represents believers gathered at the sacrament of the body and blood of the Lord; that is, the new Passover supper, which is Holy

Communion. *The dead body* is the slain Lamb. *The eagles* are disciples who gather at the Lord's table in a spiritual upper room to receive the broken bread of his body and the cup of wine that is his blood shed for the remission of sins. The high flying of eagles represents a spiritual ascent: believers soar by faith to heavenly places to discern the body of the Lord (1Co 11:29) slain upon the cross. For the body of the slain Lamb must thus be shown (1Co 2:2, 11:26). Where he is so shown, and not in secret or desert places, there believers will gather together, in spiritual flight beholding his dead body, and thereby supping with him, and also mysteriously partaking of the altar (1Co 10:16-18). See Lu 17, note (a).]

Chapter 25

The ten virgins, the talents delivered to the servants, and of the general judgment.

Then the kingdom of heaven will be likened to ten virgins who took their
lamps and went to meet the bridegroom.[a] 2 Five of them were foolish, and
five were wise. 3 The foolish took their lamps, but took no oil with them.[b]
4 But the wise took oil with them in their vessels, with their lamps also.

5 While the bridegroom tarried, all slumbered and slept. 6 And right at
midnight there was a cry made: Behold, the bridegroom comes! Go out to
meet him! 7 Then all those virgins arose and prepared their lamps. 8 And
the foolish said to the wise, Give us some of your oil, for our lamps are
going out. 9 But the wise answered, saying, Not so, lest there not be
enough for us and you;[c] but go rather to those who sell, and buy for yourselves.

10 And while they were going to buy, the bridegroom came. And those
who were ready went in with him to the wedding, and the gate was shut
up. 11 Afterwards came also the other virgins, saying, Lord, Lord, open to
us! 12 But he answered and said, Truly I say to you, I know you not.

Watch 13 Watch, therefore. For you know neither the day nor yet the hour
when the Son of man will come.

14 Likewise it will be as a certain man, ready to take his journey to a
strange country, called his servants and delivered his goods to them.
15 And to one he gave five talents, to another two, and to another one – to Lu 19:11-27.
every man according to his ability – and straightaway departed. 16 Then he
who had received the five talents went and traded with them, and won
another five talents. 17 Likewise, he who received two gained another two.
18 But he who received the one went and dug a hole in the earth, and hid
his master's money.

19 After a long season, the lord of those servants came and reckoned
with them. 20 Then came he that had received five talents, and brought
another five talents, saying, Master, you delivered to me five talents; here,
I have gained with them five talents more. 21 Then his master said to him,
Well done, good and faithful servant. You have been faithful in a little; I
will appoint you over much. Enter into your master's joy![d]

22 Also he who received two talents came and said, Master, you delivered to me two talents; here, I have won two other talents with them.
23 And his master said to him, Well done, good and faithful servant. You

have been faithful in a little; I will appoint you over much. Go in, into
your master's joy.
24 Then he who had received the one talent came and said, Master, I
considered that you were a hard man, who reaps where you did not sow
and gathers where you did not scatter, 25 and was therefore afraid, and
went and hid your talent in the earth. Here, have your talent.
26 His master answered and said to him, You evil servant, and slothful:
you knew that I reap where I did not sow, and gather where I did not
scatter? 27 You ought therefore to have put my money with the money-
changers, and then at my coming I would have received what is my own (Mk 4:24,25
with profit. 28 Take therefore the talent from him, and give it to the one (Lu 8:18; 19:26.)
(Covenant) who has ten talents. 29 For every person who has will be given more, and
((M't 13:12)) he will have abundance; and from him who has not, shall be taken away
even what he has. 30 And cast that unprofitable servant into outer dark-
ness.[e] There will be weeping and gnashing of teeth.
31 When the Son of man comes in his glory, and all the holy angels
with him, then shall he sit upon the seat of his glory. 32 And before him
shall be gathered all nations. And he will separate them one from another,
as a shepherd divides the sheep from the goats. 33 And he will set the
(Covenant) sheep on his right hand and the goats on the left. 34 Then shall the king say
to those on his right hand, Come ye blessed children of my Father, inherit
the kingdom prepared for you from the beginning of the world. 35 For I (Isa 58:7)
was hungry and you gave me food. I was thirsty and you gave me drink. I (Eze 18:7)
was homeless and you lodged me. 36 I was naked and you clothed me. I
was sick and you visited me. I was in prison and you came to me.
37 Then the righteous will answer him, saying, Master, when did we
see you hungry and feed you, or thirsty and give you drink? 38 When did
we see you homeless and lodge you, or naked and clothe you? 39 Or when
did we see you sick, or in prison, and come to you? 40 And the king will
answer and say to them, Truly I say to you, inasmuch as you did it for one
of the least of these my brethren, you did it for me.
41 Then shall the king say to those who will be on the left hand, Depart
(Covenant) from me, ye cursed, into everlasting fire, which is prepared for the devil (Ps 6:8
and his angels. 42 For I was hungry and you gave me no food. I was thirsty (Lu 13:27 Joh 5:28,29)
and you gave me no drink. 43 I was homeless and you did not lodge me. I
was naked and you did not clothe me. I was sick, and in prison, and you
did not visit me.
44 Then they also will answer him, saying, Master, when did we see
you hungry, or thirsty, or homeless, or naked, or sick, or in prison, and
did not minister* to you? 45 Then shall he answer them and say, Truly I say
to you, inasmuch as you did it not for one of the least of these, you did it
not for me. 46 And these shall go into everlasting pain, but the righteous
into life eternal.

[**To minister**: to care for, serve, or administer. Used in the New Testament in a variety of ways, it includes the sense of attending to bodily needs, as here and at M't 6:33 and 8:15]

The Notes

Kingdom of heaven (25:1)

a) In this place, the 'kingdom of heaven' signifies the whole congregation of believers being still in this life, which God governs invisibly, as at Lu 7:8.

Lamps without oil (25:3)

b) By lamps without oil understand works without faith, which cannot shine because they are without light.

Not so, lest there be not enough (25:9)

c) Note here that their own good works were not sufficient for themselves, and therefore none remained to be distributed to their fellows.

Your master's joy (25:21,23)

d) Enter into your master's joy! is as much as to say, Possess the kingdom prepared for all such as are faithful.

Outer darkness (25:30)

e) Outer darkness does not here signify hell, but trouble and pains in this world, as in Isaiah 5:30.

Chapter 26

The Magdalene anoints Christ. They eat the Passover lamb and the supper of the Lord. Christ prays in the garden. Judas betrays him. Peter strikes off Malcus' ear. Christ is accused by false witnesses. Peter denies him.

The passion foretold

Passover instituted: Ex c12.

And it came to pass, when Jesus had finished all these sayings, he said to his disciples, [2]You know that after two days will be the Passover. And the Son of man will be delivered to be crucified.

Mk 14:1,2
Lu 22:1-6
Joh 11:47-57

[3]Then the chief priests, scribes, and elders of the people assembled together at the palace of the high priest called Caiaphas [4]and held a council, how they might take Jesus by subtlety and kill him. [5]But, they said, not on the holy day, lest any uproar arise among the people.

He is anointed for burial

Mk 14:3-11
Lu 7:36-38
Joh 12:1-8

[6]When Jesus was in Bethany, in the house of Simon the leper, [7]there came to him a woman who had an alabaster jar of precious anointing oil, and poured it on his head as he sat at the board. [8]When his disciples saw that, they were indignant, saying, Why this waste? [9]This oyntment might well have been sold, and the money given to the poor. [10]When Jesus understood this he said to them, Why do you trouble the woman? She has wrought a good work upon me. [11]For you will have poor folk always with you, but me you will not have always. [12]And in that she poured this oyntment on my body, she did it to bury me with. [13]Truly I say to you, wherever this gospel is preached throughout all the world, there also will this that she has done be told, for a memorial of her.

He is sold

[14]Then one of the twelve, called Judas Iscariot, went to the chief priests [15]and said, What will you give me, and I will deliver him to you? And they agreed with him for thirty pieces of silver. [16]And from that time, he sought an opportunity to betray him.

Sweet (unleavened) bread.

[**My Passover:** Galilean Jews ate Passover supper a day before the Jerusalem Jews, probably due to a different way of reckoning the beginning of the day. Thus Jesus could celebrate his Passover on Thursday evening and then himself be offered at Jerusalem during the Friday Passover preparations there]

Mk 14:12-21
Lu 22:7-13; 21-23.
Joh 13:21-30

[17]On the first day of sweet bread the disciples came to Jesus, saying to him, Where would you have us prepare for you to eat the Passover lamb? [18]And he said, Go into the city to a certain man, and say to him, The Master says, My time is at hand; I will keep my Passover* at your place with my disciples.

[19]And the disciples did as Jesus had directed them, and made ready the Passover lamb.

[20]When the evening was come, he sat down with the twelve. [21]And as they were eating he said, Truly I say to you that one of you will betray me. [22]And they were exceeding sorrowful, and began every one of them to

say to him, Is it I, Master? 23He answered and said, He who dips his hand
with me in the dish, the same will betray me. 24The Son of man goes as it
is written of him. But woe is to that man by whom the Son of man is
betrayed. It would have been good for that man if he had never been born.
25Then Judas who betrayed him answered and said, Is it I, Master?
Jesus said to him, You have said it.
26As they were eating, Jesus took bread and gave thanks, broke it, and
The institution of the sacrament of the body and blood of the Lord.
gave it to the disciples and said, Take, eat; this is my body. 27And he took Ge 14:18
the cup, and thanked, and gave it to them, saying, Drink of it, everyone. Heb 5:6 Mk 14:22-25
28For this is my blood of the new testament, which is shed for many for Lu 22:14-20; 31-34.
the remission of sins. 29I say to you, I will not drink henceforth of this 1Co 11:23-26.
fruit of the vine until that day when I shall drink it new with you in my
Father's kingdom.
30And when they had sung praises, they went out to the Mount of
Olives. 31Then Jesus said to them, You will all fall away because of me
this night. For it is written: I will smite the shepherd, and the sheep of the Zec 13:7
flock will be scattered abroad. 32But after I am risen again, I will go Mk 14:26-42 Lu 22:39-46
before you into Galilee.
33Peter answered and said to him, Even if everyone were to fall away
because of you, yet I would never fall away. 34Jesus said to him, Truly I
say to you that this same night, before the cock crows, you will deny me
three times. 35Peter said to him, If I had to die with you, yet I would not
deny you. Likewise also said all the disciples.
36Then Jesus went with them to a place which is called Gethsemane,
and said to the disciples, Sit here while I go and pray yonder. 37And he
took with him Peter and the two sons of Zebedee, and began to be
sorrowful, and to be in an agony. 38Then said Jesus to them, My soul is
heavy, even unto death. You stay here, and watch with me.
He arms himself against the passion
39And he went a little apart and fell flat on his face and prayed, saying,
O my Father, if it be possible, let this cup pass from me; nevertheless, not
as I will, but as you will.
40And he came back to the disciples and found them asleep, and said
to Peter, What, could you not watch with me for one hour? 41Watch, and
pray that you do not fall into temptation. The spirit is willing, but the flesh
is weak.
42He went away once more and prayed, saying, O my Father, if this
cup cannot pass away from me but that I drink of it, thy will be fulfilled.
43And he came and found his disciples asleep again. For their eyes were
heavy. 44And he left them and went again and prayed the third time,
saying the same words. 45Then he came to his disciples and said to them,
Sleep on now, and take your rest![a] Take heed: the hour is at hand, and the
Son of man is betrayed into the hands of sinners. 46Arise, let us be going.
Behold, he who betrays me is at hand.
47While he was yet speaking, lo, Judas, one of the twelve, came, and
with him a large band of men bearing swords and clubs, sent by the chief Mk 14:43-50
priests and elders of the people. 48And he who betrayed him had arranged Lu 22:47-53 Joh 18:1-11 Ps 41:9

a sign, saying, Whoever I kiss, he is the one; lay hands on him. [49]And at
He is betrayed once he went up to Jesus and said, Hail, Master! and kissed him. [50]And
Jesus said to him, Friend, why have you come? Then they came and laid
hands on Jesus and took him.

[51]And at that, one of the men who were with Jesus stretched out his
hand and drew his sword, and struck a servant of the high priest and cut
off his ear. [52]Then said Jesus to him, Put your sword back in its sheath. Ge 9:6
For all who take the sword will perish by the sword. [53]Or do you think I Rev 13:10
cannot now pray to my Father, and he would send me more than twelve
legions of angels? [54]But how then would the scriptures be fulfilled? For
this is how it must be.

[55]At the same time Jesus said to the throng, You have come out as if
against a thief, with swords and clubs to take me. I sat daily teaching in
the temple among you, and you did not take me. [56]All this was done so
that the scriptures of the prophets may be fulfilled.

[57]Then all the disciples forsook him and fled.

He is taken And they took Jesus and led him to Caiaphas, the high priest, where Mk 14:53-65
the scribes and the elders were assembled. [58]And Peter followed him from Lu 22:54-55;
afar off to the high priest's palace, and went in and sat with the servants, 66-71. Joh 18:12-
to see the end of it. 14, 19-24.

[59]The chief priests and the elders and all the council sought false
witness against Jesus, in order to put him to death, [60]but found none.
He is falsely accused Though many false witnesses came forward, yet they found none. At the
last came two false witnesses, [61]and said, This fellow said, I can destroy Joh 2:19
the temple of God and build it again in three days.

[62]And the chief priest arose and said to Jesus, Do you answer nothing?
How is it that these men bear witness against you? [63]But Jesus held his
peace. And the chief priest spoke and said to him, I charge you in the
name of the living God to tell us if you are Christ, the Son of God.

[64]Jesus said to him, It is as you have said. But I say to you, hereafter
you will see the Son of man sitting on the right hand of power, and come
in the clouds of the sky.

[65]Then the high priest tore his clothes, saying, He has blasphemed!
Why do we need any more witnesses? Here, now you have heard his
blasphemy. [66]What do you think? They answered and said, He is worthy
to die. [67]Then they spat in his face and buffeted him with fists. And others
struck him with the palm of their hands on the face, [68]saying, Tell us,
Christ, who is it that hit you?

[69]Peter was sitting out in the centre courtyard. And a maidservant
came to him, saying, You also were with Jesus of Galilee. [70]But he denied Mk 14:66-72
Peter denies him it before them all, saying, I don't know what you are saying. [71]When he Lu 22:54-62
had gone out into the porch, another servant girl saw him and said to the Joh 18:15-
people who were there, This fellow was also with Jesus of Nazareth. 18, 25-27.
[72]And again Peter denied with an oath that he knew the man. [73]And after a
while, some people standing nearby came up and said to Peter, Surely you
are also one of them, for your speech gives you away.

[74]Then he began to curse, and to swear that he did not know the man.
And immediately the cock crew. [75]And Peter remembered the words of
Jesus, who had said to him, Before the cock crows, you will deny me
three times. And he went out at the doors and wept bitterly.

The Notes

Sleep on now (26:45)

a) Sleep on and take your rest: this is irony; that is, one thing spoken and another meant. In bidding them to sleep, he signified that it would have been better for them to have gone about other things than to fall to sleeping at this time.

Chapter 27

Christ is delivered to Pilate. Judas hangs himself. Christ is crucified between thieves. He dies and is buried. Watchmen guard the grave.

When the morning was come, all the chief priests and the elders of the
people held a council against Jesus, to put him to death, [2]and brought him Mk 15:1
He is delivered to Pilate — bound, and delivered him to Pontius Pilate the governor. Lu 23:1 Joh 18:28
[3]Then when Judas who had betrayed him saw that he was condemned, Acts 1:16-20
he repented, and brought back the thirty pieces of silver to the chief
priests and elders, [4]saying, I have sinned, betraying the innocent blood.
And they said, What is that to us? You see to it. [5]And Judas cast down the
silver pieces in the temple and departed, and went and hanged himself.
[6]And the chief priests took the silver pieces and said, It is not lawful to
put them into the treasury, because it is the price of blood. [7]And they took
counsel, and bought with the money a potter's field to bury strangers in.
[8]Therefore that field is called the Field of Blood until this day. [9]Then was
[**Jeremiah**: actually a free quotation from Zechariah 11:12,13] — fulfilled that which was spoken by Jeremiah the prophet,* saying: And
they took thirty silver pieces, the price of him that was sold, whom they Jer 32:6-9
bought from the children of Israel, [10]and gave them for the potter's field, Zec 11:12,13
as the Lord appointed me.
[11]Jesus stood before the governor, and the governor asked him, saying,
Are you the king of the Jews? Jesus said to him, It is as you say. [12]And
when he was accused by the chief priests and elders, he answered nothing.
[13]Then Pilate said to him, Do you not hear how many things they lay Mk 15:2-14
He holds his peace — against you? [14]And he answered him never a word, insomuch that the Lu 23:2-24 Joh 18:29-40
governor marvelled greatly.
[15]At that feast the governor was accustomed to release to the people a
prisoner, whomever they would request. [16]He had then a notable prisoner
called Barabbas. [17]And when the people were gathered together, Pilate
said to them, Which do you want me to release to you: Barabbas, or Jesus
who is called Christ? [18]For he knew well that it was for envy they had
delivered him.
[19]When he was seated to give judgment, his wife sent to him, saying,
Have nothing to do with that just man. For I have suffered many things
this day in a dream about him. [20]But the chief priests and the elders had
persuaded the people that they should ask for Barabbas and destroy Jesus.

21Then the governor spoke and said to them, Which of the two do you
The people choose Barabbas
want me to set free to you? And they said, Barabbas! 22Pilate said to them,
What shall I do then with Jesus who is called Christ? They all said to him,
Let him be crucified! 23Then said the governor, What evil has he done?
And they cried out all the more, saying, Let him be crucified!

24When Pilate saw that he was not prevailing, but that more of a
tumult was made, he took water and washed his hands before the people,
His judge declares him to be just
saying, I am innocent of the blood of this just person, and that you should
see. 25Then all the people answered and said, His blood be on us and on
our children!

He is scourged

26Then he let Barabbas go free to them, and had Jesus scourged, and
delivered him to be crucified.

27Then the governor's soldiers took Jesus to the common hall, and
gathered to him the whole company of soldiers. 28And they stripped him Mk 15:15-19
He is crowned
and put on him a purple robe, 29and plaited a crown of thorns and put it on Lu 23:25
his head, and a reed in his right hand. And they bowed their knees before Isa 50:6; 53:3-5.
him and mocked him, saying, Hail, King of the Jews! 30And they spat
upon him, and took the reed and struck him on the head.

31And when they had mocked him, they took the robe back from him
and put his own clothes on him, and led him away to crucify him. 32And
as they went out, they found a man from Cyrene named Simon; him they
compelled to bear his cross. 33And when they came to the place called Mk 15:20-32
Golgotha (which means, a place of dead mens' skulls), 34they gave him Lu 23:26-43 Joh 19:17-29
vinegar to drink mixed with gall. But when he had tasted of it, he would Ps 69:21
not drink.

He is crucified

35When they had crucified him, they parted his garments and cast lots,
to fulfil that which was spoken by the prophet: They divided my garments Ps 22:18
among them, and for my vesture did cast lots. 36And they sat and kept
watch over him there. 37And they set up over his head his accusation,
written THIS IS JESUS THE KING OF THE JEWS. 38And there were two
thieves crucified with him, one on the right hand and another on the left.

He is railed on

39The people who passed by reviled him, wagging their heads 40and
saying, You who destroy the temple of God and build it in three days,
save yourself! If you are the Son of God, come down from the cross!

41Likewise also the high priests, mocking him with the scribes and
elders, said, 42He saved others; himself he cannot save. If he really is the Ps 42:9,10
king of Israel, let him come down now from the cross, and we will believe
him. 43He trusted in God – let him deliver him now, if he will have him.
For he said, I am the Son of God.

44Also the thieves who were crucified with him cast the same in his
teeth.

[**The 6th to 9th hour**: 12:00 noon to 3:00 pm by Jewish reckoning, counting from sunrise. About 3:00 Jesus died, when Passover lambs were also being killed in Jerusalem, thus fulfilling the law and the prophets]

45From the sixth hour there was darkness over all the land until the
ninth hour.* 46And about the ninth hour, Jesus cried out with a loud voice,
saying, Eli, Eli, lama sabachthani? (which means, My God, my God, why Ps 22:1
have you forsaken me?)

47Some of the people who were standing there, when they heard that,

said, This man is calling for Elijah! 48And straightaway one of them ran
and took a sponge, and filled it full of vinegar and put it on a reed, and
gave him to drink. 49Others said, Leave him be; let us see if Elijah will
come and deliver him.

He gives up his spirit
The veil rents

50Jesus cried out again with a loud voice, and yielded up the spirit.
51And behold: the veil of the temple did tear in two, from the top to the
bottom, and the earth did quake, and the rocks did split. 52And graves did
open, and the bodies of many saints who slept arose, 53and came out of the
graves after his resurrection, and came into the holy city and appeared to
many.

Graves open

Mk 15:37-41
Lu 23:44-49
Joh 19:30
Heb 9:12; 10:19,20.

54When the centurion and those who were with him watching Jesus
saw the earthquake and those things that happened, they feared greatly,
saying, Surely this was the Son of God.

55And many women were there, watching him from afar – those who
had followed Jesus from Galilee, ministering to him. 56Among them were
Mary Magdalene, Mary the mother of James and Joses, and the mother of
Zebedee's children.

57When the evening was come, there came a rich man of Arimathea
named Joseph, which man also was Jesus' disciple. 58He went to Pilate
and requested the body of Jesus. Then Pilate commanded the body to be
delivered.

He is buried

59And Joseph took the body and wrapped it in a clean linen cloth,
60and put it in his new tomb, which he had hewn out even in the rock. He
rolled a great stone to the door of the sepulchre and departed. 61And there
were Mary Magdalene and the other Mary, sitting across from the sep-
ulchre.

Mk 15:42-47
Lu 23:50-56
Joh 19:31-42
Isa 53:9

[**The next day** was the Saturday Sabbath. Friday, the Passover, was also called the day of preparation]

62The next day,* which followed the day of preparing the Sabbath, the
high priests and Pharisees assembled before Pilate 63and said, Sir, we
remember what this deceiver said while he was still alive: After three
days, I will arise again. 64Command therefore that the sepulchre be made
secure until the third day, lest perhaps his disciples come and steal him
away, and say to the people that he is risen from the dead, and the last
error be worse than the first.

He is watched for rising again.

65Pilate said to them, Take watchmen; go and make it as secure as you
can. 66And they went and made the sepulchre secure with watchmen, and
sealed the stone.

Chapter 28

The resurrection of Christ. The high priests give the soldiers a large sum of money to say that Christ was stolen out of his grave. Christ appears to his disciples, and sends them forth to preach and to baptize.

Early Sunday morning

At the close of the Sabbath day, which is in the dawn of the morrow after
the Sabbath, Mary Magdalene and the other Mary came to see the sep-
ulchre. 2And behold, there was a great earthquake. For the angel of the
Lord descended from heaven, and came and rolled back the stone from

Mk c16
Lu 24:1-12
Joh c20

the door and sat upon it. 3His countenance was like lightening, and his
raiment white as snow. 4And for fear of him the guards were over-
whelmed, and became as dead men.
5The angel spoke and said to the women, Fear not: I know that you
seek Jesus, who was crucified. 6He is not here. He is risen, as he said.
Come and see the place where the Lord was put. 7And go quickly and tell
his disciples that he is risen from death. And behold, he will go before you
into Galilee; there you will see him. Lo, I have told you.
8And they departed quickly from the sepulchre with fear and great joy,
and did run to bring his disciples word. 9And as they went to tell his
disciples, behold, Jesus met them, saying, All Hail! And they came and
held him by the feet and worshipped him. 10Then said Jesus to them, Do
not be afraid. Go and tell my brethren[a] to go into Galilee, and there they
will see me.
11When they had gone, some of the guards went into the city and told
to the high priests all the things that had happened. 12And they gathered
them together with the elders and took counsel, and gave a large sum of
money to the soldiers, 13saying, Say that his disciples came by night and
stole him away while you slept. 14And if this comes to the governor's
ears, we will appease him and keep you out of trouble.
15And the soldiers took the money and did as they were instructed.
And this story is circulated among the Jews to this day.
16Then the eleven disciples went away into Galilee, to a mountain
where Jesus had directed them. 17And when they saw him, they wor-
shipped him. But some of them doubted.
18And Jesus came and spoke to them, saying, All power is given to me
in heaven and in earth. 19Go therefore and teach all nations, baptizing
them in the name of the Father and the Son and the Holy Spirit, 20and Mk 16:14-20 Lu 24:36-53
teaching them to observe all things, whatsoever I commanded you. And
lo, I am with you always, even until the end of the world.

Here ends the gospel
of St. Matthew.

The Notes

Tell my brethren (28:10) a) This means, tell those who believe in me, as at Romans 8:29.

A Prologue Upon the Gospel of Mark

Of Mark, also called John Mark, read in Acts 12 how Peter, after he was released from prison by the angel, went to Mark's mother's house, where many of the disciples were praying for his deliverance. And Paul and Barnabas took him with them from Jerusalem to Antioch, and when they were sent out to preach (Acts 13). He also departed from them, as it appears in the said chapter, and returned to Jerusalem again. And Paul and Barnabas were at variance about him (Acts 15), Paul not wanting to take him with them, because he forsook them in their first journey. Notwithstanding, when Paul wrote the epistle to the Colossians, Mark was with him, as he says in the fourth chapter. Of him Paul also testifies that he was both Barnabas' nephew (the son of Barnabas' sister) and Paul's fellow worker in the kingdom of God (Col 4:10). And in 2 Timothy c. 4, Paul instructs Timothy to bring Mark with him, affirming that he was needful to him, to minister to him. Finally, he was also with Peter when he wrote his first epistle, and so close that Peter calls him his son. From this you see who Mark learned his gospel from: the very apostles, whom he was with continually. You see also of what authority his writing is, and how worthy of credence. *W.T. (1534)*

[Ed: It is said that Mark's gospel may have been written in the 50s, but in any event it was before the destruction of the temple in A.D. 70, judging from comments in chapter 13.]

The Gospel of St. Mark

Chapter 1

The office of John the Baptist. The baptism of Christ, his fasting, his preaching, and the calling of Peter, Andrew, James, and John. Christ heals the man with the unclean spirit, helps Peter's mother-in-law, and cleanses the leper.

THE BEGINNING of the gospel of Jesus Christ, the Son of God, [2]as it is
written in the prophets: Behold, I send my messenger before your face, Isa 40:3
who shall prepare your way before you. [3]The voice of a crier in the wild- Mal 3:1 M't cc3,4
erness: Prepare ye the way of the Lord; make his paths straight! Lu cc3,4
[4]John baptized in the wilderness, and preached the baptism of repen- Joh c1
tance for the remission of sins. [5]And all the countryside of Judea and the
people of Jerusalem went out to him, and were all baptized by him in the
river Jordan, confessing their sins.
[6]John was clothed with camel's hair, and with a girdle of skin about
his loins. And he ate locusts and wild honey,[a] [7]and preached, saying, One
mightier than I comes after me, whose shoe latchet I am not worthy to
stoop down and loose. [8]I have baptized you with water, but he will baptize
you with the Holy Spirit.
[9]And it came to pass in those days that Jesus came from Nazareth, a
Jesus is baptized town of Galilee, and was baptized by John in the Jordan River. [10]And as
soon as Jesus came out of the water, John saw heaven open,[b] and the Holy M't 3:17 Lu 3:22
Spirit descending upon him like a dove. [11]And there came a voice from Joh 1:32
heaven: You are my dear Son, in whom I delight. 2Pe 1:16-18
[12]And immediately the Spirit drove him into the wilderness. [13]And he
was there in the wilderness forty days, and was tried by Satan, and was

with wild creatures. And the angels ministered to him.
[**Taken:** John the Baptist was imprisoned by Herod the tetrarch. See 6:14-29, and note (a) to M't c14]
[14]After John was taken,* Jesus came into Galilee, preaching the gospel M't 4:12-22
of the kingdom of God [15]and saying, The time has come, and the kingdom
of God is at hand. Repent, and believe the gospel!

[16]As he walked by the Sea of Galilee, he saw Simon and John his
brother casting nets into the sea, for they were fishermen. [17]And Jesus said
to them, Follow me, and I will make you fishers of men. [18]And straight-
away they left their nets and followed him. [19]And when he had gone a
little further, he saw James the son of Zebedee and John his brother as
they were in the boat mending their nets. [20]And right away he called them.
And they left their father Zebedee in the boat with his hired servants, and
went their way after him.

[21]And they entered into Capernaum. And straightaway on the Sabbath
days he entered into the synagogue and taught. [22]And the people mar- M't 7:29
velled at his teaching. For he taught them as one who had power with him, Lu 4:32
and not as the scribes.

[23]And there was in their synagogue a man vexed with an unclean
spirit, who cried out, [24]saying, Let us be! What have we to do with you,
Jesus of Nazareth? Have you come to destroy us? I know you, who you Lu 4:33-35
are: even the Holy One of God. [25]And Jesus rebuked him, saying, Hold
your peace and come out of him!

[26]And the unclean spirit tore the man and cried out with a loud voice,
The unclean spirit is cast out
and came out of him. [27]And they were all amazed, insomuch that they
questioned one another among themselves, saying, What thing is this?
What new doctrine is this?[c] For he commands the foul spirits with power,
and they obey him. [28]And immediately his fame spread abroad throughout
all the region bordering on Galilee.

[29]And directly, as soon as they had left the synagogue, they entered
into the house of Simon and Andrew with James and John. [30]And Simon's M't 8:14
mother-in-law lay sick of a fever. And right away they told him of her. Lu 4:38,39
[31]And he came and took her by the hand and lifted her up. And the fever
left her immediately, and she ministered to them.

[32]And in the evening, when the sun was down, people brought to him
all their sick and those that were possessed with devils. [33]And all the city
gathered together at the door. [34]And he healed many who were sick of
different diseases. And he cast out many devils, and would not permit the
devils to speak, because they knew him.

[35]And in the morning very early, Jesus arose and went out to a solitary
place, and there prayed. [36]And Simon and those who were with him
followed after Jesus. [37]And when they had found him, they said to him,
All the people are searching for you. [38] He said to them, Let us go into the
next towns so that I can preach there also; for truly, I came out for that
purpose.

[39]And he preached in their synagogues throughout all Galilee, and cast
the devils out.

[40]And there came a leper to him, beseeching him, who kneeled down

to him and said to him, If you will, you can make me clean. 41And Jesus M't 8:2-4
had compassion on him, and put forth his hand, touched him, and said to Lu 5:12-16
him, I will; be clean. 42And as soon as he had spoken, immediately the
leprosy departed from him and he was cleansed. 43And Jesus charged the
man, and sent him away directly, 44and said to him, See that you say
nothing to anyone, but go and show yourself to the priest, and offer for
your cleansing those things that Moses commanded, for a testimony to Lev 14:2
them.

45But the man (as soon as he had left) began to talk freely, and to tell
everyone what had been done, so that Jesus could no longer openly enter
into the towns, but was out in the country. And people came to him from
every quarter.

The Notes

Locusts (1:6) a) See note (a) to Matthew, chapter 3.

John saw heaven open, etc (1:10) b) That is, John had manifest confirmation of the Godhead of Christ, and was fully assured that he was the one sent by God to be the saviour of all who would believe in him. See Ezekiel 1:1 and note thereon.

What new doctrine is this? (1:27) c) It was new doctrine then, and now after 1,536 years is still new. When will it then be old? [Ed: Here we see that John Rogers penned this note in 1536. I copy it now, 476 years later, in the year of our Lord 2012.]

Chapter 2

Jesus heals the paralytic, calls Levi, the customs officer, eats with open sinners, and defends his disciples.

After a few days he entered into Capernaum again, and it was rumoured
that he was in a house. 2And soon many gathered together, insomuch that M't 9:1-8
now there was no room to receive them, no, not so much as about the Lu 5:1-26
door. And he preached the word to them. 3And there came to him people
bringing a paralytic, borne by four men. 4And because they could not
come near to him for the press, they uncovered the roof of the house
where he was. And when they had broken it open, they let down the bed
that the paralytic lay in. 5When Jesus saw their faith, he said to the
paralytic, Son, your sins are forgiven you.

6And certain of the scribes were sitting there and thinking in their
hearts, 7How does this fellow so blaspheme? Who can forgive sins, but
God only? 8And immediately, when Jesus perceived in his spirit that they
so questioned in themselves, he said to them, Why do you think such
things in your hearts? 9Which is easier to say to the paralytic: Your sins
are forgiven you, or to say, Arise, take up your bed and walk? 10But so
that you may know that the Son of man has power in earth to forgive
sins* – He spoke to the paralytic: 11I say to you, arise, and take up your
bed, and go your way into your own house. 12And at once he arose, took
up the bed, and went out before them all, so that they were all amazed and
glorified God, saying, We have never seen anything like this!

*The visible miracle would be a sign of the invisible power.

13And he went again to the sea side. And all the people gathered to

[**Levi** is also called Matthew. See M't 9:9]

him, and he taught them. 14And as Jesus was passing by, he saw Levi* the
son of Alphaeus sitting at the receipt of custom and said to him, Follow M't 9:9-13
me. And he arose and followed him. Lu 5:27-32

Publicans and sinners eat with Christ.

15And it came to pass, as Jesus sat at food in Levi's house, that many
publicans and sinners sat at food also with Jesus and his disciples. For
there were many who followed him. 16And when the scribes and Pharisees
saw him eat with publicans and sinners, they said to his disciples, How is
it that he eats and drinks with publicans and sinners? 17When Jesus heard
that, he said to them, The whole have no need of the physician, but the
sick do. I came not to call the righteous, but sinners to repentance.

18And the disciples of John and the Pharisees used to fast, and so they
came and said to him, Why do the disciples of John and of the Pharisees
fast, but your disciples do not fast? 19And Jesus said to them, Can the M't 9:14-17
children of a wedding fast while the bridegroom is with them? As long as Lu 5:33-39
they have the bridegroom with them, they cannot fast. 20But the days will
come when the bridegroom will be taken from them, and then they will

[**New cloth**: new cloth is unfulled or unshrunk]

[**Old wineskins**, being brittle, crack and split under the pressure of fermentation]

fast, in those days.[a] 21Also, no one sows a piece of new cloth* onto an old
garment, because then the new piece pulls away from the old, and the tear
is worse. 22Likewise, no one pours new wine into old wineskins,* for if he
does, the new wine bursts the skins, and the wine runs out and the vessels
are marred. But new wine must be poured into new vessels.

23And it chanced that he was walking through the grain fields in the
Sabbath days, and his disciples, as they went their way, began to pluck the
ears of grain. 24And the Pharisees said to him, Look, why are they doing M't 12:1-8 Lu 6:1-5
on the Sabbath days that which is not lawful? 1Sam 21:1-6

25And he said to them, Have you never read what David did when he
had need and was hungry, both he and those who were with him? 26How
he went into the house of God in the days of Abiathar the high priest and
did eat the hallowed loaves, which it is not lawful to eat but for the priests
only, and gave also to those who were with him?

The Sabbath was made for man. Christ is Lord over the Sabbath.

27And he said to them, The Sabbath was made for man, and not man
for the Sabbath. 28Therefore the Son of man is Lord even of the Sabbath
day.

The Notes

Then they shall fast (2:20)

a) That is, as long as I am with them, they will not feel the trouble and great persecution of the world. But when I am taken from them, then they will fast; that is, then they will mourn, for then their persecution and trouble will begin.

Chapter 3

He helps the man with the withered hand, and chooses his apostles. He casts out the unclean spirit, which the Pharisees ascribe to the devil. The brother, sister, and mother of Christ.

And he entered again into the synagogue, and there was a man there who M't 12:9-14
had a withered hand. 2And they watched him to see if he would heal him Lu 6:6-11
on the Sabbath day, so that they might accuse him. 3And he said to the

man who had the withered hand, Arise, and stand in the midst. 4And he
said to them, Is it lawful to do a good deed on the Sabbath days, or an evil
deed? To save life, or to kill? But they held their peace. 5And he looked
round about on them angrily, mourning the blindness of their hearts, and
said to the man, Stretch forth your hand. And he stretched it out, and his
hand was restored fully as whole as the other.

6Then the Pharisees departed, and straightaway assembled a council
with Herod's men against him, so that they might destroy him.

[**The sea**: the Sea of Galilee, a large freshwater lake, 13 miles long and 8 miles across at its widest]

7And Jesus withdrew with his disciples to the sea.* And great crowds M't 12:15-21
followed him from Galilee and from Judea, 8and from Jerusalem and from
Idumea and from beyond the Jordan, and also those who dwelt about Tyre
and Sidon: great crowds who, when they heard the things he did, came to
him. 9And he told his disciples that a boat should be kept at hand for him,
because of the people, lest they should throng him. 10For he had healed
many, insomuch that they pressed in upon him to touch him, as many as
had afflictions. 11And when the unclean spirits saw him, they fell down
before him and cried out, saying, You are the Son of God! 12And he
charged them strictly not to make him known.

The apostles are chosen.

13And he went up into a mountain and called to him whom he wished, M't 10:1-8
and they came to him. 14And he ordained the twelve to be with him, so Lu 6:12-16
that he might send them to preach, 15and to have power to heal sicknesses
and to cast out devils. 16And he gave Simon the name Peter. 17And he
called James, the son of Zebedee, and John, James' brother, and gave
them the name Boanerges, which means Sons of Thunder. 18And there
were Andrew and Philip, Bartholomew, Matthew, Thomas, James the son
of Alphaeus, Thaddaeus, Simon of Canaan, 19and Judas Iscariot, which
same also betrayed him.

And they came to a house. 20And the people assembled together again,
so greatly that they had no opportunity so much as to eat bread. 21And
when his family members heard of it, they set out to get him, because they
thought he would be beside himself.

Beelzebub

22And the scribes who came from Jerusalem said, He has Beelzebub, M't 9:32-34;
and by the power of the chief devil he casts out devils. 23And Jesus called 12:22-32.
them to him and spoke to them in similitudes: How can Satan drive out Lu 11:14-19
Satan? 24For if a realm is divided against itself, that realm cannot endure.
25Or if a house is divided against itself, that house cannot continue. 26So if
Satan makes insurrection against himself and is divided, he cannot con-
tinue, but is at an end. 27No one can enter into a strong man's house and
take away his goods unless he first binds the strong man, and then he
plunders his house. 28Truly I say to you, all sins may be forgiven the
children of men, and blasphemies with which they blaspheme. 29But he
who blasphemes the Holy Spirit may never have forgiveness, but is liable
to eternal condemnation. 30(For they said he had an unclean spirit.)

Of blasphemy, read M't 12, note (a).

Sent to him: that is, sent a message to him by the people.

31Then his mother and his brethren arrived and stood outside, and sent
to him* and called for him. 32The people were sitting around him, and they M't 12:46-50
said to Jesus, Your mother and your brethren are asking for you outside. Lu 8:19-21

[33]And he answered them, saying, Who are my mother and my brethren?
[34]And he looked round about on his disciples, who sat in a circle around
him, and said, Behold my mother and my brethren. [35]For whosoever does
the will of God, he is my brother, my sister, and mother.

Chapter 4

The parable of the sower. Take heed to God's word. Christ stills the tempest of the sea, which obeyed him.

And he began again to teach by the sea side. And there gathered together
unto him crowds of people, so greatly that he entered into the boat and sat Mk 3:9
in it in the sea, and all the people were by the sea side on the shore. [2]And M't 13:1-23
he taught them many things in similitudes, and said to them in his lesson: Lu 8:4-18
The sower [3]Hearken to! Behold, there went out a sower to sow. [4]And it happened as
he sowed that some seed fell by the wayside, and the fowls of the air came
and devoured it up. [5]Some fell on stony ground, where it had not much
earth, and quickly sprang up because it did not have depth of earth; [6]but as
soon as the sun was up, it caught heat, and because it did not have rooting,
withered away. [7]And some fell among the thorns, and the thorns grew up
and choked it, so that it gave no fruit. [8]And some fell upon good ground,
and yielded fruit that sprang up and grew, and brought forth: some thirty-
fold, some sixtyfold, and some a hundredfold. [9]And he said to them, He
who has ears to hear, let him hear.

[10]And when he was alone, those who were around him with the twelve
asked him about the similitude. [11]And he said to them, To you it is given Isa 6:8-10
to know the mystery of the kingdom of God. But to those who are outside, M't 13:11-15
Those who see but do not perceive or understand. all things shall be done in similitudes, [12]and when they see, they will see Lu 8:10 Joh 12:37-41
but not discern, and when they hear, they will hear and not understand, Ac 28:25-27
lest at any time they should turn; and their sins would be forgiven them. Ro 11:7-10

[13]And he said to them, Do you not understand this similitude? How
then will you understand any other similitudes? [14]The sower sows the
The sower expounded word. [15]And those who are by the wayside where the word is sown are
those to whom, as soon as they have heard it, Satan comes immediately,
and takes away the word that was sown in their hearts. [16]And likewise,
those who receive the seed on the stony ground are those who, when they
have heard the word, at once receive it with gladness, [17]yet have no roots
in themselves. And so they endure but a time, and once trouble and per-
secution arise for the word's sake, they fall immediately. [18]And those who
receive the seed among the thorns are such as hear the word, [19]but the care
of this world, and the deceitfulness of riches, and the hunger for other
things, enter in and choke the word, and it is made unfruitful. [20]And those
who received the seed in good ground are those who hear the word and
receive it, and bring forth fruit: some thirtyfold, some sixtyfold, some a
hundredfold.

[21]And Jesus said to the people, Is the candle lighted to be put under a
bushel or under the table, and not rather to be put on a candlestick? [22]For M't 5:14-16
there is nothing so hid that it will not be revealed, nor so secret but that it Lu 8:16-18

may become clear. [23]If any person has ears to hear, let him hear.
[24]And he said to them, Attend with care to what you hear. With the
same measure you give, it will be measured back to you. And to you who M't 13:12 &
hear, more will be given. [25]For to him who has, it will be given, but from note thereon.
him who has not, shall be taken away even what he has.
[26]And he said, The kingdom of God is like this: it is as if a man sows
seed in the ground, [27]and sleeps, and rises up night and day, and the seed M't 13:24-30
sprouts and grows up, he knows not how. [28]For the earth brings forth fruit
of herself: first the blade, then the ears, after that the full grain in the ears.
[29]And as soon as the fruit is brought forth, immediately the man thrusts in
the sickle, because the harvest has come.
[30]And he said, To what may we liken the kingdom of God? or what
comparison can we use? [31]It is like a grain of mustard seed, which, when M't 13:31-32
it is sown in the earth, is the least of all seeds that are in the earth. [32]But Lu 13:18,19
after it is sown, it grows up and is greatest of all shrubs, and bears great
branches, so that the birds of the air may dwell under the cover of it.
[33]And with many such similitudes he preached the word to the people, M't 13:34-35
as they were able to hear it. [34]And without similitude he spoke nothing to Ps 78:2
them. But when they were apart, he expounded all things to his disciples.
[35]And the same day, when evening was come, he said to them, Let us
pass over to the other side. [36]And they left the people and took him just as M't 8:23-27
he was in the boat. And there were also with him other boats. [37]And there Lu 8:22-25
arose a great storm of wind, and it dashed the waves into the boat so that
it was full. [38]And he was in the stern, asleep on a pillow. And they awoke
him and said to him, Teacher, do you not care if we perish?
[**Rebuked**: repressed or drove back with words] [39]And he rose up and rebuked[*] the wind, and said to the sea, Peace,
and be still! And the wind allayed, and there followed a great calm. [40]And
he said to them, Why are you so fearful? How is it that you have no faith?
[41]And they feared exceedingly, and said to one another, What manner of
man is this? For both wind and sea obey him.

Chapter 5

He delivers the possessed man from the unclean spirits, and the woman from the flow of blood, and raises the synagogue leader's daughter.

And they went over to the other side of the sea, into the country of the
Gadarenes. [2]And when he got out of the boat, there met him out of the M't 8:28-34
graves a man possessed by an unclean spirit, [3]who had his dwelling Lu 8:26-39
among the graves. And no man could bind him, no, not with chains. [4]For
he had often been bound with shackles and chains, but he pulled the
chains apart and broke the shackles in pieces. Neither could anyone quiet
him. [5]And always, both night and day, he wailed in the mountains and in
the graves, and beat himself with stones.
[6]When he saw Jesus afar off, he ran and worshipped him,[a] [7]and cried
out with a loud voice and said, What have I to do with you, Jesus Son of
the most high God? I call on you in the name of God not to torment me.

8 For Jesus had said to him, Come out of the man, you foul spirit! 9 And
Jesus asked him, What is your name? He answered, saying, My name is
Legion, for we are many. 10 And he pressed Jesus urgently not to send
them away out of the region.

Legion of spirits [see note (c) on Luke 8]

11 And there was there, near to the mountains, a great herd of swine
feeding. 12 All the devils besought him, saying, Send us into the herd of
swine, so that we may enter into them. 13 And at once Jesus gave them
leave. And the unclean spirits went out and entered into the swine. And
the herd started, and ran headlong into the sea. There were about 2,000
swine, and they were drowned in the sea.

14 And the swineherds fled and told this in the town and in the country.
And the people came out to see what had happened, 15 and came to Jesus.
They saw the man who had been vexed with the fiend and had the legion
sitting both clothed and in his right mind, and were afraid. 16 And those
who had seen it told them what had happened to the man possessed with
the devil, and also about the swine. 17 And they began to urge Jesus to
depart from their shores.

18 And when he got into the boat, the man who had been possessed
with the devil asked him if he could be with him. 19 However Jesus would
not allow him, but said to him, Go home to your own house and to your
friends, and show them what great things the Lord has done for you, and
how he had compassion on you.

20 And he departed and began to tell everywhere in the Ten Cities*
what great things Jesus had done for him. And all the people marvelled.

21 And when Jesus had crossed over again by boat to the other side,*
crowds of people gathered to him. And he was near to the sea. 22 And there M't 9:18-26
came one of the leaders of the synagogue, whose name was Jairus. And Lu 8:40-56
when he saw him, he fell down at his feet, 23 and besought him greatly,
saying, My daughter lies at the point of death. Please come and lay your
hand on her, so that she can be saved and live.

[**The Ten Cities**, also called Decapolis: a league of separate Greek municipalities under Rome's jurisdiction, most lying south of the Sea of Galilee and east of the Jordan]
[**Other side**: north-westerly to Capernaum across the lake. M't 9:1]

24 And Jesus went with him, and the crowds followed him and
thronged him. 25 And there was a certain woman who had been troubled by
a flow of blood for twelve years. 26 She had endured many things from
many physicians, and spent all that she had, and was not helped at all, but
grew worse and worse. 27 When she heard of Jesus, she penetrated the
press behind him and touched his garment. 28 For she thought, If I can but
touch his clothes, I shall be healed. 29 And straightaway her flow of blood
was dried up, and she felt in her body that she was healed of the illness.

30 And Jesus immediately felt in himself the power that went out of
him, and turned around in the press of people and said, Who touched my
clothes? 31 And his disciples said to him, You see the people thronging
you, and yet you ask, Who touched me?

32 And he looked round about to see who had done it. 33 The woman
feared and trembled (for she knew what was done within her), and she
came and fell down before him, and told him the truth of everything.
34 And he said to her, Daughter, your faith has made you whole. Go in

peace, and be healed of your affliction.

The synagogue leader's daughter

35 While he was yet speaking, certain people came from the house of
the synagogue leader and said, Your daughter is dead; why trouble the
Teacher any further? 36 As soon as Jesus heard that word spoken, he said
to the leader of the synagogue, Be not afraid; only believe.

37 And he let no one follow him other than Peter, James, and John the
brother of James. 38 And he went to the house of the synagogue leader and
saw the disturbance, and the people who wept and wailed greatly, 39 and
went in and said to them, Why do you make this ado, and weep? The
maiden is not dead, but sleeping. 40 And they laughed him to scorn.

Then he put them all out, and took the father and the mother of the
maiden and those who were with him, and entered in where the maiden
lay. 41 He took the maiden by the hand and said to her, Tabitha, cumi!
which translated is, Child, I say to you, arise. 42 And at once the maiden
arose, and she walked on her feet, for she was twelve years of age. And
they were astonished at it beyond measure. 43 And he charged them strictly
that no one should know of it, and said to give her food.

The Notes

The possessed man worshipped (5:6)

a) *To worship* here is not to give the due honour that belongs to God, but such reverence as pertains to men, as by bowing the knee, or inclining the head or body.

Chapter 6

Christ sends his apostles to heal people who were diseased. Of John and Herod. Of the five loaves and two fishes, and of the walking on the sea.

And he departed from there and went into his own country, and his dis- M't 13:53-58
ciples followed him. 2 And when the Sabbath day came, he began to teach Lu 4:16-30
in the synagogue. And many who heard him were astonished and said, Joh 4:44; 6:41-44.
Where does he have these things from? And what wisdom is this that is
given to him? And such miracles that are wrought by his hands! 3 Is this
not that carpenter – Mary's son, the brother of James and Joses, and of
Judas and Simon?[a] And are his sisters not here with us?

A prophet in his own country

And they were offended by him. 4 And Jesus said to them, A prophet is
not without honour but in his own country, and among his own kin, and
among those who are of the same household. 5 And he could show no
miracles there, except he laid his hands upon a few sick folk and healed
them. 6 And he marvelled at their unbelief.

And he went about by the towns that lay on every side, teaching. 7 And
he called the twelve and began to send them out two by two, and gave M't 10:1-15
them power over unclean spirits. 8 And he commanded them to take noth- Lu 9:1-6 Ac 13:51
ing for their journey save only a rod – no bag, no bread, no money in their
belts – 9 but to be shod with sandals, and not to put on two coats.[b] 10 And he
said to them, Wherever you enter into a house, stay there till you move on
from that town. 11 And whoever does not receive you or hear you, when
you leave there, shake off the dust that is under your feet, for a witness to

them. I say truly to you, it will be easier for Sodom and Gomorrah at the
day of judgment than for that place.

[12]And they went out and preached that the people should repent. [13]And
they cast out many devils, and anointed many who were sick with oil, and
healed them.

[14]And King Herod heard of Jesus (for his name was spread abroad)
and said, John the Baptist has risen again from death, and therefore M't 14:1-12
miracles are wrought by him. [15]Others said, It is Elijah; and some said, It Lu 3:19,20;
is a prophet, or like one of the prophets. [16]But when Herod heard of him, 9:7-9
he said, It is John whom I beheaded: he has risen back up from death.

[17]For Herod himself had sent forth and seized John, and bound him
and cast him into prison for the sake of Herodias, who was his brother
Philip's wife. For Herod had married her. [18]John said to Herod, It is not
lawful for you to have your brother's wife. [19]So Herodias was laying in
wait for him, and would have killed him. But she could not, [20]because
Herod feared John, knowing that he was a just and holy man, and gave
him reverence. And he heeded him in many things, and heard him gladly.

[21]But when an opportune day came, Herod on his birthday put on a
supper for the lords, captains, and chief personages of Galilee. [22]And the
Herodias' daughter. daughter of the said Herodias came in and danced, and pleased Herod and
those who sat with him. Then the king said to the maiden, Ask of me what
you will, and I will give it to you. [23]And he swore to her, Whatever you
ask of me, I will give it to you, even up to one half of my kingdom.

[24]And she went out and said to her mother, What should I ask for?
And she said, The head of John the Baptist. [25]And the maiden went in
straightaway with haste to the king and asked, saying, I would like you to
give me right now the head of John the Baptist on a platter.

[26]And the king was sorry. However, for his oath's sake, and because
of those who sat at supper also, he did not want to put her beside her
purpose. [27]And immediately the king sent the hangman and commanded
John's head to be brought in. And he went and beheaded him in the
John the Baptist is beheaded prison, [28]and brought his head on a platter, and gave it to the maiden, and
the maiden gave it to her mother.

[29]And when John's disciples heard of it, they came and took up his
body, and put it in a tomb.

[30]And the apostles gathered themselves together to Jesus, and told him
all things, both what they had done and what they had taught. [31]And he
said to them, Come apart into the countryside and rest awhile. For there M't 14:13-21
were so many comers and goers that they had no time so much as to eat. Lu 9:10-17
[32]And they went by boat out of the way into an isolated place. Joh 6:1-14

[33]But the people noticed them when they departed, and many recog-
nized him. And they ran there by foot out of all the towns, and got there
before them, and came together to him. [34]And Jesus went out and saw the
crowds of people, and had compassion on them, because they were like
sheep without a shepherd. And he began to teach them many things.

[35]And when the day was now far spent, his disciples came to him,

saying, This is an isolated place, and now the day is far gone. 36 Let the people depart so that they can go into the country round about and into the towns and buy themselves bread, for they have nothing to eat. 37 He answered and said to them, You give them to eat. And they said to him, Shall we go and buy two hundred denarii worth of bread and give them to eat? 38 He said to them, How many loaves do you have? Go and look. And when they had searched, they said, Five, and two fishes.

Five loaves and two fishes

39 And Jesus directed them to make all the people sit down in groups on the green grass. 40 And they sat down here a row and there a row, by hundreds and by fifties. 41 And he took the five loaves and the two fishes, and looked up to heaven, and blessed, and broke the loaves, and gave them to his disciples to put before the people. And he divided the two fishes among them all. 42 And they all did eat and were satisfied. 43 And they took up twelve baskets full of the fragments and of the fishes. 44 And those who ate were about 5,000 men.

45 And straightaway he made his disciples get into the boat and go ahead over the water to Bethsaida while he sent the people away. 46 And as soon as he had sent them away, he went apart to a mountain to pray.

M't 14:22-36
Joh 6:16-21

Jesus walks on the water

47 And when evening was come, the boat was in the middle of the sea and he was alone on the land. 48 And he saw them having trouble rowing, for the wind was contrary to them. And about the fourth quarter of the night[c] he went out to them, walking upon the sea, and would have passed by them. 49 When they saw him walking upon the sea, they supposed it was a spirit and cried out. 50 For they all saw him and were afraid. And immediately he spoke to them and said to them, Be of good cheer, it is I. Be not afraid. 51 And he went up to them into the boat, and the wind ceased; and they were greatly amazed in themselves beyond measure, and taken aback. 52 For they did not remember about the loaves, because their hearts were blinded.

[**The land of Gennesaret**: a fertile plain stretching about 3 miles (5 km) along the NW shore of the Sea of Galilee]

53 And they crossed over and went into the land of Gennesaret,[*] and drew up to anchorage. 54 And as soon as they got out of the boat, people quickly recognized Jesus, 55 and ran everywhere throughout all the region round about, and began to carry all who were sick in beds to the place where they heard he was. 56 And wherever he entered into towns, cities, or villages, they laid their sick in the streets and begged to touch even just the edge of his vesture. And as many as touched him were made well.

The Notes

Brethren (6:3)
a) Jesus, the brother of James and Joses, etc: see note on Ge 13:8 [and note (a) on John 7:3].

Nothing except a staff (6:8,9)
b) Although at Matthew 10:10 and Luke 9:3 Jesus seems to forbid them a rod, yet the text does not mean this literally, but forbids coat, shoes, staff, etc, as a figure, to the intent only that they should utterly put from themselves all care about such provisions. For if he had meant that they should have taken no such things with them, then it would not now be lawful for any preacher to have any of those things with them when they go to preach. And therefore Mark, expressing Christ's mind more plainly, gives liberty to take a rod or a walking staff to ease themselves when they are weary.

The fourth quarter (6:48)
c) The fourth quarter is the fourth watch, as in Matthew 14:25.

Chapter 7

The disciples eat with unwashed hands. The commandment of God is transgressed by man's precepts. Of the woman of Syro-Phoenicia. Of the Sabbath.

M't 15:1-20

And the Pharisees came together to him, and some of the scribes who came from Jerusalem. 2And when they saw certain of his disciples eat bread with common hands (that is to say, with unwashed hands), they complained. 3For the Pharisees and all the Jews, unless they wash their hands often, will not eat, observing the precepts of the elders. 4And when they come from the market, unless they wash, they will not eat. And there are many other things that they have taken upon themselves to observe, such as the washing of cups and pots, and of brazen vessels,* and of tables.

[**Brazen vessels**: made of brass or bronze]

5Then the Pharisees and scribes asked him, Why do your disciples not walk according to the precepts of the elders, but eat bread with unwashed hands? 6He answered and said to them, Well did Isaiah prophesy of you hypocrites, as it is written: This people honours me with their lips, but their heart is far from me. 7In vain they worship me, teaching doctrines which are nothing but the commandments of men. 8For you lay the commandment of God aside, and observe the precepts of men, such as the washing of pots and of cups. And many other suchlike things you do.

Isa 29:13

The commandments of men

9And he said to them, All too well do you cast aside the commandment of God to maintain your own precepts. 10For Moses said, Honour your father and your mother, and whosoever curses father or mother, let him die for it. 11But you say a man should say to father or mother, Corban, which is, What you ask me for, to help you with, is dedicated to God. 12And so you no longer let him do anything for his father or his mother, 13making the word of God of no effect through your own precepts, which you have established. And many such things you do.

Ex 20:12; 21:17. De 5:16 Lev 20:9 Pr 20:20 Eph 6:13

14And he called all the people to him and said to them, Hearken unto me, every one of you, and understand. 15There is nothing outside a man that can defile him when it enters into him.* But those things that proceed out of him are the things that defile a man. 16If anyone has ears to hear, let him hear.

*What goes into the mouth does not defile. [Jesus here declares all foods to be clean: a new teaching for the Jews, and difficult to accept]

17And when he went indoors, away from the people, his disciples asked him about the similitude. 18And he said to them, Are you also without understanding? Do you not yet perceive that whatever thing from without enters into a person, it cannot defile him, 19because it enters not into his heart, but into the stomach, and goes out into the drain that carries away all foods?

20And he said, What defiles a man is that which comes out of a man. 21For from within, namely out of the heart of men, proceed evil thoughts: adultery, fornication, murder, 22theft, covetousness, wickedness, deceit, uncleanness, a wicked eye, blasphemy, pride, foolishness. 23All these evil things come from within, and defile a person.

What comes out of a man defiles the person.

24From there he arose, and went into the borders of Tyre and Sidon, and entered into a house, and wanted no one to know. But he could not be hid. 25For a certain woman whose daughter had a foul spirit heard of him, and came and fell at his feet. 26The woman was a Greek out of Syro-Phoenicia, and she besought him to cast the devil out of her daughter. 27And Jesus said to her, Let the children first be fed. For it is not meet to take the children's bread and cast it to dogs. 28She answered and said to him, Quite so, Master. Nevertheless, the dogs also eat under the table of the children's crumbs. 29And he said to her, For this saying, go your way; the devil has gone out of your daughter. 30And when she arrived home, she found the devil departed, and her daughter lying on the bed.

The Syropheonician

M't 15:21-28

[**Dogs**: see note (b) to Matthew c15]

31And he departed again from the region of Tyre and Sidon, and went to the Sea of Galilee through the region of the Ten Cities. 32And some people brought to him a man who was deaf and stammered in his speech, and asked him to put his hand upon him. 33And he took him aside from the people, and put his fingers in his ears, and spat, and touched his tongue, 34and looked up to heaven and sighed, and said to him, Ephatha; that is to say, Be opened. 35And straightaway his ears were opened, and the string of his tongue was loosed, and he spoke plainly.

M't 9:32-34
Lu 11:14-23

36And Jesus directed them to tell no one. But the more he forbad them, so much the more greatly they spoke of it. 37And they were beyond measure astonished, saying, He has done all things well, and has made both the deaf to hear and the dumb to speak.

Chapter 8

The miracle of the seven loaves. The Pharisees ask for a sign. The leaven of the Pharisees and of Herod. The blind man receives his sight.

In the days when there was a great multitude, and they had nothing to eat, Jesus called his disciples to him and said to them, 2I have compassion on this people, because they have now been with me three days, and have nothing to eat. 3And if I send them away to their own houses without eating, they might faint on the way, because some of them have come from far. 4And his disciples answered him, Where could anyone obtain bread here in this remote place to satisfy all these? 5And he asked them, How many loaves do you have? They said, Seven.

M't 15:32-38

6And he directed the people to sit down on the ground. And he took the seven loaves, gave thanks, broke, and gave to his disciples to set before them. And they set them before the people. 7And they had a few small fishes, and he blessed them, and directed them also to be set before the people. 8And they ate and were filled. And they took up of the broken food that was left seven baskets full. 9And those who had eaten were in number about 4,000. And Jesus sent them away.

Seven loaves and a few fishes

10And shortly he entered into a boat with his disciples, and went into the region of Dalmanutha. 11And the Pharisees came out and began to dispute with him, seeking from him a sign from heaven, and testing him. 12And he sighed in his spirit and said, Why does this generation seek a

M't 16:1-4

sign? Truly I say to you, there will be no sign given to this generation.

13 And he left them and went into the boat again, and departed over the water.

14 And the disciples had forgotten to take bread with them, and had in the boat with them no more than one loaf. 15 And he charged them, saying, Take heed, and beware of the leaven of the Pharisees, and of the leaven of Herod. 16 And they deliberated among themselves, saying, It is because we have no bread.

Beware, leaven

M't 16:6-12

17 And when Jesus knew this, he said to them, Why are you troubled because you have no bread? Do you not yet perceive or understand? Are your hearts still blinded? 18 Do you have eyes, but not see? And do you have ears, and not hear? Do you not remember? 19 When I broke five loaves among five thousand, how many baskets full of broken pieces did you take up? They said to him, Twelve.

20 When I broke seven among four thousand, how many baskets of the leftover fragments did you take up? They said, Seven.

21 And he said to them, How is it that you do not understand?

22 And he came to Bethsaida, and people brought a blind man to him and asked him to touch him. 23 And he took the blind man by the hand and led him out of the town, and spat in his eyes, and put his hands upon him, and asked him whether he could see anything. 24 And the man looked up and said, I see the people, for I see them walk, as if they were trees. 25 After that Jesus put his hands again upon his eyes, and made him see. And his sight was restored, and he saw every person clearly. 26 And Jesus sent him home to his house, saying, Do not go into the town, nor tell anyone in town about this.

A blind man is healed

27 And Jesus went out with his disciples into the towns around the city called Caesarea Philippi. And on the way he asked his disciples, saying, Who do people say that I am? 28 And they answered, Some say that you are John the Baptist, some say Elijah, and some, one of the prophets. 29 And he said to them, But who do you say that I am? Peter answered and said to him, You are the Christ. 30 And he charged them to tell no one of it.

M't 16:13-20
Lu 9:18-22

31 And he began to teach them how the Son of man must suffer many things, and would be reproved by the elders and by the high priests and scribes, and be killed, and after three days arise again. 32 And he spoke this word plainly. But Peter took him aside and began to chide him. 33 Then he turned around and looked on his disciples, and rebuked Peter, saying, Get behind me, Satan, for you savour not the things of God, but the things of men.

M't 16:21-23

Peter is Satan [Ed: This is said to appear more severe in translation than in the original. For in the Jews' language, *satan* signifies in general any adversary, as at 2Sa 19:22. But because the devil is in the highest sense man's great adversary, the name has been appropriated to him by way of eminence, both in scripture and in common speech. Here, it is that Peter was not acting the part of a friend, as he believed, but of an adversary]

34 And he called the people to him with his disciples also, and said to them, Whoever would follow me, let him deny himself, and take up his cross and follow me. 35 For whoever would save his life, will lose it. But whoever loses his life for my sake and the sake of the gospel, shall save it. 36 What does it profit a man, if he should win all the world and lose his own soul? 37 Or what can a person give to redeem his soul? 38 Whosoever therefore is ashamed of me and of my words among this adulterous and

M't 16:24-28
Lu 9:23-27; 17:33.
Joh 12:25,26

sinful generation, of him will the Son of man be ashamed when he comes
in the glory of his Father with the holy angels.
[9:1]And he said to them, Truly I say to you, there are some standing
here who will not taste of death till they have seen the kingdom of God
come with power.

Chapter 9

The transfiguration. The frenzied boy is healed. Who should
be the greatest. Offences are forbidden.

In the MB, verse 9:1 is at the end of chapter 8.

[Fuller*: a person whose work is cleaning and thickening cloth]

[2]And after six days, Jesus took Peter, James, and John, and led them up
into a high mountain out of the way alone. And he was transfigured before
them. [3]And his raiment did shine, and was made very white, even as M't 17:1-8
snow: such a white as no fuller* can make upon the earth. [4]And there Lu 9:28-36 2Pe:16-18
appeared to them Elijah with Moses, and they talked with Jesus.
[5]And Peter spoke and said to Jesus, Rabbi, it is good for us to be here.
Let us make three tabernacles: one for you, one for Moses, and one for
Elijah. [6]And yet he did not know what he was saying, for they were
afraid. [7]And there was a cloud that covered them. And a voice came out of
the cloud, saying, This is my dear Son; hear him! [8]And suddenly, when
they looked round about them, they saw no one but Jesus with them.
[9]And as they came down from the hill, he charged them to tell no one
what they had seen until the Son of man was risen from death again. M't 17:9-13
[10]And they kept that saying with them, and wondered amongst themselves Mal 4:5,6
what rising from death again might mean. [11]And they asked him, saying,
Why then do the scribes say that Elijah must come first? [12]He answered
and said to them, Indeed, Elijah does first come, and restore all things.
And also the Son of man, as it is written, will suffer many things, and will Isa c53
be rejected. [13]Moreover I say to you that Elijah has come, and they have
done to him whatsoever pleased them, as it is written of him.
[14]And he came to his disciples and saw crowds of people about them,
and the scribes disputing with them. [15]And straightaway all the people, M't 17:14-21
when they saw Jesus, were moved with wonder, and ran to him and Lu 9:37-43
greeted him. [16]And he said to the scribes, What are you disputing with
them? [17]A man from the crowd answered and said, Teacher, I have
brought my son to you, who has a dumb spirit, [18]and whenever it takes
him, it tears him, and he foams and gnashes with his teeth, and collapses.
And I spoke to your disciples, to cast it out, but they could not.
[19]Jesus answered him and said, O generation without faith, how long
shall I be with you? How long shall I suffer you? Bring him to me. [20]And
they brought the boy to him. And as soon as the spirit saw him, it tore the
boy, and he fell down on the ground, wallowing and foaming. [21]And Jesus
asked his father, How long has this been happening to him? And he said,
Since childhood. [22]And often it casts him into the fire, and also into the
water, to kill him. But if you can do anything, have mercy on us and help
us! [23]And Jesus said to him, If you can believe, all things are possible to
him who believes. [24]And straightaway the father of the child exclaimed

Help my unbelief

with tears, saying, Lord, I believe; help my unbelief!
[25]When Jesus saw that the people came running to gather to him, he rebuked the foul spirit, saying to him, Deaf and dumb spirit, I charge you to come out of him, and enter no more into him!
[26]And the spirit cried out, and rent him badly, and came out. And the boy was as one dead, insomuch that many said, He is dead.
[27]But Jesus caught his hand and lifted him up, and he arose.

[28]And when Jesus had entered into the house, his disciples asked him privately, Why could we not cast him out?
[29]And he said to them, This kind can come out no other way but by prayer and fasting.

[30]And they left that place, and took their journey through Galilee. But Jesus did not want anyone to know of it,
[31]because he was teaching his disciples. And he said to them, The Son of man will be delivered into the hands of men, and they will kill him. And after he has been killed, he will arise again on the third day.
[32]But they did not comprehend what that saying meant, and were afraid to ask him.

M't 17:22,23
Lu 9:22

The dispute over who should be greatest.

[**Chief**: foremost in rank, authority, or honour]

[33]And they came to Capernaum. And once he was indoors, he asked them, What was it that you were disputing between yourselves along the way?
[34]And they held their peace, for on the road they had been debating among themselves who should be chief.*
[35]And he sat down and called the twelve to him and said to them, If any man desires to be first, let him be last of all, and servant to all.
[36]And he took a child and set him in the midst of them, and took him in his arms and said to them,
[37]Whosoever receives any such a child in my name, receives me. And whosoever receives me, receives not me, but him who sent me.

M't 18:5
Lu 9:48

[38]John answered him, saying, Teacher, we saw someone who does not follow us casting out devils in your name, and we told him not to, because he does not follow us.
[39]But Jesus said, Do not forbid him. For no one who does a miracle in my name can lightly speak evil of me.
[40]Whosoever is not against you, is on your side.

*__Reward__: whatever is done for Christ's sake shall be rewarded with the reward that Christ has deserved for us.

[41]And whosoever gives you a cup of water to drink for my name's sake, because you belong to Christ, truly I say to you, he will not lose his reward.*
[42]But whoever hurts one of these little ones that believe in me, it would be better for him if a millstone were hung around his neck and he were cast into the sea.
[43]Therefore if your hand causes you to offend, cut it off. It is better for you to enter into life maimed than, having two hands, to go into hell, into fire that never shall be quenched,
[44]where their worm dies not and the fire never goes out.
[45]Likewise, if your foot causes you to offend, cut it off. For it is better for you to go lame into life than, having two feet, to be cast into hell, into fire that never shall be quenched,
[46]where their worm dies not and the fire never goes out.
[47]So also if your eye causes you to offend, tear it out. It is better for you to go into the kingdom of God with one eye than, having two eyes, to be cast into hell fire,
[48]where their worm dies not and the fire never goes out.

M't 18:8-14

Isa 66:24

Fire is tribulation and **salt** is God's word.

[49]Every man therefore must be salted with fire. And every sacrifice must be seasoned with salt.*
[50]Salt is good. But if the salt is unsavoury,

what can you salt with it? See that you have salt in yourselves. And have
peace among yourselves, one with another.

Chapter 10

On divorce. The rich man questions Christ. Of the sons of
Zebedee. Bartimaeus the blind man.

And he arose from there and went into the borders of Judea, through the
region that is beyond the Jordan. And the people resorted to him afresh,
and as his custom was, he taught them again. 2And the Pharisees came
and asked him a question, whether it was lawful for a man to put away his M't 19:1-12
wife, in order to prove him. 3And he answered and said to them, What did
Moses tell you to do? 4And they said, Moses permitted us to write a
testimonial of divorce and to put her away.

5And Jesus answered and said to them, For the hardness of your
On divorce hearts, he wrote this precept for you. 6But at the first creation, God made
them man and woman. 7And for the sake of this, a man must leave his Ge 1:27; 2:24; 5:2.
father and mother, and abide by his wife, 8and the two shall be one flesh. Eph 5:22,23
So then they are now not two, but are one flesh. 9Therefore what God has 1Co 6:16
joined together, let not man separate.

10And in the house, his disciples asked him again about that matter.
11And he said to them, Whoever puts away his wife and marries another,
breaks wedlock to her. 12And if a woman forsakes her husband and is M't 5:31,32 Lu 6:18
married to another, she commits adultery.

13And they brought children to him, for him to touch them. And his
disciples rebuked the people who brought them. 14When Jesus saw that,
Suffer the children to come to him. he was displeased, and said to them, Suffer the children to come to me, M't 19:13-15 Lu 18:15-17
and forbid them not. For of such is the kingdom of God. 15Truly I say to
you, whoever does not receive the kingdom of God like a child, he shall
not enter therein. 16And he took them up in his arms, and put his hands
upon them, and blessed them.

17And when he had gone out to the road, a man came running, and
kneeled to him and asked him, Good Teacher, what should I do so that I M't 19:16-24
may inherit eternal life? 18Jesus said to him, Why do you call me good? Lu 18:18-27
There is none good but one, who is God. 19You know the commandments: Ex 20:12-17 De 5:16-21
do not break matrimony, do not kill, do not steal, bear no false witness, Lev 19:18
defraud no man, honour your father and mother. 20He answered and said
to him, Teacher, all these I have observed from my youth.

21Jesus regarded him with favour and said to him, One thing is lacking
to you. Go and sell all that you have,[a] and give to the poor, and you will
have treasure in heaven. And come and follow me, and take up the cross.

22But the man was downcast with that saying, and went away grieved,
for he had great possessions.

23And Jesus looked round about and said to his disciples, What a hard
thing it is for those who have riches to enter into the kingdom of God!
24And his disciples were astonished at his words. But Jesus spoke again
and said to them, Children, how hard is it for those who trust in riches to

Rich men, camels

enter into the kingdom of God? [25]It is easier for a camel to go through the eye of a needle than for a rich man to enter into the kingdom of God.

[26]And they were astonished out of measure, saying between themselves, Who then can be saved? [27]Jesus looked upon them and said, With men it is impossible, but not with God. For with God, all things are possible.

M't 19:25-30
Lu 18:28-30

[28]And Peter began to say to him, Lo, we have left everything and have followed you. [29]Jesus answered and said, Truly I say to you, there is no one who gives up house, or brethren, or sisters, or father, or mother, or wife, or children, or lands, for my sake and the gospel's, [30]who will not receive a hundredfold now in this life: houses and brethren and sisters and mothers and children and lands – with persecutions – and in the world to come, eternal life. [31]But many that are first will be last, and the last, first.

[**Up to Jerusalem**: *up* because the city lies on the heights of the mountain ridge that separates the Mediterranean Sea and the Dead Sea]

[32]And they were on the road going up to Jerusalem, and Jesus went before them. And they were amazed, and as they followed, were afraid. And Jesus took the twelve again, and began to tell them the things that would happen to him: [33]Behold, we are going up to Jerusalem, and the Son of man will be delivered to the high priests and to the scribes. And they will condemn him to death, and will deliver him to the Gentiles. [34]And they will mock him, and scourge him, and spit upon him, and kill him. And the third day he will rise again.

M't 20:20-28

[35]And then James and John, the sons of Zebedee, came to him, saying, Teacher, we would like you to do for us whatever we ask. [36]He said to them, What would you like me to do for you? [37]They said to him, Grant to us that we may sit one on your right hand, and the other on your left hand, in your glory. [38]But Jesus said to them, You know not what you ask. Can you drink of the cup that I must drink of, and be baptized in the baptism that I must be baptized in? [39]And they said to him, That we can. Jesus said to them, You will drink of the cup that I will drink of, and be baptized with the baptism that I will be baptized in. [40]But to sit on my right hand and on my left hand is not mine to give, but is for them for whom it is prepared.

M't 20:25-28
Lu 22:25-30

[41]And when the ten heard this, they began to be much displeased with James and John. [42]But Jesus called them to him and said to them, You know that those who are seen to bear rule among the Gentiles reign as lords over them. And those who are great among them exercise authority over them. [43]It shall not be this way among you, but whoever would be great among you shall minister to you, [44]and whoever would be chief shall be servant to all. [45]For even the Son of man came not to be served, but to serve, and to give his life for the redemption of many.

M't 20:29-34
Lu 18:35-43

Jericho; Bartimaeus the blind man.

[46]And they came to Jericho. And as he was going out of Jericho with his disciples and a great number of people, Bartimaeus the son of Timeus, who was blind, sat by the side of the high road, begging. [47]And when he heard that it was Jesus of Nazareth, he began to call out and to say, Jesus, Son of David, have mercy on me! [48]And many people admonished him to hold his peace. But he cried the more a great deal, Son of David, have

mercy on me!
[49]And Jesus stood still and directed that he be called. And they called the blind man, saying to him, Be of good comfort. Rise, he has called you.
[50]And he threw away his cloak, and rose and came to Jesus. [51]And Jesus spoke and said to him, What do you want me to do for you? The blind man said to him, Teacher, that I could see! [52]Jesus said to him, Go
Miracle of sight. your way; your faith has saved you.
And immediately the man received his sight, and followed Jesus in the road.

The Notes

Go and sell all you have (10:21) a) That is, tear your heart from all your possessions, and surrender them with all your heart, so that in your mind you sell them, and are ready also in fact to sell them, if the need of your neighbour requires it. Affection for and trust in our possessions must ever be renounced, or we are not perfect, as is said at Matthew 19:21.

Chapter 11

Christ rides into Jerusalem. The fig tree dries up. The buyers and sellers are cast out of the temple. The Pharisees question Christ.

And when they came near Jerusalem, to Bethphage and Bethany beside M't 21:1-11
the Mount of Olives, he sent forth two of his disciples [2]and said to them, Lu 19:28-38
Go your ways into the town that is in front of you. And as soon as you Joh 12:12-19
have entered into it, you will find a colt tied, on which no man ever sat.
Untie him and bring him here. [3]And if anyone asks you why you are
doing this, say that the Lord has need of him, and straightaway he will
send him here.
[4]And they went their way and found a colt tied by the door outside, in
a place where two roads met, and they untied him. [5]And some of the
people standing there said to them, What are you doing, untying the colt?
[6]And they answered just as Jesus had instructed, and the people let them
go. [7]And they brought the colt to Jesus, and cast their garments on it, and
he sat upon it. [8]And many spread their garments in the way. Others cut
down branches of the trees and strew them in the way. [9]And those who
went before, and those who followed, cried out, saying, Hosanna! Blessed Ps 118:26
is he that comes in the name of the Lord! [10]Blessed is the kingdom that
comes in the name of him who is Lord of our father David: Hosanna in
the highest![a]
[11]And the Lord entered into Jerusalem and into the temple. And when
he had looked round about upon everything, and now that evening time
was come, he went out to Bethany with the twelve.
[12]And on the morrow, when they had left Bethany, he hungered. [13]And
afar off he spotted a fig tree in leaf,[b] and went to see whether he might
find anything on it. But when he came to it, he found nothing but leaves,
for the time of figs was not yet. [14]And Jesus spoke and said to it, Never
may man eat fruit from you hereafter while the world stands. And his

disciples heard it.

15 And they came to Jerusalem. And Jesus went into the temple, and began to cast out the sellers and buyers in the temple, and overthrew the tables of the money changers, and the stools of those who sold doves, 16 and would not suffer anyone to carry a vessel through the temple. 17 And he taught, saying to them, Is it not written: My house shall be called the house of prayer for all nations? But you have made it a den of thieves! 18 And the scribes and high priests heard this, and sought how to destroy him. For they feared him, because all the people marvelled at his doctrine.

Sellers and buyers cast out

Isa 56:7
Jer 7:11
M't 21:12,13

19 And when evening came, he went out of the city. 20 And in the morning, as they passed by, they saw the fig tree dried up from the roots. 21 And Peter remembered and said to him, Rabbi, look! The fig tree that you cursed has withered away.

22 And Jesus answered and said to them, Have confidence in God. 23 Truly I say to you that whoever says to this mountain, Take yourself away and cast yourself into the sea, and who does not waver in his heart, but believes that those things which he says will come to pass – whatever he says will be done for him. 24 Therefore I say to you, whatever you ask when you pray, believe that you will have it, and it will be done for you. 25 And when you stand and pray, forgive, if you have anything against any person, so that your Father who is in heaven may also forgive you your trespasses. 26*

M't 21:18-22

Jas 1:5-8

[Verse 26 in not included in Tyndale's New Testament. In the New King James Version it reads, 'But if you do not forgive, neither will your Father in heaven forgive your trespasses.']

27 And they came again to Jerusalem. And as he walked in the temple, there came to him the high priests and the scribes and the elders, 28 and they said to him, By what authority do you do these things? And who gave you this authority, to do these things? 29 Jesus answered and said to them, I will also ask of you a certain thing. Answer me, and I will tell you by what authority I do these things. 30 The baptism of John: was it from heaven, or of men?[c] Answer me.

M't 21:23-27
Lu 20:1-8

31 They thought in themselves, saying, If we say from heaven, he will say, Why then did you not believe him? 32 But if we say of men, then we fear the people. (For everyone counted John to be a very prophet.) 33 And they answered and said to Jesus, We don't know. And Jesus answered and said to them, Neither will I tell you by what authority I do these things.

The Notes

Hosanna (11:9) a) Look in Matthew 21, note (a).

The fig tree (11:13) b) Look in Matthew 21, note (b).

Of heaven or men (11:30) c) Look in Matthew 21, note (c).

Chapter 12

[**Doctor of law**: a man learned in the Hebrew scriptures, esp. Mosaic law]

The vineyard is let out. Give to Caesar that which belongs to Caesar. Of the Sadducees and of the doctor of law.[*] Hypocrites must be eschewed. The offering of the poor widow.

And he began to speak to them in similitudes: A certain man planted a vineyard, and compassed it about with a hedge, and made a winepress,

M't 21:33-46
Lu 20:9-19
Isa 5:1-7

and built a tower in it. And he let it out on hire to husbandmen, and went into a far country. [2]And when the time came, he sent a servant to the tenants, in order to receive from the tenants some of the fruit of the vineyard. [3]And they caught him and beat him, and sent him back empty-handed. [4]And moreover he sent to them another servant, and at him they cast stones, and wounded him in the head, and sent him back utterly reviled. [5]And again he sent another, and him they killed; and many others, beating some and killing some.

The tenants persecute.

[6]He had yet one son, whom he loved tenderly. Him also he sent to them at the last, saying, They will respect my son. [7]But the tenants said amongst themselves, This is the heir; come, let us kill him, and the inheritance will be ours. [8]And they took him and killed him, and cast him out of the vineyard.

[9]What then will the lord of the vineyard do? He will come and destroy the tenants, and let out the vineyard to others. [10]Have you not read this scripture: The stone which the builders refused is made the chief stone in the corner; [11]this was done by the Lord, and is marvellous in our eyes?

Ps 118: 22, 23.
Isa 28:16
Ac 4:10-12
Ro 9:33
1Pe 2:6,8

[12]And they went about to apprehend him, but they feared the people. For they perceived that he had spoken that similitude against them. And they left him and went their way.

[13]And they sent to him certain of the Pharisees, along with Herod's servants, to take him in his words. [14]And as soon as they arrived, they said to him, Teacher, we know that you are true, and mind no man, for you do not consider the degree of men, but teach the way of God truly. Is it lawful to remit tribute to Caesar, or not? [15]Ought we to give, or ought we not to give?

M't 22:15-22
Lu 20:20-26
Ro 13:6,7

Tribute to Caesar

He understood their simulation and said to them, Why do you bait me? Bring me a denarius so that I may see it. [16]And they brought one. And he said to them, Whose image and superscription is this? And they said to him, Caesar's. [17]And Jesus answered and said to them, Then give to Caesar that which belongs to Caesar, and to God that which belongs to God. And they marvelled at him.

[18]Then the Sadducees, who say there is no resurrection, came to him. And they asked him, saying, [19]Teacher, Moses wrote to us that if any man's brother dies and leaves his wife behind him, and leaves no children, that then his brother should take his wife and raise up seed for his brother. [20]There were seven brethren. The first took a wife, and when he died left no seed behind him. [21]And the second took her, and died also not leaving any seed. And the third likewise. [22]And all seven had her, but left no seed behind them. Last of all, the wife died also. [23]In the resurrection then, when they rise again, whose wife will she be? For seven of them had her as wife.

M't 22:23-33
Lu 20:27-40
De 25:5-10

[24]Jesus answered and said to them, Are you not therefore deceived, and do not understand the scriptures, nor the power of God? [25]For when they rise again from death, people neither marry nor are married, but are as the angels who are in heaven. [26]And concerning the dead, that they will

The resurrection

rise again, have you not read in the book of Moses how, in the bush, God
spoke to him, saying, I am the God of Abraham and the God of Isaac and
the God of Jacob? 27He is not the God of the dead, but the God of the
living. You are therefore greatly deceived.
28And there came one of the scribes who had heard them disputing M't 22:34-40
together. He perceived that Jesus had answered them well, and asked him, Lu 10:25-37
Which is the first of all the commandments? De 6:5
First commandments 29Jesus answered him, The first of all the commandments is: Hear, O Lev 19:18
Israel, the Lord God is one Lord. 30And you shall love the Lord your God
with all your heart, and with all your soul, and with all your mind, and
with all your strength. This is the first commandment. 31And the second is
like it: You shall love your neighbour as yourself. There is no command-
ment greater than these.
32And the scribe said to him, Well said, Teacher. You have spoken the
truth: that there is one God, and that there is none but he. 33And to love
him with all the heart, and with all the mind, and with all the soul, and
with all the strength, and to love one's neighbour as oneself, is a greater
thing than all burnt offerings and sacrifices.
34And when Jesus saw that he answered wisely, he said to him, You
are not far from the kingdom of God.[a]
And after that, no one dared ask him any question.
35And Jesus spoke and said, teaching in the temple, How is it the M't 22:41-46
scribes say that Christ is the son of David? 36For David himself, inspired Lu 20:41-44
with the Holy Spirit, said, The Lord said to my Lord, sit on my right hand Ps 110:1
until I make your enemies your footstool. 37So David himself calls him
Lord. By what means then is he David's son?
And the crowds of people heard him gladly. 38And he said to them in M't 23:1-7;
Beware the scribes his doctrine, Beware of the scribes, who love to go about in long clothing, 14.
and love salutations in the market places, 39and the chief seats in the
synagogues, and to sit in the uppermost places at feasts; 40and who devour
widows' houses, and that under a colour of long praying. These shall re-
ceive greater damnation.
41Jesus sat across from the treasury and observed how the people put Lu 21:1-4
money into the treasury. And many who were rich cast in much. 42And
there came a certain poor widow, and she threw in two small coins worth
a pittance. 43And he called his disciples to him and said to them, Truly I
say to you that this poor widow has cast in more than all the others who
have cast into the treasury. 44For they all gave from their surplus, but she,
in her poverty, did cast in all that she had, even all her living.

The Notes

Not far from the kingdom (12:34) a) You are not far from the kingdom of God; that is, you have the true knowledge of the law and lack nothing but faith and trust in me, by which only comes everlasting life.

Chapter 13

The destruction of Jerusalem and the temple. The end of the

world; the day and the hour is unknown.

And as he went out of the temple, one of his disciples said to him, Teach-
er, see what stones and what buildings are here! 2And Jesus answered and
The destruction of the temple foretold.
said to him, Do you see these great buildings? There will not be left one *M't c24; Lu 19:41-44*
stone upon another that will not be thrown down.
3And as he sat on the Mount of Olives across from the temple, Peter
and James and John and Andrew asked him privately, 4Tell us, when will
these things be? And what will be the sign when all these things are going
to be fulfilled?
Antichrist
5And Jesus answered them and began, saying, Take heed, lest anyone *Lu 17:20-24; 21:8.*
deceive you. 6For many will come in my name saying, I am Christ, and
will deceive many.
7When you hear of war and reports of war, do not be troubled. For
such things must be. But the end is not yet. 8For nation will arise against *Lu 21:9-20*
nation, and kingdom against kingdom. And there will be earthquakes in
all quarters, and famines and troubles. These are the beginning of sorrows.
9But take heed to yourselves. For they will bring you up before the
councils and into the synagogues, and you will be beaten; yea, and will be *M't 10:16-23; Joh 16:1-4*
brought before rulers and kings for my sake, for a testimony to them.
10And the gospel must first be preached among all nations. 11But when
they lead you and present you, do not be anxious about what you will say,
The Spirit answers
nor prepare ahead. But whatever is given you at that same time, that
speak. For it will not be you who speak, but the Holy Spirit.
12Yea and brother will deliver brother to death, and the father the son;
and the children will rise against their fathers and mothers, and will put
them to death. 13And you will be hated by all men for my name's sake. *Lu 21:16*
But whosoever endures to the end, the same shall be saved.
14Moreover, when you see the abomination that betokens desolation,
of which Daniel the prophet has spoken, standing where it ought not, let
him who reads, understand.[*] Then let those who are in Judea flee to the *Da 9:27; 11:31.*
mountains. 15And let him who is on the housetop not descend down into *M't 24:15-22*
the house, neither enter in to fetch anything out of his house. 16And let *Lu 21:20-24; 19:43,44.*
him who is in the field not turn back again to those things that he left
behind him, to take his clothes with him. 17Woe shall be then to women
that are with child, and to them that give suck in those days. 18But pray
that your flight be not in the winter.[a] 19For there shall be in those days
such tribulation as was not from the beginning of creatures that God cre-
Those days are shortened for the sake of the elect.
ated to this time, nor will be again. 20And if the Lord did not shorten those
days, no one would be saved. But for the sake of the elect, whom he has
chosen, he has shortened those days.
21And then if anyone says to you, Lo, here is Christ! Lo, he is there! –
believe it not. 22For false Christs will arise, and false prophets, and they
will show miracles and wonders, to deceive if it were possible even the *M't 24:23-28; Lu 17:22-24*
elect. 23But take heed: behold, I have told you all things beforehand.
24Moreover in those days, after that tribulation, the sun will grow dark,
and the moon will not give her light, 25and the stars of heaven will fall; *Lu 21:25-28; Eze 32:7,8*

[**Who reads**: That is, who reads Daniel's prophecy. See M't 24:25. The Hebrew scriptures were kept and read in the many synagogues of Jerusalem. See the OT feature at the end of this gospel]

and the powers which are in heaven shall move. [26]And then will they see Isa c13
the Son of man coming in the clouds with great power and glory. [27]And Joe 2:1-11
then he will send his angels, and will gather together his elect from the
four winds, and from one end of the world to the other.

[28]Learn from a similitude of the fig tree. When its branches are yet
tender and it has brought forth leaves, you know that summer is near. [29]So Lu 21:29-32
also in like manner, when you see these things come to pass, understand
that it is near, even at the doors. [30]Truly I say to you that this generation
will not pass till all these things be done.

Heaven and earth shall pass

[31]Heaven and earth shall pass, but my words will not pass. [32]But of
that day and hour no one knows, no, not the angels who are in heaven, nor Lu 21:33-36
the Son himself, but the Father only.[b] [33]Take heed. Watch and pray, for
you know not when the time is. [34]It is as a man who has gone into a far
country, and has left his house, and given authority to his servants, and to
each his work, and instructed the porter to watch.

[35]Watch therefore. For you know not when the master of the house
will come – whether at evening or midnight, whether at the cock-crowing
or in the dawning – [36]lest, if he come suddenly, he should find you sleep-
ing. [37]And what I say to you, I say to all: Watch!

The Notes

Winter flight (13:18)

a) Pray that your flight be not in the winter: Look in Matthew 24 and note (a).

The Son does not know, but only the Father (13:32)

b) As concerning his manhood, Jesus was less than his Father and therefore did not know the day or the hour, though by his Godhead he knew it.

Chapter 14

Mary Magdalene anoints Christ. The Passover lamb is eaten. Christ is taken. Peter denies him, with many other things that were demanded of Christ.

After two days followed Passover, and the days of sweet bread. And the M't 26:1-5
high priests and the scribes were seeking means to apprehend Jesus by Lu 22:1-6
craft and put him to death. [2]But, they said, not in the feast day, lest any Joh 11:46-53
uproar arise among the people.

[3]When he was in Bethany, in the house of Simon the leper, even as he
sat at food, there came a woman having an alabaster jar of anointing oil
called nard, which was pure and costly. And she broke the jar and poured M't 26:6-16
Jesus is anointed. it on his head. [4]And there were some who were displeased in themselves Lu 7:36-38
and said, Why this waste of oyntment? [5]For it could have been sold for Joh 12:1-8
more than three hundred denarii, and the money given to the poor. And
they grudged against her.

[6]And Jesus said, Let her be in rest. Why do you trouble her? She has
done a good work on me. [7]For you will have the poor with you always,
and whenever you wish, you may do them good. But me you will not have
always. [8]She has done what she could: she came beforehand to anoint my
body for the burial. [9]Truly I say to you, wherever this gospel is preached
throughout the whole world, this also that she has done will be told, in

remembrance of her.
10And Judas Iscariot, one of the twelve, went away to the high priests,
He is betrayed.
to betray him to them. 11When they heard that, they were glad, and
promised that they would give him money. And he sought an opportune
way to betray him.
12And the first day of sweet bread, when people offer the Passover
lamb, Jesus' disciples said to him, Where would you like us to go and
prepare for you to eat the Passover lamb? 13And he sent forth two of his M't 26:17-29 Lu 22:7-23
disciples and said to them, Go into the city, and there a man will meet you
bearing a pitcher of water. Follow him. 14And wherever he goes in, say to
[**Guest chamber**: in Jerusalem, banqueting rooms were often borrowed or rented by visitors who came to celebrate religious festivals]
the head of the house, The Teacher asks, Where is the guest chamber
where I may eat the Passover lamb with my disciples? 15And he will show
you a large upper room furnished and prepared: there make ready for us.
16And his disciples went forth, and came to the city, and found things
as he had said to them, and made ready the Passover lamb.
17And in the evening, he came with the twelve. 18And as they sat at the
table and ate, Jesus said, Truly I say to you that one of you who eats with
me will betray me. 19And they began to mourn, and to say to him one by
one, Is it I? And another said, Is it I?
20He answered and said to them, It is one of the twelve, and the same
dips with me in the platter. 21The Son of man goes as it is written of him. Joh 13:21-30
But woe is to that man by whom the Son of man is betrayed. It would
have been good for that man if he had never been born.
The institution of the Sacrament.
22And as they ate, Jesus took bread, blessed, and broke, and gave to
them and said, Take, eat; this is my body. 23And he took the cup, gave Ge 14:18 Heb 5:6
thanks, and gave it to them, and they all drank of it. 24And he said to them, M't 26:26-29
This is my blood of the new testament, which is shed for many. 25Truly I Lu 22:14-20
say to you, I will drink no more of this fruit of the vine until that day that I 1Co 11:23-26.
drink it new in the kingdom of God.
[**Sung praises**: probably from the Psalms of praise which by tradition followed the Passover supper, being Psalms 113-118 & 136]
26And when they had sung praises,* they went out to the Mount of
Olives. 27And Jesus said to them, All of you will fall away because of me
this night. For it is written: I will smite the shepherd, and the sheep will be M't 26:36-57 Lu 22:39-54
scattered. 28But after I am risen up again, I will go into Galilee ahead of Joh 18:1-14
you. 29But Peter said to him, Even if all were to fall away, yet I would not. Zec 13:7
30And Jesus said to him, Truly I say to you, this day – even this night,
before the cock crows twice – you will deny me three times. 31And Peter
spoke more boldly: No; if I must die with you, I will not deny you. Like-
wise also said all the others.
32And they came to a place named Gethsemane. And he said to his
disciples, Sit here, while I go apart and pray. 33And he took with him
Peter, James, and John. And he began to be horrified, and to be in an
agony, 34and said to them, My soul is very heavy, even to the death. You
He arms himself against his passion.
stay here and watch. 35And he went forward a little, and fell down on the
ground and prayed that, if it were possible, the hour might pass from him.
36And he said, Abba, Father, all things are possible to you; take away this
cup from me. Nevertheless, not what I will, but what you will, be done.

37 And he came and found them sleeping and said to Peter, Simon, are
you sleeping? Could not you watch with me one hour? 38 Watch and pray,
lest you enter into temptation. The spirit is ready, but the flesh is weak.

39 And again he went away and prayed, and spoke the same words.
40 And he returned and found them asleep again, for their eyes were heavy;
neither did they know what to answer him. 41 And he came the third time,
and said to them, Sleep on now, and take your ease!* It is enough. The
hour has come. Behold, the Son of man will be delivered into the hands of
sinners. 42 Rise up, let us go. Lo, he who betrays me is at hand.

*Look in M't 26:45 and note (a) thereon.

43 And immediately, while he yet spoke, came Judas, one of the
twelve. With him was a large band of people with swords and clubs, sent
from the high priests and scribes and elders. 44 And he who betrayed him
had arranged a sign, saying, Whoever I kiss, he it is; take him and lead
him away warily.

Jesus is betrayed by Judas, who also gave them a sign to know him by.

45 And as soon as Judas had come, he went straightaway to Jesus and
said to him, Master, Master! and kissed him. 46 And they laid their hands
on him and took him. 47 And one of those who stood by drew out a sword
and struck a servant of the high priest, and cut off his ear.

48 And Jesus spoke and said to them, You have come out as if to a
thief, with swords and with clubs to capture me. 49 I was daily with you in
the temple teaching, and you did not take me. But the scriptures must be
fulfilled.

50 And they all forsook him, and ran away. 51 And he had a follower, a
certain young man clothed in linen upon the bare. And the young men
caught him, 52 but he left his linen cloth and fled from them naked.

53 And they led Jesus away to the highest priest of all, and to him came
all the high priests and the elders and the scribes. 54 And Peter followed
him a great way off, right into the palace courtyard of the high priest, and
sat with the servants, and warmed himself at the fire.

M't 26:57-68 Lu 22:54-71 Joh 18:12-14, 19-24.

55 And the high priests and all the council sought for witness against
Jesus, to put him to death, and found none. 56 Yet many bore false witness
against him, but their testimonies did not agree together. 57 And certain
men arose and brought false witness against him, saying, 58 We heard him
say, I will destroy this temple made with hands, and within three days I
will build another made without hands. 59 But their testimonies did not
agree together.

He is falsely accused.

60 And the highest priest stood up amongst them and asked Jesus,
saying, Do you answer nothing? How is it that these men bear witness
against you? 61 And he held his peace and answered nothing. Again the
highest priest asked him and said to him, Are you Christ, the Son of the
Blessed? 62 And Jesus said, I am; and you will see the Son of man sitting
on the right hand of power and coming in the clouds of heaven.

63 Then the highest priest tore his clothes and said, Why do we need
any further witnesses? 64 You have heard the blasphemy. What do you
think?

And they all gave sentence that he was worthy of death. 65 And some

He is mocked, spit on, blindfolded, and buffeted.

began to spit at him, and to cover his face, and to beat him with fists, and to say to him, Prophesy to us! And the servants struck him on the face.

[66]And as Peter was below in the interior courtyard, there came one of the servant girls of the highest priest. [67]When she saw Peter warming himself, she looked on him and said, Were you not also with Jesus of Nazareth? [68]And he denied it, saying, I do not know him, or understand what you are saying. And he went out into the porch, and the cock crew. [69]And a maidservant saw him and again began to say to those who stood by, This is one of them. [70]And he denied it again. And soon after, those standing by said again to Peter, Surely you are one of them, for you are from Galilee and your speech is the same. [71]And he began to curse and to swear, saying, I do not know this man of whom you speak. [72]And again the cock crew. And Peter remembered the word that Jesus had said to him – before the cock crows twice, you will deny me three times – and he began to weep.

Peter denies him.

M't 26:69-75
Lu 22:54-62
Joh 18:15-18, 25-27.

Chapter 15

The passion of Christ. Of his death and burial.

He is delivered to Pilate.

M't 27:1-26
Lu 23:1-25
Joh 18:28-40; 19:1-16.

And early in the dawning, the high priests consulted with the elders and the scribes and the whole council, and bound Jesus and led him away, and delivered him to Pilate.

[2]And Pilate asked him, Are you the king of the Jews? And he answered and said to him, It is as you say. [3]And the high priests accused him of many things. [4]So Pilate asked him again, saying, Do you answer nothing? Look how many things they lay to your charge. [5]But Jesus still answered never a word, so that Pilate marvelled.

[6]At that feast it was Pilate's custom to release to the people, at their pleasure, a prisoner – whomever they desired. [7]And there was one named Barabbas, who lay bound with those who had made insurrection, and in the insurrection had committed murder. [8]And the people called to Pilate and began to ask that he do as usual for them. [9]Pilate answered them and said, Do you want me to release to you the king of the Jews? [10]For he knew that the high priests had delivered him out of envy. [11]But the high priests had moved the people to have Barabbas released to them instead.

[12]And Pilate answered again and said to them, What will you have me do then with him whom you call the king of the Jews? [13]And they cried again, Crucify him! [14]Pilate said to them, What evil has he done? And they cried the more fervently, Crucify him!

He is scourged and then delivered to death.

[15]And so Pilate, choosing to appease the people, released Barabbas to them, and delivered Jesus, when had scourged him, to be crucified.

[**Common hall**: a large room in Pilate's palace, which latter is also called the Praetorium]

M't 27:27-44
Lu 23:26-43
Joh 19:17-30

[16]And the soldiers led him away into the common hall,* and called together the whole company. [17]And they clothed him with purple, and they plaited a crown of thorns and crowned him with it, [18]and began to pay mock homage to him: Hail, King of the Jews! [19]And they struck him on the head with a reed, and spat upon him, and kneeled down and worshipped him.

20 And when they had mocked him, they took the purple off him and
put his own clothes on him, and led him out to crucify him. 21 And they
compelled a man who was passing by, called Simon of Cyrene (who was
coming out of the field, and was the father of Alexander and Rufus), to
Golgotha — bear his cross. 22 And they brought him to a place named Golgotha (which
translated is, the place of dead men's skulls). 23 And they offered him wine
mingled with myrrh to drink, but he would not receive it.

24 And when they had crucified him, they parted his garments, casting
lots for them, what every man should have. 25 And it was about the third — Ps 22:18
[**The third hour**: 9 am] — hour,* and they crucified him. 26 And the notice of his accusation was writ-
ten: THE KING OF THE JEWS. 27 And they crucified with him two thieves,
one on the right hand and the other on his left. 28 And the scripture was
fulfilled which says, He was counted among the wicked. — Isa 53:12

29 And people who were going by railed on him, wagging their heads
and saying, Ah, wretch, who destroys the temple and builds it in three
days! 30 Save yourself, and come down from the cross!

31 Likewise also the high priests mocked him among themselves with
the scribes, and said, He saved other men; himself he cannot save. 32 Let
Christ the King of Israel now descend from the cross, so that we may see
and believe.

And those who were crucified with him reviled him also.

33 And when the sixth hour was come, darkness arose over all the earth
[**Sixth to ninth hour**: noon to 3:00 pm. See note on M't 27:45] — until the ninth hour. 34 And at the ninth hour Jesus cried out with a loud — M't 27:45-55; Lu 23:44-49
voice, saying, Eloi, Eloi, lama sabachthani? which is, if it be translated,
My God, my God, why have you forsaken me?

35 And some of the people who were standing by, when they heard
that, said, Look, he is calling for Elijah. 36 And one ran and filled a sponge
Vinegar is offered him to drink. — full of vinegar, and put it on a reed and gave him to drink, saying, Let him
alone. Let's see if Elijah will come and take him down.

37 But Jesus cried out with a loud voice and gave up the spirit. 38 And
He gives up the spirit; the veil rents. — the veil of the temple did tear in two pieces, from the top to the bottom.[a]
39 And when the centurion who stood before Jesus saw that he so cried out
and gave up the spirit, he said, Truly this man was the Son of God.

40 There were also women a good way off beholding him, among
whom were Mary Magdalene, Mary the mother of James the Little and of
Joses, and Mary Salome, 41 who also, when he was in Galilee, had fol-
lowed him and ministered to him, and many other women who had come
up with him to Jerusalem.

42 And now when night was come (because it was the Preparation, the
day before the Sabbath), 43 Joseph of Arimathea came, a noble councillor, — M't 27:57-60; Lu 23:50-56; Joh 20:38-42
who also looked for the kingdom of God. He went in bravely to Pilate and
requested the body of Jesus. 44 And Pilate marvelled that he was already
dead, and called for the centurion, and asked him if Jesus was already
dead. 45 And when he knew the truth from the centurion, he gave the body
to Joseph.

46 And Joseph bought a linen cloth, and took him down, and wrapped

He is buried.

him in the linen cloth, and laid him in a tomb that was hewn out of the rock, and rolled a stone to the opening of the sepulchre. [47]And Mary Magdalene and Mary Joses saw where he was laid.

The Notes

The veil of the temple (15:37)

a) This veil that tore in two pieces was a certain cloth that hung in the temple dividing the most holy place from the rest of the temple, as our cloth that is hung up during Lent divides the altar from the rest of the church. The tearing of this veil signified that the shadows of Moses' law were to vanish away at the flourishing light of the gospel.

Chapter 16

Christ is risen up again. He appears to the apostles, to whom he commits the preaching of the gospel.

M't c28
Lu c24
Joh c20

And when the Sabbath day was past, Mary Magdalene, Mary Jacobi, and Salome bought sweet spices so that they could come and anoint him. [2]And early in the morning of the day after the Sabbath day, they came to the sepulchre when the sun was risen. [3]And they said to one another, Who will roll the stone away from the opening of the sepulchre for us? [4]But when they looked, they saw that the stone had been rolled away; for it was a very great one.

[5]And they went into the sepulchre, and saw a young man clothed in a long white garment sitting on the right side, and they were afraid. [6]But he said to them, Do not be afraid. You seek Jesus of Nazareth, who was crucified. He is risen; he is not here. Behold the place where they put him. [7]But go your way, and tell his disciples, and especially Peter. He will go before you into Galilee; there you will see him, as he said to you.

[8]And they went out quickly and fled from the sepulchre. For they trembled and were amazed. And they did not say anything to anyone, because they were afraid.

Mary Magdalene is the first to see the risen Lord

[9]After Jesus had risen on the day after the Sabbath day, he appeared first to Mary Magdalene, out of whom he had cast seven devils. [10]And she went and told those who had been with him, as they mourned and wept. [11]And though they heard that he was alive and he had appeared to her, yet they did not believe it.

Lu 24:13-35

[12]After that, he appeared to two of them as a stranger when they were walking and going into the country. [13]And they went and told it to the rest, but they did not believe them either.

M't 28:19
Lu 24:47

[14]After that, he appeared to the eleven as they sat at food, and cast in their teeth their unbelief and hardness of heart, because they would not believe those who had seen him after his resurrection. [15]And he said to them, Go into all the world, and preach the glad tidings to all creatures.[a] [16]He who believes and is baptized will be saved, but he who does not believe will be damned. [17]And these signs will follow those who believe: in my name they will cast out devils, and will speak with new tongues, [18]and will kill serpents. And if they drink any deadly thing, it will not hurt them. They will lay their hands on the sick, and they will recover.

[19]So then, when the Lord had spoken to them, he was received into
heaven and sat down on the right hand of God. [20]And they went forth and
preached everywhere. And the Lord worked with them, and confirmed the
word with miracles that followed.

The end of the gospel
of St Mark

The Notes

Preach to all creatures (16:15) a) To preach the glad tidings to all creatures means to preach to all nations of the world.

Old Testament Feature - A glimpse into the Old Testament of the 1549 Matthew Bible... Daniel chapter 9, the prophecy contained in verses 26 & 27 minimally updated.

Daniel – The .ix. Chapter

...The death of Christ. The casting out of the wicked Jews.

... After these 62 weeks shall Christ be slain, and they shall have no pleasure in him. Then shall there come a people with the prince, and destroy the city and the sanctuary: and its end shall come as the water flood. But the desolation shall continue till the end of the battle.

He shall make a strong bond with many for the space of a week, and when the week is half gone, he shall put down the slain and meat offering.

And in the temple there shall be an abominable desolation, till it has destroyed all. And it is concluded that this wasting shall continue to the end.

Original text:

... After these .lxii. wekes, shal christ be slayne, and they shall have no pleasure in hym. Then shal there come a people with the Prince, and destroy the cytie and the Sanctuary: and his end shal come as the water floud. But the desolatyon shal contynue tyl the ende of the battayl.

He shall make a strong bond with many, for the space of a weke: and when the weke is half gone, he shal put downe the slayne and meatofferynge.

And in the temple there shalbe an abhomynable desolacyon/ tyll it have destroyed all. And it is concluded, that thys wastyng shall contynue unto the ende.

A Prologue Upon the Gospel of Luke

Luke was Paul's companion, at least from the 16th chapter of Acts onwards, and was with him in all his tribulation. And he went with Paul at his last trip up to Jerusalem. From there he followed Paul to Caesarea, where Paul lay two years in prison, and from Caesarea he went with Paul to Rome, where he lay two more years in prison. He was with Paul when he wrote to the Colossians, as he testifies in the fourth chapter, saying, The beloved Luke, the physician, greets you. And he was with Paul during his second Roman imprisonment, when Paul wrote 2 Timothy, as he says in the fourth chapter, saying, Only Luke is with me.

By these things you see the authority of the man, and what credence and reverence his writing is worthy of. Moreover, you see from whom he learned the story of his gospel; as he says, he learned it from and made diligent enquiries of the people who saw the events and were part of them. And as for the acts of the apostles, related by Luke in the book of the same name, he was present at the doing of them, or at least most of them, and played his part in them, and therefore wrote that account also from his own experience. *W.T. (1534)*

[Ed: Luke probably wrote his gospel in A.D. 60 or 61, when Paul was first in prison in Rome.]

The Gospel of
St. Luke

Chapter 1

The conception and birth of John the Baptist. The conception of Christ. The thankful songs of Mary and Zacharias.

SINCE MANY have taken in hand to compile an account of those things that
are known for certain among us, 2as told to us by those who were eye-
witnesses from the beginning, and ministered at the doing of them, 3I de-
termined also that, as soon as I had searched out diligently all things from
the beginning, then I would write to you, good Theophilus, 4so that you
may know the certainty of those things of which you are informed.

Zacharias and Elizabeth [**Shift of Abijah**: one of 24 groups of priests in the temple, who served by rotation]

5There was in the days of Herod, the king of Judea, a certain priest
named Zacharias, of the shift of Abijah.* And his wife was of the daught-
ers of Aaron, and her name was Elizabeth. 6Both were perfect before God,
and walked in all the laws and observances of the Lord, and no man could
find fault with them. 7And they had no child, because Elizabeth was bar-
ren, and both were well stricken in age.

8And it came to pass as he executed the priest's office before God, Ex 30:7,8
when his shift came 9according to the custom of the priest's office, the lot Heb 9:4
fell to him to burn incense. And he went into the temple of the Lord, 10and
the whole host of the people were outside in prayer while the incense was
a-burning. 11And there appeared to him an angel of the Lord standing on
the right side of the altar of incense. 12And when Zacharias saw him, he
was startled, and fear came on him.

13And the angel said to him, Fear not, Zacharias, for your prayer is
heard. And your wife Elizabeth will bear you a son, and you shall call his
Of John the Baptist
name John. 14And you will have joy and gladness, and many will rejoice
at his birth. 15For he will be great in the sight of the Lord, and shall drink
neither wine nor strong drink. And he will be filled with the Holy Spirit,

even in his mother's womb. [16]And he will turn many of the children of
Israel to their Lord God. [17]And he will go before him in the spirit and Mal 3:1, 4:5,6.
Turn the hearts: that is, to make the children have such a heart to God as Abraham and the fathers had.
power of Elijah, to turn the hearts of the fathers to the children,* and the
unbelievers to the wisdom of the just men: to make the people ready for
the Lord.

A sign is requested.
[18]And Zacharias said to the angel, How may I be sure of this, seeing
that I am old, and my wife well stricken in years?

[19]And the angel answered and said to him, I am Gabriel who stands in
the presence of God, and have been sent to speak to you and to show you
these glad tidings. [20]And behold, you shall be dumb and not able to speak
until the time that these things are performed, because you did not believe
my words, which will be fulfilled in their season.

[21]And the people waited for Zacharias, and wondered that he was so
long in the temple. [22]And when he came out, he could not speak to them,
whereby they perceived that he had seen some vision in the temple. And
he gestured to them and remained speechless.

[23]And eventually, as soon as the time of his ministration was up, he
departed home to his own house. [24]And after those days, his wife Eliza-
beth conceived, and hid herself five months, saying, [25]Thus has God dealt
with me in the days when he looked on me,[a] to take from me the disgrace
that I suffered among men.

[26]In the sixth month, the angel Gabriel was sent from God to a city of
Galilee named Nazareth, [27]to a virgin espoused to a man whose name was
Mary
Joseph, of the house of David. And the virgin's name was Mary. [28]And
the angel went in to her and said, Hail, thou full of grace![b] The Lord is
with you. Blessed are you among women.

[29]When she saw him, she was bewildered at his words, and cast in her
mind what manner of salutation this could be. [30]And the angel said to her,
Fear not, Mary, for you have found grace with God. [31]Lo, you shall con- Isa 7:14
Of Jesus
ceive in your womb, and shall bear a son, and shall call his name Jesus.
[32]He will be great, and will be called the Son of the Highest. And the Lord
God will give to him the seat of his father David, [33]and he will reign over
the house of Jacob forever, and of his kingdom shall be no end.

[34]Then said Mary to the angel, How will this be, seeing I do not know
a man?

[35]And the angel answered and said to her, The Holy Spirit shall come
upon you, and the power of the Highest shall overshadow you. Therefore
also, that holy thing which will be born of you will be called the Son of
God. [36]And behold: your cousin Elizabeth, she has also conceived a son in
her old age. And this is her sixth month, though she be called barren.
[37]For with God, nothing is impossible.

[38]And Mary said, Behold the handmaiden of the Lord! Be it unto me
even as you have said.

And the angel departed from her.

[39]And Mary arose in those days, and went into the mountains with
haste, into a town of Judea, [40]and entered into the house of Zacharias, and

greeted Elizabeth. 41And it happened, as Elizabeth heard the greeting of Mary, the babe sprang in her belly. And Elizabeth was filled with the Holy Spirit, 42and cried out with a loud voice, and said, Blessed are you among women, and blessed is the fruit of your womb! 43And how does it happen that the mother of my Lord should come to me? 44For lo, as soon as the voice of your greeting sounded in my ears, the babe sprang in my belly for joy. 45And blessed are you who believed, for those things will be performed that were told you from the Lord.

The Magnificat [ie, which magnifies. Also known as the Canticle or Song of Mary, this speech became one of the eight most ancient Christian hymns, named after its opening words in Latin, *Magnificat anima mea Dominum*: My soul doth magnify the Lord]

46And Mary said, My soul does magnify the Lord, 47and my spirit rejoices in God my saviour. 48For he has looked on the poor degree of his handmaiden. Behold, now from henceforth all generations will call me blessed. 49For he who is mighty has done great things unto me, and holy is his name. 50And his mercy is on them who fear him, throughout all generations. 51He shows strength with his arm.[c] He scatters those who are proud in the imagination of their hearts. 52He puts down the mighty from their seats, and exalts those of low degree. 53He fills the hungry with good things, and sends the rich away empty. 54He remembers mercy, and helps his servant Israel, 55even as he promised to our fathers, to Abraham and to his seed forever.

Isa 41:8-13; 30:18; 54:7. Jer 31:1-5 Ps 132

56And Mary stayed with Elizabeth about three months, and returned again to her own house.

57Elizabeth's time came to be delivered, and she brought forth a son. 58And her neighbours and her relatives heard how the Lord had shown great mercy upon her, and they rejoiced with her.

59And when it was the eighth day, they came to circumcise the child, and were calling him by the name Zacharias, after his father. 60However his mother spoke and said, Not so, but he shall be called John. 61And they said to her, There is no one in your family called by this name.

62And they made signs to his father, how he would have him called. 63And he asked for writing tablets and wrote, saying, His name is John. And they all marvelled. 64And Zacharias' mouth was opened immediately, and his tongue also, and he spoke, lauding God.

65And awe came on all those who dwelt near to them. And also these stories were spread abroad throughout all the hill country of Judea, 66and everyone who heard them laid them up in their hearts, saying, What manner of child will this be? And the hand of the Lord was with him.

The Benedictus [Song of Thanksgiving]

67And his father, Zacharias, was filled with the Holy Spirit, and prophesied, saying, 68Blessed be the Lord God of Israel, for he has visited[d] and redeemed his people. 69And he has raised up a horn of salvation for us in the house of his servant David, 70just as he promised by the mouth of his holy prophets, who have been since the world began: 71that we would be saved from our enemies and from the hands of all who hate us, 72to fulfil the mercy promised to our fathers, to remember his holy covenant, 73and to perform the oath that he swore to our father Abraham, 74to give us, so that we, delivered out of the hands of our enemies, might serve him without fear all the days of our life, 75in such holiness and

Ps 74 Jer 23:1-4; 30:7-10; 31:31-33.

righteousness as are accepted before him.
76And thou, child, shall be called the prophet of the Highest. For you
will go before the face of the Lord to prepare his ways, 77and to give
knowledge of salvation to his people for the remission of sins 78through
the tender mercy of our God, whereby the Dayspring[*] from on high has
visited us[e] 79to give light to those who sat in darkness and in the shadow
of death, and to guide our feet into the way of peace.
80And the child grew and became strong in spirit, and was out in the
wilderness till the day came when he was to show himself to the Israelites.

[**Dayspring**: an obsolete word for daybreak, ie the time when light dawns, personified to describe Christ]

The Notes

When he looked on me (1:25) a) That is, when he showed favour or grace to me.

Hail thou full of grace! (1:28) b) That is, Hail! as one to whom the Lord has shown abundant favour. [Ed: 'Hail' was used formerly in English as a respectful salutation or greeting.]

He shows strength with his arm (1:51) c) The arm is Christ, as it is expounded at Isaiah 51:9 [Awake and be strong, O thou arm of the Lord! Awake as in times past, ever and since the world began].

He has visited (1:68) d) That is, he has remembered his people, as in Genesis 50:24 & 25 [to deliver them, as in Genesis it was said God would visit his people to deliver them out of Egypt.]

The Dayspring from on high (1:78) e) Christ is the Dayspring that gives light to those who sit in the darkness of the ignorance of God.

Chapter 2

The birth and circumcision of Christ. How he was received into the temple. How Simeon and Anna prophesy of him, and how he was found in the temple among the learned instructors of the Jews.

And it happened in those days that there went out a commandment from
Augustus the Emperor that all the world should be taxed. 2And this taxing
was the first, and executed when Quirinius was governor in Syria. 3And
every man went to his own town to be taxed. 4And Joseph also ascended
from Galilee out of a town called Nazareth, into Judea to the city of David
which is called Bethlehem, because he was of the house and lineage of
David, 5to be taxed with Mary, his espoused wife, who was with child.
6And it came to pass while they were there that her time came to be
delivered. 7And she brought forth her first begotten son, and wrapped him M't 1:25
in swaddling clothes, and laid him in a manger because there was no room
for them within the inn.[*]

Christ is born.

[**The inn**: in old English this could mean a public place of lodging or a room in the home of a relative or other person]

8And there were in the same region shepherds abiding in the field and
watching their flock by night. 9And lo, the angel of the Lord stood right
by them, and the brightness of the Lord shone round about them, and they
were very afraid. 10But the angel said to them, Be not afraid. For behold, I
bring you tidings of great joy, which will come to all the people. 11For
unto you is born this day in the city of David a saviour, who is Christ the
Lord. 12And take this for a sign: you will find the child swaddled and laid
in a manger.
13And suddenly there was with the angel a multitude of heavenly

soldiers, lauding God and saying, 14 Glory be to God on high, and peace on
earth,[a] and to men rejoicing.

15 And it so was, as soon as the angels had gone away from them into
heaven, the shepherds said to one another, Let us go straight to Bethlehem
and see this thing that has happened, which the Lord has shown to us.
16 And they went with haste and found Mary and Joseph, and the babe laid
in a manger.

17 And when they had seen this, they proclaimed everywhere the
message that had been given them concerning that child. 18 And all who
heard it wondered at those things the shepherds told them. 19 But Mary laid
up all those sayings, and pondered them in her heart. 20 And the shepherds
returned, praising and lauding God for all that they had heard and seen,
even as it had been told to them.

21 And when the eighth day came and the child was to be circumcised, Lev 12:3
Christ is circumcised. his name was called Jesus, which was the name given by the angel before
he was conceived in the womb.

22 And when the time of their purification according to the law of
Moses came, they brought him to Jerusalem, to present him to the Lord Ex 13:1,2; 34:19.
23 (as it is written in the law of the Lord: every man-child that first opens Lev 12:6-8
the womb shall be called holy to the Lord), 24 and to offer (as it is said in Nu 8:15-18
the law of the Lord) a pair of turtledoves or two young pigeons.

Simeon

25 And behold, there was a man in Jerusalem whose name was Simeon.
And the same man was just, and feared God, and longed for the consola-
tion of Israel, and the Holy Spirit was in him. 26 And a revelation had been
given him by the Holy Spirit that he would not see death before he had
seen the Lord's Christ. 27 And he came by inspiration into the temple. And
when the father and mother brought in the child Jesus, to do for him
according to the custom of the law, 28 then he took him up in his arms and
said, 29 Lord, now let your servant depart in peace according to your prom-
ise. 30 For my eyes have seen the saviour sent from you, 31 whom you have
prepared before the face of all people – 32 a light to give sight to the Gen-
tiles, and the glory of your people Israel.

Nunc Dimittis ['Now you dismiss': the Song of Simeon, named from its initial words in the Vulgate, was part of daily prayers from the 4th century]

33 And his father and mother marvelled at those things that were spo-
ken of him. 34 And Simeon blessed them and said to Mary, his mother, Isa 8:14; 28:16.
Behold, this child shall be the fall and the resurrection of many in Israel, Ro 9:33
and a sign that shall be spoken against. 35 And moreover, the sword will 1Pe 2:6-10
pierce your soul,[b] so that the thoughts of many hearts may be revealed.[c]

Anna the prophetess.

36 And there was a prophetess, one Anna, the daughter of Phanuel, of
the tribe of Asher. She was of a great age, having lived with a husband
seven years from her virginity, 37 and been a widow for about eighty-four
years. She never went out of the temple, but served God with fasting and
prayer night and day. 38 And she came forth also that same hour, and
praised the Lord, and spoke of him to all who looked for redemption in
Jerusalem.

39 And as soon as they had performed all things according to the law of
the Lord, they returned into Galilee to their own town, Nazareth. 40 And

the child grew and became strong in spirit, and was filled with wisdom,
and the grace of God was with him.

41 Now his father and mother went to Jerusalem every year at the feast
of the Passover. 42 And when he was twelve years old, they went up to
Jerusalem, according to the custom of the feast. 43 And when the days had
come to an end, as they turned back for home, the child Jesus remained
still in Jerusalem, unbeknownst to his father and mother. 44 For they
supposed he would be with the caravan. And therefore they went a day's
journey, and were searching for him among their kinsfolk and compan-
ions. 45 When they did not find him, they went back again to Jerusalem
and searched for him. 46 And eventually, after three days, they found him
in the temple, sitting in the midst of the doctors,* both listening to them
and asking them questions. 47 And everyone who heard him marvelled at
his understanding and answers.

Christ is found disputing in the temple. [**Doctors**: instructors of Jewish biblical law]

48 When his parents saw him, they were astonished. And his mother
said to him, Son, why have you dealt with us this way? Look, your father
and I have been searching for you, sorrowing.

49 And he said to them, How is it that you were searching for me? Did
you not know that I must go about my Father's business?

50 But they did not understand what he was saying to them.

51 And he went with them, and came to Nazareth, and was obedient to
them. And his mother kept all these things in her heart. 52 And Jesus
increased in wisdom and age, and in favour with God and man.

The Notes

Peace on earth (2:14)

a) Here *peace* signifies reconciliation and the remission of our sins, as Paul called Christ our peace at Ephesians 2:14.

The sword will pierce your soul (2:35)

b) That is, because the Son of God whom you have rejoiced to bear, the truth he will preach, and the people who will put their faith in him, will all be gainsaid by the wicked, the sword of great grief and sorrow will pierce your soul; that is, yourself.

The thoughts of many hearts (2:35)

c) So that the thoughts of many hearts may be revealed, etc: The unbelieving do gainsay him, and the faithful are thrust through with the sword of sorrowfulness when he is gainsaid. And so by this sign of Christ are the different thoughts and dispositions of people revealed and made manifest, both of the wicked and of the faithful.

Chapter 3

The preaching, baptism, and imprisonment of John. The baptism of Christ. A recital of the lineage of the fathers.

Tetrarch: look in Matthew 14, note (a).

The preaching of John the Baptist

In the fifteenth year of the reign of Tiberius the Emperor (Pontius Pilate
being governor of Judea, Herod being tetrarch of Galilee, his brother
Philip tetrarch in Iturea and in the region of Trachonitis, and Lysanias
tetrarch of Abilene), 2 when Annas and Caiaphas were the high priests, the
word of God came to John the son of Zacharias in the wilderness. 3 And he
came into all the country about the Jordan River preaching the baptism of
repentance for the remission of sins, 4 as it is written in the book of the
sayings of Isaiah the prophet, which says: The voice of a crier in the

wilderness: Prepare ye the way of the Lord; make his paths straight!
5 Every valley shall be filled, and every mountain and hill shall be brought
low. And crooked things shall be made straight, and the rough ways shall
be made smooth. 6 And all flesh shall see the saviour sent by God.

Isa 40:3-5
Mal 3:1
M't c3
Mk1:1-11
Joh 1:15-34;
3:22-36.

7 Then he said to the people who came to be baptized by him, O
offspring of vipers, who has taught you to flee from the wrath to come?
8 Bring forth the due fruits of repentance, and do not begin to say in
yourselves, We have Abraham for our father. For I say to you, God is able
of these stones to raise up children unto Abraham. 9 And now also is the
axe laid to the root of the trees, so that every tree that does not bring forth
good fruit shall be hewn down and cast into the fire.

10 And the people asked him, saying, What should we do then? 11 He
answered and said to them, He who has two coats, let him share with him
who has none; and he who has food, let him do likewise.

12 Then there came publicans to be baptized, who asked him, Master,
what should we do? 13 And he said to them, Require no more than that
which is appointed to you.

14 The soldiers likewise enquired of him, saying, And what should we
do? And he said to them, Do violence to no man, neither trouble any man
wrongfully, but be content with your wages.

15 And as the people were in expectation, and all musing in their hearts
about John, whether he was the Christ, 16 John answered and said to them
all, I baptize you with water, but one stronger than I is coming after me,
whose shoe latchet I am not worthy to loose. He will baptize you with the
Holy Spirit and with fire. 17 He has his fan in his hand, and will purge his
floor, and will gather the wheat into his barn; but the chaff he will burn
with fire that never shall be quenched.

The chaff he will burn: look in Matthew 3, note (b).

18 And with many other exhortations, John preached to the people.

19 Then Herod the tetrarch (when he was rebuked by him concerning
Herodias, his brother Philip's wife, and for all the evils that Herod had
done) 20 added this above all, and shut up John in prison.

Mk 6:17

Jesus Christ baptized by John: the beginning of his ministry.

21 And it came to pass, as all the people were receiving baptism, and
when Jesus was baptized and did pray, that heaven was opened, 22 and the
Holy Spirit came down in a bodily shape like a dove upon him, and a
voice came from heaven saying, You are my dear Son; in you I do delight.

M't 3:13-17
Mk 1:9-11
Joh 1:29-34
2Pe 1:16-18

Geneology

23 And Jesus himself was about thirty years of age when he began,
being as men supposed the son of Joseph, who was the son of Heli, 24 who
was the son of Matthat, who was the son of Levi, who was the son of
Melchi, who was the son of Janna, who was the son of Joseph, 25 who was
the son of Mattathiah, who was the son of Amos, who was the son of
Nahum, who was the son of Esli, who was the son of Naggai, 26 who was
the son of Maath, who was the son of Mattathiah, who was the son of
Semei, who was the son of Joseph, who was the son of Judah, 27 who was
the son of Joannas, who was the son of Rhesa, who was the son of
Zerubbabel, who was the son of Shealtiel, who was the son of Neri, 28 who
was the son of Melchi, who was the son of Addi, who was the son of

Cosam, who was the son of Elmodam, who was the son of Er, [29]who was
the son of Jose, who was the son of Eliezer, who was the son of Jorim,
who was the son of Matthat, who was the son of Levi, [30]who was the son
of Simeon, who was the son of Judah, who was the son of Joseph, who
was the son of Jonan, who was the son of Eliakim, [31]who was the son of
Melea, who was the son of Menan, who was the son of Mattathah, who
was the son of Nathan, who was the son of David, [32]who was the son of
Jesse, who was the son of Obed, who was the son of Boaz, who was the
son of Salmon, who was the son of Nahshon, [33]who was the son of
Amminadab, who was the son of Ram, who was the son of Hezron, who
was the son of Perez, who was the son of Judah, [34]who was the son of
Jacob, who was the son of Isaac, who was the son of Abraham, who was
the son of Terah, who was the son of Nahor, [35]who was the son of Serug,
who was the son of Reu, who was the son of Peleg, who was the son of
Eber, who was the son of Shelah, [36]who was the son of Cainan, who was
the son of Arphaxad, who was the son of Shem, who was the son of Noah,
who was the son of Lamech, [37]who was the son of Methuselah, who was
the son of Enoch, who was the son of Jared, who was the son of
Mahalalel, who was the son of Cainan, [38]who was the son of Enos, who
was the son of Seth, who was the son of Adam, who was the son of God.

Chapter 4

Jesus is led into the wilderness and fasts all the time of his temptation. He overcomes the devil, and goes into Galilee to preach. At Nazareth the Jews despise him. In Capernaum the devils recognize and identify him, he enters Peter's house and heals his mother-in-law, and does great miracles.

Jesus, then full of the Holy Spirit, returned from the Jordan, and was
Jesus fasts 40 days. carried by the Spirit [2]into the wilderness, and was for forty days tempted M't 4:1-11
by the devil. And during those days he ate nothing. And when they were Mk 1:12,13
ended, he was afterwards hungered. [3]And the devil said to him, If you are De 8:3
the Son of God, command this stone to be made bread. [4]And Jesus
answered him, saying, It is written: Man shall not live by bread alone, but
by every word of God.

[5]And the devil took him up into a high mountain and showed him all
the kingdoms of the world, even in the twinkling of an eye. [6]And the devil
said to him, All this power I will give you, every whit, and the glory of
these kingdoms. For it has been delivered to me, and to whomever I wish,
I give it. [7]If you therefore will worship me, they shall all be yours.

[8]Jesus answered him and said, Away from me, Satan! For it is written: De 6:13;
You shall honour the Lord your God, and him only serve. 10:12-21

[9]And the devil carried him to Jerusalem, and set him on a pinnacle of
the temple and said to him, If you are the Son of God, cast yourself down
from here. [10]For it is written: He will give his angels charge over you, to
keep you, [11]and with their hands they will hold you up so that you do not
dash your foot against a stone. Ps 91:11,12

12 Jesus answered and said to him, It is said: You shall not tempt the
Lord your God.
13 And as soon as the devil had ended all his temptations, he departed
from him for a season.
14 Jesus returned by the power of the Spirit into Galilee, and there went
a renown of him throughout all the region round about. 15 And he taught in M't 4:12-25
their synagogues, and was commended by all. Mk 1:14-45
16 And he went to Nazareth, where he had been brought up, and as his
custom was, went into the synagogue on the Sabbath days, and stood up M't 13:53-58
to read. 17 And there was delivered to him the book of the prophet Isaiah. Mk 6:1-6
And when he had opened the scroll, he found the place where it was Joh 4:43,44
written: 18 The Spirit of the Lord is upon me, because he has anointed me. Isa 61:1,2
To preach the gospel to the poor he has sent me, and to heal the broken-
hearted; to preach deliverance to the captive, and sight to the blind, and
[**Acceptable**: welcome, freely to set at liberty those who are bruised, 19 and to preach the accept-
pleasing, propitious] able year of the Lord.*
20 And he rolled up the scroll and returned it to the minister, and sat
down. And the eyes of everyone in the synagogue were fastened on him.
21 And he began and said to them, This day this scripture is fulfilled in
your ears.
22 And they all witnessed him, and wondered at the gracious words that
Joseph's son. proceeded out of his mouth, and said, Is this not Joseph's son?
23 And he said to them, You may very well say to me this maxim: Phy-
sician, heal thyself; the things that we heard were done in Capernaum, do
the same here likewise in your own country.
No prophet is accepted by his 24 And he said, Truly I say to you, no prophet is accepted in his own Joh 4:44
own. country. 25 But I tell you of a truth, many widows were in Israel in the days
of Elijah, when heaven was shut for three years and six months, when
great famine was throughout all the land; 26 but to none of them was Elijah 1Ki 17:9
sent save into Sarepta, a city of Sidon, to a woman who was a widow. 2Ki 5:1-14
27 And many lepers were in Israel in the time of Elisha the prophet, and yet Ja 5:13-16
none of them was healed except Naaman of Syria.
28 And as many as were in the synagogue, when they heard that, were
filled with wrath. 29 And they rose up and thrust him out of the city, and
led him even to the edge of the hill on which their town was built, to cast
him down headlong. 30 But he went his way even through the midst of
them, 31 and descended into Capernaum, a city of Galilee, and there taught
them on the Sabbath days. 32 And they were astonished at his instruction,
for his preaching was with power.
33 And in the synagogue there was a man who had a spirit of an un-
clean devil, who cried with a loud voice, saying, 34 Let me alone! What Mk 1:23-26
have you to do with us, Jesus of Nazareth? Have you come to destroy us?
I know you, who you are: even the Holy One of God.
35 And Jesus rebuked him, saying, Hold your peace and come out of
The unclean spirit is cast out. him! And the devil threw the man in the midst of them and came out of
him, and did not hurt him.

[36]And fear came on them all, and they spoke among themselves, saying, What manner of thing is this? For with authority and power he commands the foul spirits, and they come out. [37]And the news of him spread abroad through all places of the country round about.

M't 7:28
Mk 6:2

Simon's mother-in-law.

[38]And he rose up and departed from the synagogue, and entered into Simon's house. And Simon's mother-in-law was taken with a great fever, and they made intercession to him for her. [39]And he stood over her and rebuked the fever, and it left her. And immediately she arose and ministered to them.

M't 8:14,15
Mk 1:29-31

Laid his hands on them.

[40]When the sun was down, all the people that had sick folk taken with different diseases brought them to him, and he laid his hands on every one of them and healed them. [41]And devils also came out of many of them, crying out and saying, You are Christ, the Son of God!

M't 8:16,17
Mk 1:32-34

But he rebuked the devils, and would not permit them to speak, for they knew that he was Christ.

[42]As soon as it was day, he departed and went away into an isolated place. And the people sought him out and came to him, and kept him from leaving them. [43]But he said to them, I must preach the kingdom of God to other places also, for that is why I have been sent.

Mk 1:35

[44]And he preached in the synagogues of Galilee.

Chapter 5

Christ preaches in the boat. The disciples leave everything and follow him. He cleanses the leper, heals the paralytic, calls Matthew, the customs officer, and eats with open sinners.

[**Lake of Gennesaret**: another name for the Sea of Galilee, derived from the plain of Gennesaret, a fertile region on the NW shore]

It came to pass, as the people pressed in upon him to hear the word of God, that he was standing by the lake of Gennesaret* [2]and saw two boats standing by the lake side. But the fishermen were gone out of them and were washing their nets. [3]And he entered into one of the boats, which belonged to Simon, and asked him to thrust out a little from the land. And he sat down and taught the people out of the boat.

M't 13:2
Mk 4:1

[4]When he had left speaking, he said to Simon, Launch out into the deep, and let slip your nets to make a catch. [5]And Simon answered and said to him, Master, we have laboured all night and have caught nothing. But at your word, I will loose forth the net.

A haul of fish

[6]And when they had so done, they netted a great multitude of fishes. And their net was tearing, [7]but they made signs to their fellow fishermen who were in the other boat to come and help them. And they came and filled both the boats, so that they were sinking back.

[8]When Simon Peter saw this, he fell down at Jesus' knees, saying, Lord, go from me, for I am a sinful man. [9]For he was utterly astonished, as was everyone with him, at the haul of fish that they took; [10]and so also were James and John, the sons of Zebedee, who were partners with Simon. And Jesus said to Simon, Fear not; from henceforth you shall catch men.

[11]And they brought the boats to land, and left everything, and fol-
lowed him.
[12]And it happened, as he was in a certain town, behold, there was a M't 8:2-4
The leper man full of leprosy. And when he saw Jesus, he fell on his face and Mk 1:40-45
besought him, saying, Lord, if you will, you can make me clean. [13]And
Jesus stretched forth his hand and touched him, saying, I will; be clean.
And immediately the leprosy departed from him. [14]And Jesus told him not
to tell anyone, but to go and show himself to the priest, and to make an
offering for his cleansing as Moses had commanded, for a witness to Lev 14:2
them. [15]But word of him went abroad all the more, and crowds of people
came together to hear him and to be healed by him of their infirmities.
[16]And he kept himself apart in the remote places, and gave himself to
prayer.
[17]And it happened on a certain day that he was teaching, and there sat
the Pharisees and doctors of the law, who had come out of all the towns of M't 9:1-8 Mk 2:1-26
Galilee, Judea, and Jerusalem. And the power of the Lord was to heal the
people. [18]And behold, some men brought a man lying in his bed, who was
taken with paralysis, and were trying to find a way to bring him in and to
lay him before Jesus. [19]And when they could not find a way to bring him
[**The press**: the crowd of people pressing in] in, because of the press,* they went up on the top of the house and let him
down through the tiling, bed and all, in the midst before Jesus. [20]When he
saw their faith, he said to him, Man, your sins are forgiven you. [21]And the
scribes and the Pharisees began to think, saying, What fellow is this, who
speaks blasphemy? Who can forgive sins, but God only?
[22]When Jesus perceived their thoughts, he answered and said to them,
What are you thinking in your hearts? [23]Which is easier to say: Your sins
are forgiven you, or to say, Rise and walk? [24]But so that you may know
that the Son of man has power to forgive sins on earth – He said to the
paralytic, I say to you, arise; take up your bed and go home to your house.
[25]And immediately he rose up before them, took up the bed he laid on,
and departed to his own house, praising God.
[26]And they were all amazed, and they lauded God and were filled with
fear, saying, We have seen strange things today.
[27]And after that, Jesus went out and saw a publican named Levi sit-
Levi (Matthew) is called. ting at the receipt of custom, and said to him, Follow me. [28]And he left all,
rose up, and followed him. [29]And that same Levi gave for Jesus a great M't 9:9-13 Mk 2:14-17
feast at home in his own house. And there was a great company of publi-
cans and of others that sat at food with him.
[30]And the scribes and Pharisees murmured against his disciples, say-
Publicans and sinners. ing, Why do you eat and drink with publicans and sinners? [31]Jesus an-
swered and said to them, The whole have no need for the physician, but
the sick do. [32]I came not to call the righteous, but sinners, to repentance.
[33]Then they said to him, Why do the disciples of John fast often, and
pray, and the disciples of the Pharisees also, but yours eat and drink?
[34]And he said to them, Can you make the children of the wedding fast
while the bridegroom is present with them? [35]The days will come when M't 9:14-17 Mk 2:18-22

the bridegroom will be taken away from them. Then they will fast, in
those days.
[36]Then he spoke to them in a similitude: No one patches a piece of a
New and old do not agree. new garment into an old vesture, because if he does, then he will have cut
up the new, and the piece that was taken out of the new does not agree
with the old. [37]Also, no one pours new wine into old wineskins, because if
he does, the new wine bursts the vessels and runs out, and the vessels are Job 32:19
[**Destroyed**: gases formed during the fermentation of wine create pressure that bursts dry or brittle skins] destroyed.* [38]But new wine must be poured into new vessels, and both are M't 9:14-17 Mk 2:18-22
preserved. [39]Also, no one who drinks old wine can straightaway abide the
new, for he says the old is pleasanter.

Chapter 6

He defends the disciples that pluck the ears of grain. He heals the man with the withered hand, chooses his twelve apostles, gives a sweet sermon, and teaches to do good for evil.

It happened on an after-Sabbath that Jesus went through the grain field,
and his disciples plucked the ears of grain and ate, rubbing them in their M't 12:1-8
hands. [2]And certain of the Pharisees said to them, Why do you do that Mk 2:23-28
The Sabbath day is broken. which is not lawful to do on the Sabbath days? [3]And Jesus answered them
and said, Have you not read what David did when he himself was hungry,
and those who were with him? [4]How he went into the house of God, and 1Sam 21:1-6
took and ate the loaves of hallowed bread, and gave also to those who
were with him – which bread it was not lawful to eat, but for the priests
only? [5]And he said to them, The Son of man is Lord of the Sabbath day.
[6]And it came about in another Sabbath also that he entered into the
synagogue and taught. And there was there a man whose right hand was M't 12:9-14
withered. [7]And the scribes and Pharisees watched Jesus to see if he would Mk 3:1-6
heal on the Sabbath day, to find an accusation against him. [8]But he knew
their thoughts, and said to the man that had the withered hand, Rise up,
and stand forth in the midst. And he arose and stepped forth. [9]Then Jesus
said to them, I will ask you a question: whether it is lawful on the Sabbath
days to do good, or to do evil; to save life, or to destroy it? [10]And he
looked around at them all and said to the man, Stretch forth your hand.
And he did so, and his hand was restored and made as whole as the other.
[11]And they were filled full of madness, and conferred with each other,
what they might do to Jesus.
[12]And it came to pass in those days that he went out into a mountain to
pray, and continued all night in prayer to God. [13]And as soon as it was
day, he called his disciples. And of them he chose twelve, whom he also M't 10:1-4
The twelve are chosen. called apostles: [14]Simon, whom he named Peter, and Andrew his brother; Mk 3:13-19
James and John; Philip and Bartholomew; [15]Matthew and Thomas; James
the son of Alpheus, and Simon called Zelotes; [16]Judas, James' son; and
Judas Iscariot, which same was the traitor.
[17]And he came down with them, and stood in the open field with the
company of his disciples and a great crowd of people out of all parts of
Judea and Jerusalem, and from the sea-coast of Tyre and Sidon, who came

to hear him and to be healed of their diseases, [18]and people also who were
vexed with foul spirits, and they were healed. [19]And all the people pressed
in to touch him, because power went out of him and healed them all.

[20]And he lifted up his eyes upon the disciples and said, Blessed are
you who are poor,[a] for yours is the kingdom of God. [21]Blessed are you M't 5:1-12
who hunger now, for you shall be satisfied. Blessed are you who weep
now, for you will laugh. [22]Blessed are you when men hate you and thrust
you out of their company, and rail, and abhor your name as an evil thing,
for the Son of man's sake. [23]Rejoice then, and be glad, for behold, your
reward is great in heaven. Likewise did their fathers treat the prophets.

[24]But woe is to you who are rich,[b] for you have therein your conso-
lation. [25]Woe to you who are full, for you shall hunger. Woe to you who Am c6
now laugh, for you will wail and weep. [26]Woe to you when all men praise Ec'us 31:1-4
you, for likewise did their fathers praise the false prophets.

[27]But I say to you who hear: Love your enemies. Do good to those M't 5:43-48
who hate you. [28]Bless those who curse you, and pray for those who
wrongfully trouble you. [29]And to him that strikes you on the one cheek,
offer also the other. And him that takes away your gown, forbid not to
take your coat also. [30]Give to every man that asks of you. And of him who
Do unto others as you would have them do unto you
takes away your goods, ask not for them back. [31]And as you would have M't 7:12
others do unto you, so do unto them likewise.

[32]If you love those who love you, what credit are you worthy of? For
the very sinners love their friends. [33]And if you do good to those who do
good to you, what credit are you worthy of? For the very sinners do even
the same. [34]If you lend to people from whom you hope to receive, what
credit should you have? For the very sinners lend to sinners, to receive as
much in return. [35]Therefore love your enemies, do good, and lend, looking
for nothing in return; and your reward will be great, and you will be the
children of the Highest. For he is kind to the unkind and to the evil.

[36]Be therefore merciful, as your Father is merciful. [37]Judge not, and
Covenants
you will not be judged. Condemn not, and you will not be condemned. M't 7:1-5
Forgive, and you will be forgiven. [38]Give, and it will be given to you: a Ro 2:1
good measure pressed down, shaken together, and running over will men
give into your bosoms. For the measure that you use will be measured
back to you.

[39]And he put forth a similitude to them: Can the blind lead the blind?
Do they not both then fall into the ditch? [40]The disciple is not above his
master, but everyone will be formed even as his teacher is.

[41]Why do you see a speck in your brother's eye, and not consider the
beam that is in your own eye? [42]Or how can you say to your brother,
Brother, let me pull out the speck that is in your eye – when you do not
perceive the beam that is in your own eye? Hypocrite! First cast the beam
out of your own eye, and then you will see clearly to pull the speck out of
your brother's eye.

[43]It is not a good tree that brings forth bad fruit, nor is that a bad tree
The tree is known by its fruit.
that brings forth good fruit. [44]For every tree is known by its fruit. Neither

is it from thorns that men gather figs, nor from bushes that they gather
grapes. [45]A good man, out of the good treasure of his heart, brings forth
that which is good. And an evil man, out of the evil treasure of his heart, M't 12:33-35 Mk 7:20-23
brings forth that which is evil. For out of the abundance of the heart, his
mouth speaks.*

[Luther had 'What fills the heart overflows the mouth.' This became a popular saying in 16th century Germany]

[46]Why do you call me Master, Master, and yet not do as I bid you?
[47]Whoever comes to me and hears my sayings and does them, I will show M't 7:24-27
you whom he is like: [48]he is like a man who built a house, and dug deep,
and laid the foundation on a rock. When the waters rose, the flood beat
upon that house, and could not move it. For it was grounded upon a rock.
[49]But the person who hears and does not is like a man who built a house
without a foundation upon the soil, against which the flood beat, and it
fell immediately. And the fall of that house was great.

To build on rock or sand.

The Notes

Blessed are you who are poor (6:20)

a) Christ calls *the poor* those persons who are poor in spirit; that is, who trust in no worldly things and are forsaken and little regarded by others, being poor and contrite in heart. Such people often do not prosper in the world, because they lead a godly life and put their whole trust and confidence in God, as in Matthew 5:3.

Woe to the rich (6:24)

b) Such riches are spoken of at Matthew 19:16-26.

Chapter 7

He heals the centurion's servant, raises up the widow's son from death to life, and answers the disciples that John the Baptist sent to him. He commends John, and reproves the Jews for their unfaithfulness. He eats with the Pharisee. The woman washes his feet with her tears, and he forgives her her sins.

When Jesus had ended all his sayings in the hearing of the people, he
entered into Capernaum. [2]And a certain centurion's servant was sick and
ready to die, whom he made much of. [3]And when the centurion* heard of M't 8:5-13
Jesus, he sent to him the elders of the Jews, beseeching him to come and
heal his servant. [4]And they came to Jesus and besought him urgently,
saying, He is worthy that you should do this for him, [5]for he loves our
nation, and has built us a synagogue.

Centurion: a captain over a hundred men.

[6]And Jesus went with them. And when he was not far from the house,
the centurion sent friends to him, saying to him, Lord, do not trouble
yourself, for I am not worthy that you should come under my roof.
[7]Therefore I did not think myself worthy to come to you. But speak the
word only, and my servant shall be healed. [8]For I likewise am a man
under authority, and have under me soldiers. And I say to one, Go, and he
goes; and to another, Come, and he comes; and to my servant, Do this,
and he does it.

[9]When Jesus heard this, he marvelled at him, and turned about and
said to the people that followed him, I say to you, I have not found such
great faith, no, not in Israel.

10 And those that had been sent turned back home again, and found the
servant that had been sick, whole.
11 And it happened after that, that he went into a town called Nain. And
many of his disciples went with him, and crowds of people. 12 When he
came near to the gate of the town, behold, there was a dead man being
carried out. He had been the only son of his mother, and she was a widow,
and a large group of townsfolk were with her. 13 And when the Lord saw
her, he had compassion on her and said to her, Weep not. 14 And he went 1Ki 17:23
The dead man is raised. and touched the bier, and those who were bearing it stood still. And he 2Ki 4:36
said, Young man, I say to you, arise. 15 And the dead man sat up, and
began to speak. And Jesus delivered him to his mother.
16 And there came a fear upon them all. And they glorified God, say-
ing, A great prophet is risen among us, and God has visited his people.
17 And this talk of him went forth throughout all Judea, and throughout
all the regions that lie round about.
18 And the disciples of John reported to him about all these things.
John the Baptist sends to 19 And John called to him two of his disciples, and sent them to Jesus, M't 11:2-6
Christ. saying, Are you he that was to come, or should we look for another?
20 When the men came to Jesus, they said, John the Baptist sent us to
you, saying, Are you he that was to come, or should we wait for another?
21 And at that same time, Jesus cured many people of their infirmities
and diseases, and of evil spirits; and to many who were blind, he gave
sight. 22 And Jesus answered and said to John's disciples, Go your ways,
and tell John what things you have seen and heard – how the blind see, the
lame walk, the lepers are cleansed, the deaf hear, the dead arise. To the Isa c60
poor, the glad tidings are preached; 23 and happy is he who is not offended
by me.[a]
24 When the messengers of John had departed, Jesus began to speak to
the people about John. What did you go out into the wilderness to see?
Did you go to see a reed shaken with the wind? 25 But what did you go out
to see? A man clothed in soft raiment? Behold, those who are gorgeously
apparelled and live delicately are in kings' courts. 26 But what did you go
out to see? A prophet? Yea, I say to you, and more than a prophet. 27 This
is he of whom it is written: Behold, I send my messenger before your Isa 40:3
face, to prepare your way before you. 28 For I say to you, among the chil- Mal 3:1; 4:5. M't 11:7-11
dren of women there is no greater prophet than John. Nevertheless, one Mk 1:1-9
who is less in the kingdom of God, is greater than he.[b]
Publicans justify God. 29 And all the people who heard, and the publicans, justified God, and
Pharisees despise the counsel were baptized with the baptism of John. 30 But the Pharisees and scribes
of God. rejected the counsel of God against themselves, and were not baptized by
him.
31 And the Lord said, To what shall I liken the people of this gen- M't 11:16-20
eration, and what are they like? 32 They are like children sitting in the and note (b)
marketplace and calling one to another, and saying, We have piped to
you, and you have not danced; we have mourned to you, and you have not
wept. 33 For John the Baptist came neither eating bread nor drinking wine,

and you say he has the devil. [34]The Son of man has come, and eats and
drinks, and you say, Here is a man who is a glutton and a drinker of wine,
a friend of publicans and sinners. [35]Yet wisdom is justified by her chil-
dren.

[36]And one of the Pharisees invited him to eat with him. And he went
Mary of Bethany. into the Pharisee's house and sat down to food. [37]And behold, a woman in M't 26:6-13 Mk 14:1-11 Joh 12:1-8
that town who was a sinner, as soon as she knew that Jesus sat at food in
the Pharisee's house, brought an alabaster jar of oyntment. [38]And she
stood at his feet behind him, weeping, and began to wash his feet with
tears, and wiped them with the hair of her head, and kissed his feet, and
anointed them with oyntment.

[39]When the Pharisee who had invited him saw this, he spoke within
himself, saying, If this man were a prophet, he would surely know who
and what manner of woman this is that touches him; for she is a sinner.
[40]And Jesus responded and said to him, Simon, I have something to say to
you. And he said, Teacher, say on.

[41]There was a certain lender who had two debtors. One owed five
[**Denarii**: a denarius was a Roman coin, and a day's wage for a Roman soldier]
hundred denarii,* and the other fifty. [42]When they had nothing to pay, he
forgave them both. Which of them, tell me, will love him most?

[43]Simon answered and said, I suppose the one that was forgiven most.

And he said to him, You have truly judged.

[44]And Jesus turned to the woman and said to Simon, Do you see this
woman? I entered into your house, and you gave me no water for my feet,
but she has washed my feet with tears, and wiped them with the hair of
her head. [45]You gave me no kiss, but she, since the time I came in, has not
ceased to kiss my feet. [46]My head with oil you did not anoint, but she has
anointed my feet with oyntment. [47]Therefore I say to you, many sins are
Love is the sign that the sins are forgiven her.
forgiven her, for she loved much.[d] But he who is forgiven less, loves less.

[48]And he said to her, Your sins are forgiven you.

[49]And those who sat at food with him began to say within themselves,
Who is this, who forgives sins in this way?

[50]And he said to the woman, Your faith has saved you. Go in peace.

The Notes

Happy is he who is not offended by me (7:23)

a) To be offended in Christ is to be determined not to acknowledge Christ, nor yet to believe in him. Not to be offended in him is to receive him and to acknowledge by a perfect faith that he is our saviour.

Less in heaven (7:28)

b) One that is less in the kingdom of heaven is greater than he: look in M't 11:11.

Wisdom is justified (7:35)

c) Wisdom is justified by her children: look in M't 11:19 and note (c) thereon.

Many sins are forgiven her (7:47)

d) Many sins are forgiven her, because she loved much: It is not that her love obtained remission of her sins, but the faith out of which her love proceeded, and therefore Christ openly affirms, Your faith has saved you. For as Saint Paul says, without faith it is impossible to please God (Hebrews 11:6).

Chapter 8

Christ, with his apostles, goes from town to town and preaches, explains the parable of the seed, says who is his mother and his brother, and stills the raging of the sea. He delivers the possessed man and drives the devils into the herd of swine, and helps the sick woman and Jairus' daughter.

And it happened after that, that he went throughout cities and towns,
preaching and proclaiming the kingdom of God. And the twelve were
with him, [2]and also certain women who had been healed of evil spirits and
infirmities: Mary called Magdalene, out of whom went seven devils, [3]and
Joanna the wife of Chuza, Herod's steward, and Susanna, and many
others, who ministered to them from their substance.
[4]When crowds of people were gathered together, having come to him
out of all places, he spoke by a similitude: [5]A sower went out to sow his
The sower. seed. And as he sowed, some fell by the wayside, and it was trodden M't 13:3-23
under foot, and the fowls of the air devoured it up. [6]And some fell on Mk 4:2-20
stone, and as soon as it had sprung up, it withered away, because it lacked
moisture. [7]And some fell among thorns, and the thorns grew up with it
and choked it. [8]And some fell on good ground, and sprang up, and bore
fruit a hundredfold.
And as he said these things, he called: He who has ears to hear, let
him hear!
[9]His disciples asked him, saying, What manner of similitude is this? Isa 6:8-10
Secrets of the kingdom: to whom revealed, to whom they remain hid. [10]And he said, To you it is given to know the secrets of the kingdom of M't 13:11-15 Mk 4:11,12
God. But to others they remain in similitudes, so that when they see, they Joh 12:37-41 Ac 28:25-27
will not see, and when they hear, they will not understand. Ro 11:7-10
[11]The similitude is this: The seed is the word of God. [12]Those who are
beside the way are the people that hear, but afterward the devil comes and
takes away the word out of their hearts, lest they should believe and be
saved. [13]Those on the stones are people who, when they hear, receive the
word with joy. But these have no roots, and for a while believe, but in
time of trial go away. [14]As for that which fell among thorns, this is those
who hear and go forth, but are choked with cares, and with riches and
[**Voluptuous living**: a way of life characterized by the gratification of sensual desires, esp. luxurious tastes] voluptuous living,[*] and bring forth no fruit. [15]As for that in the good
ground, this is those who with a good and pure heart hear the word, and
keep it, and bring forth fruit with patience.
[16]No man lights a candle and covers it under a vessel, neither puts it
under the table, but sets it on a candlestick, so that those who enter in may M't 5:14-16; 13:12.
see the light. [17]Nothing is in secret that may not become clear, nor any- Mk 4:21-23
thing hid that may not be known and come to light. [18]Take heed therefore
how you hear. For whosoever has, to him will be given, and whosoever
has not, from him shall be taken even that same which he supposes that he
has.[a]
[19]Then Jesus' mother and his brethren came looking for him, but could M't 12:46-50
not come in to him because of the press of people. [20]And they told him, Mk 3:31-35
Mother and brethren. saying, Your mother and your brethren are standing outside and want to
see you. [21]He answered and said to them, My mother and my brethren are
these who hear the word of God and do it.
[22]And it happened on a certain day that he got into a boat, and his

Jesus sleeps in the boat.

M't 8:23-27
Mk 4:35-41

disciples also, and he said to them, Let us go over to the other side of the lake. And they launched forth. 23And as they sailed, he fell asleep. And there arose a storm of wind on the lake, and they were filled with water and were in jeopardy. 24And the disciples went to him and awoke him, saying, Master, Master, we are lost! Then he arose and rebuked the wind and the tempest of water, and they ceased, and it became calm. 25And he said to them, Where is your faith?

They feared and wondered, saying one to another, What manner of man is this? For he commands both the winds and water, and they obey him.

Gadarenes [also called the Gergesenes in Matthew]

M't 8:28-34
Mk 5:1-20

26And they sailed to the region of the Gadarenes, which is across from Galilee. 27And as he went out to land, there met him a certain man from the place, who had for a long time had a devil. And he wore no clothes; neither did he live in a house, but among graves. 28When he saw Jesus, he cried out and fell down before him, and with a loud voice said, What have I to do with you, Jesus, Son of the God Most High? I beseech you, torment me not! 29For Jesus commanded the foul spirit to come out of the man. For it often affected him violently, and he was bound with chains and kept with shackles, but he broke the bonds, and was carried by the fiend into wilderness areas.

30And Jesus asked him, saying, What is your name? And he said, Legion[b] (because many devils were entered into him). 31And the devils besought Jesus not to command them to go out into the deep. 32There was nearby a herd of many swine feeding on a hill, and the devils besought him to suffer them to enter into the swine. And he suffered them. 33Then the devils went out of the man and entered into the swine. And the herd took their course and ran headlong into the lake, and were drowned.

34When the herdsmen saw what had happened, they fled and told it in the town and in the villages. 35And people came out to see what had been done, and came to Jesus, and found the man out of whom the devils were departed sitting at the feet of Jesus, clothed and in his right mind; and they were afraid. 36Those also who had witnessed it told them how the demon-possessed man was healed. 37And all the whole population from the country of the Gadarenes besought Jesus to depart from them, for they were taken with great fear.

And he got into the boat and turned back again. 38Then the man from whom the devils were departed asked him if he could be with him. But Jesus sent him away, saying, 39Go home again into your own house, and show what great things God has done for you.

And the man went his way, and preached throughout all the city about the great things Jesus had done for him.

40And it came to pass that, when Jesus arrived back again, the people received him gladly, for they were all awaiting him. 41And behold, there came a man named Jairus (and he was a leader of the synagogue), and he fell down at Jesus' feet and besought him to come to his house. 42For he had but a daughter only, about twelve years of age, and she lay dying.

M't 9:18-26
Mk 5:21-43

And as he went, the people thronged him. [43]And a woman who had for
Issue of blood
twelve years had an issue of blood (who had spent all her substance on
physicians, but could not be helped by any) [44]came behind him and
touched the hem of his garment, and immediately her issue of blood was
stanched. [45]And Jesus said, Who is it that touched me? When everyone
denied it, Peter and those who were with him said, Master, the people
throng you and crowd you, and you say, Who touched me? [46]And Jesus
said, Somebody touched me. For I can tell that power has gone out of me.

[47]When the woman saw that she was not hid, she came trembling and
fell at his feet, and told him before all the people the reason why she had
touched him, and how she was healed immediately. [48]And he said to her,
Daughter, be of good comfort. Your faith has made you whole. Go in
peace.

[49]While he was yet speaking, a person from the house of the synagogue leader came and said to him, Your daughter is dead; don't trouble
the Master. [50]When Jesus heard that, he spoke to the father, saying, Fear
not; only believe, and she shall be made whole.

[51]And when he came to the house, he allowed no one to go in with
him except Peter, James, and John, and the father and the mother of the
maiden. [52]Everybody wept and sorrowed for her. And he said, Weep not,
for she is not dead, but sleeping. [53]And they laughed him to scorn, because they knew that she was dead. [54]And he put them all out, and took
her by the hand and called, saying, Maiden, arise! [55]And her spirit came
Jairus' daughter is raised.
back, and she rose up straightaway. And he said to give her food. [56]And
her father and mother were astonished. But he charged them to tell no one
what had been done.

The Notes

Whosoever has (8:18)

a) Whosoever has, to him will be given, but from who has not, will be taken away: look in Matthew 13:12 and note (a) thereon. [Ed> In verses 4-18, Jesus is speaking about spiritual hearing and seeing; that is, understanding the secrets of the kingdom of God referred to in verse 10. By hearing we enter into the house (M't 5:15), and by the light of the word and Spirit we receive understanding. Therefore things 'hid' and 'secret' mean here in these verses the mysteries of the kingdom, which the Lord promises to make known to us as we take heed how we hear (v18).]

Legion (8:30)

b) According to Vegetius, a legion comprises at the least 6,732. [Ed: P.F. Vegetius Renatus was a writer on military matters during the late Roman Empire. Mark says there were about 2,000 swine, all possessed by spirits that left the man (Mk 5:13).]

Chapter 9

He sends out the twelve apostles to preach. Herod hears about him. He feeds 5,000 men with five loaves and two fishes. The disciples confess him to be the Son of God. He transfigures himself upon the mount, delivers the possessed, and teaches his disciples to be lowly. They desire vengeance, but he reproves them.

Then he called the twelve together and gave them power and authority

over all devils, and to heal diseases. 2And he sent them to preach the M't 10:1-15
The twelve are sent. kingdom of God and to cure the sick. 3And he said to them, Take nothing Mk 6:7-13
to support you along the way; neither staff nor bag, nor bread, nor money;
neither have two coats.[a] 4And whatever house you enter into, there make
your stay, and from there take your leave. 5And whoever will not receive
you, when you go out of that city, shake off the very dust from your feet,
for a testimony against them.

6And they went out, and went through the towns preaching the gospel
and healing everywhere.

7And Herod the tetrarch[b] heard of all that was done by Jesus, and was
disconcerted because it was said by some that John was risen again from Mk 6:14-16
death, 8and by some that Elijah had appeared, and by some that one of the
old prophets was risen up again. 9And Herod said, John I have beheaded; M't 14:10
who then is this of whom I hear such things? And he desired to see him.

10And the apostles returned and told Jesus what great things they had
done. And he took them and went aside into a solitary place near to a
town called Bethsaida. 11But the people knew of it, and followed him.
And he received them, and spoke to them of the kingdom of God, and
healed those who had need of healing. 12And when the day began to wear M't 14:15-21 Mk 6:30-44
away, then the twelve came and said to him, Send the people away, so
that they can go into the towns and villages round about and find lodging
and get food, for we are in a remote place here. 13But he said to them, You
give them to eat. And they said, We have no more than five loaves and
two fishes, unless we go and buy food for all these people.

14And there were about 5,000 men. And he said to his disciples, Have
Five loaves and two fishes. them sit down in groups of fifty. 15And they did so, and made them all sit
down. 16And he took the five loaves and the two fishes, and looked up to
heaven, and blessed them, and broke, and gave to the disciples to set
before the people. 17And they ate and were all satisfied. And there were
taken up of what remained to them twelve baskets full of leftovers.

18And it so was, as he was apart praying, that his disciples were with
him, and he asked them, saying, Who do the people say I am? 19They
answered and said, John the Baptist, or some say Elijah, and some say one M't 16:13-23
of the old prophets is risen again. 20He said to them, Who do you say that Mk 8:27-33
I am? Peter answered and said, You are the Christ of God. 21And Jesus
warned and instructed them that they should tell no one this thing,
22saying that the Son of man must suffer many things, and be reproved by
the elders and by the high priests and scribes, and be slain, and the third
day rise again.

23And he said to them all, if any person would come after me, let him
Passion foretold. deny himself, and take up his cross daily and follow me. 24Whosoever M't 16:24-28
would save his life shall lose it,[c] but whosoever loses his life for my sake, Mk 8:34-38 Lu 17:33
he will save it. 25For what does it profit a man to win the whole world, if Joh 12:25,26
Christ's disciple. he loses himself, or runs in harm's way? 26For whoever is ashamed of me
and of my sayings, of him will the Son of man be ashamed when he
comes in his own glory, and in the glory of his Father, and of the holy

angels. 27 And I tell you truly, there are some standing here who will not taste of death till they see the kingdom of God.[d]

M't 17:1-9
Mk 9:2-10

Transfiguration.

28 And it followed, about eight days after those sayings, that Jesus took Peter, James, and John, and went up into a mountain to pray. 29 And as he prayed, the fashion of his countenance was changed, and his garment was white and shone. 30 And behold, two men talked with him; and they were Moses and Elijah, 31 who appeared gloriously, and spoke of his departing from this life, which he was to carry through to the end at Jerusalem.

32 Peter and those who were with him were heavy with sleep. And when they awoke, they saw his glory, and two men standing with him. 33 And as the men were departing from him, Peter said to Jesus, Master, it is good for us, being here. Let us make three tabernacles: one for you, and one for Moses, and one for Elijah. But he did not know what he was saying. 34 While he thus spoke, there came a cloud that covered them, and they were afraid when they came under the cloud. 35 And there came a voice out of the cloud, saying, This is my dear Son. Hear him!

Hear him!

36 And as soon as the voice was past, Jesus was found alone. And they kept it close, and told no one in those days any of those things that they had seen.

M't 17:14-21
Mk 9:14-29

37 And the next day, as they came down from the hill, a large crowd met him. 38 And a man from the crowd cried out, saying, Teacher, I beg you, look upon my son, for he is all that I have. 39 And see, a spirit takes him, and suddenly he shouts out. And it tears him, so that he foams at the mouth, and with much pain departs from him when he has battered him. 40 And I begged your disciples to cast it out, but they could not.

41 Jesus answered and said, O generation without faith and perverse, how long shall I be with you and suffer you? Bring your son here.

The spirit of the falling sickness is cast out.

42 And as the boy was yet coming, the fiend rent him and tore him. 43 And Jesus rebuked the unclean spirit, and healed the child, and delivered him to his father. And they were all amazed at the mighty power of God.

The Passion again foretold.

While everyone marvelled at all the things that he did, he said to his disciples, 44 Let these words sink down into your ears: the time will come when the Son of man will be delivered into the hands of men. 45 But they did not comprehend what that saying meant. It was hid from them, so that they did not understand it. And they were afraid to ask him about it.

M't 18:1-5
Mk 9:33-37
Lu 22:26

46 Then there arose a dispute among them, who should be the greatest. 47 When Jesus perceived the thoughts of their hearts, he took a child and set him close by himself 48 and said to them, Whoever receives this child in my name, receives me. And whoever receives me, receives him who sent me. For he that is least among you all, the same shall be great.

49 And John answered and said, Master, we saw a man casting out devils in your name, and we told him not to, because he does not follow with us. 50 And Jesus said to him, Forbid him not. For whoever is not against us, is with us.

51 And it followed, when the time was come that he should be received up, then he set his face to go to Jerusalem, and sent messengers before

him. 52And they went and entered into a city of the Samaritans, to make
ready for him. 53But the Samaritans would not receive him, because his
face was set toward Jerusalem. 54When his disciples James and John saw
Fire from heaven. that, they said, Lord, would you have us call fire down from heaven to
consume them, even as Elijah did?

55Jesus turned about and rebuked them, saying, You know not what
manner of spirit you are of. The Son of man has not come to destroy
men's lives, but to save them.

56And they set off for another town. 57And as he walked in the road, a
certain man said to him, I will follow you wherever you go. 58Jesus said to M't 8:19-22
him, Foxes have holes, and birds of the air have nests, but the Son of man
has nowhere to lay his head.

59And he said to another, Follow me. And the man said, Lord, allow
me first to go and bury my father. 60Jesus said to him, Let the dead bury
their dead;[e] but as for you, go and preach the kingdom of God.

61And another said, I will follow you, Lord, but let me first go and bid
farewell to the people who are at home at my house. 62Jesus said to him,
No one who puts his hand to the plow and looks back is fit for the kingdom of God.

The Notes

Neither staff nor bag (9:3) a) Look in Mark 6, note (a).

Herod the tetrarch (9:7) b) *Tetrarch* is expounded at Matthew 14, note (a).

Who would save his life (9:24) c) Whosoever would save his life, etc; that is, whoever (in this world) so regards his life that he will not put it in jeopardy for me when the time requires, the same shall lose his life eternally, etc.

There are some standing here (9:27) d) Some standing here will not taste of death till they see the kingdom of God: This kingdom of God, which Mark in the 8th chapter at the last verse [v 9:1 in later versions] writes will come with power, is the kingdom of Christ, which some of them did then see – namely Peter, John, and James, when they saw the cloud and the glory of Christ transformed, and heard the testimony and witness of the Father of heaven, and of Moses and Elijah. For then all these things did abundantly testify that Christ was a king and the Son of God.

Let the dead bury their dead (9:60) e) Let the dead bury their dead; that is, let the infidels alone with their infidelity. Follow me; that is, believe in me, etc., and go and preach the kingdom of God, etc.

Chapter 10

He sends the seventy on before him to preach, and instructs them how to conduct themselves. He prays to his heavenly Father, answers the scribe that tested him, and by the example of the Samaritan, shows who is our neighbour. Martha receives the Lord into her house. Mary Magdalene is fervent in hearing his word.

After these things, the Lord appointed seventy others also, and sent them Nu 11:16-29
two by two before him into every city and place where he himself would
come. 2And he said to them, The harvest is great, but the labourers are
Seventy are sent, lambs among wolves. few. Pray therefore the Lord of the harvest to send forth labourers into his
harvest. 3Go your ways. Behold, I send you forth as lambs among wolves. M't 10:16

4Carry no wallet, nor bag, nor shoes, and address no man by the way.
5Into whatever house you enter, first say, Peace be to this house. 6And if a
child of peace be there, your peace will rest upon him; if not, it will return
to you again. 7And in the same house remain, eating and drinking such
Faith ministers all. things as they have. For the labourer is worthy of his reward. Go not from
house to house.

8And into whatever town you enter, if they receive you, eat such
things as are set before you, 9and heal the sick that are there, and say to
them, The kingdom of God is come nigh upon you! 10But into whatever
town you enter, if they do not receive you, go your ways out into the M't 10:14
streets of the same and say, 11Even the very dust that cleaves on us from
your city, we wipe off against you. But yet mark this, that the kingdom of
God came nigh upon you.

12Yea and I say to you that it shall be easier in that day for Sodom than M't 10:15
Chorazin, Bethsaida, Tyre, for that town. 13Woe is to you, Chorazin! Woe to you, Bethsaida! For if
Sidon, Capernaum. the miracles had been done in Tyre and Sidon that have been done in you,
they would have repented a great while ago, sitting in sackcloth and ashes.
14But it will be easier for Tyre and Sidon at the judgment than for you.
15And you, Capernaum, who are exalted to heaven, will be thrust down to
hell.

16He who hears you, hears me; and he who rejects you, rejects me; and M't 10:40,41
he who rejects me, rejects him who sent me. Joh 13:20

17And the seventy returned back again with joy, saying, Lord, even the
very devils are subject to us through your name! 18And he said to them, I
saw Satan, like lightning as it were, fall down from heaven. 19Behold, I
give to you power to tread on serpents and scorpions, and over all manner
of power of the enemy, and nothing shall hurt you. 20Nevertheless, do not
rejoice in this, that the spirits are under your power, but rejoice because
your names are written in heaven.

21At the same time, Jesus rejoiced in the Spirit and said, I confess unto
you, Father, Lord of heaven and earth, that you have hid these things from
the wise and learned, and revealed them to the babes. Even so, Father, for
so pleased it you. 22All things are given me by my Father. And no man
Only the person who is taught knows who the Son is except the Father, nor who the Father is except the
by Christ knows the Father. Son, and the person to whom the Son will show him.

23And he turned to his disciples and said privately, Happy are the eyes M't 13:16,17
that see what you see. 24For I tell you that many prophets and kings have
desired to see those things that you see, and have not seen them, and to
hear those things that you hear, and have not heard them.

25And a certain doctor of the law stood up and tested him, saying,
Teacher, what must I do to inherit eternal life? 26Jesus said to him, What
is written in the law? How do you read it? 27And he answered and said, M't 22:34-40
Love your Lord God with all your heart, and with all your soul, and with Mk 12:28-34
all your strength, and with all your mind; and your neighbour as yourself. De 6:5 Lev 19:18

28And Jesus said to him, You have answered right. This do, and you
shall live. 29But he, wanting to justify himself,[a] said to Jesus, Who then is

my neighbour?
30 Jesus answered and said, A certain man descended from Jerusalem
to Jericho, and fell into the hands of thieves, who robbed him of his
clothing, and wounded him, and departed leaving him half dead. 31 And by
chance there came a certain priest that same way. And when he saw him,
he passed by. 32 And likewise a Levite, when he came near to the place,
The good Samaritan. went and looked on him, and passed by. 33 Then a certain Samaritan, as he
journeyed, came near to him, and when he saw him had compassion on
him, 34 and went and bound up his wounds, and poured in oil and wine.
And he put him on his own animal and brought him to a common inn, and
made provision for him. 35 And when he departed the next day, he took out
two denarii and gave them to the innkeeper, and said to him, Take care of
him; and whatever more you spend, when I come back, I will recompense
you. 36 Which now of these three do you think was neighbour to the man
that fell into the thieves' hands?
37 And the doctor of law said, He that showed mercy on him.
Then Jesus said to him, Go then and do likewise.
38 It happened as they journeyed that he entered into a certain village,
Martha and Mary. and a certain woman named Martha received him into her house. 39 And
this woman had a sister called Mary, who sat at Jesus' feet and heard his
preaching. 40 But Martha was distracted with much work of serving, and
stood and said, Master, do you not care that my sister has left me to
minister alone? Tell her therefore that she should help me. 41 And Jesus
answered and said to her, Martha, Martha, you care and are troubled about
many things. 42 Truly one is needful, and Mary has chosen that good part, Joh 6:27
which shall not be taken away from her.[b]

The Notes

Wanting to justify himself (10:29)

a) That is, wanting to show himself as just and as a learned man, the doctor of the law said, Who is my neighbour, etc.

Mary has chosen that good part (10:42)

b) That is, Mary has chosen the hearing of the word of God, which endures forever and is the only way to everlasting life.

Chapter 11

He teaches his disciples to pray, drives out a devil, and rebukes the blasphemous Pharisees. They require signs and tokens. He eats with the Pharisee, and reproves the hypocrisy of the Pharisees, scribes, and hypocrites.

The paternoster [ie, the Lord's Prayer, so-called after the Latin for the first two words, 'Our Father']

And it happened as he was praying in a certain place, that when he ceased,
one of his disciples said to him, Master, teach us to pray, as John taught
his disciples. 2 And he said to them, When you pray, say, Our Father who M't 6:7-14
art in heaven, hallowed be thy name. Thy kingdom come. Thy will be
done, even in earth as it is in heaven. 3 Give us our daily bread evermore.
4 And forgive us our sins, for even we forgive every person that trespasses
against us. And lead us not into temptation, but deliver us from evil.
5 And he said to them, If any of you had a friend, and went to him at

midnight and said to him, Friend, lend me three loaves, [6]because a friend
of mine has come from a journey to me and I have nothing to set before
him, [7]and the man inside were to answer and say, Don't trouble me; the
door is now shut, and my servants are with me in the chamber; I cannot
rise and give them to you – [8]I say to you, though he would not arise and
give him a loaf because he is his friend, yet because of his importunity he
would rise and give him as many as he needed. [9]And so I say to you: ask, M't 7:7-11;
Covenant. and it shall be given you; seek, and you shall find; knock, and it shall be 21:21,22.
opened unto you. Joh 16:23,24 Jas 1:5

[10]For everyone that asks, receives, and he that seeks, finds, and to him
who knocks, it will be opened. [11]If the son asks for bread from any of you
that is a father, will he give him a stone? Or if he asks for fish, will he
give him a serpent for a fish? [12]Or if he asks for an egg, will he offer him
a scorpion? [13]If you then who are evil can give good gifts to your chil-
Prayer, what it does. dren, how much more will the Father of heaven give a holy spirit to those
who desire it of him?

[14]And he was a casting out a devil that was dumb. And it followed, M't 9:32-34
when the devil was gone out, the dumb man spoke. And the people were Mk 7:31-37
filled with wonder. [15]But some of them said, He casts out devils by the
power of Beelzebub, the chief of the devils.[a] [16]And others challenged him,
seeking from him a sign from heaven.

[17]But Jesus knew their thoughts and said to them, Every kingdom
divided within itself will be brought to desolation, and one house will fall
upon another. [18]So if Satan is divided within himself, how shall his king-
dom endure? For you say that I cast out devils by the power of Beelzebub.
Beelzebub [19]If I cast out devils by the power of Beelzebub, by whom do your chil- M't 12:24-28 Mk 3:22-30
dren cast them out? Therefore they will be your judges. [20]But if I with the
finger of God[b] cast out devils, without question the kingdom of God has
come upon you.

[21]When a strong man armed guards his house, that which he possesses
is in peace. [22]But when one stronger than he comes upon him and over-
comes him, he takes from him his weapons in which he trusted, and di-
vides up his goods. [23]He who is not with me, is against me. And he who
does not gather with me, scatters.

[24]When the unclean spirit has gone out of a man, he walks through
waterless places, seeking rest. And when he finds none, he says, I will
return again to my house from which I came out. [25]And when he comes
back, he finds it swept and set in order. [26]Then he goes and gets seven M't 12:43-45
Seven worse than himself. other spirits worse than himself, and they enter in and dwell there, and the
end of that man is worse than the beginning.

[27]And it happened, as he spoke those things, a certain woman of the
company lifted up her voice and said to him, Happy is the womb that bore
you, and the paps that gave you suck. [28]But he said, Yea, happy are those
who hear the word of God and keep it.

[29]When the people were gathered thick together, he began and said,
This is an evil nation. They seek a sign, but no sign will be given to them

except the sign of Jonah the prophet. 30 For as Jonah was a sign to the Jon 1:17;
Ninevites, so will the Son of man be to this nation. 31 The queen of the 3:5-10.
south will rise at the judgment with the men of this generation and con- 1Ki 10:1-13 2Ch 9:1-12
demn them, for she came from the end of the world to hear the wisdom of M't 12:38-42
Solomon, and behold, one greater than Solomon is here. 32 The men of
Nineveh will rise at the judgment with this generation and condemn them,
for they repented at the preaching of Jonah, and behold, one greater than
Jonah is here.

[**Bushel**: the old bushel was a container holding approx 8 gallons. Used to measure grains, poorer folk turned it end up for use as a low table.] [**Single eye**: see note (e) on M't 6]

33 No man lights a candle and puts it in a concealed place, nor under a
bushel,* but on a candlestick, so that those who come in may see the light.
34 The light of your body is the eye. Therefore when your eye is single,* M't 5:14-16 Mk 4:21-23
then is all your body full of light. But if your eye is bad, then shall all Lu 18:16-18
your body be full of darkness. 35 Take heed therefore that the light which is
in you be not darkness. 36 For if all your body is lighted, having no part
dark, then shall all be full of light, even as when a candle lights you with
its brightness.

37 And as he spoke, a certain Pharisee asked him to dine with him, and
Jesus went in and sat down to food. 38 When the Pharisee saw that, he was
shocked that he had not first washed before dinner. 39 And the Lord said to
The outside of the cup.
him, Now you Pharisees make clean the outside of the cup and the platter, M't 23:23-33 Mk 12:38-40
but your inward parts are full of greed and wickedness. 40 O foolish men,
did not he who made the outside also make that which is within? 41 But
rather give alms of what you have, and behold, all is clean to you. 42 But
woe is to you Pharisees. For you tithe mint and rue and all manner of
herbs, but pass over justice and the love of God. These you ought to have
done, but yet not have left the others undone.

Uppermost seats: Pharisees, scribes, and doctors of the law are rebuked.

43 Woe to you, Pharisees, for you love the uppermost seats in the syna-
gogues, and greetings in the markets. 44 Woe to you, scribes and Pharisees,
hypocrites! For you are like graves that are not seen, and the men who
walk over them are not aware of them.

45 Then one of the wise men of the law answered and said to him,
Teacher, by so saying, you put us to rebuke also.

46 Then he said, Woe is to you also, doctors of the law. For you load
men with burdens grievous to be borne, and you yourselves do not touch
the packs with one of your fingers. 47 Woe to you! You build the sepul-
chres of the prophets, and your fathers killed them; 48 truly you bear wit-
ness that you accept the deeds of your fathers, for they killed them, and
you build their sepulchres. 49 Therefore the wisdom of God spoke: I will
send them prophets and apostles, and some they will slay, and some per-
secute, 50 so that the blood of all the prophets, which was shed from the
beginning of the world, may be required of this generation, 51 from the
blood of Abel to the blood of Zechariah, who perished between the altar Ge 4:8
and the temple. Truly I say to you, it shall be required of this nation. 2Ch 24:20, 21.

52 Woe to you, doctors of the law, for you have taken away the key of
knowledge. You yourselves did not enter in, and those who came in, you
opposed.

[**Stop his mouth**: obstruct his speaking, harass him with questions]
[53]When he spoke this way to them, the teachers of the law and the
Pharisees began to hound him, and to stop his mouth[*] with many ques-
tions, [54]laying wait for him, and attempting to catch something out of his
mouth that they could use to accuse him.

The Notes

Beelzebub (11:15) a) Of Beelzebub, read note (a) to Matthew 10.

Finger of God (11:20) b) If I by the finger of God cast out devils, etc; that is, if I by the power of God cast them out, etc.

Chapter 12

The leaven of the Pharisees. Christ strengthens his disciples against persecution, and warns them to beware of covetousness by the similitude of a certain rich man. He does not want them to hang upon earthly things, but to watch and to be ready for his coming.

As there gathered together an innumerable multitude of people (insomuch
that they trod on one another), he began and said to his disciples, First of M't 16:6-12
Leaven all, beware of the leaven of the Pharisees, which is hypocrisy.[a] [2]For there Mk 8:15
is nothing covered that will not be uncovered, nor hid that will not be
known. [3]For whatever you have spoken in darkness, that same shall be
heard in the light. And that which you have spoken in the ear, even in M't 10:26-33
secret places, shall be declared even on the top of the houses.
[4]I say to you, my friends, do not be afraid of those who kill the body,
and after that have no more that they can do. [5]But I will show you whom
Who is to be feared. you should fear: fear him who, after he has killed, has power to cast into
hell. Yea, I say to you: him fear!
[6]Are not five sparrows bought for two copper coins? And yet not one
of them is forgotten by God. [7]Indeed, even the very hairs of your heads M't 6:26
are numbered. Fear not, therefore. You are of more value than many
sparrows.
[8]I say to you, whoever confesses me before men, him also shall the
Covenants Son of man confess before the angels of God. [9]And he who denies me
before men shall be denied before the angels of God. [10]And whoever M't10:32,33;
speaks a word against the Son of man, it may be forgiven him;[b] but to him 12:31-33.
who blasphemes the Holy Spirit, it will not be forgiven. Mk 3:28,29
[11]When they bring you before the synagogues, and before the rulers
and officers, take no thought how or what thing to answer, or what you
A promise that the Spirit shall teach us. will say. [12]For the Holy Spirit will teach you in that same hour what you
ought to say.
[13]A man in the company said to him, Master, tell my brother to divide
the inheritance with me. [14]And he said to him, Man, who made me a judge
or a divider over you? [15]And he said to them, Take heed, and beware of
Beware of covetousness covetousness. For no man's life stands in the abundance of the things that
he possesses.
[16]And he put forth a similitude to them, saying, The ground of a cer-

tain rich man brought forth fruits plenteously, [17]and he thought in him-
self, saying, What should I do, since I have no room to store my fruits?
[18]And he said, This I will do: I will pull down my barns, and build bigger Ec 11:9
ones, and there I will store all my fruits and my goods. [19]And I will say to
my soul, Soul, you have goods enough laid up in store for many years;
take your ease; eat, drink, and be merry! [20]But God said to him, You fool,
this night they will call away your soul back from you. Then whose will
be those things that you have laid up?

[21]This is how it is with him who gathers riches, but is not rich in God.

[22]And he spoke to his disciples: Therefore I say to you, do not be
anxious about your life, what you will eat; neither for your body, what
you will put on. [23]Life is more than food, and the body is more than cloth- M't 6:25-34
Ravens ing. [24]Consider the ravens. For they neither sow nor reap, and have neither
storehouse nor barn, and yet God feeds them. How much more of value
are you than the birds? [25]Which of you, with taking thought, can add one
cubit to his stature? [26]If you then are not able to do that which is least,
why be anxious about the rest? [27]Consider the lilies, how they grow: they
do not labour, they do not spin, and yet I say to you that Solomon in all
his royalty was not clothed like one of these. [28]If God so clothes the grass
that is today in the field and tomorrow will be cast into the furnace, how
much more will he clothe you, O ye of little faith? [29]And ask not what
you shall eat or what you shall drink, neither climb up on high. [30]For all
such things the heathen people of the world seek for. Your Father knows
that you have need of such things. [31]Therefore seek the kingdom of God,
and all these things will be ministered unto you.

Little flock [32]Fear not, little flock, for it is your Father's pleasure to give you a
kingdom. [33]Sell what you have, and give alms,[c] and make yourselves
pouches that won't wear out, and treasure that won't fail in heaven, where M't 6:19-21
no thief comes or moth destroys. [34]For where your treasure is, there will
your hearts be also.

[35]Let your loins be girded about, and your lights burning, [36]and you
yourselves like men waiting for their master, for when he will return from
a wedding, so that as soon as he comes and knocks, they can open to him.
[37]Happy are those servants whom the Lord, when he comes, finds watch-
ing. Truly I say to you, he will gird himself about and make them sit down
to food, and walk by and minister to them. [38]And if he comes in the sec-
ond watch, yea if he comes in the third watch, and finds them so, happy
are those servants. [39]This understand: if the householder knew what hour
the thief would come, he would surely watch, and not allow his house to
Watch be broken into. [40]Be prepared therefore, for the Son of man will come at M't 24:44
an hour when you think not.

[41]Then Peter said to him, Master, do you speak this similitude to us, or
to all men? [42]And the Lord said, If there be any servant faithful and wise,
whom his lord appoints over his household to give them their portion of
food at due season, [43]happy is that servant whom his master, when he
comes, finds so doing. [44]Of a truth I say to you, he will appoint him over

all that he has. 45 But if the evil servant says in his heart, My master will
defer his coming, and begins to smite the menservants and maidservants,
and to eat and drink and to be drunken, 46 the lord of that servant will come
in a day when he thinks not, and at an hour when he is not aware, and will
separate him, and will give him his reward with the unbelievers.

47 The servant that knew his master's will and did not prepare himself,
nor do according to his will, shall be beaten with many stripes. 48 But he
who did not know, and yet committed things worthy of stripes, will be
beaten with few stripes. For to whom much is given, of him will much be
required. And to whom men commit much, the more will they ask of him.

49 I have come to send fire on earth. And what is my desire, but that it
were already kindled? 50 But I must be baptized with a baptism – and how
I am pained till it be ended! 51 Do you suppose that I have come to send
Division peace on earth? I tell you no, but rather division.[d] 52 For from henceforth
there will be five in one house, divided three against two, and two against
three. 53 The father will be divided against the son, and the son against the
father; the mother against the daughter, and the daughter against the
mother; the mother-in-law against her daughter-in-law, and the daughter- M't 10:34-37
in-law against her mother-in-law.

54 Then he said to the people, When you see a cloud rise out of the
west, straightaway you say we will have a rain shower, and so it is. 55 And
when you see the south wind blow, you say we will have heat, and it M't 16:1-4
comes to pass. 56 Hypocrites, you know how to interpret the aspect of the Mk 8:11,12
earth and of the sky, but why is it that you cannot interpret this present
time?

57 Yea, and why do you not judge for yourselves what is right? 58 When
Adversary you go with your adversary to the magistrate, as you are in the way, be
diligent to be delivered from him, lest he bring you to the judge, and the M't 5:25,26
judge commit you to the jailer, and the jailer cast you into prison. 59 I tell
you, you will not get out of there until you have made good the last mite.[e]

The Notes

Leaven of the Pharisees (12:1)
a) What leaven the faithful must beware of is more clearly explained in Matthew 16, where by 'leaven' is understood the teaching and inventions of the Pharisees, and of all other men who are likewise disposed. Here such leaven is denoted by the name of hypocrisy because it is deceitful, false, and ungodly, and makes hypocrites of all who are enamoured of it.

Against the Son of man (12:10)
b) To speak a word against the Son of man is to be offended with the humanity or manhood of Jesus Christ because of his humble and low degree, as were many of the Jews. (John 7, Matthew 12:32)

Sell all (12:33)
c) Of this, look in Mark 10:21 and note (a) thereon.

I came to send not peace, but division (12:51)
d) I did not come to send on the earth such peace as is loved by this world, which is at peace when people's appetites and desires are satisfied, and when the evil agree with the evil. But I came with the words of very peace to destroy the peace of this world. For since the doctrine of the gospel (which teaches peace to all) will be resented by many, it cannot be but that strife will arise, even among the greatest friends, as long as those who love this world would sooner exercise cruelty toward those they love best than leave the vices they have been accustomed to. And again, those whom the fire of the charity belonging to the gospel

has touched, will by no means suffer themselves to be parted from that which they have begun to cleave to. Between such persons [says the Lord] I have not come to send peace, but division.

The last mite (12:59) e) Of this, look in Matthew 5, note (h).

Chapter 13

Of the Galileans whom Pilate slew, and of those that died in Siloam. The similitude of the fig tree. Christ heals the sick woman. The parables of the mustard seed and leaven. Few enter into the kingdom. Christ reproves Herod and Jerusalem.

There were present at that same time people who told him of the Galileans
whose blood Pilate mingled with their own sacrifice. [2]And Jesus answered
and said to them, Do you suppose these Galileans were greater sinners
than all the other Galileans, because they suffered such punishment? [3]I tell
you no, but unless you repent, you will all likewise perish. [4]Or those
Tower of Siloam. eighteen upon whom the tower in Siloam fell and slew them, do you think
they were sinners above all who dwell in Jerusalem? [5]I tell you no, but
unless you repent, you will all likewise perish.

[6]He put forth this similitude: A certain man had a fig tree planted in
his vineyard, and he came and sought fruit on it, and found none. [7]Then
he said to the dresser of his vineyard, Look, for three years I have come
seeking fruit on this fig tree, and find none. Cut it down. Why is it taking
up space on the ground? [8]And he answered and said to him, Lord, let it
alone this year also, till I dig round about it and dung it to see whether it
will bear fruit. [9]And if it does not bear then, after that cut it down.

[10]And he taught in one of their synagogues on the Sabbath days. [11]And
behold, there was a woman who had had a spirit of infirmity for eighteen
The woman that was bowed together. years, and was stooped over, and could not lift herself up at all. [12]When
Jesus saw her, he called her to him and said to her, Woman, you are
delivered from your disease. [13]And he laid his hands on her, and im-
mediately she was made straight and glorified God. [14]But the leader of the
synagogue responded with indignation because Jesus had healed on the
Sabbath day, and he said to the people, There are six days in which men
ought to work; in them come and be healed, and not on the Sabbath day.

[15]Then the Lord answered him and said, Hypocrite, does not each one
of you on the Sabbath day loose his ox or his donkey from the stall and
lead it to the water? [16]And ought not this daughter of Abraham, whom
Satan has bound now eighteen years, be loosed from this bond on the
Sabbath day?

[17]And when he said this, all his adversaries were ashamed. But all the
people rejoiced for all the tremendous deeds that were done by him.

[18]Then he said, What is the kingdom of God like? or to what shall I M't 13:31,32
compare it? [19]Is is like a grain of mustard seed that a man took and sowed Mk 4:30-32
in his garden; and it grew, and developed into a great tree, and the birds of
the air made nests in its branches.

[20]And again he said, To what may I liken the kingdom of God? [21]It is

[Luther>here **leaven** is faith, the gift and inward good that, with time, works inwardly to purge the sin to which it is opposed (*Ag. Latomus*)]

like leaven[*] that a woman took and hid in three bushels of flour until it M't 13:33
was leavened right through.
22 And he went through all manner of cities and towns, teaching and
journeying towards Jerusalem.
23 Then someone said to him, Lord, are there few that will be saved?

The strait gate.

And he said to them, 24 Strive with yourselves to enter in at the strait M't 7:13-23; 25:1-12. Ps 6:8
gate. For many, I say to you, will seek to enter in, and will not be able.
25 When the master of the house has risen up and has shut the door to, you
all will begin to stand outside and to knock at the door, saying, Lord,
Lord, open to us! And he will answer and say to you, I know you not,
where you are from. 26 Then you will begin to say, We have eaten and
drunk in your presence, and you have taught in our streets. 27 And he will
say, I tell you, I do not know you, where you are from; depart from me, all
you workers of iniquity![a]
28 There will be weeping and gnashing of teeth when you see Abraham
and Isaac and Jacob and all the prophets in the kingdom of God, and
yourselves thrust out at the doors. 29 And people will come from the east
and from the west, and from the north and from the south, and will sit
down in the kingdom of God. 30 And behold, there are last who will be
first, and there are first who will be last.
31 That same day, certain of the Pharisees came and said to him, Get
yourself out of the way, and depart from here, because Herod wants to kill
you. 32 And he said to them, Go and tell that fox, behold, I cast out devils
and heal the people today and tomorrow, and the third day I make an end
of it. 33 Nevertheless, I must be going on my way today and tomorrow and M't 20:18,19
the day following, for it cannot be that a prophet should perish anywhere
other than at Jerusalem.

Jerusalem kills prophets.

34 O Jerusalem, Jerusalem, who kills the prophets and stones those who M't 23:37-39 Ps 118:26
are sent to you! How often would I have gathered your children together,
like the hen gathers her nest under her wings! But you would not. 35 Be-
hold, your habitation shall be left to you desolate. For I tell you, you will
not see me until the time comes that you say, Blessed is he that comes in
the name of the Lord.

The Notes

Lord, Lord! (13:25-27)

a) When the covenant made in the blood of Christ is hidden from our understanding, then people pain themselves with holy works, trusting thereby to enter in, but all in vain.

Chapter 14

Jesus eats with the Pharisee, heals a man with dropsy on the Sabbath, teaches to be lowly, tells of the great supper, and warns people who would follow him to first determine what it will cost them. The salt of the earth.

[**Dropsy**: an excess of watery fluid in the cavities of the body, also called edema]

And it happened that he went into the house of one of the chief Pharisees
to eat bread[a] on a Sabbath day, and they were watching him. 2 And there
was before him a man who had the dropsy.[*] 3 And Jesus addressed the

wise men of law and the Pharisees, asking, Is it lawful to heal on the
Sabbath day? 4But they held their peace. And he took the man and healed
him, and let him go. 5And he spoke to them, saying, Which of you, having
a donkey or an ox fallen into a pit, would not straightaway pull him out on
the Sabbath day? 6And they could not answer him in reply to that.

7He put forth a similitude to the guests, when he observed how they
sought out the seats of honour, and said to them, 8When you are invited to
a wedding by anyone, do not sit down in the highest place, lest a more
honourable man than you be bidden by him, 9and he who invited both him
and you come and say to you, Make place for this man – and you then
begin with shame to take the lowest seat. 10But rather, when you are Pr 25:6,7
invited, go and sit in the lowest seat, so that when he who invited you M't 23:11,12
comes, he may say to you, Friend, sit up higher. Then you will have Lu 18:4
honour in the presence of those who sit at food with you. 11For whoever
exalts himself will be brought low, and he who humbles himself will be
exalted.

12Then he said also to the man who had asked him to dinner, When
you give a dinner or a supper, do not call your friends or your brethren, Tob 4:7-11
neither your kinsfolk or rich neighbours, lest they return the invitation and
Feast the poor. a recompense be made you. 13But when you put on a feast, call the poor,
the maimed, the lame, and the blind, 14and you will be happy; for they
cannot recompense you, but you shall be recompensed at the resurrection
of the just.

15When one of those who sat at food also heard that, he said to Jesus,
Happy is he who eats bread in the kingdom of God!

The great supper. 16Then Jesus said to him, A certain man prepared a great supper and M't 22:1-14
invited many people. 17And he sent his servant at supper time to say to Rev 19:7-9
those who were bidden, Come, for all things are now ready. 18And they all
at once began to make excuse. The first said to him, I have bought a farm,
and I need to go and see it; I pray you, have me excused. 19And another
said, I have bought five yoke of oxen and I'm going to inspect them; I
pray you, have me excused. 20The third said, I have married a wife, and
therefore I cannot come.

21And the servant went and brought his master word of this. Then was
the lord of the house displeased, and said to his servant, Go out quickly
into the streets and quarters of the city, and bring in here the poor and the
maimed and the lame and the blind.

22And the servant said, Lord, it is done as you ordered, and still there
is room. 23And the lord said to the servant, Go out into the highways and
hedges, and compel the people to come in, so that my house may be filled.
24For I say to you that none of those men that were bidden shall taste of
my supper.

25A great number of people went with Jesus, and he turned and said to
them, 26If a person comes to me and does not hate his father and mother, M't 8:19-22;
wife, and children, and brethren and sisters, and moreover his own life, he 16:24,25.
cannot be my disciple. 27And whoever does not bear his cross and come Mk 8:34,35

after me, cannot be my disciple. [28]Which of you, thinking of building a
tower, would not sit down first and count the cost, whether he has suffi-
cient to complete it?– [29]lest after he has laid the foundation and is not able
to complete it, all who see it begin to mock him, [30]saying, This man began
to build, and was not able to finish it. [31]Or, what king goes to make battle
against another king, and does not sit down first and cast in his mind
whether he is able with 10,000 to meet him who comes against him with
20,000? [32]If not, while the other is yet a great way off, he will send am-
bassadors and seek peace. [33]So now then, none of you who will not re-
Christ's disciples. nounce all that he has can be my disciple.

[34]Salt is good. But if salt has lost her saltness, what can be seasoned M't 5:13
with it? [35]It is neither good for the land, nor yet for the dunghill, but men Mk 9:50
cast it out at the doors. He who has ears to hear, let him hear.

The Notes

To eat bread (14:1) a) To eat bread is to dine or take refreshments, as at Genesis 43:25.

Chapter 15

The loving mercy of God is openly seen in the parables of
the hundredth sheep and of the son that was lost.

Publicans and sinners. Then all the publicans and sinners sought him out, in order to hear him. M't 9:9-13
[2]And the Pharisees and scribes murmured, saying, He receives sinners Mk 2:15-17
into his company, and eats with them. [3]Then Jesus put forth this similitude Lu 5:27-32
to them, saying, [4]What man of you, having a hundred sheep, if he loses
one of them, does not leave the ninety-nine in the countryside and go after
the one that is lost until he finds him? [5]And when he has found him, he
puts him on his shoulders with joy. [6]And as soon as he comes home, he
calls together his friends and neighbours, saying to them, Rejoice with
me, for I have found my sheep that was lost! [7]I say to you that likewise
there will be joy in heaven over one sinner that repents more than over
ninety-nine just persons who need no repentance.

[**Drachma**: a silver coin roughly equivalent to the Roman denarius, and a day's pay for a common labourer]

[8]Or what woman who has ten drachmas,* if she loses one, does not
light a lamp, and sweep the house, and search diligently till she finds it?
[9]And when she has found it, she calls her friends and her neighbours,
saying, Rejoice with me, for I have found the drachma that I had lost.
[10]Likewise I say to you, there is joy in the presence of the angels of God
over one sinner that repents.

[11]And he said, A certain man had two sons, [12]and the younger of them
said to his father, Father, give me the part of the goods that belongs to me.
And he divided the substance of his wealth between them. [13]And not long
after, the younger son gathered all that he had together, and took his Pr 29:3
journey into a far country. And there he wasted his goods with riotous
living. [14]And when he had spent all that he had, there arose a great dearth
throughout all that same land, and he began to be in want. [15]And he went
and attached himself to a citizen of that same country, who sent him to his

[**Pods**: the bean pods of carob or locust trees, used as food for animals and by the poor]

field to keep his swine. [16]And he would gladly have filled his belly with the pods* that the swine ate, but no man gave to him.

[17]Then he came to himself and said, How many hired servants at my father's have bread enough, and I am dying of hunger? [18]I will arise and go to my father, and will say to him, Father, I have sinned against heaven and before you, [19]and am no longer worthy to be called your son. Make me like one of your hired servants.

[20]And he arose and went to his father. And when he was yet a great way off, his father saw him, and had compassion, and ran and fell on his neck, and kissed him. [21]And the son said to him, Father, I have sinned against heaven and in your sight, and am no longer worthy to be called your son. [22]But his father said to his servants, Bring forth that best garment, and put it on him; and put a ring on his hand and shoes on his feet. [23]And bring here the fatted calf, and kill it, and let us eat and be merry. [24]For this my son was dead, and is alive again; he was lost, and is now found. And they began to be merry.

[25]The elder brother was in the field, and when he came and drew near to the house, he heard music and dancing, [26]and called one of his servants and asked what those things meant. [27]And the servant said to him, Your brother is come, and your father had the fatted calf killed, because he has received him safe and sound.

[28]And the elder brother was angry, and would not go in. Then his father came out and entreated him. [29]He answered and said to his father, Lo, these many years I have served you, and not once broken your commandment, and yet you never gave me so much as a kid to make merry with my friends. [30]But as soon as this your son comes, who has devoured your goods with harlots, you have for his pleasure killed the fatted calf!

[31]And the father said to him, Son, you were always with me, and all that I have is yours. [32]It was right to make merry and be glad, for this your brother was dead, and is alive again, and was lost, and is found.

Chapter 16

The parable of the wicked mammon. Not one tittle of God's word shall perish. Of the rich man and poor Lazarus.

The unrighteous steward. [**Wasting his goods**: causing or allowing loss or damage]

And he said also to his disciples, There was a certain rich man who had a steward that was accused of wasting his goods.* [2]And he summoned him and said to him, How is it that I hear this of you? Give accounts of your stewardship, for you may no longer be steward.

[3]The steward said within himself, What can I do? For my master will take away from me the stewardship. I cannot dig, and to beg I am ashamed. [4]I know what to do, so that when I am put out of the stewardship, people may receive me into their houses.

[5]Then he called all his master's debtors, and said to the first, How much do you owe to my master? [6]And he said, A hundred tons of oil. And the steward said to him, Take your bill, and sit down quickly and write fifty. [7]Then he said to another, What do you owe? And he said, A hundred

quarters of wheat. The steward said to him, Take your bill and write
eighty.
8 And the lord commended the unjust steward because he had done
wisely. For among their own, the children of this world are wiser than the
children of light. 9 And I say also to you, make friends for yourselves with
Mammon — the wicked mammon,[a] so that when you depart this world, they may re-
ceive you into everlasting habitations.
10 He who is faithful in that which is least, the same is faithful in much.
And he who is unfaithful in the least is unfaithful also in much. 11 So then,
if you have not been faithful in the wicked mammon, who will believe
you in that which is true? 12 And if you have not been faithful in another
man's business, who will give you your own?
13 No servant can serve two masters. For either he will hate the one and — M't 6:24
love the other, or else he will lean to the one and neglect the other. You
cannot serve both God and mammon.
14 All these things the Pharisees also heard, who were covetous; and
they mocked him. 15 And he said to them, You are those who justify your-
selves before men,[b] but God knows your hearts. For that which is highly
esteemed among men, is abominable in the sight of God.
16 The law and the prophets reigned until the time of John; and since
that time, the kingdom of God is preached, and everyone strives to go in. — M't 11:12
17 Sooner can heaven and earth perish, than one tittle of the law can — M't 5:17-20;
pass away. 18 Whosoever forsakes his wife and marries another, breaks — 5:32. Mk 10:11,12
Of the law of matrimony Genesis 2:24 — matrimony, and every man who marries her that is divorced from her — 1Co 7:10,11
husband, commits adultery also.
19 There was a certain rich man that was clothed in purple and fine
The rich glutton and Lazarus. [Of the law of love for our neighbour. Lev 19:18] — linen, and fared deliciously every day. 20 And there was a certain beggar
named Lazarus who lay at his gate, full of sores, 21 longing to be relieved
of hunger with the crumbs which fell from the rich man's table. However,
the dogs came and licked his sores.
22 And it came to pass that the beggar died, and was carried by the
angels into Abraham's bosom.[c] The rich man also died, and was buried;
23 and being in hell, in torments, he lifted up his eyes and saw Abraham
afar off, and Lazarus in his bosom. 24 And he cried out and said, Father
Abraham, have mercy on me, and send Lazarus so that he may dip the tip
of his finger in water and cool my tongue! For I am tormented in this
flame.
25 But Abraham said to him, Son, remember that you in your lifetime
received your pleasure, and contrariwise Lazarus pain. Now therefore he
is comforted, and you are punished. 26 Beyond all this, between all of you
and us there is a great space set, so that those who would desire to go
from here to you cannot, and none may come from there to us.
27 Then he said, I pray you therefore, Father, send him to my father's
house, 28 for I have five brethren, to warn them, lest they also come into
this place of torment.
29 Abraham said to him, They have Moses and the prophets. Let them

hear them.
30 And he said, Nay, Father Abraham, but if one came to them from the
dead, they would repent.
*Moses and the prophets is the Old Testament.
31 He said to him, If they do not hear Moses and the prophets,* neither
will they believe though one rose from death again.

The Notes

Make friends with the wicked mammon (16:9)

a) This word *mammon* is a word of Syrian speech and signifies riches. Therefore the text means, bestow your riches according to the word of God, so that God is pleased with your doings, not deceitfully like this fellow did.

You justify yourselves 16:15)

b) This is spoken of above at note (a) to chapter 10.

Abraham's bosom (16:22)

c) By *Abraham's bosom* some understand the faith of Abraham. Some also understand it of the place where the elect and chosen, who follow the faith of Abraham, rest after their death. But where that place is (because the scripture does not expressly determine it), we cannot tell, and therefore no man may be so bold as to define it.

Chapter 17

Christ teaches his disciples to avoid occasions of evil, to forgive one another, steadfastly to trust in God, and that no one should presume in his own works. He heals the ten lepers, and speaks of the latter days, and of the end of the world.

Then Jesus said to his disciples, It cannot be avoided but that offences will
come. Nevertheless, woe be to him through whom they come. 2 It would M't c18 Mk 9:41-50
be better for him that a millstone were hung about his neck and that he Lev 19:16-18.
were cast into the sea, than that he should hurt one of these little ones.
3 Take heed to yourselves. If your brother trespasses against you, Ec'us 20:2
rebuke him; and if he repents, forgive him. 4 And even if he sins against
you seven times in a day, and seven times in a day turns again to you
saying, I am sorry – forgive him.
5 And the apostles said to the Lord, Increase our faith. 6 And the Lord
said, If you had faith like a grain of mustard seed and were to say to this
[**Sycamine tree**: a fast-growing tree with bitter fruit]
sycamine tree,* Pluck yourself up by the roots and plant yourself in the
sea, it would obey you.
7 Who among you, if he had a servant plowing or feeding sheep, would
say to him when he came in from the field, Go quickly, and sit down to
food? 8 And not rather say to him, Prepare for me to sup, and gird yourself
[**Gird up**: literally, tuck a robe up into a belt to free the legs; fig, to prepare oneself]
up*, and serve me till I have eaten and drunk, and afterward you shall eat
and drink? 9 Does he thank that servant because he did that which was
commanded of him? I think not. 10 So likewise you, when you have done
all the things that are commanded of you, say, We are unprofitable ser-
vants; we have done that which was our duty to do.*
*In works may no faith be put, for by them no man is justified before God, but by Christ's blood only.
11 And it so was that, as he journeyed to Jerusalem, he passed through
Samaria and Galilee. 12 And as he entered into a certain town, there met
him ten men that were lepers, who stood afar off, 13 and put forth their
voices and said, Jesus, Master, have mercy on us!

14When he saw them, he said to them, Go and show yourselves to the
priests. And it came to pass that as they went, they were cleansed. 15And
one of them, when he saw that he was cleansed, turned back again and
with a loud voice praised God, 16and fell down on his face at Jesus' feet,
and gave him thanks. And he was a Samaritan.

[**Stranger**: the man was a Samaritan, and thus an alien or stranger in the eyes of Israel]

17And Jesus answered and said, Were there not ten cleansed? But
where are the other nine? 18There are not found any that returned again to
give God praise, save only this stranger.* 19And he said to the man, Arise
and go your way; your faith has made you whole.

*The kingdom of God is to love God with all your heart, and to put your whole trust in him, according to the covenant made in Christ; and for Christ's sake, to love your neighbour as Christ loved you. And all this is within you.

20When he was asked by the Pharisees when the kingdom of God
would come, he answered them and said, The kingdom of God does not
come with watching for it. 21Neither may men say, See here, look there!
For behold, the kingdom of God is within you.*

22And he said to the disciples, The days will come when you will
desire to see one day of the Son of man, and you will not see it. 23And
they will say to you, See here, see there! Do not go after them or follow
them. 24For as the lightning that appears out of the one part of the heaven M't 16:21
and shines to the other part of heaven, so shall the Son of man be in his Mk 8:31
days. 25But first he must suffer many things, and be refused by this nation. Lu 18:31-34

26As it happened in the time of Noah, so shall it be in the time of the
Son of man: 27they ate, they drank, they married wives, and were married, M't c24 Ge cc6,7
right up to the same day that Noah went into the ark; and the flood came
and destroyed them all. 28Likewise also as it happened in the days of Lot:
they ate, they drank, they bought, they sold, they planted, they built. Ge c19
29And even the same day that Lot went out of Sodom, it rained fire and
brimstone from heaven, and destroyed them all. 30After these examples
shall it be in the day when the Son of man appears.

31At that day, let him who is on the house-top, with his stuff in the
house, not come down to take it out. And likewise, let not him who is in
the fields turn back again to what he left behind. 32Remember Lot's wife.
33Whosoever would go about to save his life, shall lose it, and whosoever
will lose his life, shall save it. 34I tell you, in that night there will be two in
one bed; the one will be received, and the other will be left. 35Two will
also be a-grinding together; the one will be received, and the other left.36*

[v36 of later versions is not included in the MB. In the KJV v36 reads 'Two *men* shall be in the field; the one shall be taken, and the other left.' Ed]

37And they answered and said to him, Where Lord? And he said to
them, Wherever the body is, there will the eagles resort.[a]

The Notes

Wherever the body is, there will the eagles resort (17:36)

a) That is, there as the Son of man shall be to judge the world, shall all gather together to me. [Ed>This does not agree with Cranmer's interpretation of the eagles proverb in M't 24:28 (note c). In Matthew, the Greek word rendered 'dead body' (Tyndale had 'carcase') is *ptoma,* which means a lifeless, slain, or fallen body. But in Luke, the word translated 'body' (as Tyndale had it) is *soma,* which can be applied to living persons and is perhaps a clue to Luke. The gospels do variously apply some sayings. Compare Luke 14:34 with Matthew 5:13, regarding salt that has lost its saltness. Also at Luke 12:2, the saying "things hid that will be known" refers to the secrets of men, but at Mark 4:22 and Luke 8:17, the secrets of the kingdom of God. However, the difference may be due to different Eucharist theologies.]

Chapter 18

He teaches to be fervent in prayer continually. Of the Pharisee and the publican. The kingdom of God belongs to children. Christ answers the ruler, and promises reward to all who suffer loss for his sake and follow him. The blind man is restored to his sight.

And he put forth a similitude to them, signifying that men ought always to
pray, and not to be weary of it, [2]saying, There was a judge in a certain city
The wicked judge. who neither feared God nor regarded man. And there was a certain widow
in the same city, who came to him, [3]saying, Avenge me of my adversary!
[4]And he would not for a while. But afterward he said to himself, Though I
do not fear God or care about people, [5]yet because this widow is troubling
me, I will avenge her, lest she wear me out with nagging.
[6]And the Lord said, Hear what the unrighteous judge says. [7]And will
God not avenge his elect who cry day and night to him – yea, though he
defer them? [8]I tell you, he will avenge them, and that quickly. Nevertheless, when the Son of man comes, do you suppose he will find faith on
the earth?
[9]And he put forth this similitude to certain people who trusted in
The Pharisee and the publican. themselves, that they were righteous, and despised others: [10]Two men
went up into the temple to pray, the one a Pharisee and the other a publican. [11]The Pharisee stood and prayed thus within himself: God, I thank
you that I am not like other men are: extortioners, unjust, adulterers – or
like this publican. [12]I fast twice in the week; I give tithes of all that I
possess. [13]But the publican stood afar off, and would not lift up his eyes to
heaven, but smote his breast, saying, God be merciful to me, a sinner. [14]I
tell you, this man departed home to his house justified more than the
other. For everyone who exalts himself will be brought low, and he who M't 23:11,12
humbles himself will be exalted. Lu 14:11
[15]They brought to him also babes, so that he could touch them. When
his disciples saw that, they rebuked the people. [16]But Jesus called them to
him and said, Allow the children to come to me, and do not forbid them.
For of such is the kingdom of God. [17]Truly I say to you, whoever does not M't 19:13-14
receive the kingdom of God like a child, he shall not enter therein. Mk 10:13-16
[18]And a certain ruler asked him, saying, Good Master, what ought I to M't 19:16-25
do to obtain eternal life? [19]Jesus said to him, Why do you call me good? Mk 10:17-31
None is good, save God only. [20]You know the commandments: You shall & note (a) to
not commit adultery, you shall not kill, you shall not steal, you shall not Mk 10.
bear false witness, honour your father and your mother. Ex 20:12-17 De 5:16-21 Lev 19:18
[21]And he said, All these I have kept from my youth.
[22]When Jesus heard that, he said to him, You lack yet one thing. Sell
all that you have, and distribute it to the poor, and you will have treasure
in heaven; and come, and follow me.
[23]When the man heard that, he was downcast, for he was very rich.
[24]When Jesus saw him grieve, he said, With what difficulty do those
Camel. who have riches enter into the kingdom of God! [25]It is easier for a camel

to go through the eye of a needle than for a rich man to enter into the
kingdom of God. [26]Then said those who heard that, And who then can be
saved? [27]And he said, Things that are impossible with men, are possible
with God.

[28]Then Peter said, Lo, we have left everything and have followed you.
Covenant. [29]And he said to them, Truly I say to you, there is no man who leaves M't 19:25-30
house, or father and mother, or brethren, or wife, or children, for the Mk 10:28-31
kingdom of God's sake, [30]who will not receive much more in this world,
and in the world to come, everlasting life.

[31]He took the twelve and said to them, Behold, we are going up to M't 16:21
Passion foretold. Jerusalem, and all things will be fulfilled that are written by the prophets Mk 8:31 Lu 17:25
concerning the Son of man. [32]He will be delivered to the Gentiles, and
will be mocked, and will be despitefully abused, and will be spit upon.
[33]And when they have scourged him, they will put him to death. And the
third day, he will arise again.

[34]But they understood none of these things. This saying was hid from
them, and they could not perceive the things that were spoken.

[35]And it came to pass, as he came near to Jericho, a certain blind man M't 20:29-34
Blind man. sat by the wayside, begging. [36]And when he heard the people pass by, he Mk 10:46-52
asked what it meant. [37]And they said to him that Jesus of Nazareth was
passing by. [38]And he called out, saying, Jesus, Son of David, have mercy
on me! [39]And the people who were in front admonished him to hold his
peace. But he cried all the more, Son of David, have mercy on me!

[40]And Jesus stood still, and directed him to be brought to him. And
when he had come near, Jesus asked him, saying, [41]What do you want me
to do for you? And he said, Lord, that I may receive my sight! [42]Jesus said
to him, Receive your sight; your faith has saved you. [43]And immediately
he saw, and followed him, praising God. And all the people, when they
saw it, gave laud to God.

Chapter 19

Of Zaccheus, and of the ten servants to whom the minas were delivered. Christ rides to Jerusalem and weeps over it.

And he entered in and went through Jericho. [2]And there was a man named
Zaccheus Zaccheus, who was a chief publican, and was rich also. [3]And he made
efforts to see Jesus, who he was. But due to the press of people, he could
not, because he was of a low stature. [4]And so he ran ahead and climbed up
into a wild fig tree in order to see him, for he would be coming that way.

[5]And when Jesus came to the place, he looked up and saw him, and
said to him, Zacche, come down at once, for today I must stay at your
house. [6]And he came down hastily, and brought him home joyfully. [7]And
when the people saw that, they all murmured, saying, He has gone in to
stay with a man that is a sinner.

[8]And Zacche stood forth and said to the Lord, Behold, Lord: half of
my goods I give to the poor, and if I have done any man wrong, I will
restore him fourfold. [9]And Jesus said to him, This day salvation has come

to this house, seeing that he also has become the child of Abraham. 10For the Son of man has come to seek and to save that which was lost.

11As the people listened to these things, he added a similitude, because he was nearing Jerusalem, and also because they thought that the kingdom of God would shortly appear. 12He said therefore, A certain nobleman went into a far country to receive a kingdom for himself, and then to return. 13And he called his ten servants and gave them ten minas,[*] saying to them, Trade with these till I come. 14But his citizens hated him and sent messengers after him, saying, We will not have this man to reign over us.

Parable of the minas.

[**Mina**: a valuable ancient coin, probably worth about three months' wages]

M't 25:14-30

15And it came to pass, when the nobleman returned and had received his kingdom, he commanded those servants to whom he had given his money to be called to him, to find out how each had done. 16Then came the first, saying, Lord, your mina has increased ten minas. 17And he said to him, Well done, good servant; because you were faithful in a very little thing, you shall have authority over ten cities. 18And the other came, saying, Lord, your mina has increased five minas. 19And to him he said, You also shall be over five cities.

20And the third came and said, Lord, here is your mina, which I have kept in a napkin. 21For I feared you, because you are a hard man. You take where you did not invest, and reap what you did not sow.

22And his lord said to him, By your own mouth I judge you, you evil servant. You knew that I am a hard man, taking where I did not invest and reaping what I did not sow? 23Why then didn't you put my money into the bank, so that at my coming I could have claimed what is my own with profit?

24And he said to those who stood by, Take from him that mina, and give it the one who has ten minas. 25And they said to him, Lord, he has ten minas!

26I say to you that to all those who have, it will be given, and from him who has not, even that which he has will be taken from him.[a] 27Moreover, those my enemies who did not want me to reign over them, bring them here and slay them before me.

To him that has, it shall be given.

M't 25:29, Mk 4:24,25

28And when Jesus had thus spoken, he went on ahead, ascending up to Jerusalem. 29And it so was, when he came near Bethphage and Bethany at the Mount of Olives, he sent two of his disciples, 30saying, Go into the town which is in front of you, in which, as soon as you enter, you will find a colt tied, on which no man ever yet sat. Untie him and bring him here. 31And if anyone asks you why you are untying him, thus say to him: The Lord has need of him.

M't 21:1-9
Mk 11:1-11

32Those who were sent went their way and found it just as he had said to them. 33And as they were untying the colt, the owners said to them, Why are you untying the colt? 34And they said, Because the Lord has need of him.

35And they brought him to Jesus. And they cast their cloaks on the colt and set Jesus thereon. 36And as he went, people spread their cloaks in the way. 37And when he came now to where he was to descend from the

King on a colt.

Mount of Olives, the whole number of the disciples began to rejoice, and
to laud God with a loud voice for all the miracles that they had seen, Joh 12:12-19
[38]saying, Blessed be the king that comes in the name of the Lord! Peace in Ps 118:26
heaven and glory in the highest!
[39]And some of the Pharisees in the company said to him, Teacher,
rebuke your disciples. [40]He answered and said to them, I tell you, if these
held their peace, the stones would cry out.
[41]And when he came near, he beheld the city and wept on it, [42]saying,
If only you had known those things that belong to your peace, at this your
very time![b] But now they are hid from your eyes. [43]For the days will come M't c24 Mk c13
upon you that your enemies will cast up a siege-mound about you, and
compass you around, and hem you in on every side, [44]and lay you level
with the ground, with your children who are in you. And they will not
leave in you one stone upon another, because you did not acknowledge
the time of your visitation.
[45]And he went into the temple and began to cast out those who sold
Traders in the temple are cast out. therein, and those who bought, [46]saying to them, It is written: My house is Isa 56:7 Jer 7:11
the house of prayer. But you have made it a den of thieves.
[47]And he taught daily in the temple. The high priests and the scribes
and the chief men of the people went about to destroy him, but could not
find what to do, [48]because all the people stayed close by him, and listened
attentively to him.

The Notes

It will be given (19:26) a) To him who has, it will be given: look in Matthew 13:12 and note (a).

Your peace (19:42) b) The things that belong to your peace: here *peace* is taken for wellbeing, as may be seen in Isaiah 48:18.

Chapter 20

They ask Christ one question, and he asks them another. The parable of the vineyard. Of tribute to be given to Caesar, and how Christ stops the mouths of the Sadducees.

And it happened in one of those days, as he taught the people in the
temple and preached the gospel, the high priests and the scribes came with
the elders [2]and spoke to him, saying, Tell us by what authority you do M't 21:23-27 Mk 11:27-33
these things. Or who is it that gave you this authority? [3]He answered and
said to them, I also will ask you a question, and answer me. [4]The baptism
Whence John's baptism? of John: was it from heaven, or of men?[a]
[5]And they thought within themselves, saying, If we say from heaven,
he will say, Why then did you not believe him? [6]But if we say of men, all
the people will stone us, because they are persuaded that John is a proph-
et. [7]And they answered that they did not know where it was from.
[8]And Jesus said to them, Neither will I tell you by what authority I do
Whence Jesus' authority? these things.
[9]Then he began and put forth to the people this similitude: A certain
man planted a vineyard and let it out to farmers, and went himself into a

far country for a great season. [10]And when the time came, he sent a M't 21:33-45
Vineyard parable. servant to his tenants, so that they would give him some of the fruits of Mk 12:1-12
the vineyard. But the tenants beat him, and sent him away empty-handed. Isa 5:1-7
[11]And again he sent yet another servant. And they beat him and grievously
used him also, and sent him away empty-handed. [12]Moreover he sent a
third too, and him they wounded and cast out.

[13]Then said the lord of the vineyard, What shall I do? I will send my
dear son; him perhaps they will respect, when they see him. [14]But when
the farmers saw him, they thought in themselves, saying, This is the heir;
come, let us kill him so that the inheritance can be ours. [15]And they cast
him out of the vineyard and killed him. Now, what will the lord of the
vineyard do to them? [16]He will come and destroy these farmers, and will
let out his vineyard to others.

When they heard that, they said, God forbid!

[17]And he looked upon them and said, What then does this mean that is Ps 118:22
written: The stone that the builders refused, the same is made the head Isa 8:14,15; 28:16,17.
cornerstone; [18]whosoever stumbles at that stone will be broken, but on Ac 4:10,11
whomever it falls, it will grind him to powder? Ro 9:30-33

[19]And the high priests and the scribes in that same hour went about to
lay hands on him, but they feared the people. For they perceived that he
had spoken this similitude against them.

[20]And they watched him, and sent forth spies who would pretend to be
sincere, to take him in his words, and to deliver him to the power and M't 22:15-22
authority of the governor. [21]And they asked him, saying, Teacher, we Mk 12:13-17
know that you say and teach right, and do not consider any man's degree, Ro 13:6,7
Tribute to Caesar. but teach the way of God truly. [22]Is it lawful for us to pay tribute to Cae-
sar, or no?

[23]He perceived their craftiness and said to them, Why do you bait me?
[24]Show me a denarius. Whose image and superscription does it have?

They answered and said, Caesar's.

[25]And he said to them, Give then to Caesar that which belongs to Cae-
sar, and to God that which belongs to God.

[26]And they could not reprove his saying before the people. But they
marvelled at his answer, and held their peace.

[27]Then there came to him certain of the Sadducees, who deny that M't 22:15-22
there is any resurrection. [28]And they asked him, saying, Teacher, Moses Mk 12:18-27
wrote to us that if any man's brother dies, leaving a wife but no issue, De 25:5-10
then his brother should take his wife and raise up seed for his brother.
[29]There were seven brethren, and the first took a wife, and died without
children. [30]And the second took the wife, but he died childless. [31]And the
third took her, and so on likewise the rest of the seven, leaving no children
behind them, and died. [32]Last of all, the woman died also. [33]Now at the
At the resurrection. resurrection, whose wife will she be of the brothers? For seven had her as
wife.

[34]Jesus answered and said to them, The children of this world marry
and are married, [35]but those who will be made worthy to enjoy that world,

and the resurrection from death, neither marry, nor are married, 36 nor yet
can die any more. For they are like the angels, and are the sons of God,
inasmuch as they are the children of the resurrection. 37 And that the dead
shall rise again, even Moses signified in his account of the bush, when he Ex 3:1-6,15.
calls the Lord the God of Abraham, and the God of Isaac, and the God of
Jacob. 38 For he is not the God of the dead, but of the living. For all live in
him.

39 Then certain of the Pharisees answered and said, Teacher, you have
well said. 40 And after that they dared not ask him any question at all.

41 Then he said to them, How is it they say that Christ is David's son?
42 And David himself says in the book of the Psalms, The Lord said to my M't 22:41-46 Mk 12:35-37
Lord, Sit on my right hand, 43 till I make your enemies your footstool. Ps 110:1
44 Seeing David calls him Lord, how is he then his son?

45 Then, in the hearing of all the people, Jesus said to his disciples,
46 Beware of the scribes, who desire to go around in long clothing, and M't 23:1-7;
love greetings in the markets, the highest seats in the synagogues, and the 14.
places of honour at feasts; 47 who devour widows' houses, and that under a Mk 12:38-40
colour of long praying. The same shall receive greater damnation.

The Notes

Of men or of God? (20:4) a) Look in Matthew 21:25 and note (c).

Chapter 21

Christ commends the poor widow. He tells of the destruction of Jerusalem, of false teachers, of the signs and troubles to come, of the end of the world, and of his own coming.

As he looked on, he saw the rich, how they cast their offerings into the
treasury. 2 And he saw also a certain poor widow who cast in two small
coins, 3 and he said, Of a truth I say to you, this poor widow has put in
more than all of them. 4 For they all have added to the offering to God out Mk 12:41-44
of their surplus, but she, of her penury, has cast in all the substance that
she had.

5 When some were speaking about the temple, how it was adorned with
beautiful stones and jewels, Jesus said, 6 The days will come when of these
Destruction of the temple foretold. things that you see, there will not be left stone upon stone that shall not be
thrown down. 7 And they asked him, saying, Teacher, when will these
things be? And what sign will there be when such things are about to
happen?

8 And he said, Take heed that you be not deceived. For many will
come in my name, saying, I am he. And the time draws near. You must M't c24
not follow them therefore. 9 But when you hear of war and dissension, do Mk c13
not be afraid. For these things must come first. But the end will not follow
immediately.

10 Then he said to them, Nation will rise against nation, and kingdom
against kingdom. 11 And great earthquakes will be in all quarters, and
hunger and pestilence, and fearful things. And there will be great signs

from heaven. 12But before all these, they will lay their hands on you and
persecute you, delivering you up to the synagogues and into prison, and
will bring you before kings and rulers for my name's sake. 13And this will
happen to you for a testimony.

14Let it therefore stick fast in your hearts not once to concern your-
A promise. selves beforehand what to answer, 15for I will give you a mouth and wis-
dom against which none of your adversaries will be able to speak or resist.

16Yea and you will be betrayed by your fathers and mothers, and by
your brethren and kinsmen and friends, and some of you they will put to
death. 17And you will be hated by all men for my name's sake. 18Yet not
one hair of your heads shall perish. 19With your patience possess your
souls.[a]

[In the Table of Principal Matters of the MB, under 'Abomination,' it is explained that the abomination standing in the holy place is Jerusalem besieged by her enemies, as here described, with reference also to Matthew xxiiii.g. and Mark iii.b. Ed]

20And when you see Jerusalem besieged with a host, then understand
that its desolation is near. 21Then let the people who are in Judea flee to
the mountains, and let those who are in the city get out. And let not those
who are in other countries enter in. 22For these are the days of vengeance, Lu 19:43,44
to fulfil all the things that are written. 23But woe will be to women who
are with child and to those who give suck in those days, for there will be
great trouble in the land, and wrath over all this people. 24And they will
fall on the edge of the sword, and will be led captive into all nations. And Dan 9:26
Jerusalem will be trodden under foot by the Gentiles, until the time of the
Gentiles is fulfilled.

25And there will be signs in the sun and in the moon and in the stars,
and in the earth the people will be in such perplexity that they will not
know which way to turn. The sea and the waters will roar, 26and men's Isa 13:4-10
hearts will fail them for fear, and for the dread of those things which shall
come on the earth. For the powers of heaven shall move. 27And then shall
they see the Son of man come in a cloud, with power and great glory.
28When these things begin to come to pass, then look up, and lift up your
heads,[b] for your redemption draws near.

29And he told them a similitude: Consider the fig tree, and all other
trees. 30When they shoot forth their buds, you see and can tell for your
own selves that summer is then nigh at hand. 31So likewise, when you see
these things come to pass, understand that the kingdom of God is near.
32Truly I say to you, this generation shall not pass till all be fulfilled.
33Heaven and earth shall pass, but my words shall not pass.

[Ambrose>A spare diet keeps under lust and carnality]

34Take heed to yourselves, lest your hearts be overcome with excess of
eating, and drunkenness, and worldly cares, and that day come on you
unawares. 35For as a snare shall it come upon all who sit on the face of the
earth. 36Watch therefore continually, and pray that you may obtain grace
to escape all this that is to come, and that you may stand before the Son of
man.

37In the daytime he taught in the temple, and at night he went out and
stayed on the Mount of Olives. 38And all the people came to him in the
morning in the temple, to hear him.

The Notes

With patience possess your souls (21: 19) — a) The soul is possessed (that is, the soul does not perish, but is saved) by patience, if through faith in Christ it patiently suffers all adversities.

Lift up your heads (21:28) — b) To lift up the head is to have remembrance or to rejoice.

Chapter 22

Christ is betrayed. They eat the Passover lamb. The institution of the sacrament. They dispute who should be greatest; he reproves them. He prays three times upon the mount. They seize him and bring him to the high priest's house. Peter denies him three times, and they bring Jesus before the council.

[**Sweet bread**: others have here 'unleavened bread'] The feast of sweet bread* drew near, which is called the Passover. 2And M't 26:3-5; 14-16.
the high priests and scribes were seeking how to kill Jesus, but they feared Mk 14:1,2; 10,11.
the people. 3Then Satan entered into Judas, whose surname was Iscariot Joh 13:2
(who was of the number of the twelve), 4and he went his way and com-
muned with the high priests and officers, how he might betray Jesus to
them. 5And they were glad, and promised to give him money. 6And he
accepted, and sought an opportunity to betray Jesus to them when the
people were away.
7Then came the day of sweet bread, when of necessity the Passover
Passover lamb — lamb must be offered. 8And Jesus sent Peter and John, saying, Go and M't 16:17-19 Mk 14:12-17
prepare for us the Passover lamb so that we may eat. 9They said to him,
Where would you like us to prepare it? 10And he said to them, When you
have entered into the city, there a man bearing a pitcher of water will meet
you. Follow him into the same house that he enters in, 11and say to the
head of the house, The Master says to you, where is the guest chamber,
where I may eat my Passover lamb with my disciples? 12And he will show
you a large upper room furnished. There make ready.
13And they went and found things as he had said to them, and made
ready the Passover lamb.
14And when the hour was come, he sat down, and the twelve apostles
with him. 15And he said to them, I have inwardly desired to eat this
Passover lamb with you before I suffer. 16For I say to you, henceforth I
will not eat of it any more until it is fulfilled in the kingdom of God.
17And he took the cup and gave thanks and said, Take this, and divide it
among you. 18For I say to you, I will not drink of the fruit of the vine until
the kingdom of God has come.
The sacrament is instituted. — 19And he took bread, gave thanks, and gave to them, saying, This is M't 26:20-29
my body, which is given for you. This do in the remembrance of me. Mk 14:17-22 Ge 14:18
20Likewise also, when they had supped, he took the cup, saying, This cup Heb 5:6
is the new testament in my blood, which shall be shed for you. 21Yet 1Co 11:23-26.
behold, the hand of him who betrays me is with me on the table. 22And the
Son of man goes as it is appointed; but woe be to that man by whom he is
betrayed.
23And they began to enquire among themselves which of them it could

be that would do that.

[24]And there was a dispute among them, which of them should be taken
for the greatest. [25]And he said to them, The kings of the Gentiles reign
over them, and those who bear rule over them are called gracious lords.
[26]But you shall not be like this. Rather, he who is greatest among you M't 20:25-28 Mk 10:42-45
shall be as the youngest, and he who is chief shall be as the servant. [27]For
who is greater: he who sits at food, or he that serves? Is it not he who sits
at food? But I am among you as he that serves. [28]And you are those who
have stayed with me in my trials. [29]And I appoint unto you a kingdom, as
my Father has appointed to me, [30]so that you may eat and drink at my
table in my kingdom, and sit upon seats, and judge the twelve tribes of
Israel.

Simon Peter's faith will not fail [These verses are emended to show singular and plural number, lost in modern English 2nd person pronouns]

[31]And the Lord said, Simon, Simon, behold: Satan has desired you all,
to sift you like wheat. [32]But I have prayed for you, Simon, that your faith M't 26:33-35
should not fail. And when you have turned back again, strengthen your Mk 14:29-31 Joh 18:15-
brethren. [33]And Peter said to him, Lord, I am ready to go with you into 18,25-27.
prison, and to death. [34]And he said, I tell you, Peter, the cock will not
crow this day till you have three times denied that you knew me.

[35]And he said to them, When I sent you out without wallet or bag or
shoes, did you lack anything? And they said, No. [36]And he said to them,
But now, let him who has a wallet take it up, and likewise his bag. And he
who has no sword, let him sell his coat and buy one. [37]For I say to you
that that which is written must yet be performed in me: Even with the Isa 53:12
wicked was he numbered. For those things which are written of me have
their fulfilment.

[38]And they said, Lord, see, here are two swords.

And he said to them, It is enough.

[39]And he came out, and went, as was his custom, to the Mount of
Olives. And the disciples followed him. [40]And when he came to the place,
he said to them, Pray, lest you fall into temptation. [41]And he went apart by
himself, about a stone's throw from them, and kneeled down and prayed,
saying, [42]Father, if you will, withdraw this cup from me. Nevertheless, not
my will, but yours be fulfilled.

Christ arms himself against his passion.

An angel comforts him.

[43]And there appeared to him an angel from heaven, comforting him.
[44]And he was in an agony, and prayed somewhat longer. And his sweat
was like drops of blood trickling down to the ground.

He sweats blood.

[45]And he rose up from prayer, and came to his disciples, and found
them sleeping for sorrow, [46]and said to them, Why do you sleep? Rise and
pray, lest you fall into temptation.

[47]While he was yet speaking, behold, there came a band of men, and M't 26:47-75
he who was called Judas, one of the twelve, was leading them. And he Mk 14:43-72
pressed near to Jesus to kiss him. [48]And Jesus said to him, Judas, do you Joh 18:1-27
betray the Son of man with a kiss?

[49]When those who were with Jesus saw what would follow, they said
to him, Lord, shall we smite with swords? [50]And one of them struck a
servant of the most high priest, and cut off his right ear. [51]But Jesus

Ear is struck off.

answered and said, Let it come to this. And he touched the servant's ear
and healed him.
52 Then Jesus said to the high priests and officers of the temple, and the
elders who had approached him, Have you come out as if to a thief, with
swords and clubs? 53 When I was daily with you in the temple, you did not
stretch forth hands against me. But this is even your very hour, and the
power of darkness.
54 Then they took him and led him, and brought him to the home of the
high priest. And Peter followed afar off.
55 When they had kindled a fire in the centre courtyard of the palace M't 26:69-75
and were sitting together, Peter also sat down among them. 56 And one of Mk 14:66-72
the servant girls saw him as he sat by the fire, and took a good look at him Joh 18:15-
and said, This man was also with him. 57 Then he denied him, saying, 18, 25-27.
Peter denies. Woman, I know him not. 58 And after a little while another saw him and
said, You are also one of them. And Peter said, Man, I am not. 59 And
about the space of an hour afterwards, another affirmed, saying, Surely
this fellow was with him, for he is from Galilee. 60 And Peter said, Man, I
don't know what you are talking about.
And immediately, while he yet spoke, the cock crew. 61 And the Lord
turned back and looked upon Peter. And Peter remembered the words of
the Lord, how he said to him, Before the cock crows, you will deny me
three times. 62 And Peter went out and wept bitterly.
Christ is mocked. 63 And the men that stood about Jesus mocked him and beat him, 64 and M't 26:57-68
blindfolded him, and struck his face. And they asked him, saying, Mk 14:53-65
Prophesy! Who it is that hit you? 65 And they said many other things de- Joh 18:12-
spitefully against him. 14, 19-24.
66 And as soon as it was day, the elders of the people and the high
priests and scribes came together, and they led him into their council,
saying, 67 Are you the very Christ? Tell us.
And he said to them, If I tell you, you will not believe. 68 And also if I
ask you, you will not answer me or let me go. 69 Hereafter shall the Son of
man sit on the right hand of the power of God.
70 Then they all said, Are you then the Son of God?
He said to them, As you say, I am.
71 Then they said, Why do we need any further testimony? We our-
selves have heard from his own mouth.

Chapter 23

Jesus is brought before Pilate and Herod. The women make lamentation for him. He prays for his enemies, forgives the thief upon his right hand, and dies on the cross and is buried.

And the whole number of them arose, and led Jesus to Pilate. 2 And they
He is delivered to Pilate. began to accuse him, saying, We have found his fellow upsetting the M't 27:2; 11-
people, and forbidding to pay tribute to Caesar, saying that he is Christ, a 32.
king. 3 And Pilate questioned him, saying, Are you the king of the Jews? Mk 17:1-21 Joh 18:28-
He answered him and said, It is as you say. 40; 19:1-16.

4 Then Pilate said to the high priests and to the people, I find no fault in
this man. 5 But they were all the more fierce, saying, He stirs up the
people, teaching throughout Judea, beginning at Galilee, and even to this
place.
6 When Pilate heard mention of Galilee, he asked whether the man was
from Galilee. 7 And as soon as he knew he was of Herod's jurisdiction, he
He is sent before Herod. sent him to Herod, who was also at Jerusalem in those days.
8 And when Herod saw Jesus, he was exceedingly glad. He had desired
to see him for a long time, because he had heard many things about him,
and trusted to see some miracle done by him. 9 Then he questioned him
He holds his peace. concerning many things, but Jesus answered him not one word. 10 The
high priests and scribes stood forth and accused him vehemently. 11 And
Herod with his men of war derided him and mocked him, and arrayed him
in white, and sent him again to Pilate.
Pilate and Herod become friends. 12 And that same day, Pilate and Herod were brought together as
friends. For before, they were at variance.
13 And Pilate called together the high priests, the rulers, and the people,
14 and said to them, You have brought this man to me as one who incited
uprising among the people. But I have examined him before you, and
have found no fault in this man concerning those things you accuse him
of. 15 No, nor did Herod; for I sent you all to him, and lo, nothing worthy
of death was determined against him. 16 I will therefore chastise him and
let him go. 17 (For custom constrained Pilate to release one prisoner to
them at that feast.)
18 And all the people cried out at once, saying, Away with him, and
Barabbas. release Barabbas to us! 19 (who for insurrection made in the city and for
murder had been cast into prison).
20 Pilate spoke again to them, wanting to let Jesus go free. 21 But they
shouted, saying, Crucify him! Crucify him!
22 He said to them the third time, What evil has he done? I find no
cause of death in him. I will therefore chastise him and release him.
23 But they called with loud voices for him to be crucified.
And the voice of the people and of the high priests prevailed, 24 and
Pilate gave sentence that it should be as they required, 25 and released to
them the one who for insurrection and murder had been cast into prison,
whom they desired, and delivered Jesus to do with him what they would.
Simon of Cyrene. 26 And as they led him away, they caught one Simon of Cyrene coming out
of the field, and on him they laid the cross, to bear it after Jesus.
27 And there followed him a great company of people, and of women,
which women bewailed and lamented him. 28 But Jesus turned back to
them and said, Daughters of Jerusalem, weep not for me, but weep for
yourselves and for your children. 29 For behold, the days will come when Isa 54:1
men will say, Happy are the barren, and the wombs that never bore, and Ga 4:22-27 Wis 3:13,14
the paps that never gave suck. 30 Then will they begin to say to the moun-
tains, Fall on us! and to the hills, Cover us! 31 For if they do this to a green Isa 2:19 Hos 10:8
tree, what shall be done to the dry? Rev 6:16

[**Calvary**: Tyndale took this word from the Latin *calvarium*, meaning 'skull,' which the Latin Vulgate used to translate the Greek *kranion* (2898). This place of public execution outside Jerusalem, the exact location of which is uncertain, had come to be known as The Skull (in Aramaic, Golgotha)]

M't 27:33-56
Mk 15:22-41
Joh 19:17-37

32 And there were two evil-doers led with him to be slain. 33 And when they came to the place that is called Calvary,* there they crucified him, and the evil-doers also, one on right hand and the other on the left. 34 Then said Jesus, Father, forgive them, for they know not what they do.

And they divided up his garments and cast lots for them. 35 And the people stood and looked on. And the leaders mocked him with them, saying, He helped other men; let him help himself, if he is Christ, the chosen of God. 36 The soldiers also mocked him, and came and gave him vinegar, 37 and said, If you are the king of the Jews, save yourself. 38 And a superscription was written over him in Greek, in Latin, and Hebrew: THIS IS THE KING OF THE JEWS.

39 And one of the evil-doers who hung there railed on him, saying, If you are the Christ, save yourself and us. 40 But the other answered and rebuked him, saying, Do you not fear God, seeing that you are under the same sentence? 41 We are rightly punished, for we receive according to our deeds, but this man has done nothing amiss. 42 And he said to Jesus, Lord, remember me when you come into your kingdom. 43 And Jesus said to him, Truly I say to you, today you shall be with me in Paradise.[a]

[**6th - 9th hour**: noon to 3:00 pm. See note on M't 27:45]
The veil is torn.

44 And it was about the sixth hour. And there came a darkness over all the land until the ninth hour,* 45 and the sun was darkened. And the veil of the temple did tear, right through the middle. 46 And Jesus cried with a great voice and said, Father, into your hands I commit my spirit. And when he had thus spoken, he gave up the spirit.

47 When the centurion saw what had happened, he glorified God, saying, Surely this was a just man. 48 And all the people who came together to that sight, beholding the things that were done, smote their breasts and returned home. 49 And all those who knew him, and the women who had followed him from Galilee, stood afar off beholding these things.

Joseph of Arimathea.

M't 27:57-61
Mk 15:42-47
Joh 19:38-42

50 And there was a man named Joseph, a member of the council, and he was a good man and just. 51 He had not consented to their counsel and deed. He was from Arimathea, a city of the Jews, and he was also waiting for the kingdom of God. 52 He went to Pilate and requested the body of Jesus, 53 and took it down, wrapped it in a linen cloth, and laid it in a tomb hewn out in stone, in which no man had ever before been laid. 54 And that day was the day of preparation; and the Sabbath drew on.

55 The women who had come with Jesus from Galilee followed after, and saw the sepulchre and how his body was laid. 56 And they returned and prepared spices and oyntments, but rested on the Sabbath day according to the commandment.

The Notes

Paradise (23:43)

a) By *Paradise* (as Erasmus affirms in his annotations upon this text) is understood a place of singular quietness and pleasure.

Chapter 24

The women come to the grave. Christ appears to the two

disciples on their way to Emmaus, stands in the midst of his
disciples, opens their understanding in the scriptures, gives
them a charge, and ascends up to heaven.

The eighth day.

M't 28:1-15
Mk 16:1-12
Joh 20:1-18

On the morrow after the Sabbath, early in the morning, the women went
to the tomb, bringing the spices they had prepared and other women with
them. [2]And they found the stone rolled away from the sepulchre, [3]and
went in, but did not find the body of the Lord Jesus. [4]And it happened as
they wondered at this, behold, two men stood by them in shining vestures.

[5]And as the women became afraid and bowed down their faces to the
earth, they said to them, Why do you seek the living among the dead? He
is not here, but is risen. [6]Remember how he spoke to you when he was yet
with you in Galilee, [7]saying that the Son of man must be delivered into
the hands of sinful men and be crucified, and the third day rise again?

[8]And they remembered his words, [9]and returned from the sepulchre,
and told all these things to the eleven, and to all the rest. [10]It was Mary
Magdalene, Joanna, Mary Jacobi, and others that were with them, who
told these things to the apostles. [11]But their words seemed to them like
vain things, and they did not believe them.

The linen cloths are left there.

Lev 16:23

[12]Then Peter arose and ran to the sepulchre, and stooped in and saw
the linen cloths laid by themselves. And he departed, wondering in him-
self at that which had happened.

The road to Emmaus.
[**Sixty furlongs**: about 7 miles]

Mk 16:12,13

[13]And behold, two of them set out that same day for a town called
Emmaus, which was about sixty furlongs* from Jerusalem, [14]and they
talked together about all these things that had happened. [15]And it so was,
as they conversed together and discussed, that Jesus himself drew near,
and went alongside them. [16]But their eyes were held,* so they could not
know him. [17]And he said to them, What sort of conversations are these
that you are having with each other as you walk and are sad?

[**Held**: Coverdale>The Lord holds their eyes so they do not know him, so that by this means they themselves through their own words can see and confess their doubtful wavering and weakness of faith, and he may give the right medicine for their unbelief: the kindling of their desires, their doubtfulness taken away, and their weak faith strengthened (*Pearl*)]

[18]And the one named Cleopas answered and said to him, Are you only
a stranger in Jerusalem, and do not know about the things that have hap-
pened there in these days?

[19]Jesus said to them, What things?

And they said to him, Of Jesus of Nazareth, who was a prophet
mighty in deed and word before God and all the people, [20]and how the
high priests and our rulers delivered him to be condemned to death, and
have crucified him. [21]But we trusted that it was he who would deliver
Israel. And regarding all these things, today is just the third day since they
happened. [22]Yea, and also certain women of our company have us
mystified. They went early to the sepulchre, [23]but did not find his body,
and came saying that they had seen a vision of angels who said that he
was alive. [24]And some of those who were with us went their way to the
sepulchre and found it just as the women had said, but they did not see
him.

[25]And he said to them, O foolish ones, and slow of heart to believe all
that the prophets have spoken! [26]Ought not the Christ to have suffered
these things, and to enter into his glory?

[27]And he began at Moses and at all the prophets, and interpreted to
them all the scriptures that were written about him. [28]And they drew near
the town they were headed to, and Jesus made as though he would have
gone further. [29]But they constrained him, saying, Stay with us, for it is
drawing towards night, and the day is far past. And he went in to stay with
them.

[30]And it came to pass, as he sat at food with them, he took bread,
[He is known in the breaking of bread: an object lesson concerning Holy Communion]
blessed it, broke, and gave to them. [31]And their eyes were opened, and
they knew him; and he vanished out of their sight. [32]And they said be-
tween themselves, Did not our hearts burn within us while he talked with
us along the road, and as he opened to us the scriptures?

[33]And they rose up the same hour, and returned again to Jerusalem.
And they found the eleven gathered together, and those who were with
them, [34]who said, The Lord is risen indeed, and has appeared to Simon!

[35]And the two told what things had happened along the road, and how
they knew him in the breaking of bread.

[36]As they were thus speaking, Jesus himself stood in the midst of them
and said to them, Peace be with you. [37]And they were startled and afraid, Mk 16:14 Joh 20:19-29
supposing they saw a spirit. [38]And he said to them, Why are you troubled,
and why do doubts arise in your hearts? [39]Behold my hands and my feet,
that it is even I myself. Handle me and see. For spirits do not have flesh
and bones, as you see me to have.

[40]And when he had thus spoken, he showed them his hands and his
feet. [41]And while they still could not believe for joy and wonderment, he
said to them, Have you any food here? [42]And they gave him a piece of
broiled fish and some honeycomb. [43]And he took it and ate it before them.

[44]And he said to them, These are the things that I told to you while I
was still with you: that all must be fulfilled that was written about me in
the law of Moses, and in the Prophets, and in the Psalms.

He gives the keys.
[45]Then he opened their wits to understand the scriptures, [46]and said to
them, Thus it is written, and thus it was necessary for Christ to suffer, and
to rise again from death the third day, [47]and that repentance and remission
of sins should be preached in his name among all nations, and must begin
at Jerusalem. [48]And you are witnesses of these things. [49]And behold, I will
send the promise of my Father upon you. But stay in the city of Jerusalem Ac 1:4,5; 2:1-4.
until you are endued with power from on high.

[50]And he led them out into Bethany, and lifted up his hands and
blessed them. [51]And it came to pass, as he blessed them, he departed from
them, and was carried up into heaven.

[52]And they worshipped him, and returned to Jerusalem with great joy,
[53]and were continually in the temple, praising and lauding God.

Amen.

Here ends the gospel
of Saint Luke.

A Prologue Upon the Gospel of John

John, who he was, is manifest by the three first evangelists. First he was Christ's apostle, and that one of the chief. Then Christ's near kinsman, and for his singular innocency and softness, singularly beloved, and of singular familiarity with Christ, and ever one of the three witnesses of the most secret things.

The cause of his writing was certain heresies that arose in his time, and namely two, of which one denied Christ to be very man and to be come in the very flesh and nature of man. [The second presumably was that which denied the deity of Christ. Ed.] Against which two heresies he wrote both in his gospel and also his first epistle, and in the beginning of his gospel says that the word or thing was at the beginning, and was with God, and was also very God, and that all things were created and made by it, and that it was also made flesh; that is to say, became very man. And he dwelt among us (he says), and we saw his glory.

And in the beginning of his epistle, he says, We show you of the thing that was from the beginning, which also we heard, saw with our eyes, and our hands handled. And again, we show you everlasting life, that was with the father and appeared to us, and we heard and saw, and etc. In that he says that it was from the beginning, that it was eternal life, and that it was with God, he affirms him to be very God. And in that he says, We heard, saw, and felt, he witnesses that he was very man also.

John wrote last of all, and therefore did not touch on the story that the other evangelists had compiled. But he writes most of the faith and promises and of the sermons of Christ. *W.T. (1534)*

[Ed: It is believed on the authority of early church fathers that John wrote this, his 'spiritual gospel,' at an advanced age, between 80-90 A.D., being about fifty years after he walked with Jesus our Lord.]

The Gospel of
St. John

Chapter 1

The everlasting birth of Christ, and how he became man. The testimony of John. The calling of Andrew, Peter, etc.

IN THE BEGINNING was the word, and the word was with God, and the
word was God. [2]The same was in the beginning with God. [3]All things
were made by it, and without it was made nothing that was made. [4]In it
was life, and the life was the light of men. [5]And the light shines in the
darkness, but the darkness comprehended it not.[a]

[6]There was a man sent from God, whose name was John. [7]This man
came as a witness to bear witness of the light, so that all through him
might believe. [8]He was not that light, but was sent to bear witness of the
light [9]that was the true light, who lights all men that come into the world.
[10]He was in the world, and the world was made by him, and yet the world
knew him not.[b]

*Own is his own people

[11]He came among his own,* and his own received him not. [12]But as
many as received him, to them he gave power to be the children of God,
in that they believed on his name – [13]who were born not of blood, nor of
the will of the flesh, nor yet of the will of man, but of God.

Faith makes us the children of God

[14]And the word was made flesh and dwelt among us. And we saw the
glory of it, as the glory of the only begotten Son of the Father, which M't 1:18 Lu 1:35
word was full of grace and truth. [15]John bore witness of him and cried out,

[v15 is emended and updated from Cranmer 1539]

saying, This was he of whom I spoke, who, though he came after me, went before me, because he was before me. 16And of his fullness we have all received, even grace for grace.[c] 17For the law was given by Moses, but grace and truth came by Jesus Christ.

18No man has seen God at any time.[d] The only begotten Son, who is in the bosom of the Father, he has declared him.

19And this is the witness of John, when the Jews sent priests and Levites from Jerusalem to ask him, Who are you? 20He acknowledged, and did not deny, but said plainly, I am not the Christ.

21And they asked him, What then? Are you Elijah?

And he said, I am not.

Are you a prophet?

And he answered, No.

22Then said they to him, Who are you, so that we may give an answer to those who sent us: what do you say about yourself?

Voice: That is, I am what I say, a preacher sent to prove you sinners, and to cry on you to amend, so that you may receive Christ and his grace.

23He said, I am the voice of a crier in the wilderness, Make straight the way of the Lord! as the prophet Isaiah said.[*]

Isa 40:3
Mal 3:1

24And those who were sent were of the Pharisees. 25And they asked him and said to him, Why do you baptize then, if you are not the Christ, nor Elijah, nor a prophet?

26John answered them, saying, I baptize with water, but one is come among you whom you do not know. 27He it is that comes after me, who was before me, whose shoe latchet I am not worthy to loose.

28These things were done in Bethabara beyond the Jordan, where John did baptize.

Behold the Lamb of God.

29The next day, John saw Jesus coming to him, and said, Behold the Lamb of God, who takes away the sin of the world! 30This is he of whom I said, after me comes a man who went before me, because he was before me. 31And I did not know him. But in order that he should be declared to Israel, I have come baptizing with water.

32And John bore witness, saying, I saw the Spirit descend from heaven like a dove and rest upon him. 33And I did not know him, but he who sent me to baptize in water, the same said to me, Upon whom you see the Spirit descend and remain still on him, the same is he who baptizes with the Holy Spirit. 34And I saw and bore witness that this is the Son of God.

M't 3:11-17
Mk 1:1-11
Lu 3:1-22
2Pe 1:16-18

35The next day after, John was standing again with two of his disciples. 36And he saw Jesus as he walked by, and said, Behold the Lamb of God! 37And the two disciples heard him speak, and followed Jesus.

38And Jesus turned about and saw them following and said to them, What are you seeking? They said to him, Rabbi (which means, Teacher), where are you staying? 39He said to them, Come and see.

They went and saw where he was lodging, and stayed with him that day. For it was about the tenth hour.

Andrew

40One of the two who heard John speak and followed Jesus was Andrew, Simon Peter's brother. 41He found his brother Simon first and said to him, We have found the Messiah! (which translated is, the Anointed).

[42]And he brought him to Jesus. And Jesus regarded him and said, You are
Peter Simon, the son of Jonah. You shall be called Cephas (which translated is,
a rock).
[43]The day following, Jesus decided to go into Galilee. And he found
Philip Philip and said to him, Follow me. [44]Philip was from Bethsaida, the town
Nathanael of Andrew and Peter. [45]And Philip found Nathanael and said to him, We
have found him of whom Moses in the law and the prophets did write:
Jesus, the son of Joseph of Nazareth. [46]And Nathanael said to him, Can
any good thing come out of Nazareth? Philip said to him, Come and see.
[47]Jesus saw Nathanael coming to him and said of him, Behold a right
Israelite, in whom there is no guile. [48]Nathanael said to him, Where did
you know me? Jesus answered and said to him, Before Philip called you,
when you were under the fig tree, I saw you. [49]Nathanael answered and
said to him, Rabbi, you are the Son of God, you are the king of Israel!
[50]Jesus answered and said to him, Because I said to you, I saw you
under the fig tree, you believe. You will see greater things than these.
[51]And he said to him, Truly truly I say to you, hereafter you shall see
heaven open, and the angels of God ascending and descending over the
Son of man.

The Notes

The light shines in the darkness (1:5)
a) By *the light* understand Christ, and by *the darkness*, ungodly and unbelieving people, among whom Christ came, and they did not receive him, as at Ephesians 4:17-19.

World knew him not (1:10)
b) Here *the world* means the people of the world, as in John 7:7 and Mark 16:15.

Grace for grace (1:16)
c) By *grace* understand favour. The meaning is, for the favour that God the Father has to his son Christ, he has received us into favour, so that just as Christ is beloved by his Father, so are we beloved for his sake. Romans 5:15. [Chrysostom> Under the new covenant we have received new grace for old, the reality for the type (*Hom/John*)]

No man has seen God at any time, etc (1:17)
d) No bodily eye can behold the majesty of God in his excellent nature as he is, as we have declared to us in Exodus 33:20.

Chapter 2

Christ turns the water into wine, and drives the buyers and sellers out of the temple.

And the third day there was a marriage in Cana, a village of Galilee, and
the mother of Jesus was there. [2]And Jesus was invited also, and his
disciples, to the marriage. [3]And when the wine failed, Jesus' mother said
to him, They have no wine. [4]Jesus said to her, Woman, what have I to do
with you? My hour is not yet come. [5]And his mother said to the servants,
Whatever he says to you, do it.
[6]And there were standing there six waterpots of stone, for the puri-
fication rites of the Jews, containing twenty or thirty gallons apiece. [7]And
Jesus said to them, Fill the waterpots with water. And they filled them up
to the brim. [8]And he said to them, Draw some out now, and bring it to the
master of the feast. And they brought it.
[9]When the master of the feast tasted the water that was turned to wine,

and did not know where it was from (but the servants who had drawn the
Water into wine
water knew), he called the bridegroom 10 and said to him, All men at the
beginning set out good wine, and when people have drunk,[a] then that
which is worse. But you have kept back the good wine until now.
11 This beginning of miracles Jesus did in Cana of Galilee, and showed
his glory, and his disciples believed on him. 12 After that, he descended
into Capernaum with his mother and his brethren[b] and his disciples, but
continued not many days there.
13 And the Jews' Passover was near at hand. And Jesus went up to
Jerusalem, 14 and found sitting in the temple those who sold oxen and M't 21:12,13
sheep and doves, and the money-changers. 15 And he made a scourge of Mk 11:15-17
Sellers in the temple cast out.
small cords and drove them all out of the temple with the sheep and oxen,
and poured out the changers' money, and overthrew the tables, 16 and said
to those who sold doves, Take these things away from here, and do not
make my Father's house a house of merchandise! 17 And his disciples re-
membered that it was written: The zeal of your house has consumed me. Ps 69:9
18 Then the Jews said to him, What sign can you show to us, seeing
that you do these things? 19 Jesus answered and said to them, Destroy this
temple, and in three days I will rear it up again.
20 Then the Jews said, This temple was forty-six years in building, and
will you rear it up in three days?
21 But he was speaking of the temple of his body. 22 As soon therefore
as he was risen up again from death, his disciples remembered that he had
said this. And they believed the scripture, and the words that Jesus had
spoken.
23 When he was at Jerusalem, at Passover in the feast, many believed
on his name when they saw the miracles that he did. 24 But Jesus did not
put himself in their hands, 25 because he knew all men, and needed not that
anyone should testify of man. For he knew what was in man.

The Notes

Drunk (2:10) a) When people have drunk: that is, when they are filled and satisfied.

Brethren (2:12) b) Jesus' brethren: See note (a) on John c7.

Chapter 3

The conversation of Christ with Nicodemus. The teaching and baptism of John, and what witness he bears of Christ.

[**Nicodemus** may have been a member of the Sanhedrin, the ruling council with supreme executive, legislative, and judicial power over the Jewish faith and lifestyle, within limits imposed by Rome]

There was a man of the Pharisees named Nicodemus, a ruler among the
Jews.* 2 He came to Jesus by night and said to him, Rabbi, we know that
you are a teacher come from God. For no man could do such miracles as
you do unless God were with him.
3 Jesus answered and said to him, Truly truly I say to you, unless a man
be born anew, he cannot see the kingdom of God.
4 Nicodemus said to him, How can a man be born when he is old? Can
he enter into his mother's womb and be born again?
5 Jesus answered, Truly truly I say to you, unless a man be born of

water and of the Spirit, he cannot enter into the kingdom of God. 6That
which is born of the flesh is flesh, and that which is born of the Spirit is
spirit. 7Marvel not that I said to you, you must be born anew.[*] 8The wind
blows where it will, and you hear its sound, but cannot tell from whence it
comes and where it goes. That is how it is with everyone that is born of
the Spirit.

[**Born anew**: or born *from above,* as the Greek *anothen* (509) may also be understood. Most bible versions have 'born again' here and at v3:3]

9And Nicodemus answered and said to him, How can these things be?
10Jesus answered and said to him, Are you a teacher in Israel, and do
not know these things? 11Truly truly I say to you, we speak what we
know, and testify what we have seen, and you people do not receive our
witness. 12If when I tell you all earthly things, you do not believe, how
will you believe if I tell you of heavenly things? 13And no man ascends up
to heaven but he who came down from heaven; that is to say, the Son of
Serpent lifted up. man who is in heaven.[a] 14And as Moses lifted up the serpent in the wil- Nu 21:9
derness, even so must the Son of man be lifted up, so that no one who
believes in him will perish, but will have eternal life.

15For God so loves the world that he has given his only Son, 16so that
none who believe in him should perish, but should have everlasting life.
17For God did not send his Son into the world to condemn the world, but 1Jo 4:14
so that the world through him could be saved.[b] 18Whoever believes on him
shall not be condemned. But whoever does not believe is condemned al-
ready, because he does not believe in the name of the only Son of God.
19And this is the condemnation: that light has come into the world, and
men loved darkness more than light, because their deeds were evil. 20For
everyone who does evil hates the light, and does not come to the light, lest
his deeds should be reproved. 21But whoever does truth comes to the light,
so that his deeds may be known, that they are wrought in God.

22After these things, Jesus and his disciples went into the Judean
countryside, and there he spent time with them and baptized. 23And John
also was baptizing in Aenon near Salim, because there was much water
there, and people came and were baptized. 24For John had not yet been
cast into prison.

25And there arose a question between John's disciples and the Jews
about purifying. 26And they came to John and said to him, Rabbi, he who
was with you beyond the Jordan, of whom you bear witness, behold, he is
baptizing, and everyone is going to him.

27John answered and said, A man can receive nothing at all unless it is
given to him from heaven. 28You yourselves are witnesses that I said I am
not the Christ, but have been sent before him. 29He who has the bride is
the bridegroom. But the friend of the bridegroom, who stands by and
hears him, rejoices greatly to hear the bridegroom's voice. Therefore this
my joy is fulfilled. 30He must increase in renown, and I must decrease.

31He who comes from on high is above all. He who is of the earth is
earthly, and speaks of the earth. He who comes from heaven is above all,
32and what he has seen and heard, that he testifies; but no one receives his
testimony. 33However, the person who has received his testimony has set

to his seal that God is true.[c] [34]For he whom God has sent speaks the words
of God. For God does not give the Spirit by measure (to him).[d] [35]The
Father loves the Son, and has given all things into his hand. [36]The person 1Jo 5:12
who believes on the Son has everlasting life, and the person who does not
believe the Son shall not see life, but the wrath of God abides on him.

The Notes

Into heaven (3:13) a) No man ascends into heaven but he that came from heaven, etc: That is, no man can come in heaven but by Christ the Son of God who came from heaven, etc. Only by his righteousness must we ascend.

So the world be saved (3:17) b) Here *the world* signifies only the chosen and those that do believe.

His seal (3:33) c) Has set to his seal that God is true: That is, has it printed in his belief, as it were with a seal.

Not by measure (3:34) d) God does not give the Spirit by measure (to Christ): How the Spirit or the gifts of the Spirit are given by measure, read at Romans 12 and 1 Corinthians 12. And this is how the Spirit is given throughout all Christendom by measure. But to Christ, who alone has put away all sins and death, the Spirit was given above measure, as in Titus 3:6.

Chapter 4

The loving conversation of Christ with the woman from Samaria by the well's side. How he heals the ruler's son.

As soon as the Lord knew that the Pharisees had heard how Jesus made
and baptized more disciples than John [2](though Jesus himself did not
baptize, but his disciples), [3]he left Judea and went back to Galilee. [4]And it
so was that he had to go through Samaria. [5]Then he came to a village of Ge 33:19;
Samaria called Sychar, near the parcel of land that Jacob gave to his son 48:22.
Joseph. [6]And there was Jacob's well. Jos 24:32

Jesus, then wearied in his journey, sat on the well. And it was about
the sixth hour,[a] [7]and there came a woman of Samaria to draw water. And
Jesus said to her, Give me to drink. [8]For his disciples had gone away to
The woman of Samaria. the town to buy food. [9]Then the woman of Samaria said to him, How is it
that you, being a Jew, ask drink of me, a Samaritan? (For the Jews will
have nothing to do with the Samaritans.)

[10]Jesus answered and said to her, If you knew the gift of God, and who
it is that says to you, Give me to drink, you would have asked of him, and
he would have given you the water of life.

[11]The woman said to him, Sir, you have nothing to draw with, and the
well is deep. Where then do you have that water of life from? [12]Are you
greater than our father Jacob who gave us the well, and he himself drank
from it, and his children and his animals?

[13]Jesus answered and said to her, Whoever drinks of this water will
thirst again. [14]But whoever drinks of the water that I give him shall never
more thirst, but the water that I give him will be in him a well of water
springing up into everlasting life.

[15]The woman said to him, Sir, give me of that water so that I may not
thirst, nor come here to draw. [16]Jesus said to her, Go and call your hus-

band, and come here. [17]The woman answered and said to him, I have no husband. Jesus said to her, You have well said, I have no husband. [18]For you have had five husbands, and he whom you now have is not your husband. This you have said truly.

[19]The woman said to him, Sir, I perceive that you are a prophet. [20]Our fathers worshipped in this mountain, but you Jews say that in Jerusalem is the place where people ought to worship.

[21]Jesus said to her, Woman, believe me, the hour is coming when you will neither in this mountain, nor yet at Jerusalem, worship the Father. [22]You Samaritans worship you know not what. We know what we worship, for salvation comes of the Jews. [23]But the hour comes, and now is, when the true worshippers shall worship the Father in spirit and in truth.

God must be worshipped in spirit and truth.

For indeed, the Father seeks such to worship him. [24]God is a spirit, and those who worship him must worship him in spirit and truth. 2Co 3:17

[25]The woman said to him, I know well the Messiah will come, who is called Christ. When he is come, he will tell us all things.

[26]Jesus said to her, I who speak to you am he.

[27]And at that point his disciples came, and were surprised that he talked with the woman. Yet no one said to him, What are you asking? or, Why are you talking with her? [28]The woman then left her water-pot, and went her way into the village and said to the people, [29]Come see a man who told me all that I ever did. Is he not the Christ? [30]Then they went out of the village and came to him.

[31]And in the meanwhile his disciples urged him, saying, Rabbi, eat! [32]He said to them, I have food to eat that you know not of.[b] [33]Then the disciples said between themselves, Has anyone brought him food?

[34]Jesus said to them, My food is to do the will of him who sent me, and to finish his work. [35]Do you not say, There are yet four months, and then comes the harvest? Behold, I say to you, lift up your eyes and look

Fields white for harvest.

on the fields, for they are already white for harvest. [36]And he who reaps receives reward, and gathers fruit unto life eternal, so that both he who sows and he who reaps may rejoice together. [37]And this saying is true, that one sows and another reaps. [38]I sent you to reap that whereon you bestowed no labour. Other men laboured, and you have entered into their labours.

[39]Many of the Samaritans of that village believed on him because of the word of the woman who testified, He told me all that I ever did. [40]Then when the Samaritans had come to him, they besought him to stay with them. And he stayed there two days. [41]And many more believed because of his own words, [42]and said to the woman, Now we believe, not because of what you said, but because we have heard him ourselves, and know that this is even indeed Christ, the Saviour of the world.

[43]After two days he departed from there and went away into Galilee. [44]And Jesus himself testified that a prophet has no honour in his own country. [45]Then as soon as he came into Galilee, the Galileans received him, having seen all the things that he did at Jerusalem at the feast. For

M't 13:57
Mk 6:4
Lu 4:24

they had also gone to the feast day.

46 And Jesus came again into Cana of Galilee, where he had turned the Lu 4:31
water into wine. And there was a certain nobleman whose son was sick at
Capernaum. 47 As soon as he heard that Jesus had come out of Judea into
Galilee, he went to him, and besought him to come down and heal his son,
for he was even ready to die. 48 Then Jesus said to him, Unless you see
signs and wonders, you cannot believe. 49 The nobleman said to him, Sir,
come away before my child dies! 50 Jesus said to him, Go your way, your
son lives.

And the man believed the words that Jesus had spoken to him, and
went his way. 51 And as he was going down, his servants met him and told
him, saying, Your child lives. 52 Then he enquired of them the hour when
the child began to recover. And they said to him, Yesterday at the seventh
hour the fever left him. 53 And the father knew that it was the same hour in
which Jesus had said to him, Your son lives. And he believed, and all his
household. 54 This is again the second miracle that Jesus did after he had
come out of Judea into Galilee.

The Notes

About the 6th hour, etc (4:6)

a) The Jews reckoned the hours of their day from the sun rising to the sun setting, so that the sixth hour was 6 hours after sunrise, or, at that time of the year, about noon. [Ed: see also notes on M't 27:45 and Mk 15:25.]

I have food to eat, etc (4:32)

b) His food is to do the will of his Father, and the chief thing of his Father's will is to preach the gospel to all the world. Which thing was even now at hand to be done, just as when the wheat is ripe, men must fall to harvest (John 4:35).

Chapter 5

He heals the man who had been sick for 38 years. The Jews accuse him. He answers for himself and reproves them.

*The Greek has 'sheep house,' a place where they killed the animals that were offered.

After that, there was a feast of the Jews, and Jesus went up to Jerusalem.
2 And there is at Jerusalem, by the slaughterhouse,* a pool called in the
Hebrew tongue Bethseda,[a] having five porches, 3 in which lay a great
number of sick folk, of the blind, lame, and paralyzed, waiting for the
moving of the water. 4 For an angel went down at a certain time into the
pool and stirred up the water. Whoever then first after the stirring of the
water stepped in, was made whole of whatever disease he had.

5 And a certain man was there who had been diseased 38 years. 6 When
Jesus saw him lying there, and knew that for a long time now he had been
diseased, he said to him, Do you want to be made whole? 7 The sick man
answered him, Sir, I have no one to put me into the pool when the water is
stirred up. But in the meantime, when I am about to come, another steps
down before me. 8 And Jesus said to him, Rise, take up your bed, and
walk. 9 And immediately the man was made whole, and took up his bed,
and walked.

And that day was the Sabbath day. 10 The Jews therefore said to him
who had been healed, It is the Sabbath day; it is not lawful for you to

carry your bed. 11 He answered them, The man who made me whole said to me, Take up your bed and walk. 12 Then they asked him, What man is it that said to you, Take up your bed and walk? 13 But the man that was healed did not know who it was. For Jesus had gotten himself away, because there was a press of people in the place.

14 And after that, Jesus found the man in the temple and said to him, Behold, you are made whole. Sin no more, lest a worse thing happen to you. 15 The man departed and told the Jews that it was Jesus who had made him whole. 16 And therefore the Jews persecuted Jesus, and sought means to slay him, because he had done these things on the Sabbath day.

17 And Jesus told them, My Father works until now, and I work.[b]

18 Therefore the Jews sought all the more to kill him, not only because he had broken the Sabbath, but said also that God was his Father, and made himself equal with God.

19 Then Jesus said to them, Truly truly I say to you, the Son can do nothing of himself, but that which he sees the Father do. For whatsoever he does, that the Son does also. 20 For the Father loves the Son, and shows him all things, whatever he himself does. And he will show him greater works than these, because you should marvel. 21 For likewise as the Father raises up the dead and gives them life, even so the Son gives life to whom
he will. 22 Neither does the Father judge any man, but has committed all
Christ is judge over all. judgment to the Son, 23 because all should honour the Son fully as they
honour the Father. He who does not honour the Son, does not honour the
Father who has sent him. 24 Truly truly I say to you, he who hears my
Faith. words and believes on him who sent me, has everlasting life, and shall not
come into damnation, but is escaped from death to life.

25 Truly truly I say to you, the time shall come, and now is, when the
The dead shall hear. dead shall hear the voice of the Son of God.[c] And those who hear will
live. 26 For as the Father has life in himself, so likewise has he given to the
Son to have life in himself, 27 and has given him power also to judge, in
that he is the Son of man. 28 Do not be surprised at this. And the hour shall M't 25:31-46
come in which all who are in the graves will hear his voice, 29 and will
come forth – those who have done good to the resurrection of life, and
those who have done evil, to the resurrection of damnation.

30 I can of my own self do nothing at all. As I hear, I judge. And my judgment is just, because I seek not my own will, but the will of the Father who has sent me.

31 If I bear witness of myself, my witness is not true. 32 There is another
The witness of John. who bears witness of me, and I know that the witness he bears of me is M't 3:11
true: 33 you sent to John, and he bore witness to the truth. 34 But I do not
[**Do not receive**: that is, I need it not. See Rogers' note on chapter 15 (a)] receive the testimony of man.[*] Nevertheless, I say these things so that you
might be saved. 35 He was a burning and a shining light, and you were
willing for a season to enjoy his light.

36 But I have greater witness than the witness of John. For the works
The witness of the works. which the Father has given me to finish, the same works that I do, bear
witness of me, that the Father sent me.

The witness of the Father. 37And the Father himself who has sent me bears witness of me. You M't 3:17
have not heard his voice at any time, nor have you seen his nature, 38and
his words you do not have abiding in you. For whom he has sent, him you
do not believe.

Search the scriptures. 39Search the scriptures, for in them you think you have eternal life,
and it is they that testify of me. 40And yet you will not come to me so that
you might have life. 41I do not receive praise from men, 42but I know you,
that you do not have the love of God in you. 43I have come in my Father's
name, and you do not receive me. If another comes in his own name, him
you will receive. 44How can you believe, who receive honour from one
another, and do not seek the honour that comes from God only?

45Do not think that I will accuse you to my Father. There is one who
accuses you: even Moses, in whom you trust. 46For had you believed
Moses, you would have believed me. For he wrote of me. 47But seeing
you do not believe his writing, how will you believe my words?

The Notes

Pool called Bethseda (5:2)

a) Bethseda, or as some write it, Bethesda, is as much as to say an infirmary or hospital where the poor who are sick go, which place was by a pool where the sheep that were offered in the temple were kept. And the sick remained there looking for the moving of the water, etc.

My Father works, etc (5:17)

b) My Father works until now, and I work: That is, my Father does not keep the Sabbath day, nor do I, but my Father is occupied in no common business on the Sabbath, and neither am I.

The dead shall hear the voice of the Son of God, etc. (5:25)

c) The dead shall hear, etc: Here he speaks of the resurrection of justification whereby the wicked person arises from his wickedness, and whereby the sinner is brought from the death of his sins into the life of righteousness – and especially of the calling of the Gentiles, which was done after the coming of the Holy Spirit. For the Gentiles are reputed as dead men in comparison to the Jews. And afterward, at v29, when he says that all who are in the graves shall hear the voice of the Son of man, he means the general resurrection which will be in the last day.

Chapter 6

Jesus feeds 5,000 men, goes away in order that they should not make him king, and reproves the fleshly hearers of his word. The carnal are offended at him.

After these things, Jesus went his way over the sea of Galilee, near to a
city called Tiberias. 2And a great number of people followed him, because
they had seen the miracles he did on people who were diseased. 3And
Jesus went up into a mountain, and there he sat with his disciples. 4And
Passover, a feast of the Jews, was near. 5Then Jesus lifted up his eyes and
saw a great crowd coming to him, and said to Philip, Where will we buy M't 14:13-21
bread so that these people can eat? 6This he said to prove him, for he Mk 6:35-44 Lu 9:10-17
himself knew what he would do.

7Philip answered him, two hundred denarii worth of bread is not suf-
ficient for them, so that everyone has a little. 8Then one of his disciples,
Andrew, Simon Peter's brother, said to him, 9There is a lad here who has

five barley loaves and two fishes, but what is that among so many? [10]And Jesus said, Make the people sit down.

There was much grass in the place. And the men sat down, in number about 5,000. [11]And Jesus took the bread, and gave thanks, and gave to the disciples, and his disciples to them that were seated. And likewise of the fishes, as much as they desired.

[12]When they had eaten enough, he said to his disciples, Gather up the leftover food that remains, so that nothing is lost. [13]And they gathered it together, and filled twelve baskets with the pieces of the five barley loaves left over from those who had eaten. [14]Then the people, when they had seen the miracle that Jesus did, said, This is of a truth the prophet that was to come into the world.

[15]When Jesus perceived that they wanted to come and take him up to make him king, he departed again into a mountain himself alone.

[**The sea**: Lake Galilee, also called the Sea of Galilee, though it is a fresh water lake]

[**25 or 30 furlongs**: three or four miles]

M't 14:22-36
Mk 6:47-50

[16]And when evening was come, his disciples went to the sea,* [17]and entered into a boat, and went over the sea to Capernaum. And soon it was dark, and Jesus had not come to them. [18]And the sea arose with a great wind that blew. [19]And when they had rowed about 25 or 30 furlongs,* they saw Jesus walking on the sea and drawing near to the ship, and were afraid. [20]And he said to them, It is I; be not afraid.

[21]Then they willingly received him into the boat, and the boat was immediately at the land where they were going.

[22]The day following, the people who stood on the other side of the sea saw that there had been no other boat there except the one his disciples had entered into, and that Jesus had not got in the boat with his disciples, but that his disciples had gone away alone. [23]However, other boats from Tiberias came near to the place where they had eaten bread, when the Lord had blessed. [24]Then when the people saw that Jesus was not there, nor his disciples, they also set off in boats, and went to Capernaum, seeking for Jesus.

[25]And when they found him on the other side of the sea, they said to him, Rabbi, when did you come here? [26]Jesus answered them and said, Truly truly I say to you, you seek me not because you saw the miracles, but because you ate of the loaves, and were filled. [27]Labour not for the food that perishes, but for the food that endures unto everlasting life, which food the Son of man will give to you. For him has God the Father sealed.*

Sealed: that is, he has put the mark of the Holy Spirit on him, which testifies with miracles what he is.

[28]Then they said to him, What should we do so that we can work the works of God? [29]Jesus answered and said to them, This is the work of God: to believe on him whom he has sent.

Ex 16:15
Nu 11:6-9
Ps 78

[30]They said to him, What sign will you show then, so that we can see and believe you? What work do you do? [31]Our fathers ate manna in the desert, as it is written: He gave them bread from heaven to eat.

[32]Jesus said to them, Truly truly I say to you, Moses did not give you bread from heaven, but my Father gives you the true bread from heaven. [33]For the bread of God is he who comes down from heaven and gives life

to the world.[a]

34 Then they said to him, Lord, give us this bread forevermore.

35 And Jesus said to them, I am that bread of life. He who comes to me
He is the bread of life. shall not hunger, and he who believes on me shall never thirst. 36 But I said
to you that you have seen me, and yet do not believe. 37 All whom the
Father gives me shall come to me, and him who comes to me, I cast not
away. 38 For I came down from heaven not to do my own will, but the will
of him who has sent me. 39 And this is the will of the Father who has sent
me: that of everything that he has given me, I should lose nothing, but
should raise it up again at the last day. 40 And this is the will of him who
sent me: that every person who sees the Son and believes on him should
have everlasting life. And I will raise him up at the last day.

41 The Jews then murmured at him, because he said, I am that bread
that has come down from heaven. 42 And they said, Is this not Jesus the M't 13:55-57
son of Joseph, whose father and mother we know? How is it then that he
says, I came down from heaven?

43 Jesus answered and said to them, Do not murmur between your-
selves. 44 No one can come to me unless the Father who has sent me draws
him. And I will raise him up at the last day. 45 It is written in the prophets Isa 54:13
that they will all be taught by God. Everyone therefore who has heard and Jer 31:33
has learned from the Father, comes to me. 46 Not that anyone has seen the
Father, except he who is of God; the same has seen the Father.

47 Truly truly I say to you, he who believes on me has everlasting life.
48 I am that bread of life. 49 Your fathers ate manna in the wilderness, but
are dead. 50 This is the bread that comes from heaven, so that one may eat
of it and not die. 51 I am that living bread that came down from heaven. If
anyone eats of this bread, he will live forever. And the bread that I will
give is my flesh, which I will give for the life of the world.

52 And the Jews strove among themselves, saying, How can this fellow
give his flesh to eat?

53 Then Jesus said to them, Truly truly I say to you, unless you eat the
flesh of the Son of man, and drink his blood, you shall not have life in
you. 54 Whoever eats my flesh and drinks my blood has eternal life, and I
will raise him up at the last day. 55 For my flesh is food indeed, and my
blood is drink indeed. 56 He who eats my flesh and drinks my blood dwells
in me, and I in him. 57 As the living Father has sent me, even so do I live
by my Father, and he that eats me, shall live by me. 58 This is the bread
which came from heaven – not as your fathers ate manna, and are dead.
He who eats of this bread shall live forever.

59 These things he said in the synagogue as he taught in Capernaum.
60 Many therefore of his disciples, when they heard this, said, This is a
hard saying. Who can abide the hearing of it?

61 Jesus knew in himself that his disciples murmured at it, and said to
His disciples are offended. them, Does this offend you?[b] 62 What if you see the Son of man ascend up
to where he was before? 63 It is the Spirit that quickens. The flesh profits
nothing: the words that I speak to you, are spirit and life. 64 But there are

some of you who do not believe. (For Jesus knew from the beginning who
they were that did not believe, and who would betray him.) 65And he said,
Therefore I said to you that no one can come to me, unless it be given to
him by my Father.

66From that time, many of his disciples went back and walked no more
with him. 67Then Jesus said to the twelve, Will you also go away? 68Then
Simon Peter answered, Lord, to whom shall we go? You have the words M't 16:16 Mk 8:29
of eternal life, 69and we believe and know that you are Christ, the Son of Lu 9:20
the living God.

70Jesus answered them, Have I not chosen you twelve? And yet one of
you is a devil. 71He spoke this of Judas Iscariot, the son of Simon. For it
was he who would betray him, and was one of the twelve.

The Notes

The bread of God (6:33) a) The bread of God is he who comes down from heaven, etc: The word of the gospel (which is Christ) is the true and living bread of heaven that gives life to the whole world.

Offend (6:61) b) Does this offend you? That is, if my words do so offend you, what then will the performance of them do, when the Son of man actually does what he has now spoken?

Chapter 7

Jesus comes to Jerusalem at the feast, teaches the Jews, and reproves them. There are different opinions of him among the people. The Pharisees rebuke the temple officers because they have not seized him, and chide Nicodemus for taking his part.

After that, Jesus went about in Galilee, and would not go about in Judea,
because the Jews were seeking to kill him. 2The Jews' tabernacle feast
was at hand. 3His brethren therefore said to him, Go on, and go into Judea,
so that your disciples can see the works that you do. 4For there is no man
who does anything secretly when he himself seeks to be known openly. If
you do such things, show yourself to the world. 5(For as yet his brethren
did not believe in him.)

6Then Jesus said to them, My time is not yet come, but your time is
always at hand. 7The world cannot hate you, but me it hates, because I tes-
tify of it that its works are evil. 8You go up to this feast. I will not go up
yet to this feast, for my time is not yet full come.

9These words he said to them, and remained still in Galilee. 10But as
soon as his brethren[a] had gone up, then he also went up to the feast, not
openly, but as it were, privately.

11Then the Jews were looking for him at the feast, and said, Where is
he? 12And there was much murmuring concerning him among the people.
Some said, He is good, and others said, No, but he deceives the people.
13However no one spoke openly about him, for fear of the Jews.

14Midway through the feast, Jesus went up into the temple and taught.
15And the Jews marvelled, saying, How does he know the scriptures,
seeing that he was never taught?

16Jesus answered them and said, My doctrine is not mine, but his who
sent me. 17If any person desires to do his will, he will know concerning
the doctrine, whether it is of God or whether I speak of myself. 18He who
speaks of himself seeks his own glory. But he who seeks the glory of the
one who sent him, such a person is true, and no unrighteousness is in him.
19Did not Moses give you a law? And yet none of you keeps the law.[b]
Why are you going about to kill me?
20The people answered and said, You have a devil. Who is going
about to kill you?
[**One work**: ie, healed a man on the Sabbath. John 5:1-16]
21Jesus answered and said to them, I have done one work,* and you are
all troubled. 22Moses gave you circumcision, not because it is from Mo- Ge 17:9-14
ses, but from the fathers. And yet you on the Sabbath day circumcise a Lev 12:3
man. 23If a man on the Sabbath day may receive circumcision without
breaking the law of Moses, do you take offence at me, because I have
made a man every whit whole on the Sabbath day? 24Do not judge ac-
cording to the outward appearance, but judge with righteous judgment.
25Then some of the people of Jerusalem said, Is this not the man they
are going about to kill? 26Look, he speaks boldly, but they say nothing to
him. Do the rulers know indeed that this is the very Christ? 27But we
know this man, where he is from, and when Christ comes, no one will
know where he is from.
28Then Jesus cried out in the temple as he taught, saying, You know
me; and where I am from, you know. And yet I am not come of myself,
but he who sent me is true, whom you do not know. 29I know him, for I
am of him, and he has sent me.
30Then they would have apprehended him, but no man laid hands on
him, because his time was not yet come. 31Many of the people believed on
him and said, When Christ comes, will he do more miracles than this man
has done?
32The Pharisees heard that the people rumoured such things about him.
So then the Pharisees and high priests sent officers forth to seize him.
33Then Jesus said to them, Yet a little while I am with you, and then I go
to him who sent me. 34You will seek me, and will not find me; and where
I am, there you cannot come.
35Then the Jews said between themselves, Where will he go, that we
will not find him? Will he go among the Gentiles, who are scattered all
abroad, and teach the Gentiles? 36What manner of saying is this that he
said: You will seek me, and will not find me, and where I am, there you
cannot come?
If anyone thirsts, let him come.
37In the last day, the great day of the feast, Jesus stood and cried out,
saying, If anyone thirsts, let him come unto me and drink. 38He who be- Isa 12:3; 43:20; 44:3; 55:1.
lieves on me, as says the scripture, out of his belly shall flow rivers of the
water of life.
39He spoke this of the Spirit, which those who believed on him would
receive. For the Holy Spirit was not yet there, because Jesus was not yet
glorified. 40Many of the people, when they heard this saying, said, Of a

truth, this is a prophet. [41]Others said, This is the Christ. Some said, Will the Christ come out of Galilee? [42]Does the scripture not say that Christ will come of the seed of David, and out of the town of Bethlehem, where David was? Mic 5:2 M't 2:5,6

[43]So was there dissension among the people about him. [44]And some of them wanted to seize him, but no man laid hands on him.

[45]Then the officers went to the high priests and Pharisees, who said to them, Why have you not brought him? [46]The officers answered, Never did any man speak as this man does. [47]Then the Pharisees answered them, Are you also deceived? [48]Do any of the rulers or of the Pharisees believe on him? [49]But the common people who do not know the law are cursed.

Rulers and Pharisees believe not.

[50]Nicodemus (he who had come to Jesus by night, and was one of them) said to them, [51]Does our law judge any man before it hears him and knows what he has done? [52]They answered and said to him, Are you also of Galilee? Search and look, for no prophet arises out of Galilee.

[53]And every man went to his own house.

The Notes

His brethren (7:10)

a) The Hebrews understand by this word *brother* [plural *brethren*] all descendants, relations not immediate, neighbours, and all who are of one stock. Genesis 13:8, Romans 9:3. [Ed: Rogers believed in the perpetual virginity of Mary. He wishes to show how the 'brethren' of Jesus may mean his half brothers or more distant relations.]

Of keeping the law (7:19)

b) None of you keeps the law, etc: Of the keeping of the law, see Matthew 5:19 & 20.

Chapter 8

A woman is caught in adultery. Christ delivers her. The freedom of those who follow Christ. They accuse him of having the devil with him, and go about to stone him.

And Jesus went to the Mount of Olives, [2]and early in the morning came again into the temple. And all the people came to him, and he sat down and taught them. [3]And the scribes and Pharisees brought to him a woman caught in adultery, and set her in the midst, [4]and said to him, Teacher, this woman was caught in adultery, even in the act. [5]Moses in the law commanded us that such should be stoned. What therefore do you say? Lev 20:10

[6]And they said this to bait him, to have something to accuse him of.

Jesus stooped down, and with his finger wrote on the ground. [7]And while they continued asking him, he lifted himself up and said to them, Let him who is without sin among you, cast the first stone at her. [8]And again he stooped down and wrote on the ground. De 17:7

[9]And as soon as they heard that, they went out one by one, the eldest first. And Jesus was left alone, and the woman standing in the centre. [10]When Jesus lifted up himself again and saw no one but the woman, he said to her, Woman, where are they, your accusers? Has no one condemned you? [11]She said, No one, Lord. And Jesus said, Neither do I condemn you. Go, and sin no more.[a]

Go and sin no more.

[12]Then Jesus spoke to them again, saying, I am the light of the world.

He who follows me shall not walk in darkness, but will have the light of 1Jo 1:5-7
life. [13]The Pharisees said to him, You bear witness of yourself; your wit-
ness is not true.

[14]Jesus answered and said to them, Though I bear witness of myself,
yet my witness is true, for I know where I came from and where I am
going. But you do not know where I come from or where I am going.
[15]You judge after the flesh. I judge no one; [16]and yet if I do judge, my
judgment is true. For I am not alone, but it is I and the Father who sent De 17:6;
me. [17]It is also written in your law that the testimony of two men is true. 19:15.
[18]I am one who bears witness of myself, and the Father who sent me bears M't 18:16 2Co 13:1
witness of me.

[19]Then they said to him, Where is your father?

Jesus answered, You know neither me, nor yet my Father. If you had
Christ is his doctrine. known me, you would have known my Father also.

[20]These words Jesus spoke in the treasury, as he taught in the temple.
And no man laid hands on him, for his time was not yet come.

[21]Then Jesus said again to them, I go my way; and you will seek me,
and will die in your sins. Where I go, there you cannot come.

[22]Then the Jews said, Will he kill himself? For he says, Where I go,
there you cannot come.

[23]And he said to them, You are from beneath. I am from above. You
are of this world. I am not of this world. [24]I said therefore to you that you
will die in your sins. For unless you believe that I am he, you will die in Ro 3:25
your sins.

[25]Then they said to him, Who are you? And Jesus said to them, Even
the very same thing that I say to you. [26]I have many things to say, and to
judge of you. Yea, and he who sent me is true. And I speak in the world
those things that I have heard from him.

[27]However, they did not understand that he was speaking of his Fa-
ther. [28]Then Jesus said to them, When you have lifted up on high the Son
of man, then you will know that I am he, and that I do nothing of myself,
but as my Father has taught me, even so I speak. [29]And he who sent me is
with me. The Father has not left me alone, for I do always those things
that please him.

[30]As he spoke these words, many believed on him. [31]Then Jesus said
to those Jews who believed on him, If you continue in my words, then you
are my very disciples, and shall know the truth; [32]and the truth shall make
you free.

Abraham's seed. [33]They answered him, We are Abraham's seed, and were never bond
to any man. Why do you say then, You shall be made free?

[34]Jesus answered them, Truly truly I say to you that whoever commits
sin, is the servant of sin. [35]And the servant does not abide in the house Ro 6:16
forever. But the Son abides forever. [36]If the Son therefore makes you free,
then you are free indeed. [37]I know that you are Abraham's seed. But you
seek means to kill me, because my sayings have no place in you. [38]I speak
that which I have seen with my Father, and you do that which you have

seen with your father.

[39]They answered and said to him, Abraham is our father.

The deeds of Abraham.

Jesus said to them, If you were Abraham's children, you would do the deeds of Abraham. [40]But now you are going about to kill me, a man who has told you the truth, which I have heard from God. This Abraham did not do. [41]You do the deeds of your father.

Then they said to him, We were not born of fornication. We have one Father, who is God.

They do not know his speech.

[42]Jesus said to them, If God were your Father, then you would love me. For I proceeded forth and come from God. Neither did I come of myself, but he sent me. [43]Why do you not know my speech? Even because you cannot abide the hearing of my words. [44]You are of your father, the devil, and your will is to follow the desires of your father. He was a murderer from the beginning, and did not abide in the truth, because there is no truth in him. When he speaks a lie, he speaks of his own nature. For he is a liar, and the father of lies. [45]And because I tell you the truth, therefore you do not believe me. [46]Which of you can rebuke me of sin? If I speak the truth, why do you not believe me? [47]He who is of God, hears God's words. You therefore do not hear them, because you are not of God.

1Jo 3:8

Christ called a Samaritan and a devil.

[48]Then the Jews answered and said to him, Are we not right to say that you are a Samaritan and have a devil?

[49]Jesus answered, I have no devil. But I honour my Father, and you have dishonoured me. [50]I do not seek my own glory, but there is one who seeks and judges. [51]Truly truly I say to you, if a person keeps my sayings,* he shall never see death.

[**Keeps my sayings** or words: Chrysostom>this refers not only to keeping faith, but also a pure life (*Hom/John*)]

[52]Then said the Jews to him, Now we know that you have a devil. Abraham is dead, and also the prophets, and yet you say, If anyone keeps my sayings, he will never taste of death. [53]Are you greater than our father Abraham, who is dead? And the prophets are dead. Who do you make yourself out to be?

[54]Jesus answered, If I honour myself, my honour is of no value. It is my Father who honours me, whom you say is your God, [55]and yet you have not known him. But I know him. And if I said I did not know him, I would be a liar like you. But I know him, and keep his word. [56]Your father Abraham was glad to see my day, and he saw it and rejoiced.[b]

[57]Then the Jews said to him, You are not yet fifty years old, and have you seen Abraham?

[58]Jesus said to them, Truly truly I say to you, before Abraham was, I am.

[59]Then they took up stones to cast at him. But Jesus hid himself, and went out of the temple.

The Notes

Go and sin no more (8:11)

a) The gospel does not preach remission of sins to us so that we will continue in sin, but so that we will change our life and walk in a new life of the Spirit, never purposing to sin any more.

Abraham was glad to see my day (8: 56)

b) All the holy fathers that were before the coming of Christ, from the beginning of the world, had the same faith in Christ that we have who are called Christian.

Chapter 9

Christ makes the man who was born blind able to see.

And as Jesus passed by, he saw a man who was blind from his birth. [2]And
his disciples asked him, saying, Master, who did sin: this man, or his
father and mother, that he was born blind? [3]Jesus answered, Neither has
this man sinned, nor yet his father and mother, but it is so that the works
of God may be shown on him. [4]I must work the works of him that sent me
while it is day. The night comes, when no man can work.* [5]As long as I
am in the world, I am the light of the world.

The night is when the true knowledge of Christ, how he only justifies, is lost. Then no man can work a good work in the sight of God, however glorious his works appear.

[6]As soon as he had thus spoken, he spat on the ground and made clay
of the spittle, and rubbed the clay on the eyes of the blind man, [7]and said
to him, Go and wash in the pool of Siloam (which translated, means Sent).
He went his way and washed, and came back seeing. [8]The neighbours and
people that had seen him before, how he was a beggar, said, Is this not the
man who sat and begged? [9]Some said, This is the man. Others said, He is
like him. But he himself said, I am he.

The blind man and the pool of Siloam.

[10]They said to him, How were your eyes opened then? [11]He answered
and said, The man that is called Jesus made clay and anointed my eyes,
and said to me, Go to the pool Siloam and wash. And I went and washed,
and received my sight.

[12]They said to him, Where is he? He said, I do not know.

The man that was blind is brought before the Pharisees.

[13]Then they brought to the Pharisees the man who a little before had
been blind. [14]For it was the Sabbath day when Jesus had made the clay
and opened his eyes. [15]Then again the Pharisees also asked him how he
had received his sight. He said to them, He put clay upon my eyes, and I
washed, and do see. [16]Then some of the Pharisees said, This man is not of
God, because he does not keep the Sabbath day. Others said, How can a
man who is a sinner do such miracles? And there was disagreement a-
mong them. [17]Then they spoke to the blind man again: What do you say
about him, since he has opened your eyes? And he said, He is a prophet.

[18]But the Jews did not believe concerning the fellow, that he had been
blind and received his sight, until they called the father and mother of him
who had received his sight. [19]And they asked them, saying, Is this your
son, whom you say was born blind? How then does he now see?

The blind man's parents are questioned.

[20]His father and mother answered them and said, We know well that
this is our son, and that he was born blind. [21]But by what means he now
sees, that we do not know. Or who has opened his eyes, we do not know.
He is old enough; ask him. Let him answer for himself.

[22]His father and mother spoke such words because they feared the
Jews. For the Jews had decided already that if anyone confessed that Jesus
was the Christ, he would be excommunicated out of the synagogue.
[23]Therefore his father and mother said, He is old enough; ask him.

[24]Then again they called the man who had been blind and said to him,

Give God the praise. We know that this man is a sinner.

[25]He answered and said, Whether he is a sinner or not, I do not know. One thing I am sure of: I was blind, and now I see.

[26]Then they said to him again, What did he do to you? How did he open your eyes?

[27]He answered them, I told you already, and you did not hear. Why do you want to hear it again? Do you also want to be his disciples?

[28]Then they berated him and said, You are his disciple. We are Moses' disciples. [29]We are sure that God spoke with Moses. This fellow, we do not know where he is from.

[30]The man answered and said to them, This is a marvellous thing, that you do not where he is from, seeing he has opened my eyes. [31]For we are sure that God does not hear sinners.[a] But if anyone is a worshipper of God and does his will, him he hears. [32]Since the world began it has never been heard that any man opened the eyes of someone that was born blind. [33]If this man were not of God, he could have done nothing.

The man who had been blind is excommunicated.

[34]They answered and said to him, You are altogether born in sin, and do you teach us? And they cast him out.

[35]Jesus heard that they had excommunicated the man, and as soon as he found him, he said to him, Do you believe on the Son of God? [36]He answered and said, Who is it, Lord, so that I can believe on him? [37]And Jesus said to him, You have seen him, and he it is who talks with you.

[38]And he said, Lord, I believe! and worshipped him.

Judgment: blindness.

[39]Jesus said, I have come for judgment into this world, so that those who do not see may see, and those who see, may be made blind.

The Pharisees say that they see, and therefore their sin remains.

[40]And some of the Pharisees who were with him heard these words and said to him, Are we then blind? [41]Jesus said to them, If you were blind, you would have no sin. But now you say, We see. Therefore your sin remains.

The Notes

God hears not sinners (9:31)

a) That is, God hears none who do not repent or intend to leave their evil life.

Chapter 10

Christ is the true shepherd, and the door of the sheep. Some say Christ has a devil and is mad. Some say he does not speak the words of a man that has a devil. Because he tells the truth, the Jews take up stones to cast at him, call his preaching blasphemy, and go about to take him.

Truly truly I say to you, He who does not enter into the sheepfold by the door, but climbs up some other way, the same is a thief and a robber. [2]He who goes in by the door is the shepherd of the sheep; [3]to him the porter opens, and the sheep hear his voice, and he calls his own sheep by name and leads them out. [4]And when he has sent forth his own sheep, he goes before them, and the sheep follow him, for they know his voice. [5]A stranger they will not follow, but will flee from him. For they know not the voice of strangers.

6 This similitude Jesus spoke to them, but they did not understand the things that he was saying to them.

Christ is the door.

7 Then Jesus spoke to them again: Truly truly I say to you, I am the door of the sheep. 8 All, even as many as came before me, are thieves and robbers; but the sheep did not hear them. 9 I am the door. If anyone enters in by me, he will be safe, and will go in and out, and find pasture. 10 The thief comes not but to steal, kill, and destroy. I have come so that they may have life, and have it more abundantly.

Christ is the good shepherd.

11 I am the good shepherd. The good shepherd gives his life for the sheep. 12 But a hired servant who is not the shepherd, neither are the sheep his own, sees the wolf coming and leaves the sheep and flees, and the wolf catches them and scatters the sheep. 13 The hired servant flees because he is a hired servant and does not care for the sheep.

Isa 40:11
Eze c34
Zec 11:16,17

14 I am the good shepherd, and know my own, and am known by my own. 15 As my Father knows me, even so do I know my Father. And I give my life for the sheep. 16 And other sheep I have who are not of this fold. Them also must I bring, so that they may hear my voice, and so that there may be one flock and one shepherd.

17 Therefore does my Father love me: because I put my life from me so that I may take it back again. 18 No man takes it from me, but I put it away of myself. I have power to put it from me, and have power to take it again. This commandment I have received from my Father.

19 And there was dissension again among the Jews because of these sayings, 20 and many of them said, He has a devil, and is mad. Why do you listen to him? 21 Others said, These are not the words of a man that has a devil. Can a devil open the eyes of the blind?

[**Feast of the Dedication**: now called Hanukkah, instituted in 165 BC to commemorate the re-consecration of the temple in Jerusalem after it had been desecrated during persecutions under Antiochus Epiphanes]

22 And it was at Jerusalem the feast of the Dedication,* 23 and it was winter. And Jesus walked in Solomon's porch. 24 Then the Jews came round about him and said to him, How long are you going to keep us in doubt? If you are the Christ, tell us plainly.

1Macc 4

25 Jesus answered them, I told you, and you do not believe. The works that I do in my Father's name, they bear witness of me. 26 But you do not believe, because you are not of my sheep. 27 As I said to you, my sheep hear my voice, and I know them, and they follow me, 28 and I give to them eternal life. And they shall never perish, neither shall any man pluck them out of my hand. 29 My Father who gave them to me is greater than all, and no one is able to take them out of my Father's hand. 30 And I and my Father are one.

31 Then the Jews again took up stones, to stone him. 32 Jesus answered them, Many good works have I shown you from my Father. For which of them would you stone me? 33 The Jews answered him, saying, We do not stone you for your good works, but for your blasphemy, and because you, being a man, make yourself God.

34 Jesus answered them, Is it not written in your law: I say, you are gods? 35 If he called them gods to whom the word of God was spoken (and

Ps 82:6

the scripture cannot be broken), [36]do you then say to him whom the Father has sanctified and sent into the world, You blaspheme, because I said I am the Son of God? [37]If I do not the works of my Father, believe me not. [38]But if I do, then though you do not believe me, yet believe the works, so that you may know and believe that the Father is in me, and I in him.

Believe the works.

[39]Again they went about to seize him, but he escaped out of their hands. [40]And he went away again beyond the Jordan, into the place where John before had baptized, and stayed there. [41]And many people resorted to him and said, John did no miracle, but all the things that John spoke about this man are true.

[42]And many believed on him there.

Chapter 11

Christ raises Lazarus from death. The high priests and Pharisees gather a council against him. He gets himself out of the way.

A certain man was sick, named Lazarus of Bethany, the town of Mary and her sister Martha. [2]It was that Mary who anointed Jesus with oyntment and wiped his feet with her hair whose brother Lazarus was sick. [3]And his sisters sent to him, saying, Lord, behold, he whom you love is sick.

[4]When Jesus heard that, he said, This infirmity is not unto death, but for the laud of God, so that the Son of God may be praised by reason of it.

[5]Jesus loved Martha and her sister and Lazarus. [6]Then, after he had heard that he was sick, he remained still two days in the same place where he was. [7]Then after that, he said to his disciples, Let us go into Judea again. [8]His disciples said to him, Master, lately the Jews tried to stone you, and will you go there again?

[9]Jesus answered, Are there not twelve hours in the day? If a man walks in the day, he does not stumble, because he sees the light of this world. [10]But if a man walks in the night, he stumbles, because there is no light in him.

[11]This he said, and after that, he said to them, Our friend Lazarus sleeps, but I go to wake him out of sleep. [12]Then his disciples said, Lord, if he sleeps, he will do well enough. [13]However Jesus was speaking of his death. But they thought that he had spoken of the natural sleep. [14]Then Jesus said to them plainly, Lazarus is dead. [15]And I am glad for your sakes that I was not there, so that you may believe. But let us go to him.

[**Didymus**: the Twin]

[16]Then Thomas who is called Didymus* said to the disciples, Let us also go, so that we may die with him.

[**Fifteen furlongs**: about two miles]

[17]Then Jesus went, and found that Lazarus had lain in his grave four days already. [18]Bethany was near Jerusalem, about fifteen furlongs* off, [19]and many of the Jews had come to Martha and Mary to comfort them over their brother. [20]Martha, as soon as she heard that Jesus was coming, went and met him, but Mary sat still in the house.

[21]Then Martha said to Jesus, Lord, if you had been here, my brother would not be dead. [22]But nevertheless, I know that whatever you ask of

God, God will give you. 23 Jesus said to her, Your brother will rise again.
24 Martha said to him, I know that he will rise again in the resurrection at
the last day.

25 Jesus said to her, I am the resurrection and the life. He who believes
on me, yea though he be dead, yet shall he live.[a] 26 And whoever lives and
believes on me, shall never die. Do you believe this?

27 She said to him, Yes, Lord. I believe that you are Christ, the Son of
God who was to come into the world.

28 And as soon as she had so said, she went her way and called Mary
her sister quietly, saying, The Teacher has come and is calling for you.
29 And Mary, as soon as she heard that, arose quickly and went to him.

30 Jesus had not yet come into the town, but was in the place where
Martha met him. 31 Then the Jews that were with Mary in the house and
comforting her, when they saw that she rose up hastily and went out, fol-
lowed her, saying, She is going to the grave, to weep there.

32 Then when Mary arrived where Jesus was and saw him, she fell
down at his feet, saying to him, Lord, if you had been here, my brother
would not be dead.

33 When Jesus saw her weep, and the Jews who came with her also
weep, he groaned in the spirit, and was troubled in himself, 34 and said,
Where have you laid him? They said to him, Lord, come and see. 35 And
Jesus wept. 36 Then the Jews said, See how he loved him! 37 And some of
them said, Could not he who opened the eyes of the blind, have made also
that this man should not have died? 38 Jesus again groaned in himself, and
came to the grave. It was a cave, and a stone lay against it. 39 And Jesus
said, Take away the stone.

Martha, the sister of him who was dead, said to him, Lord, by this
time he will smell, for he has been dead four days. 40 Jesus said to her, Did
I not say to you that if you believed, you would see the glory of God?

41 Then they took away the stone from the place where the dead man
was laid. And Jesus lifted up his eyes and said, Father, I thank you, be-
cause you have heard me. 42 I know that you hear me always. But because
of the people that stand by, I said this – so that they may believe that you
have sent me.

Lazarus is raised from death.

43 And when he thus had spoken, he cried with a loud voice, Lazarus,
come forth! 44 And he that was dead came forth wrapped hand and foot
with grave bonds,* and his face was bound about with a head-cloth.

[**Grave bonds**: cloth wrappings for burial]

Jesus said to them, Loose him and let him go.

45 Then many of the Jews who had come to Mary and seen the things
that Jesus did, believed on him. 46 But some of them went their ways to the
Pharisees and told them what Jesus had done.

47 Then the high priests and the Pharisees gathered a council and said,
What should we do? This man does many miracles. 48 If we let him go on
this way, everyone will believe on him, and the Romans will come and
take away our country and the people.

49 And one of them named Caiaphas, who was the high priest that same

year, said to them, You perceive nothing at all, [50]nor yet consider that it is
better for us that one man die for the people, and not that all the people
perish. [51]This he spoke not of himself, but, being high priest that same
year, he prophesied that Jesus would die for the people – [52]and not for the
people only, but that he would gather together in one the children of God
that were scattered abroad.

[53]From that day forth they took counsel together about how to put him
to death. [54]Jesus therefore no longer walked openly among the Jews, but
went his way from there to a region near to a wilderness, into a village
called Ephraim, and there continued with his disciples.

[55]And the Jews' Passover was at hand, and many people went out of
the country up to Jerusalem before the Passover, to purify themselves.
[56]Then they sought for Jesus, and spoke between themselves as they stood
in the temple: What do you think, seeing he is not coming to the feast?
[57]The high priests and Pharisees had given a commandment that if anyone
knew where he was, they should report it, so that they might seize him.

The Notes

I am the resurrection and the life (11:25)

a) That is, I am the author of resurrection and life, for those who believe in me I will raise up at the last day into life everlasting, and those who are dead shall live by me, because they believe in me.

Chapter 12

Mary anoints Christ's feet. Judas murmurs. Christ defends her, and rides into Jerusalem.

Then, six days before the Passover, Jesus went to Bethany, where Lazarus
was who had been dead, and whom Jesus raised from death. [2]There they
made him a supper, and Martha served. Lazarus was one of those who sat
at the table with him. [3]Then Mary took a pound of oyntment called nard,
perfect and precious, and anointed Jesus' feet, and wiped his feet with her
hair. And the house was filled with the fragrance of the oyntment.

[4]Then one of his disciples, named Judas Iscariot (Simon's son, who M't 26:6-16
afterward betrayed him), said, [5]Why was this oyntment not sold for three Mk 14:3-11 Lu 7:36-38
hundred denarii, and given to the poor? [6]He said this, not because he
cared for the poor, but because he was a thief, and kept the bag, and car-
ried that which was given. [7]Then Jesus said, Let her alone. She kept it for
the day of my burial. [8]The poor you will always have with you, but me
you will not always have.

[9]A great many of the Jews learned that he was there, and they went to
Bethany, not for Jesus' sake only, but also to see Lazarus, whom he had
raised from death. [10]The high priests therefore held a council, how they
could put Lazarus to death also, [11]because on his account many of the
Jews went away and believed on Jesus.

[12]On the next day, many people who had come to the feast, when they
heard that Jesus was coming to Jerusalem, [13]took branches of palm trees,
Hosanna and went and met him, and cried, Hosanna! Blessed is he that comes in

the name of the Lord, the king of Israel! [14]And Jesus got a young donkey and sat on it, according to that which was written: [15]Fear not, daughter of Zion. Behold, your king comes, sitting on a donkey's colt.

Isa 62:11 Zec 9:9 M't 21:1-11 Mk 11:1-10 Lu 19:28-38

[16]These things his disciples did not understand at the first. But when Jesus was glorified, then they remembered that such things were written of him, and that people had done such things to him.

[17]The people that had been with Jesus when he called Lazarus out of his grave and raised him from death were speaking about it. [18]Therefore the crowd met him, because they heard that he had done such a miracle. [19]The Pharisees therefore said among themselves, See how we are accomplishing nothing? Look, the world is going away after him.

[**Bethsaida**: a fishing village, the home of Peter, Andrew, and Philip]

[20]There were among them certain Greeks who came to pray at the feast. [21]They came to Philip, who was of Bethsaida, a village in Galilee, and asked him, saying, Sir, we would like to see Jesus. [22]Philip went and told Andrew, and in turn Andrew and Philip told Jesus.

The wheat seed must die to bring forth fruit.

[23]And Jesus answered them, saying, The hour is come that the Son of man must be glorified. [24]Truly truly I say to you, unless the wheat seed falls into the ground and dies, it remains alone. If it dies, it brings forth much fruit. [25]He who loves his life will destroy it, and he who hates his life in this world will keep it unto life eternal.[a] [26]If anyone serves me, let him follow me, and where I am, there also shall my servant be. And if anyone serves me, him will my Father honour.

1Co 15:36

M't 16:24-28 Mk 8:34-38 Lu 9:32-27; 17:33.

[27]Now is my soul troubled, and what shall I say? Father, deliver me from this hour? But for this cause I have come to this hour. [28]Father, glorify your name.

Then there came a voice from heaven: I have glorified it, and will glorify it again. [29]Then the people that stood by and heard said, It thundered! Others said an angel spoke to him.

[When he is lifted up, he will draw unto him people from all nations]

[30]Jesus answered and said, This voice came not because of me, but for your sakes. [31]Now is the judgment of this world; now shall the prince of this world be cast out. [32]And I, if I be lifted up from the earth, will draw all peoples unto me.

[33]This Jesus said, signifying what death he would die.

[34]The people answered him, We have heard out of the law that Christ endures forever, so how do you say then that the Son of man must be lifted up? Who is that Son of man?

Isa 40:8

[35]Then Jesus said to them, Yet a little while is the light with you. Walk while you have light, lest the darkness come on you. He who walks in the dark does not know where he is going. [36]While you have light, believe on the light, so that you may be the children of the light.

These things Jesus spoke and departed, and hid himself from them. [37]And though he had done so many miracles before them, yet they did not believe on him, [38]so that the saying of Isaiah the prophet might be fulfilled, what he spoke: Lord, who believes our message? and to whom is the arm of the Lord revealed? [39]Therefore they could not believe, because Isaiah says again: [40]He has blinded their eyes and hardened their hearts, so

He has blinded their eyes and hardened their hearts.

Isa 53:1

that they will not see with their eyes and understand with their hearts and be reformed, and I would heal them. [41]Such things Isaiah said when he saw his glory and spoke of him.

Isa 6:8-10
M't 13:11-15
Mk 4:11,12
Lu 8:10
Ac 28:25-27
Ro 11:7-10

[42]Nevertheless, among the chief rulers many believed on him. But because of the Pharisees, they would not acknowledge it, lest they should be excommunicated. [43]For they loved the praise that is given by men more than the praise that comes of God.

[44]And Jesus cried out and said, He who believes on me, believes not on me, but on him who sent me. [45]And he who sees me, sees him who sent me. [46]I am come a light into the world, so that whosoever believes on me will not remain in darkness. [47]And if a person hears my words and does not believe, I do not judge him. For I came not to judge the world, but to save the world. [48]He who refuses me, and does not receive my words, has one that judges him. The words that I have spoken, they will judge him in the last day. [49]For I have not spoken of myself, but the Father who sent me, he gave me a commandment, what I should say and what I should speak. [50]And I know that this commandment is life everlasting. Whatsoever I speak therefore, even as the Father has said to me, so I speak.

The Notes

He who hates his life, etc. (12:25)

a) That is, he who can be content to lose his temporal life in this world for Christ's sake and his word, shall live forever, as is said in Matthew 10:37-39, Mark 8:34-38, Luke 9:23-26, etc.

Chapter 13

Christ washes the disciples' feet, tells them of Judas the traitor, and commands them to love one another earnestly.

Before the feast of Passover, when Jesus knew that his hour had come to depart out of this world to the Father, having loved his own who were in the world, to the end he loved them. [2]And when supper was ended, after the devil had put in the heart of Judas Iscariot, Simon's son, to betray him, [3]Jesus, knowing that the Father had given all things into his hands, and that he had come from God and was going to God,[4] arose from supper and laid aside his upper garments, and took a towel and girded himself. [5]After that, he poured water into a basin and began to wash his disciples' feet, and to wipe them with the towel with which he was girded.[a]

M't 26:14-16
Mk 14:10
Lu 22:3

Jesus washes his disciples' feet.

[6]Then he came to Simon Peter. And Peter said to him, Lord, shall you wash my feet? [7]Jesus answered and said to him, What I am doing, you do not understand now, but you will know hereafter. [8]Peter said to him, You shall not wash my feet while the world stands! Jesus answered him, If I do not wash you, you will have no part with me. [9]Simon Peter said to him, Lord, not my feet only, but also my hands and my head! [10]Jesus said to him, He who is washed needs not but to wash his feet, and is clean every whit. And you my disciples are clean – but not all. [11]For he knew his betrayer. Therefore he said, you are not all clean.

[V10 is emended to show the plural number of 'you' when Jesus answered Simon Peter]

[12]After he had washed their feet, and received his clothes and was

seated again, he said to them, Do you understand what I have done to
you? 13You call me Teacher and Lord, and you say well, for so I am. 14If I
then, your Lord and Teacher, have washed your feet, you also ought to
wash one another's feet. 15For I have given you an example, so that you
will do as I have done to you. 16Truly truly I say to you, the servant is not M't 10:24
greater than his master, nor the messenger greater than he who sent him. Lu 6:40
17If you understand these things, happy are you if you do them.

18I am not speaking of you all. I know whom I have chosen. But so
that the scripture may be fulfilled, he who eats bread with me has lifted up
his heel against me.[b] 19Now I tell you before it happens, so that when it Ps 41:9
has come to pass, you may believe that I am he. 20Truly truly I say to you,
he who receives whomever I send, receives me. And he who receives me, M't 10:40,41
receives him who sent me. Lu 10:16

21When Jesus had said these things, he was troubled in the spirit and
testified, saying, Truly truly I say to you, that one of you will betray me. M't 26:20-25

22And then the disciples looked on one another, doubting of whom he Mk 14:17-21
spoke. 23There was one of his disciples who leaned on Jesus' bosom,
whom Jesus loved. 24Simon Peter motioned to him, that he should ask of
whom he spoke. 25He then, as he leaned on Jesus' breast, said to him,
[**Sop**: a piece of bread for dipping in wine or some other liquid, or for scooping food] Lord, who is it? 26Jesus answered, It is he to whom I give a sop when I
have dipped it. And he wet a sop and gave it to Judas Iscariot, Simon's
son. 27And after the sop, Satan entered into him.[c]

Then Jesus said to him, What you are going to do, do quickly.

28But no one at the table understood for what intent he spoke to him.
29Some of them thought that because Judas had the bag, Jesus had said to
him, Buy those things that we need for the feast, or that he should give
something to the poor.

30As soon then as he had received the sop, Judas went immediately
Judas leaves the Supper. out. And it was night. 31When he had gone out, Jesus said, Now is the Son
of man glorified, and God is glorified by him. 32If God is glorified by him,
God will also glorify him in himself, and will straightaway glorify him.

33Dear children, yet a little while I am with you. You will seek me,
and as I said to the Jews, where I am going, you cannot come. 34Also I say
to you now, a new commandment I give to you: to love together. As I 1Jo 2:3-11
have loved you, so also should you love one another. 35By this shall all
men know that you are my disciples, if you have love for one another.

36Simon Peter said to him, Lord, where are you going? Jesus answered
him, Where I am going you cannot follow me now, but you will follow M't 26:33-35 Mk 14:29-31
me afterwards. 37Peter said to him, Lord, why can I not follow you now? I Lu 22:33
will give my life for your sake. 38Jesus answered him, Will you give your
life for my sake? Truly truly I say to you, the cock will not crow till you
have denied me three times.

The Notes

The washing of the disciples' feet (13:5) a) He washes their feet to declare that he came to minister to others, and not to be ministered to; and further, to teach by this washing that his ministration was to purge and wash away the dirt and defilement of sin, which is done by the shedding of his blood. For the blood of Christ, sprinkled into our hearts by the word of his gospel and received by faith, cleanses us from all sin.

To lift up his heel (13:18) b) This is to cast down by violence. For whomever you kick or trip with the heel, you throw to the ground.

After the sop, Satan entered (13:27) c) Satan was entered into Judas before, as this evangelist affirms in the beginning of this chapter (13:2). But now he began more to exert his strength, and more openly to show himself. In a similar way, the apostles had the Holy Spirit before Christ's resurrection, when they believed in him, when they confessed him to be the Son of God, etc. But then they evidently received him when Christ was ascended (Acts 2:1-4). [Ed> Here Rogers compares Satan's inner suggestion to Judas (John 13:2) with the Holy Spirit's teaching of the disciples, who "had" the Spirit before Christ's resurrection; both do put thoughts on our hearts. Rogers then concludes that what is expressed as the later entry of Satan into Judas at v13:27 may be likened to the disciples later "evidently" (openly, visibly) receiving the Spirit, presumably at Pentecost. The wording is a little ambiguous, but the thrust of this note seems to be to deny that the Holy Spirit later entered the disciples to indwell them in any different way or measure than before, because they always "had him," and after the ascension the Spirit began simply to be more active in them. But at John 14:17 in the Matthew Bible, Jesus says that the Holy Spirit was then *with* the disciples and would later be *in* them, which indicates something different. This issue is examined in *The Story of the Matthew Bible.*]

Chapter 14

He arms his disciples with consolation against trouble, and promises them the Holy Spirit, the Spirit of Comfort.

Let not your hearts be troubled. And he said to his disciples, Let not your hearts be troubled. Believe in
God, and believe in me. [2]In my Father's house are many rooms. If it were
not so, I would have told you. I go to prepare a place for you. [3]And if I go
to prepare a place for you, I will come again and receive you unto myself,
so that where I am, there you may be also. [4]And where I go, you know;
and the way, you know.
[5]Thomas said to him, Lord, we do not know where you are going.
How then is it possible for us to know the way?
[6]Jesus said to him, I am the way, the truth, and the life. And no one
comes to the Father except by me. [7]If you have known me, you have
known my Father also. And now you know him, and have seen him.
[8]Philip said to him, Lord, show us the Father, and it is enough for us.
[9]Jesus said to him, Have I been so long a time with you, and yet you
have not known me? Philip, he who has seen me has seen the Father. And
how do you say then, Show us the Father? [10]Do you not believe that I am
in the Father, and the Father in me? The words that I speak to you, I do
not speak of myself, but the Father who dwells in me is he who does the
works. [11]Believe me, that I am in the Father, and the Father in me. At the
least, believe me for the very works' sake. [12]Truly truly I say to you, He
who believes on me, the works that I do, he also will do; and greater
works than these he will do, because I go to my Father. [13]And whatever M't 7:7-11;
you ask in my name, that I will do, so that the Father may be glorified by 21:22.
A promise. the Son.[a] [14]If you ask anything in my name, I will do it. Mk 11:23-25 Joh 16:24

[**Comforter**: who strengthens, encourages, helps, and gives comfort]

15 If you love me, keep my commandments. 16 And I will pray the Fa-
ther, and he will give you another Comforter,* so that he may be with you
forever, 17 which is the Spirit of Truth[b] – whom the world cannot receive,
because the world neither sees him nor knows him. But you know him.
For he dwells with you and shall be in you. 18 I will not leave you comfort-
less, but will come to you.

19 Yet a little while, and the world will see me no more. But you will
see me. For I live, and you will live. 20 That day you will know that I am in
my Father, and you in me, and I in you.

By keeping the commandments a person is known, that he loves God.

21 He who has my commandments and keeps them, that is he who
loves me. And he who loves me shall be loved by my Father, and I will
love him and will show my own self to him.

22 Judas said to him (not Judas Iscariot), Lord, what is the reason that
you will show yourself to us, and not to the world?

23 Jesus answered and said to him, If a person loves me and will keep
my sayings, my Father also will love him, and we will come to him and
will dwell with him. 24 He who does not love me, does not keep my say-
ings. And the words that you hear are not mine, but the Father's who sent
me.

25 This I have spoken to you being yet present with you. 26 But the
Comforter, which is the Holy Spirit (whom my Father will send in my
name), he will teach you all things, and bring all things to your remem-
brance, whatsoever I have told you.

27 Peace I leave with you; my peace I give to you. Not as the world
gives do I give to you. Let not your hearts be troubled, and do not fear.
28 You have heard how I said to you, I am going away, and coming again
to you. If you loved me, you would indeed rejoice because I said I am
going to the Father. For the Father is greater than I. 29 And now I have told
you before it comes, so that when it has come to pass, you may believe.

30 Hereafter I will not speak many words to you. For the ruler of this
world comes. And he has nothing in me, 31 but so that the world may know
that I love the Father, therefore as the Father gave me commandment,
even so I do. Arise, let us go from here.

The Notes

Glorified by the Son (14:13)

a) That the Father might be glorified by the Son, etc: The Father is glorified by the Son when we confess and give thanks that he gave his Son for us, to save us.

The Spirit of Truth (14:17)

b) He is called the Spirit of Truth not only because he is true, but because he makes the people into whom he enters true. But without the Spirit, there is nothing but lies.

Chapter 15

The true vine. The husbandman and the branches. A doctrine of love. A sweet comfort against persecutions.

[**Husbandman**: one who practices husbandry, a farmer]

I am the true vine, and my Father is the husbandman.* 2 Every branch that
does not bear fruit in me, he will take away. And every branch that bears
fruit he will prune, so that it may bring forth more fruit. 3 Now you are

Clean through the words spoken: abide therein.

clean through the words that I have spoken to you. 4Abide in me, and let
me abide in you. As the branch cannot bear fruit of itself, unless it abides
in the vine, no more can you unless you abide in me.
5I am the vine, and you are the branches. He who abides in me, and I
in him, the same brings forth much fruit. For without me you can do
nothing. 6If a person does not abide in me, he is cast forth like a branch,
and is withered; and men gather it and cast it into the fire, and it burns. 7If
you abide in me, and my words also abide in you, ask what you will, and
it shall be done for you. 8In this is my Father glorified: that you bear much 1Jo 3:22
fruit, and be made my disciples.

Covenant. To keep the law makes us to continue in the love and favour of Christ.

9As the Father has loved me, even so have I loved you. Continue in
my love. 10If you keep my commandments, you will abide in my love,
even as I have kept my Father's commandments, and abide in his love.
11These things I have spoken to you so that my joy may remain in you,
and so that your joy may be full. 12This is my commandment: that you Eph 5:2
love together, as I have loved you. 13Greater love than this has no man, 1Th 4:9
than to bestow his life for his friends. 14You are my friends, if you do 1Jo3:18; 4:7.
whatsoever I command you. 15Henceforth I do not call you servants, for
the servant knows not what his lord does, but I have called you friends.
For all that I have heard from my Father, I have made known to you.
16You have not chosen me, but I have chosen you, and ordained you,
that you should go and bring forth fruit, and that your fruit should endure;
that whatever you ask of the Father in my name, he should give it to you.
17This I command you: love one another. 18If the world hates you, you
know that it hated me before it hated you. 19If you were of the world, the
world would love its own. However because you are not of the world, but
I have chosen you out of the world, therefore the world hates you. 20Re-
member the saying that I said to you: the servant is not greater than his
lord. If they have persecuted me, so will they persecute you. If they have
kept my sayings, so will they keep yours. 21But they will do all these
things to you for my name's sake, because they have not known him who
sent me. 22If I had not come and spoken to them, they would not have had
sin. But now they have nothing to cloak their sin with.
23He who hates me, hates my Father. 24If I had not done works among M't c23
them which no other man did, they would not have sin. But now they have
seen, and yet have hated both me and my Father, 25even so that the saying Ps 69:4
is fulfilled that is written in their law: They hated me without a cause. Lu 24:44
26But when the Comforter is come, whom I will send to you from the
Father, which is the Spirit of truth who proceeds of the Father, he will
testify of me. 27And you shall bear witness also,[a] because you have been
with me from the beginning.

The Notes

Witness of Christ (15:27)

a) Whereas at John 5:34 Christ says he receives no witness of man, it is to be understood that for his own part he needed none. But for our sakes it was necessary that his disciples should testify his truth to us, and therefore he says here, You shall bear witness of me also.

Chapter 16

Consolation for trouble. Prayers are heard through Christ.

These things I have said to you so that you are not made to stumble. [2]They will excommunicate you; yea, the time shall come that whoever kills you will think that he does God service. [3]And such things they will do to you because they have not known the Father, nor me. [4]But I have told you these things so that when that hour comes, you may remember them, that I told you so.

M't 24:9

I did not say these things to you at the beginning, because I was present with you. [5]But now I go my way to him who sent me, and none of you asks me, Where are you going? [6]But because I have said such things to you, your hearts are full of sorrow. [7]Nevertheless, I tell you the truth: it is better for you that I go away. For if I do not go away, the Comforter will not come to you. But if I depart, I will send him to you. [8]And when he is come, he will rebuke the world of sin, and of righteousness, and of judgment: [9]of sin, because they do not believe on me;[a] [10]of righteousness, because I go to my Father and you will see me no more; [11]and of judgment, because the chief ruler of this world is judged already.

Sin. Righteousness. Judgment.

[12]I have yet many things to say to you, but you cannot receive them now. [13]However, when he is come (I mean the Spirit of truth), he will lead you into all truth. He will not speak of himself, but whatever he hears, that he will speak, and he will show you things to come. [14]He will glorify me, for he will receive of mine and will show it to you. [15]All things that the Father has are mine. Therefore I said to you that he will take of mine and show it to you.

[16]After a while you will not see me, and again after a while you will see me, because I go to the Father.

[17]Then some of his disciples said between themselves, What is this that he says to us, After a while you will not see me, and again after a while you will see me? and, Because I go to the Father? [18]They said therefore, What is this that he says, After a while? We cannot understand what he says.

[19]Jesus perceived that they wanted to question him and said to them, You enquire about this between yourselves, that I said, After a while you will not see me, and again after a while you will see me. [20]Truly truly I say to you, you will weep and lament, and the world will rejoice. You will sorrow; but your sorrow will be turned to joy.

[**When she travails**: that is, labours in childbirth]

[21]A woman when she travails has sorrow, because her hour is come. But as soon as she is delivered of the child, she remembers no more the anguish, for joy that a man is born into the world. [22]And you now are in sorrow. But I will see you again, and your hearts will rejoice, and no one will take your joy from you. [23]And in that day you will ask me no question. Truly truly I say to you, whatever you ask the Father in my name, he will give you. [24]Until now you have asked nothing in my name. Ask, and you will receive, so that your joy may be full.

M't 7:7-11; 21:22. Mk 11:23-25 Joh 14:14 Jas 1:6

Promise

[25]These things I have spoken to you in parables. The time will come

when I will speak no more to you in figures, but I will show you plainly
from my Father. 26At that day, you will ask in my name. And I say not to
you that I will speak to my Father for you. 27For the Father himself loves
you, because you have loved me, and have believed that I came out from
God. 28I went out from the Father and came into the world; and I leave the
world again and go to the Father.

29His disciples said to him, Lo, now you speak plainly, and you use no
parable. 30Now we know that you understand all things, and there is no
need for anyone to ask you any question. Therefore we believe that you
came from God.

31Jesus answered them, Now you do believe. 32Behold, the hour draws
near, and is already come, that you shall be scattered every man his ways,
and will leave me alone. And yet I am not alone, because the Father is M't 26:31 Mk 14:27
with me.

33These words I have spoken to you so that in me you may have
peace. For in the world you will have tribulation. But be of good cheer: I
have overcome the world.

The Notes

The Holy Spirit will rebuke of sin (16:9)

a) Of sin because they do not believe on me: unbelief is the sin that condemns the world. (By *the world*, understand here the wicked, reproved, and unfaithful, not all the creatures that are in the world.) And faith is the righteousness of believers. This the world and natural reason will not accept, but would be justified and saved by their own works. This is the thing of which the Holy Spirit will rebuke the world, and show that it shall be justly condemned.

Chapter 17

The most hearty and loving prayer of Christ to his Father for all those who receive the truth.

These words Jesus spoke, and lifted up his eyes to heaven, and said,
Father, the hour is come. Glorify your Son, so that your Son may glorify
you. 2For you have given him power over all flesh, so that he may give
Eternal life. eternal life to as many as you have given him. 3This is life eternal: to
know you, the only true God, and Jesus Christ whom you have sent.

4I have glorified you on the earth. I have finished the work that you
gave me to do. 5And now glorify me, Father, with your own self – with
the glory that I had with you before the world was. 6I have declared your
name to the men that you gave me out of the world.[a] Yours they were, and Ps 22:22
you gave them to me, and they have kept your sayings. 7Now they know
that all things, whatsoever you have given me, are of you. 8For I have
given to them the words that you gave me, and they have received them,
and know surely that I came out from you, and do believe that you did
send me.

9I pray for them – and pray not for the world,[b] but for those whom you
He prays for his own. have given me. For they are yours. 10And all mine are yours, and yours
are mine, and I am glorified in them. 11And now I am no longer in the
world, but they are in the world, and I come to you. Holy Father, keep in

your own name those whom you have given me, so that they may be one, as we are. [12]While I was with them in the world, I kept them in your name. Those whom you gave me I have kept, and none of them is lost, except that lost child, so that the scripture may be fulfilled.

Ps 41:9; 109:8.

[13]Now I come to you. And I speak these words in the world so that they may have my joy full in them. [14]I have given them your words. And the world has hated them, because they are not of the world, just as I am not of the world. [15]I ask not that you take them out of the world, but that you keep them from evil. [16]They are not of the world, as I am not of the world. [17]Sanctify them with your truth. Your word is truth. [18]As you sent me into the world, so have I sent them into the world. [19]And for their sakes I sanctify myself, so that they also may be sanctified through the truth.

[20]I pray not for them alone, but also for those who will believe on me through their preaching: [21]that they all may be one, as you, Father, are in me, and I in you; that they may also be one in us, so that the world may believe that you have sent me. [22]And the glory that you gave me, I have given them, so that they may be one as we are one, [23]I in them and you in me, so that they may be made perfect in one, and so that the world may know that you have sent me, and have loved them as you have loved me.

[24]Father, I will that those whom you have given me be with me where I am, that they may see the glory that you have given me. For you loved me before the making of the world. [25]O righteous Father, the very world has not known you, but I have known you, and these have known that you have sent me. [26]And I have declared to them your name, and will declare it, so that the love with which you have loved me may be in them, and so that I may be in them.

The Notes

I have declared your name (17:6)

a) That is, I have manifested and made known your renown and glory, that you are merciful, forgive sins for my sake, are good and righteous, etc.

I pray not for the world (17:9)

b) That is, I pray for the chosen, not for the wicked, froward, and unbelievers.

Chapter 18

Christ is betrayed. The words of his mouth smite the officers to the ground. Peter strikes off Malchus' ear. Jesus is brought before Annas, Caiaphas, and Pilate.

When Jesus had spoken these words, he went forth with his disciples over the brook Kidron, where there was a garden into which he entered with his disciples. [2]Judas who betrayed him also knew the place, for Jesus often resorted there with his disciples. [3]Judas then, after he had received a band of men, and officers of the high priests and Pharisees, went there with lanterns and firebrands* and weapons.

M't c26 Mk c14 Lu c22

[**Firebrands**: wooden sticks kindled at the fire, used in ancient times for light]

[4]Then Jesus, knowing all things that would come on him, went forth and said to them, Whom do you seek? [5]They answered him, Jesus of Nazareth. Jesus said to them, I am he.

Judas who betrayed him also stood with them. [6]But as soon as Jesus
had said to them, I am he, they went backwards and fell to the ground.
[7]And he asked them again, Whom do you seek? They said, Jesus of
Nazareth. [8]Jesus answered, I said to you, I am he. If you seek me, let these
go their way. [9]This was to fulfil the saying that he had spoken: Of those Joh 6:39; 17:12.
whom you gave me, I have not lost one.

Malchus' ear.

[10]Simon Peter had a sword, and drew it and struck the high priest's
servant, and cut off his right ear. The servant's name was Malchus. [11]Then
Jesus said to Peter, Put up your sword into the sheath. Shall I not drink of
the cup which my Father has given me?

[12]Then the company of men and the captain and the officers of the
Jews took Jesus and bound him, [13]and led him away to Annas first. For he
was the father-in-law of Caiaphas, who was the high priest that same year.
[14]Caiaphas was the one who gave counsel to the Jews that it was good that
one man should die for the people.

[15]And Simon Peter followed Jesus, and so did another disciple. That
disciple was known to the high priest, and went in with Jesus into the
palace of the high priest. [16]But Peter stood at the door outside. Then that
other disciple, who was known to the high priest, went out and spoke to M't 26:33-35
the maid that kept the door, and brought Peter in. [17]Then the maid that Mk 14:29-31 Lu 22:55-62
kept the door said to Peter, Are you not one of this man's disciples? He Joh 18:25-27

Peter begins to deny his Lord.

said, I am not. [18]The servants and the officers were standing there, and
had made a fire of coals, for it was cold and they were warming them-
selves. Peter also stood among them and warmed himself.

[19]The high priest asked Jesus about his disciples and about his teach-
ing. [20]Jesus answered him, I spoke openly in the world. I always taught in
the synagogue and in the temple where all the Jews come together, and in
secret I have said nothing. [21]Why do you ask me? Ask those who heard
me what I said to them. They can tell what I said.

[22]When he had thus spoken, one of the officers who stood by struck
Jesus on the face, saying, Is this how you answer the high priest?

[23]Jesus answered him, If I have spoken wrongly, bear witness of the
wrong. If I have spoken well, why do you hit me?

[24]And Annas sent him bound to Caiaphas, the high priest.

[25]Simon Peter was standing and warming himself, and they said to
him, Are you not also one of his disciples? He denied it and said, I am
not. [26]One of the servants of the high priest (a relative of the man whose
ear Peter cut off) said to him, Did I not see you in the garden with him?
[27]Peter denied it again; and immediately, the cock crew.

[28]Then they led Jesus from Caiaphas into the hall of judgment. It was
the morning, and they themselves did not go into the judgment hall lest

Fear of defilement.

they should be defiled, but so that they could eat the Passover lamb.

[Nonetheless, the hypocrites defile themselves with malice and false dealing]

[29]Pilate then went out to them and said, What accusation do you bring
against this man? [30]They answered and said to him, If he were not an evil-
doer, we would not have delivered him to you. [31]Then Pilate said to them,
You take him, and judge him according to your own law.

Then the Jews said to him, It is not lawful for us to put any man to death. [32]This was to fulfil the words of Jesus, which he spoke signifying how he would die.[a]

[33]Then Pilate entered into the judgment hall again, and called Jesus and said to him, Are you the king of the Jews? [34]Jesus answered, Do you say that of yourself, or did others tell you this about me?

M't 27:11-26
Mk 15:2-15
Lu 23:1-25

[35]Pilate answered, Am I a Jew? Your own nation and high priests have delivered you to me. What have you done?

[36]Jesus answered, My kingdom is not of this world.[b] If my kingdom were of this world, then my servants would surely fight so that I would not be delivered to the Jews. But now my kingdom is not from here.

[37]Pilate said to him, Are you a king then?

Jesus answered, You say rightly that I am a king. For this cause I was born, and for this cause I came into the world: that I should bear witness to the truth. And all who are of the truth hear my voice.

What is truth?

[38]Pilate said to him, What is truth?

And when he had said that, Pilate went out again to the Jews and said to them, I find in him no fault at all. [39]You have a custom that I should set one prisoner free to you at Passover. Do you want me to release to you the king of the Jews?

[40]Then they all cried out again, saying, Not him, but Barabbas!

Now that Barabbas was a robber.

The Notes

To fulfil Jesus' words (18:32)

a) This was to fulfil the words of Jesus, etc: He had said that he would be crucified by the Gentiles. Therefore Pilate must pass sentence on him, and not the Jews, for the performance of his word.

My kingdom is not of this world (18:36)

b) That is, my kingdom is not a worldly kingdom, which consists in strength, in armour, in men, in the sword, and in taking dominion over things of this material or worldly realm. But my kingdom is spiritual, and is in the hearts of the faithful, who are ruled not by the sword, but by the gospel.

Chapter 19

Christ is crucified. He commits his mother to John's care, sheds his blood, and is buried.

Then Pilate took Jesus and scourged him. [2]And the soldiers wound a crown of thorns and put it on his head. And they put on him a purple garment, [3]and said, Hail, King of the Jews! And they struck him on the face.

M't c27
Mk c15
Lu c23

His judge finds no fault in him.

[4]Pilate went forth again and said to the people, Look, I am bringing him out to you so that you may know that I find no fault in him. [5]Then Jesus came forth wearing the crown of thorns and the robe of purple. And Pilate said to them, Behold the man!

The people call for Jesus to be crucified.

[6]When the high priests and officers saw him, they cried out, saying, Crucify him, crucify him! Pilate said to them, You take him and crucify him, for I find no fault in him. [7]The Jews answered him, We have a law,

and by our law he ought to die, because he made himself the Son of God.
8When Pilate heard these words, he was the more afraid, 9and went
again into the judgment hall and said to Jesus, Where are you from? But
Jesus gave him no answer. 10Then Pilate said to him, Will you not speak
to me? Do you not know that I have the power to crucify you, and have
the power to set you free?

11Jesus answered, You could have no power at all against me unless it
were given you from above. Therefore he who delivered me to you is
more in sin.

12And from then on Pilate sought means to release him. But the Jews
cried out, saying, If you let him go, you are not Caesar's friend! For who-
ever makes himself a king, is against Caesar.

[**Day before the Sabbath**: Friday, the Passover, also called the day of preparation] [**Sixth hour**: About 6:00 am. John reckons time here by the Roman method of the day beginning at midnight. See note on M't 27:45 concerning Jewish reckonings of time]

13When Pilate heard that saying, he brought Jesus forth and sat down
to give sentence in a place called The Pavement, but in the Hebrew
tongue, Gabbatha. 14It was the day before the Sabbath* that falls in the
Passover feast, and about the sixth hour.* And he said to the Jews, Behold
your king! 15They cried, Away with him, away with him, crucify him!
Pilate said to them, Shall I crucify your king? The high priests answered,
We have no king but Caesar.

16Then Pilate delivered him to them, to be crucified.

He is crucified.

17And they took Jesus and led him away. And he bore his cross, and
went out to a place called the Place of Dead Men's Skulls, which is
named in Hebrew, Golgotha. 18There they crucified him, and two others
with him, one on either side, and Jesus in the middle. 19And Pilate wrote
his title and put it on the cross. The writing was, JESUS OF NAZARETH,
KING OF THE JEWS. 20Many of the Jews read this title, because the place
where Jesus was crucified was near the city. And it was written in He-
brew, Greek, and Latin.

21Then the high priests of the Jews said to Pilate, Do not write King of
the Jews, but that he said, I am King of the Jews. 22Pilate answered, What
I have written, I have written.

23Then the soldiers, when they had crucified Jesus, took his garments
and made four parts, to every soldier a part; and also his coat. The coat
was without seam, woven throughout, 24and they said to one another, Let
us not tear it, but cast lots who should have it. This was to fulfil the
scripture that says: They parted my garments among them, and for my Ps 22:18
coat did cast lots. 25And the soldiers did such things indeed.

Then there stood by the cross of Jesus his mother, and his mother's
sister Mary, the wife of Cleophas, and Mary Magdalene. 26When Jesus
saw his mother and the disciple whom he loved standing by, he said to his
mother, Woman, behold your son. 27Then he said to the disciple, Behold
your mother. And from that hour, the disciple took her for his own.

Vinegar: the sour fruit of the vineyard, which the Lord receives at the last, and all is finished. Coverdale> His bitter drink is unto us a blessed medicine (*Fruitful*)]

28After that, when Jesus perceived that all things were performed, so
that the scripture would be fulfilled, he said, I thirst! 29There was standing Ps 22:15; 69:21.
nearby a vessel full of vinegar, and they filled a sponge with vinegar,* and
wound it about with hyssop, and put it to his mouth. 30As soon as Jesus

had received of the vinegar, he said, It is finished! And he bowed his head
and gave up the spirit.
[31]The Jews then, because it was the day before the Sabbath, in order
that the bodies should not remain upon the cross on the Sabbath day (for
that Sabbath day was a high day), requested Pilate that their legs might be
broken and that they might be taken down. [32]Then the soldiers came and
broke the legs of the first man and of the other that was crucified with
Jesus. [33]But when they came to Jesus and saw that he was dead already,
they did not break his legs. [34]But one of the soldiers thrust him in the side
with a spear, and immediately there came out blood and water.
[35]And he who saw it has borne witness, and his testimony is true. And
he knows that he speaks the truth, so that you may believe also. [36]These Ex 12:46
things were done so that the scripture would be fulfilled: Not one of his Nu 9:12 Ps 34:20
bones shall be broken. [37]And again another scripture says: They shall look Zec 12:10
on him whom they pierced.
[38]After that, Joseph of Arimathea (who was a disciple of Jesus, but
secretly for fear of the Jews) asked Pilate if he could take down the body
of Jesus. And Pilate gave him permission.
[39]And Nicodemus came also, who at the beginning had gone to Jesus
His body is prepared for by night, and brought myrrh and aloes mingled together, about a hundred
burial. pound weight. [40]Then they took the body of Jesus and wound it in linen
cloths with the spices, as the custom of the Jews is to bury. [41]And in the
place where Jesus was crucified was a garden, and in the garden a new
sepulchre, in which no man had ever been laid. [42]There they laid Jesus,
because of the Jews' Sabbath eve. For the sepulchre was near at hand.

Chapter 20

The resurrection of Christ, who appears to Mary Magdalene
and to all his disciples, to their great comfort.

Mary Magdalene The morrow after the Sabbath day, Mary Magdalene came early to the
sepulchre when it was still dark, and saw the stone taken away from the
tomb. [2]Then she ran and went to Simon Peter, and to the other disciple M't c28 Mk c16
whom Jesus loved, and said to them, They have taken away the Lord out Lu c24
of the tomb, and we do not know where they have laid him.
[3]Peter went out, and that other disciple, and came to the sepulchre.
[4]They ran both together, and the other disciple outran Peter and came first
to the sepulchre. [5]And he stooped down and saw the linen cloths lying
there, but did not go in. [6]Then came Simon Peter following him, and went
The head linen. into the sepulchre and saw the linen cloths lying there, [7]and the cloth that
had been around his head not lying with the linen cloth, but wrapped
together in a place by itself. [8]Then that other disciple went in also, who
had come first to the sepulchre; and he saw and believed.[a] [9]For as yet they
did not know not the scriptures, that he must rise again from death. [10]And
the disciples went away again to their own homes.
[11]Mary stood outside at the sepulchre, weeping. And as she wept, she
bowed herself into the sepulchre [12]and saw two angels in white sitting, the

one at the head and the other at the feet, where they had laid the body of Jesus. [13]And they said to her, Woman, why do you weep? She said to them, Because they have taken away my Lord, and I do not know where they have laid him.

[14]When she had said this, she turned herself back, and saw Jesus standing, but did not know that it was Jesus. [15]Jesus said to her, Woman, why do you weep? Whom are you seeking?

She, supposing he was a gardener, said to him, Sir, if you have carried him away, tell me where you have laid him so that I may get him.

[16]Jesus said to her, Mary!

She turned herself about and said to him, Rabboni! (which is to say, Teacher!).

[17]Jesus said to her, Do not touch me, for I am not yet ascended to my Father.[b] But go to my brethren and say to them, I am ascending to my Father and your Father, to my God and your God.

[18]Mary Magdalene went and told the disciples that she had seen the Lord, and that he had spoken such things to her.

Jesus appears to his disciples.

[19]The same day at night, which was the day after the Sabbath day, when the doors were shut where the disciples were assembled together for fear of the Jews, Jesus came and stood in their midst, and said to them, Peace be with you. [20]And when he had so said, he showed to them his hands and his side. Then were the disciples glad, when they saw the Lord.

[21]Then Jesus said to them again, Peace be with you. As my Father sent me, so I also send you.

[22]And when he had said that, he breathed on them and said to them, Receive the Holy Spirit. [23]Whosever sins you remit, they are remitted to them, and whosever sins you retain, they are retained.[c]

[24]But Thomas (called Didymus), one of the twelve, was not with them when Jesus came. [25]The other disciples said to him, We have seen the Lord! And he said to them, Unless I see in his hands the print of the nails, and put my finger in the marks of the nails, and put my hand into his side, I will not believe.

Jesus appears again to the disciples.

[26]And after eight days his disciples were again inside, and Thomas with them. Then Jesus came when the doors were shut, and stood in their midst and said, Peace be with you.

[27]After that he said to Thomas, Bring your finger here, and see my hands, and bring your hand and put it into my side; and be not faithless, but believing.

[28]Thomas answered and said to him, My Lord and my God!

[29]Jesus said to him, Thomas, because you have seen me, therefore you believe. Happy are those who have not seen, and yet believe! 1Co 15:3-8

[30]And Jesus did many other signs in the presence of his disciples, which are not written in this book. [31]These are written so that you may believe that Jesus is Christ, the Son of God, and so that in believing you may have life through his name.

The Notes

And he believed (20:8) a) Chiefly, he believed that Christ was taken out of the sepulchre, as Mary Magdalene had told him before.

Touch me not (20:17) b) That is, because you do not believe that I am risen very God, but am carnal as I was before I suffered death, therefore do not touch me.

Whose sins, etc (20:23) c) Whose sins you remit, are remitted: Look in Matthew 18:18 and note (a) thereon.

Chapter 21

He appears to his disciples again by the Sea of Tiberias, and commands Peter earnestly to feed his sheep.

[The **Sea of Tiberius** is an alternate name for the sea or lake of Galilee]

After that, Jesus showed himself again to the disciples at the Sea of
Tiberias. And this is how he showed himself: 2there were together Simon
Peter, and Thomas who is called Didymus, and Nathanael of Cana (a town
of Galilee), and the sons of Zebedee, and two others of the disciples.
3Simon Peter said to them, I'm going fishing. They said to him, We also
will go with you.

They went their way and entered into a boat straightaway, and that
night they caught nothing. 4But when the morning was now come, Jesus
stood on the shore. Nevertheless, the disciples did not know that it was
Jesus. 5Jesus said to them, Sirs, do you have any fish? They answered
him, No. 6And he said to them, Cast out the net on the right side of the
boat, and you will find some.

They cast out, and then they were not able to draw the net in for the number of fishes.

[**Girded his mantle**: ie tied or belted his mantle, a loose, sleeveless cloak]

7Then the disciple whom Jesus loved said to Peter, It is the Lord!
When Simon Peter heard that it was the Lord, he girded his mantle* to
him (for he had stripped down), and sprang into the sea.

8The other disciples came by boat – for they were not far from land,
but about a hundred yards – and they drew in the net with fishes. 9As soon
as they had come to land they saw hot coals, and fish laid on them, and
bread. 10Jesus said to them, Bring some of the fish that you have now
caught. 11Simon Peter stepped forth and drew the net to land full of great
fishes, a hundred and fifty-three. And for all there were so many, yet the
net was not torn.

12Jesus said to them, Come and eat. And none of the disciples ven-
tured to ask him, Who are you? because they knew that it was the Lord.
13Jesus then came and took bread, and gave it to them, and the fish
likewise.

14And this is now the third time that Jesus appeared to his disciples after he was risen again from death.

15When they had eaten, Jesus said to Simon Peter, Simon son of Jonah, do you love me more than these?

He said to him, Yes, Lord, you know that I love you.

*He loves Christ who feeds his lambs and sheep.

Jesus said to him, Feed my lambs.* 16He said to him again the second
time, Simon son of Jonah, do you love me?

He said to him, Yes, Lord, you know that I love you.

Jesus said to him, Feed my sheep. [17]He said to him the third time,
Simon, do you love me?

And Peter sorrowed because he said to him the third time, Do you
love me? And he said to him, Lord, you know all things. You know that I
love you.

Jesus said to him, Feed my sheep. [18]Truly truly I say to you, when you
were young, you girded yourself and walked where you wished. But when
you are old, you will stretch forth your hands, and another will gird you
and lead you where you do not wish. 2Pe 1:14

[19]He spoke this signifying by what death Peter would glorify God.
And when he had said this, he said to him, Follow me.

[20]Peter turned about and saw the disciple whom Jesus loved following,
who also had leaned on his breast at supper and said, Lord, who is it that
will betray you? [21]When Peter saw him he said to Jesus, Lord, what about
this man?

[22]Jesus said to him, If I desire him to remain till I come, what is that to
you? Follow me.

[23]Then there went out a saying among the brethren that that disciple
would not die. But Jesus did not say to him that he would not die, but, If I
desire him to remain till I come, what is that to you?

[24]The same disciple is he who testifies of these things and wrote these
His testimony is true. things. And we know that his testimony is true.

[25]There are also many other things that Jesus did, which, if they were
written every one, I suppose the world could not contain the books that
would be written.[a]

Here ends the gospel
of Saint John.

The Notes

The world could not contain the books (21:25) a) This is figurative speech, which signifies that there were many things more to write about. But as Erasmus affirms in his paraphrases upon this place, there remains enough written as is necessary and sufficient for our salvation.

[Luke probably wrote this account in 60-62 AD, before the end of Paul's first Roman imprisonment]

The Acts
of the Apostles,
written by Saint Luke the Evangelist, who was present at the doings of them.

Chapter 1

The ascension of Christ. Matthias is chosen in Judas' place.

IN THE FORMER TREATISE (dear friend Theophilus), I have written of all
that Jesus began to do and teach [2]until the day in which he was taken up,
after he through the Holy Spirit had given commandments to the apostles
whom he had chosen. [3]To them also he showed himself alive after his
passion by many certain proofs, appearing to them during forty days and
speaking of the kingdom of God. [4]And he gathered them together and
instructed them not to depart from Jerusalem, but to wait for the promise Lu 24:49
of the Father – Of which (he said) you have heard from me; [5]for John bap- Joh 1:33
tized with water, but you will be baptized with the Holy Spirit, and that Ac 11:16
within this few days.

[6]When they had come together, they asked him, saying, Lord, will you
at this time restore again the kingdom to Israel? [7]And he said to them, It is
not for you to know the times or the seasons which the Father has put in
his own power. [8]But you will receive power from the Holy Spirit, who
shall come on you. And you will be my witnesses in Jerusalem, and in all
Judea and Samaria, and even to the world's end.

[9]After he had spoken these things, while they looked on, he was taken
up, and a cloud received him out of their sight. [10]And while they looked Mk 16:19 Lu 24:51
steadfastly up to heaven as he went, behold, two men stood by them in
white apparel, [11]who also said, Men of Galilee, why do you stand gazing
up into heaven? This same Jesus, who is taken up from you into heaven,
He will come back. will come back in the same way as you have seen him go into heaven.

[12]Then they returned to Jerusalem from the Mount of Olives, which is
near Jerusalem a Sabbath day's journey.[a] [13]And when they had come in,
they went up into an upper room where abode both Peter and James, John
and Andrew, Philip and Thomas, Bartholomew and Matthew, James the
son of Alphaeus, Simon the Zealot, and Judas, James' son. [14]These all
continued with one accord in prayer and supplication with the women,
and with Mary the mother of Jesus, and with his brethren.

[15]And in those days Peter stood up in the midst of the disciples (the
number of names that were together was about a hundred and twenty),
and said, [16]Men and brethren, this scripture had to be fulfilled, which the
Holy Spirit spoke before through the mouth of David concerning Judas,
who was a guide to those who took Jesus. [17]For he was numbered with us
and had obtained fellowship in this ministry. [18]And this Judas has now Ps 41:9
possessed a plot of ground with the reward of iniquity, and when he was Joh 18:3
hanged, burst in the middle, and all his bowels gushed out. [19]And this is
known to all the inhabiters of Jerusalem, insomuch that this field is called

in their mother tongue Akel Dama; that is to say, the Field of Blood. M't 27:3-10
[20]It is written in the book of Psalms: Let his habitation be void, and let
no one dwell in it; and his bishopric, let another take. [21]Therefore of these Ps 69:25
men who have been with us all the time that the Lord Jesus went in and Ps 109:8
out among us, [22]beginning at the baptism of John to the same day that he
was taken up from us, one must bear witness with us of his resurrection.

[23]And they proposed two: Joseph called Barsabas (whose surname
was Justus) and Matthias. [24]And they prayed, saying, You, Lord, who
know the hearts of all men, show which of these two you have chosen,
[25]so that one may take the place in this ministry and apostleship from
which Judas by transgression fell, that he might go to his own place.

Matthias is chosen

[26]And they cast their lots, and the lot fell on Matthias, and he was
counted with the eleven apostles.

The Notes

Sabbath day's journey (1:12)

a) A Sabbath day's journey was about a mile. See Mathew 24:20 and note (a).

Chapter 2

The coming of the Holy Spirit. The sermon of Peter before the crowds of people at Jerusalem, and the increase of the faithful.

[**The fiftieth day,** or Day of Pentecost in the Feast of Weeks or Feast of Harvest, one of 3 annual feasts that brought the Jews to Jerusalem]

[**With other tongues**: that is, in other languages, as further described in verses 8-12]

When the fiftieth day was come, they were all with one accord together in Ex 34:22
one place. [2]And suddenly there came a sound from heaven like the Lev 23:16
coming of a mighty wind, and it filled all the house where they sat. [3]And
there appeared to them cloven tongues, as if of fire, which sat upon each
of them. [4]And they were all filled with the Holy Spirit, and began to speak Ac 4:31;
with other tongues,* even as the Spirit gave them utterance. 19:6.

[5]And there were dwelling at Jerusalem Jews, devout men, who were
from all nations under heaven. [6]Hearing of this, a large crowd came to-
gether. And the people were astonished, because everyone heard them
speak his own tongue. [7]They all wondered and marvelled, saying among
themselves, Are not all these who speak from Galilee? [8]And how is that
we hear each his own tongue in which he was born? [9]Parthians, Medes,
and Elamites, and the inhabiters of Mesopotamia, of Judea, and of Cappa-
docia, of Pontus and Asia, [10]Phrygia, Pamphylia, and of Egypt, and of the
parts of Libya adjoining Cyrene, and strangers from Rome, Jews and
converts,* [11]Greeks and Arabians: we have heard them speak with our
own tongues about the great works of God. [12]They were all amazed, and
wondered, saying to one another, What does this mean? [13]Others mocked
them, saying, They are full of new wine.

*__Converts__: that is, heathen or Gentiles converted to the Jews' faith.

[14]But Peter stepped forth with the eleven, and lifted up his voice and
said to them, Men of Judea, and all ye who inhabit Jerusalem, let this be
known to you, and with your ears hear my words. [15]These are not drunk,
as you suppose, for it is yet but the third hour of the day. [16]But this is that
which was spoken by the prophet Joel: [17]It shall be in the last days, says
God, I will pour out of my Spirit upon all flesh.* And your sons and your

[**All flesh**: that is, not just Israel, but people from all nations and tongues]

daughters shall prophesy, and your young men shall see visions, and your
old men shall dream dreams. [18]And on my servants and on my hand-
maidens I will pour out of my Spirit in those days, and they will prophesy.
[19]And I will show wonders in heaven above, and signs in the earth be-
neath: blood and fire, and the vapour of smoke. [20]The sun shall be turned
into darkness, and the moon into blood, before that great and notable day Joe 2:31
of the Lord comes. [21]And it shall be that whosoever calls on the name of
the Lord, shall be saved. Ro 10:13 Joe 2:32

[22]Ye men of Israel, hear these words. Jesus of Nazareth was a man
accredited by God among you with miracles, wonders, and signs that God
did by him in the midst of you, as you yourselves know. [23]Him you have
taken by the hands of unrighteous persons, after he was delivered by the
determinate counsel and foreknowledge of God, and have crucified and
Sorrows of death loosed. slain. [24]But God has raised him up, and loosed the sorrows of death,
because it was impossible that he should be held by it. [25]For David speaks
of him: I foresaw God always before me. For he is on my right hand, that
I should not be shaken. [26]Therefore my heart rejoiced and my tongue was Ps 16:8-11
glad. Moreover also, my flesh shall rest in hope, [27]because you will not
leave my soul in hell, nor suffer your Holy One to see corruption. [28]You
The ways of life. have shown me the ways of life, and will make me full of joy with your
countenance.

[29]Men and brethren, let me freely speak to you of the patriarch David.
For he is both dead and buried, and his sepulchre remains with us to this
day. [30]Therefore, seeing he was a prophet, and knew that God had sworn
with an oath to him that the fruit of his loins would sit on his seat, [31]in that
Christ would rise again in the flesh, he saw beforehand and spoke of the 1 Ki 2:4
The promised resurrection. resurrection of Christ – that his soul would not be left in hell, nor would
his flesh see corruption. [32]This Jesus, God has raised up – whereof we are
all witnesses.

[33]Since now he is exalted by the right hand of God, and has received
The promised Spirit. from the Father the promise of the Holy Spirit, he has shed forth that
which you now see and hear. [34]For David did not ascend into heaven, but Ps 8:6
he said: The Lord said to my Lord, Sit on my right hand [35]until I make Ps 110:1
your enemies your footstool. [36]So therefore, let all the house of Israel 1Co 15:25-28.
know most certainly that God has made this same Jesus, whom you Heb 1:13; 2:8;10:13.
crucified, both Lord and Christ.

[37]When they heard this, they were pricked in their hearts and said to
Peter and to the other apostles, Men and brethren, what shall we do?

[38]Peter said to them, Repent and be baptized, every one of you, in the
name of Jesus Christ, for the remission of sins, and you shall receive the
gift of the Holy Spirit. [39]For the promise was made to you and to your
children, and to all that are afar off, even as many as the Lord our God
will call.

[40]And with many other words he bore witness and exhorted them,
saying, Save yourselves from this perverse generation. [41]Then those who
gladly received his preaching were baptized, and the same day there were

added to them about three thousand souls.

42 And they continued in the apostles' doctrine and fellowship, and in breaking of bread and in prayer. 43 And fear came over every soul. And many wonders and signs were shown by the apostles. 44 And all who believed kept themselves together and had all things common, 45 and sold their possessions and goods and distributed them to all, as anyone had need. 46 And they continued daily with one accord in the temple, and broke bread in every house and ate their food together, with gladness and singleness of heart praising God, 47 and had favour with all the people. And the Lord added to the congregation daily such as were to be saved.

All things had in common.

Chapter 3

The crippled man is restored to his feet. Peter preaches Christ to the people.

Peter and John went up together into the temple at the ninth hour of prayer. 2 And there was a certain man crippled from his mother's womb, whom they brought and laid at the temple gate called Beautiful, to ask alms of the people that entered into the temple. 3 Which man, when he saw Peter and John about to go into the temple, requested alms. 4 And Peter fastened his eyes on him with John and said, Look on us. 5 And he gave heed to them, trusting to receive something from them. 6 Then said Peter, Silver and gold I do not have, but such as I have, I give you. In the name of Jesus Christ of Nazareth, rise up and walk! 7 And he took him by the right hand and lifted him up. And immediately his feet and anklebones received strength. 8 And he sprang up, stood, and also walked, and entered with them into the temple, walking and leaping and lauding God.

Healing.

9 And all the people saw him walk and laud God. 10 And they knew him, that it was the man who sat and begged at the Beautiful Gate of the temple. And they were filled with wonder and astonishment at what had happened to him. 11 And as the lame man who was healed held Peter and John, all the people ran amazed to them in Solomon's porch.

12 When Peter saw this, he spoke to the people: Men of Israel, why do you marvel at this? Or why do you look so steadfastly on us, as though by our own power or holiness we had made this man walk? 13 The God of Abraham, Isaac, and Jacob, the God of our fathers, has glorified his Son Jesus, whom you delivered up and denied in the presence of Pilate when he had determined to release him. 14 But you denied the Holy and Just One, and asked for a murderer to be given to you, 15 and killed the Lord of Life – whom God has raised from death, of which we are witnesses.[a] 16 And his name, through the faith of his name, has made this man sound, whom you see and know. And the faith which is by him has given this man health in the presence of you all.

M't 27
Mk 15:12-15
Lu 23
Joh 18:39-40

17 And now, brethren, I know well that you did it through ignorance, as did also your leaders. 18 But those things that God before had shown by the mouth of all his prophets, how the Christ would suffer, he has fulfilled this way. 19 Repent therefore, and turn,[b] so that your sins may be put away

[Verse 20 is emended partly from Coverdale 1535]

when the time of refreshing comes, which we will have from the presence
of the Lord, [20]and when God will send him who now before is preached to
you; that is to say, Jesus Christ, [21]who must receive heaven until the time
that all things, which God has spoken by the mouth of all his holy
prophets since the world began, are restored again.

[22]For Moses said to the fathers: The Lord your God will raise up a
prophet for you, even from among your brethren, as he did me. Him you
must hear, in all things whatsoever he says to you. [23]For the time will
come that every soul who will not hear that same prophet, shall be de-
stroyed from among the people. [24]Also all the prophets from Samuel on-
wards, as many as have spoken, have likewise told of these days.

De 18:15, 18,19. Ac 7:37

[25]You are the children of the prophets, and of the covenant that God
made to our fathers, saying to Abraham: Even in your seed shall all the
kindreds of the earth be blessed. [26]First unto you has God raised up his
Son Jesus, and him he has sent to bless you, that every one of you should
turn from your wickedness.

Ge 22:18; 26:4; 28:14.

The Notes

The Lord of life, etc (3:15)

a) The Lord of life is even he who first did rise from death to life, and by whom all we must rise and live, etc.

Repent (3:19)

b) Repent and turn: look in Matthew 4:17 and note (a) thereon.

Chapter 4

The apostles are taken and brought before the council. They are forbidden to preach, but they turn themselves to prayer, and are more obedient to God than to men.

*In Jesus: that he was risen, and all would rise by him.

As they spoke to the people, the priests and the chief warden of the temple
and the Sadducees came upon them, [2]taking it grievously that they taught
the people and preached in Jesus the resurrection from death.* [3]And they
laid hands on them and put them in custody until the next day, for it was
now evening. [4]However, many of those who heard the word believed, and
the number of the men was about five thousand.

[5]And it happened on the next day that their rulers and elders and
scribes, [6]as Annas the chief Priest, and Caiaphas and John and Alexander,
and as many as were of the kindred of the high priests, gathered together
at Jerusalem, [7]and set the apostles before them and asked, By what power
or in what name have you done this, Sirs?

Peter speaks.

[8]Then Peter, full of the Holy Spirit, said to them, Ye rulers of the
people, and elders of Israel, [9]if we this day are examined concerning the
good deed done to the sick man, how he has been made whole, [10]let it be
known to you all, and to the people of Israel, that in the name of Jesus
Christ of Nazareth – whom you crucified, and whom God raised again
from death – even by him does this man stand here present before you,
healed. [11]Jesus is the stone cast aside by you builders, which is set in the
chief place of the corner. [12]Neither is there salvation in any other, nor yet
also is there any other name given to mankind in which we can be saved.

Jesus is the stone cast aside by the builders. Salvation.

Ps 118:22 M't 21:42 Mk 12:10,11 Lu 20:17,18 Ro 9:33

[13]When they saw the boldness of Peter and John, and understood that
they were unlearned men and lay people, they marveled. And they knew
them, that they had been with Jesus. [14]And seeing also the man that was
healed standing with them, they could not speak against it. [15]But they
ordered them to go aside out of the council, and conferred among them-
selves, [16]saying, What shall we do with these men? For a manifest sign
has been done by them, and is openly known to all who dwell in Jeru-
salem, and we cannot deny it. [17]But so that it spreads no further among the
people, let us threaten them, and charge them to speak to no one in this
name from now on.

[18]And they called them and ordered them not to speak or teach at all in
the name of Jesus. [19]But Peter and John answered them and said, Whether
God is more to be obeyed than man. it is right in the sight of God to obey you more than God, you judge. [20]For
we cannot but speak that which we have seen and heard.

[21]So they threatened them and let them go, and found no way to
punish them, because of the people. For all the people lauded God for the
miracle that was done. [22]For the man was over forty years old on whom
this miracle of healing had been shown.

[23]As soon as they were let go, they went to their companions and told
them all that the high priests and elders had said to them. [24]And when they
heard that, they lifted up their voices to God with one accord and said,
Lord, you are God who has made heaven and earth, the sea, and all that is
in them, [25]who by the mouth of your servant David has said: Why did the
heathen rage, and the people imagine vain things? [26]The kings of the earth Ps 2:1,2
stood up, and the rulers came together against the Lord and against his
Christ. [27]For of a truth, against your holy child Jesus, whom you have
anointed, both Herod and also Pontius Pilate, with the Gentiles and the
people of Israel, gathered themselves together, [28]to do whatever your hand
and your counsel determined before to be done. [29]And now, Lord, look
upon their threatenings, and grant to your servants to speak your word
with all confidence, [30]and stretch forth your hand so that healing and signs
and wonders may be done by the name of the holy child Jesus.

[31]And as soon as they had prayed, the place moved where they were
assembled together, and they were all filled with the Holy Spirit, and they
spoke the word of God boldly.

[32]And the whole number of those who believed were of one heart and
of one soul. Also, none of them said that any of the things that he pos-
All things in common. sessed was his own, but had all things in common. [33]And with great
power the apostles gave witness of the resurrection of the Lord Jesus. And
great grace was with them all. [34]Neither was there any among them that
lacked, for as many as possessed lands or houses sold them, and brought
the money from the things that were sold, [35]and laid it down at the
apostles' feet. And distribution was made to every person according to his
need. [36]And Joses, who was also called Barnabas by the apostles (which
means, son of consolation), who was a Levite of the country of Cyprus,
[37]had land and sold it, and laid the money down at the apostles' feet.

Chapter 5

The dissembling of Ananias and Sapphira is punished. Miracles are done by the apostles, who are seized, but the angel of God brings them out of prison. They are brought before the council. The advice of Gamaliel. The apostles are beaten. They rejoice in trouble.

Ananias and Sapphira.

A certain man named Ananias, with Sapphira his wife, sold some property, [2]and kept back part of the money (his wife also knowing of it), and brought a certain part and laid it down at the apostles' feet. [3]Then Peter said, Ananias, how is it that Satan has so filled your heart that you would lie to the Holy Spirit and keep away part of the proceeds of the land? [4]Did it not belong to you alone? And after it was sold, was the money not at your own disposal? How is it that you have conceived this thing in your heart? You have not lied to men, but to God.

[5]When Ananias heard these words, he fell down and gave up the spirit. And great fear came on all them that heard these things. [6]And the young men rose up, and put Ananias apart, and carried him out and buried him.

[7]And then, about the space of three hours after, his wife came in, unaware of what had happened. [8]And Peter said to her, Tell me, did you sell the land for so much? And she said, Yes, for so much. [9]Then Peter said to her, Why have you agreed together to tempt the Spirit of the Lord? Behold, the feet of those who have buried your husband are at the door, and will carry you out.

[10]Then she fell down straightaway at his feet and yielded up the spirit. And the young men came in and found her dead, and carried her out and buried her by her husband.

[11]And great fear came on all the congregation, and on as many as heard these things.

[12]By the hands of the apostles many signs and wonders were shown among the people. And they were all together with one accord in Solomon's porch. [13]And none of the rest dared join himself to them; nevertheless, the people held them in high regard.

The shadow of Peter.

[14]The number of those who believed in the Lord, both of men and women, grew more and more, [15]insomuch that they brought the sick into the streets and laid them on beds and pallets so that at least the shadow of Peter, when he came by, might fall on some of them. [16]Many people also came from the towns round about Jerusalem, bringing sick folks and those who were vexed with unclean spirits. And they were healed, every one.

[**Sadducees**: a Jewish party of the intertestamental period, consisting of a traditional ruling class of priests who rejected important doctrines, including retribution in a future life and the existence of angels]

[17]Then the chief priest rose up, and all they that were with him (which is the sect of the Sadducees*), and were full of indignation, [18]and laid hands on the apostles, and put them in the common prison. [19]But the angel of the Lord opened the prison doors by night, and brought them out and said, [20]Go; step forth, and speak in the temple to the people all the words of this life. [21]When they heard that, they entered into the temple early in the morning and taught.

The chief priest came, and those who were with him, and called a

council together with all the elders of the children of Israel, and sent to the
prison to fetch the apostles. 22When the officers came and did not find
them in the prison, they returned and reported, saying, 23We found the
prison shut as securely as was possible, and the guards standing outside
before the doors. But when we opened up, we found no one within.

24When the most chief priest and the chief warden of the temple and
the high priests heard these things, they were fearful about them, what this
might grow into. 25Then someone came and told them, Behold, the men
that you put in prison are standing in the temple and teaching the people.

26Then the chief warden of the temple went with officers, and brought
them without violence, because they feared to be stoned by the people.

27And when they had brought the apostles, they set them before the
council. And the chief priest asked them, 28saying, Did we not strictly
order you not to teach in this name? And look, you have filled Jerusalem
with your teaching, and you intend to bring this man's blood upon us.

29Peter and the other apostles answered and said, We ought more to Ge 26:5
God must be obeyed. obey God than men. 30The God of our fathers raised up Jesus, whom you Ex 15:17
slew, hanging him on a tree. 31Him God has lifted up with his right hand, De 11:8
to be a ruler and a saviour, to give repentance to Israel, and forgiveness of
sins. 32And we are his witnesses concerning these things, and so also is
the Holy Spirit, whom God has given to those who obey him.

33When they heard this, they were cut to the heart, and thought to kill
Gamaliel speaks. them. 34Then one in the council stood up, a Pharisee named Gamaliel, a
doctor of law greatly respected among all the people, and directed that the
apostles be put apart for a little while, 35and said to them, Men of Israel,
take heed to yourselves, what you intend to do regarding these men.
36Before these days, one Theudas rose up, claiming himself to be some-
body, and a number of men joined him – about four hundred. But he was
slain, and all the people who believed him were scattered abroad, and
brought to nothing. 37After this man, Judas of Galilee arose, in the time
when tribute began, and he drew away many people after him. He also
perished, and all, even as many as followed him, are scattered abroad.
38And now I say to you, restrain yourselves concerning these men. Let
them alone. For if the counsel of this work is of men, it will come to
nothing. 39But if it is of God, you cannot destroy it, and you might even be
found to be striving against God.

40And they agreed with him, and called the apostles, and beat them,
and ordered them not to speak in the name of Jesus, and let them go.

41And they departed from the council, rejoicing that they were counted
worthy to suffer rebuke for his name. 42And daily in the temple and in
every house they did not cease teaching and preaching Jesus Christ.

The Notes

Laid it down at the apostles' feet (5:2)

a) By the casting of his money at the apostles' feet, Ananias would have been counted to be one of the Christian congregation, and that one of the chief. But in holding part back, he demonstrated outwardly what he was; that is, subtle, and a very hypocrite, doubting the Holy

Spirit – which thing Peter, because he would in no case have it among that group, therefore punished so seriously.

Chapter 6

Ministers (or deacons) are ordained in the congregation to do service in necessary things of the body so that the apostles may attend only to the word of God. Stephen is accused.

In those days, as the number of the disciples grew, there arose a grudge
among the Greeks against the Hebrews, because their widows were
neglected in the daily distribution. 2Then the twelve called all of the
disciples together and said, It is not right that we should leave the word of
God and serve at the tables. 3Therefore, brethren, choose from among you
seven men of good reputation, and full of the Holy Spirit and wisdom,
whom we may appoint to this needful business. 4But we will give our-
selves continually to prayer and to the ministry of the word.
5And this proposal pleased the whole assembly. And they chose
Stephen, a man full of faith and of the Holy Spirit, and Philip, Prochorus,
Nicanor, Timon, Parmenas, and Nicolas, a convert from Antioch. 6These
they set before the apostles, and they prayed and laid their hands on them.
7And the word of God advanced, and the number of the disciples mul-
tiplied in Jerusalem greatly, and a great company of the priests accepted
the faith. 8And Stephen, full of faith and power, did great wonders and
miracles among the people.

[**Freedmen**: or Libertines, as older versions have, were persons who had earned or been granted freedom from slavery]

9Then some of those who were of the synagogue of the Freedmen* (as
it was called), and Cyrenians, and some from Alexandria and Cilicia and
Asia, arose and disputed with Stephen. 10But they could not resist the
wisdom and the spirit with which he spoke. 11Then they sent in men who
said, We have heard him speak blasphemous words against Moses and
against God. 12And they moved the people and the elders and the scribes,
and came upon him and caught him, and brought him to the council.
13And they brought forth false witnesses who said, This man does not
cease to speak blasphemous words against this holy place and the law,
14for we heard him say that this Jesus of Nazareth will destroy this place,
and will change the ordinances that Moses gave us.
15And all who sat in the council looked steadfastly on him, and saw
his face as it were the face of an angel.

Chapter 7

Stephen makes answer to his accusation, rebukes the hard-necked Jews, and is stoned to death.

Then the chief priest said, Is it really so?
2And Stephen said, Men, brethren and fathers, hearken to: The God of

The sermon of Stephen

glory appeared to our father Abraham while he was yet in Mesopotamia,
before he dwelt in Haran, 3and said to him, Come out of the country and Ge 12:1
away from your kindred, and come into the land that I will show you.

[4]Then he came out of the land of Chaldea and dwelt in Haran. And
after that, as soon as his father was dead, God brought him into this land
in which you now dwell. [5]And he gave him no inheritance in it, no not the
breadth of a foot, but promised that he would give it to him to possess, Ge 13:14,15;
and to his seed after him, when as yet he had no child. 17:8.

[6]God spoke in this way: that his seed would be a dweller in a strange
land, and that they would keep them in bondage and ill-treat them for four
hundred years. [7]But the nation to whom they will be in bondage, I will Ge 15:14
judge, said God. And after that, they will come forth and serve me in this Ex 3:12
place. [8]And he gave Abraham the covenant of circumcision. And Abra-
ham begat Isaac, and circumcised him the eighth day. And Isaac begat Ge 35:23-26
Jacob, and Jacob the twelve patriarchs.

[9]And the patriarchs, having indignation, sold Joseph into Egypt. But
God was with him, [10]and delivered him out of all his adversities, and gave
him favour and wisdom in the sight of Pharaoh, king of Egypt, who made
him governor over Egypt and over all his household.

[11]Then there came a dearth over all the land of Egypt and Canaan, and
great affliction, and our fathers found no sustenance. [12]But when Jacob
heard that there was wheat in Egypt, he sent our fathers a first time, [13]and Ge 41:54,
then a second time when Joseph made himself known to his brethren and cc42-47.
Joseph's kindred was made known to Pharaoh. [14]Then Joseph sent and
caused his father to be brought, and all his kin: seventy-five souls.[a] [15]And
Jacob descended into Egypt. And he died, both he and our fathers, [16]and
were carried back into Shechem, and were put in the sepulchre that Abra-
ham bought for money from the sons of Hamor at Shechem.

[17]When the time of the promise drew near (which God had sworn to
Abraham), the people grew and multiplied in Egypt, [18]till another king
arose who did not know of Joseph. [19]This king dealt treacherously with
our kindred, and ill-treated our fathers, and compelled them to cast out
[v20 is emended after their young children so that they would not remain alive. [20]At this time
Wycliffe 1380] Moses was born, and was loved by God.* He was nursed in his father's
house for three months. [21]When he was cast out, Pharaoh's daughter took
him up and reared him as her own son. [22]And Moses was learned in all the
wisdom of the Egyptians, and was strong in deeds and in words.

[23]And when he was fully forty years old, it came into his heart to visit
his brethren, the children of Israel. [24]And when he saw one of them suffer
wrong, he defended him, and avenged the quarrel of him who had the
harm done to him, and killed the Egyptian. [25]For he supposed his brethren
would understand that God by his hands would save them. But they did
not understand.

[26]And the next day, he appeared to them as they were fighting, and
[**Set them at one again**: that would have set them at one again,* saying, Sirs, you are brethren; why do
is, reconciled them] you hurt one another? [27]But the man who was doing his neighbour wrong
thrust him away, saying, Who made you a ruler and a judge among us? Ex 2:14
[28]What, will you kill me like you did the Egyptian yesterday?

[29]Then at those words, Moses fled, and was a sojourner in the land of

Midian, where he begat two sons.
30 And when forty years were expired, there appeared to him in the
wilderness of Mount Sinai an angel of the Lord, in a flame of fire in a Ex 3:2
bush. 31 When Moses saw it, he wondered at the sight. And as he drew
near to look, the voice of the Lord came to him: 32 I am the God of your
fathers – the God of Abraham, the God of Isaac, and the God of Jacob. Ex 3:6,15
Moses trembled and dared not look. 33 Then said the Lord to him, Put off
your shoes from your feet, for the place where you stand is holy ground. Jos 5:15

God came down to deliver his people from their affliction.

34 I have well seen the affliction of my people in Egypt, and I have heard
their groaning, and have come down to deliver them. And now, come, and Ex 3:5,7,8,10
I will send you into Egypt.
35 This Moses – whom they refused, saying, Who made you a ruler and Ex 2:14
a judge? – is the one God sent both a ruler and deliverer by the hands of
the Angel who appeared to him in the bush. 36 And this Moses brought
them out, showing wonders and signs in Egypt and in the Red Sea and in
the wilderness for forty years. 37 This is that Moses who said to the children
of Israel: The Lord your God will raise up for you a prophet like me from De 18:15 Ac 3:22
your brethren. Him you must hear.
38 This is he who was in the congregation in the wilderness, with the
Angel who spoke to him on Mount Sinai and with our fathers. This man
received the word of life to give to us – 39 to whom our fathers could not

But the people turned back to Egypt in their hearts.

pay heed, but cast it from them, and in their hearts turned back again into
Egypt, 40 saying to Aaron, Make us gods to go before us! As for this Mo-
ses who brought us out of the land of Egypt, we do not know what has Ex 32:1,23
become of him.
41 And they made a calf in those days, and offered sacrifice to the idol,
and rejoiced in the works of their own hands.

Then God gave them up to worship stars and idols.

42 Then God turned himself and gave them up to worship the stars of
the sky, as it is written in the book of the prophets: O ye of the house of
Israel, did you give to me sacrifices and offerings during forty years in the
desert? 43 And you took to yourself the tabernacle of Moloch,* and the star
of your god Remphan, figures that you made, to worship them. And I will Am 5:25-27
send you away beyond Babylon.
44 Our fathers had the tabernacle of witness in the wilderness, as he had
appointed them, telling Moses to make it according to the pattern that he
had seen. 45 Which tabernacle our fathers received and brought with Josh-
ua into the lands held by the Gentiles, whom God drove out before the
face of our fathers, to the time of David. 46 David found favour before
God, and desired to make a tabernacle for the God of Jacob. 47 But Solo-
mon built him a house.
48 However, he that is highest of all does not dwell in temples made
with hands, as says the prophet: 49 Heaven is my seat, and earth is my foot-
stool. What house will you build for me, says the Lord? Or what place is
it that I should rest in? 50 Has not my hand made all these things? Isa 66:1,2
51 You stiff-necked people, and of uncircumcised hearts and ears! You
have always resisted the Holy Spirit. As your fathers did, so do you.

Moloch [Rogers' note on Leviticus 20: Under this name 'Moloch' is forbidden all manner of idolatry, especially the offering of children, for that is abominable before the Lord. Moloch was an idol of the children of Ammon, whose image was hollow, having in it seven chambers. One was to offer therein fine flour, another was for turtle doves, the third for a sheep, the fourth for a ram, the fifth for a calf, the sixth for an ox. And for those who would offer their son, the seventh chamber was opened. And the face of this idol was like the face of a calf, his hands made open, ready to receive from the people that stood by]

[52]Which of the prophets did your fathers not persecute? And they
killed those who told before of the coming of the Just One, whom you
have now betrayed and murdered. [53]And you also have received a law by
the ordinance of angels, and have not kept it.
[54]When they heard these things, they were cut to the heart, and they
gnashed on him with their teeth. [55]But he, being full of the Holy Spirit,
looked up steadfastly with his eyes into heaven and saw the glory of God,
and Jesus standing on the right hand of God. [56]And he said, Behold, I see
the heavens open, and the Son of man standing on the right hand of God!
[57]Then they gave a shout with a loud voice, and stopped their ears, and
ran upon him all at once, [58]and cast him out of the city, and stoned him.
And the witnesses laid down their clothes at the feet of a young man
named Saul. [59]And they stoned Stephen, who was calling on the Lord and
saying, Lord Jesus, receive my spirit! [60]And he kneeled down and cried
with a loud voice, Lord, lay not this sin to their charge! And when he had
thus spoken, he fell asleep.

The Notes

Seventy-five souls (7:14) a) Souls are men and women, as at Genesis 12:5 and 14:21.

Chapter 8

Saul persecutes the Christians. The apostles are scattered abroad. Philip comes into Samaria. Simon Magus is baptized; he dissembles. Philip baptizes the chamberlain.

Saul had pleasure in Stephen's death. And at that time there was a great
persecution against the congregation that was at Jerusalem, and they were
all scattered abroad throughout the regions of Judea and Samaria, except
the apostles.
[2]Then devout men arranged Stephen's burial, and made great lamenta-
tion over him. [3]But Saul made havoc of the congregation, and entered into Ph'p 3:6
every house, and drew out both men and women, and thrust them into
prison.
[4]However, those who were scattered abroad went everywhere preach-
ing the word. [5]Then Philip went into a city of Samaria and preached
Christ to them. [6]And the people gave heed to the things that Philip spoke
with one accord when they heard and saw the miracles that he did. [7]For
unclean spirits, crying with loud voice, came out of many who were pos-
sessed by them. And many who were paralyzed, and many who limped,
were healed. [8]And there was great joy in that city.
Simon Magus. [9]And there was a certain man called Simon, who had previously prac-
ticed witchcraft and magic in that same city, and had bewitched the people
of Samaria, saying that he was a man who could do great things. [10]They
regarded him highly, from the least to the greatest, saying, This fellow is
the great power of God! [11]And they set much store by him, because for a
long time he had taken them in with magic.
[12]But as soon as they believed Philip's preaching of the kingdom of

God and of the name of Jesus Christ, they were baptized, both men and
women. [13]Then Simon himself believed also and was baptized, and con-
tinued with Philip; and he marvelled, seeing the miracles and signs that
were shown.

[14]When the apostles who were at Jerusalem heard that Samaria had
received the word of God, they sent Peter and John to them, [15]who, when
they arrived, prayed for them to receive the Holy Spirit. [16]For as yet he
had come on none of them, but they had only been baptized in the name
of Christ Jesus. [17]Then they laid their hands on them, and they received
the Holy Spirit.[a]

Laying on of hands.

[18]When Simon saw that through the laying on of the apostles' hands
the Holy Spirit was given, he offered them money, [19]saying, Give me also
this power, so that whomever I lay hands on may receive the Holy Spirit.

[20]Then Peter said to him, May your money perish with you, because
you thought that the gift of God might be obtained with money. [21]You
have neither part nor fellowship in this work, for your heart is not right in
the sight of God. [22]Repent therefore of this your wickedness, and pray
God that the thought of your heart may be forgiven you. [23]For I perceive
that you are full of bitter gall and wrapped in iniquity.

[24]Then Simon answered and said, Pray to the Lord for me that none of
these things that you have spoken will fall on me.

[25]And when they had testified and preached the word of the Lord,
Peter and John returned toward Jerusalem, and preached the gospel in
many villages of the Samaritans.

[26]Then the angel of the Lord spoke to Philip, saying, Arise and go to-
ward the south, to the road that goes down from Jerusalem to Gaza, which
is in the desert. [27]And Philip arose and went on. And behold, a man of
Ethiopia who was a chamberlain,* and of great authority with Candace,
queen of the Ethiopians, and in charge of all her treasure, had come to
Jerusalem to pray. [28]And as he returned home again sitting in his chariot,
he was reading Isaiah the prophet.

[**Chamberlain**: an officer who manages the household of a monarch or noble]

[29]Then the Spirit said to Philip, Go near and overtake that chariot.
[30]And Philip ran to him and heard him reading the prophet Isaiah, and
said, Do you understand what you are reading? [31]And he said, How can I,
unless I have a guide? And he asked Philip to come up and sit with him.
[32]The tenor of the scripture that he was reading was this: He was led as a
sheep to be slain, and like a lamb dumb before his shearer, so he opened
not his mouth. [33]Because of his humbleness, he was not esteemed.* But Isa 53:7,8
who can number his descendants? For his life is taken from the earth.

*Because he was of such a low degree in this world – but a poor carpenter, who humbled himself to all men and was obedient even to the most vile death of the cross – therefore the Jews cannot esteem him as the very Messiah.

[34]The chamberlain said to Philip, I ask you, of whom does the prophet
speak this? of himself, or of some other man? [35]And Philip opened his
mouth and began at the same scripture, and preached Jesus to him.

[36]And as they went on their way, they came to some water, and the
chamberlain said, See, here is water. What is to keep me from being
baptized? [37]Philip said to him, If you believe with all your heart, you may
be. He answered and said, I believe that Jesus Christ is the Son of God.

38
And he commanded the chariot to stand still. And they both went
down into the water, both Philip and also the chamberlain, and he bap-
tized him.
39
And as soon as they had come out of the water, the Spirit of the Lord
caught Philip away, and the chamberlain saw him no more. And he went
on his way rejoicing.
40
But Philip was found at Azotus, and he walked
throughout the country preaching in their towns till he came to Caesarea.

The Notes

They received the Holy Spirit (8:17)
[**Whitsunday**: the Feast of the Descent of the Holy Spirit upon the apostles on the 50th day after Easter; Pentecost]

a) Understand they received the Holy Spirit in a manifest and visible sign, as the apostles themselves received it on the fiftieth day, or (as we call it) Whitsunday,* which thing at that time was necessary for the furtherance and validation of the preaching of the gospel, although not needful for salvation. But now that the preaching of the gospel is sufficiently confirmed, this visible miracle is ended. However, that remains which was confirmed by the miracle; that is, by the preaching of the gospel the Holy Spirit is ministered, although our bodily eyes do not see it; and by the Holy Spirit faith comes, which receives Christ to be our righteousness, sanctification, and redemption (1Cor 1:21).

Chapter 9

Paul is converted & confounds the Jews. Peter raises Tabitha.

And Saul, still breathing out threats and murder against the disciples of
the Lord, went to the high priest,
2
and desired of him letters to Damascus,
to the synagogues, so that if he found any who were of this Way, whether
they were men or women, he could bring them bound to Jerusalem.
3
But
as he journeyed and came near to Damascus, suddenly there shone round
about him a light from heaven.
4
And he fell to the earth and heard a voice
saying to him, Saul, Saul, why do you persecute me?
5
And he said, Who
are you Lord? And the Lord said, I am Jesus, whom you persecute. It is
hard for you to kick against the prick.* And he, both trembling and aston-
ished, said, Lord, what will you have me to do? And the Lord said to him,
6
Arise and go into the city, and it will be told you what you must do.
7
The men who journeyed with him stood amazed, for they heard a
voice, but saw no one.
8
And Saul arose from the ground and opened his
eyes, but saw no one. Then they led him by the hand and brought him into
Damascus.
9
And he was three days without sight, and neither ate nor
drank.
10
And there was a certain disciple at Damascus named Ananias, and to
him the Lord said in a vision, Ananias! And he said, Behold, I am here,
Lord.
11
And the Lord said to him, Arise, and go to the street that is called
Straight, and inquire at the house of Judas for one called Saul of Tarsus.
For he is praying,
12
and has seen in a vision a man named Ananias coming
in to him and putting his hands on him so that he may receive his sight.
13
Then Ananias answered, Lord, I have heard by many of this man,
how much evil he has done to your saints at Jerusalem,
14
and here he has
authority from the high priests to arrest all who call on your name.
15
The Lord said to him, Go your way. For he is a chosen vessel of

Gal 1:13,14
1Co 15:8,9
2Co 12:1-4
Ph'p 3:6

Ac 8:1; 22:3-16; 26:9-18.

[A **prick** or goad is a stick for prodding cattle and horses. The expression *kick against the prick(s)* means to offer vain and perilous or ruinous resistance]

Saul is converted.

Ananias the disciple.

mine, to bear my name before the Gentiles, and kings, and the children of Israel. [16]For I will show him what great things he must suffer for my name's sake.

[17]Ananias went his way, and entered into the house, and put his hands on him and said, Brother Saul, the Lord who appeared to you on the road as you came has sent me, so that you may receive your sight and be filled with the Holy Spirit. [18]And immediately there fell from his eyes as it were scales, and he received sight and arose, and was baptized, [19]and took food, and was comforted.

Paul preaches Christ.

Then Saul spent some days with the disciples who were at Damascus. [20]And straightaway he preached Christ in the synagogues, that he was the Son of God. [21]All who heard him were amazed and said, Is this not the man that ravaged those who called on this name in Jerusalem, and came here intending to bring them as prisoners to the high priests?

[22]But Saul increased in strength, and confounded the Jews who dwelt at Damascus, affirming that Jesus was the very Christ.

Paul is persecuted.

[23]And after a good while the Jews took counsel together, to kill him. [24]But Paul knew they were laying in wait. And they watched at the gates day and night, to kill him. [25]Then the disciples took him by night, and put him through the wall and let him down in a basket.

2Co11:32,33

[26]And when Saul got to Jerusalem, he tried to join himself with the disciples. But they were all afraid of him, and did not believe that he was a disciple. [27]But Barnabas took him and brought him to the apostles, and explained to them how he had seen the Lord on the road and had spoken with him, and how bold he had been at Damascus in the name of Jesus.

[28]And Saul had his intercourse with them at Jerusalem, [29]and acquitted himself boldly in the name of the Lord Jesus. And he spoke and disputed with the Greeks, and they went about to kill him. [30]But when the brethren knew of this, they brought him to Caesarea and sent him forth to Tarsus.

The congregations are strengthened and grow

[31]Then the congregations had rest throughout all Judea and Galilee and Samaria, and were strengthened, and walked in the fear of the Lord, and multiplied by the comfort of the Holy Spirit.

[32]And it chanced that as Peter walked throughout all the country, he came to the saints who dwelt at Lydda. [33]And there he found a certain man named Eneas, who had been confined to his bed sick for eight years, paralyzed. [34]Then Peter said to him, Eneas, may Jesus Christ make you whole! Arise and make your bed. And he arose immediately. [35]And all who dwelt at Lydda and Sharon saw him, and turned to the Lord.

Dorcas in Greek and **Tabitha** in Aramaic both mean deer or gazelle]

[36]There was at Joppa a certain woman, a disciple named Tabitha (which translated is Dorcas*). She was full of good works and alms-deeds that she did. [37]And it happened in those days that she became sick and died. When they had washed her, they laid her in a chamber. [38]Because Lydda was near Joppa, and the disciples had heard that Peter was there, they sent to him, imploring him not to be grieved to come to them.

[39]Peter arose and went with them. And when he arrived, they brought him into the chamber. And all the widows stood round about him, weep-

ing and showing the coats and the garments that Dorcas had made while she was with them. 40And Peter put them all out, and kneeled down and prayed, and turned to the body and said, Tabitha, arise! And she opened her eyes, and when she saw Peter, sat up. 41And he gave her his hand and lifted her up, and called the saints and widows, and showed her alive.

42And this was known throughout all Joppa, and many believed on the Lord. 43And it came about that Peter stayed many days in Joppa with one Simon, a tanner.

Chapter 10

The vision that Peter saw. How he was sent to Cornelius. The heathen also receive the Spirit, and are baptized.

There was a certain man in Caesarea called Cornelius, a captain of the soldiers of Italy, 2a devout man, and one who feared God with all his household. He gave many alms[*] to the people, and prayed to God always. 3The same man saw in a vision clearly, about the ninth hour of the day, an angel of God coming in to him and saying to him, Cornelius! 4When he looked on him, he was afraid, and said, What is it, Lord? He said to him, Your prayers and your alms have come up into remembrance before God.[a] 5And now, send men to Joppa, and call for one Simon, named also Peter. 6He lodges with one Simon a tanner, whose house is by the seaside. 7He will tell you what you ought to do.

[**Alms**: charitable gifts]

When the angel who spoke to Cornelius had departed, he called two of his household servants and a devout soldier from among those that waited on him, 8and told them all the matter, and sent them to Joppa.

9On the next day, as they went on their journey and drew near to the city, Peter went up upon the top of the house to pray, about the sixth hour. 10Then he grew hungry and wanted to eat. But while they made ready, he fell into a trance, 11and saw heaven opened, and a certain vessel come down to him, like a great sheet knit at the four corners. And it was let down to the earth. 12In it were all manner of four-footed animals of the earth, and wild beasts, and reptiles, and birds of the air. 13And there came a voice to him: Rise, Peter; kill and eat! 14But Peter said, God forbid, Lord, for I have never eaten anything that is common or unclean. 15And the voice spoke to him again the second time: What God has cleansed, do not judge common. 16This was done three times, and the vessel was received up again into heaven.

Peter's vision.

17While Peter mused in himself what this vision that he had seen might mean, behold, the men sent from Cornelius had made inquiry for Simon's house, and were standing before the door. 18And one called out and asked whether Simon who was also called Peter was lodged there. 19While Peter thought on the vision, the Spirit said to him, Behold, three men are seeking you. 20Arise therefore; go down and go with them, and do not doubt. For I have sent them.

21Peter went down to the men that were sent to him from Cornelius and said, I am the one you are seeking. What is the reason for your visit?

[22]And they said to him, Cornelius the captain, a just man, and one who fears God, and is of good report among all the people of the Jews, was told by a holy angel to send for you to come into his house, and to hear words from you.

[23]Then he invited them in and lodged them. And the next day, Peter went away with them, and certain brethren from Joppa accompanied him. [24]And the third day, they entered into Caesarea.

Peter goes in to Cornelius.

Cornelius was waiting for them and had called together his relatives and special friends. [25]And as Peter entered, Cornelius met him, and fell down at his feet and worshipped him. [26]But Peter took him up, saying, Stand up. For even I myself am a man.

[27]And as he talked with him, he went in and found many who had come together. [28]And he said to them, You know that it is an unlawful thing for a man that is a Jew to keep company or visit with a foreigner. But God has shown me that I should not call any man common or unclean. [29]Therefore I came to you, without saying no, as soon as I was sent for. I ask therefore, why have you sent for me?

[30]And Cornelius said, Four days ago now I had been fasting, and at the ninth hour I was praying in my house. And behold, a man stood before me in bright clothing, [31]and said, Cornelius, your prayer has been heard, and your alms-deeds are remembered in the sight of God. [32]Send therefore to Joppa, and call for Simon who is also called Peter. He is lodged in the house of one Simon, a tanner by the seaside. [33]As soon as he has come, he will speak to you. Then I sent for you immediately, and you have done well to come. Now we are all here present before God, to hear all the things that are commanded to you by God.

[34]Then Peter opened his mouth and said, Of a truth I perceive that God is not partial, [35]but among all peoples, whoever fears him and works righteousness is accepted with him.

De 10:17
2Ch 19:7
Job 34:19
Ec'us 35:12
Ro 2:11
Ga 2:6
Eph 6:9
Col 3:25
1Pe 1:17

[36]You know the preaching that God sent to the children of Israel, preaching peace by Jesus Christ, who is Lord over all things. [37]This preaching was proclaimed throughout all Judea, and began in Galilee after the baptism that John preached – [38]how God had anointed Jesus of Nazareth with the Holy Spirit, and with power. Which Jesus went about doing good, and healing all who were oppressed by the devils. For God was with him. [39]And we are witnesses of all the things that he did in the land of the Jews and at Jerusalem. But they slew him and hung him on a tree. [40]But God raised him up on the third day, and showed him openly – [41]not to all the people, but to us witnesses chosen before by God, who ate and drank with him after he arose from death. [42]And he commanded us to preach to the people, and to testify that it is he who is ordained by God to be judge of the quick* and the dead. [43]To him all the prophets give witness: that through his name, all who believe in him shall receive remission of sins.

[**The quick**: the living]

Faith is the remission of sins.

Jer 31:34
Mic 7:19,20

The Holy Spirit comes without laying on of hands.

[44]While Peter was still speaking these words, the Holy Spirit fell on all those who heard the preaching. [45]And the men of the circumcision who

The apostles were here first taught and convinced by the Holy Spirit of the conversion of the Gentiles.

believed were astonished, as many as came with Peter, because the gift of
the Holy Spirit was also shed out on the Gentiles. [46]For they heard them
speak with tongues and magnify God. Then Peter said, [47]Can any man
forbid water to baptize these people, who have received the Holy Spirit as
well as we? [48]And he directed them to be baptized in the name of the
Lord. Then they asked him to stay a few days.

The Notes

Your prayers and alms have come up into remembrance before God. (10:4)

a) Inasmuch as no man can be saved by works – as the psalmist openly affirms: In your sight none who live can be justified (Ps 143:2); and again: If you look on our iniquities, Lord, who will be able to bear them? (Ps 130:3) – no Christian should be so bold as to attribute the salvation of this man Cornelius to his prayer and fasting. For first you see he was a Gentile, uncircumcised, not keeping the law or once thinking on it, and therefore must be justified by faith that came by hearing the glad tidings preached in Christ (Ro 10:17). And therefore you must look to the words of Luke in the beginning of this chapter, where he says that Cornelius feared God. This he could not have done – no, nor yet have prayed or given alms – unless he had believed. For how could he have called on him on whom he does not believe? Thus we must ascribe his calling to faith, from which these fruits of prayer and fasting proceeded.

The Christian then, and those who desire the scripture to be true in all places, and to so expound one text that another may agree with it, do right well know that our calling and salvation are freely given by God for his son Christ's sake, and not for the merit of our works. And because faith can receive this great and free gift from God, and believe it to be true, but works neither can believe it nor yet earn it, therefore salvation is ascribed to faith, and not to works.

If prayer or fasting or the holiest work under heaven could save, Christ would never have needed to suffer such grievous pains, but died in vain. Neither would God freely choose us, but our works would choose him. Understand therefore that Cornelius was not called by his works, but by his faith, out of which his works grew – which faith God freely gave him, and by it freely called him, as he calls and saves us all.

Good works we must do, as this man did, and that with all love and earnestness. And we are bound to do them, and without them it cannot be known if we are truly Christian or not, any more than we can know a tree to be good and never taste its fruit. But we may in no case ascribe justification or salvation to works, for as Christ says (Luke 17:10), when you have done all you can do, say you are unprofitable servants. But we must ascribe justification and salvation to faith, which alone can receive the benefit of Christ and believe that he alone has won forgiveness for the sins of the whole world (John 1:29 and 1 John 2:2).

Chapter 11

Peter explains the reason why he went in to the heathen. Barnabas and Paul preach to the heathen. Agabus prophesies of the famine to come.

And the apostles and the brethren that were throughout Judea heard that
the heathen had also received the word of God. [2]And when Peter came up
to Jerusalem, those of the circumcision contended with him, [3]saying, You
went in to uncircumcised men and ate with them!

[4]Then Peter began and explained the matter in order to them, saying,
[5]I was in the city of Joppa, praying, and in a trance I saw a vision, a cer-
tain vessel descend, like a large linen cloth let down from heaven by the

*The Jews called that **common** which is impure and unclean, and which they were forbidden by the law (Lev 11).

four corners; and it came to me. [6]When I looked into it, I considered and
saw four-footed animals of the earth, and wild beasts and reptiles and
birds of the air. [7]And I heard a voice saying to me, Arise, Peter; kill and
eat. [8]And I said, God forbid, Lord, for nothing common* or unclean has at
any time entered into my mouth. [9]But the voice answered me again from
heaven: Do not judge common those things that God has cleansed.

[10]And this was done three times, and everything was taken up again
into heaven.

[11]And behold, immediately three men came to the house where I was,
sent from Caesarea to me. [12]And the Spirit said to me that I should go
with them, without doubting. Moreover, the six brethren accompanied me.
And we entered into the man's house. [13]And he described to us how he
had seen an angel in his house, who stood and said to him, Send men to
Joppa, and call for Simon, named also Peter. [14]He will speak words to you
whereby both you and all your house shall be saved.

[15]And as I began to preach, the Holy Spirit fell on them, as he did on
us at the beginning. [16]Then I remembered the words of the Lord, how he Joh 1:33 Ac 1:5
said John baptized with water, but you will be baptized with the Holy
Spirit. [17]Inasmuch then as God gave them the same gift as he did to us
when we believed on the Lord Jesus Christ, who was I, that I should have
withstood God?

To the Gentiles also is granted repentance unto life.

[18]When they heard this, they held their peace, and glorified God, say-
ing, Then God has granted repentance unto life to the Gentiles also.

[19]Those who were scattered abroad through the affliction that arose
about Stephen walked throughout till they came to Phoenicia and Cyprus
and Antioch, preaching the word to no one but the Jews only. [20]But some
of them were men of Cyprus and Cyrene, who when they came to Antioch
spoke to the Greeks, and preached the Lord Jesus. [21]And the hand of the
Lord was with them, and a great number believed and turned to the Lord.

Barnabas is sent to Antioch.

[22]Reports of these things came to the ears of the congregation that was
in Jerusalem, and they sent Barnabas to go to Antioch. [23]When he arrived
and had seen the grace of God, he was glad, and exhorted them all, that
with purpose of heart they should continually cleave unto the Lord. [24]For
he was a good man, and full of the Holy Spirit and of faith. And a great
number of people were brought to the Lord.

Barnabas seeks Paul.

[25]Then Barnabas departed to Tarsus, to seek Saul. [26]And when he had
found him, he brought him to Antioch. And it came about that for a whole
year they were with the congregation there, and taught many people. And
the disciples of Antioch were the first that were called Christian.

[**Dearth**: a time of famine, scarcity, great lack]

[27]In those days, prophets came from Jerusalem to Antioch. [28]And one
of them, named Agabus, stood up and signified by the Spirit that there Ac 21:10,11
would be great dearth* throughout all the world, which came to pass in the
days of the Emperor Claudius. [29]Then the disciples, everyone according to
his ability, determined to send aid to the brethren who dwelt in Judea.
[30]Which thing they also did, and sent it to the elders by the hands of
Barnabas and Saul.

Chapter 12

Herod persecutes the Christians, kills James the brother of John, and puts Peter in prison, whom the Lord delivers by an angel. The shameful death of Herod.

In that time Herod the king stretched forth his hand to persecute some of the congregation. 2And he killed James, the brother of John, with the sword. 3And because he saw that it pleased the Jews, he proceeded further and took Peter also. This was during the days of sweet bread.* 4And when he had caught Peter, he put him in prison, and delivered him to four quaternions* of soldiers to be kept, intending after the Passover to bring him forth to the people.

[**Days of sweet bread**: ie of unleavened bread, during the Passover feast days] **Quaternions of soldiers** is four companies of 4 soldiers [who rotated the watch]

5Then Peter was kept in prison. But prayer for him was made to God without ceasing by the congregation. 6And when Herod was about to bring him out to the people, that night Peter slept between two soldiers, bound with two chains; and the guards before the door kept the prison.

7And behold, the angel of the Lord was there present, and a light shone in the jail. And he struck Peter on the side and awoke him, saying, Rise up quickly! And his chains fell off from his hands. 8And the angel said to him, Gird yourself, and bind on your sandals.* And so he did. And the angel said to him, Cast your mantle around you and follow me.

Sandals are soles to be bound under the feet.

9And Peter came out and followed him, and did not know that it was really being done by the angel, but thought he had seen a vision. 10When they were past the first and the second guard, they came to the iron gate that leads to the city, which opened to them by its own accord. And they went out and passed down one street, and immediately the angel departed from him.

Peter is released.

11And when Peter came to himself, he said, Now I know for certain that the Lord has sent his angel and has delivered me out of the hand of Herod, and from all the Jews were waiting for. 12And as he considered the matter, he came to the house of Mary, the mother of one John who was also called Mark,* where many were gathered together in prayer.

*This John is the same Mark that wrote the gospel of Mark.

13As Peter knocked at the entry door, a maidservant named Rhoda came forth to listen. 14And when she recognized Peter's voice, she did not open the entry door for gladness, but ran in and said that Peter was standing before the entry. 15And they said to her, You are mad. But she insisted that it was really so. Then they said, It is his angel. 16But Peter continued knocking, and when they opened the door and saw him, they were astonished. 17And he motioned to them with his hand to hold their peace, and told them by what means the Lord had brought him out of the prison. And he said, Go and tell these things to James and to the brethren.

And he departed, and went to another place.

18As soon as it was day, there was no little ado among the soldiers about what had become of Peter. 19When Herod had called for him, but not found him, he examined the guards and commanded them to depart. And he descended from Judea to Caesarea, and stayed there.

20Now Herod had been displeased with the people of Tyre and Sidon.

And they came all at once and made intercession to Blastus, the king's chamberlain, and requested peace, because their country was supplied with food by the king's land. [21]And upon a day appointed, Herod arrayed himself in royal apparel, and sat in his seat and made a speech to them. [22]And the people gave a shout, saying, It is the voice of a god, and not of a man!

Herod is slain and eaten by worms.

[23]And immediately the angel of the Lord struck him down, because he did not give God the honour. And he was eaten by worms and gave up the spirit.

[V25 is emended after Coverdale 1535]

[24]And the word of God grew and multiplied. [25]As for Barnabas and Paul, they went again to Jerusalem and delivered the relief, and took with them John, who was also called Mark. Ac 11:29,30

Chapter 13

Paul and Barnabas are called to preach among the heathen. Of Sergius Paulus and Elymas the magician. Paul preaches at Antioch.

Barnabas and Paul are sent to preach.

There were in the congregation at Antioch certain prophets[a] and teachers, such as Barnabas, and Simeon called Niger, and Lucius of Cyrene, and Manaen, who had been brought up with Herod the tetrarch, and Saul. [2]As they worshipped the Lord and fasted, the Holy Spirit said, Separate unto me Barnabas and Saul for the work to which I have called them. [3]Then they fasted and prayed, and put their hands on them, and let them go. [4]And they, after they were sent by the Holy Spirit, went down to Seleucia, and from there they sailed to the island of Cyprus. [5]And when they had come to Salamis, they preached the word of God in the synagogues of the Jews. And they had John Mark to assist them.

[**Proconsul of the province**: appointed to govern Cyprus, then a province of the Roman Empire]

[6]When they had gone throughout the isle to the city of Paphos, they found a certain magician, a false prophet who was a Jew named Bar-Jesus.[b] [7]He was with the proconsul of the province,[*] one Sergius Paulus, a man of understanding. This man called to him Barnabas and Saul, and desired to hear the word of God. [8]But Elymas the magician (for so was his name by translation) withstood them, and sought to turn the proconsul away from the faith.

[9]Then Saul, who also is called Paul,[c] being full of the Holy Spirit, set his eyes on him [10]and said, O full of all subtlety and deceitfulness, child of the devil and enemy of all righteousness, you cease not to pervert the straight ways of the Lord. [11]And now behold, the hand of the Lord is upon you, and you will be blind and not see the sun for a season.

And immediately there fell on him a mist and a darkness, and he went about seeking someone to lead him by the hand. [12]Then the proconsul, when he saw what had happened, believed, and wondered at the doctrine of the Lord.

Mark the evangelist, otherwise called John, breaks company.

[13]When those who were with Paul departed from Paphos by ship, they went to Perga, a city of Pamphylia; but there John Mark left them and returned to Jerusalem. [14]But they wandered through the districts from

Perga to Antioch, a city of the province of Pisidia, and went into the syn-
agogue on the Sabbath day, and sat down. [15]And after the law and the
prophets were read, the leaders of the synagogue sent to them, saying,
Men and brethren, if you have any sermon to exhort the people, do speak.

[16]Then Paul stood up and beckoned with his hand and said, Men of De 7:6-8
Israel and you who fear God, listen! [17]The God of this people chose our
fathers, and exalted the people when they dwelt as strangers in the land of
Egypt, and with a mighty arm brought them out of it. [18]And for the time Ex c13; 14:8.
of about forty years he suffered their ways in the wilderness. [19]And he
destroyed seven nations in the land of Canaan, and divided their land to Jos 14:1,2 J'g 2:16
them by lot. [20]And afterward he gave them judges for about 450 years, 1Sa 8:5; 10:20-24;
until the time of Samuel the prophet.[d] [21]And after that they desired a king, c16.
and God gave to them Saul the son of Kish, a man of the tribe of Ben-
jamin, for 40 years. [22]And after he had put him down, he set up David to
be their king, of whom he reported, saying: I have found David the son of Ps 89:20 1Sa 13:14
Jesse to be a man after my own heart. He will fulfil all my will.

[23]From this man's seed, God (according to his promise) brought forth
to the people of Israel a saviour, one Jesus, [24]when John, before his com-
ing, had first preached the baptism of repentance to Israel. [25]And when Lu 3:3 M't 3:11
John was finishing his course, he said, He whom you think that I am, I am Mk 1:7
not. But behold, there comes one after me, the shoes of whose feet I am Jo 1:27
not worthy to loose.

[26]Men and brethren, children of the stock of Abraham, and whoever
among you fears God, to you is this word of salvation sent. [27]The in-
They do not know him, nor the voices of his prophets. habiters of Jerusalem and their rulers, because they did not know him, nor
yet the voices of the prophets that are read every Sabbath day, have ful-
filled the prophets in condemning him. [28]And when they found no cause M't cc27,28
of death in him, yet they asked Pilate to kill him. [29]And when they had Mk cc15,16
fulfilled all the things that were written of him, they took him down from Lu cc23,24 Joh cc18-21
the tree and put him in a sepulchre. [30]But God raised him again from
death, [31]and he was seen during many days by those who came with him
from Galilee to Jerusalem, who are his witnesses to the people.

[32]And we declare to you that the promise made to the fathers, [33]God
has fulfilled unto us, their children, in that he raised up Jesus again, even
as it is written in the second psalm: You are my Son; this same day I have Ps 2:7 Heb 1:5
begotten you. [34]As concerning that he raised him up from death, now no
more to return to corruption, he said thus: The holy promises made to
David, I will give faithfully to you. [35]Therefore he says also in another Isa 55:3
place: You shall not suffer your Holy One to see corruption. [36]However Ps 16:10
David, after he had in his time fulfilled the will of God, slept, and was laid
with his fathers, and saw corruption. [37]But he whom God raised again saw
no corruption.

[38]Be it known to you therefore, men and brethren, that through this
man the forgiveness of sins is preached to you, [39]and that by him all who
Faith justifies, and not the law. believe are justified from all things from which you could not be justified
by the law of Moses. [40]Beware, therefore, lest that fall on you which is

spoken of in the prophets: 41Behold, ye despisers, and wonder, and perish!
For I do a work in your days that you will not believe, though a man were Hab 1:5
to declare it to you.

42When they came out of the synagogue of the Jews, the Gentiles
urged them to preach the word to them between the Sabbath days. 43When
the congregation broke up, many of the Jews and virtuous converts fol-
lowed Paul and Barnabas, who spoke to them and exhorted them to con-
tinue in the grace of God. 44And the next Sabbath day, almost the whole
city came together to hear the word of God.

45When the Jews saw the people, they were full of indignation, and
spoke against those things that were said by Paul, contradicting and
railing on it. 46Then Paul and Barnabas were bold and said, It was fitting
that the word of God should first have been preached to you. But seeing
you put it from you, and think yourselves unworthy of everlasting life, lo,
we turn to the Gentiles. 47For so has the Lord commanded us: I have made Isa 49:6
you a light to the Gentiles, to be salvation to the end of the world.

48The Gentiles heard, and were glad, and glorified the word of the
Lord, and believed – even as many as were appointed to eternal life.
49And the word of the Lord went abroad throughout all the region.

50But the Jews moved the devout and honourable women and the chief
men of the city, and raised persecution against Paul and Barnabas, and M't 10:14
expelled them from their district. 51And they shook off the dust from their Mk 6:11
feet against them, and went to Iconium. 52And the disciples were filled Lu 9:5
with joy and with the Holy Spirit.

The Notes

Prophets (13:1) a) Prophets: Look in chapter 15, verse 32.

Bar-Jesus (13:6) b) Bar-Jesus is by interpretation the son of Jesus [or, son of Joshua, signifying *the son of salvation*]. Even this name had the magician gotten to himself, to blind the world with and deceive the people.

Saul also called Paul (13:9) c) Many disagree concerning Paul's name, but the most accepted opinion is that he was called Saul by the Hebrews, and after the manner of speech of the Gentiles and Romans, he was called Paul.

450 years (13:20) d) These 450 years must be counted from their coming forth from Egypt (Exodus 12) and not from their first judge (Othniel, Judges 3:9).

Chapter 14

Paul and Barnabas preach at Iconium. Some believe, some stir up a revolt. At Lystra the people want to make sacrifice to Barnabas and Paul, who refuse it, and exhort the people to worship the true God. Paul is stoned. After that, he goes to Derbe, and again to Lystra, Iconium, and Antioch.

And it happened in Iconium that Paul and Barnabas went both together
into the synagogue of the Jews, and so spoke that a great number both of
the Jews and also of the Greeks believed. 2But the unbelieving Jews
stirred up and disquieted the minds of the Gentiles against the brethren.

[3]They remained there a long time, and acquitted themselves boldly with the help of the Lord, who bore witness to the word of his grace, causing signs and wonders to be done by their hands.

[4]The people of the city were divided: part held with the Jews, and part with the apostles. [5]When an assault was planned, both by the Gentiles and also by the Jews with their leaders, to put them to shame and to stone them, [6]they were aware of it, and fled to Lystra and Derbe in Lycaonia and to the region that lies round about, [7]and there preached the gospel.

A lame man is healed.

[8]And at Lystra there sat a certain man weak in his feet, being crippled from his mother's womb, who had never walked. [9]This man heard Paul preach. Paul looked at him and perceived that he had faith to be whole, [10]and said with a loud voice, Stand upright on your feet! And he started up and walked.

[11]And when the people saw what Paul had done, they lifted up their voices, saying in the speech of Lycaonia, Gods have come down to us in the likeness of men! [12]And they called Barnabas Jupiter, and Paul Mercurius, because he was the preacher. [13]Then the priest of Jupiter, who dwelt in front of their city, brought oxen and garlands to the temple porch, and wanted to make sacrifice with the people.

Paul and Barnabas abhor to have oxen and garlands offered to them.

Ps 146:6
Rev 14:7

[14]But when the apostles Barnabas and Paul heard this, they tore their clothes and ran in among the people, crying out and saying, [15]Sirs, why do you do this? We are mortal men like you, and preach to you that you should turn from these vanities to the living God, who made heaven and earth and the sea, and all that is in them – [16]who in times past suffered all nations to walk in their own ways. [17]Nevertheless, he did not leave himself without witness, in that he showed his goodness in giving us rain from heaven and fruitful seasons, filling our hearts with food and gladness. [18]And with these words, they barely refrained the people from making sacrifice to them.

Paul is stoned.

[19]But certain Jews from Antioch and Iconium came there, and they won the people over, and stoned Paul and drew him out of the city, supposing him to be dead. [20]However as the disciples stood round about him, he rose up and went into the city.

Tribulation.

Prayer and fasting go together.

And the next day, Paul departed with Barnabas to Derbe. [21]After they had preached to that city and had taught many, they returned again to Lystra, and to Iconium and Antioch, [22]and strengthened the disciples' souls, exhorting them to continue in the faith, affirming that we must through much tribulation enter into the kingdom of God. [23]And they appointed elders by election in every congregation, and prayed and fasted, and committed them to God on whom they believed.

[24]And they went through Pisidia, and came into Pamphylia. [25]And when they had preached the word of God in Perga, they descended into Attalia, [26]and from there returned by ship to Antioch, where they had been committed to the grace of God for the work that they had completed. [27]When they arrived and had gathered the congregation together, they described all that God had done by them, and how he had opened the door

of faith to the Gentiles. [28]And they remained there a long time with the
disciples.

Chapter 15

Disagreement about circumcision. The apostles bring peace to the matter at Jerusalem, and Paul and Barnabas preach at Antioch.

Then certain men came from Judea and taught the brethren, Unless you
Circumcision. [v 2 is emended after Coverdale 1535] are circumcised as observed by Moses, you cannot be saved. [2]And when Ga 5:1-6
dissension arose, and Paul and Barnabas had set themselves hard against
them, they determined that Paul and Barnabas and certain others of them
should go up to Jerusalem, to the apostles and elders, about this question.
[3]And after they were brought on their way by the congregation, they
passed over Phoenicia and Samaria, telling about the conversion of the
Gentiles, and they brought great joy to all the brethren.

[4]And when they got to Jerusalem, they were welcomed by the congre-
gation, and by the apostles and elders. And they described what things
God had done by them. [5]Then there rose up certain men of the sect of the
Pharisees who believed, saying that it was necessary to circumcise the
Gentiles, and to enjoin them to keep the law of Moses. [6]And the apostles
and elders came together to consider this matter.

[7]And when there was much disputing, Peter rose up and said to them,
Men and brethren, you know that a good while ago God chose among us
that the Gentiles by my mouth should hear the word of the gospel and Ac c10
believe. [8]And God, who knows the heart, bore witness to them, and gave
to them the Holy Spirit, even as he did to us. [9]And he put no difference Ac 10:44
between them and us, but with faith purified their hearts.[a] [10]Now therefore
why do you tempt God, and put a yoke on the disciples' necks that neither
The grace of Christ saves. our fathers nor we were able to bear? [11]But we believe that through the
grace of the Lord Jesus Christ we shall be saved, as they do.

[12]Then all the company was silent and listened to Barnabas and Paul,
who told what signs and wonders God had shown among the Gentiles by
them.

[13]And afterward, while they held their peace, James spoke, saying,
Men and brethren, listen to me. [14]Simon told how God at the beginning
visited the Gentiles and took out of them people for his name. [15]And to
this the words of the prophets agree, as it is written: [16]After this I will
return, and will build again the tabernacle of David, which has fallen
down; and that which is fallen into decay of it, I will build again; and I
will set it up, [17]so that the rest of mankind may seek after the Lord, even
all the Gentiles upon whom my name is named,[b] [18]says the Lord who does Am 9:11,12
all these things.

Known to God are all his works from the beginning of the world.
[19]Therefore my recommendation is that we not trouble those who from
among the Gentiles are turned to God, [20]but that we write to them to keep
themselves from the defilement of idols, from fornication, from things

strangled,[c] and from blood. [21]For Moses since ancient times has had those
who preach him in every city, and he is read in the synagogues every
Sabbath day.

[22]Then it pleased the apostles and elders with the whole congregation
to send men chosen from their own company to Antioch (in Syria) with
Paul and Barnabas. They sent Judas, called also Barsabas, and Silas, who
were chief men among the brethren, [23]and gave them letters in their hands
as follows:

The apostles, elders, and brethren send greetings to the brethren who
are of the Gentiles in Antioch, Syria, and Cilicia. [24]Since we have heard
that certain men who departed from us have troubled you with words, and
unsettled your minds, saying you must be circumcised and keep the law –
to whom we gave no such instruction – [25]it seemed therefore to us a good
thing, when we came together with one accord, to send chosen men to you
with our beloved Barnabas and Paul, [26]men who have risked their lives for
the name of our Lord Jesus Christ. [27]We have therefore sent Judas and
Silas, who will also tell you the same things by mouth. [28]For it seemed
good to the Holy Spirit and to us to put no greater burden upon you than

Idols.
Fornication.
Blood.
Things strangled.

these necessary things, [29]that is to say, to abstain from things offered to
idols, from blood, from things strangled, and fornication. From which, if
you keep yourselves, you will do well. So fare ye well.

[30]When they departed, they went to Antioch, and gathered the whole
community together and delivered the epistle. [31]When they had read it, the
people were glad of that consolation. [32]And Judas and Silas, being proph-
ets,* exhorted the brethren with much preaching, and strengthened them.
[33]And after they had stayed there a little while, they were let go in peace
from the brethren to the apostles. [34]Notwithstanding, it pleased Silas to
remain there still. [35]Paul and Barnabas continued in Antioch, teaching and
preaching the word of the Lord with many others.

*Here and in diverse other places of the New Testament, **prophets** are taken as expounders of the scripture.

[36]But after some days, Paul said to Barnabas, Let us go again and visit
our brethren in every place where we have preached the word of the Lord,
and see how they are doing. [37]And Barnabas gave counsel to take with
them John, called also Mark. [38]But Paul did not think it good to take him
into their company, who had departed from them at Pamphylia, and not

Dispute about Mark the evangelist.

gone with them to the work. [39]And the dissension was so sharp between
them that they separated one from the other. Barnabas took Mark and
sailed to Cyprus, [40]and Paul chose Silas and departed, committed by the
brethren to the grace of God. [41]And he went through all Syria and Cilicia,
strengthening the congregations.

The Notes

Faith purified their hearts (15:9)

a) Their hearts were purified with faith because they received by faith that their sins were not imputed to them, but forgiven for Christ's blood's sake.

My name is named (15:17)

b) Upon whom my name is named, etc; that is, those that shall be named with my name, as are those that are called the people of God and the servants of the Lord, or the congregation of Christ, or the Christian company.

Things strangled (15:20)

c) Things strangled are those creatures that die and do not have their blood shed.

Chapter 16

Timothy is circumcised. Paul preaches at Phillipi, and there he is put in prison.

Then Paul went to Derbe and to Lystra. And a certain disciple was there named Timothy, the son of a woman who was a Jewess and believed, but his father was a Greek. 2The brethren of Lystra and of Iconium spoke well of Timothy. 3Paul wanted him to go forth with him, and took and circumcised him because of the Jews that were in those quarters, for they all knew that his father was a Greek. 4As they went through the towns, they delivered to them the decrees to keep, as resolved by the apostles and elders who were at Jerusalem. 5And so the congregations were strengthened in the faith, and increased in number daily.

6When they had gone throughout Phrygia and the region of Galatia, and were forbidden by the Holy Spirit to preach the word in Asia, 7they came to the region of Mysia, and sought to go into Bithynia. But the Spirit would not permit them. 8Then they went over Mysia and down to Troas. 9And a vision appeared to Paul in the night: there stood a man from Macedonia who appealed to him, saying, Come into Macedonia and help us! 10After he had seen the vision, immediately we prepared to go into Macedonia, persuaded that the Lord had called us to preach the gospel to them. 11Then we set sail from Troas, and with a straight course went to Samothrace, and the next day to Neapolis, 12and from there to Philippi,* which is the chief city in the parts of Macedonia, and a Roman colony.

[**Philippi**: the first European city to receive the gospel]

We were in that city for several days. 13And on the Sabbath days we went out of the city, beside a river where people were accustomed to pray. And we sat down and spoke to the women who gathered there. 14And a certain woman named Lydia, a seller of purple from the city of Thyatira who worshipped God, listened to us, and the Lord opened her heart so that she attended to the things that Paul said. 15When she was baptized, and her household, she invited us, saying, If you think that I believe on the Lord, come into my house and stay there. And she constrained us.

Lydia the seller of purple.

16And it happened as we went to prayer that a certain girl possessed with a spirit that prophesied* met us, who brought her masters much income by prophesying. 17She followed Paul and us, and cried out, saying, These men are the servants of the most high God, who show to us the way of salvation! 18And she did this many days. But Paul, not pleased, turned about and said to the spirit, I command you in the name of Jesus Christ to come out of her! And it came out the same hour.

[**Spirit that prophesied**: a demon that told fortunes and revealed matters. See OT feature at the end of the book of Acts]

Lev 20:27
De 18:10-14
1Sa 28:3-19

The spirit is cast out.

19And when her master and mistress saw that the hope of their gains was gone, they caught Paul and Silas and drew them into the marketplace to the authorities, 20and brought them to the magistrates, saying, These men are troubling our city. They are Jews, and preach customs 21that are not lawful for us to receive nor to observe, seeing we are Romans.

22And the people ran on them, and the magistrates tore their clothes and ordered them to be beaten with rods. 23And when they had beaten them sore, they cast them into prison, charging the jailer to keep them

2Co 11:25

securely. [24]Which jailer, when he had received such direction, thrust them
into the inner prison and made their feet fast in the stocks.

[25]At midnight, Paul and Silas were praying and lauding God, and the
A great earthquake. prisoners heard them. [26]And suddenly there was a great earthquake, so
that the foundation of the prison was shaken. And immediately all the
doors opened, and every man's bonds were loosed. [27]When the keeper of
the prison awoke out of his sleep and saw the prison doors open, he drew
out his sword and would have killed himself, supposing the prisoners had
escaped. [28]But Paul called out with a loud voice, saying, Do yourself no
harm, for we are all here!

[29]Then he called for a light and rushed in, and came trembling, and
fell down before Paul and Silas, [30]and brought them out and said, Sirs,
what must I do to be saved? [31]And they said, Believe on the Lord Jesus,
and you shall be saved, and your household. [32]And they preached the
word of the Lord to him and to all who were in his house. [33]And he took
them the same hour of the night and washed their wounds, and was bap-
tized with all who belonged to him straightaway. [34]When he had brought
The joy of new faith. Paul and Silas into his house, he set food before them, and rejoiced that he
with all his household believed on God.

[35]And when it was day, the magistrates sent their officers, saying, Let
those men go. [36]The keeper of the prison told this to Paul, saying, The
magistrates have sent word to release you; now therefore take your leave,
and go in peace.

[37]Then Paul said to them, They have beaten us openly, without a trial,
for all that we are Romans, and have cast us into prison. And now would
they send us away quietly? No, not so, but let them come themselves and
get us out.

[38]When the officers told these words to the magistrates, they feared,
hearing that Paul and Silas were Romans, [39]and came and entreated them,
and brought them out, and desired them to depart out of the city. [40]And
they went out of the prison and entered into the house of Lydia. And when
they had seen the brethren, they comforted them and departed.

Chapter 17

Paul goes to Thessalonica, where the Jews set the city on a roar. Paul escapes and goes to Athens, where he preaches the true and unknown God.

As they made their journey through Amphipolis and Apollonia, they came
to Thessalonica, where there was a synagogue of the Jews. [2]And Paul, as
his custom was, went in to them, and for three Sabbath days reasoned
with them out of the scriptures, [3]explaining and showing that the Christ
must necessarily have suffered and risen again from death, and that this Lu 24:26,27
Jesus was Christ, whom (said he) I preach to you. [4]And some of them
believed, and came and kept company with Paul and Silas; also of the
honourable Greeks a great number, and of the chief women not a few.

[5]But the Jews who did not believe, being indignant, took some evil

men that were vagabonds, and gathered a company, and set all the city on
a roar, and attacked the house of Jason, and intended to bring Paul and
Silas out to the people. [6]But when they did not find them, they drew Jason
and certain brethren to the officials of the city, shouting, Those men that
trouble the world have come here also, [7]and Jason took them in. And Joh 19:12
these people all go contrary to the decrees of Caesar, affirming another
king, one Jesus!

[8]And the people and the officials of the city were troubled when they
heard these things. [9]But when they were sufficiently answered by Jason
and by the others, they let them go.

[10]And the brethren immediately sent away Paul and Silas by night to
Berea. When they arrived there, they entered into the synagogue of the
Jews. [11]These were the noblest of birth among those of Thessalonica, and 1Th 1:6,7
Search the scriptures, for by them ye may try all doctrine.
received the word with all diligence of mind, and searched the scriptures
daily, whether those things were so. [12]And many of them believed; also
noble women who were Greek, and men not a few.

[13]When the Jews of Thessalonica learned that the word of God was
preached by Paul at Berea, they came and stirred up the people there.
[14]And then immediately the brethren sent Paul away to go to the sea, but
Silas and Timothy remained there still. [15]And the men who guided Paul
Paul at Athens.
brought him to Athens, and were given a message for Silas and Timothy
to come to him at once, and went their way.

[16]While Paul waited for them at Athens, his spirit was moved in him,
to see the city given to the worship of idols. [17]Then he spoke at length in
[**Epicures** denied the afterlife and held that God was not involved in the affairs of mankind. **Stoics** taught self-mastery through indifference to pain or pleasure]
[**New devils**: some have 'new' or 'foreign gods.' The Gk allows for either. Many ancient peoples purposely worshiped demons, doing them honour in order to appease their evil wrath. St Augustine in the 4th century wrote about this in his book *City of God*]
the synagogue with the Jews and with the devout persons, and in the
market daily with those who came to him. [18]Certain philosophers of the
Epicures* and of the Stoics* debated with him. And there were some who
said, What will this babbler say? Other said, He seems to be a preacher of
new devils,* because he preached Jesus and the resurrection to them.
[19]And they took him and brought him into Mars Street, saying, May we
not know what this new doctrine is of which you speak? [20]For you bring
strange tidings to our ears. We would like to know therefore what these
things mean. [21](For all the Athenians and foreigners who were there gave
themselves to nothing else but either to tell or to hear new things.)

[22]Paul stood in the middle of Mars Street and said, Ye men of Athens,
I perceive that in all things you are too superstitious. [23]For as I passed by
and saw how you worship your gods, I found an altar on which was
written, TO THE UNKNOWN GOD. Him then, whom you worship without
knowledge, I proclaim to you. [24]God, who made the world and everything
that is in it, seeing that he is Lord of heaven and earth, dwells not in
temples made with hands. [25]Neither is he worshipped with men's hands,
as though he needed anything, seeing he himself gives life and breath to
all people everywhere. [26]And he has made from one blood all nations of
men to dwell on all the face of the earth, determining beforehand how
long, and also the bounds of their habitation, [27]desiring them to seek God,
if they might feel after and find him – though he is not far from any one of

us. 28For in him we live and move and have our being, as certain of your own poets have said. For we are also his offspring.[a] 29Since then we are the offspring of God, we ought not to think that the godhead is as gold, silver, or stone, graven by the craft and imagination of man.

30And God overlooked the time of this ignorance. But now he bids all people everywhere to repent, 31because he has appointed a day in which he will judge the world according to righteousness by that man whom he has appointed. And he has offered faith to all peoples, after raising him from death.[b]

32When they heard of the resurrection from death, some mocked, but others said, We would like to hear you again concerning this matter.

[This **council** was called the Areopagus, named after the hill northwest of ancient Athens where the council met]

33Leaving it there, Paul departed from the assembly. 34However, certain men joined with Paul and believed, among whom was Dionysius, a member of the aristocratic council,[*] and a woman named Damaris, and others with them.

The Notes

The offspring of God (17:28)

a) We are his offspring, etc: that is, we are come of him, as of our Father and Maker.

He has offered faith to all peoples (17:31)

b) Faith is here taken for the promises of mercy, which through faith save us – which promises, after the resurrection of Christ, God commanded to be preached to all nations, and not to the Jews only, as before.

Chapter 18

Paul preaches at Corinth, continuing there a year and a half. He goes again into Syria, and to Ephesus, Caesarea, and Antioch. Of Aquila and Priscilla, and Apollos.

[**Corinth:** a coastal city, busy commercial centre, and capital of the Roman province of Achaia in southern Greece]

Tentmakers.

After that, Paul departed from Athens and went to Corinth.[*] 2And he met a certain Jew named Aquila, born in Pontus, lately come from Italy with his wife Priscilla, because the Emperor Claudius had commanded all Jews to depart from Rome. And he fell in with them. 3And because he was of the same craft, he stayed with them and worked; their craft was to make tents. 4And he preached in the synagogue every Sabbath day, and exhorted the Jews and the Gentiles.

5When Silas and Timothy had come from Macedonia, Paul was constrained by the Spirit to testify to the Jews that Jesus was the very Christ. 6And when they contradicted and reviled him, he shook out his clothing and said to them, Your blood is upon your own heads, and from henceforth I go blameless to the Gentiles. 7And moving on from there, he entered into the house of a certain man named Justus, a worshipper of God whose house adjoined the synagogue. 8However one Crispus, the chief ruler of the synagogue, believed on the Lord with all his household, and many of the Corinthians listened and believed and were baptized.

9Then the Lord spoke to Paul in the night by a vision: Do not be afraid, but speak; and do not hold your peace. 10For I am with you, and no man will attack you that will hurt you. For I have many people in this city.

11And Paul continued there a year and six months, and taught the 1,2 Co people the word of God.

More persecutions against Paul.

[12]When Gallio was ruler of the province of Achaia, the Jews made a united attack against Paul, and brought him to the judgment seat, [13]saying, This fellow counsels the people to worship God contrary to the law. [14]And as Paul was about to open his mouth, Gallio said to the Jews, If it were a matter of wrong, or an evil deed, O ye Jews, I should by reason hear you. [15]But if it is a question of words, or of names, or of your law, look to it yourselves. For I will be no judge in such matters. [16]And he drove them from the seat. [17]Then all the Greeks took Sosthenes, the chief ruler of the synagogue, and beat him outside the judge's seat. And Gallio cared about none of these things.

[18]After this, Paul remained there yet a good while, and then took his leave of the brethren and set sail for Syria, Priscilla and Aquila accompanying him. And he shaved his head in Cenchrea, for he had made a vow.[a] [19]And he came to Ephesus, and left Priscilla and Aquila there; but he himself entered into the synagogue and reasoned with the Jews.

Here Paul went to Jerusalem.

[20]When they asked him to stay longer with them, he did not consent, [21]but bid them farewell, saying, I must be in Jerusalem at the coming feast. But I will return again to you, if God so wills. And he sailed from Ephesus, [22]and landed at Ceasarea, and ascended to Jerusalem, and briefly visited the congregation.

Paul descends to Antioch, and passes then over all Galatia.

And he went down to Antioch (in Syria). [23]And when he had stayed there a while, he departed and went over all the region of Galatia and Phrygia systematically, strengthening all the disciples.

Apollos.

[24]And a certain Jew named Apollos, born at Alexandria, went to Ephesus. He was an eloquent man, and strong in the scriptures. [25]He was informed in the way of the Lord, and spoke fervently in spirit, and taught diligently the things of the Lord; but he knew only the baptism of John. [26]And he began to speak boldly in the synagogue. When Aquila and Priscilla heard him, they took him to themselves and expounded to him the way of God more perfectly. [27]And when he wanted to go into Achaia, the brethren wrote exhorting the disciples to receive him. After he got there, he greatly helped those who had believed through grace. [28]And with strong arguments he overcame the Jews, and that openly, showing by the scriptures that Jesus was the Christ.

The Notes

Shaved his head (18:18)

a) He shaved his head and kept his vow according to the law of abstinence, as you may read at Numbers 6:2-5.

Chapter 19

Of the twelve men that Paul baptized at Ephesus, and what miracles were done by him. Demetrius incites riot in the city.

It came about, while Apollos was at Corinth, that Paul passed through the upper regions and went to Ephesus, and found certain disciples, [2]and said to them, Have you received the Holy Spirit since you believed? And they

said to him, No, we have not heard whether there is a Holy Spirit or not.
[3]And he said to them, With what then were you baptized? And they said,
With John's baptism. [4]Then Paul said, John baptized with the baptism of
repentance, saying to the people that they should believe on him who was
to come after him; that is, on Christ Jesus.

[5]When they heard that, they were baptized in the name of the Lord
Jesus. [6]And Paul laid his hands upon them, and the Holy Spirit came on
them, and they spoke with tongues* and prophesied. [7]And the men were
about twelve in all.

[**Tongues**: The Gk *glossa* (1100) means literally the tongue, and by implication a human language. The Anglo-Saxon word *tongue* was used similarly when Tyndale wrote, but in modern non-literal use is replaced by *language*, a word of classical origin. To speak in other tongues or languages was a sign that God was calling other nations]

[8]And he went into the synagogue, and spoke boldly for the space of
three months, teaching and giving them exhortations of the kingdom of
God. [9]When some grew hardhearted and did not believe, but spoke evil of
the Way, and that before the assembly, he departed from them and with-
drew the disciples. And he held discussions daily in the school of one
called Tyrannus. [10]And this continued for two years, so that all those who
dwelt in Asia heard the word of the Lord Jesus, both Jews and Greeks.

[11]And God worked no small miracles by the hands of Paul. [12]Napkins
or partlets* were even brought from his body to the sick, and their diseases
departed from them, and the evil spirits went out of them.

[**Partlet**: an item of clothing worn over the neck and upper part of the chest]

[13]Then certain of the vagabond Jews, exorcists, took upon themselves
to call the name of the Lord Jesus over those who had evil spirits, saying,
We exorcise you by Jesus whom Paul preaches! [14]And there were seven
sons of one Sceva, a Jew and chief of the priests, who did this. [15]And the
evil spirit answered and said, Jesus I know, and Paul I know, but who are
you? [16]And the man in whom the evil spirit was ran on them and over-
came them, and so prevailed against them that they fled out of that house
with their clothes torn off, and wounded. [17]And this became known to all,
both the Jews and Greeks that dwelt at Ephesus. And fear came on them
all, and they magnified the name of the Lord Jesus.

[18]And many who believed came and confessed, and showed their
works. [19]Many of those who had been involved in occult practices brought
their books and burned them openly. They estimated the value of them,
and found it fifty thousand silverlings.* [20]Thus the word of God grew
mightily and prevailed.

[**Silverlings**: pieces of silver. One silverling was a day's wage for a common labourer. This indicates the extent and lucrative nature of magic and occult practices in Ephesus]

[21]After these things were accomplished, Paul purposed in the Spirit to
pass over Macedonia and Achaia, and to go to Jerusalem, saying, After I
have been there, I must also see Rome. [22]And he sent into Macedonia two
of those who assisted him, Timothy and Erastus; but he himself remained
in Asia for a season.

[23]At that time there arose no little ado about the Way. [24]For a certain
man named Demetrius, a silversmith who made silver shrines for Diana,*
brought no little income to the craftsmen. [25]He called these men together,
with the workmen of related occupations, and said, Sirs, you know that
we profit from this trade. [26]Moreover, you see and hear that not only at
Ephesus, but almost throughout all Asia, this Paul has persuaded and
turned away many people, saying that things made with hands are not

[**Diana**: a goddess also called Artemis. Her temple at Ephesus is one of the Seven Wonders of the Ancient World]

gods. [27]As a result, not only is this our craft at risk of being discredited, but also the temple of the great goddess Diana may fall into disrepute, and her magnificence be destroyed, whom all Asia and the world worship.

[28]When they heard this, the men were full of wrath and cried out, saying, Great is Diana of the Ephesians! [29]And all the city was on a roar, and the people rushed into the public theatre with one assent and caught Gaius and Aristarchus, men of Macedonia, Paul's companions.

[30]When Paul would have entered in to the people, the disciples prevented him. [31]Also, certain of the leading Asians that were his friends sent to him, urging him not to press into the theatre. [32]Some cried one thing and some another, and the crowd was all out of order, and the majority did not know why they had come together.

[33]Some of the crowd drew Alexander out, the Jews thrusting him forward. Alexander motioned with his hand and wanted to give the people an answer. [34]But when they knew that he was a Jew, there arose a shout for almost two hours, everyone crying, Great is Diana of the Ephesians!

[35]When the town clerk had quieted the people, he said, Men of Ephesus, what man is it that does not know that the city of the Ephesians is a worshipper of the great goddess Diana and of the image that came from heaven?[a] [36]Seeing then that no one here denies this, you ought to be quiet, and do nothing rashly. [37]For you have brought here these men who are neither robbers of temples nor blasphemers of your goddess. [38]And so if Demetrius and the craftsmen that are with him have any charge against anyone, the court is open, and there are deputies. Let them bring complaints against one another. [39]If you have any other matter, it may be determined in a lawful assembly. [40]For we are at risk of charges being made against us for this day's uproar, since there is no good reason we can give to account for this mob of people.

[41]And when he had thus spoken, he let the assembly depart.

The Notes

Image from heaven (19:35)

a) For their own greater advantage, the craftsmen who made idols among the Greeks pretended that they were sent out of heaven from Jupiter, and that they were not mortal or subject to death.

Chapter 20

Paul goes into Macedonia and into Greece. At Troas he raises up a dead body. At Ephesus he calls the elders of the congregation together, commits the keeping of God's flock to them, warns them of false teachers, makes his prayer with them, and departs by ship.

After the tumult was calmed, Paul called the disciples to him and took his leave of them, and departed to go into Macedonia. [2]And when he had gone over those parts and given the people many exhortations, he went into Greece, [3]and was there three months. And when the Jews laid wait for him as he was about to sail into Syria, he decided to return through

Macedonia.
[4]There accompanied him into Asia, Sopater of Berea, and from Thes-
salonica, Aristarchus and Secundus, and Gaius of Derbe, and Timothy;
and from Asia, Tychicus and Trophimus. [5]These went on ahead and
waited for us at Troas. [6]And we sailed away from Philippi after the Pass-
over holy days, and in five days came to them at Troas, where we stayed
seven days.

[The morrow after the Sabbath day: Sunday, or as some have it, 'the first day of the week']

[Lamps: the heat of the lamps together with the late hour are considered to have caused the young man to be overcome with sleep]

[7]And on the morrow after the Sabbath day,* the disciples came to-
gether to break bread. Paul, who was ready to depart on the next day,
preached to them, and continued preaching until midnight. [8]And there
were many lamps in the upper chamber where they were gathered to-
gether. [9]And a certain young man named Eutychus sat in a window, fall-
ing into a deep sleep. And as Paul spoke on, he was the more overcome
with sleep, and fell down from the third story, and was taken up dead. 1Ki 17:17-22
[10]Paul went down and fell on him, and embraced him and said, Don't be 2Ki 4:20-37
troubled, for his life is in him.
[11]When Paul had gone upstairs again, he broke bread and ate, and
talked a long while, even till the morning, and so departed. [12]And they
brought in the young man alive, and were not a little comforted.
[13]And we went on to the ship and set sail for Assos, there to take Paul
on board. For so he had arranged, and would himself go afoot. [14]When he
came to us at Assos, we took him in and went to Mitylene. [15]And we
sailed from there and arrived the next day off Chios. And the next day we
arrived at the island of Samos and stayed at Trogyllium. The next day we
went on to Miletus, [16]for Paul had determined to pass by Ephesus as they
sailed, because he did not want to spend the time in Asia. For he hastened
to be (if he could possibly) at Jerusalem for the day of Pentecost. [17]And so
from Miletus he sent to Ephesus and summoned the elders of the con-
gregation.

The sermon of Paul to the Ephesians.

[18]And when they had come to him, he said to them, You know how,
from the first day that I came to Asia, I have been with you at all seasons,
[19]serving the Lord with all humbleness of mind, and with many tears and
trials that happened to me through the plots of the Jews; [20]and how I kept
back nothing that was profitable, but have shown you and taught you
openly and at home in your houses, [21]witnessing both to the Jews and also

Repentance and faith.

to the Greeks repentance toward God and faith toward our Lord Jesus.
[22]And now behold, I go bound in the spirit to Jerusalem, not knowing
what will come on me there, [23]but that the Holy Spirit witnesses in every
city, saying that bonds and trouble await me. [24]But none of those things
move me. I do not count my life dear to myself, so that I may finish my
course with joy, and the ministry that I have received from the Lord Jesus
to testify the gospel of the grace of God.
[25]And now behold, I am sure that henceforth you all (among whom I
have gone preaching the kingdom of God) shall see my face no more.
[26]And so I call you as witnesses this same day, that I am clear of the blood 2Sa 3:28
of all men. [27]For I have kept nothing back, but have spoken to you all the

counsel of God. 28Take heed therefore to yourselves, and to all the flock
whereof the Holy Spirit has made you overseers, to shepherd the con-
gregation of God, which he has purchased with his blood. 29For I am sure M't 10:16
Grievous wolves. of this, that after my departing, grievous wolves will enter in among you, 1Ti 4:1-3
who will not spare the flock. 30Moreover, from among your own selves 2Co 11:12-20.
men will rise up speaking perverse things, to draw disciples after them. 2Pe 2:1-3
31Therefore awake, and remember that for the space of three years I did Jude 1:17-19
not cease to warn every one of you, both night and day, with tears.
32And now, brethren, I commit you to God, and to the word of his
grace, which is able to build further and to give you an inheritance among
all those who are sanctified. 33I have desired no man's silver, gold, or 1Co 9:12
clothing. 34You know well that these hands have provided for my needs 1Th 2:4-10
and for those who were with me. 35I have shown you in every way how, 2Th 3:8,9
by so labouring, you ought to help the weak, and to remember the words
of the Lord Jesus, that he said it is more blessed to give than to receive.
36When he had thus spoken, he kneeled down and prayed with them
all. 37And they all wept abundantly, and fell on Paul's neck and kissed
him, 38sorrowing most of all for the words that he spoke, that they would
see his face no more. And they accompanied him to the ship.

Chapter 21

Paul's journey by ship. Of Philip the evangelist, and of Agabus the prophet, who warned Paul not to go to Jerusalem. He remains steadfast in his purpose, and is taken in the temple.

And once we had launched forth and drawn away from them, we went
with a straight course to Cos, and the day following to Rhodes, and from
there to Patara. 2And we found a ship ready to sail to Phoenicia, and went
aboard and set sail. 3Then we came in sight of Cyprus, and we passed it
on the left hand and sailed to Syria. We put in at Tyre, because the ship
was to unload her cargo there. 4And when we found brethren, we stayed
there seven days. And they told Paul through the Spirit that he should not
go up to Jerusalem.
5And when the days were ended, we departed and went our ways; and
they all brought us on our way, with their wives and children, till we got
to the outskirts of the city. And we kneeled down on the shore and prayed.
And when we had taken our leave of one another, 6we boarded ship, and
they returned home again.
7When we had completed the voyage from Tyre, we went on to
Ptolemais and greeted the brethren, and stayed with them one day. 8The
next day, we who were of Paul's company departed and went to Caesarea.
And we entered into the house of Philip the evangelist, who was one of
Philip. the seven deacons, and stayed with him. 9This man had four daughters,
virgins who prophesied.
10And while we tarried there a good many days, there came a certain
Agabus. prophet from Judea named Agabus. 11When he had come to us, he took Ac 11:28
[**Girdle**: a belt or sash] Paul's girdle* and bound his hands and feet, and said, Thus says the Holy

Spirit: in this manner the Jews at Jerusalem will bind the man that owns
this girdle, and will deliver him into the hands of the Gentiles.
12When we heard this, both we and others of the same place besought
Paul not to go up to Jerusalem. 13Then Paul answered and said, What are
you doing, weeping and breaking my heart? I am ready not only to be
bound, but also to die at Jerusalem for the name of the Lord Jesus.
14When we could not turn his mind, we gave up, saying, May the will
of the Lord be fulfilled.
15After those days we made ourselves ready and went up to Jerusalem.
16There went with us also certain of the disciples of Caesarea, and they
brought with them one Mnason of Cyprus, an old disciple, with whom we
would lodge. 17And when we got to Jerusalem, the brethren received us
gladly. 18And on the morrow, Paul went in with us to James. And all the
elders came together. 19And when he had greeted them, he told in order all
the things that God had wrought among the Gentiles through his ministry.
20And when they heard it, they glorified the Lord and said to him, You
see, brother, how many thousand Jews there are who believe, and they are
all zealous over the law.* 21And they are informed of you that you teach
all the Jews who are among the Gentiles to forsake Moses, and say that
they ought not to circumcise their children, nor live according to the
customs. 22What then? This group is bound to get together, because they
will hear that you have come. 23Do therefore what we say to you: We Nu 6:2,13,18
have four men who are under a vow. 24Take them, and purify yourself
with them, and bear their expenses so that they can shave their heads, and
everyone will know that those things that they have heard concerning you
are nothing, but that you yourself also walk keeping the law. 25For con-
cerning the Gentiles who believe, we have written and concluded that they
need observe no such things, but should keep themselves from things
offered to idols, from blood, from things strangled, and from fornication.
26Then the next day Paul took the men and purified himself with them,
and entered into the temple, declaring that he was observing the days of
purification until an offering should be offered for every one of them.
27And as the seven days were almost ended, the Jews of Asia, when
they saw Paul in the temple, moved all the people, and laid hands on him,
28crying, Men of Israel, help! This is the man that teaches everyone every-
where against the people and the law and this place. Moreover, he has
also brought Greeks into the temple, and has defiled this holy place. 29(For
they had seen one Trophimus, an Ephesian, with him in the city, and they
supposed Paul had brought him into the temple.)
30And all the city was moved, and the people swarmed together. And
they took Paul and drew him out of the temple, and immediately the doors
were shut to.
31As they went about to kill him, a report came to the high captain of
the soldiers that all Jerusalem was in an uproar. 32He immediately took
soldiers and centurions* and ran down to them. When they saw the high
captain and the soldiers, the people stopped beating Paul. 33Then the

*Zealous is jealous, as a man is over his wife.

[**Centurion**: captain of a 'century,' or 100 soldiers, and subordinate to the high captain. A century formed part of a 'legion' of 6000 men] captain came near and took him, and commanded him to be bound with two chains, and demanded who he was and what he had done. 34And one shouted this and another that among the people. And when he could not ascertain the facts due to the tumult, the captain commanded Paul to be taken into the castle. 35And when Paul came to a flight of stairs, he had to be carried by the soldiers, because of the violence of the people. 36For the crowd of people followed after, crying, Away with him!

The people cry to be rid of Paul.

37And as Paul began to be led into the castle, he said to the high captain, May I speak to you? He said, Can you speak Greek? 38Are you not that Egyptian who before these days caused a riot, and led out into the wilderness four thousand men that were murderers?

39But Paul said, I am a Jew of Tarsus, a city in Cilicia, a citizen of no mean city. I beseech you, allow me to speak to the people.

40When he had given him leave, Paul stood on the steps and beckoned with his hand to the people, and there was a great silence. And he spoke to them in the Hebrew tongue, saying,

Chapter 22

Paul answers to the Jews, is scourged, and is put in prison again.

Men, brethren and fathers, hear my answer, which I make to you.

2When they heard that he spoke in the Hebrew tongue to them, they kept the more silence.

Paul addresses the crowd.

And he said, 3I am indeed a Jew, born in Tarsus, a city in Cilicia, but brought up in this city at the feet of Gamaliel, and thoroughly taught in the law of the fathers. And I was fervent-minded toward God, as you all are this same day. 4And I persecuted this Way to the death, binding and delivering into prison both men and women, 5as the chief priest bears me witness, and all the elders – from whom also I received letters to the brethren, and went to Damascus to bring those who were there as prisoners to Jerusalem, to be punished.

Ac 8:1; 9:1-19; 26:9-18.

6But it came to pass, as I made my journey and had come near to Damascus about noon, that suddenly a great light from heaven shone round about me. 7And I fell to the earth and heard a voice saying to me, Saul, Saul, why do you persecute me? 8And I answered, Who are you, Lord? And he said to me, I am Jesus of Nazareth, whom you persecute.

9And those who were with me saw a light, and were afraid, but they did not hear the voice of him that spoke with me. 10And I said, What shall I do Lord? And the Lord said to me, Arise and go into Damascus, and there it will be told you all the things that are appointed for you to do.

11And when I could not see anything due to the brightness of the light, I was led by the hand by those who were with me, and came into Damascus. 12And one Ananias, a godly man, and as pertaining to the law having a good report among all the Jews who dwelt there, 13came to me. And he stood and said to me, Brother Saul, look up! And that same hour I received my sight, and could see him. 14And he said, The God of our

Ananias restores Paul's sight and declares Paul's mission.

fathers has fore-ordained you to know his will, and to see that which is rightful, and to hear the voice of his mouth. 15For you shall be his witness to all people of those things that you have seen and heard. 16And now, why tarry? Arise and be baptized, and wash away your sins, in calling on the name of the Lord.

Be baptized.

17And it happened, when I returned again to Jerusalem and was praying in the temple, that I was in a trance, 18and saw him saying to me, Make haste, and get quickly out of Jerusalem, for they will not receive the witness that you bear of me.

19And I said, Lord, they know that I imprisoned and beat in every synagogue those who believed on you. 20And when the blood of your witness Stephen was shed, I also stood by and consented to his death, and minded the garments of those who slew him. 21Then he said to me, Depart, for I will send you far from here, to the Gentiles.

22The people listened to him until these words, and then lifted up their voices and said, Away with such a fellow from the earth! It is a pity that he should live! 23And as they cried out and cast off their clothes and threw dust into the air, 24the high captain ordered him to be brought into the castle, and commanded him to be scourged and examined in order to find out why the people cried out so against him. 25And as they bound him with thongs, Paul said to the centurion that stood by, Is it lawful for you to scourge a man that is a Roman, and without a trial? 26When the centurion heard that, he went and told the high captain, saying, What do you intend to do? This man is a Roman.

27Then the high captain came and said to him, Tell me, are you a Roman? He said, Yes. 28And the captain answered, With a great sum I obtained this freedom. And Paul said, I was free born.*

[**Free born**: because he was born a citizen of Rome, Paul was exempt from brutal methods of interrogation. Roman citizenship was not officially for sale, but might be obtained by bribing corrupt officials]

29Then the soldiers who were to have examined him straightaway drew back from him. And the high captain also was afraid, after he knew that he was a Roman, because he had bound him.

30On the day following, because he wanted to know exactly what Paul was accused of by the Jews, the captain released him from his bonds, and commanded the high priests and all the council to come together, and brought Paul and set him before them.

Chapter 23

Paul comes before the council. Debate arises among the people. The high captain delivers him. God comforts him.

Paul beheld the council and said, Men and brethren, I have lived in all good conscience before God until this day. 2Then the high priest Ananias commanded those who stood by to strike him on the mouth.

3Then Paul said to him, God smite you, you whitewashed wall! Do you sit and judge me according to the law, and command me to be struck contrary to the law?

4And those who stood by said, Do you revile God's high priest?

5Then Paul said, I did not know, brethren, that he was the high priest.

For it is written: You shall not curse the ruler of your people. Ex 22:28
Sadducees and Pharisees. [6]When Paul perceived that the one part were Sadducees and the other
Pharisees, he cried out in the council, Men and brethren, I am a Pharisee, Ph'p 3:5
the son of a Pharisee. It is concerning the hope and resurrection from
death that I am on trial.
[7]And when he had said this, there arose a quarrel between the Phar-
isees and the Sadducees, and the assembly was divided. [8]For the Sad-
ducees say that there is no resurrection, and also no angels or spirits. But M't 22:23-32
the Pharisees grant both. [9]And there arose a great cry, and the scribes who
were of the Pharisees' party arose and protested, saying, We find no evil
in this man. And if a spirit or an angel has appeared to him, let us not
strive against God.
[10]And when great controversy arose, the captain, fearing lest Paul
should be pulled apart by them, commanded the soldiers to go down and
take him from among them, and to bring him into the castle. [11]The night
following, the Lord stood by him and said, Be of good cheer, Paul. For as
you have testified of me in Jerusalem, so must you bear witness at Rome.

[**The Lord stood by**: Tyndale had *God* stood by. The Great Bible (1539) followed him, but Wycliffe, the Rheims, the KJV, and most others have *the Lord.* Ed]

[12]When day came, certain of the Jews gathered themselves together
and made a vow, saying that they would neither eat nor drink till they had
killed Paul. [13]There were about forty who conspired this together. [14]And
they went to the chief priests and elders and said, We have bound our-
selves with a vow that we will eat nothing until we have slain Paul. [15]Now
therefore, petition the high captain and the council to bring him forth to us
tomorrow, as though we want to better understand something concerning
him. But we, before he comes near, are ready meanwhile to kill him.
Paul's nephew warns him. [16]When the son of Paul's sister heard of their plan to lie in wait, he
went and entered into the castle and told Paul. [17]And Paul called one of
the centurions to him and said, Bring this young man to the high captain,
because he has a certain thing to tell him. [18]And he brought him and said,
Paul the prisoner called me to him, and asked me to bring this young man
to you, who has a certain matter to tell you of.
[19]The high captain took him by the hand and went apart with him
privately, and asked him, What have you to say to me? [20]And he said, The
Jews have resolved to ask you to bring forth Paul tomorrow into the
council, as though they want to make further enquiries of him. [21]But do
not go along with them, because there will be more than forty men lying
in wait for him, who have bound themselves with a vow that they will
neither eat nor drink till they have killed him. And now they are ready and
waiting for your word.
[22]The high captain let the young man depart, and instructed him, See
Things are made ready to bring Paul safe to Felix the governor in Caesarea. you tell no one that you have told these things to me. [23]And he called to
him two centurions, saying, Make ready 200 soldiers to go to Caesarea,
and 70 horsemen and 200 spearmen, at the third hour of the night. [24]And
provide horses to put Paul on, and bring him safe to Felix, the governor.[a]
[25]And he wrote a letter in this manner:
[26]Claudius Lysias to the most noble Governor Felix, sends greetings.

27This man was taken by the Jews and was near to being killed by them. Then I came with soldiers and rescued him, and learned that he was a Roman. 28And when I wished to know the offence for which they accused him, I brought him forth into their council. 29There I could see that he was accused concerning questions of their law, but was not guilty of anything worthy of death or of bonds. 30Afterward, when it was reported to me that the Jews were lying in wait for the man, I sent him straightaway to you, and directed his accusers, if they had anything against him, to tell it to you. Farewell.

31Then the soldiers, as it was commanded them, took Paul and brought him by night to Antipatris. 32The next day they left horsemen to go with him, and returned to the castle.

Paul is presented before Governor Felix.

33When the horsemen got to Caesarea, they delivered the epistle to the governor and presented Paul before him. 34When the governor had read the letter, he asked what province he was from. And when he understood that he was from Cilicia, he said, 35I will hear you when your accusers have come also.

And he commanded him to be kept in Herod's palace.

The Notes

Bring him safe to Felix (23:24)

a) [Ed: In the Great Bible of 1539 (also sometimes called the Cranmer Bible) we find added at verse 24 an explanation why the captain took such care to deliver Paul safely to Felix: *"For he did fear lest haply the Jews should take him away and kill him, and he himself should be afterward blamed, as though he would take money."* Wycliffe (1380) and the Rheims (1582) added similar words.]

Chapter 24

Paul is accused before Felix. He answers for himself.

After five days, Ananias the high priest descended with elders and with a certain orator named Tertullus, and made representations to the governor concerning Paul. 2When Paul was called forth, Tertullus began the case against him, saying,

Seeing that we live in great quietness owing to you, and that many good things are done for this nation through your prudent government, 3we receive and acknowledge it ever and in all places, most noble Felix, with all thanks. 4But in order that I not be tedious to you, I pray that you would kindly hear a few words from us.

Paul is spoken against.

5We have found this man a pestilent fellow, and a mover of conflict among all the Jews throughout the world, and a maintainer of the sect of the Nazarites, 6who has also taken in hand to profane the temple. We took him and would have judged him according to our law, 7but the high captain Lysias came upon us and with great force took him away out of our hands, 8commanding his accusers to come to you. You may, if you wish to enquire, ascertain from him the facts concerning all these things of which we accuse him.

Pr 15:7; 29:9.

9The Jews maintained likewise, saying that it was even so.

Paul answers for himself.

10 Then Paul (after the governor himself had indicated to him that he should speak) answered, I shall with a more quiet mind answer for myself, 11 since I understand that for many years you have been a judge to this people, in order that you may know that it is yet only twelve days since I went up to Jerusalem to pray, 12 and they neither found me in the temple disputing with anyone, nor inciting the people, either in the synagogues or in the city. 13 Nor can they prove the things they accuse me of.

14 But this I confess to you: that in accordance with the Way, which they call heresy, so do I worship the God of my fathers, believing all things that are written in the law and the prophets. 15 And I have hope in God that the same resurrection of the dead that they themselves look for also will come, both of the just and the unjust. 16 And therefore I strive to have a clear conscience toward God, and toward man also.

17 But after many years I came, bringing alms and offerings to my people, 18 in the course of which they found me purified in the temple, neither with a lot of people, nor making a disturbance. However, there were certain Jews out of Asia, 19 who ought to be here present before you and accuse me if they have anything against me. 20 Or else let these men here say if they have found any wrongdoing in me, while I stand here in the council – 21 unless it be for this one statement that I made standing among them: It is concerning the resurrection from death that I am on trial before you this day.

Felix adjourns the hearing.

22 When Felix heard these things, he adjourned the hearing – for he knew very well of that Way – and said, When Lysias the captain arrives, I will hear the last of your matters. 23 And he commanded a centurion to keep Paul, and that he should have rest, and not to forbid any of his friends to minister to him* or come to him.

[**Minister to him**: provide for him; attend to his wants, needs, and comforts]

[**Temperance**: moderation or abstinence as befits holiness]

24 And after some time, Felix and his wife Drusilla, who was a Jewess, came and called for Paul, and heard him concerning the faith that is toward Christ. 25 And as he preached of righteousness, temperance,* and the judgment to come, Felix trembled and answered, That is enough at this time; depart. When I have a convenient time, I will send for you. 26 He hoped also that Paul would give him money to set him free, so he called for him often and conversed with him.

27 But after two years, Festus Porcius succeeded Felix. And Felix, wanting to please the Jews, left Paul bound in prison.

Chapter 25

The Jews accuse Paul before Festus. Paul appeals to the Emperor, and is sent to Rome.

Festus Porcius.

When Festus had arrived in the province, after three days he ascended from Caesarea to Jerusalem. 2 Then the high priests and the chief men of the Jews made submissions to him about Paul. And they entreated him, 3 and requested his indulgence concerning Paul, that he would send for him to come to Jerusalem. And they planned to lay wait for him along the way, to kill him.

[4]But Festus answered that Paul should be kept at Caesarea, but that he himself would shortly go there. [5]Therefore (said he) let those among you who are able to do it come down with us, and bring your case against him there, if there be any fault in the man.

[6]When he had been in Jerusalem more than ten days, Festus departed to Caesarea. And the next day he sat down in the judgment seat and commanded Paul to be brought. [7]When he appeared, the Jews that had come from Jerusalem came about him, and laid many and grievous complaints against Paul – which they could not prove, [8]as long as he answered for himself that he had not offended against the law of the Jews, nor against the temple, nor yet against Caesar, in anything at all.

[9]Festus, wanting to please the Jews, answered Paul and said, Will you go to Jerusalem and be judged there before me concerning these things? [10]Then Paul said, I stand at Caesar's judgment seat, where I ought to be judged. To the Jews I have done no harm, as you very well know. [11]If I have hurt them, or committed anything worthy of death, I do not refuse to die. If none of these things are so, of which they accuse me, no one ought to deliver me to them. I appeal to Caesar!

Paul appeals to Caesar.

[12]Then Festus spoke with deliberation and answered, You have appealed to Caesar: to Caesar you shall go.

King Agrippa and Bernice.

[13]After some days had passed, King Agrippa and Bernice came to Caesarea to pay their respects to Festus. [14]And when they had been there a good season, Festus described Paul's case to the king, saying, There is a certain man left in prison by Felix, [15]against whom the high priests and elders of the Jews informed me when I went to Jerusalem, and asked to have judgment against him. [16]To whom I answered, It is not the practice of the Romans to deliver any man to die before he has his accusers before him, and has the opportunity to answer for himself concerning the charge made against him. [17]When they came here, without delay I sat the next day to give judgment, and commanded the man to be brought forth.

[18]When the accusers stood up, they brought no accusation against him of such things as I supposed, [19]but had certain questions against him concerning their own superstition, and about one Jesus who was dead, whom Paul affirmed to be alive. [20]And because I was uncertain of such questions, I asked him if he would go to Jerusalem and be judged there concerning these matters. [21]Then, when Paul appealed to be held for hearing by Caesar, I commanded him to be kept till I could send him to Caesar.

[22]Agrippa said to Festus, I would also like to hear the man myself.

Tomorrow (said he) you shall hear him.

[23]And the next day, when Agrippa and Bernice came with great pomp, and had entered into the council house with the high captains and chief men of the city, at Festus' commandment Paul was brought forth. [24]And Festus said, King Agrippa, and everyone here present with us, you see this man, about whom all the Jews have been calling upon me, both at Jerusalem and also here, complaining that he ought not to live any longer. [25]Yet I found nothing worthy of death committed by him. Nevertheless,

seeing that he has appealed to Caesar, I have determined to send him. 26But I have nothing certain to write to my lord about him. Therefore I have brought him before you all, and especially before you, King Agrippa, so that after examination I might have something to write. 27For it seems to me unreasonable to send a prisoner and not to specify the complaints that are laid against him.

Chapter 26

King Agrippa hears Paul, who describes his calling from the beginning.

Agrippa said to Paul, You are permitted to speak for yourself. Then Paul stretched forth his hand and answered for himself:

2I think myself fortunate, King Agrippa, because I may answer this day before you to all the things I am accused of by the Jews, 3especially because you are expert in all the customs and questions that are among the Jews. Therefore I beseech you to hear me patiently.

Paul again recounts his conversion.

He was always law-abiding.

4My life from my childhood, which was at first among my own nation at Jerusalem, all the Jews 5who knew me from the beginning know, if they would testify it. For in accordance with the most strict sect of our religion, I lived as a Pharisee. 6And now I stand and am judged for the hope of the promise made by God to our fathers, 7to which promise our twelve tribes, earnestly serving God day and night, hope to attain. For which hope's sake, King Agrippa, I am accused by the Jews. 8Why should it be thought a thing incredible to you, that God should raise the dead up again?

Paul was sincerely, and violently, opposed to Christianity before his conversion.

9I also truly thought in myself that I ought to do many things to utterly oppose the name of Jesus of Nazareth – 10which things I also did in Jerusalem, where I shut up many of the saints in prison, having received authority from the high priests. And when they were put to death, I joined in giving the sentence. 11And I punished them often in every synagogue, and compelled them to blaspheme, and was even more mad upon them, and persecuted them even to distant cities.

Ac 9:1-19; 22:3-16.

His conversion experience.

12In going about these things, as I was going to Damascus with leave and authority from the high priests, 13at midday, O King, I saw in the road a light from heaven, brighter than the sun, shining round about me and those who were journeying with me. 14When we had all fallen to the earth, I heard a voice speaking to me and saying in the Hebrew tongue, Saul, Saul, why do you persecute me? It is hard for you to kick against the pricks. 15And I said, Who are you, Lord? And he said, I am Jesus, whom you persecute. 16But rise and stand up on your feet. For I have appeared to you for this purpose: to make you a minister and a witness both of those things you have seen, and of those things in which I will appear to you, 17delivering you from the people, and from the Gentiles to whom I now send you, 18to open their eyes so that they may turn from darkness to light, and from the power of Satan to God, and may receive forgiveness of sins, and an inheritance among those who are sanctified by faith in me.

Faith sanctifies.

19And so, King Agrippa, I was not disobedient to the heavenly vision,

Paul becomes a preacher and begins to suffer persecution.

[20]but preached first to those of Damascus, and then at Jerusalem, and
throughout all the country of Judea, and then to the Gentiles, that they
should repent and turn to God, and do the right works of repentance.
[21]Because of this, the Jews caught me in the temple and went about to kill
me. [22]Nevertheless, I obtained help from God, and continue to this day
witnessing both to small and to great, speaking of no other things than
those which the prophets and Moses did say would come: [23]that Christ
would suffer, and that he would be the first to rise from death, and would
show light to the people and to the Gentiles.

[24]As he thus answered for himself, Festus said with a loud voice, Paul,
you are beside yourself! Much learning has made you mad.

[25]And Paul said, I am not mad, most dear Festus, but speak the words
of truth and soberness. [26]The king knows of these things, before whom I
speak freely. I do not think any of these things are hidden from him. For
this was not done in a corner. [27]King Agrippa, do you believe the proph-
ets? I know well that you believe.

[28]Agrippa said to Paul, You bring me in mind somewhat to become a
Christian.

[29]And Paul said, I would to God that not only you, but also all who
hear me today, were not only somewhat, but altogether such as I am,
except for these bonds.

He desires that all would turn.

[30]And when he had thus spoken, the king rose up with the governor
and Bernice and those who sat with them. [31]And when they had gone
apart, they talked between themselves, saying, This man does nothing
worthy of death, nor of bonds. [32]Then Agrippa said to Festus, This man
might have been released, if he had not appealed to Caesar.

Chapter 27

Paul begins the voyage toward Rome. The centurion Julius treats him graciously. They suffer shipwreck.

When it was concluded that we should sail into Italy, they delivered Paul
and certain other prisoners to one named Julius, a centurion* of Caesar's
soldiers. [2]And we entered into a ship of Adramyttium and put out from
land, appointed to sail by the coasts of Asia. One Aristarchus, a Mace-
donian from Thessalonica, was with us. [3]And the next day we came to
Sidon. And Julius treated Paul graciously, and gave him liberty to go to
his friends and to refresh himself. [4]And from there we put out to sea, and
sailed hard by Cyprus, because the winds were contrary. [5]Then we sailed
over the sea that is off Cilicia and Pamphylia, and came to Myra, a city in
Lycia.

[**Centurion**: Tyndale had *undercaptain* for *centurion* here and elsewhere in Acts. Skilled and often noble men, centurions might be deployed on varying tasks, as here to escort Paul to Rome]

They set sail for Italy.

[6]And there the centurion found a ship of Alexander ready to sail to
Italy, and put us in it. [7]And when we had sailed slowly many days, and
with difficulty arrived off Cnidus (because the wind was against us), we
sailed hard by the coast of Crete off Salmone. [8]With much work we sailed
beyond Salmone, and came to a Cretan port called Fair Havens, near
which was a city called Lasea. [9]When much time had passed, and sailing

[**The Fast** of the Day of Atonement (Lev 23:27) occurred in late September or early October]

was now risky, and also because we had fasted too long,[*] Paul gave them
warning 10and said to them, Sirs, I can see that this voyage will be with
injury and much loss, not of the cargo and ship only, but also of our lives.
11But the centurion believed the steersman and the shipmaster over
those things that were spoken by Paul. 12And because the port was not
good to winter in, many were minded to depart, if by any means they
might reach Phoenix, a harbour of Crete that serves to the southwest and
northwest wind, and winter there.
13When the south wind blew, they, expecting to achieve their purpose,
raised anchor and sailed past all Crete. 14But soon after, there arose a

A storm arises.

contrary squall of wind out of the northeast. 15And when the ship was
caught and could not resist the wind, we let her go, and drove with the
weather.
16And we came to an isle named Clauda, and with much effort ob-
tained a skiff, 17which they hoisted up. And we had help undergirding the
ship, fearing to fall into the Syrtis Sands.[a] And we floated an anchor, and
so were carried.
18The next day, when we were tossed with an exceeding tempest, they
lightened the ship. 19And the third day, we cast the ship's tackle overboard
with our own hands. 20When at the last neither sun nor star appeared for
many days, and no small tempest lay upon us, all hope that we would be
saved was then taken away.
21Then, after long forbearance, Paul stood forth in the midst of them

Paul reports a message from an angel that the men will be saved, but the ship lost.

and said, Sirs, you should have listened to me, and not set out from Crete,
and brought to us this harm and loss. 22But now I exhort you to be of good
cheer. For there shall be no loss of any man's life among you, but of the
ship only. 23For there stood by me this night an angel of the God whose I
am, and whom I serve, 24saying, Fear not, Paul, for you must be brought
before Caesar. And lo, God has given to you all those who sail with you.
25Therefore, Sirs, be of good cheer. For I believe God, that it will be
just as it was told me. 26However, we must be cast onto a certain island.
27But when the fourteenth night came, as we were carried about in the
Adriatic Sea, at about midnight the sailors suspected some land was near.
28And they took soundings, and found it twenty fathoms. And when they
had gone a little further, they took soundings again, and found fifteen
fathoms. 29Then, fearing to hit some rock, they cast four anchors out of
the stern, and wished for the day.
30Then, as the sailors were about to escape out of the ship, and had let
the skiff down into the sea under the pretence of casting anchors out of the
foreship, 31Paul said to the centurion and the soldiers, Unless these men
remain in the ship, you cannot be safe.
32Then the soldiers cut the rope off of the skiff, and let it fall away.
33And in the meantime, between that and day, Paul besought them all
to take food, saying, This is the fourteenth day that you have been waiting
and continued without eating, taking nothing at all. 34So I urge you to take
food for your health. For not a hair shall fall from the head of any of you.

[35]And when he had thus spoken, he took bread and gave thanks to God in the presence of them all, and broke it and began to eat. [36]Then they were all of good cheer, and they also took food. [37]We were altogether in the ship 276 souls. [38]And when they had eaten enough, they lightened the ship and cast out the wheat into the sea.

[39]When it was day, they did not recognize the land, but they spotted a certain inlet with a bank, into which they were minded (if it were possible) to thrust in the ship. [40]And when they had taken up the anchors, they committed themselves to the sea, loosed the rudder bonds, hoisted up the mainsail to the wind, and drew to land. [41]They chanced on a shallow
They thrust the ship in to land. sandbank and thrust in the ship. And the forepart stuck fast, and did not 2Co 11:25
move, but the stern broke with the violence of the waves.

[42]The soldiers' counsel was to kill the prisoners, lest any of them, when he had swum out, should flee away. [43]But the centurion, wanting to save Paul, kept them from their purpose, and commanded that those who could swim should cast themselves first into the sea and escape to land. [44]And the others he commanded to go, some on boards and some on broken pieces of the ship. And so it came to pass that they all came safe to
All come safe to land. land.

The Notes

Fearing the Syrtis Sands (27:17)

a) The Syrtis Sands are a perilous sandy place in the Mediterranean Sea around the coasts of Africa, where whirlpools occur. [Ed: known as a ships' graveyard, these shallow waters contain dangerous cross currents. The undergirding of the ship probably involved winching cables tight around the hull, a procedure called frapping, to help the ship endure battering by wind and waves.]

Chapter 28

The viper does not hurt Paul's hand. He heals Publius' father, and preaches Christ at Rome.

And when they had escaped, then they learned that the island was called Malta. [2]And the people of the island showed us no little kindness, for they kindled a fire, and took us in every one, because of the falling rain and because of the cold.

[3]And when Paul had gathered a bundle of sticks and put them into the fire, there came a viper out of the heat, which leapt upon his hand. [4]When the islanders saw the venomous snake hanging on his hand, they said among themselves, This man must be a murderer, whom, though he has escaped the sea, yet vengeance suffers not to live. [5]But he shook the snake off into the fire and felt no ill effect. [6]However, they waited for him to swell up or fall down dead suddenly. But after they had waited a great while and saw no harm come to him, they changed their minds and said that he was a god.

[7]In the same region, the chief man of the island, whose name was
Publius receives them. Publius, had a lordship. He received us and kindly lodged us for three
days. [8]And it happened that the father of Publius lay sick of a fever and of

Laying on of hands.

dysentery. Paul entered in to him and prayed, and laid his hands on him
and healed him. 9When this was done, others also who had diseases in the
isle came and were healed. 10And they honoured us greatly; and when we
departed, they brought on board such things as were necessary.

11After three months, we departed in a ship of Alexandria that had
wintered in the island, whose figurehead was Castor and Pollux.[a] 12And
when we came to Syracuse, we stayed there three days. 13And from there
we made a circuit and came to Rhegium.

And after one day, the south wind blew. And we came the next day to
Puteoli, 14where we found brethren and were invited to stay with them
seven days; and so we went on toward Rome.

Paul arrives in Rome.

15And from Rome, when the brethren heard of us, they came out as far
as Appii Forum and the Three Taverns to meet us. When Paul saw them,
he thanked God and gained courage. 16And when he reached Rome, the
centurion delivered the prisoners to the chief captain of the host. But Paul
was allowed to dwell by himself, with one soldier to guard him.

17And it came about after three days that Paul called the chief Jews
together. And when they were assembled, he said to them, Men and
brethren, though I have committed nothing against the people or laws of
our fathers, yet I was delivered a prisoner from Jerusalem into the hands
of the Romans, 18who, when they had examined me, would have let me
go, because they found no cause of death in me. 19But when the Jews
cried out against this, I was constrained to appeal to Caesar – not because
I had anything to accuse my people of. 20So I have called for you in order
to see you and to speak with you, because it is for the hope of Israel that I
am bound with this chain.

21And they said to him, We have not received any letters out of Judea
concerning you, nor did any of the brethren who came here report or
speak any ill of you. 22But we will hear from you what you think. For we
have heard of this sect, that everywhere it is spoken against.

Paul preaches to the Roman Jews.

23And when they had appointed him a day, many came to him at his
lodging. To them he expounded and testified the kingdom of God, and
preached to them of Jesus, both out of the law of Moses and also out of
the prophets, even from morning to night.

Dull of heart and hearing, certain of them have closed their eyes and their ears.

Isa 6:8-10
M't 13:11-15
Mk 4:11,12
Lu 8:10
Joh 12:37-41
Ro 11:7-10

24And some believed the things that were spoken, and some did not
believe. 25So in disagreement among themselves they departed, after Paul
had spoken one word: Well did the Holy Spirit speak by Isaiah the proph-
et to our fathers, saying, 26Go to this people and say, With your ears you
will hear and will not understand, and with your eyes you will see and not
perceive. 27For the heart of this people has become dull, and their ears are
hard of hearing. And their eyes have they closed, lest they should see with
their eyes, and hear with their ears, and understand with their hearts, and
should be converted; and I would heal them. 28Let it be known to you,
therefore, that this salvation of God is sent to the Gentiles, and they will
hear it.

29And when he had said that, the Jews departed, and had great dis-

Paul dwells two full years in his lodgings in Rome.

putations among themselves.
30 And Paul dwelt two full years in his lodging, and welcomed all who
came to him, 31 preaching the kingdom of God and teaching those things
that concerned the Lord Jesus with all confidence, unforbidden.

Here ends the Acts
of the apostles.

The Notes

Castor and Pollux (28:11)

a) In the old time, Castor and Pollux were esteemed as gods who, if they appeared both together, were counted favourable and lucky to mariners and such as travelled the seas, but if one after another, or but one alone, unfortunate and cruel. The owner of the ship carried the figurehead of the two with confidence, thinking that these two gods would prosper his voyages because he honoured them with the carrying of the figurehead.

Old Testament Feature - A glimpse into the Old Testament of the 1549 Matthew Bible...
Verses concerning spiritism and divination, minimally updated:

Deuteronomy: The .xviii. Chapter (verses 10-14)

Let there not be found among you any who makes his son or daughter to go through the fire, or who practices witchcraft [marginal note: or magic arts], or a chooser of days, or who regards the flying of souls, or a sorcerer, or a charmer, or one who counsels with spirits, or a prophesier, or one who asks the advice of the dead. For all who do such things are abominable to the Lord. And because of these abominations, the Lord your God does cast them out before you.

Be pure therefore with the Lord your God. For these nations that you shall conquer hearken to choosers out of days and prophesiers. But the Lord your God does not permit this to you.

William Tyndale's Prologue Upon the Epistle of Saint Paul to the Romans

(Matthew's Version Abridged)

William Tyndale first published this in his 1534 New Testament, and John Rogers then incorporated it in the Matthew Bible with some modifications. Tyndale largely followed and expanded Martin Luther's prologue, and also added the last section, 'Sum and Whole Cause of the Epistle.' Here it is updated, organized, and abridged, removing much repetition, though it remains a lengthy foreword.

SEEING AS this epistle is the principal and most excellent part of the new testament, and most pure evangelion – that is to say, glad tidings, and that which we call the gospel – and is also a light and a way into the whole scripture, I think it meet that every Christian not only know it by memory, but also exercise himself in it continually, as with the daily bread of the soul. No one can read it too often or study it too well. For the more it is studied, the easier it is, and the more it is chewed, the pleasanter it is, and the more thoroughly it is searched, more precious things are found in it, so great a treasure of spiritual things lies hid herein.

I will therefore bestow my labour and diligence through this little prologue to prepare a way in to it, so far forth as God may give me grace, so that everyone may understand it. It has been darkened by false commentary, but nevertheless is of itself a bright light, sufficient to illumine all the scripture.

First we must mark diligently the manner of speaking of the apostle, and above all things know what Paul means by the words *law, sin, grace, faith, righteousness, flesh,* and *spirit.*[1] Otherwise, no matter how often you read it, you will but lose your labour.

The law and what it requires

This word *law* may not be understood here the usual way (or to use Paul's term, after the manner of men, or after man's ways), so that you would say that the law here is nothing but regulation that sets out what ought to be done and what ought not to be done. This is how it is with man's law, which is fulfilled with outward works only, even if the heart be ever so far off. But God judges the ground of the heart, yea and the thoughts and the secret movings of the mind.

And therefore his law requires the ground of the heart, and love from the bottom of the heart. It is not satisfied by the external work only, but rebukes most of all those works which do not spring of love from the ground and low bottom of the heart, even if they appear outwardly ever so honourable and good, as Christ in the gospel rebukes the Pharisees above all others who were open sinners. He calls them hypocrites, which is to say dissemblers, and white-washed tombs. Which Pharisees lived among men most purely insofar as the outward deeds and works of the law were concerned. Yea, and Paul in the 3rd chapter of his epistle to the Philippians says of himself that concerning the law he was such a one as no man could complain of, and yet notwithstanding was a murderer of the Christians, persecuted them, and tormented them so terribly that he compelled them

[1] There is some ambiguity in the use of 'spirit' in this prologue. At times it is not certain if the human spirit after regeneration is intended, or the Holy Spirit, or both together. Consider John 3:6. This editor has carefully considered when it seemed best to capitalize according to the context, though ambiguity remains.

to blaspheme Christ. He was altogether merciless, as many who now pretend to outward good works are.

But no one keeps the law from the ground of the heart, nor can so keep it, even if he appears outwardly full of good works, because all men are naturally inclined to evil. We find in ourselves disinclination and distaste to do good, but a bent and a taste to do evil. Now where there is no free inclination or desire to do good, there the bottom of the heart does not fulfil the law. And there no doubt also is sin, and wrath is deserved before God, even if there is an outward appearance of good living.

Moreover, the law increases sin, as he says in the fifth chapter, inasmuch as it requires so many things clean contrary to man's nature. A person becomes more and more an enemy of the law the more it demands of him what he cannot or does not wish to do.

And so he says in the seventh chapter that the law is spiritual, as if saying, if the law were fleshly and but man's discipline, it could be fulfilled, satisfied, and reconciled with bodily deeds. But the law is spiritual, and no one fulfils it unless all that he does springs of love from the bottom of the heart. Such a new heart, and an eager dedication to the law, you can never come by of your own strength and effort, but only by the operation and working of the Spirit.

For only the Spirit of God makes a man spiritual and conformable to the law, so that now henceforth he or she does nothing out of fear, or for money or advantage, or for vainglory, but of a free heart and of inward desire. The law is spiritual, and demands to be both loved and fulfilled by a spiritual heart, and therefore of necessity requires the Spirit, which makes a person's heart free, and disposes him in spirit to love and serve the law. Where such a spirit is not, there remains sin, grudging, and enmity against the law – which law nevertheless is good, righteous, and holy.

To fulfil the law is to do the work of the law, and whatever it commands, with love, desire, inward affection, and real pleasure. And it is to live godly and well freely, willingly, and without the compulsion of the law, even as if there were no law at all. Such willingness and free liberty to love the law come only by the working of the Spirit in the heart.

Now the Spirit is not otherwise given than by faith alone, in that we believe the promises of God – that he is true, and will fulfil all his good promises toward us for the sake of Christ's blood. I am not ashamed, says Paul, of Christ's glad tidings, for it is the power of God for salvation to as many as believe (Romans 1:16). For at once, simultaneously as we believe the glad tidings preached to us, the Holy Spirit enters into our hearts and breaks the bonds of the devil, who before possessed our hearts in captivity, and held them so that we could have no desire for the will of God in the law.

And as the Spirit comes by faith alone, even so faith comes by hearing the word or glad tidings of God when Christ is preached: that he is God's Son, and man also, dead and risen again for our sakes, as Paul says in the third, fourth, and tenth chapters. All our righteousness then comes by faith, and faith and the Spirit come of God, and not of us.[2]

---

[2] Here are removed problematic sentences that were added to Tyndale's prologue between 1534 (as it is contained in David Daniell's modern spelling edition) and 1537, when John Rogers brought it into the Matthew Bible. It was asserted that the Holy Spirit is ever present in us, even before faith, and the author attempted then to explain how we may say nonetheless that "faith brings the Spirit." This editor does not know if Rogers added these sentences of his own accord, or if it was a revision that Tyndale later made, or one that Rogers felt he would desire. (This is considered more closely in *The Story of the Matthew Bible.*)

From this it comes that faith alone justifies, makes righteous, and fulfils the law. For it brings the Spirit through the merits of Christ. The Spirit then brings desire, unbinds the heart, makes it free, sets it at liberty, and gives it strength to work the deeds of the law with love, as the law requires. Then at the last, out of the same faith so working in the heart, spring all good works of their own accord. This is what he means in the third chapter. For after he has cast away the works of the law, such that it seems as if he would break and nullify the law through faith, he answers possible objections, saying that we do not destroy the law through faith, but we maintain, further, or establish the law through faith. That is to say, we fulfil the law through faith.

Sin

Sin in the scripture is not only the outward work or deed that the body does. It includes everything that is involved, including whatever accompanies, moves, or stirs to the outward deed, and that from which the works spring, such as unbelief, and proneness and readiness to do the deed in the ground of the heart, with all the powers, affections, and appetites with which we can but sin. When a person sins, he is carried away headlong into it, thus showing all that he is, due to the poison inclination and corrupt nature in which we are conceived and born. For there is no outward sin committed unless a person be carried away altogether, with nature, soul, heart, body, will, and mind, to do it.

The scripture looks singularly to the heart, and to the root and original source of all sin, which is unbelief in the bottom of the heart. For as faith alone justifies us and brings the Spirit and predisposition to perform the outward good works, even so unbelief alone damns us, exalts the flesh, and stirs up the will to do evil outward works, as happened to Adam and Eve in Paradise (Genesis 3).

And so Christ calls unbelief sin, and that notably at John 16:9. The Spirit, says he, will rebuke the world of sin, because they do not believe in me. And at John 8:12 he says, I am the light of the world. And therefore in the twelfth chapter of John he bids them, while they have light, to believe in the light, so that they may be the children of light. For he who walks in darkness does not know where he goes. Now, as Christ is the light, so is the ignorance of Christ the darkness that he speaks of, in which he who walks does not know where he goes; that is, he does not know how to work a good work in the sight of God, or what a good work is. And therefore in the ninth he says, As long as I am in the world, I am the light of the world, but the night comes, when no man can work. Which night is but the ignorance of Christ, in which no one can please God.

And Paul at Ephesians 4:17 exhorts them not to walk as other Gentiles, who are strangers from the life of God through the ignorance that is in them. And again in the same chapter (Ephesians 4:22) he says, Put off the old man, which is corrupt through the lusts of error, that is to say, ignorance. And Romans 13:12: Let us cast away the deeds of darkness; that is to say, of ignorance and unbelief. And 1Peter 1:14: Do not fashion yourselves to your old lusts of ignorance. And 1John 2:10,11: He who loves his brother dwells in light, but he who hates his brother walks in darkness, and does not know where he goes, because the darkness has blinded his eyes. By *light* he means the knowledge of Christ, and by *darkness* the ignorance of Christ. For it is impossible that he who knows Christ truly should hate his brother.

Furthermore, to perceive this thing more clearly, understand that it is impossible to sin any sin at all unless a person first breaks the first commandment: You shall love your

Lord God with all your heart, with all your soul, with all your power, and with all your might. The whole reason why I sin against any inferior precept is that this love is not in my heart.

Therefore, before all good works as good fruits, there must be faith in the heart from whence they spring. And before all bad deeds as bad fruits, there must be unbelief in the heart, being the root, source, pith, and strength of all sin. Which unbelief and ignorance is called the head of the serpent and of the old dragon, which the seed of the woman, Christ, must tread underfoot, as it was promised to Adam.

Grace, gift

Grace and gift have this difference: *Grace* properly is God's favour, benevolence, or kind mind, which of his own self, without our deserving, he bears to us, and whereby he was moved and inclined to give Christ to us, with all his other gifts of grace. *Gift* is the Holy Spirit and his working, whom God pours into the hearts of those on whom he has mercy and whom he favours.

Though the gifts of the Spirit increase in us daily, and have not yet their full perfection – yea and though evil desires and sin that fight against the Spirit remain in us, as he says here in the seventh chapter and at Galatians 5:17, and also as it was spoken before at Genesis 3:15 of the strife between the woman's seed and the seed of the serpent – yet nevertheless, God's favour or grace is so great and so strong over us for Christ's sake, that we are counted fully whole and perfect before God. For his favour toward us is not incremental, increasing little by little like the gifts do, but he receives us wholly and immediately, in full love, for the sake of Christ, our intercessor and mediator, and because the gifts of the Spirit, and the battle between the Spirit and evil lusts, are begun in us already.

Of this now understand the seventh chapter, where Paul accuses himself as a sinner, and yet in the eighth chapter says that there is no damnation to those who are in Christ, and that because of the Spirit, and because the gifts of the Spirit are begun in us. Sinners we are, because the flesh is not full killed and mortified. Nevertheless, inasmuch as we believe in Christ, and have the earnest and beginning of the Spirit, and would very gladly be perfect, God is so loving and favourable to us that he will not look on such sin, neither will count it as sin, but will deal with us based on our belief in Christ, and according to the promises that he has sworn to us, until sin be full slain and mortified by death.

Faith

Faith is not man's opinion and dream, as some imagine, and form their own ideas when they hear the story of the gospel. The cause is that when they hear the gospel or glad tidings, they fashion by their own strength certain imaginations and thoughts in their hearts, saying, I have heard the gospel; I remember the story; lo, I believe! And this they count true faith – which nevertheless, since it is but man's imagination and assumption, does not profit. Neither do good works or a lasting amendment of life follow.

But true faith is a thing wrought by the Holy Spirit in us, which changes us, transforms our nature, begets us anew in God, and makes us the children of God, as you read in the first of John. A faith that is genuine kills the old Adam, and makes us altogether new in the heart, mind, will, desire, and in all our affections and powers of the soul, and brings the Holy Spirit with her.

Faith is a living thing, mighty in working, courageous and strong, ever doing, ever fruitful, so that it is impossible that the person endued with faith should not work good works. A person of faith does not ask whether good works are to be done or not, but has done them already, before mention be made of them. And he is always doing, for such is his nature now: a living faith in his heart, and the active moving of the Spirit, constrain him and stir him to this. Whoever does not do good works is an unbelieving person, and faithless, and looks around groping after faith and good works, but does not know what faith or good works are, even when he talks ever so much about faith and good works.

Faith is then a living and steadfast trust in the favour of God, whereby we commit ourselves altogether to God. And that trust is so surely grounded and sticks so fast in our hearts that a man would not once doubt of it, though he should die a thousand times for it. And such trust wrought by the Holy Spirit through faith makes a person glad, joyful, cheerful, and true-hearted, toward God and toward all creatures. And thus he or she is willingly and without compulsion glad and ready to do good to all, to render service to all, to suffer all things, so that God who has given him such grace may be loved and praised. So it is impossible to separate good works from faith, even as it is impossible to separate heat and burning from fire.

Therefore take heed to yourself. Beware of your own suppositions and imaginations, which to judge of faith and good works will seem wise, but indeed are blind, and of all things most unwise. Pray God that he will assent to work faith in your heart, or you will remain evermore faithless, however much you surmise, imagine, strengthen your resolve, wrestle with yourself, or do what you will or can.

Righteousness

Righteousness is even the faith spoken of above, which is the righteousness of God, or the righteousness that is of value before God. For it is God who gives it, and it alters a person, and gives him a new spiritual nature, and makes him free and generous to pay every one his due. For through faith a person is purged of his sins and becomes eager for God's law, by which he honours God, and pays him what he owes him; and he serves people willingly whenever he can, and pays each his due. Such righteousness nature, free will, or our own strength, can never bring to pass.

Flesh, spirit, spiritual

Flesh and spirit may not be understood here as if flesh denotes only that which pertains to unchastity, and the spirit that which pertains to the inward heart. But Paul considers flesh here, as Christ does in John 3, all that is born of flesh – the whole person, with life, soul, body, wit, will, reason, and whatever he is within himself and whatever he does outwardly. For these all, and all that is in man, lean to the world and the flesh. Consider flesh therefore whatever (as long as we are without the Spirit of God) we think or speak of God, of faith, of good works, and of spiritual matters. Call flesh also all works that are done without grace and without the working of the Spirit, however good, holy, and spiritual they seem to be, as you may see in the fifth chapter to the Galatians.

Likewise on the other hand, consider spiritual the person who is renewed in Christ, and also all deeds that spring of faith, seem they ever so common, such as the washing of the disciples' feet done by Christ, and Peter's fishing after the resurrection.

Review of the epistle

1st chapter

Since it becomes the preacher of Christ's glad tidings to begin with an exposition of the law, to prove all men sinners, and children of wrath by inheritance, and how to sin is their nature, and that by nature they cannot help but sin, and so to humble the pride of man, and bring him to the knowledge of himself and of his misery and wretchedness, so that he might desire help, likewise does Saint Paul. He begins in the first chapter to rebuke unbelief and the gross sins that everyone can see, as the idolatry and the obvious sins of the heathen were, and as the sins now are of all who live in ignorance without faith and without the favour of God.

And he says that through the gospel is revealed the wrath of the God of heaven upon all mankind, for their ungodly and unholy living. For though it is known and daily understood by the creatures that there is but one God, yet human nature of itself, without the Spirit and grace, is so corrupt and so poisoned that it cannot thank him, nor worship him, nor give him his due honour, but blinds itself, and falls continually into a worse case – even until people come to the worshipping of idols and the working of shameful sins that are abominable and against nature. And moreover, they suffer the same sins unrebuked in others, having delight and pleasure in them.

2nd chapter

In the second chapter, he proceeds further, and rebukes all those holy people also who, without desire and love for the law, live well outwardly in the face of the world, or sin secretly and condemn others gladly.

It is the nature of hypocrites to think themselves pure and yet hate the law inwardly, and to be full of covetousness, envy, and all uncleanness (Matthew 23). They it is who despise the goodness of God, and according to the hardness of their hearts heap together for themselves the wrath of God. Furthermore, Saint Paul, as a true expounder of the law, suffers no one to be without sin, but declares that all are under sin who would live well by free will and by nature, and suffers them not to be better than the open sinners; yea, he calls them hard-hearted, and such as cannot repent.

3rd chapter

In the third chapter he lumps together both the Jews and the Gentiles and says that one is as the other: both sinners, with no difference between them, except only that the Jews had the word of God committed to them. And though many of them did not believe on it, yet God's truth and promise are not thereby hurt or diminished. And he makes an aside to quote the saying of the 51st Psalm, that God remains true in his words, and overcomes when he is judged. After that he returns to his thesis again, and proves by the scripture that all without difference or exception are sinners, and that by the works of the law no one is justified, but that the law was given only to show and reveal sin.

Then he begins and shows the true way to righteousness, and how man must be made righteous and safe. He says all are sinners, and without praise before God. They must therefore, without any regard to their own merit, be made righteous through faith in Christ, who has merited such righteousness for us. He has become to us God's mercy-stool for the remission of sins that are past, thereby proving that Christ's righteousness alone helps us, which comes on us through faith. Which righteousness, Paul says, is now declared through the gospel, and was testified of before by the law and the prophets.

Furthermore (says he), the law is helped and furthered through faith, though the works of the law, with all their boast, are brought to nothing, and are proved not to justify.

4th chapter

After sins have been revealed for what they are in the first three chapters, and the way of faith to righteousness laid, Paul begins to answer certain objections and criticisms. First, if faith only justifies, why does a person need to be occupied in doing good works? He puts forth Abraham as an example, saying, What did Abraham accomplish with his works? Was all in vain? Did his works not profit? And he concludes that Abraham, without and before he did any works, was justified and made righteous by faith alone, insomuch that even before the 'work' of circumcision, he was praised in the scripture and considered righteous for his faith alone (Genesis 15).

So Abraham did not perform the work of circumcision to be helped to righteousness – which work God yet commanded him to do, and it was a good work of obedience. Likewise, surely no other works help at all for justification. But just as Abraham's circumcision was an outward sign, by which he demonstrated the righteousness that he had by faith, and his obedience and readiness to do the will of God, even so are all other good works outward signs, and the outward fruit of faith and of the Spirit, which do not justify a man, but demonstrate that a man is justified already before God inwardly in the heart, through faith and through the Spirit purchased by Christ's blood.

Here now Saint Paul reinforces his teaching on faith, previously set out in the third chapter, and brings also the testimony of David in the 32nd Psalm, which calls a man blessed, not for works, but in that his sin is not brought into account, and in that faith is imputed for righteousness – though he will not continue afterwards without good works, once he is justified.

After that, he extends his example to all other works of the law, and concludes that the Jews cannot be Abraham's heirs because of blood and kindred only, and much less by the works of the law. Rather, they must inherit Abraham's faith if they will be the true heirs of Abraham. For it was before both the law of Moses and the law of circumcision that Abraham was made righteous by faith, and called the father of all who believe. He was not called the father of those who do works.

Moreover, Paul says that the law causes wrath, since no one can fulfil it with love and eagerness. As long as grudging, hate, or indignation against the law remain in the heart, not being taken away by the Spirit that comes with faith, then surely it shows us that the wrath of God is upon us, and not favour.

Therefore faith alone receives the grace promised to Abraham. And these examples were not written for Abraham's sake only, says Paul, but also for us, to whom, if we believe, faith shall be reckoned likewise for righteousness, as he says in the end of the chapter.

5th chapter

In the fifth chapter, he commends the fruits and works of faith: peace, joy, inward love to God and man; moreover boldness, trust, confidence, courage, and steadfast hope in tribulation and suffering. For all such follow where the faith is genuine, through and for the abundant grace and gifts of the Spirit that God has given us in Christ, in that he gave him to die for us when we were yet his enemies. Now then, we see that faith alone, before any good works, justifies. And yet it does not follow that therefore we should do no good works. Rather, properly performed works do not lag behind, but accompany faith, even as brightness does the sun, and are called by Paul the fruits of the Spirit. Where the Spirit is, it is always summer, and there we may always find good fruits; that is to say, good works.

This is Paul's order: that good works grow out of the Spirit, the Spirit comes by faith, and faith comes by hearing the word of God, when the glad tidings and promises that God has made to us in Christ are preached truly, and received in the ground of the heart. Of this – God's Spirit and his fruit – our holy hypocrites have not once known, nor yet tasted how sweet they are, though they invent many good works out of their own imagination, in order to be justified thereby. In their works there is not one crumb of true faith or spiritual love, or of inward joy, peace, or quietness of conscience, seeing they do not have the word of God for them, that such works please God. But they are even the rotten fruits of a rotten tree.

After that, Paul breaks forth and unfolds the big picture, and shows from whence sin and righteousness, death and life, come. And he compares Adam and Christ, reasoning and arguing that Christ necessarily came as a second Adam, in order to make us heirs of his righteousness through a new spiritual birth without our prior merit, even as the first Adam made us heirs of sin through the bodily birth without our prior fault. Whereby it is obvious and proved absolutely that no one can bring himself out of sin to righteousness, any more than he could have prevented his bodily birth.

And Paul shows here that the very law of God, which should have helped if anything could help, not only came and brought no help, but even increased sin, because our evil and poisoned nature is offended and displeased with the law. And the more it is constrained by the law, the more it is provoked to satisfy its own desires. Therefore by the law we see that we need Christ to justify us by his grace, and to help nature.

6th chapter

In the sixth, Paul sets forth the chief and principal work of faith: the battle of the Spirit against the flesh – how the Spirit labours and makes us strong to kill the sin and the wrongful motions and desires that remain in the flesh after our justification. And this chapter teaches us that we are not so free from sin through faith that we may go up and down idly from now on, careless and sure of ourselves, as if there were now no more sin in us. Yes, there is sin remaining in us. But it is not counted against us, because of faith and the Spirit, which fight against it.

Therefore we have enough to do all our lives long to tame our bodies, and to compel the members to obey the Spirit, and not the appetites, so that we may conform to Christ's death and resurrection, and may fulfil our baptism, which signifies the mortifying of sins and the new life of grace. For this battle does not end in us until the last breath, until sin be utterly slain by the death of the body.

This thing – I mean to tame the body and so on – we are able to do (says he) because we are under grace, and not under the law. What it is not to be under the law, he himself explains. For not to be under the law does not mean that you may satisfy yourself as you please. But not to be under the law is to have a free heart renewed with the Spirit, so that you have the inner desire, of your own accord, to do what the law commands, without compulsion – yea, even as if there were no law. For grace – that is to say, God's favour – brings us the Spirit and makes us love the law, so that there is now no more sin through opposition to the law. Neither is the law against us any more. Rather, it agrees with us, and we with it.

But to be under the law is to contend with the works of the law, and is to work without the Spirit and grace. As long as this is the case, surely sin reigns in us through the law – the law is revealing that we are under sin, which has power and dominion over us because we cannot consent to the law. Which thing is great sin, because the law is the will of God.

So then, this is the true freedom and liberty from sin and from the law, of which Paul writes to the end of this chapter. It is a freedom to do only good with eagerness, and to live well without the compulsion of the law. Therefore this freedom is a spiritual freedom. It does not suspend the law, but supplies that which the law requires and with which it is fulfilled, namely love and a willing heart (Romans 3:31). Where these are, the law is silenced, and accuses us no more, compels us no more, neither has anything more to demand of us.

But it is not as though we ourselves could pay sin's debt to the law. If you were in debt to a man and were not able to pay, there are two ways you might be released. One way would be for the man to require nothing of you and to write off the debt. Another way would be if some other good man paid the debt for you and gave you what you need to satisfy your obligation; this is how Christ has made us free from the penalty of the law. And therefore this is no wild fleshly freedom that should do nothing, but it does all things, and yet is free from the demand and debt of the law.

7th chapter

In the seventh, Paul considers the foregoing with an analogy drawn from the state of matrimony. Then he declares more largely the nature of sin and of the law, and confirms that the law reveals sin and brings us to the knowledge of ourselves.

Furthermore, he declares how the Spirit [or spirit, as in our renewed spirit] and flesh fight against each other, and makes an example of himself. The flesh drives and fights against the Spirit and will have its desires satisfied, and on the other side the Spirit drives and fights against the flesh, and will have its desires satisfied. This fight endures in us as long as we live: in some people more, and in some less.

8th chapter

In the eighth chapter, he comforts such fighters so that they will not despair because of the flesh, nor think that they are less in favour with God. And he shows how it is that the sin that remains in us does not hurt, because there is no danger to those who are in Christ, who do not walk after the flesh, but fight against it. And he expounds more largely the nature of the flesh and of the Spirit, and how the Spirit comes by Christ. Which Spirit makes us spiritual, tames, subdues, and mortifies the flesh, and assures us that we are nevertheless the children of God, and also beloved, though sin rage ever so much in us, as long as we follow the Spirit and fight against sin, to kill and mortify it.

And because nothing is as effective for the mortifying of the flesh as the cross and tribulation, which yet are difficult to bear, Paul comforts us in our passions and afflictions. He confirms the assistance of the Spirit, who makes intercession to God for us mightily with groanings that pass man's utterance, so that man's speech cannot express or contain them; and he mentions the mourning of the creatures with us, out of the great desire that they have that we be freed from sin and the corruption of the flesh.

So see we that these three chapters – the sixth, seventh, and eighth – drive us to the true work of faith, which is to kill the old man and mortify the flesh.

9th, 10th and 11th chapters

In the ninth, tenth, and eleventh chapters, Paul treats of God's predestination, by which is determined entirely whether we will believe or not believe, be set free from sin or not be set free, and by which our justification and salvation are taken completely out of our hands and put in the hands of God alone. And this is most necessary, because we are so weak and so uncertain. If it depended on us, there would of a truth be no one saved; the devil would surely deceive and overcome us. But now God is true, unchanging, and utterly to be relied upon. His predestination cannot prove false. Nor can anyone resist or oppose him. Therefore we have hope and trust against sin.

But follow the order of this epistle. First, make Christ your study and concern. Learn what the law and the gospel are, and the office of both, so that you may in the one know yourself, that you have of yourself no strength but to sin, and in the other know the grace of Christ. And then see that you fight against sin and the flesh, as the first seven chapters teach you. After that, when you come to the eighth chapter, and are under the cross and suffering of tribulation, the necessity of predestination will be sweet, and you will feel how precious a thing it is. For unless you have borne the cross of adversity and temptation, and have felt yourself brought to the very brim of desperation, yea and to hell's gates, you cannot come to grips with the doctrine of predestination. For it will not be possible for you to think that God is righteous and just. Therefore the old Adam must be well mortified, and fleshly reason destroyed, before you can accept and drink such strong wine.

Take heed to yourself therefore, not to drink wine while you are yet but a babe. For all learning is progressive, and has its time, measure, and age. In Christ there is a certain childhood in which one must be content with milk for a season, until he or she is stronger and able to eat stronger meat.

12th chapter

In the twelfth chapter, he gives exhortations. For Paul observes this method in all his epistles. First he teaches Christ and the faith. Then he exhorts to good works and to continual mortifying of the flesh. So here he teaches good works indeed, and the true serving of God. He makes all men priests to offer up not money and animals, as was the way in the time of the law, but their own bodies, by killing and mortifying the desires and affections of the flesh.

After that, he describes the social intercourse of Christians: how they ought to govern themselves in spiritual things; how to teach, preach, and rule in the congregation of Christ; to serve one another; to suffer all things patiently; and to commit retribution and vengeance to God – in conclusion, how a Christian ought to conduct himself toward all people, be they friend, foe, or whatever. These are the true works of a Christian, which arise from faith.

13th chapter

In the thirteenth, he teaches us to honour the worldly and temporal sword; that is, the police and the secular authorities. They are appointed for the aid of the commonwealth: to maintain peace, to punish evildoers, and to defend the good. Therefore the good ought to honour the temporal sword, though as concerning themselves they do not need it, but would abstain from evil of their own accord.

Finally, he knits up all in love, and sets forth Christ as an example to us.

14th chapter

In the fourteenth chapter, he teaches to deal discreetly with the consciences of those who are weak in the faith, who do not yet understand the liberty of Christ perfectly enough, and to indulge them out of Christian love, and not to use the liberty of the faith harmfully.

There should be consideration for the weak, because where such consideration is not, arguments follow, and rejection of the gospel. It is better therefore to bear with the weak a while, until they become stronger, than that the teaching of the gospel should come altogether underfoot. And such work is singular work of love, and where love is perfect, there will certainly be such a regard for the weak – a thing that Christ commanded and charged to be had above all things.

15th chapter

In the fifteenth chapter, he sets Christ forth again as an example, to be longsuffering with others who are weak, including those who fall repeatedly, open sinners, the unlearned, the inexperienced, and people with offensive ways and manners. We ought not to cast them away at once, but to bear with them until they become better, and exhort them in the meantime. For that is how Christ was in the gospel, and now deals with us daily, bearing with our imperfections, weakness, behaviours, and ways not yet conformed to the teaching of the gospel, but smelling of the flesh – yea, and sometimes breaking out into carnal deeds.

After that, he wishes them increase of faith, peace, and joy of conscience, praises them, and commits them to God. He also seeks aid from them for the poor saints who were at Jerusalem.

16th chapter

The last chapter is a chapter of recommendations, wherein Paul adds a good admonition to beware of the precepts and doctrines of men, who beguile the simple with sophistry and with teaching that is not in accordance with the gospel, and draw them away from Christ. Compare therefore all teachings to the scripture, and see whether they agree or not. And commit yourself wholly and altogether to Christ, and so shall he with his Holy Spirit and with all his fullness dwell in your soul.

Sum and whole cause of the epistle

The sum and whole cause of the writing of this epistle is to prove that man is justified by faith alone. Whoever denies this proposition, to him not only is this epistle and all that

Paul writes, but also the whole scripture, so locked up that he can never understand it to his soul's health. To bring us to the understanding and conviction that faith alone justifies, Paul proves that the whole nature of man is so poisoned and so corrupt, yea and so dead concerning godly living or godly thinking, that it is impossible for a human being to keep the law in the sight of God – that is, to love it, and of love and eagerness keep it as naturally as one eats or drinks – until the soul is quickened and healed through faith.

And by justification, understand reconciliation with God, restoration to his favour, and forgiveness of your sins. And when I say that faith alone justifies, understand that only faith and trust in the truth of God and in the mercy promised to us in Christ Jesus, and him crucified, obtains this reconciliation with God, confers Christ's innocence upon us so that we are pronounced righteous, and assures our consciences that our sins are forgiven, and we in the full favour of God.

When I say God justifies us, understand by this that only for the sake of Christ, and only for his merits, and because he earned it, does God receive us to his mercy, favour, and grace, and forgive us our sins. And when I say Christ justifies us, understand thereby that Christ has redeemed us, bought and delivered us out of the wrath of God and damnation, and has with his work alone, bearing in his own body the punishment for our sins, purchased for us the mercy, favour, and grace of God, and the forgiveness of our sins.

Furthermore, set before your eyes the works of Christ and your own works. Christ's works alone justify and make satisfaction for your sin, and your own works do not. Nor can your own works quiet your conscience and make you sure that your sins are forgiven you. For the promise of mercy is made you for the sake of what Christ did, and not for what you do or have done.

Now go to, reader, and according to the order of Paul's writing, so proceed. First, behold yourself diligently in the law of God, and see there your just damnation. Second, turn your eyes to Christ, and see there the exceeding mercy of your most kind and loving Father. Third, remember that Christ did not make this atonement in order that you should anger God again. Nor did he die for your sins in order that you should still live in them, nor cleanse you so that you may return as a swine to your old puddle again, but in order that you should be a new creature, and live a new life in accordance with the will of God, and not of the flesh. And be diligent, lest through your own negligence and unthankfulness you should lose this favour and mercy again.

Farewell,
W. T. (1534)
with also R. M. D. (2015)

[Paul likely wrote this epistle while in Corinth, toward the close of his third missionary journey in 56 AD]

The Epistle of the Apostle Saint Paul to the
Romans

Chapter 1

Paul declares his love for the Romans, shows what the gospel is with the fruit of it, and reproves the base nature of the flesh.

PAUL, the servant of Jesus Christ called to be an apostle, put apart to
preach the gospel of God – 2the gospel that he promised before by his
prophets in the holy scriptures 3that speak of his Son, who was begotten
of the seed of David as to the flesh, 4and was with power identified as the
Son of God by the Holy Spirit, who sanctifies since the time that Jesus
Christ our Lord rose up from death. 5By him we have received grace and
apostleship to bring all manner of heathen peoples to the obedience of
faith, which is in his name. 6Of such peoples you are a part also, who are
Jesus Christ's by calling.

7To all you of Rome, beloved of God and saints by calling.[a] Grace be
with you and peace from God our Father and from the Lord Jesus Christ.[b]

8First, truly I thank my God through Jesus Christ for you all, because
your faith is spoken of throughout all the world. 9For God is my witness,
whom I serve with my spirit in the gospel of his Son, that without ceasing
I make mention of you always in my prayers, 10asking that at one time or
another a successful journey (by the will of God) might enable me to go
to you. 11For I long to see you, so that I may bestow among you some
spiritual gift to strengthen you with; 12that is, so I may have consolation
together with you through the common faith, which both you and I have.

13I want you to know, brethren, that I have often hoped to go to you
(but have been prevented so far) to have some fruit among you, as I have
among other of the Gentiles. 14For I am a debtor both to the Greeks and to
those who are not Greek, to the learned and also to the unlearned. 15So
then, as much as is in me, I am ready to preach the gospel to you of Rome
also. 16For I am not ashamed of the gospel of Christ, because it is the
power of God for salvation to all who believe, namely to the Jew and also
to the Gentile. 17For by it the righteousness which comes from God is Hab 2:4
unveiled,[c] from faith to faith.[d] As it is written: The just shall live by faith. Ga 3:11

18For the wrath of God appears from heaven against all ungodliness Heb 10:38
and unrighteousness of men, who suppress the truth in unrighteousness,
19seeing that what may be known of God is manifest among them. For
God did show it unto them. 20For his invisible things – that is to say, his Ps 9:17;19:1
eternal power and Godhead – are understood and seen from the works of Job c38 Ac 7:42
the creation of the world. So they are without excuse, 21inasmuch as when 2Th 2:6,7
they knew God,* they did not glorify him as God, neither were thankful,
but increased full of vain imaginations, and their foolish hearts were
blinded. 22When they counted themselves wise, they became fools, 23and
turned the glory of the immortal God into the similitude of the image of

[**When they knew God**: there is archaeological evidence that monotheism was the early religion of mankind, which had awareness of the one true God, but fell into polytheism and lost it. Psalm 9:17, written about 1000 BC, refers to the heathen who forget God]

mortal man, and of birds, and four-footed animals, and serpents.
24For this God likewise gave them up to their heart's lusts, unto un-
cleanness, to defile their own bodies between themselves – 25those who
turned his truth to a lie, and venerated and served created things more
than the Maker, who is blessed forever. Amen. 26For this cause God gave
them up to shameful lusts. For even their women turned from the natural
way to the unnatural. 27And likewise also the men left the natural way
with a woman, and burned in their lusts for one another. And man with
man wrought uncleanness, and received in themselves the reward of their
error accordingly.

What follows when people know the truth, but love it not.

28And as it did not seem good to them to acknowledge God, so God
delivered them up to a reprobate mind, to do those things which were not
right, 29being full of all unrighteous doing: of fornication, wickedness,
covetousness, vice; full of envy, murder, debate, deceit; evil-natured,
whisperers, 30backbiters, haters of God, doers of wrong, proud, boasters,
inventors of evil things, disobedient to father and mother, 31without un-
derstanding, covenant breakers, unloving,* truce breakers, and merciless.
32Which people, though they knew the righteousness of God, that those
who do such things are worthy of death, yet not only do the same, but also
have pleasure in those who do them.[e]

[**Unloving**: the Gk *astorgos* (794) means hardhearted toward family, without natural care and affection]

The Notes

Saints by calling (1:7)

a) *Saints by calling* is as much as to say, called to be saints: called to holiness and holy living. For the custom of scripture is to call those who are alive saints, and it ought to be one and the same thing to say 'a saint' and 'a Christian.'

Grace be with you and peace (1:7)

b) By *grace*, here understand the favour of God with which he freely forgives sins, and by *peace*, the tranquillity of conscience proceeding therefrom.

The righteousness that comes from God unveiled (1:17)

c) By the preaching of the gospel, the imputation of righteousness, whereby God reputes and pronounces us righteous freely through mercy, is openly declared.

From faith to faith (1:17)

d) That is, from an imperfect faith to a perfect faith, from a weak faith to a stronger, and from one battle of faith to another. As we escape one jeopardy by faith, another invades us, through which we must wade by the help of faith also. [Ed: See note (c) on John c1. Some understand this to refer to the unveiling of the old testament faith by the new, thus passing from figure to fulfilment (Chrysostom, *Hom/ John*).]

Other people's sins (1:32)

e) To have pleasure in another person's sins is greater evil than to sin yourself.

Chapter 2

Paul rebukes the Jews, who as concerning sin are like the heathen; yea, worse than they.

Therefore you are inexcusable, O man, whoever you are who judge.[a] For
in the same thing that you judge another, you condemn yourself. For you
who judge do even the same things. 2But we are sure that the judgment of
God is according to truth against those who commit such things.
3Do you think, O man, you who judge others who do such things, and
yet do even the very same, that you will escape the judgment of God? 4Or
do you think nothing of the riches of his goodness, patience, and long-

1Co 4:5
M't 7:1-5
Lu 6:37
Joh 8:7
Jas 4:12

suffering? And remember not how it is that the kindness of God leads you to repentance?

5But you, after your hard heart that cannot repent, heap together against yourself the treasure of wrath for the day of vengeance, when the righteous judgment of God will be revealed. 6He will reward every person according to his deeds;[b] 7that is to say, praise, honour, and immortality to those who continue in doing good and seek eternal life; 8but to those who are rebellious, and reject the truth, and follow iniquity, will come indignation and wrath – 9tribulation and anguish upon the soul of every person who does evil: of the Jew first, and also of the Gentile. 10To everyone who does good will come praise, honour, and peace: to the Jew first, and also to the Gentile. 11For there is no partiality with God. 12But whoever has sinned without law will perish without law, and as many as have sinned under the law will be judged by the law.

*Deeds are an outward righteousness before the world and testify what a person is within, but do not justify the heart before God, nor assure the conscience that the earlier sins are forgiven.

13For before God they are not righteous who hear the law, but the doers* of the law will be justified.[c] 14For if the Gentiles who have no law do by nature the things contained in the law, then they, having no law, are a law unto themselves. 15They show the deeds of the law written in their hearts, while their conscience bears witness to them, and also their thoughts, accusing one another or defending, 16on the day when God will judge the secrets of men by Jesus Christ, as my gospel declares.

17Behold, you are called a Jew, and trust in the law, and put confidence in God, 18and know his will, and have confirmation of good and bad in that you are instructed by the law. 19And you believe that you yourself are a guide to the blind, a light to those who are in darkness – 20an instructor of those who lack wisdom and a teacher of the unlearned, who has the example of that which ought to be known, and of the truth, in the law. 21But you who teach another, do not teach yourself. You preach that a person should not steal, and yet you steal. 22You say a person should not commit adultery, and you break wedlock. You abhor images, and rob God of his honour. 23You boast in the law, and through breaking the law dishonour God. 24For the name of God is ill spoken of among the Gentiles because of you, as it is written.

Isa 52:5
Eze 36:20-22

25Circumcision indeed avails, if you keep the law. But if you break the law, your circumcision is made uncircumcision. 26Therefore if the uncircumcised man keeps the righteous things contained in the law, shall his uncircumcision not be counted for circumcision? 27And shall not uncircumcision which is by nature, if it keeps the law, condemn you who, being under the letter and circumcision, do transgress the law? 28For he is not a Jew who is a Jew outwardly. Neither is that thing circumcision which is outward in the flesh. 29But he is a Jew who is hid within, and the circumcision of the heart is the true circumcision, which is in the Spirit,* and not in the letter; whose praise is not from men, but from God.

[**In the Spirit**: or perhaps, in the spirit; ie, of the person]

Jer 4:4

The Notes

Wrongful judgment (2:1-3)

a) *To judge* here (as in many other places) means to condemn others and esteem yourself righteous [which is wrong, for we also are fallen (M't 7:5; Lu 6:37; Joh 8:7). But we are called to judge right and wrong, and to judge doctrine (De 13:1-3; Ro 16:17; 1Co 2:15, 5:12; 2Co 6:17; Eph 5:6; Col 2:8; 1Ti:3,4; 2Ti 2:16; 2Pe c2; 2Jo 7-11, etc.) while avoiding strife (M't 15:14; Ro 14:1; 2Ti 2:14,23).]

Who will reward every person according to his deeds (2:6)

b) This saying may no one understand as though works justify before God, because that would make false this whole epistle, which labours especially to prove that our sins are forgiven freely through mercy for what Christ has done, and not for our merits or works. Understand therefore that Paul does not here ascribe justification to works, but is describing people who are righteous by what follows; that is, by their fruits, what their fruits are. That God will reward every person, etc, means that to the righteous he will give life, and to the unrighteous, pain.

Not those who hear, but the doers of the law will be justified before God (2:13)

c) Those who do the law will be justified; that is, they will be pronounced just and righteous. This passage is only spoken to the rebuke of the Jews, who set no small store by themselves as to the law, but yet did not keep it. This Paul lays to their charge thusly: it is not enough for you, O Jew, to hear the law only, and to profess it and rely upon it. But if you really want to be justified and made righteous in the sight of God by the law, as you so greatly boast, then you must keep it, not only hear it. Now this you do not do, but you are guilty of breaking it. Therefore you need another way to become righteous in the sight of God than by the keeping of the law. That way, as the whole epistle both before and after plainly establishes, is faith that firmly believes sins to be forgiven freely through Christ, and not for our works or merits, no, not even when we have done the best that we can (Luke 13).

And likewise does St. Ambrose [c 339-397, Bishop of Milan], writing on this same text, expound Paul. He says the righteous are not those who hear the law, but those who believe in Christ whom the law promised, affirming plainly that to believe in him is to do the law.

Chapter 3

Paul shows what preferment the Jews have, and that both Jews and Gentiles are under sin, and are justified only by the grace of God in Christ.

What preferment, then, has the Jew? Or what advantage from circum-
cision? 2Surely very much. The word of God was committed first to them.
3What, then, if some of them did not believe? Does their unbelief make
the promise of God without effect? 4God forbid. Let God be true and all
men liars, as it is written: That you may be justified in your words, and Ps 51:4;
should overcome when you are judged. 116:11.
5If our unrighteousness makes the righteousness of God more ex-
cellent, what shall we say? Is God unrighteous, who takes vengeance? I
speak after the manner of men. 6God forbid, for how then will God judge
the world? 7If the truth of God appears more excellent through my lie,* to
his glory, why am I still judged as a sinner? 8And why not say rather (as
some ill report of us, and as some allege we say), let us do evil, so that
good may come of it? Their condemnation is just.

[**Lie**: the Gk *pseusma* (5582) means a fabrication, ie falsehood: anything not of truth]

9What are we saying then? Are we better than they? No, not in any
way. For we have already established that both Jews and Gentiles are all
under sin, 10as it is written: There is none righteous, no, not one. 11There Ga 3:22
is no one who understands. There is no one who seeks after God. 12They Ro 11:32
are all gone out of the way. They are all unprofitable. There is no one who Isa 53:6;
does good: no, not one. 13Their throat is an open sepulchre. With their 59:1-15.

There is no one who does good [See OT feature at the end of this epistle]

tongues they have deceived. The poison of asps is under their lips. [14]Their
mouths are full of cursing and bitterness. [15]Their feet are swift to shed Ps 5:9; 14:1-3; 36:1-4; 53:1-3.
blood. [16]Destruction and wretchedness are in their ways, [17]and the way of
peace they have not known. [18]There is no fear of God before their eyes.
[19]Yea and we know that whatever the law says, it says to those who
are under the law, so that all mouths may be stopped, and all the world be
subdued to God, [20]because no flesh can be justified in the sight of God by
the deeds of the law. For by the law comes the knowledge of sin.

The law justifies no one before God, but reveals sin only. [Luther>Through the knowledge of sin comes humility, and through humility, grace is acquired. Thus an action which is alien to God's nature results in a deed belonging to his very nature: he makes a person a sinner so that he may make him righteous (*Heid. Disp.*)]

[21]But now is manifested the righteousness that comes of God without
the fulfilling of the law, yet having the witness of the law, and of the
prophets. [22]Without doubt, the righteousness which is good before God
comes by the faith of Jesus Christ, to all and upon all who believe.
There is no difference. [23]For all have sinned and fall short of the glory Ga 2:16; 3:11.
of God, [24]but are justified freely by his grace, through the redemption that
is in Christ Jesus.[a] [25]Him God has made a seat of mercy, through faith in
his blood, to show the righteousness that is of value before him, in that he
forgives the sins that are past. [26]These God suffered in order to show at
this time the righteousness that is granted by him, so that he may be
counted just, and a justifier of the person who believes on Jesus.
[27]Where then is self-righteousness? It is excluded. By what law? By
the law of works? No, but by the law of faith.
[28]Therefore we hold that a man is justified by faith without the deeds
of the law. [29]Is he the God of the Jews only? Is he not also the God of the
Gentiles? Yes, even of the Gentiles also. [30]For there is one God, who jus-
tifies circumcision which is of faith, and uncircumcision through faith.

*Faith maintains the law because by it we obtain power to love and keep the law.

[31]Do we then destroy the law through faith?* God forbid. But we
rather maintain the law.

The Notes

Justified freely by his grace (3:24+)

a) This saying does St. Ambrose expound as follows: Those who do no works, neither return one whit to God, are justified by faith alone, by the gift of God. This word *alone* (though many are unjustly offended by it) is also clearly reflected by Paul himself in these words: *freely*, *without the law*, *without works*, *it is a gift*, and such like. You must mark these words, for they are all at one with the exposition of St. Ambrose, that by faith alone we are justified, which is to say as much. Only by the belief that the mercy of God granted in Christ's blood saves us are we pronounced righteous. This word *alone* excludes works. Not that you should not do them, for you are bound to all good works commanded in the scripture, and called to walk in them, and must earnestly study and exert yourself to leave none of them undone. But in no case should you think that you are thereby justified or made righteous before God.

Chapter 4

Paul shows by the example of Abraham that faith justifies, and not the law or the works of the law.

What shall we say then that Abraham, our father as to the flesh, did find?
[2]If Abraham were justified by deeds, then he has wherein to glory, but not

with God. [3]For what does the scripture say? Abraham believed God, and it Ge 15:6
was counted to him for righteousness. [4]To him who works, the reward is
not reckoned from favour, but as his due. [5]To him who does not work, but
believes on him who justifies the ungodly, his faith is counted for righ-
teousness. [6]It is just as David describes the blessedfulness of the person to
Blessedfulness: what it is. whom God ascribes righteousness apart from deeds: [7]Blessed are those
whose unrighteousnesses are forgiven, and whose sins are covered; [8]bless- Ps 32:1,2
ed is that man to whom the Lord does not impute sin.

[9]Did this blessedness come then upon the circumcised, or upon the
uncircumcised? We say that faith was reckoned to Abraham for righteous-
ness. [10]How then was it reckoned? In the time of circumcision, or in the
time before he was circumcised? Not in the time of circumcision, but
when he was yet uncircumcised.

[11]And he received the sign of circumcision as a seal of the righteous-
ness that is by faith. This faith he had when still uncircumcised, to the
intent that he should be the father of all who believe, though they are not
circumcised, so that righteousness may be ascribed to them also; [12]and to
the intent that he should be the father of the circumcised, not only because
they are circumcised, but because they walk also in the steps of that faith
that was in our father Abraham before the time of circumcision.

[13]For the promise that he would be the heir of the world was not given
to Abraham or to his seed through the law, but through the righteousness
The promise comes by faith. that comes by faith. [14]For if those who are of the law are the heirs, then
The law causes wrath. faith is but vain, and the promise of no effect. [15]Because the law causes
wrath.

[**No law, no transgression**: As dead concerning the law (7:4), and no longer under it (6:15), and set free from it (7:6), we are not under wrath for our sins. Now the promise of life everlasting may be effective through simple faith, by the grace of God]

But where no law is, there is no transgression.* [16]Therefore it is by
faith that the inheritance is given, so that it may come by favour, and so
the promise may be sure to all the seed[a] – not only to those who are of the
law, but also to those who are of the faith of Abraham, who is the father
of us all. [17]As it is written: I have made you a father to many nations, even Ge 17:5
before God whom you have believed, who gives life to the dead, and calls
those things which are not, as though they were.

[18]This Abraham, contrary to hope, believed in hope that he would be Ge 15:5
the father of many nations, according to that which was spoken: Thus
shall your seed be. [19]And he fainted not in the faith, nor yet considered his
own body (which was now dead inasmuch as he was almost a hundred
years old), nor yet that Sarah was past childbearing. [20]He staggered not at
the promise of God through unbelief, but was made strong in the faith and
gave honour to God, [21]fully persuaded that what he had promised, that he
was able to make good. [22]And therefore it was reckoned to him for righ- Ge 15:6
teousness.

[23]It is not written for him only that faith was reckoned to him for righ-
teousness, [24]but also for us, to whom it will be credited as righteousness if
we believe on him who raised up Jesus our Lord from death, [25]who was
Christ justifies us delivered for our sins, and rose up again to justify us.

The Notes

It is by faith (4:16)

a) Therefore it is by faith, so the promise may be sure to all the seed, etc: that is, therefore you are pronounced righteous by faith (by which understand the mercy of God received by faith) so that the conscience may be assured of the will of God and of the promises of the gospel (remission of sins; reconciliation, or being reputed righteous; and everlasting life): that these things will be performed. Assurance would not be possible if the promises depended upon our works. For then the conscience would be unsure, doubting whether we had works enough, whether God would be merciful, whether the law that we know we have transgressed would condemn us, etc. Now when doubtfulness remains in us, there remains also fearfulness, by which come giving up and death. For as long as the law shows us the anger of God, fear and death cannot be overcome. Therefore we must hold only to faith in the merciful promises of God, steadfastly assured that they will be fulfilled although our works are undeserving. [Ed: But where God's law is not, neither is there fear of him, nor of his judgment. See Tyndale's prophecy in his prologue to 2 Peter.]

Chapter 5

The power of faith, hope, and love. How death reigned from Adam to Christ, by whom only we have forgiveness of sins.

[Verses 2 & 3 are partly emended from Coverdale 1535]

*We are not ashamed of our hope, for we are sure by the death of Christ that God loves us and will bring our hope to pass.

Because therefore we are justified by faith, we are at peace with God[a]
through our Lord Jesus Christ, 2by whom we have a way in through faith,
to this grace wherein we stand and rejoice in the hope of the glory to
come, which shall be given by God. 3Not only that, but we also rejoice in
tribulation. For we know that trouble brings patience, 4patience brings
experience, and experience brings hope. 5And our hope makes not ash- Jas 1:2-4
amed,* because the love of God is shed abroad in our hearts by the Holy
Spirit, who is given to us.
6For when we were yet weak, according to the time, Christ died for us
who were ungodly. 7Yet scarcely will anyone die for a righteous person;
perhaps for a good person a man might dare to die. 8But God sets out the
love that he has for us in that while we were yet sinners, Christ died for
us. 9Much more then now, seeing we are justified in his blood, will we be
saved from wrath through him. 10For if when we were enemies, we were Heb 9:11-15
reconciled to God by the death of his Son, much more, seeing we are rec-
onciled, will we be preserved by his life. 11Not only this, but we also joy
in God by the means of our Lord Jesus Christ, by whom we have received
reconciliation.
12 And so it is just as sin entered into the world through one man, and
death by means of sin; and in this way death went over all people,
inasmuch as all people sinned. 13For even to the time of the law, sin was
in the world. But where no law is, there sin is not regarded. 14Never-
theless, death reigned from Adam to Moses, even over those also who did
not sin with such a transgression as did Adam, who is the similitude of
him who is to come.
15But the gift is not like the sin. For if through the sin of one, many are
dead, much more lavish upon many was the grace of God and gift by
grace, which grace was given by one man: Jesus Christ.

[V13 is emended after Coverdale 1535]

*Adam's disobedience damned us all before we ourselves worked any evil, and Christ's obedience saves us all before we ourselves work any good.

[16]And the gift is not over only one sin, as death came through one sin of one man who sinned. For the sentence of condemnation came from one sin.[*] But the gift came to justify from many sins. [17]For if by the sin of one, death reigned by the means of one, much more will those who receive of abundant grace and of the gift of righteousness reign in life by the means of one; that is to say, Jesus Christ.

[18]Likewise then, just as by the sin of one, condemnation came on all men, so also by the justifying of one comes the righteousness that brings life upon all men. [19]For just as by one man's disobedience many became sinners, so by the obedience of one shall many be made righteous.

[20]But the law in the meantime entered in, that sin should increase.[b] Nevertheless, where there was much sin, there was more abundance of grace, [21]so that as sin had reigned unto death, so also grace could reign through righteousness unto eternal life by the help of Jesus Christ.

The Notes

At peace with God (5:1)

a) To be at peace with God is no other thing than to have tranquillity and rest in our hearts toward God, knowing assuredly that we are accepted by him and do please him. This we find by faith only, in that it receives forgiveness of sins and the bestowal of life everlasting by mercy obtained at Christ's blood. Our own works can bring no such tranquillity, because they are unsure and engender doubt, from which follows casting off, and from it, judgment.

That sin should increase (5:20)

b) The law increases sin, and makes our nature more greedy to do ill, because she gives no power or desire to do what she bids, nor to refrain from what she forbids (Ga c3).

Chapter 6

Since we have been delivered from sin through Christ, we must fashion ourselves to live as the servants of God, not following our own desires. The different rewards of righteousness and sin.

What shall we say then? Shall we continue in sin, so that there may be an abundance of grace? [2]God forbid. How can we, who are dead as regards sin, live any longer in it? [3]Do you not remember that all we who are baptized in the name of Jesus Christ, are baptized to die with him? [4]We are buried with him by baptism in order to die, so that in the same way as Christ was raised up from death by the glory of the Father, we also may walk in a new life.[*] [5]For if we are grafted in death like him, so also must we be in the resurrection. [6]We must remember that our old man is crucified with him also, so that the body of sin may utterly be destroyed, to the intent that henceforth we will not be servants of sin. [7]For he who is dead, is justified from sin.

Ga 3:27
Heb 12:2
1Pe 2:4
Eph 4:17-24
Col 3:5

[Walking in new life in the resurrection: this refers to the new life now, after the resurrection of the soul in Christ. That Paul is speaking of the present is evident from the context. We are to walk in the holiness of the Lord's resurrection life. See also 1Jo 5:12, references to being risen in Christ in Colossians 2 & 3, and Rogers' note (c) on John 5 concerning the resurrection of justification]

[8]And so if we are dead with Christ, we believe that we are to live with him – [9]remembering that Christ, once raised from death, dies no more. Death no longer has power over him. [10]For concerning that he died, he died as to sin once. And concerning that he lives, he lives unto God. [11]Think of yourselves also in the same way: that you are dead concerning sin,[a] but are alive unto God through Jesus Christ our Lord. [12]Therefore let

not sin reign in your mortal bodies, so that you bow to it in its affections and lusts. [13]Neither give your members as instruments of unrighteousness unto sin. But give yourselves unto God as people who are alive from death, and give your members as instruments of righteousness unto God. [14]Let not sin have power over you. For you are not under the law, but under grace.

[15]What then? Shall we sin because we are not under the law, but under grace? God forbid. [16]Do you not consider that whomever you commit yourselves to, as servants to obey, his servants you are? – whomever you bow to, whether it be through sin to death, or through obedience to righteousness. [17]But God be thanked that, though you were once the servants of sin, you have conformed with heart to the model of instruction unto which you were delivered. [18]You are then made free from sin, and have become the servants of righteousness.

Joh 8:34-36
2Pe 2:19

[19]I will speak plainly, because of the infirmity of your flesh. Just as you once gave your members* as servants to uncleanness and to iniquity, from iniquity to iniquity, so now give your members as servants to righteousness so that you may be sanctified. [20]For when you were the servants of sin, you were not under righteousness. [21]What fruit had you then, in those things that you are now ashamed of? For the end of those things is death. [22]But now you are delivered from sin, and made the servants of God, and have as your fruit to be sanctified, and the end everlasting life. [23]For the reward of sin is death, but eternal life is the gift of God through Jesus Christ our Lord.

[**Members**: your limbs, minds, ears, and eyes. Use all in righteousness. Keep from that which defiles or condemns. Guard the heart; from it come the issues of life. Pr 4:23]

Eternal life is what Christ merits and has earned for us.

The Notes

Dead concerning sin (6:11)

a) To die to sin is not to serve the concupiscence of sin; [that is, the evil inclination and nature of the old Adam, which entice us to sin and the world. J Rogers, Table of P. Matters]

Chapter 7

Christ has delivered us from the law and death. Paul shows what the flesh and natural man is, and calls it the law of the members.

Do you not consider, brethren (I speak to people who know the law), that the law has dominion over a person as long as it endures? [2]For the woman who is under a husband is bound by the law to the man as long as he lives. But if the husband is dead, she is released from the law of the husband. [3]So then, if while the husband is alive she couples herself with another man, she will be counted a wedlock breaker. But if the husband is dead, she is free from the law, so that she is no wedlock breaker if she couples herself with another man.

1Co 7:39

[4]In a similar way, my brethren, you are dead concerning the law by the body of Christ,[a] in order to be coupled to another (I mean, to him who is risen again from death), so that we will bring forth fruit unto God. [5]For when we were in the flesh, the lusts of sin, which were stirred up by the law, reigned in our members to bring forth fruit unto death. [6]But now we

1Co 6:17

are delivered from the law, and dead to that to which we were in bondage,
in order to serve in a new life of the Spirit, and not in the old life of the
letter.
7What shall we say then? Is the law sin? God forbid. But I would not
have known what sin meant, if not by the law. For I would not have
known what coveting meant unless the law had said, You shall not covet.
8But sin took occasion by the means of the commandment, and wrought
in me all manner of inordinate desire. For without the law, sin was dead.
9I once lived without law. But when the commandment came, sin revived,
and I was dead. 10And the very same commandment that was ordained for
life, was found to be to me an occasion of death. 11For sin took occasion
by the means of the commandment, and thus deceived me, and by the
same commandment slew me. 12Therefore the law is holy, and the com- 1Ti 1:8
mandment holy, just, and good.

Law makes sin to be known **[I would not have known**: Chrysostom> Paul is not here speaking of an absolute want of knowledge, but of the more accurate knowledge that came by the law of Moses and added to nature's law. *Hom/Ro*]

13Was then that which is good, made death to me? God forbid. No, sin
was death to me, so that it could appear how sin, by the means of that
which is good, had wrought death in me; so that sin which is under the
commandment might be out of measure sinful. 14For we know that the
law is spiritual. But I am carnal, sold under sin,[b] 15inasmuch as I know not
what I do.* For what I would, I do not, but what I hate, that I do. 16If I
would rather not do that which I do, I grant to the law that it is good. 17So
then now it is not I who do it, but sin that dwells in me. 18For I know that
in me (that is to say, in my flesh) dwells no good thing. To will is present Ga 5:17
with me, but I find no means to perform that which is good. 19For I do not
that good thing which I would, but I do the evil that I would not. 20Finally,
if I do what I do not want, then it is not I who do it, but sin that dwells in
me does it.
21I find then by the law that when I want to do good, evil is present
with me. 22I delight in the law of God as far as the inner man is con-
cerned, 23but I see another law in my members, rebelling against the law
of my mind, and subduing me to the law of sin that is in my members. 24O
wretched man that I am! Who shall deliver me from this body of death?
25I thank God through Jesus Christ our Lord. So then, I myself in my
mind serve the law of God, and in my flesh the law of sin.

*Or rather, dislike what I do.

The Notes

Dead concerning the law (7:4)

a) To be dead concerning the law is to be made free from the law and from the burden of it, and to receive the Spirit by which we are able to do according to the law. And the same is to be delivered from the law of death. [Ed> We may say that the Lord took Israel as a bride, and died to set her free. However we also understand that, unlike the earthly wife, Israel's new life is with the departed Lord himself.]

Sold under sin (7:14)

b) To be sold under sin is to be made a bondservant to the will of sin only.

Chapter 8

The law of the Spirit gives life. The Spirit of God makes us God's children and heirs with Christ. We cannot be separated from the abundant love of God.

There is then no damnation to those who are in Christ Jesus – who walk not after the flesh, but after the Spirit. [2]For the law of the Spirit that brings life through Jesus Christ has delivered me from the law of sin and death. [3]For what the law could not do, inasmuch as it was weak because of the flesh, God has performed. He sent his Son in the similitude of sinful flesh, and by sin* punished sin in the flesh, [4]so that the righteousness required by the law may be fulfilled in us, who walk not after the flesh, but after the Spirit. [5]For those who are carnal are carnally minded. But those who are spiritual are spiritually minded. [6]To be spiritually minded is life and peace. But to be carnally minded is death, [7]because the fleshly mind is enmity against God. For it is not obedient to the law of God, neither can be. [8]So then, those who are given to the flesh cannot please God.[a]

Sin is taken here for a sin-offering after the use of the Hebrew tongue.

Isa 53:5-12
Joh 1:29

[9]But you are not given to the flesh, but to the Spirit, if it so be that the Spirit of God dwells in you. If there is any person who does not have the Spirit of Christ, the same is none of his. [10]If Christ is in you, the body is dead because of sin, but the Spirit is life for righteousness' sake. [11]And so if the Spirit of him who raised up Jesus from death dwells in you, he who raised up Christ from death will give life to your mortal bodies, because his Spirit dwells in you.

[If *Christ* is in you, the *Spirit* is life, and the *Spirit of God* who raised up Jesus from death dwells in you: Here is the Holy Trinity manifest]

[12]Therefore, brethren, we are now debtors – not to the flesh, to live after the flesh. [13]For if you live after the flesh, you must die. But if you put to death the deeds of the body by the help of the Spirit, you will live. [14]For as many as are led by the Spirit of God, they are the sons of God. [15]For you have not received the spirit of servanthood to fear again, but you have been given the Spirit of adoption, whereby we cry, Abba, Father! [16]The Spirit himself bears witness with our spirit that we are the children of God. [17]If we are children, we are also heirs – the heirs, I mean, of God; and joint heirs with Christ, if so be that we suffer together so that we may be glorified together.[b] [18]For I suppose that the afflictions of this life are not worthy of the glory that will be shown upon us.

[**Spirit of servanthood**: ie to the covenant of works, esp the Mosaic law. Ex 20:18] **Adoption**; that is, the inheritance promised by grace.

Ga 4:6,7

[19]Also, the fervent desire of the creatures endures, looking for when the sons of God will appear, [20]because the creatures are subdued to vanity against their will, but for the will of him who subjects them in hope. [21]For the very creatures will be delivered from the bondage of corruption into the glorious liberty of the children of God. [22]For we know that every creature groans with us also, and travails in pain, even to this time.

[23]Not only they, but we also who have the first fruits* of the Spirit mourn in ourselves, and await the adoption, and look for the deliverance of our bodies. [24]For we are saved by hope.[c] But hope that is seen is no hope. For how can a person hope for that which he sees? [25]But if we hope for that which we do not see, then with patience we await it.

First fruits: a taste and a certain portion, and not the full gift of the Spirit.

1Pe 1:3
Tit 3:7

[26]Furthermore, the Spirit also relieves our infirmities. For we know not what to pray as we ought, but the Spirit makes intercession mightily for us, with groanings which cannot be expressed by tongue. [27]And he who searches the hearts knows what is the intent of the Spirit, for he

makes intercession for the saints according to the pleasure of God. [28]For
we know that all things work for the best for those who love God, who
also are called according to his purpose. [29]For those whom he knew
God chooses by his own goodness and mercy, calls through the gospel, justifies through faith, and glorifies through good works. before, he also ordained before to be fashioned to the image of his Son, so
that he may be the firstborn among many brethren. [30]Moreover, those
whom he appointed before, them he also called; and whom he called,
them he also justified; and whom he justified, them he also glorified.

[31]What shall we say then to these things? If God is on our side, who
can be against us? [32]He who did not spare his own Son, but gave him for
us all, how would he not also give us all things with him? [33]Who shall lay
anything to the charge of God's chosen ones? It is God who justifies;
[34]who then shall condemn? It is Christ who is dead – yea rather, risen a-
gain, who is also on the right hand of God, and makes intercession for us.

[35]Who can separate us from the love of God? Can tribulation? or an-
guish? or persecution? or hunger? or nakedness? or peril? or sword? [36]As
it is written: For your sake we are killed all day long, and are counted as Ps 56:11; 44:22.
sheep appointed to be slain. [37]Nevertheless, in all these things we over-
come strongly through the help of him who loved us. [38]Yea, and I am sure
that neither death, nor life, nor angels, nor rule, nor power, nor things
present, nor things to come, [39]nor height, nor depth, nor any other thing in
creation, will be able to separate us from the love of God shown in Christ
Jesus our Lord.

The Notes

Given to the flesh (8:9+) a) To be given to the flesh is to live in the works of the flesh, which works are recited at Galatians 5:19-21. [See also Ro 1:29 & 30, 13:13; 2Co 12:20 &21.]

Suffer with Christ (8:17) b) We must suffer with Christ if we will reign with him in glory.

We are saved by hope (8:24) c) That is, we hope to be delivered out of the corruption of our bodies into the glory that Christ is now in, and therefore do not faint in our tribulations.

Chapter 9

Paul complains upon the hard hearts of the Jews who would not receive Christ. How the heathen are chosen in their stead.

I speak the truth in Christ, and do not lie, regarding that of which my
conscience bears me witness in the Holy Spirit. [2]I have great heaviness
and continual sorrow in my heart. [3]For I have wished myself to be cursed
What love does. from Christ for my brethren and my kinsmen according to the flesh, [4]who
Adoption is an inheritance by grace. are the Israelites. To them pertain the adoption and the glory, and the
covenants, and the law that was given, and the service of God, and the
promises. [5]Theirs also are the fathers, and those from whom (as to the
flesh) Christ came, who is God over all things blessed forever. Amen.

[6]I do not say these things as though the words of God had taken no
effect. For not all who come from Israel are Israelites. [7]Nor are they all
children just because they are the seed of Abraham, but: In Isaac shall Ge 21:12
your seed be called. [8]That is to say, the children of the flesh are not the Ga 4:21-31 Ro c11; 2:28
children of God, but the children of promise are counted the seed. [9]For Ge 18:10,14

this is a word of promise: About this time I will come, and Sarah shall
have a son. [10]Neither was it so with her only, but also when Rebecca was
pregnant with twins by one – I mean, by our father Isaac. [11]Before the
children were born, when they had done neither good nor bad, so that the
purpose of God which is by election would stand, it was said to her, not
by reason of works, but by the grace of the caller: [12]The elder shall serve Ge 25:23
the younger. [13]As it is written: Jacob he loved, but Esau he hated. Mal 1:2,3

[14]What shall we say then? Is there any unrighteousness with God?
God forbid. [15]For he says to Moses: I will show mercy to whom I show
mercy, and will have compassion on whom I have compassion. [16]So then, Ex 33:19
it lies not in a man's will or running, but in the mercy of God. [17]For the
scripture says to Pharaoh: For this very purpose I have stirred you up, to Ex 9:16
show my power on you, and so that my name may be declared throughout
all the world. [18]Therefore he has mercy on whom he will have mercy, and
whom he will, he makes hardhearted.

The fleshly and proud mind that would be as wise as God must be mortified to learn to fear God and obey him, and to stop disputing with him.

[19]You will say to me then, So why does he still blame us? For who
can resist his will? [20]But, O man, what are you to dispute with God? Shall Isa 29:16;
the work say to the workman, Why have you made me this way? [21]Does 45:9. Jer 18:6
the potter not have power over the clay, to make out of the same lump one
vessel unto honour, and another unto dishonour? [22]Accordingly God,
intending to show his wrath and to make his power known, suffered with
long patience the vessels of wrath fitted to damnation, [23]in order to show
the riches of his glory on the vessels of mercy, which he had prepared for
glory – [24]that is to say, us, whom he called not from the Jews only, but
also from the Gentiles.

[25]As he says in Hosea: I will call them my people who were not my Ho 2:23;
people, and her beloved who was not beloved. [26]And: It will come to pass 1:10.
in the place where it was said to them, You are not my people, that there 1Pe 2:10
the children of the living God shall be called. [27]But Isaiah cries con-
cerning Israel: Though the number of the children of Israel be as the sand Isa 10:22,
of the sea, yet shall but a remnant be saved. [28]He carries out the word* to 23; 1:9.
the end, and makes it short in righteousness. For a short word will God
make on earth. [29]And as Isaiah said before: If the Lord of Sabaoth* had
not left us a seed, we would have been made as Sodom, and would have
been likened to Gomorrah.

[**Word**: the Gk *logos* (3056) is often rendered 'word', as Tyndale put in these places]
[**Lord of Sabaoth**: a military epithet of God, sometimes rendered Lord of hosts (armies), or Lord All-powerful]

[30]What shall we say then? We say that the Gentiles, who did not
follow righteousness, have found righteousness; I mean the righteousness
which comes of faith. [31]But Israel, who followed the law of righteousness,
could not attain to the law of righteousness. [32]And why not? Because they
sought it not by faith, but as if it were by the works of the law. For they
have stumbled at the stumbling stone. [33]As it is written: Behold, I put in Isa 8:14;
Zion a stumbling stone, and a rock that will make men fall. But none who 28:16.
believe on him will be ashamed.

Chapter 10

The unfaithfulness of the Jews. Two kinds of righteousness.

Brethren, my heart's desire and prayer to God for Israel is that they might
be saved. 2For I can attest that they have a fervent heart for God, but not
according to knowledge. 3For they are ignorant of the righteousness that is
admitted before God, and go about to establish their own righteousness,
and therefore give no heed to the righteousness that is of value before
The law drives to Christ to be justified. God. 4For Christ is the end of the law,[a] to justify all who believe.
5Moses describes the righteousness which comes of the law, how the
person who does the things of the law will live therein. 6But the righteous- Le 18:5
ness that comes by faith speaks this way: Say not in your heart, who shall Eze 20:11
ascend into heaven? (which is nothing else than to fetch Christ down), 7or, Ga 3:12
who shall descend into the deep? (which is nothing else than to fetch
Christ up from death). 8But what does the scripture say? The word is near
you, even in your mouth and in your heart. This word is the word of faith
that we preach. 9For if you acknowledge with your mouth that Jesus is the De 30:11-14
Lord, and believe with your heart that God raised him up from death, you
will be safe. 10For the belief of the heart justifies, and to acknowledge
with the mouth makes a man safe.[b] 11For the scripture says: Whoever be-
lieves on him, will not be ashamed.
12There is no difference between the Jews and the Gentiles. For there Isa 28:16
is one Lord over all, who richly blesses all who call on him. 13For: Who-
soever calls upon the name of the Lord, shall be saved. 14But how can Pr 18:10
people call on him, on whom they have not believed? How can they be- Joe 2:32
lieve on him, if they have not heard of him? How can they hear without a Ac 2:21 Isa 52:7
preacher? 15And how can men preach, unless they be sent?[c] As it is writ- Na 1:15
ten: How beautiful are the feet of those who bring glad tidings of peace,
and bring glad tidings of good things.
16But they have not all hearkened to the gospel. For Isaiah says: Lord, Isa 6:9, 53:1
who believes our message? 17So then, faith comes by hearing, and hearing Joh 12:38
comes by the word of God. 18But, I ask, have they not heard? No doubt: Ps 19:4
Their sound went out into all lands, and their words into the ends of the
world.
19But I demand whether Israel did know, or not? First Moses says: I
will provoke you to envy by those who are not a people, and by a foolish De 32:21
nation I will anger you. 20Isaiah after that is bold and says: I am found by Isa 65:1,2
those who were not seeking me, and have appeared to those who were not
asking for me. 21And against Israel he says: All day long I have stretched
out my hands to a people that does not believe, but speaks against me.

The Notes

Christ is the end of the law (10:4)

a) That is, Christ is the fulfilment of the law, so that whoever has him and believes that he with the shedding of his blood has washed away sins, and therewith overcome death and hell, and has obtained the favour of his Father for all who so believe, is counted righteous, though he does not by his own deeds satisfy the law.

To acknowledge makes safe (10:10)

b) Though faith justifies from sin, and though Christ has won the reward promised, yet the promise is made on the condition that we embrace Christ's doctrine and confess him in word and deed. So it is that we are justified in order to do good works, and in them to walk to the salvation promised.

Unless they be sent (10:15)

c) That is, unless the word be given to them by God. You will ask, by whom would they be sent? Of course, by him who is the owner of the gospel; that is, God. By him are sent the men who preach Christ truly and purely, without the desire for glory or gain. In the same way does Christ prove that he was sent by his Father. He spoke to the glory of his Father, not of himself (John 7). But those who, under the pretence of preaching the gospel, preach men's precepts whereby they seek praise for themselves, are false apostles, and sent by Antichrist, not by Christ.

Chapter 11

All the Jews are not cast away. Therefore Paul warns the Gentiles who are called not to be high-minded or despise the Jews. For the judgments of God are deep and secret.

I say then, has God cast away his people? God forbid. For even I of
course am an Israelite, of the seed of Abraham and of the tribe of Ben-
jamin. [2]God has not cast away his people whom he foreknew. Or do you
not know what the scripture says by the mouth of Elijah, how he makes
intercession to God against Israel, saying, [3] Lord, they have killed your 1Ki 19:10-
prophets and dug down your altars, and only I am left, and they seek my 18
life? [4]But what is the answer of God to him in response? – I have reserved
for myself seven thousand who have not bowed the knee to Baal. [5]Like-
wise also there is at this time a remnant left through the election of grace.
[6]If it is by grace, then it is not by works, for then grace would not be grace
any more. And if it is by works, then it is not grace any more, for then de-
serving would no longer be deserving.
[7]What then? Israel has not obtained what it sought. No, but yet the
chosen ones have obtained it. The rest are blinded, [8]as it is written: God De 29:4
has given them the spirit of unquietness: eyes so that they cannot see, and Isa 6:8-10 M't 13:11-15
ears so that they cannot hear, until this day. [9]And David says, Let their Mk 4:11,12
table be made a snare to take them with, and an occasion to fall, and a Lu 8:10 Joh 12:37-41
reward to them. [10]Let their eyes be blinded so that they do not see, and Ac 28:25-27
ever bow down their backs.[a] Ps 69:22,23
[11]I say then, have they therefore stumbled, only but to fall? God for-
bid. But through their fall, salvation has come to the Gentiles, to rally
them at the same time. [12]And so if their fall is the riches of the world, and
their diminishment the riches of the Gentiles, how much greater the riches
if they all believed? [13]I preach to you Gentiles, inasmuch as I am the apos-
tle to the Gentiles. I will magnify my office,* [14]so that I might rally those
who are my flesh, and might save some of them. [15]For if the casting away
of them is the reconciling of the world, what is the receiving of them, but
life again from death? [16]For if one piece is holy, the whole lump is holy.
And if the root is holy, the branches are holy also.
[17]Though some of the branches are broken off, and you, being a wild
olive tree, are grafted in among them and made partaker of the root and
sap of the olive tree, [18]do not boast against the branches. For if you boast,
remember that you do not bear the root, but the root bears you. [19]You will
say then that the branches are broken off so that you may be grafted in.

Magnify my office: do my work with all diligence.

[20]Well said: because of unbelief they are broken off, and you stand stead-
fast in faith. Be not high-minded, but fear, [21]seeing that God spared not
the natural branches, lest perhaps he also not spare you.

[22]Behold the kindness and severity of God: on those who fell, severity,
but towards you, kindness – if you continue in his kindness. Otherwise,
you will be hewn off. [23]And they, if they do not persist in unbelief, will be
grafted in again. For God is of power to graft them in again. [24]For if you
were cut out of a naturally wild olive tree, and were grafted contrary to
nature into a true olive tree, how much more may the natural branches be
grafted into their own olive tree again?

[25]I would not that this mystery be hid from you, my brethren (lest you
be wise in your own estimations), that, with respect to a part, blindness is
upon Israel, until the fullness of the Gentiles be come in; [26]and in this
way, all Israel will be saved. As it is written: There will come out of Zion Isa 59:20,21
he who does deliver, and who will turn away ungodliness from Jacob. Lu 21:24
[27]And: This is my covenant to them, when I take away their sins. [28]Con-
cerning the gospel, they are enemies for your sakes; but as for the chosen
ones, these are loved for the fathers' sakes. [29]For indeed, the gifts and
calling of God are such that he cannot change his mind about them.

[30]For look, just as you in time past did not believe God, and yet have
now obtained mercy through their unbelief, [31]in the same way now they
have not believed the mercy that has come to you, so that they also may
obtain mercy. [32]God has wrapped all nations in unbelief in order that he Ga 3:22
may have mercy on all.

[33]O the deepness of the riches of the wisdom and knowledge of God!
How unsearchable are his judgments, and his ways past finding out. [34]For Jer 23:18 Isa 40:13
who has known the mind of the Lord? Or who has been his counsellor? E'cus 42:21
[35]Or who has given to him first, that he should be recompensed? [36]For
from him, and through him, and for him, are all things. To him be glory
forever. Amen.

The Notes

Bow down their backs (11:10)

a) To bow down their backs does not only signify that they would be brought under by the Gentiles and oppressed with all kinds of misfortune, but that they would not once look up to call on the Lord with sure belief of heart.

Chapter 12

The sweet living, love, and works of the people who believe in Christ.

The true serving of God is bringing the body into obedience to the law of God.

I beseech you therefore, brethren, by the mercifulness of God, to make
your bodies a living sacrifice, holy and acceptable to God, which is your Ph'p 4:8,9
reasonable serving of God. [2]Do not fashion yourselves to this world, but
be changed in your nature by the renewing of your mind, so that you may
prove what is that good, that acceptable, and perfect will of God.

[3]For I say by the grace that is given to me, to everyone among you,
that no one should think of himself more than it behoves him to think, but

should soberly judge of himself, as God has given to each the measure of
faith. 4Just as we have many members in one body, and all members do Eph 4:7
not have the same service, 5so we, being many, are one body in Christ,
and everyone among us one another's members. 6Seeing that we have dif- 1Co c12
ferent gifts, according to the grace that is given to us, if one has the gift of Eph 4:11-13
prophecy,* let him have it agreeing to the faith. 7Let him who has an
office attend to his duty. Let him who teaches take heed to his doctrine.
8Let him who exhorts give heed to his exhortation. If anyone gives, let
him do it with sincerity. Let him who governs do it with diligence. If any-
one shows mercy, let him do it with cheerfulness.

Here, **prophecy** means the expounding of the scriptures, which in dark places must be expounded to agree to the clear places and the general articles of the faith.

9Let love be without dissembling. Hate that which is evil, and cleave
unto that which is good. 10Be kind to one another, with brotherly love.
Honour others before yourselves. 11Let not the work that you have in hand Am 5:14,15
be tedious to you. Be fervent in the Spirit. Apply yourselves to the time. Eph 4:2 Heb 13:1
12Rejoice in hope. Be patient in tribulation. Continue in prayer. 13Give to 1Pe 4:8
meet the needs of the saints, and be ready to take people in.

14Bless those who persecute you; bless, but curse not. 15Be merry with
those who are merry. Weep with those who weep. 16Be of equal affection
one towards another. Be not high-minded, but make yourselves equal to
the lowly. Do not be wise in your own opinions. 17Repay no one evil for
evil. Provide beforehand for things that are honourable in the sight of all
people. 18If it is possible, as for your part, have peace with all people.

19Dearly beloveds, do not avenge yourselves, but leave room for the
wrath of God. For it is written: Vengeance is mine, and I will reward, says De 32:35
the Lord. 20Therefore: If your enemy hungers, feed him, and if he thirsts, Pr 25:21,22
give him drink. For in so doing, you will heap coals of fire on his head. 1Pe 3:8-17 Heb 12:14
21Do not be overcome by evil, but overcome evil with goodness.

Coals: Thus you will kindle him and make him to love.

Chapter 13

The obedience of people to governing powers. Love fulfils the law. It is now no time to follow the works of darkness.

Let every soul submit himself to the authority of the higher powers. For
there is no power except from God. The powers that be are ordained by
God. 2Therefore whoever resists authority, resists the ordinance of God.
And those who resist will bring retribution on themselves, 3for rulers and
authorities are not to be feared for good works, but for bad. Would you be
without fear of the authority? Do well then, and you will be commended 1Pe 2:13-17
by the same. 4For he is the minister of God for your welfare. But if you do M't 22:21
wrong, then fear. For he does not bear a sword for nothing, but is the
minister of God to take vengeance on those who do evil. 5Therefore you
must obey – not for fear of vengeance only, but also because of con-
science.[a] 6And also for this reason, pay tribute.* For the Roman authorities
are God's ministers, serving for the same purpose.

[**Tribute**: payment to a foreign ruler; here, Rome]

7Give to all persons therefore that which is due to them: tribute to
whom tribute belongs, custom to whom custom is due, fear to whom fear
belongs, honour to whom honour pertains. 8Owe nothing to anyone, but to

love one another. For he who loves another, fulfils the law. [9]For these
commandments – you shall not commit adultery, you shall not kill, you Ex c20
shall not steal, you shall not bear false witness, you shall not covet, and so De c5 Le 19:18
forth (if there be any other commandment) – are all comprehended in this M't 22:39
saying: Love your neighbour as yourself. [10]Love does no harm to his Mk 12:31
neighbour. Therefore love is the fulfilling of the law.

Love is the fulfilling of the law.

[11]This also we know – I mean the season, that it is time now to awake
out of sleep. For our salvation is nearer now than when we first believed.[b]
[12]The night has passed, and the day has come near. Let us therefore cast
away the deeds of darkness, and let us put on the armour of light.[c] [13]Let us
walk honourably, as in the daylight: not in revelry and drunkenness, nor in
sleeping around and wantonness, nor in strife and envying, [14]but put on
the Lord Jesus Christ. And do not make provision for the flesh, to fulfil its
lusts.

The Notes

Because of conscience (13:5)

a) Even if you were able to resist the authorities, you would be condemned in your conscience if you did so, because it is against God's commandment.

Our salvation is nearer (13:11)

b) Christ, who is our salvation, is nearer now than when we looked for him in the Old Testament.

The armour of light (13:12)

c) The armour of light is faith, hope, love, the fear of God, truth – all that the light of God's word teaches.

Chapter 14

The weak ought not to be held in disdain. No person should occasion harm to another's conscience. Again, no one should condemn another for outward things.

However weak we may be, we are Christ's, and therefore to be favoured for his sake. [Ed: Here Paul considers the weak faith of Jewish Christians who still felt bound by Mosaic ceremonial laws governing diet and other Old Covenant observances. In 1Co 8, Paul considers former pagans who had superstitious fears of eating food dedicated to idols]

Him who is weak in the faith,[a] receive to yourselves – not in disputing and
troubling his conscience. [2]One believes that he may eat all things. An-
other, who is weak, eats vegetables. [3]Let not him who eats look down on
him who does not. And let not him who abstains judge one who eats. For
God has received him. [4]Who are you to judge another man's servant? Jas 4:12
Whether he stands or falls pertains to his master; yea, he will stand, be-
cause God is able to make him stand.
[5]This man distinguishes between day and day. Another counts all days Compare
alike. See to it that no one wavers in his own purpose: [6]he who observes Ga 4:9, Isa 1:13,14.
one day over another does it for the Lord's pleasure, and he who does not
observe one day over another, does it also to please the Lord. He who eats
does it to please the Lord, for he gives God thanks; and he who does not
eat, abstains to please the Lord at the same time, and gives God thanks.
[7]For none of us lives as his own servant, and neither does any of us die his
own servant. [8]If we live, we live to be at the Lord's will, and if we die, we
die at the Lord's will. Therefore whether we live or die, we are the Lord's.
[9]It is for this that Christ died and rose up and recovered life: to be Lord of
both the dead and the living.
[10]But why do you then judge your brother? Or why do you despise

your brother? We shall all be brought before the judgment seat of Christ.
[11]For it is written: As surely as I live, says the Lord, all knees will bow to Isa 45:23
me, and all tongues will acknowledge God. [12]So then, every one of us will
give an account of himself to God. [13]Therefore let us not judge one
another any more, but determine rather that no one shall put a stumbling
block or an occasion to fall in his brother's way. [14]For I know, and am
Common: that is to say, unclean.
fully assured in the Lord Jesus, that there is nothing common* of itself. Ac 10:15
But for him who judges it to be common, to him it is common. [15]If your Tit 1:15 1Co c8
brother is grieved by your food, now you are not walking charitably. Do
not destroy by your food a person for whom Christ died. [16]Give no reason
Our treasure is our knowledge.
for your treasure* to be ill spoken of. [17]For the kingdom of God is not
food and drink, but righteousness, peace, and joy in the Holy Spirit. [18]For
whosoever serves Christ in these things, pleases God well, and is commended by men. [19]Let us follow those things that make for peace, and
things whereby one may support another.

[20]Do not undo the work of God for the sake of a little food. All these
things are pure, but it is wrong for that person who eats with harm to his
conscience. [21]It is good not to eat flesh, nor drink wine, nor do anything
whereby your brother stumbles, or falls, or is made weak. [22]Do you have
Makes conscience: To do against conscience is culpable. [Hooker>Here **faith** means a full persuasion that what we do is well done (*2nd Book*)]
faith? Have it within yourself before God. Happy is he who does not condemn himself by what he allows. [23]For he who makes conscience is guilty
if he eats,* because he does not do it of faith. For whatsoever is not of
faith,* that same is sin.

The Notes

The weak brother or sister (14:1)

a) He is weak who is soon offended and has made little progress in the knowledge and liberty of Christ, which thing he got with his blood. And he is strong who knows the liberty of a Christian – that to the clean, all things are clean – and who does not doubt. St. Ambrose, writing on this chapter, says that all things which are ordained for man's use are to be eaten, which he proves by the clear text of Genesis that says all things God made are exceedingly good. From this he argues that they are not to be refused. He adds moreover that neither Enoch, who first pleased God, nor Noah, who alone at the flood was found righteous, nor Abraham the friend of God, nor Isaac or Jacob, righteous men and God's friends, amongst whom was also Lot, nor other righteous men, were ready to have abstained from these (meaning meats, whether fish or flesh).

Chapter 15

The infirmity and frailness of the weak should be borne with all love and kindness, after the example of Christ.

He is strong who can bear another person's weakness.

We who are strong ought to bear the frailness of those who are weak, and
not to stand in our own understanding. [2]Let everyone please his neighbour
for his well-being and encouragement. [3]Christ did not please himself, but,
as it is written: The rebukes of those who rebuked you, fell on me. [4]The Ps 69:9
things that were written aforetime were written for our instruction, so that
we, through patience and comfort from the scripture, might have hope.

[5]May the God of patience and consolation grant to every one of you to

have such a mind towards one another, after the example of Christ Jesus,
[6]in order that you all, in harmony together, may with one mouth praise 1Co 1:10
God, the Father of our Lord Jesus. [7]So then, receive one another as Christ
received us, to the glory of God.

[8]And I say that Jesus Christ was a minister of the circumcision for the
truth of God, to confirm the promises made to the fathers. [9]And let the
Gentiles praise God for his mercy, as it is written: For this cause I will Ps 18:49 2Sa 22:50
praise you among the Gentiles, and sing in your name. [10]And again he Ps 117:1
says: Rejoice, ye Gentiles, with his people! [11]And again: Praise the Lord, De 32:43 Isa 11:10
all ye Gentiles, and laud him, all nations! [12]And in another place Isaiah Rev 22:16
says: The root of Jesse is to come, he who will rise to reign over the
Gentiles; in him shall the Gentiles trust. [13]May the God of hope fill you
with all joy and peace in believing, so that you may be rich in hope
through the power of the Holy Spirit.

[14]I myself am confident of you, my brethren, that you yourselves are
full of goodness, and filled with all knowledge, and are able to exhort one
another. [15]Nevertheless, brethren, I have somewhat boldly written to you,
as one who puts you in mind through the grace that is given to me by God
[16]to be the minister of Jesus Christ among the Gentiles, and to minister the
So that the Gentiles may be an acceptable offering sanctified by the Holy Spirit. glad tidings of God so that the Gentiles may be an acceptable offering Ph'p 2:17
sanctified by the Holy Spirit. [17]I have therefore something I can make
claim to in Christ Jesus, in those things that pertain to God. [18]For I shrink
to speak of anything Christ has not wrought by me, to make the Gentiles
obedient, with word and deed, [19]in mighty signs and wonders, by the
power of the Spirit of God, so that from Jerusalem and the coasts round
about to Illyricum, I have filled all countries with the glad tidings of
Christ. [20]Thus have I exerted myself to preach the gospel – not where
Christ was already named, lest I should have built on another man's foun- 2Co 10:16
dation, [21]but as it is written: People who have not been told of him, they Isa 52:15
will see, and those who have not heard will understand.

[22]For this cause, I have often been prevented from going to you all.
[23]But now, seeing I have no more to do in these countries, and also having
wanted for many years to go to you, [24]when I take my journey into Spain,
I will go to you. I trust to see you in my journey, and that you will help
me on my way after I have enjoyed your company for a while.

[25]Now I am going to Jerusalem, to minister to the saints. [26]For it has
pleased the people of Macedonia and Achaia to send aid to the poor saints 2Co 9:2
at Jerusalem. [27]It has genuinely pleased them. And they are their debtors,
for if the Gentiles are made partakers of their spiritual things, their duty is
to minister to them in carnal things. [28]When I have completed this, and
have brought them this fruit sealed, I will come back again by you on my
way into Spain. [29]And I am sure that when I come, I will come with an
abundance of the blessing of the gospel of Christ.

[30]I beseech you, brethren, for our Lord Jesus Christ's sake, and for the
love of the Spirit, to help me in my concerns, with your prayers to God
for me – [31]that I may be delivered from those in Judea who do not believe,

and that this, my service to Jerusalem, may be accepted by the saints, [32]so that I may come to you with joy, by the will of God, and may with you be refreshed. [33]The God of peace be with you. Amen.

Chapter 16

A chapter of greetings. He warns them to beware of false teachers who bring men's doctrine, and commends to them certain godly men and women who were friends and brethren in the truth.

I commend to you our sister Phoebe, who ministered to the congregation of Cenchrea. [2]Receive her in the Lord as is worthy of a saint, and assist her in whatever way she needs your help. For she has assisted many, including me.

Ac 18:2

[3]Greet Priscilla and Aquila, my helpers in Christ Jesus, [4]who have for my life laid down their own necks – to whom not only I give thanks, but also the congregation of the Gentiles. [5]Likewise, greet the congregation that is in their house.

First fruit: the first converted to God in Achaia.

Greet my well-beloved Epaenetus, who is the first fruit* among those of Achaia. [6]Greet Mary, who bestowed much labour upon us.

[7]Greet Andronicus and Junia, my kinsmen, who were prisoners with me also, who are well regarded among the apostles, and were in Christ before me. [8]Greet Amplias, my beloved in the Lord. [9]Greet Urbanus, our helper in Christ, and Stachys, my beloved. [10]Greet Apelles, tried and true in Christ. Greet those of Aristobulus' household. [11]Greet Herodion, my kinsman. Greet those of the household of Narcissus who are in the Lord.

[12]Greet Tryphena and Tryphosa, which women did labour in the Lord. Greet the beloved Persis, who laboured much in the Lord. [13]Greet Rufus, chosen in the Lord, and his mother, also a mother to me. [14]Greet Asyncritus, Phlegon, Hermas, Patrobas, Hermes, and the brethren who are with them. [15]Greet Philologus and Julia, Nereus and his sister, and Olympas, and all the saints who are with them. [16]Greet one another with a holy kiss. The congregations of Christ send greetings to you.

[17]I beseech you, brethren, to mark those who cause division, and give occasion to evil, contrary to the doctrine that you have been taught, and avoid them. [18]For such people do not serve the Lord Jesus Christ, but their own interests, and with sweet preaching and flattering words deceive the hearts of the simple and unlearned. [19]For your duty to listen extends to all men.* Without question I am pleased with you, but still, I want you to be wise in that which is good, and to be innocent concerning evil.

*Paul would have the lay people to be learned, able to judge the prophets [pastors, priests, teachers], and to heed them only according to true knowledge.

[20]May the God of peace tread Satan under your feet shortly. The grace of our Lord Jesus Christ be with you.

[21]Timothy my work-fellow, and Lucius and Jason and Sosipater, my kinsmen, greet you. [22]I, Tertius, who wrote this letter in the Lord, greet you. [23]Gaius, my host and the host of all the congregations, greets you. Erastus, the chamberlain of the city, greets you. And Quartus, a brother, greets you. [24]The grace of our Lord Jesus Christ be with you all. Amen.

The mystery is now unveiled.

25Now to him who is of power to establish you by my gospel and
preaching of Jesus Christ, whereby is revealed the mystery that was kept
secret since the world began, 26but now is unveiled through the scriptures
of prophecy at the commandment of the everlasting God, to stir up
obedience to the faith proclaimed among all nations – 27to the same God,
who alone is wise, be glory through Jesus Christ forever. Amen.

To the Romans. Sent from Corinth by the hand of Phoebe, she who ministered to the congregation at Cenchrea.

Old Testament Feature - A glimpse into the Old Testament of the 1549 Matthew Bible... Isaiah 59:1-15, minimally updated:

Isaiah: The .lix. Chapter

The Lord is mighty to save, and ready to hear our requests.

Behold, the Lord's hand is not so shortened that it cannot help, neither is his ear so stopped that it may not hear. But your misdeeds have separated you from your God, and your sins hide his face from you, so that he hears you not. For your hands are defiled with blood, and your fingers with unrighteousness. Your lips speak lies, and your tongue sets out wickedness. No man regards righteousness, and no man judges truly. Every man hopes in vain things, and imagines deceit, conceives weariness, and brings forth evil.

They breed cockatrice eggs, and weave the spider's web. Whoso eats of their eggs, dies. But if one treads upon them, there comes up a serpent. Their web makes no cloth, and they may not cover themselves with their labour.

Their deeds are the deeds of wickedness, and the work of robbery is in their hands. Their feet run to evil, and they make haste to shed innocent blood. Their counsels are wicked counsels: harm and destruction are in their ways. But the way of peace they know not. In their goings is no equity. Their ways are so crooked, that whosoever walks therein, knows nothing of peace.

[Corinth was a city in southern Greece. This epistle was probably written in late 54 or early 55 AD]

The First Epistle of Saint Paul the Apostle to the Corinthians

Chapter 1

He recalls God's grace to the Corinthians, exhorts them to be of one mind, and rebukes the division that was among them. The wisdom of the world is foolishness before God; yea, there is no wisdom but in the despised cross of God.

PAUL, by calling an apostle of Jesus Christ through the will of God, and brother Sosthenes.

[2]To the congregation of God which is at Corinth. To those who are sanctified in Christ Jesus, saints by calling, with all who in every place call on the name of our Lord Jesus Christ, their Lord and ours.

[3]Grace be with you and peace from God our Father and from the Lord Jesus Christ.

[4]I thank my God always in your behalf, for the grace of God which is
given you by Jesus Christ – [5]that in all things you are made rich by him,
in all learning and in all knowledge, [6]even as the testimony of Jesus Christ
was confirmed in you, [7]so that you are behind in no gift, and wait for the
appearing of our Lord Jesus Christ. [8]He will strengthen you to the end, so
that you may be blameless in the day of our Lord Jesus Christ. [9]For God 1Th 5:23,24
is faithful, by whom you are called to the fellowship of his Son, Jesus
Christ our Lord.

[10]I beseech you, brethren, in the name of our Lord Jesus Christ, to all Ro 12:16
speak one thing, and that there be no dissension among you, but be knit
together in one mind and in one purpose. [11]It is reported to me about you,
my brethren, by those who are of the house of Chloe, that there is strife
among you. [12]And this is what I mean: that commonly among you one
says, I hold to Paul; another, I hold to Apollos; the third, I hold to Cephas;
the fourth, I hold to Christ. [13]Is Christ divided? Was Paul crucified for
you? Or were you baptized in the name of Paul? [14]I thank God that I
christened none of you except Crispus and Gaius, [15]lest anyone should say
that I had baptized in my own name. [16](I baptized also the household of
Stephanas. Beyond this, I do not remember if I baptized anyone or not.)

[17]For Christ sent me not to baptize, but to preach the gospel – not with
wisdom of words, lest the cross of Christ should have been made of no
effect. [18]For the preaching of the cross is foolishness to those who are
The preaching of the cross is the power of God.
perishing, but to us who are saved it is the power of God. [19]For it is writ-
ten: I will destroy the wisdom of the wise, and will cast away the under-
standing of the learned. [20]Where is the wise man? Where is the scribe? Isa 29:14
Where is the philosopher of this world? Has not God made the wisdom of
this world foolishness?

[21]For when the world through wisdom did not know God, in the wis-

dom of God, it pleased God to save those who believe through the fool-
ishness of preaching. [22]For the Jews require a sign, and the Greeks seek
after wisdom. [23]But we preach Christ crucified: to the Jews an occasion of
falling, and to the Greeks foolishness, [24]but to those who are called, both
of the Jews and the Greeks,[a] we preach Christ the power of God and the
wisdom of God. [25]For the foolishness of God is wiser than men, and the
weakness of God is stronger than men.

Christ is the power and wisdom of God.

[26]Brethren, look on your calling, how it is that not many who are wise
according to the flesh, not many powerful, not many of high degree, are
called. [27]But God has chosen the foolish things of the world, to confound
the wise. And God has chosen the weak things of the world, to confound
things which are strong. [28]And low things of the world, and things which
are despised, God has chosen, yea and things of no reputation, to bring to
nothing things of reputation, [29]so that no flesh may glory in his presence.
[30]And to him you belong in Christ Jesus, who by God is made wisdom to
us, and also righteousness and sanctifying and redemption, [31]so that as it
is written, he who glories will glory in the Lord.[b] Jer 9:23,24

Christ is wisdom. To him only should we hold, and in him only, boast.

The Notes

The Greeks (1:24)

a) References to the Greeks sometimes signify their own nation only, as at Acts 6:1, and sometimes all the Gentiles, as here and at Romans 1:14 and 1:16.

To glory in the Lord (1:31)

b) He who glories in the Lord knows with certainty that God wills him good and favours him, so long as the thing which he does pleases God, and that what he does not do as he should is forgiven him, and not imputed to him (Jer 9:24; Ro 8:15,16).

Chapter 2

It is not eloquence and glorious painted words of worldly wisdom that can edify and convert souls to Christ, but the plain words of the scripture. For they tell of him and his cross.

And I, brethren, when I came to you, came not in gloriousness of words or
of wisdom declaring to you the testimony of God. [2]Nor did I show myself Ac c18
to know anything among you except Jesus Christ, and him crucified. [3]And
I was among you in weakness and in fear, and in much trembling. [4]And
my words and my preaching were not with enticing words of man's
wisdom, but in the demonstration of the Spirit and of power, [5]so that your
faith would not stand in the wisdom of men, but in the power of God.

[V2:2 follows Wycliffe 1380, as did the Rheims and KJV]

[6]That which we speak of is wisdom among those who are sound:[*] not
the wisdom of this world, nor of the rulers of this world (who come to
nothing), [7]but we speak the wisdom of God, which is in secret and lies
hid, which God ordained before the world for our glory. [8]Which wisdom
none of the rulers of this world knew, for had they known it, they would
not have crucified the Lord of Glory. [9]But as it is written: The eye has not
seen and the ear has not heard, neither have entered into the heart of man, Isa 64:4
the things that God has prepared for those who love him.
[10]But God has revealed them to us by his Spirit. For the Spirit searches

*[*] **Sound**: they are sound who understand the law, faith, and works truly, and profess them.*

all things, yea, the bottom of God's secrets. 11 For what man knows the
things of a man, except the spirit of a man which is within him? In the
same way, the things of God are known by no man, but by the Spirit of
God. 12 And we have not received the spirit of the world, but the Spirit
which comes of God, in order to know the things that are given to us by
God – 13 which things also we speak, not in the wise words of man's wis-
dom, but with the wise words of the Holy Spirit, making spiritual com-
parisons of spiritual things. 14 For the natural man does not perceive the
things of the Spirit of God. For they are but foolishness to him. Nor can
he perceive them, because they are spiritually examined. 15 But he who is
spiritual evaluates all things. Yet he himself is judged by no man. 16 For Isa 40:13
who knows the mind of the Lord, or who shall inform him? But we under- Jer 23:18 Ro 11:34
stand the mind of Christ.

The Spirit understands the things of God. The natural man, not renewed in Christ, cannot perceive the things of God.

Chapter 3

Paul rebukes the sects, and authors of sects. Christ is the foundation of his church. We must take heed how we build on this foundation. No one ought to glory in men, but in God.

And I could not speak to you brethren as to spiritual people, but as to
carnal; even, as it were, to babes in Christ. 2 I gave you milk to drink, and
not meat. For you were not strong then, no, neither are you yet. 3 For you
are yet carnal. For as long as there is among you envying, strife, and
dissension, are you not carnal, and walking after the manner of men? 4 As
long as one says, I hold to Paul, and another, I'm for Apollos, are you not
carnal? 5 What is Paul? What is Apollos? Only ministers they are, by
whom you believed, even as the Lord gave grace to each one. 6 I have
planted, Apollos watered, but God gave the increase. 7 So then, neither is
he who plants anything, nor he who waters, but God who gives the in-
crease. 8 He who plants and he who waters are neither better than the other.
Each will receive his reward according to his labours. Ps 62:12

9 We are God's labourers. You are God's husbandry, you are God's Ga 6:7 1Pe 2:5
building. 10 By the grace of God given to me, as a wise builder I have laid Eph 2:19-22
the foundation, and another built on it. But let everyone take heed how he
builds upon it. 11 For no other foundation can anyone lay than that which is
laid, which is Jesus Christ. 12 And whether anyone builds on this foun-
dation gold, silver, precious stones, wood, hay, or stubble, 13 his work will
be seen for what it is. For the day will reveal it, and it will be shown in
fire. And the fire shall try every person's work, what it is. 14 If what some-
one has built remains, he will receive a reward. 15 If anyone's work burns,
he will suffer loss; but he will be saved himself, nevertheless yet as it
were through fire.[a]

Christ is the foundation that bears all.

16 Are you not aware that you are the temple of God, and that the Spirit
of God dwells in you? 17 If anyone defiles the temple of God, God will 1Co 6:19 2Co 6:16
destroy him. For the temple of God is holy, which temple you are. 18 Let
no one deceive himself.

If any man seems wise among you, let him be a fool in this world so that he may be wise. [19]For the wisdom of this world is foolishness with God. For it is written: He compasses the wise in their craftiness. [20]And again: God knows the thoughts of the wise, that they are vain.

Job 5:13 Ec'cus 27:25-27. Ps 94:11

[21]Therefore let no one glory in men. For all things are yours – [22]whether it be Paul or Apollos or Cephas, whether it be the world or life or death, whether they be things present or things to come. All are yours, [23]and you are Christ's, and Christ is God's.

In the kingdom of God we are subject to none save to Christ and his doctrine.

The Notes

The day will reveal it, etc (3:13-15)

a) *Day* signifies here the time when God brings to light the thing that is hid. By *fire* understand carefully searched out and perfect true judgment, which, when it reveals the fault and error, is followed by the affliction of renouncing and repenting. St. Paul so teaches here of preachers who came after him when he had departed from the Corinthians. He had laid a good foundation. Let others take heed, he says, what they build thereon. If they build things worthy of Christ, their work will remain and abide even when it is seen in the light, which he means when he says that the day will reveal it. But if they bring in Jewish ways, they may perhaps deceive for a time, but at length their deception will be seen, as soon as it is begun to be examined with true and sincere judgment, which is signified by this word 'fire.' Thus does Erasmus expound this place, in his annotation upon these words *day* and *stubble*, proving also by the authority of St. Ambrose and Jerome, and other old authorities, that it makes nothing for purgatory, though many have wrongfully laboured to wrest it to that purpose.

Chapter 4

Those who preach are but servants. Judgment belongs to God only.

Let people esteem us this way: as the ministers of Christ, and stewards of
the secrets of God. [2]Furthermore, it is required of the stewards that they
be found faithful.* [3]With me it is but a very small thing if I am judged by
you, or by man's day.* No, I do not judge my own self. [4]I know nothing
against myself, yet I am not thereby justified. It is the Lord who judges
me. [5]Therefore judge nothing before the time, until the Lord comes, who
will shed light on things that are hid in darkness, and reveal the counsels
of the hearts. And then shall each have praise from God.

*He who is **faithful** preaches his master, not himself. **Man's day** is man's wisdom.

[6]Brethren, I have explained these things with reference to myself and
Apollos for your sakes, so that you might learn from us: so that no one
accounts of himself beyond what is written above, so that no one swells
against another for any man's cause. [7]For who prefers you? What do you
have that was not given to you? If you have received it, why do you glory
as though you had not received it? [8]Now you are full, now you are made
rich; you reign as kings without us. And I would to God you did reign, so
that we might reign with you.

The fashion of true apostles.

[9]It seems to me that God has set forth us who are apostles as the low-
est of all – men appointed to death, as it were. For we are a gazing stock
to the world, and to the angels, and to men. [10]We are fools for Christ's Job 17:6
sake, but you are wise through Christ. We are weak, and you are strong.
You are honourable, and we are dishonoured. [11]Even to this day we both

hunger and thirst, and are clothed in rags, and are buffeted with fists, and
have no certain dwelling place, [12]and labour, working with our own
hands. We are reviled, and yet we bless. We are persecuted, and suffer it. Ac 20:33-35
[13]We are ill spoken of, and we pray. We are made as if the refuse of the 1Th 2:9 2Th 3:7,8
world, the off-scouring of all things, even to this time.

[14]I do not write these things to shame you, but as my beloved children
I warn you. [15]For though you have ten thousand instructors in Christ, yet
you do not have many fathers. In Christ Jesus I have begotten you through
the gospel. [16]So then, I want you to follow me. [17]For this reason I have
sent to you Timothy, who is my dear son and faithful in the Lord. He will
remind you of my ways, which I have in Christ, even as I teach every-
where in all congregations.

[18]Some swell, as though I will not be coming to you any more. [19]But I
will come to you shortly, if God so wills, and will know not the words of
those who swell, but the power. [20]For the kingdom of God is not in words,
but in power. [21]What would you have? Shall I come to you with a rod, or
in love and in the spirit of gentleness?

Chapter 5

How Paul curses the man who committed fornication with
his stepmother.

There is a report abroad that there is fornication among you, and such
fornication as is not once named among the Gentiles: that a man should Le 18:6-8
have his father's wife. [2]And you swell, and have not rather sorrowed, so
that he who has done this deed might be put out from among you. [3]For
indeed I, as absent in body yet present in spirit, have determined already Col 2:5
(as though I were present) concerning him who has done this thing, [4]in the
name of our Lord Jesus Christ, when you are gathered together, and my
spirit, with the power of the Lord Jesus Christ, [5]to deliver him to Satan for
the destruction of the flesh, so that the spirit may be saved in the day of
the Lord Jesus.*

*Excommunication is to destroy fleshly wisdom so that the spirit may be found in the doctrine of Christ.

[6]Your complacency is not good. Do you not know that a little leaven Ga 5:9
sours the whole lump of dough? [7]Purge therefore the old leaven, so that
you may be new dough, as you are sweet bread. For Christ our Passover
lamb is offered up for us. [8]Therefore let us keep holy day – not with old
leaven, neither with the leaven of immorality and wickedness, but with
the sweet bread of pureness and truth.

[9]I wrote to you in an epistle that you should not keep company with
fornicators. [10]And I did not at all mean the fornicators of this world, or the
covetous, or swindlers, or idolaters, because then you would need to go
out of the world. [11]But now I write to you not to keep company together
with anyone called a brother who is a fornicator, or covetous, or a wor-
shipper of images, or a railer,* or a drunkard, or a swindler. With such a
one, see that you do not eat.* [12]For what have I to do with judging those
who are outside? Do you not judge those who are within? [13]Those who
are without, God will judge. Put away from among you that evil person.

[**Railer:** one who curses or uses reviling, harsh, or insolent language]
***Such a one**: If anyone like this professes Christ, no true Christian can bear his company.

Chapter 6

He rebukes them for going to law against each other before the heathen, and reproves uncleanness.

How dare one of you, having a problem with another, go to law under the unrighteous, and not rather under the saints? [2]Do you not know that the saints will judge the world? If the world will be judged by you, are you not good enough to judge small trifles? [3]Do you not know that we will judge the angels? How much more may we judge things that pertain to this life? [4]If you have trials of worldly matters, take those who are least esteemed in the congregation and make them judges. [5]This I say to your shame. Is there really no wise man among you? What, no one at all who can judge between brother and brother? [6]But one brother goes to law against another, and that under the unbelievers?

[7]Now therefore there is utterly a failing among you, because you go to law one with another. Why not rather suffer wrong? Why not rather suffer yourselves to be robbed? [8]Nay, you yourselves do wrong, and rob – and that the brethren.

These and suchlike have no part in Christ.

[**Cursed speakers**: Tyndale put 'railer' for the same Greek word at 5:11. E'cus 28:13: The slanderer and double-tongued man is cursed]

[9]Do you not know that the unrighteous will not inherit the kingdom of God? Be not deceived. For neither fornicators, nor worshippers of images, nor whoremongers, nor effeminates, nor abusers of themselves with the male sex, [10]nor thieves, nor the covetous, nor drunkards, nor cursed speakers,* nor swindlers, will inherit the kingdom of God. [11]And such were some of you. But you are washed, you are sanctified, you are justified by the name of the Lord Jesus and by the Spirit of our God.

[**All things**: Hooker> Paul speaks here for the maintenance of liberty in things indifferent; ie, not unlawful. (*2nd Book*)]

Our bodies are the members of Christ.

He who is of Christ, has his Spirit.

[12]All things are lawful to me,* but all things are not profitable. I may do all things, but I will be brought under no man's power. [13]Foods are for the belly, and the belly for foods, but God will destroy both it and them. Let not the body be given to fornication, but to the Lord, and the Lord to the body. [14]God has raised up the Lord, and will raise us up by his power. [15]Or do you not consider that your bodies are the members of Christ? Shall I now take the members of Christ and make them the members of a harlot? God forbid. [16]Do you not understand that he who couples himself with a harlot has become one body with her? For two (says he) shall be one flesh. [17]But he who is joined to the Lord is one spirit with him.

Ge 2:24

[**Fornication**: understand any form of sexual immorality or impurity.]

[18]Flee fornication.* All sins that a man does are outside the body, but he who is a fornicator sins against his own body. [19]Or do you not know that your bodies are the temple of the Holy Spirit, who is in you, whom you have of God, and that you are not your own? [20]For you are dearly bought. Therefore glorify God in your bodies and in your spirits, for they are God's.

1Co 3:16
1Pe 1:18,19

Chapter 7

Of marriage, virginity, and widowhood.

As for the things you wrote to me about: it is good for a man not to touch a woman. [2]Nevertheless, to avoid fornication, let every man have his wife,

[**Right over the body of the other**: Chrysostom> Their bodies belong to each other, and each is servant to the other (*Hom/ 1Cor*)]

and let every woman have her husband. [3]Let the man give due affection to
his wife; likewise also the wife to the man. [4]The wife does not have right
over her own body, but the husband, and likewise the husband does not
have right over his own body, but the wife.* [5]Do not withdraw yourselves
one from another, unless it be with consent for a time to give yourselves
to fasting and prayer. And afterward, come again to the same thing, lest
Satan tempt you through your lack of self control.

[6]This I say by way of concession, and not of commandment. [7]For I
would that all men were as I myself am. But every one has his own gift
from God – one of this kind, another of that. [8]I say to the unmarried men
and widows that it is good for them if they remain just as I do. [9]But if they
cannot abstain, let them marry. For it is better to marry than to burn.[a]

[10]To the married command not I, but the Lord, that the wife should not M't 5:31,32
separate herself from the man. [11]But if she separates herself, let her Mk 10:9
remain unmarried or be reconciled to her husband again. And let not the Lu 16:18
husband put his wife away from him.

[12]To the rest I, and not the Lord, speak. If any brother has a wife who
does not believe, if she is content to dwell with him, let him not put her
away. [13]And the woman who has an unbelieving husband, if he consents
to dwell with her, let her not put him away. [14]For the unbelieving husband
is sanctified by the wife, and the unbelieving wife is sanctified* by the
husband. Otherwise your children would be unclean; but now they are
pure.[b] [15]But if the unbeliever departs, let him depart. A brother or a sister
is not bound to such. God has called us in peace. [16]For how do you know,
O woman, whether you will save that man or not? Or how do you know,
O man, whether you will save that woman or not? – [17]but even as God has
granted to each.

[**Sanctified:** Tyndale>The unbeliever is sanctified for the (limited) purpose of marriage]

As the Lord has called every person, so let him walk; and I so ordain
in all the congregations. [18]If a man is called when circumcised, let him
add nothing to it. If a man is called when uncircumcised, let him not be
circumcised. [19]Circumcision is nothing, uncircumcision is nothing, but the
keeping of the commandments of God is everything. [20]Let every person
abide in the same state in which he was called. [21]Are you called when a
servant? Care not for it. But if you may be free, avail yourself of it rather. 1Ti 6:1,2
[22]For he who is called in the Lord when a servant, is the Lord's free man.
Likewise, he who is called when free is Christ's servant. [23]You are dearly
bought; do not be men's servants.[c] [24]Brethren, let each, in whatever state 1Co 6:20
he is called, abide therein with God. 1Pe 1:18,19

To keep the commandments of God is everything.

[25]Concerning virgins I have no commandment from the Lord, yet I
give counsel as one who has obtained mercy from the Lord to be faithful.
[26]I suppose that it is good for the present necessity. For it is good for a
man so to be.

[27]Are you bound to a wife? Seek not to be released. Are you released
from a wife? Do not seek a wife. [28]But if you take a wife, you do not sin.
Likewise, if a virgin marries, she does not sin. Nevertheless, the married
will have trouble in their flesh. But I make allowance for you.

The time is short: the things of this world are passing away.

29 This I say, brethren: the time is short. It remains that those who have
wives should be as though they had none, 30 and those who weep should be
as though they wept not, and those who rejoice should be as though they
did not rejoice. And those who buy should be as though they did not
possess, 31 and those who are occupied in this world should be as not con-
sumed in it. For the fashion of this world is passing away.
32 I would have you be without preoccupation. The single man cares
for the things of the Lord, how he may please the Lord. 33 But he who is
married cares for the things of the world, how he may please his wife.
34 There is a difference between a virgin and a wife. The single woman
cares for the things of the Lord, that she may be pure both in body and
also in spirit. But she who is married cares for the things of the world,
how she may please her husband. 35 This I say for your profit – not to
tangle you in a snare, but for that which is fitting and agreeable for you,
and so that you may quietly cleave unto the Lord without hindrance.
36 If any man thinks that it is not best for his virgin, if she is passing the
time of marriage and if need so requires, let him do what he wishes. He
does not sin; let them be coupled in marriage. 37 Nevertheless, he who
purposes surely in his heart, having no need, but has power over his own
will, and has thus determined in his heart that he will keep his virgin, does
well. 38 So then, he who joins his virgin in marriage does well, but he who
does not join his virgin in marriage does better.
39 The wife is bound to the law as long as her husband lives. If her
husband sleeps, she is at liberty to marry whomever she wishes, only in Ro 7:1-3
the Lord. 40 But she is happier if she remains as she is, in my judgment.
And I think indeed that I have the Spirit of God.

The Notes

Better to marry than burn (7:9)

a) To burn, according to St. Ambrose, is when the will consents to the lust of the flesh.

Now they are pure (7:14)

b) It is not that children are by nature clean and pure, for that would go against the apostle himself, who proves (Romans 5) that all are under original sin, and naturally the children of God's wrath. See also Ephesians 2. But his meaning here is that just as all things are clean to the clean (Titus 1:15), so the unchristian wife is clean to the Christian man. Thus he can be with her and not offend, and their children are not to be considered unlawful and unclean.

Do not be men's servants (7:23)

c) To be the servants of men means here to do anything to earn the favour of men. By this, people fall from the favour of God; disesteeming Christ, they hang on men, and regard men's precepts and ordinances more than the very institutions of God – yea, more than God himself. This St. Paul forbids here. He is not saying that we should refuse to be servants to our civil masters, to whom we are bound according to the appointed order of things in society. Them we are strictly commanded in various places of scripture to obey with love and diligence, in all things that agree with God's holy word.

Chapter 8

He rebukes those who use their freedom to the detriment of others, and shows how people ought to behave towards the weak.

Now to speak of things dedicated to idols. We are sure that we all have

A little love is better than much knowledge.

knowledge. Knowledge makes a man swell, but love edifies. 2If anyone
thinks he knows anything, he knows nothing yet as he ought to know.
3But if anyone loves God, the same is known by him.

4To speak of meat dedicated to idols: we are sure that an idol is
nothing in the world, and that there is no other God but one. 5And though
there be what are called gods, whether in heaven or in earth (as there be
gods many and lords many), 6yet to us there is but one God, who is the
Father, of whom are all things, and we in him; and one Lord Jesus Christ,
by whom are all things, and we by him. 7But not everyone has knowledge.
For some still suppose that an idol really is something, and eat a thing as
offered to the idol, and so their consciences, still being weak, are defiled.

In all our deeds we must have regard to our neighbour's well being.

8Meat does not make us acceptable to God. We are neither the better if
we eat, nor the worse if we do not. 9But take heed that your liberty does
not cause the weak to fall. 10For if someone sees you who have know-
ledge sitting at food in the idol's temple, might not the conscience of him
who is weak be emboldened to eat those things that are offered to the
idol? 11And so through your knowledge shall the weak brother perish, for
whom Christ died. 12When you sin so against the brethren, and wound Ro 14:19-23; 15:1-6.
their weak consciences, you sin against Christ. 13Therefore if meat hurts
my brother, I will eat no flesh while the world stands, because I do not
want to hurt my brother.

Charity: what it does.

Chapter 9

Love forgoes the thing that she may do according to the law. Paul exhorts them to keep on running in the course that they have begun.

Paul proves himself an apostle equal to the best, in that the Spirit bears witness to his preaching, and as many were converted by him as by the other apostles.

Am I not an apostle? Am I not free? Have I not seen Jesus Christ our
Lord? Are you not my work in the Lord? 2If I am not an apostle to others,
yet I am to you. For you in the Lord are the seal of my apostleship.

3My answer to those who ask me is this: 4Do we not have the right to
eat and to drink? 5Or do we not have the right to have with us a sister as
wife, as well as the other apostles, and the brethren of the Lord, and
Cephas? 6Or do only Barnabas and I not have the right to do this?

Who goes to war any time at his own expense? 7Who plants a vine-
yard, and eats not of the fruit? Who feeds a flock, and drinks not of the
milk? 8Do I say these things after the manner of men, or does the law not
say the same also? 9For it is written in the law of Moses: You shall not De 25:4
muzzle the mouth of the ox that treads out the grain. Is God taking 1Ti 5:18
thought for oxen, 10or does he say it not altogether for our sakes? For our
sakes no doubt this is written, because he who ploughs should plough in
hope, and because he who threshes in hope should be partaker of his
hope. 11If we sow spiritual things unto you, is it a great matter if we reap
your carnal things? 12If others are partakers of this right over you, why not
rather we? Nevertheless, we have not exercised this right, but endure all
things, lest we hinder the gospel of Christ.

13Do you not understand that those who minister in the temple have their provision from the temple? And those who wait at the altar are partakers with the altar? [14]Likewise also did the Lord ordain that those who preach the gospel should live from the gospel. [15]But I have availed myself of none of these things. Neither have I written these things so that it would be done so for me. For it would be better for me to die than for anyone to take this claim from me.

De 18:1-8

The preacher has right to claim sustenance for his labour.

[16]In that I preach the gospel, I have nothing to boast of, for necessity is put upon me; woe it is to me, if I do not preach the gospel! [17]If I do it with a good will, I have a reward. But if I do it against my will, an office is committed to me. [18]What is my reward then? Truly, that when I preach the gospel, I make the gospel of Christ free: that I do not misuse my authority in the gospel.

[19]For though no man is my master, yet I have made myself a servant to all, so that I might win the more. [20]To the Jews I became as a Jew, to win the Jews. To those who were under the law, I was as though under the law, to win those who were under the law. [21]To those who were without law, I became as though I were without law (when I was not without law as pertaining to God, but under a law as concerning Christ), to win those who were without law. [22]To the weak I became as weak, to win the weak. In all things I fashioned myself to all men, to save at least some. [23]And this I do for the gospel's sake, so that I may have my part in it.

What love makes a man do.

[24]Do you not perceive that of those who run in a race, all run, yet but one receives the reward? So run that you may prevail. [25]Athletes who compete discipline themselves in all things. And they do it to obtain a corruptible crown, but we to obtain an incorruptible crown. [26]I therefore run accordingly: not as at an uncertain thing. I fight accordingly: not as one who beats the air, [27]but I tame my body, and bring it into subjection, lest after I have preached to others, I myself should be a castaway.

Chapter 10

He puts them in fear with examples from the Old Testament, and exhorts them to lead godly lives. Of the Lord's Supper.

Brethren, I would not want you to be ignorant of this: that our fathers were all under a cloud, and all passed through the sea, [2]and were all baptized under Moses in the cloud and in the sea, [3]and did all eat of the same spiritual food, [4]and did all drink of the same spiritual drink. And they drank of that spiritual rock that followed them, which rock was Christ. [5]But in many of them, God had no delight. For they were overthrown in the wilderness. [6]These are examples for us, so that we will not lust after evil things like they did.

As it went in the old Testament, so will it go in the new.

Ex 13:21,22; 14:19-23; 14:29. Nu 26:65

[7]Neither be worshippers of images, like some of them were, as it is written: The people sat down to eat and drink, and rose up again to play. [8]Neither let us commit fornication, as some of them committed fornication, and in one day 23,000 were destroyed. [9]Neither let us tempt Christ, as some of them did, and were destroyed by serpents. [10]Neither murmur, as some of them murmured, and were destroyed by the destroyer.

Ex 32:6
Nu 25:1-9

11All these things happened to them for examples, and were written to
make us mindful – we upon whom the ends of the world have come. Nu 21:6-9 Ex 16:2
12Therefore let him who thinks he stands, take heed lest he fall. Nu 14:37
13No trial has taken you, but such as follows the nature of man. But
God is faithful, who will not suffer you to be tried above your strength,
but will in the midst of the trial make a way to escape out.
14And so, my dear beloveds, flee from the worshipping of idols. 15I

The Lord's Supper

speak as to people who have discernment. Judge what I say. 16Is not the
cup of blessing that we bless, partaking of the blood of Christ? Is not the
bread that we break, partaking of the body of Christ? 17Because we,
though we be many, yet are one bread and one body, inasmuch as we are

[**Partakers of the altar**: carnal or national Israel was a type or figure of spiritual Israel. When Paul wrote, the temple still stood in Jerusalem, and the Jews were still offering on the altar the Old Covenant sacrifices that prefigured Jesus, the New Covenant Lamb. Looking to Old Testament practice, Paul teaches about him who was offered on the altar of the New Covenant, and what it means to partake of this altar in Holy Communion]

all partakers of one bread. 18Observe Israel which walks carnally; are not
those who eat of the sacrifice, partakers of the altar?*
19What am I saying then? That the idol is anything? or that what is
offered to idols is anything? 20No, but I say that these things that the
Gentiles offer, they offer to devils, and not to God. And I do not want you
to have fellowship with the devils. 21You cannot drink of the cup of the
Lord and of the cup of the devils. You cannot be partakers of the Lord's
Table and of the table of devils. 22Or shall we provoke the Lord? Are we
stronger than he?
All things are lawful to me, but all things are not helpful. 23All things
are lawful to me, but all things do not edify. 24Let no one seek his own
profit, but let each seek the welfare of the other. 25Whatever is sold in the
market, eat it, and ask no questions, for conscience' sake. 26For the earth
is the Lord's, and all that is in it. 27If any unbelievers invite you to a feast,
and if you are disposed to go, eat whatever is set before you, asking no 1Co 6:12
question, for conscience' sake. 28But if anyone says to you, This is dedi-
cated to idols, then do not eat of it – for the sake of the one who told you,
and for injury of conscience.
The earth is the Lord's, and all that is in it. Ps 24:1
29Conscience, I say: not yours, but the conscience of that other. For
why should my liberty be judged by another man's conscience? 30For if I
share in the meal with thanks, why am I ill spoken of for the thing I give
thanks for?[a] 31Whether therefore you eat or drink, or whatever you do, do Col 3:17
all to the glory of God. 32See that you give no occasion of evil, neither to
the Jews, nor yet to the Gentiles, nor to the congregation of God – 33even

Love seeks her neighbour's profit.

as I please all men in all things, not seeking my own profit, but the profit
of many, so that they might be saved. 11:1Follow me, as I do Christ.

The Notes

Why am I ill spoken of... (10:30)

a) We should be so full of love and so circumspect as to give no occasion to the ignorant to speak ill of us for our liberty, and for doing that which we may lawfully do before God.

Chapter 11

He rebukes them for abuse and for disorder concerning the sacrament of the body and blood of Christ, and brings them again to the first institution.

[Verse 11:1 is at the end of chapter 10 in the MB]

[2]I commend you, brethren, that you remember me in all things, and keep the observances even as I delivered them to you.

[3]I would that you understood that Christ is the head of every man. And the man is the woman's head. And God is Christ's head. [4]Every man praying or prophesying, having anything on his head, dishonours his head. [5]Every woman who prays or prophesies bare-headed dishonours her head, for it is one and the very same thing as if she were shaven. [6]If the woman is not covered, let her also be shorn. If it is dishonourable for a woman to be shorn or shaven, let her cover her head.

[7]A man ought not to cover his head, since he is the image and glory of God. The woman is the glory of the man, [8]for the man is not of the woman, but the woman of the man. [9]Neither was the man created for the woman's sake, but the woman for the man's sake. [10]For this reason, the woman ought to have a sign of authority on her head* – for the angels' sakes. [11]Nevertheless, neither is the man independent of the woman, nor the woman independent of the man in the Lord. [12]For as the woman is of the man, even so is the man by the woman; but all is of God.

Ge 2:21-23

*As a sign that the woman is under headship.

[13]Judge in yourselves if it is befitting that a woman pray to God bare-headed. [14]Or does not nature teach you that it is discreditable for a man if he has long hair,* [15]and brings praise to a woman if she has long hair? For her hair is given her to cover her with. [16]If there is anyone among you who is inclined to argue, let him know that we have no such custom, nor do the congregations of God.

[**Has long hair:** the Gk *komeo* (2863) means to wear tresses of hair. Paul discusses head covering as custom, not law]

[17]Now this I warn you of, and do not commend: that you come together not for the better, but for the worse. [18]First of all, when you come together in the congregation, I hear that there is dissension among you. And I believe it as to some, [19]for there must be sects among you, so that those who are sound among you may be known.

[20]When you come together, a person cannot eat the Lord's Supper, [21]because everyone begins ahead to eat his own supper. And one is hungry, and another is drunk. [22]Do you not have houses to eat and drink in? Or do you think nothing of the congregation of God, and shame those who have not? What shall I say to you? Shall I praise you? In this I do not praise you.

The institution of the Lord's Supper. [Coverdale>He that would sit now at the table of the High King, let him diligently consider what he receives in his soul through faith, namely, the body and blood of Jesus Christ, which feeds and nourishes him to eternal life (*Fruitful*)]

[23]That which I delivered to you, I received from the Lord. For the Lord Jesus, the same night in which he was betrayed, took bread, [24]and thanked, and broke, and said, Take ye, and eat; this is my body which is broken for you. This do in the remembrance of me. [25]In the same manner he took the cup when supper was done, saying, This cup is the new testament in my blood; this do as oft as you drink it, in remembrance of me.

M't 26:26-29
Mk 14:22-25
Lu 22:17-20

[26]For as often as you eat this bread and drink this cup, you show the Lord's death till he comes. [27]Therefore whosoever eats of this bread or drinks of this cup unworthily, shall be guilty of the body and blood of the Lord. [28]Let a person therefore examine himself, and thus let him eat of the

bread and drink of the cup. [29]For he who eats or drinks unworthily, eats
and drinks his own damnation, because he does not discern the Lord's
body. [30]For this reason many are weak and sick among you, and many
sleep. [31]If we truly judged ourselves, we would not be judged. [32]But when
we are judged by the Lord, we are chastened, so that we may not be
condemned with the world.*

[**Condemned with the world**: Chrysostom>we receive punishment in this life in order that we will not be judged with the world in the next. Coverdale>and to bring us to meekness, repentance, and a right fear of God]

[33]Therefore my brethren, when you come together to eat, wait for one
another. [34]If anyone is hungry, let him eat at home, so that you do not
come together unto condemnation.

Other things I will set in order when I come.

Chapter 12

The diversity of the gifts of the Holy Spirit, which are given for the comfort and edifying of one another, as the members of a person's body serve one another.

In spiritual things, brethren, I would not have you ignorant. [2]You know
that you were Gentiles, and went your ways to dumb idols even as you
were led. [3]Therefore I tell you that no one speaking in the Spirit of God
repudiates Jesus. Also, no one can say that Jesus is the Lord but by the
Holy Spirit.

Only the Spirit teaches that Christ is the Lord.

[4]There are different gifts indeed, yet but one Spirit. [5]And there are
different offices, and yet but one Lord. [6]And there are different works,
and yet but one God, who works all things that are wrought in all crea-
tures. [7]The gifts of the Spirit are given to each person to profit the congre-
gation. [8]To one is given, through the Spirit, the utterance of wisdom. To
another is given the utterance of knowledge by the same Spirit. [9]To an-
other is given faith by the same Spirit, to another the gifts of healing by
the same Spirit, [10]to another power to do miracles, to another prophecy, to
another judgment of spirits, to another divers tongues, to another the
interpretation of tongues. [11]And the very same Spirit works all these, giv-
ing to each person particular gifts as he so wills.

The gifts of the Spirit are given to us to do service to our brethren.

[12]For as the body is one, and has many members, and all the members
of a body, though they be many, yet are but one body, even so is Christ.
[13]For in one Spirit we are all baptized to make one body – whether we be
Jews or Gentiles, whether we be bond* or free – and we have all drunk of
one Spirit. [14]For the body is not one member, but many.

[**Bond**: bound or bonded as slaves or servants to a master]

[15]If the foot were to say, I am not the hand, therefore I am not of the
body, is it therefore not of the body? [16]And if the ear said, I am not the
eye, therefore I am not of the body, is it therefore not of the body? [17]If all
the body were an eye, where would the ear be? If all were hearing, where
would the smelling be? [18]But now God has set the members, every one of
them, in the body at his own pleasure. [19]If they were all one member,
where would the body be?

[20]Now there are many members, and yet but one body. [21]And the eye
cannot say to the hand, I have no need of you; nor again the head to the
feet, I have no need of you. [22]Yea rather, to a great extent those members

of the body that seem to be most feeble, are most necessary. [23]And those members of the body that we think least presentable, we clothe with more respectability, and our unattractive parts with more beauty. [24]For our respectable members do not need it. But God has thus disposed the body, and has given more honour to that part which lacked, [25]lest there should be any schism in the body, but so that the members will care impartially for one another. [26]And if one member suffers, all suffer with him; if one member is had in honour, all members are glad also. [27]You are the body of Christ, and members of one another.

[28]And God has also set in the congregation, first the apostles, secondarily prophets, thirdly teachers, then those who do miracles; after that are the gifts of healing, helpers, governors, diversity of tongues. [29]Are all apostles? Are all prophets? Are all teachers? Do all work miracles? [30]Do all have the gifts of healing? Do all speak with tongues? Do all interpret? [31]Covet the best gifts. And yet, I show you a more excellent way.

Chapter 13

The nature and attributes of love.

Though I spoke with the tongues of men and angels, and yet had no love, I would be even as sounding brass, or as a ringing cymbal. [2]And though I could prophesy and understand all mysteries and all knowledge – yea if I had all faith,* so that I could move mountains out of their places – and yet had no love, I would be nothing. [3]And if I bestowed all my goods to feed the poor, and even if I gave my body to be burned, and yet had no love, it profits me nothing.

All faith is as much as to say 'such a strong faith'.

[4]Love suffers long, and is kind. Love does not envy. Love is not contrary, does not swell up, [5]does not deal dishonourably, seeks not her own, is not provoked to anger, thinks no evil; [6]does not take pleasure in iniquity, but rejoices in the truth; [7]suffers all things, believes all things, hopes all things, endures in all things. [8]Though prophesying fail, or tongues cease, or knowledge vanish away, yet love never falls away.

[9]For our knowledge is imperfect, and our prophesying is imperfect. [10]But when that which is perfect has come, then that which is imperfect shall be put away. [11]When I was a child, I spoke as a child, I understood as a child, I imagined as a child. But as soon as I was a man, I put away childishness. [12]Now we see in a glass, even in a dark speaking,* but then we shall see face to face. Now I know imperfectly, but then I shall know even as I am known. [13]Now faith, hope, and love, these three things abide, but the chief of these is love.[a]

[**A glass**: Some say this refers to a poor mirror (ie looking glass); others, to a perspective glass that imperfectly brings distant things into the reach of sight. **Dark speaking**: the Gk noun *ainigma* (135) means an obscure saying, an enigma]

The Notes

The chief of these is love (13:13)

a) This does not concern justification, but the applying of all things to the profit of the congregation. Nothing prevents some one particular thing variously referred to from being now inferior, now superior, to another. As far as providing for the need of your neighbour is concerned, love is chief and is above faith. But concerning the obtaining of justification and salvation, faith exceeds love.

Chapter 14

Paul shows that the gift of prophecy (that is, of interpreting or preaching) excels the gift of languages, and how they both ought to be used.

To prophesy means here to expound. [Like the old English *prophesy,* the Gk *propheteuo* (4395) could mean either to expound or to foretell]

Labour for love, and covet spiritual gifts, and most chiefly to prophesy.* [2]For he who speaks in an unknown tongue speaks not to people, but to God, for no one understands him. However, in the Spirit he speaks mysteries. [3]But he who prophesies speaks to people, for edifying, for exhortation, and for comfort. [4]He who speaks in an unknown tongue, profits himself; he who prophesies, edifies the congregation.

[5]I would that you all spoke with tongues, but rather that you prophesied. For greater is he who prophesies than he who speaks with tongues – unless he expounds it also, so that the congregation may have edifying. [6]Now brethren, if I come to you speaking with tongues, how do I profit you, unless I speak to you either by revelation, or by knowledge, or by instruction?

Words that are not understood do not benefit.

[7]Moreover, when things without life give sound, whether it be a pipe or a harp, unless they make a distinction in the sounds, how can it be known what is piped or harped? [8]And also, if the trumpet gives an uncertain call, who will prepare himself to fight? [9]So also likewise, when you speak with tongues, unless you speak words that have meaning, how can it be understood what is spoken? For you will be but speaking in the air.

[10]Many kinds of voices are in the world, and none of them are without signification. [11]If I do not know what the voice means, I will be as a foreigner to him who speaks, and he who speaks will be a foreigner to me. [12]So then, since you covet spiritual gifts, seek to have them in plenty for the edifying of the congregation.

[13]Therefore let him who speaks in an unknown tongue pray such that he may interpret also.[14]If I pray in an unknown tongue, my spirit prays, but my understanding brings no one fruit. [15]What is it then? I will pray with the spirit, and will pray with the meaning also.[a] I will sing with the spirit, and will sing with the meaning also. [16]For otherwise, when you bless with the spirit, how can the person who is unlearned say Amen at your giving of thanks, seeing he does not understand what you say? [17]You give thanks well, but the other is not edified. [18]I thank my God that I speak with tongues more than you all, [19]yet in the congregation I would rather speak five words with my meaning for the information of others, than ten thousand words in an unknown tongue.

[20]Brethren, do not be children in understanding. As concerning evil, be children, but in understanding be mature. [21]In the law it is written: With other tongues* and with other lips I will speak to this people, and yet for all that, they will not hear me, says the Lord. [22]Therefore tongues are for a sign, not to those who believe, but to those who believe not. On the other hand, prophesying serves not for those who don't believe, but for those who believe.

Isa 28:11,12 Ac 2:4; 10:46; 19:6.

*Or rather, with different tongues. [Ed: The Anglo-Saxon word *tongue* has been replaced in modern use by *language,* a word of classical origin. To speak or prophesy in other languages was a sign that God was now calling people of other nations and languages to be his people, a thing difficult for the Jews to accept]

[23]If therefore when all the congregation has come together and all
speak with tongues, there come in people who are unlearned, or those
who do not believe, will they not say that you are out of your minds?
[24]But if all prophesy and there comes in one who does not believe, or one
unlearned, he is convicted by everyone, and is judged by everyone. [25]And
in this way the secrets of his heart are opened, and so he falls down on his
face and worships God, and says that God is with you indeed.

[26]How is it then, brethren? When you come together, each one has his
song, has his word, has his tongue, has his revelation, has his inter-
pretation. Let all things be done for edifying. [27]If any man speaks with
tongues, let it be two in all, or at the most three in all, and that by turn;
and let another interpret it. [28]But if there is no interpreter, let him keep
silence in the congregation, and let him speak to himself and to God.

[29]Let the prophets speak two in all, or three in all, and let the others
judge. [30]If any revelation is made to another who sits by, let the first hold
his peace. [31]For you may all prophesy one by one, so that all may learn,
and all may have comfort. [32]For the spirits of the prophets are in the
control of the prophets. [33]For God is not the author of confusion, but of
peace, as he is in all other congregations of the saints.

[34]Let your wives keep silence in the congregations. For it is not per-
mitted to them to speak, but let them be under obedience, as the law says. 1Ti 2:11-15
A woman must be in submission to her husband.
[35]If they wish to learn anything, let them ask their husbands at home. For
it is unseemly for women to speak in the congregation.

[36]Did the word of God come forth from you? Or did it come to you
only? [37]If anyone thinks himself a prophet, or spiritual, let him understand
the things I write to you. For they are the commandments of the Lord.
[38]But if anyone is ignorant, let him be ignorant.

[39]And so, brethren, desire to prophesy, and do not forbid to speak with
tongues. [40]And let all things be done decently and in order.

The Notes

To speak with tongues, spirit or meaning (14:13, etc.)

a) To speak with tongues or with the spirit is to speak in such a way that others do not understand, as priests say their service. To speak with the understanding or meaning is to speak so that others can understand, as when the preacher preaches. [Ed: When Rogers wrote this note in 1537, priests said the service in Latin, a tongue or language that people for the most part could not understand. The reference to preachers is evidently to those who preached or taught in the language of the people. Chapter 14 is somewhat emended after Coverdale's 1535 bible for its greater clarity.]

Chapter 15

The resurrection of the dead.

Brethren, as pertaining to the gospel that I preached to you, which you
have also accepted, and in which you continue, [2] by which also you are
saved, I call to your mind how I preached to you – if you keep it, unless
That Christ died for our sins is the first principle of our faith.
you have believed in vain. [3]For first of all I delivered to you that which I
received: how Christ died for our sins, agreeing to the scriptures; [4]and that Isa 53:4,5

he was buried, and that he rose again the third day in accordance with the Jon 1:17
scriptures; 5and that he was seen by Cephas, then by the twelve. 6After Ho 6:1-3
that he was seen by more than 500 brethren at once, of whom many Joh 20:14
remain to this day, and many have fallen asleep. 7After that he appeared
to James, then to all the apostles.

8And last of all he was seen by me, as by one who was born out of due
time. 9For I am the least of all the apostles, and am not worthy to be called Ac 9:1,2
an apostle, because I persecuted the congregation of God. 10But by the Eph 3:1-3
grace of God I am what I am. And his grace in me was not in vain, but I
laboured more greatly than them all – yet not I, but the grace of God
which is with me. 11Whether then it was I or they, so we preach, and so
you have believed.

12If Christ is preached that he rose from the dead, how is it that some
of you say there is no resurrection of the dead? 13If there is no rising again
of the dead, then Christ is not risen. 14If Christ is not risen, then our
preaching is in vain, and your faith is also in vain. 15Yea, and we are
found to be false witnesses of God, for we have testified of God that he
raised up Christ, whom he did not raise up if it be so that the dead rise not
again. 16For if the dead do not rise again, then Christ is not risen again.
17And if it be so that Christ did not rise, then your faith is in vain, and you
are still in your sins. 18And moreover, those who have fallen asleep in
Christ have perished. 19If it is in this life only that we believe on Christ,
then we are of all men the most miserable.

Christ the first fruits.

20But now Christ is risen from the dead, and has become the first fruits
of those who sleep. 21For by a man came death, and by a man came the Rev 1:18
resurrection of the dead. 22For as through Adam all die, even so through 1Th 4:14
Christ shall all be made alive, 23and each one in his own order. The first is
Christ, then those who are Christ's at his coming. 24Then comes the end,
when he has delivered up the kingdom to God the Father, when he has put
down all rule, authority, and power. 25For he must reign till he has put all
his enemies under his feet. 26The last enemy that will be destroyed is Ps 8:6
death. 27For he has put all things under his feet. But when he says all Ps 110:1
things are put under him, it is evident that he who put all things under him Ac 2:34-36
is excepted. 28When all things are subdued to him, then shall the Son also Heb 1:13; 2:8;10:13.
himself be subject to him who put things under him, so that God may be
all in all things.

29Or else what are the people who are baptized over the dead doing, if
the dead do not rise at all? Why are they then baptized over the dead?[a]
30Yea, and why do we stand in danger every hour? 31As sure as our confi-
dence which I have in Christ Jesus our Lord, I am dying day by day.
32That I have fought with beasts at Ephesus, after the manner of men,
what does it gain me if the dead rise not again? Let us eat and drink, for Isa 22:13
tomorrow we shall die!

33Be not deceived: unwholesome talk corrupts good ways. 34Awake
truly out of sleep, and do not sin. For some have not the knowledge of
God. I speak this to your reproach.

[35]But someone will say, How do the dead arise? With what bodies do they come in? [36]Foolish one, that which you sow is not quickened to life unless it dies. [37]And what do you sow? You sow not the body that will be, but bare seed (I mean, of wheat or something else), [38]and God gives it a body at his pleasure – to every seed a particular body.

[39]All flesh is not of the same kind, but there is one kind of flesh of men, another kind of flesh of animals, another kind of flesh of fishes, and another of birds. [40]There are celestial bodies and there are terrestrial bodies. But the glory of the celestial is one, and the glory of the terrestrial is another. [41]There is one kind of glory of the sun and another glory of the moon – and another glory of the stars, for one star differs from another in glory.

[42]So also is the resurrection of the dead. The body is sown in corruption, and rises again in incorruption. [43]It is sown in dishonour, and rises in honour. It is sown in weakness, and rises in power. [44]It is sown a natural body, and rises a spiritual body. [45]There is a natural body and there is a spiritual body; as it is written, the first man Adam was made a living soul, and the last Adam was made a life-giving spirit. [46]However, the spiritual is not first, but the natural, and then that which is spiritual.

Ge 2:7

[47]The first man is of the earth, earthy. And the second man is the Lord from heaven. [48]As is the earthy, such are those who are earthy. And as is the heavenly, such are those who are heavenly. [49]And as we have borne the image of the earthy, so shall we bear the image of the heavenly.

[50]This I say, brethren: that flesh and blood cannot inherit the kingdom of God.[b] Neither does corruption inherit incorruption. [51]Behold, I show you a mystery: we shall not all sleep, but we shall all be changed, [52]and that in a moment and in the twinkling of an eye, at the sound of the last trumpet. For the trumpet will blow, and the dead will rise incorruptible, and we shall be changed. [53]For this corruptible must put on incorruptibility, and this mortal must put on immortality.

[54]When this corruptible has put on incorruptibility, and this mortal has put on immortality, then shall be brought to pass the saying that is written: Death is consumed into victory.

Isa 25:8
Ho 13:14
Heb 2:14,15

[55]Death, where is your sting? Hell, where is your victory? [56]The sting of death is sin, and the strength of sin is the law. [57]But thanks be to God, who has given us victory through our Lord Jesus Christ. [58]Therefore my dear brethren, be steadfast and unmoveable, always rich in the works of the Lord, because you know that your labour is not in vain in the Lord.

The law is the strength of sin.

The Notes

Baptized over the dead (15:29)

a) Some men say that, in token of the general resurrection, certain Christians were baptized over dead men's graves, signifying that they would rise again.

Flesh and blood cannot inherit the kingdom of God (15:50)

b) Our belief is that there will be a general resurrection of the flesh, believers and unbelievers, according to the scripture (Isa 26:19; Dan 12:2; Job 19:26; Joh 5:28,29; M't 25:31-46). Nevertheless it shall be purged of all corruption, and be changed to immortality, for it must be an incorrupt flesh to inherit the kingdom of God.

Chapter 16

He reminds them about the gathering for the poor Christians at Jerusalem, and concludes his letter with the greetings of certain loving brethren.

Of the gathering for the saints: as I have arranged in the congregations of
Galatia, let you do the same. 2Upon some Sunday, let every one of you
put aside at home and lay up whatever he thinks meet, so that there will
be no gatherings when I come. 3When I have come, whomever you may
approve by your letters, them I will send to bring your gift to Jerusalem.
4And if it seems that I should go, they may go with me.

5I want to come to you after I have gone over Macedonia, for I will be
going throughout Macedonia. 6Perhaps I will stay with you a while, or
over the winter, so that you may bring me on my way wherever I go. 7I do
not want to see you now in passing, but I trust to stay a while with you, if
God permits. 8I will remain at Ephesus until Pentecost,* 9for a great door,
and fruitful, is opened to me, and there are many adversaries.

[**Pentecost**: Tyndale had 'whitsontyde,' or Whitsuntide, as in the Church calendar.]

10If Timothy comes, see that he be without fear with you. For he
works the work of the Lord, as I do. 11Let no one dishonour him, but send
him onwards in peace, so that he may come to me. For I am waiting for
him with the brethren.

12To speak of brother Apollos: I greatly urged him to go to you with
the brethren, but his mind was not at all to go at this time. However, he
will go when he has the opportunity.

13Watch, stand fast in the faith, acquit yourselves like men, and be
strong. 14Let all you do be done in love.

15Brethren, you know the house of Stephanas, how they are the first
fruits of Achaia, and that they have devoted themselves to minister to the
saints. 16I beseech you to show regard for such persons, and to all who
help and labour. 17I am glad of the coming of Stephanas, Fortunatus, and
Achaicus, for that which was missing on your part, they have supplied.
18They have comforted my spirit and yours. See therefore that you ack-
nowledge such people.

19The congregations of Asia greet you. Aquila and Priscilla greet you
heartily in the Lord, and so does the congregation that is in their house.
20All the brethren greet you. Greet one another with a holy kiss.

21The greeting of me, Paul, with my own hand. 22If anyone does not
love the Lord Jesus Christ, the same be anathema maranatha.* 23The grace
of the Lord Jesus Christ be with you all. 24My love be with you all in
Christ Jesus. Amen.

*Let him be accursed at the Lord's coming, or as some will, let him be excommunicate and accursed to death.

The end of the first epistle to the Corinthians, sent from
Philippi by the hands of Stephanas and
Fortunatus and Achaicus
and Timotheus.

[This epistle was likely written in late 55 or early 56 AD]

The Second Epistle of Saint Paul the Apostle to the Corinthians

Chapter 1

The consolation of God in trouble. The love of Paul toward the Corinthians, and his reason for not going to them earlier.

PAUL, an apostle of Jesus Christ by the will of God, and brother Timothy.

To the congregation of God which is at Corinth, with all the saints who are in all Achaia.* [2]Grace be with you and peace from God our Father and from the Lord Jesus Christ.

[**Achaia**: a Roman province, of which Corinth was the capital]

[3]Blessed be God the Father of our Lord Jesus Christ, the Father of mercy and the God of all comfort, [4]who comforts us in all our tribulation, insomuch that we are able to comfort others who are troubled, in whatsoever tribulation it may be, with the same comfort that we ourselves are comforted with by God. [5]For as the afflictions* of Christ are plentiful in us, so also is our consolation plentiful by Christ.

Afflictions or passions of Christ are such sufferings as Christ suffered.

[6]Whether we are troubled regarding your consolation and salvation, which salvation shows her power in that you suffer the same afflictions that we also suffer, or whether we are comforted regarding your consolation and salvation, [7]yet our hope is steadfast for you, inasmuch as we know that as you have your part in afflictions, so shall you be partakers of consolation.

[8]Brethren, I would not have you unaware of the trouble that happened to us in Asia. For we were grieved out of measure passing strength, so greatly that we despaired even of life. [9]Also, we received an answer of death in ourselves, and that because we should not put our trust in ourselves, but in God, who raises the dead to life again, [10]and who delivered us from so great a death, and does deliver. On whom we trust that yet hereafter he will deliver, [11]by the help of your prayer for us, so that by reason of many deliverances thanks may be given by many for us, for the grace given to us.

Ac 19:23

[12]Our assurance is this: the testimony of our conscience, that in sincerity and godly purity, and not in fleshly wisdom, but by the grace of God we have conducted ourselves in the world, and most of all toward you. [13]We write no other things to you than what you read and also know. Yea and I trust you will find us to the end [14]just as you have found us so far. For we are your delight and joy, even as you are ours in the day of the Lord Jesus.

[15]And in this confidence I was minded the other time to have gone to you, so that you might have had yet one pleasure more, [16]and to have passed by you on the way to Macedonia, and to have come again out of Macedonia to you, and to have been led on my way toward Judea by you. [17]When I was so minded, was it lightly? Or do I think carnally the things that I think, such that with me there should be yea, yea, and nay, nay?[a]

18God is faithful. For our preaching to you was not yea and nay. 19For
God's Son Jesus Christ, who was preached among you by us (that is to
say, by me and Silvanus and Timothy) was not yea and nay, but in him
was yea. 20For all the promises of God* in him are yea, and are in him
Amen,* to the laud of God through us. 21For it is God who established us
and you in Christ, and has anointed us; 22who has also sealed us, and has
given the earnest of the Spirit into our hearts.

All the promises of God are given to us only for Christ's sake.
[**Amen**: firm, reliable, true: a transliteration from Hebrew]
[Verses 23 & 24 are in the next chapter in the MB]

The Notes

Yea, yea, and nay, nay (1:17)

a) This is put here for unstableness, inconstancy, or feigning or frivolous words.

Chapter 2

He explains the reason for his absence. He exhorts them to forgive the man who was fallen, and to receive him again with love.

1:23I call God as a witness to my soul that it was to favour you that I did
not go any more to Corinth. 24Not that we are lords over your faith, but
are helpers of your joy. 2:1For by faith you stand. But I determined in my-
self that I would not come again to you in heaviness. 2For if I make you
sorrowful, who is it that should make me glad, but the same who are made
sorrowful by me? 3And I wrote this same epistle to you lest, if I went, I
should be made sad by those of whom I ought to rejoice. Certainly this
confidence I have in you all: that my joy is the joy of you all. 4For in great
affliction and anguish of heart I wrote to you, with many tears – not to
make you sorrowful, but so that you might perceive the love that I have
most specially for you.

5But if any man has caused grief, he has not grieved me but in part –
lest I should overburden you all. 6It is enough for the same man that he 1Co c5
was rebuked by many. So now, instead, you ought to forgive him, and
comfort him, 7lest that same person should be swallowed up with over-
much heaviness. 8Therefore I exhort you, so that love may have the power
over him.

9For this reason also I wrote: to know the proof of you, whether you
would be obedient in all things.

10Whomever you forgive for anything, I forgive also. And if I forgive
a person anything, I forgive it for your sakes in the place of Christ, 11lest
Satan should get the advantage of us. For his devices are not unknown to
us.

12When I had come to Troas for the sake of Christ's gospel (and a
great door was opened to me by the Lord), 13I had no rest in my spirit, Ac 16:8-10
because I did not find Titus my brother. So I took my leave of them and
went away into Macedonia – 14thanks be to God, who always gives us the
victory in Christ, and opens the savour of the knowledge of him by us in
every place. 15For we are for God the sweet savour of Christ, both among
those who are saved and also among those who are perishing. 16To the one
part we are the savour of death unto death, and to the other part we are the

The savour of Christ

savour of life unto life.
And who is fit for these things? [17]For we are not as many are, who
tamper with the word of God. But it is out of pureness, and by the power
of God, and in the sight of God, that we speak in Christ.

Chapter 3

Paul praises the preaching of the gospel above the preaching of the law.

[The Spirit writes his law in our hearts. See OT feature at the end of this epistle]

We begin to praise ourselves again. Do we like some others need letters of
recommendation to you? or letters of recommendation from you? [2]You
are our letter written in our hearts, which is understood and read by all
people, [3]in that it is known that you are the epistle of Christ through our Jer 31:33
work – and written not with ink, but with the Spirit of the living God, and Eze 36:25-27 Heb 8:10;
not in tablets of stone, but in fleshly tablets of the heart. 10:16.
[4]Such confidence we have through Christ in God. [5]It is not that we are
competent in and of ourselves, so as to think a good thought, as it were,
by ourselves. But our ability comes from God, [6]who has made us able to
minister the new testament – not of the letter, but of the Spirit. For the Ro c4
letter kills, but the Spirit gives life.[a]
[7]If the ministration of death through the letters figured in stones was
so glorious that the children of Israel could not behold the face of Moses Ex 34:30
for the glory of his countenance (which glory nevertheless is done away
with), [8]why shall not the ministration of the Spirit be much more glori-
ous? [9]For if the ministering of condemnation is glorious, much more does
the ministration of righteousness exceed in glory. [10]For without doubt,
that which was there glorified is not once glorified[*] in relation to this sur-
passing glory. [11]So then, if that which is destroyed was glorious, much
more will that which remains be glorious.
[12]Seeing then that we have such confidence, we speak boldly, [13]and do
not do as Moses, who put a veil over his face so that the children of Israel
could not see the purpose served by that which is abolished. [14]But their
minds were blinded. For until this day, the same covering remains un-
removed in the old testament when they read it, which in Christ is put
away. [15]But even to this day, when Moses is read, the veil hangs before
their hearts. [16]Nevertheless, when they turn to the Lord, the veil shall be
taken away.
[17]The Lord no doubt is a Spirit. And where the Spirit of the Lord is,
there is liberty. [18]And we all behold the glory of the Lord with his face
revealed,[*] and are changed into his likeness from glory to glory, even by
the Spirit of the Lord.

[In the scriptures the giving of the law, which was glorified at Mt Sinai, is **not once glorified** relative to the giving of the Spirit, which was prophesied and its superiority explained at Jer 31:31-34]

[**His face revealed,** or *his face open,* as Tyndale had, who evidently took this to mean that when the veil is removed from our hearts through faith, the Lord's face is revealed]

The Notes

The letter kills (3:6)

a) *The letter* here, and at Romans 2:27, and in divers other places of the scripture, means the law, or old testament. *The Spirit* means the gospel, or new testament. And this is how St. Augustine expounds them in various places of his book which he wrote concerning the letter and the Spirit. So also does Erasmus, both in his paraphrase and Annotations.

Because the law finds us guilty, and on this finding condemns us, therefore the apostle says rightfully that it kills. But the gospel, because it pronounces us righteous by Christ, and shows us that by him we are justified from all things from which we could not be justified by the law (Acts 13:39), does therefore bring life.

As for the teaching that 'the letter' means the literal sense, and 'the Spirit' means the spiritual sense, no Christian of understanding could accept this. For the words *letter, ministration of death, ministering of condemnation* and *that which is destroyed,* all signify one and the same thing. And the words *Spirit, ministration of the Spirit, ministration of righteousness* and *that which remains,* are opposing things. Now words meaning the same thing must have the same interpretation. But from some of the first group of words, no literal sense could be understood, and from some of the second group, no spiritual sense could be understood – and therefore not from 'letter' or 'Spirit' either. For 'letter' is one in meaning with the first group, and 'Spirit' with the second.

Chapter 4

A true preacher is diligent. He does not corrupt the word of God. He does not preach himself, but seeks the honour of Christ – yea though it be at the risk of his life.

Therefore seeing that we have such an office, even as mercy has come on
us, we faint not, [2]but have cast from us the cloaks of dishonesty, and do
not walk in craftiness. Neither do we corrupt the word of God, but walk in
open truth, and appeal to every man's conscience in the sight of God. [3]If
our gospel be yet hid, it is hid among those who are lost, [4]in whom the
god of this world[a] has blinded the minds of those who do not believe, lest
the light of the glorious gospel of Christ, who is the image of God, should
shine unto them.

[5]For we preach not ourselves, but Christ Jesus to be the Lord, and our-
selves your servants for Jesus' sake. [6]For it is God who commanded the
light to shine out of darkness, which has shone in our hearts to give the
light of the knowledge of the glory of God in the face of Jesus Christ.[b]

Treasure in earthen vessels. [7]But we have this treasure in earthen vessels so that the surpassing
power of it may be seen to be of God, and not of us. [8]We are troubled on
every side, yet we are not without means. We are in poverty, but not
utterly bereft. [9]We are persecuted, but are not forsaken. We are cast down,
nevertheless we do not perish. [10]And we always bear in our bodies the
dying of the Lord Jesus so that the life of Jesus may appear in our bodies.
[11]For we who live are always delivered to death for Jesus' sake, so that Ph'p 1:20,21
the life also of Jesus may appear in our mortal flesh. [12]So then, death
works in us, and life in you.

[13]Seeing then that we have the same spirit of faith as is written of – I
believed, and therefore I have spoken – we also believe, and therefore Ps 116:10
speak. [14]For we know that he who raised up the Lord Jesus will raise us 1Co c15
up also by the means of Jesus, and will set us with you. [15]For I do all
things for your sakes, so that the abundant grace, through thanks given by
many, may redound to the glory of God.

[16]And so we are not wearied, but though our outward man perish,[c] yet
the inward man is renewed day by day. [17]For our exceeding tribulation,

which is momentary and light, prepares an exceeding and an eternal weight of glory for us, [18]while we look not on the things that are seen, but on the things which are not seen. For the things that are seen are temporal, but the things which are not seen, are eternal.

The Notes

The god of this world (4:4)

a) Satan is God's servant, and can do no more than what God appoints him to do. Nevertheless, Christ calls him the prince of this world (John 14:30), and the apostle Paul calls him the god of this world because the world does commonly forsake the true God and serve him. For whomever we bow to, him we make our god, much as Paul says the belly is the god of those who are earthly-minded and serve their own belly (Ph'p 3:19). [And see Ro 6:16.]

In the face of Jesus Christ (4:6)

b) This is to say, in the knowledge of Jesus Christ, and not in the face of Moses, which is the knowledge of the law. For by Christ we come to the knowledge of God (Matthew 11:27; John 1:1-4, 6:32-58).

The outward man (4:16)

c) What Paul calls here *the outward man* he sometimes calls *the old man* [inclusive of both sexes in accordance with the custom of his time], and sometimes *the flesh*. What is meant by 'the flesh' you will find in the prologue to Romans.

Chapter 5

The reward for suffering trouble.

We know surely that if our earthly abode, the tabernacle we now dwell in, were destroyed, we have an abode prepared by God: a habitation not made with hands, but eternal in heaven. [2]And for this we sigh, desiring to be clothed with our dwelling which is from heaven – [3]if yet we be found clothed, and not naked. [4]For as long as we are in this tabernacle, we sigh and are grieved. For we would not be unclothed, but would be clothed upon, so that mortality may be swallowed up by life.

Isa 61:10
M't 22:11
Rev 16:15

[**Earnest** (of the Spirit): part payment given in advance to confirm the covenant]

[5]He who has ordained us for this thing is God, the very same who has given to us the earnest of the Spirit.[*] [6]Therefore we are always of good cheer. And we know well that as long as we are at home in the body, we are away from God. [7]For we walk in faith, and see not. [8]Nevertheless, we are of good comfort – and yet would rather be away from the body, and be present with the Lord.

Ph'p 1:23

[9]And so whether we are at home or away from home, we endeavour to please him. [10]For we must all appear before the judgment seat of Christ, so that every person may receive the works of his body, according to what he has done, whether it be good or bad. [11]Seeing then that we know how the Lord is to be feared, we fare fair[*] with men.[a] For we are known well enough to God.

Ro 2:16; 14:10,12. Eph 6:8

[**Fare fair**: deal fairly, well, decently, with people]

I trust also that we are known in your consciences. [12]We are not praising ourselves again to you, but give you reason to have confidence in us, so that you may have something to answer to those who put confidence in the face, and not in the heart. [13]For if we are too fervent, it is for God that we are too fervent. If we are restrained, it is for your sakes that we show restraint.

[14]For the love of Christ constrains us, because we judge this way: if

one is dead for all, then all are dead; [15]and that he died for all so that those
who live should henceforth live not for themselves, but for him who died
for them and rose again.* [16]And so henceforth we know no man after the
flesh, insomuch that even if we have known Christ after the flesh, now
henceforth we know him this way no more. [17]Therefore if any person is in
Christ, he is a new creature. Old things have passed away: behold, all
things are become new.

*Christ's servants seek Christ's will, and live not at their own pleasure, but at his.

[18]Nevertheless, all things are of God, who has reconciled us to himself
by Jesus Christ, and has given to us the office to preach the atonement.*
[19]For God was in Christ, and made agreement between the world and
himself, and did not impute people's sins to them. And he has committed
to us the preaching of the atonement. [20]Now then, we are messengers in
the place of Christ, even as though God did beseech you through us. So
we entreat you in Christ's stead to be at one with God. [21]For he has made
him who knew no sin to be sin[b] for us, so that we by means of him should
be that righteousness which is accepted before God.

*It is the office of the apostles to preach the atonement, which is between God and man in Christ.

A sin offering.

The Notes

We fare fair with men (5:11)

a) That is, we do not play the tyrant with cursings and excommunications, nor use malicious force among the people, but fear God, and entreat the people lovingly in order to draw them to Christ. [Tyndale>We give all diligence that no one be hurt or led astray by us or by our example.]

To be sin for us (5:21)

b) 'To be sin' means to be a sacrifice or offering for sins, a sin offering. 'Sin' in the scripture is sometimes taken as the *sacrifice for sin*, as at Hosea 4:8 (the priests eat the *sins* of the people) and Romans 8:3 (by *sin* he punished sin in the flesh).

Chapter 6

An exhortation to receive the word of God with thankfulness and amendment of life. The diligence of Paul in the gospel, and how he warns them to avoid the company of the heathen.

We as helpers therefore exhort you, so that you do not receive the grace of
God in vain.* [2]For he says: I have heard you in a time accepted, and in the 2Co 1:24
day of salvation I have succoured you. Behold, now is that well-accepted
time; behold, now is that day of salvation. [3]Let us give no one occasion Isa 49:8
for evil, so that in our service no fault may be found, [4]but in all things let
us behave ourselves as the ministers of God in much patience – in afflictions, in hardship, in anguish, [5]in stripes, in prison, in strife, in labour,
in sleeplessness, in hunger; [6]in pureness, in knowledge, in long-suffering,
in kindness, in the Holy Spirit, in love unfeigned, [7]in the words of truth; in
the power of God, with the armour* of righteousness on the right hand and
on the left; [8]in honour and dishonour, in evil report and good report, as 1Co c4
deceivers and yet true, [9]as unknown and yet known. As dying, and behold,
we live yet; as chastened, and not killed; [10]as sorrowing, and yet always
merry; as poor, and yet making many rich; as having nothing, and yet
possessing all things.

[11]O ye Corinthians, our mouth is open unto you.* Our heart is made

In vain, such that the word sown in your heart be fruitless, to your greater condemnation.

Armour of righteousness: the word of God with hope, love, fear, etc., which Paul calls the armour of light at Ro 13:12.

[**Mouth open** etc: possibly meaning, congruent with an old English expression, we pursue you with many words]

***A strait in your own bowels**: that is, the restraint is in your own feelings.

large. 12You are in no strait in us, but are in a strait in your own bowels.*
13I promise you like reward with me, as to my children. So set yourselves
free, 14and bear not a stranger's yoke with the unbelievers. For what fel-
lowship has righteousness with unrighteousness? What communion has
light with darkness? 15What concord has Christ with Belial? Or what part
has he who believes with an infidel? 16How does the temple of God agree
with idols? And you are the temple of the living God, as God said: I will
dwell among them and walk among them, and will be their God, and they
shall be my people. 17Therefore: Come out from among them, and sep-
arate yourselves (says the Lord), and touch no unclean thing, and I will Eze 37:26,27 Lev c26
receive you, 18and will be a father to you, and you will be my sons and Isa 52:11
daughters, says the Lord Almighty.

Chapter 7

He exhorts them to receive the promises of God thankfully. The Corinthians are commended for their obedience and love toward Paul.

Seeing that we have such promises, dearly beloveds, let us cleanse our-
selves from all defilement of the flesh and spirit, and grow up to full
holiness in the fear of God. 2Understand us: we have hurt no one, we have
corrupted no one, we have defrauded no one. 3I do not say this to con-
demn you, for I have told you before that you are in our hearts, to die and
live with you. 4I make very much of you, and rejoice greatly in you.

I am filled with comfort and am exceedingly joyous in all our tribu-
lations. 5For when we had come into Macedonia, we had no rest in our
flesh, but we were troubled on every side. Outwardly was conflict, in-
wardly was fear. 6Nevertheless, God, who comforts the abject, comforted
us at the coming of Titus. 7And not with his coming only, but also with
the consolation that he was comforted with by you. For he told us of your
longing, your mourning, your fervent heart for me, so that I now rejoice
the more. 8Therefore, though I made you sorrowful with a letter, I do not
regret it – though I did have regrets. For I realize that the letter made you
sorrowful, though it was but for a season. 9But now I am happy – not that
you were sorrowful, but that you so sorrowed that you repented. For your
sorrow was godly, so that in nothing were you hurt by us. 10For godly sor-
row causes repentance unto salvation, not to be regretted, while worldly
sorrow causes death.

11Behold what diligence this godly sorrow that you felt has wrought in
you. Yea, it caused you to clear yourselves: it led to indignation, it led to
fear, it led to desire, it led to a fervent mind, it led to punishment. For in
every point you have shown yourselves to be clear in that matter. 12So
although I wrote to you, I did it not for the sake of him who did the injury,
nor for the sake of him who was injured, but so that our good mind that
we have toward you in the sight of God might appear to you.

13Therefore we are comforted because you are comforted. Yea and we
rejoiced much more for the joy that Titus had, because his spirit was

refreshed by you all. [14]I am therefore not now ashamed, though I boasted
to him of you. For just as all the things that I preached to you are true, so
also the boasts that I made to Titus are found true. [15]And now his inward
affection for you is greater when he remembers the obedience of every
one of you, how with fear and trembling you received him. [16]I rejoice that
I may be reassured about you in every point.

Chapter 8

He reminds them to help the poor saints in Jerusalem, as the
Macedonians did. He sends Titus ahead.

I want you to understand, brethren, of the grace of God that is given in the
congregations of Macedonia, [2]how the greatness of their joy is in that they
are tried with much tribulation. And moreover, though they were very
poor, yet they have given very liberally, and that in sincerity. [3]For as they
were able (I am witness), yea and beyond their ability, they were willing
of their own accord, [4]and insisted that we take their gift and let them be
partakers with others in ministering to the saints. [5]And this they did not as
we looked for, but gave their own selves first to the Lord, and after to us
by the will of God. [6]So we could not but desire Titus to accomplish the
same work of grace among you too, even as he had begun.

[7]Now therefore, as you are rich in all respects – in faith, in word, in
knowledge, in all ferventness, and in love, which you have to us – so also
see to it that you contribute generously to this gift. [8]I say this, not as
commanding, but, seeing others are so fervent, to prove your love also,
whether it be perfect or no. [9]You know the munificence of our Lord Jesus
Christ, who, though he was rich, yet for your sakes became poor, so that
you through his poverty could be made rich.

[10]And I give counsel in the matter because to do this is proper for you,
who began not only to do, but also to will, a year ago. [11]Now therefore
perform the deed, so that as there was in you a ready willingness, so also
you follow through, out of what you have. [12]For if there is first a willing
mind, it is accepted according to what a person has, and not according to
what he does not have.

[13]It is not my mind that others be set at ease and you be burdened,
[14]but, so that there be equality now at this time, that your abundance may
[*Also hereafter* is added following Coverdale's 1535 NT to avoid anachronism]
relieve their lack, and that their abundance also hereafter* may supply
your lack – so that there may be equality, [15]agreeing to that which is writ-
ten: He who gathered much had nothing over, and he who gathered little Ex 16:18
had no lack.

[16]Thanks be to God, who put in the heart of Titus the same good mind
toward you. [17]For he accepted the request; yea rather, he was so well
willing, that of his own accord he has gone to you. [18]And we have sent
with him that brother whose renown is in the gospel throughout all the
congregations. [19]And not only this, he has also been chosen by the con-
gregations to be a fellow traveler with us in our journey concerning this
gift, which is ministered by us for the praise of the Lord, and to stir up

your ready mind. [20]For we want to guard against anyone finding fault with
us in this large distribution that we are attending to, [21]and therefore pro-
vide for things to be beyond reproach, not only in the sight of God, but
also in the sight of men. [22]And we have sent with them a brother of ours
whom we have often found eager to help in many things, but now much
more eager.

The great confidence that I have in you has caused me to do this –
[23]partly for the sake of Titus, who is my fellow and helper concerning you
all, and partly because of others who are our brethren, and the messengers
of the congregations, and the glory of Christ. [24]Therefore show them the
proof of your love, and of our boasting about you, so that the congre-
gations may see it.

Chapter 9

In this chapter he does the same that he did in the chapter going before; that is, moves them to help the poor brethren in Jerusalem.

Of the ministering to the saints, it is more than I need do to write to you.
[2]For I know your readiness of mind, of which I boast to the Macedonians,
and say that Achaia was prepared a year ago, and your ferventness has
inspired many. [3]Nevertheless, I have sent these brethren lest our boasting
over you should be in vain in this respect, and so that you (as I have said)
will prepare yourselves – [4]lest perhaps, if some of the Macedonians come
with me and find you unprepared, the boast I made in this matter should
be an embarrassment to us, not to mention to you.

[5]Therefore I thought it necessary to exhort the brethren to go before-
hand to you, to arrange for the good blessing you promised earlier, so it
could be ready – so that it is a blessing, and not a defrauding. [6]Remember
this: he who sows little will reap little, and he who sows plentifully will Pr 11:25
reap plentifully. [7]And let every person do as he has purposed in his heart – Ec'cus 35:10
not grudgingly, or under constraint. For God loves a cheerful giver.

[8]God is able to make you rich in all grace, so that you, in all things
having sufficient to the utmost, may be rich for all manner of good works.
[9]As it is written: He who dispersed abroad and has given to the poor, his Ps 112:9
righteousness remains forever.

[10]He who gives the sower seed will provide bread for food, and will Isa 55:10
multiply your seed, and increase the fruits of your righteousness, [11]so that
in everything you may be made rich, in all generosity – which raises
through us thanksgiving to God. [12]For the work of this ministry not only
supplies the need of the saints, but is also fruitful in that for this laudable
ministering, thanks may be given to God by many, [13]who glorify God for
the obedience of your profession of the gospel of Christ, and for your gen-
erosity in distributing to them and to all people. [14]And in their prayers to
God for you they long after you, for the abundant grace of God given to
you. [15]Thanks be to God for his indescribable gift.

Chapter 10

He refers to the false apostles, and defends his authority and calling.

I Paul myself beseech you, by the meekness and softness of Christ – I who when I am present among you am of no reputation, but am bold toward you when absent. [2]I beseech you so that I need not to be bold when I am present (with that same confidence that I am supposed to be bold with) toward some who consider us as though we walked carnally. [3]Nevertheless, though we walk encompassed with the flesh, we do not war after the flesh. [4]For the weapons of our warfare are not carnal things, but things mighty in God to cast down strongholds, [5]with which we overthrow imaginations and every high thing that exalts itself against the knowledge of God, and bring into captivity all understanding to the obedience of Christ, [6]and are ready to take vengeance on all disobedience, when your obedience might come to an end. [7]Do you look on things after the outward appearance?

If anyone trusts in himself that he is Christ's, let him also consider that as he is Christ's, so also are we Christ's. [8]And if I were to claim somewhat more concerning the authority that the Lord has given us – to build up,* and not to break you down – it would not be to my discredit. [9]I say this so that I do not seem as though I went about to make you afraid with letters. [10]For the epistles (says he) are strong, but his bodily presence is weak, and his speech is poor. [11]Let such a man think of it this way: that as we are in words by letters when we are absent, such are we in deeds when we are present.

[**Build up**: WT had 'edify' in the obsolete sense of rearing or building up, esp through fortifying in the faith. Paul alludes here to prophecies at Jeremiah 24:6 and 42:10]

Jer 24:6; 42:10. 2Co 13:10

[12]For we cannot find it in our hearts to make ourselves of their number, or to compare ourselves with those who praise themselves. Nevertheless, while they measure themselves with themselves, and compare themselves with themselves, they understand nothing. [13]But we will not boast unduly, but according to the measure of the work that God has assigned to us – a work that reaches even to you. [14]For we are not overrating ourselves, as if we had not reached to you, because we did reach you with the gospel of Christ. [15]And we do not claim undue credit for other men's labours. Yea and we hope, when your faith is increased among you, to be advanced further in our work, [16]and to preach the gospel in those regions that are beyond you – and not to boast of that which is prepared already by another man's work.

Eph 4:11

[17]But let him who boasts, boast in the Lord.* [18]For he who praises himself is not accepted, but he whom the Lord praises.

*Let everyone boast in that Christ died for him, and not in the holiness of his own works.

Ro 15:20

Chapter 11

Paul (with reluctance) commends himself, and defends his authority against the false prophets.

I would you could suffer me a little in my foolishness, yea and I ask you to bear with me. [2]For I am jealous over you with godly jealousy. For I

espoused you to one man, to present you a chaste virgin to Christ.* [3]But I
fear that, as the serpent beguiled Eve through his subtlety, so your minds
might be corrupted from the simplicity that is in Christ. [4]For if he who
comes preaches another Jesus than him whom we preached, or if you are
given another spirit than that which you were given, or another gospel
than that which you were given, you might right well be content.

*We are married to Christ, and not to the preacher.

[5]I suppose that I was not behind the chief apostles. [6]Though I be poor
in speaking, yet I am not so in knowledge. However, among you we are
known to the utmost, who we are in all things. [7]Did I sin, because I
humbled myself so that you could be exalted, and because I preached to
you the gospel of God free? [8]I robbed other congregations, and took
support from them in order to serve you. [9]And when I was present with
you and had need, I was a burden to no one, for that which was lacking to
me, the brethren who came from Macedonia supplied. And in all things I
kept myself so that I would not be burdensome to you. And I will con-
tinue so to keep myself. [10]If the truth of Christ is in me, this claim will not
be taken from me in the regions of Achaia. [11]Why? Because I do not love 2Co 12:14
you? God knows. [12]Nevertheless, what I do, that I will continue to do, so
as to cut away occasion from those who desire occasion to seem like us in
the things that they claim.

[13]For the false apostles are deceitful workers, and fashion themselves
to be like the apostles of Christ. [14]And no wonder, for Satan himself is
changed into the fashion of an angel of light. [15]Therefore it is no great
thing if his ministers fashion themselves as though they were the ministers
of righteousness – whose end shall be according to their deeds.

[16]I say again, lest anyone think that I am foolish, or else even now take
me as a fool if I boast a little, [17]that what I am saying I do not say after the
ways of the Lord, but as it were foolishly, since we have now come to
boasting. [18]Seeing that many boast after the flesh, I will boast also. [19]For
you suffer fools gladly, because you yourselves are wise. [20]For you oblige
even if a man brings you into bondage,* if a man devours, if a man takes,
if a man exalts himself, if a man strikes you on the face. [21]I speak by way
of rebuke. As if we were weak!

*Too much meekness and obedience is not acceptable in the kingdom of God, but all must be according to knowledge.

However, in any point a man dares to presume (I speak foolishly), I
dare to presume also: [22]they are Hebrews; so am I. They are Israelites; so Ph'p 3:4-6
am I. They are the seed of Abraham; so am I. [23]They are the ministers of
Christ (I speak like a fool); I am more so: in labours more abundant, in Acts cc 14, 16, 27.
stripes above measure, in prison more frequently, in death often.

[24]Five times from the Jews I received every time forty stripes less one.
[25]Three times I was beaten with rods. I was once stoned. I suffered ship-
wreck three times. Night and day I have been in the deep of the sea, [26]of-
ten journeying, in danger in rivers, in danger from robbers, in danger from
my own nation, in danger among the heathen. I have been in danger in
cities, in danger in the countryside, in danger on the sea, in danger among
false brethren, [27]in labour and travail, in sleepless nights often, in hunger,
in thirst – going without food often, in cold and without clothing.

[28]And besides the things that outwardly happen to me, I am daily
concerned, and do care for all the congregations. [29]Who is sick, and I am
not sick? Who is hurt in the faith, and my heart does not burn? [30]If I must
boast, I will boast of my infirmities. [31]The God and Father of our Lord
Jesus Christ, who is blessed forevermore, knows that I am not lying.

[32]In the city of Damascus, the governor of the people under king Ac 9:23-25
Aretas laid watch in the city of the Damascenes, and would have captured
me. [33]But at a window I was let down in a basket through the wall, and so
escaped his hands.

Chapter 12

Paul is taken up into the third heaven and hears words not to
be spoken of.

No doubt it is not seemly for me to boast. Nevertheless, I will come to
visions and revelations from the Lord. [2]I know a man in Christ, about
fourteen years ago (whether he was in the body I cannot tell, or whether
he was out of the body I cannot tell, God knows), who was taken up into Ac 9:1-7
the third heaven. [3]And I know the same man (whether in the body or out
of the body I cannot tell, God knows), [4]how he was taken up into Paradise
and heard words not to be spoken, which no man can utter. [5]Of this man I
will boast. Of myself I will not boast, unless it be of my infirmities. [6]And
yet if I chose to boast, I would not be a fool, because I would be speaking
the truth. Nevertheless, I refrain, lest anyone should think of me above
what he sees me to be, or hears from me.

[7]And lest I should be unduly lifted up through the greatness of the
revelations, there was given to me unquietness of the flesh, the messenger
of Satan to buffet me[a] – because I should not be unduly lifted up. [8]For this
thing I besought the Lord three times, to put it from me. [9]And he said to
me, My grace is sufficient for you, for my strength is made perfect
through weakness. Very gladly therefore will I rest in my weakness, so
that the strength of Christ may dwell in me. [10]Therefore I am content in
infirmities, in reproach, in need, in persecutions, in anguish, for Christ's
sake. For when I am weak, then I am strong.

[11]I am made a fool in going on about myself. You have compelled me.
I ought to have been commended by you. For in nothing was I inferior to
the chief apostles. Though I am nothing, [12]yet the signs that mark an
apostle were wrought among you with all patience – with miracles, and
wonders, and works of power.* [13]For in what were you less favoured than
other congregations? – unless it is in that I was not burdensome to you.
Forgive me this wrong done to you! [14]And now the third time I am ready
to come to you, and still I will not be a burden to you. For I seek not
yours, but you. Also, the children ought not to lay up for the fathers and 2Co 11:9
mothers, but the fathers and mothers for the children. [15]I will very gladly
give, and will be given, for your souls – though the more I love you, the
less I am loved in return.

*Paul proved by signs that his authority was as great as the authority of the high apostles.

[16]But granted that I did not impose upon you, nevertheless, I was

crafty, and took you with guile –[17]Did I make any gain from you by any
of those whom I sent to you? [18]I asked Titus, and with him I sent a
brother. Did Titus defraud you of anything? Did we not walk in the same
spirit? Did we not walk in like steps? [19]Again, do you think that we are
justifying ourselves to you? We speak in Christ, in the sight of God.

But we do all things, dearly beloveds, for your upbuilding. [20]For I fear
lest it come to pass that, when I come, I will not find you such as I would
like, and you will find me such as I would not want. I fear lest there be
found among you debate, envying, anger, rivalry, backbiting, whisperings,
swelling, and discord. [21]I fear that, when I come again, God may bring me
low among you, and I may be constrained to bewail many of those who
have sinned already, and have not repented of the uncleanness, fornication, and wantonness that they have committed.

The Notes

Unquietness of the flesh, the messenger of Satan to buffet me (12:7)

a) Unquietness of the flesh is here the forceful withstanding and gainsaying, and even the persecuting, of evil men, who continually troubled Paul and argued against his preaching. This was the minister of Satan that, as if with buffeting, vexed him. His adversaries, who with their blasphemous and contrary teaching disquieted and tormented him, destroying as quickly as he edified, were the very thorn and disquietness of the flesh from which he asked the Lord to be delivered. [Ed> Others say the unquietness was a physical disfigurement or ailment. God knows. But that it was lust ('concupiscence,' Geneva Bible) and related to Paul's lament at Romans 7:19, must be wrong; is not Paul's cry in Romans as Isaiah's at Isaiah 6:5? And see Jeremiah 17:9 and Psalm 51:3.]

Chapter 13

He promises to come to them, and he exhorts them to get themselves in order so that he may find them perfect and in harmony.

Now I am coming the third time to you. In the mouth of two or three De 19:15
witnesses shall everything be established. [2]I told you before, and I am M't 18:16 Joh 8:17
warning you now, and as I said when I was present with you the second
time, so I write now being absent to those who in time past have sinned,
and to all others: if I come again, I will not spare, [3]seeing that you seek
proof of Christ who speaks in me – who among you is not weak, but is
mighty in you. [4]And indeed, though it came of weakness that he was cru-
cified, yet he lives through the power of God. And we no doubt are weak
in him, but we shall live with him by the might of God among you.

[5]Prove yourselves, whether you are in the faith or not. Examine your Heb 10:16
own selves. Do you not know your own selves that Jesus Christ is in you?
– unless you are castaways. [6]I trust that you will realize that we are not
castaways.

[7]I desire before God that you do no evil – not that we should seem
commendable, but that you should do that which is honourable. And let us
be counted as uncommendable persons.

[8]We can do nothing against the truth, only for the truth. [9]We are glad

when we are weak and you strong. This also we wish for: even that you
were perfect. [10]Therefore I write these things being absent, lest when I am
present I must use sharpness, according to the power that the Lord has Jer 24:6; 42:10. 2Co 10:8
given me – to build up, and not to break down.

[11]Finally, brethren, fare ye well. Be perfect, be of good comfort, be of
one mind, live in peace, and the God of love and peace will be with you.

[12]Greet one another in a holy kiss. [13]All the saints send greetings to
you. [14]May the grace of our Lord Jesus Christ, and the love of God, and
the fellowship of the Holy Spirit, be with you all. Amen.

The end of the second epistle to the Corinthians.
Sent from Philippi, a city in
Macedonia, by the
hands of Titus
and Lucas.

Old Testament Feature - A glimpse into the Old Testament of the 1549 Matthew Bible...
Jeremiah 31:31-33, prophesy of the new covenant, minimally updated.

Jeremiah – The .xxxi. Chapter

...The new testament and covenant is prophesied.

... Behold, the days come (says the Lord) that I will make a new covenant with the house of Israel and with the house of Judah: not like the covenant that I made with their fathers, when I took them by the hand and led them out of the land of Egypt. Which covenant they broke, for which I punished them sorely, says the Lord.

But this shall be the covenant that I will make with the house of Israel after those days, says the Lord: I will plant my law in the inward parts of them, and write it in their hearts, and will be their God, and they shall be my people.

Original text:

... Beholde, the dayes come (sayth the Lorde) that I wyll make a newe couenaunte with the house of Israell and withe the house of Juda: not after thee couenaunt that I made with theyr fathers, when I toke them by the hande, and led them oute of the land of Egypte: which couenaunt they brake, wherefore I punished them sore, sayth the lord. But this shalbe the couenaunt that I wyll make with the house of Israel after those dayes, sayth the Lorde: I wyl plante my lawe in the inwarde partes of them, and write it in theyr hertes, and wyll be theyr God, and they shalbe my people.

The Epistle of Saint Paul the Apostle to the
Galatians

[**Galatia**: a district in what is now modern Turkey, then occupied by Celtic (Gallic) peoples. These Gentile congregations were being Judaized. Most scholars date this letter shortly after the Jerusalem council in 49 AD, referred to in Acts 15]

Chapter 1

Paul rebukes them because they had fallen away from the gospel. He recounts his own life, emphasizes his office and apostleship, and declares himself to be equal with the high apostles.

PAUL, an apostle not of men, neither by man, but by Jesus Christ, and by God the Father who raised him from death,* [2]and all the brethren who are with me.

* Paul, though he came long after the apostles, yet did not have his authority from Peter or from any who went before him. Nor did he bring with him letters of recommendation or bulls of confirmation. But the confirmation of his apostleship was the word of God, conscience of men, and the power of the Spirit, which testified with him by miracles and manifold gifts of grace.

To the congregations of Galatia.

[3]Grace be with you and peace from God the Father, and from our Lord Jesus Christ, [4]who gave himself for our sins to deliver us from this present evil world according to the will of God our Father, [5]to whom be praise for ever and ever. Amen.

[6]I marvel that you are so soon turned away from him who called you in the grace of Christ to another gospel – [7]which is nothing other than that there are some who trouble you and intend to pervert the gospel of Christ. [8]Nevertheless, even if we ourselves or an angel from heaven preach any gospel to you other than that which we have preached to you, hold him as accursed. [9]As I said before, so I say now again: if anyone preaches any other thing to you than that which you have received, hold him as accursed. [10]Do I preach man's doctrine, or God's? Or do I go about to please men? If I sought to please men, I would not be the servant of Christ.

[11]I tell you, brethren, that the gospel I preached was not after the manner of men. I neither received it from man, [12]nor was I taught it, but I received it by the revelation of Jesus Christ. [13]For you have heard of my conduct in time past, in the ways of the Jews – how beyond measure I persecuted the congregation of God, and ravaged it, [14]and prevailed in the law of the Jews above many of my companions who were of my own nation, and was a much more fervent maintainer of the precepts of the elders.

Paul's gospel was not confirmed by the authority of man, but by the miracles of the Spirit.

[15]But when it pleased God, who separated me from my mother's womb and called me by his grace, [16]in order to declare his Son by me, to preach him among the heathen, I did not immediately commune of the matter with flesh and blood,[a] [17]nor return to Jerusalem to those who were apostles before me, but went my ways into Arabia, and returned again to Damascus. [18]Then after three years I went up to Jerusalem to see Peter, and remained with him fifteen days. [19]I did not see any of the other apostles except James, the Lord's brother. [20]The things that I write, lo, God knows I am not lying.

[21]After that, I went into the regions of Syria and Cilicia. [22]I was not personally known to the congregations of Judea that were in Christ, [23]but

they only heard that he who persecuted them in time past, now preaches the faith that before he destroyed. [24]And they glorified God in my behalf.

The Notes

Flesh and blood (1:16)

a) *Flesh and blood* here signify men or men's counsel.

Chapter 2

He withstands Peter to his face, and asserts that the law and circumcision are not necessary to salvation.

Paul defends the liberty of the gospel.

Then fourteen years after that, I went up again to Jerusalem with Barnabas, and took with me Titus also. [2]Yea, and I went up by revelation, and discussed with them the gospel that I preach among the Gentiles (but between ourselves, with those who were counted chief), lest it be thought that I should run or had run in vain.

Ac c15

[3]Also Titus who was with me, though he was a Greek, was not compelled to be circumcised. [4]The issue arose because of incomers, being false brethren, who came in among others to spy out the liberty that we have in Christ Jesus, so that they might bring us into bondage. [5]To whom we gave no ground, no, not for the space of an hour, as concerning to be brought into subjection – and that in order that the truth of the gospel may continue with you.

The circumcision are the Jews and **the uncircumcision** are the Gentiles.

Paul is of as high authority as Peter, James, or John.

[6]Of those who seemed to be great (what they were in time past does not matter to me; God looks on no man's person) – nevertheless, those who seemed great contributed nothing to me. [7]But contrariwise, when they saw that the gospel over the uncircumcision was committed to me, as the gospel over the circumcision* was to Peter [8](for he who was mighty in Peter in the apostleship over the circumcision was mighty in me among the Gentiles), [9]and when they perceived the grace that was given to me, then James, Cephas, and John, who seemed to be pillars, gave to me and Barnabas the right hands, and agreed with us that we should preach among the heathen, and they among the Jews – [10]warning only that we should remember the poor, which thing also I was diligent to do.

2Ch 19:7
Job 34:19
Wis 6:7
Ro 2:11
Eph 6:8,9
1Pe 1:17

Paul rebukes Peter in the face.

[11]And when Peter came to Antioch, I withstood him to the face. For he was worthy to be blamed. [12]For before certain men came from James, he ate with the Gentiles. But when they came, he withdrew and separated himself, fearing those who were of the circumcision. [13]And the other Jews dissembled likewise, insomuch that Barnabas was brought into their simulation also.

Deeds of the law do not justify, but faith justifies.

[14]But when I saw that they did not go the right way after the truth of the gospel, I said to Peter before them all, If you being a Jew live according to the customs of the Gentiles, and not as do the Jews, why do you compel the Gentiles to live as do the Jews? [15]We who are Jews by nature, and not sinners of the Gentiles, [16]know that a person is not justified by the deeds of the law, but by the faith of Jesus Christ. And therefore we have believed on Jesus Christ, so that we may be justified by the faith of Christ,

Ro 3:20
Ga 3:11

and not by the deeds of the law – because no flesh can be justified by the
deeds of the law.
[17]If then, while we seek to be made righteous by Christ, we ourselves
are found to be sinners, is Christ then the minister of sin? God forbid.
[18]For if I build again that which I destroyed, then I make myself a tres-
passer. [19]But I through the law am dead to the law,[a] so that I may live unto
God. [20]I am crucified with Christ. I live indeed – yet now not I, but Christ
lives in me. For the life that I now live in the flesh, I live by the faith of
the Son of God, who loved me and gave himself for me. [21]I do not set
aside the grace of God. For if righteousness comes by the law, then Christ
died in vain.

The Notes

Dead to the law, etc. (2:19)

a) But I through the law am dead to the law; that is, by the law of liberty and grace granted in Christ, I am delivered from the law of bondage ministered by Moses, and from the burden and curse of it.

Chapter 3

He rebukes the unsteadfastness of the Galatians. He shows the imperfection of the law, but declares nevertheless that it was not given for nothing.

O foolish Galatians! Who has bewitched you, such that you should not be-
lieve the truth – you to whom Jesus Christ was described before the eyes,
and among you crucified?*

[**Among you crucified**: portrayed as crucified and known in their hearts]

[2]This only would I learn from you: did you receive the Spirit by the
deeds of the law, or by the preaching of the faith? [3]Are you so unwise that
after you have begun in the Spirit, you would now end in the flesh? [4]So
many things then you have suffered in vain, if that be vain! [5]He who
ministered to you the Spirit and works miracles among you, does he do it
through the deeds of the law, or by preaching of the faith? [6]It is even as
Abraham believed God, and it was ascribed to him for righteousness. Ge 15:6
[7]Understand therefore that it is those who are of faith who are the children Ro 4:1-3
of Abraham. Jas 2:23
[8]For the scripture foresaw that God would justify the heathen through Ge 12:3;
faith, and therefore showed beforehand glad tidings to Abraham: In you 18:18; 22:18;
shall all nations be blessed. [9]So then, those who are of faith are blessed 26:4; 28:14.
with faithful Abraham. [10]For as many as are under the deeds of the law
are under malediction. For it is written: Cursed is every one who does not
continue in all the things that are written in the book of the law, to fulfil Ga 2:16
them. Ro 3:20

The law curses, but faith blesses. For only faith makes the conscience alive.

Hab 2:4
[11]That no man is justified by the law in the sight of God is evident, Ro 1:17
Heb 10:38
for: The just shall live by faith. [12]The law is not of faith. (But: The man Lev 18:5
who fulfils the things contained in the law, will live in them.[a]) [13]But
Christ has delivered us from the curse of the law, and was made accursed
for us* – for it is written, cursed is everyone that hangs on a tree – [14]so De 21:23
that the blessing of Abraham may come on the Gentiles through Jesus

Christ was accursed for our sakes: that is, he was punished and slain for our sins.

Christ, and so that we may receive the promise of the Spirit through faith.
15Brethren, I will speak with reference to the custom of men. Though
it be but a man's last will and testament, yet no one sets it aside or adds
anything to it once it is confirmed. 16To Abraham and his seed were the Ge 22:18;
promises made. He does not say, In the seeds, as in many, but, In your 12:3,7;
seed,* as in one, which is Christ. 17This I say: the law, which began after- 13:15; 24:7.
wards (over 430 years), does not nullify the testament that was confirmed
before by God in Christ, so as to make the promise of no effect. 18For if
the inheritance comes by the law, it does not come by promise. But God
gave it to Abraham by promise.

[**In your seed**: in the original, this reads 'in thy sede']

19For what then does the law serve? The law was added because of
transgressions* (till the seed came to whom the promise was made), and it
was instituted by angels in the hand of a mediator. 20A mediator is not a By angels:
mediator of one. But God is one. 21Is the law then against the promise of Ac 7:53
God? God forbid. However, if there had been a law given that could have Heb 2:2
given life, then no doubt righteousness would have come by the law. 22But
the scripture included all things under sin so that the promise, by the faith
of Jesus Christ, should be given to those who believe.

[**Because of transgressions**: Chrysostom>the law served as a bridle to keep the Jews in check until Jesus came, and also to probe their wounds and make them long for a physician (*Hom/Gal*). Tyndale> the law makes sin to be known (Ro 7:7)]

23Before faith came, we were kept and shut up under the law, with a
view to the faith that would afterward be declared. 24Therefore the law
was our schoolmaster to the time of Christ, so that we may be made righ-
teous by faith. 25But now that faith has come, we are no longer under a
schoolmaster.[b]

26For you are all the sons of God* by the faith which is in Christ Jesus.
27For all you who are baptized have put on Christ. 28Now there is neither
Jew nor Gentile, there is neither bond nor free, there is neither man nor Col 3:11
woman, but you are all one thing in Christ Jesus. 29If you are Christ's, Ac 10:15
then you are Abraham's seed, and heirs by promise.

*Faith makes us sons or children, and of the nature of Christ, and binds each to have others in the same reverence that he has Christ.

The Notes

The man who fulfils the law, etc. (3:12)

a) [Ed: In The Matthew Bible, brackets were inserted in verse 12 as follows: 'The lawe is not of fayth: but the man that fulfilleth the thĩges contayned yn the lawe (shall lyve in them).' I have emended to a full parenthesis. Tyndale stressed that obedience to God's law brings temporal reward and blessing; this is 'life' in another sense. He wrote, 'The keeping of God's commandment is the life of a man, as well in this world as in the world to come' (*Sundry*). If God rewards obedience both here and in the world to come, and if faith is made perfect by deeds (James 2:23), we will live by fulfilling the things of the law, though we are not thereby justified (Romans 10:5).]

The law a schoolmaster (3:24)

b) To be under a schoolmaster and to be under the law are the same thing, and are expounded in the prologue to the Romans.

Chapter 4

Paul shows that through Christ we are delivered from the law, and he rebukes the unthankfulness of the Galatians.

[**Governors** (obsolete): in charge of a young man's education and pastimes, esp of a young prince or noble]

And I say that the heir, as long as he is a child, does not differ from a
servant, though he be lord of all, 2but is under tutors and governors* until

the time appointed by the father. 3Likewise we, as long as we were children, were in bondage under the ordinances of the world. 4But when the time was full come,[a] God sent his Son, born of a woman and made bond to the law, 5to redeem those who were under the law, in order that we through election could receive the inheritance that belongs to the natural sons. 6Because you are sons, God has sent the Spirit of his Son into our hearts, who cries, Abba, Father! 7Therefore now you are not a servant, but a son. If you are a son, you are also the heir of God through Christ.

Ro 8:15-17

8Notwithstanding, when you did not know God, you served them which by nature are no gods. 9But now, seeing you know God (yea rather, are known by God), how is it that you turn backward to the weak and poor rudiments,[b] to which again you desire afresh to be in bondage? 10You observe days and months and times and years. 11I fear for you, lest I have bestowed on you labour in vain. 12Brethren, I beseech you, be as I am, for I am as you are.

Infirmity and adversity are persecution, rebuke, and the cross.

You have not hurt me at all. 13You know how through infirmity of the flesh I preached the gospel to you at the first. 14And the adversity I suffered by reason of my flesh, you did not turn away or shrink from, but you received me as an angel of God, yea as Christ Jesus. 15How happy were you then? For I can attest that, if it had been possible, you would have plucked out your own eyes and given them to me. 16Have I therefore become your enemy, because I tell you the truth?

17They are fervent over you amiss. Yea, they intend to exclude you so that you will be fervent for them. 18It is good always to be fervent, provided it be in a good thing, and not only when I am present with you.

The allegory of the two women, who represent two testaments: one concerning Mount Sinai, which is in bondage, and the other concerning the Jerusalem which is above and is free.

19My little children, for whom I travail in birth again until Christ be fashioned in you, 20I wish I were with you now, and could change my tone. For I am in doubt concerning you. 21Tell me, you who desire to be under the law, have you not heard of the law? 22For it is written that Abraham had two sons, the one by a bondmaid, the other by a free woman. 23Yea, and the son of the bondwoman was born after the flesh, but the son of the free woman was born by promise, 24which things contain an allegory. For these women are two testaments. The one is from Mount Sinai, which engenders bondage, which is Hagar. 25For Mount Sinai is called Hagar in Arabia, and corresponds to the city that is now Jerusalem and is in bondage with her children. 26But the Jerusalem that is above is free, which is the mother of us all. 27For it is written: Rejoice, O barren, who bears no children! Break forth and shout, you who travail not! For the desolate has many more children than she who has a husband.

Isa 54:1

28Brethren, we are like Isaac: children of promise. 29But just as then he who was born carnally persecuted him who was born spiritually, so also is it now. 30Nevertheless, what does the scripture say? Put away the bondwoman and her son. For the son of the bondwoman will not be heir with the son of the free woman. 31So then, brethren, we are not children of the bondwoman, but of the free woman.

Ge 21:10
Ro 9:6-10

The Notes

The time full come (4:4)

a) This was the time of Christ's coming, which made an end of the law, and delivered us from the burden of it.

Why do you turn back to the weak and poor rudiments? (4:9)

b) [The Galatians were not Jews, and therefore could not have been turning back to Mosaic observances. What then? Lightfoot> It is clear from the context that here the apostle is not speaking of the Jewish race alone, but of the heathen world also before Christ. He distinctly refers to their previous idolatrous worship (v8) and describes their adoption of Jewish ritualism as a return to the weak and beggarly discipline of childhood...Heathenism had been, with respect to the ritualistic element, which is the meeting-point of Judaism and heathenism, a disciplinary training like Judaism (G.A. note 101, Chrysostom, *Hom/Gal*).]

Chapter 5

He labours to draw them away from circumcision. He shows them the battle between the Spirit and the flesh, and the fruits of them both.

Every person ought to stand by the liberty and freedom that we have in Christ.

Stand fast therefore in the liberty whereby Christ has made us free, and do
not wrap yourselves again in a yoke of bondage. [2]Behold, I Paul say to
you that if you are circumcised, Christ will profit you nothing at all. [3]I
testify again to every man who gets circumcised that he is bound to keep
the whole law. [4]You are gone quite from Christ, as many of you as would
be justified by the law, and are fallen from grace. [5]We look for and hope
in the Spirit to be justified through faith. [6]For in Jesus Christ neither is
circumcision worth anything, nor yet uncircumcision, but faith which by
love is mighty in operation. De 10:16

[7]You were running well. Who got in your way, that you should not
follow the truth? [8]This counsel is not of him who called you. [9]A little
leaven does leaven the whole lump of dough.

[10]I am confident of you in the Lord, that you will not be otherwise
minded. He who troubles you will bear his judgement, whoever he is.
[11]Brethren, if I still preach circumcision, why do I then yet suffer persec-
ution? For then the offence that the cross gives is put away. [12]I would to
God they were separated from you, those who trouble you. Ac 21:21-36

*Christ's liberty is a liberty of conscience and not of the flesh.

[13]Brethren, you were called into liberty – only let not your liberty be
an occasion for the flesh,* but in love serve one another. [14]For all the law Lev 19:18
is fulfilled in one word, which is this: You shall love your neighbour as M't 22:39 Mk 12:31
yourself. [15]If you bite and devour one another, take heed lest you be con- Ro 13:9,10 Jas 2:8
sumed by one another.

[16]I say then, walk in the Spirit, and do not fulfil the lusts of the flesh. 1Pe 2:11
[17]For the flesh lusts contrary to the Spirit, and the Spirit resists the flesh. Jas 4:5
These are contrary one to the other, so that you cannot do that which you Ro 7:14-25
would. [18]But if you are led by the Spirit, then are you not under the law.

Deeds of the flesh: to commit such deeds makes us under the damnation of the law.

[19]The deeds of the flesh are manifest, which are these: adultery, for-
nication, uncleanness, wantonness, [20]idolatry, witchcraft, hatred, dissen-
sion, ambition, anger, rivalry, factious uprisings, sects, [21]envying, murder,
drunkenness, gluttony, and suchlike – of which I warn you, as I have told
you in time past, that people who commit such things will not inherit the

Fruit of the Spirit: these testify that we are not under the damnation of the law. [**Temperance**: self-control, restraint, moderation]

kingdom of God. [22]But the fruit of the Spirit is love, joy, peace, long- Col 3:12,13
suffering, gentleness, goodness, faithfulness, [23]meekness, temperance.*
Against such there is no law.
[24]Those who are Christ's have crucified the flesh with the appetites
and lusts. [25]If we live in the Spirit, let us walk in the Spirit. [26]Let us not be 1Pe14-16
vainglorious, provoking one another and envying one another.

Chapter 6

He exhorts them to brotherly love, and to bear with one another. In the end, he warns them to beware of circumcision.

The duty of every Christian.

Brethren, if anyone has fallen by chance into any fault, you who are spir-
itual should help to amend him, in the spirit of humility – considering
yourself, lest you also be tempted. [2]Bear one another's burden, and so
fulfil the law of Christ.
[3]If any person seems to himself to be something, when indeed he is
nothing, the same deceives himself in his imagination.
[4]Let each prove his own work, and then he will have rejoicing in his
own self, and not in another. [5]For every person will reap for himself. 1Co 3:8
[6]Let him who is taught in the word minister to the one who teaches
him, in all good things. [7]Be not deceived: God is not mocked.* For what-
ever a man sows, that he will reap. [8]He who sows to his flesh will from
the flesh reap corruption. But he who sows to the Spirit will from the
Spirit reap life everlasting. [9]Let us not be weary of well-doing. For when 2Th 3:13
the time comes, we will reap without weariness. [10]Therefore, while we
have time, let us do good to all men, and especially to them who are of the
household of faith.
[11]See how large a letter I have written to you with my own hand.
[12]Those who desire to please carnally by outward appearances con-
strain you to be circumcised only because they do not want to suffer per-
secution with the cross of Christ. [13]For they themselves who are circum-
cised do not keep the law, but desire to have you circumcised so that they
may glory in your flesh.
[14]God forbid that I should glory but in the cross of our Lord Jesus
Christ, whereby the world is crucified to me, and I to the world. [15]For in
Christ Jesus neither does circumcision avail anything at all, nor uncircum-
cision, but a new creature. [16]And as many as walk according to this rule,
peace be on them, and mercy, and upon the Israel that belongs to God.
[17]From henceforth let no one put me to trouble. For I bear in my body
the marks of the Lord Jesus. [18]Brethren, may the grace of our Lord Jesus
Christ be with your spirit. Amen.

*The covenant of mercy in Christ is made only to those who will work.

Nothing helps save to be a new creation.

To the Galatians.
Written from
Rome.

[Ephesus, a city in modern Turkey, was then the capital of the Roman province of Asia. This is one of the prison epistles, written by Paul some time between 60-62 AD while he was imprisoned at Rome]

The Epistle of Saint Paul the Apostle to the
Ephesians

Chapter 1

The everlasting ordinance and election of God in saving all races through Christ Jesus his Son. We are to be saints and without blame. The dominion of Christ.

PAUL, an apostle of Jesus Christ by the will of God. To the saints who are
at Ephesus, and to those who believe on Jesus Christ.
[2]Grace be with you and peace from God our Father and from the Lord
Jesus Christ.
[3]Blessed be God the Father of our Lord Jesus Christ, who has blessed 1Pe 1:2
us with all manner of spiritual blessings in heavenly things by Christ, [4]ac- 2Co 1:3
cordingly as he had chosen us in him before the foundation of the world
was laid, to be holy and without blame before him through love. [5]And he
predestined us through Jesus Christ to be his heirs, in accordance with his
pleasure and will, [6]to the praise of the glory of the grace with which he
has made us accepted in the Beloved, [7]by whom we have redemption
through his blood; that is, the forgiveness of sins, consonant with the
riches of his grace, [8]which grace he shed on us abundantly in all wisdom
and understanding.

Redemption is the forgiveness of sins.

*__Mystery__ is secret counsel.

[9]And as it pleased him, he has made known to us the mystery* of his
will, [10]and purposed in himself to have it declared when the time was full
come – namely that all things, both the things that are in heaven and also
the things that are in earth, will be gathered together in Christ; [11]that is to
say, in him in whom we are made heirs. To this we were predestined ac-
cording to the purpose of him who works all things after the counsel of his
own will, [12]so that we who before believed* in Christ will be to the praise
of his glory. [13]In him also you (after you heard the word of truth, I mean
the gospel of your salvation, in which you believed) were sealed with the
Holy Spirit of promise, [14]which is the earnest of our inheritance to redeem
the purchased possession, and that to the laud of his glory.

[**Before believed**: before the consummation of all things described in v 10]

[**Earnest**: part payment given in advance, esp to confirm a promise]

*Where there is faith in Christ, there is love for all who are sanctified in his blood.

[15]Therefore I (after I heard of the faith that you have in the Lord Jesus
and love to all the saints),* [16]cease not to give thanks for you, making
mention of you in my prayers. [17]I ask the God of our Lord Jesus Christ
and the Father of glory to give to you the spirit of wisdom, and to open to
you the knowledge of himself, [18]and to enlighten the eyes of your minds,
so that you may know what that hope is to which he has called you, and
what the riches of his glorious inheritance is upon the saints, [19]and what is
the exceeding greatness of his power in us who believe pursuant to the
working of that his mighty power, [20]which he wrought in Christ when he
raised him from the dead and set him on his right hand in heavenly things, Col 2:12
[21]above all rule, power, and might, and dominion, and above all names
that are named, not in this world only, but also in the world to come.
[22]And he has put all things under his feet, and has made him above all

Faith is the work of God alone, fully as the raising up of Christ was. Col 2:12.

things, the head of the congregation, [23]which is his body, and the fullness of him who fills all in all things.

Col 1:17,18; 2:9.

Chapter 2

Paul shows them what manner of people they were before their conversion, and what they are now in Christ. We are ordained for good works.

Col 1:21; 2:13.

Eph 4:18

We are all by nature the children of wrath and heirs of damnation.

And you he has quickened to life also, who were dead in trespass and sin, [2]in which you walked in time past according to the course of this world, and followed the prince that rules in the air – the spirit that now works in the children of unbelief, [3]among whom we also had our living in time past, in the lusts of our flesh, and fulfilled the will of the flesh and of the mind, and were naturally the children of wrath fully as well as others.

Col 1:13,14. Rev 20:4

Isa 19:25

[4]But God, who is rich in mercy, through his great love that he loved us with [5]even when we were dead by sin, has quickened us to life together in Christ (for by grace you are saved), [6]and has raised us up together, and made us sit together in heavenly things through Christ Jesus, [7]in order to show in times to come the exceeding riches of his grace, in kindness toward us in Christ Jesus. [8]For by grace you are saved, through faith – and that not of yourselves. For it is the gift of God, [9]and does not come by works, lest any man should boast. [10]For we are his workmanship, created in Christ Jesus for good works, to which God ordained us before, that we should walk in them.[a]

[11]And so remember that you (being in time past Gentiles in the flesh, and called uncircumcision by those who are called the circumcision in the flesh, which circumcision is made by hands) – [12]remember, I say, that you were at that time without Christ, and were reputed aliens from the community of Israel, and were strangers to the testaments of promise, and had no hope,[b] and were without God in this world. [13]But now, in Christ Jesus, you who a while ago were afar off, are made near by the blood of Christ.

Reconciliation between Jew and non-Jew.

Reconciliation between man and God.

[14]For he is our peace, who has made of both one, and has broken down the wall that was a partition between us,[c] [15]and has also put away through his flesh the cause of hatred (that is to say, the law of observances contained in the written law[d]), to make of the two one new man in himself, so making peace, [16]and to reconcile both to God in one body through his cross. And he slew hatred thereby, [17]and came and preached peace to you who were afar off and to those that were near. [18]For through him we both have an open way in, in one Spirit, to the Father.

[19]Now therefore you are no longer strangers and foreigners, but citizens with the saints, and of the household of God. [20]And you are built upon the foundation[e] of the apostles and prophets, Jesus Christ being the head cornerstone, [21]in whom every structure coupled together grows into a holy temple[f] in the Lord – [22]in whom you also are built together, and made a habitation for God in the Spirit.

The Notes

Created for good works (2:10)

a) The promises of mercy in Christ's blood are made to us on the condition that we keep the law and love one another as Christ loved us. [Ed: Tyndale means that we are bound to keep God's moral, or natural law. He divided Moses' law in 3 parts. One was the ceremonial laws or observances of the Old Testament, which were signs of spiritual things (Col 2:16,17), and have been fulfilled in and put away by the cross. Second was the civil and criminal law, which was binding upon the Jews only. Third was the moral, or what Tyndale called the natural law, which is summarized in the Ten Commandments and elaborated in Moses' writings, and which is and always has been binding upon all men (*Practice*). This is the orthodox view: see Article VII of the Articles of Religion in the Book of Common Prayer. Therefore when the scriptures speak of the law, one must consider from the context what is meant.]

Had no hope (2:12)

b) Until Christ came, the Gentiles were not under the covenant of mercy, but the Jews only.

Wall of partition (2:14)

c) Moses' law, which was the wall and cause of hate between the Jews and the Gentiles, is taken away. In its stead love has come, for us to love one another as Christ loved us.

Cause of hatred (2:15)

d) The cause of hatred between the heathen and the Jews: by the law [that is, the ceremonial observances of the Mosaic law] the Jews would be better than the heathen. But now that both have one Spirit through Christ without the law, the hatred has an end, and one is equally as the other in Christ.

Foundation (2:20)

e) You are built upon the foundation of the apostles and prophets: *Foundation* is the word of God.

A holy temple (2:21)

f) *Temple* in the epistles of the apostles signifies the congregation of faithful, holy, and virtuous believers. Sometimes it signifies the heart of every Christian, as in 1 Corinthians 3:16 and 6:19, and 2 Corinthians 6:16.

Chapter 3

He explains the cause of his imprisonment, and more of the revelation of the mystery of Christ. He desires them not to faint because of his trouble, and prays God to make them steadfast in his Spirit.

Paul was an apostle to the heathen and learned his gospel by revelation.

[**Paul's understanding**: see above, Eph 1:9-12]

For this then I, Paul, am in the bonds of Jesus Christ, for the sake of you
who are heathen – [2]if you have heard of the ministration of the grace of
God that is given to me for you. [3]For by revelation he showed this mys-
tery to me, as I wrote above in a few words, [4]from which, when you read,
you may know my understanding in the mystery of Christ.* [5]This mystery
was not in times past opened to the sons of men as it is now revealed to
his holy apostles and prophets by the Spirit: [6]that the Gentiles should be
inheritors also, and of the same body, and partakers of his promise that is
in Christ by the means of the gospel – [7]of which gospel I am made a
minister by the gift of the grace of God given to me through the working
of his power. [8]To me, the least of all saints, is this grace given, to preach
among the Gentiles the unsearchable riches of Christ, [9]and to make all
men see what the fellowship of the mystery is.

This mystery has from the beginning of the world been hid in God,
who made all things through Jesus Christ, [10]to the intent that now, through
the congregation, the manifold wisdom of God may be made known to the
rulers and powers in heaven, [11]according to the eternal purpose which he
purposed in Christ Jesus our Lord, [12]by whom we are bold to draw near in

the confidence that we have by faith on him.
[13]Therefore I desire that you faint not because of my tribulations for
your sakes, which are worthy to be glorified by you. [14]For this I bow my
knees to the Father of our Lord Jesus Christ, [15]who is Father over all that
is called father in heaven and in earth. [16]I pray that he would grant you,
according to the riches of his glory, to be strengthened with power by his
Spirit in the inner man, [17]and that Christ may dwell in your hearts by faith,
so that you, being rooted and grounded in love,* [18]may be able to compre-
hend with all the saints what is that breadth and length, depth and height,
[19]and to know what is the love of Christ, which love passes knowledge;
that you might be filled with every kind of fullness that comes of God.
[20]Now to him who is able to do exceeding abundantly above all that
we ask or think by the power that works in us, [21]be praise in the congrega-
tion by Jesus Christ throughout all generations, world without end.
Amen.

*Where true faith in Christ is, there is love to the neighbour. And faith and love make us understand all things. Faith understands the secrets of God, and the mercy that is given her in Christ. And love knows her duty to her neighbour, and can interpret all laws and ordinances, and knows how far forth they are to be kept, and when to be dispensed with.

Chapter 4

He exhorts them to meekness and longsuffering, to love and peace. Everyone is to serve and edify the other with the gift that God has given him, to beware of strange doctrine, to lay aside the old life of greedy desires, and to walk in a new life.

I, therefore, who am in bonds for the Lord's sake, exhort you to walk
worthy of the calling wherein you are called, [2]in all humbleness of mind,
and meekness and long-suffering, forbearing one another through love;
[3]and to be diligent to keep the unity of the Spirit in the bond of peace, Ro 12:10,16.
[4]being one body and one spirit, even as you are called in one hope of your
calling. [5]Let there be but one Lord, one faith, one baptism: [6]one God and
Father of all, who is above all, through all, and in you all.

One God. One Lord. One faith. One baptism.

[7]To every one of us grace is given according to the nature and scope
of the gift of Christ. [8]Therefore he says: He ascended up on high, and has
led captivity captive, and has given gifts to men. [9]That he ascended, what
does it mean but that he also descended first, into the lowest parts of the Ps 68:18 Ro 12:1-8
earth? [10]He who descended is the same also who ascended up, even above 1Co c12 2Co 12:13
all heavens, to fulfil all things. [11]And the very same made some apostles,
some prophets, some evangelists, some shepherds, and some teachers,
[12]so that the saints may have all things necessary to work and minister for
the edifying of the body of Christ, [13]until we every one (in the unity of
faith and the knowledge of the Son of God) grow up to be perfect in the
maturity of the fullness of Christ;* [14]so that we henceforth would no
longer be children, wavering and carried with every wind of doctrine by
the wiliness of men, and craftiness whereby they lay in wait for us, to
deceive us.

*It is to this end and purpose that the true ministers of the congregation serve: to make us perfect in the full knowledge of Christ.

[15]But let us follow the truth in love, and in all things grow in him who
is the head; that is to say, Christ. [16]In him all the body is coupled and knit
together in every joint, and one ministers to another (according to the Col 2:19
divine working, as every part has its role), and advances the body for the

edifying of itself in love.

[17]I say therefore, and testify in the Lord, that henceforth you must not walk like other Gentiles walk, in vanity of their mind, [18]blinded in their understanding, being alienated from the life that is in God through the ignorance that is in them because of the blindness of their hearts; [19]who, being past repentance, have given themselves over to wantonness, to work all manner of uncleanness, even with greediness. [20]But you have not so learned Christ – [21]if it so be that you have heard him, and are taught in him, inasmuch as the truth is in Jesus. [22]So then, as concerning the former lifestyle, lay away from you that old man, which is corrupt through deceptive desires and affections, [23]and be renewed in the spirit of your minds, [24]and put on that new man, which is shapen in the image of God in righteousness and true holiness.

Ignorance is the root cause of bad living.

Ro c6
Col 3:7-11
Heb c12
1Pe 2:1
Ps 4:4

[25]Therefore put away lying, and let every person speak truth to his neighbour, seeing as we are members of one another. [26]Be angry, but sin not.[a] Let not the sun go down upon your wrath; [27]neither give place to the backbiter. [28]Let him who stole steal no more, but let him rather do good work with his hands, so that he may have something to give to him who has need.

Avenge not.

[29]Let no unwholesome talk proceed out of your mouths, but that which is good to edify when needful, so that it may find favour with the hearers. [30]And grieve not the Holy Spirit of God, by whom you are sealed for the day of redemption. [31]Let all bitterness, fierceness, and wrath, shouting and cursing, be put away from you, with all maliciousness. [32]Be kind to one another, and merciful, forgiving one another, even as God for Christ's sake forgave you.

Those who have the Spirit of God are grieved to hear such things.

The Notes

Be angry, and sin not (4:26)

a) Christ was angry at the blindness of the Jews (M't 23). And so was Moses at the idolatry of the Israelites (Ex 32:19), and at the sedition of Korah, Dathan, and Abiram (Nu 16:15). Nevertheless, this anger or wrath was but a very zeal for the law of God, as you may see by Phinehas (Nu 25:1-11) and by Mattathias (I Maccabees c2). As for malice, or unlawful wrath, it is forbidden, as it follows here in this chapter.

Chapter 5

He exhorts them to love. He warns them to beware of uncleanness, covetousness, foolish talking, and false counsel; to be circumspect, to avoid drunkenness, to rejoice and to be thankful to God, and to submit themselves one to another. He teaches how women should obey their husbands, and how lovingly men ought to treat their wives.

Be followers of God as dear children, [2]and walk in love, even as Christ loved us and gave himself for us, an offering and a sacrifice of a sweet savour to God.

[**Fornication** in scripture may include any manner of sexual licence or immorality]

[3]As for fornication* and all uncleanness or covetousness, let them not be once named among you, as it becomes saints. [4]Nor should there be

Ungodly talk strengthens the flesh against the Spirit.

These have no part with Christ.

coarseness, or foolish talking, or jestings which are not fitting, but rather giving of thanks. [5]For this you know, that no whoremonger or unclean person, or covetous person (who is an idolater), has any inheritance in the kingdom of Christ and of God.

[6]Let no man deceive you with vain words. For through such things comes the wrath of God upon the children of unbelief. [7]Therefore do not be companions with them. [8]You were once darkness, but are now light in the Lord. Walk as children of light. [9]For the fruit of the Spirit is in all goodness, righteousness, and truth. [10]Accept that which is pleasing to the Lord, [11]and have no fellowship with the unfruitful works of darkness, but rather rebuke them. [12]For it is shameful even to name those things that are done by them in secret. [13]But all things, when they are rebuked by the light, are manifest. For whatsoever is manifest, that same is light. [14]Therefore he says, Awake, you who sleep, and stand up from death, and Christ will give you light.

M't 24:11
Mk 13:22
Lu 21:8
2Th 2:3-12

Isa 26:19, 60:1-3.

Redeeming the time: that is, spending the time well.

[15]Take heed therefore that you walk circumspectly – not as fools, but as wise, [16]redeeming the time.* For the days are evil. [17]Therefore be not unwise, but understand what the will of the Lord is. [18]And be not drunk with wine, wherein is excess, but be fulfilled with the Spirit, [19]speaking to yourselves in psalms and hymns and spiritual songs, singing and making melody to the Lord in your hearts, [20]giving thanks always for all things to God the Father in the name of our Lord Jesus Christ, [21]and submitting yourselves to one another in the fear of God.

[22]Women, submit yourselves to your own husbands, as to the Lord. [23]For the husband is the head of the wife, even as Christ is the head of the congregation, and he is the saviour of the body. [24]Therefore as the congregation is subject to Christ, so also let the wives be subject to their husbands in all things.

1Co 11:3
Col 3:18
1Pe 3:1

[25]Husbands, love your wives, even as Christ loved the congregation and gave himself for it [26]to sanctify it, and cleansed it in the fountain of water through the word, [27]to make it for himself a glorious congregation, without spot or wrinkle or any such thing, but to be holy and without blame. [28]This is how men ought men to love their wives: as their own bodies.

Col 3:19

He who loves his wife loves himself. [29]For no man ever yet hated his own flesh, but cares for and cherishes it, even as the Lord does the congregation. [30]For we are members of his body, of his flesh and of his bones. [31]On this account must a man leave father and mother, and continue with his wife, and the two will be made one flesh. [32]This is a great mystery, but I speak as between Christ and the congregation. [33]Nevertheless, see to it that every one of you loves his wife truly, even as himself. And let the wife see that she fears her husband.*

[**Fears**: Chrysostom> not as a slave, but as a free woman who does not contradict, rebel, or seek preeminence, but loves and honours her husband (*Hom/Eph*)]

Ge 2:24
M't 19:3-7
Mk 10:2-9
1Co 6:16

Chapter 6

How children should behave toward their fathers and mothers; likewise fathers toward their children, servants toward their masters, and masters toward their servants. An exhortation to the spiritual battle, and what weapons Christians should fight with.

Children, obey your fathers and mothers in the Lord, for this is right.
[2]Honour your father and mother (which is the first commandment that has
any promise with it), [3]so that you may prosper and live long on the earth.
[4]And ye fathers, do not move your children to wrath, but bring them up in
the nurture and admonition of the Lord.

Col 3:20,21 Ex 20:12 De 5:16 Ec'cus 3:3-16. M't 15:4-6 Mk 7:10-13

[**Eye-service**: the action of an 'eye-servant,' who only works when under the master's eye]

[5]Servants, be obedient to your carnal masters with fear and trembling,
in singleness of heart, as to Christ – [6]not with eye-service,* as men-
pleasers, but as the servants of Christ, doing the will of God from the
heart with good will: [7]serving the Lord, and not men. [8]And remember,
whatever good thing anyone does, that he will receive back again from the
Lord, whether he be bond or free.

Col 3:22-25;4:1. Tit 2:9,10 1Pe 2:18-20

[9]And ye masters, do the same toward your servants, putting away
threatenings. And remember that even your master also is in heaven;
neither is there any respect of person with him.

[Verse 12 is adapted in part from Coverdale 1535. Ed]

[10]Finally, my brethren, be strong in the Lord, and in the power of his
might. [11]Put on the armour of God so that you are able to stand steadfast
against the crafty assaults of the devil. [12]For we wrestle not against flesh
and blood, but against rule, against power; namely against the rulers of the
world, of the darkness of this world; against spiritual wickedness, for
heavenly things. [13]So then take up the armour of God, so that you are able
to resist in the evil day, and to stand perfect in all things.

2Co 10:4

The armour of God: truth and truthfulness; the shoes of a steadfast purpose to follow the gospel; faith, by which our conscience is at peace after it has once known Christ; the helmet of salvation, which is hope; the word of God, which is the sword; etc. [This gloss is the combined thought of William Tyndale in 1534 and John Rogers in 1549. Ed]

[14]Stand therefore, your loins girt about with truth, having on the
breastplate of righteousness, [15]and shod with shoes prepared by the gospel
of peace. [16]Above all, take up the shield of faith, with which you will be
able to quench all the fiery darts of the evil one. [17]And take the helmet of
salvation, and the sword of the Spirit, which is the word of God. [18]And
pray always with every sort of prayer and supplication, and that in the
Spirit. And keep vigil also with all perseverance and supplication for all
the saints – [19]and for me: that utterance may be given to me; that I may
open my mouth boldly to utter the mystery of the gospel, [20]for which I am
a messenger in bonds; that I may speak freely therein as I ought to speak.

Col 4:2-4

[21]But so that you may also know how I am and what I am doing,
Tychicus, my dear brother and faithful minister in the Lord, will tell you
everything, [22]whom I sent to you for this same purpose: so that you could
know what circumstances I stand in, and so that he could comfort your
hearts.

[23]Peace be with the brethren, and love with faith, from God the Father
and from the Lord Jesus Christ. [24]Grace be with all those who love our
Lord Jesus Christ in pureness. Amen.

Sent from Rome to the Ephesians
by the hand of
Tychicus.

[**Philippians**: the Christians living in Philippi, a Roman colony. Paul wrote this letter during his first imprisonment at Rome in 60-62 AD, which he describes herein]

The Epistle of Saint Paul the Apostle to the **Philippians**

Chapter 1

He exhorts them to increase in love, in knowledge, and in experience of divine things, makes mention of his imprisonment at Rome, is glad to hear Christ preached, and is content either to die or live. He prays them to lead a godly life, to be of one mind, and to fear no persecution.

Bishops
Deacons

Of Paul's greeting see note (a) to Ro c1.

PAUL AND TIMOTHY, the servants of Jesus Christ, to all the saints in Christ Jesus who are at Philippi, with the bishops and deacons.

[2]Grace be with you and peace from God our Father and from the Lord Jesus Christ.

[3]I thank my God with every remembrance of you, [4]always in all my prayers for you, and pray with gladness, [5]because of the fellowship that you have had in the gospel from the first day until now. [6]And I am confident of this: that he who began a good work in you will go forth with it until the day of Jesus Christ – [7]as it is fitting for me so to judge of you all, because I have you in my heart, and have you also every one companions of grace with me, even in my bonds, as I defend and establish the gospel.

[8]For God is my witness how greatly I long after you all from the very heart root in Jesus Christ. [9]And this I pray: that your love may increase more and more in knowledge and in all experience, [10]that you may accept the things of most value, that you may be pure, and such as would hurt no man's conscience until the day of Christ – [11]filled with the fruits of righteousness, which fruits come by Jesus Christ for the glory and laud of God.

[12]I would you understood, brethren, that my trouble has served for the great furthering of the gospel. [13]For my bonds in Christ are manifest throughout all the judgment hall and in all other places, [14]and many of the brethren in the Lord are emboldened through my bonds, and dare to more freely speak the word without fear. [15]Some there are who preach Christ out of envy and rivalry, and some of goodwill. [16]The one part preach Christ out of rivalry, and not purely, supposing to add more adversity to my bonds, [17]but the other part out of love, because they see that I am set to defend the gospel. [18]What then? If only Christ be preached – whatever the way, whether through opportunism or of a true intent – I rejoice.

[19]Yea, and I will rejoice, because I know that these circumstances will bear toward my salvation (through your prayer and ministering of the Spirit of Jesus Christ, [20]as I heartily look for), and hope that in nothing I will be ashamed, but that with all confidence, as always in times past, so now Christ may be magnified in my body, whether it be through life or death. [21]For Christ is to me life, and death is to me gain.

[22]If it happens that I live in the flesh, it means fruitful work for me, and what to choose I do not know. [23]I am constrained by two things: I

desire to be released and to be with Christ, which thing is best of all. [24]Nevertheless, to remain in the flesh is more needful for you. [25]And this I am sure of: that I will abide, and continue with you all for the furtherance and joy of your faith, [26]so that you may more abundantly rejoice in Jesus Christ through me, by my coming to you again.

[27]Only be sure that you live worthy of the gospel of Christ, so that whether I come and see you or am absent, I may yet hear of you that you continue in one spirit and in one soul, labouring as we do to maintain the faith of the gospel – [28]and in nothing fearing your adversaries, which is to them a sign of perdition, but to you of salvation, and that from God. [29]For to you it is given not only to believe on Christ, but also to suffer* for his sake, [30]and to have even the same fight which you saw me have and now hear of me.

* Tribulation is a sign of salvation to the true believers.

Chapter 2

He exhorts them to unite in brotherly love, and to beware of rivalry and vainglory. For a trustworthy example, he sets Christ before them.

If there is among you any consolation in Christ, if there is any comforting love, if there is any fellowship of the Spirit, if there is any compassion or mercy, [2]fulfil my joy and all draw one way, having one love and being of one accord and of one mind. [3]Let nothing be done through rivalry or vainglory,* but in meekness of mind let everyone esteem the other better than himself. [4]And look not every person on his own things, but every person on the things of others.[a]

[**Rivalry or vainglory**: Tyndale> from hate or disdain one of another, or out of affection for himself, to seem glorious. *Doctrinal*]

[5]Let the same mind be in you that was in Christ Jesus, [6]who, being in the form of God, counted it not a prize to be equal to God, [7]but made himself of no reputation, and took on him the form of a servant, and became like humankind, [8]and was found in his appearance as a man. He humbled himself and became obedient unto death, even the death of the cross. [9]For this God has exalted him, and given him a name above all names, [10]so that in the name of Jesus every knee will bow, both of things in heaven and things in earth, and things under the earth, [11]and so that all tongues will confess that Jesus Christ is the Lord, to the glory of God the Father.

To follow Christ is our profession, and to likewise humble ourselves so that we may be likewise exalted.

Heb 2:9
Isa 45:23
Dan 7:14
Ro 14:11

[12]Therefore my dearly beloveds, as you have always obeyed, not only when I was present, but now much more in my absence, even so work out your own salvation with fear and trembling.* [13]For it is God who works in you both the will and also the deed, of his own good will.

As you are saved from sin through faith, so work according to the covenant, until you come to the salvation of glory. For if you cease working, the Spirit is quenched, and you cease to be partakers of the promise.

[14]Do all things without murmuring and disputing, [15]so that you may be faultless and pure, and the children of God without rebuke in the midst of a corrupt and perverse nation – among whom see that you shine as lights in the world, [16]holding fast the word of life, so that I may rejoice in the day of Christ that I have not run in vain, have not laboured in vain. [17]Yea, and even if I am offered up upon the offering and sacrifice of your faith, I am glad, and rejoice with you all.[b] [18]And you also, be glad for the same

Ro 15:16

cause, and rejoice with me.
[19]I trust in the Lord Jesus to send Timothy to you shortly, so that I also
may be of good comfort when I know your state. [20]For I have no man who
is minded so like me, who with such pure affection cares for your matters.
[21]For all others seek their own, and not that which is Jesus Christ's. [22]You
know the proof of him, how as a son with the father he bestowed his
labour upon the gospel with me. [23]I hope to send him as soon as I know
how it will go with me. [24]I trust in the Lord that I also myself may come
shortly.
[25]I supposed it necessary to send to you brother Epaphroditus, my
companion in labour and fellow-soldier – your apostle, and my minister at
my need. [26]For he longed after you, and was full of heaviness because you
had heard that he was sick. [27]And without question he was sick, and that
near to death. But God had mercy on him – not on him only, but on me
also, lest I should have sorrow upon sorrow. [28]I sent him therefore the
more quickly, so that when you saw him you might rejoice again, and I
might be less sorrowful. [29]Receive him therefore in the Lord with all glad-
ness. And make much of such a one, [30]because for the work of Christ he
went so far that he was near to death, and regarded not his life, to provide
that service which was lacking on your part toward me.

The Notes

Look not on your own (2:4)
If I am offered, etc. (2:17)

a) Look not on your own gifts or profit, but on love and unity.

b) Paul counts here two offerings or sacrifices. One is the faith of those he offered to Christ. The other is himself, if while he is working to offer the offering aright to God, he should be put to death and himself become an offering – which thing he does not refuse, if only he may bring to pass to make them worthy of God.

Chapter 3

He warns them to beware of false teachers, whom he calls dogs, evil workers, and enemies of Christ. He reproves man's own righteousness.

[**Dissension**: The Gk *katatome* (2699) means a cutting off. Tyndale evidently took this to refer to dissenting or heretical teaching, which divides, or which 'cuts off' from the body. The Greek may contain a double or triple entendre, warning also against Judaizers who require fleshly circumcision, or, more generally, the Jews. Other early English bibles also have 'dissension' at v2]

Moreover, my brethren, put your trust in the Lord. It grieves me not to
write the same thing often to you, for to you it is a safeguard. [2]Beware of
dogs. Beware of evil workers. Beware of dissension.*
[3]For we are the circumcision, who worship God in the Spirit, and trust
in Christ Jesus, and have no confidence in the flesh[a] – [4]though I have
whereof I might be confident in the flesh. If any other man thinks that he
has reason to trust in the flesh, I have much more: [5]circumcised the eighth
day, of the kindred of Israel, of the tribe of Benjamin, a Hebrew born of 2Co 11:21-23.
the Hebrews; as concerning the law, a Pharisee, [6]and as concerning fer-
ventness, I persecuted the congregation And as for the righteousness that
is in the law, I was unrebukable.
[7]But the things that were of advantage to me, I counted worthless for
Christ's sake. [8]Yea, I think all things worthless for the sake of the su-
preme and precious knowledge of Christ Jesus, my Lord. For him I have

counted all things a waste, and do judge them but dung, so that I may win
Christ, [9]and may be found in him – not having my own righteousness,
which is of the law, but that which is of the faith that is in Christ. I mean
the righteousness which comes from God through faith, [10]in knowing him,
and the power of the resurrection, and the fellowship of his passions, so
that I may be conformable to his death,* [11]if by any means I might attain Job 19:25-27
to the resurrection of the dead.

Death: we must die with Christ if we would live with him.

[12]It is not as if I had already attained to it, or were already perfect. But
I press on, if so be that I may lay hold of that for which Christ Jesus laid
hold of me. [13]Brethren, I do not count myself as having gotten it. But one
thing I say: I forget that which is behind, and reach for that which is
ahead, [14]and press on to that mark appointed, to obtain the reward of the
high calling of God in Christ Jesus. [15]Let us therefore, as many as are
sound in the faith, be so minded. And if you are otherwise minded, I pray
God would open this to you.

[16]Nevertheless, in that to which we have come, let us proceed by one
rule so that we may be of one accord. [17]Brethren, be followers of me, and
observe those who walk in the same way, since you have us for an ex-
ample. [18]For many walk (of whom I have told you often, and now tell you
weeping) as enemies of the cross of Christ, [19]whose end is damnation,
whose god is their belly, and whose glory is to their shame – who are Ro 16:18
worldly-minded. [20]But our citizenship is in heaven, from whence we look 2Co 11:15 Ho 4:7
for a saviour, even the Lord Jesus Christ, [21]who will change our lowly
bodies so that they may be fashioned like his glorious body, by the power 1Co c15
with which he is able to subdue all things to himself.

If we be like Christ in our living, we shall be like him in glory.

The Notes

Worship in the Spirit; no confidence in the flesh (3:3)

a) We worship God in the Spirit through faith and love. We trust that Christ has redeemed us, and do not trust in our works. Christ only is our righteousness, and for his sake our sins are forgiven us. And for his sake our good works are accepted, which works would otherwise be blameworthy for the sin that is in them.

Chapter 4

He greets certain of them, exhorts them to live and bear themselves honourably, and thanks them for the provision that they made for him in prison.

Therefore my brethren dearly beloved and longed for, my joy and crown,
continue in such a way in the Lord, beloveds. [2]I pray Euodias and beseech
Syntyche to be of one accord in the Lord. [3]Yea and I beseech you, faithful
yokefellow, help the women who laboured with me in the gospel, and
with Clement* also, and with my other labour-fellows whose names are in
the book of life.[a]

[**Clement**: later a bishop of Rome, after Nero died]

[4]Rejoice in the Lord always; and again I say, rejoice! [5]Let your gentle-
ness be known to all men.

The Lord is at hand. [6]Be anxious for nothing, but in all things let your Mt 6:25-34
requests be made known to God, in prayer and supplication with giving of

thanks. [7]And may the peace of God, which passes all understanding, keep your hearts and minds in Christ Jesus.

[8]Furthermore, brethren, whatever things are true, whatever things are honourable, whatever things are just, whatever things are pure, whatever things belong to love, whatever things are of good report, if there be any virtuous thing, if there be any praiseworthy thing: these same have in your minds. [9]The things you have both learned and received, heard and also seen in me, those things do, and the God of peace will be with you.

Ro 12:1,2

[10]I rejoice in the Lord greatly, that now at the last you have come around again to care for me, where you had been concerned, but you lacked opportunity. [11]I am not speaking out of need. For I have learned, in whatever state I am, therewith to be content. [12]I can both cast myself down and I can also prosper. Everywhere and in all things I am taught both to be full and to be hungry, to have plenty and to suffer need. [13]I can do all things with the help of Christ, who strengthens me. [14]Notwithstanding, you have done well to bear part with me in my tribulation.

[15]You of Philippi know that in the beginning of the gospel, when I departed from Macedonia, no congregation bore part with me (as regards giving and receiving) but you only. [16]For when I was in Thessalonica, you sent once and afterward again to supply my needs – [17]not that I desire gifts, but I desire abundant fruit on your parts. [18]I welcomed all, and have plenty. I was filled after I received from Epaphroditus that which came from you, an odour that smells sweet, a sacrifice accepted and pleasing to God.

[**Emperor's household**: the Roman court of Nero, including courtiers, soldiers, princes, servants, cooks, etc. Nero was emperor from 54-68 AD. Others have 'Caesar's household' at v.22. *Caesar* became a title for Roman emperors after Julius Caesar (101- 44 BC). Paul requested trial before Nero, and so went to Rome a prisoner (Acts 25:11,12). He was probably acquitted, but later re-arrested and martyred during Roman persecutions under Nero]

[19]May my God fulfil all your needs through his glorious riches in Jesus Christ. [20]To our God and Father be glory forevermore. Amen.

[21]Greet all the saints in Christ Jesus. The brethren who are with me greet you. [22]All the saints greet you, and most of all those who are of the Emperor's household.* [23]The grace of our Lord Jesus Christ be with you all. Amen.

Sent from Rome by the hand
of Epaphroditus.

The Notes

The book of life (4:3)

a) The book of life is spoken of at Psalm 69:28.

[Colosse was a city in Roman Asia, now part of Turkey. This is one of the prison epistles, written in 60-62 AD]

The Epistle of Saint Paul the Apostle to the Colossians

Chapter 1

He gives thanks to God for their faith, love, and hope, and prays for their increase. He explains how we are the kingdom of God won by Christ, who is the head of the congregation.

PAUL, an apostle of Jesus Christ by the will of God, and brother Timothy. 2To the saints who are at Colosse and brethren who believe in Christ.

Grace be with you and peace from God our Father and from the Lord Jesus Christ.

3We give thanks to God the Father of our Lord Jesus Christ, always praying for you 4since we heard of the faith that you have in Christ Jesus, and of the love that you bear to all the saints, 5for the sake of the hope that is laid up in store for you in heaven – of which hope you heard before by the true word of the gospel, 6which has come to you in the same way as it has into all the world, and is fruitful among you in the same way since the first day you heard it and had experience of the grace of God in the truth, 7when you learned from Epaphras, our dear fellow servant. He is for you a faithful minister of Christ. 8He also described to us the love that you have in the Spirit.

The hope that is laid up in store for us in heaven, of which we hear and learn by the true word of the gospel.

9For this reason we also, since the day we heard of it, have not ceased praying for you, and asking that you be fulfilled with the knowledge of his will in all wisdom and spiritual understanding, 10so that you may walk worthy of the Lord in all things that please him, being fruitful in all good works and increasing in the knowledge of God, 11strengthened with all might through his glorious power to have all patience and longsuffering with joyfulness, 12and giving thanks to the Father, who has made us fit to be partakers of the inheritance of saints in light. 13He has delivered us from the power of darkness, and has translated us into the kingdom of his dear Son, 14in whom we have redemption through his blood; that is to say, the forgiveness of sins. Eph 1:7

Our redemption is the forgiveness of our sins.

15He is the image of the invisible God, and the first begotten of all creatures. 16For by him were all things created: things that are in heaven and things that are in earth, things visible and things invisible, whether they be majesty, or lordship, or rule, or power. All things are created by him and in him, 17and he is before all things, and in him all things have their being.

18And he is the head of the body; that is to say, of the congregation. He is the beginning and first begotten of the dead,* so that in all things he may have the pre-eminence. 19For it pleased the Father that in him all fullness should dwell, 20and by him to reconcile all things to himself, and to set at peace by him, through the blood of his cross, both things in heaven and things in earth.

*He is the first to have the glory and new life of the resurrection.

21And you, who were in times past strangers and enemies because Eph 2:1-3

your minds were set in evil works, he has now reconciled [22]in the body of
his flesh through death, to make you holy, unblameable, and without fault
in his own sight – [23]if you continue grounded and established in the faith,
and be not moved away from the hope of the gospel, of which you have
heard how it is preached among all creatures under heaven, and of which
I, Paul, am made a minister.

*The sufferings or **passions of Christ** are the passions that we must suffer for his sake. For we have professed and are appointed to suffer with Christ. At John 20:21 Jesus said, As my Father sent me, so do I send you.

[24]Now I joy in the sufferings that I suffer for you, and fill up that
which I lack of the passions of Christ* in my flesh, for the sake of his
body, which is the congregation. [25]I am made a minister thereof according
to the ordinance of God, which ordinance was given to me for you, in
order to fulfil the word of God, [26]that mystery hid since the world began Eph 1:9-12
and since the beginning of generations, but which is now opened to his
saints, [27]to whom God desired to make known the glorious riches of this
mystery among the Gentiles. These riches are Christ in you, the Hope of
Glory [28]whom we preach, warning all people and instructing all people in
all wisdom, to make all men perfect in Christ Jesus. [29]For this I also
labour and strive,* even as far forth as his working works in me mightily.

*A true apostle would have all men perfect in the knowledge of Christ and of his doctrine.

Chapter 2

What great care Paul took for all congregations. He exhorts them to be steadfast in Christ, and to beware of false teachers and worldly wisdom. He describes the false prophets.

I would you knew what fighting I have for your sakes and for the people
of Laodicea, and for as many as have not seen me in the flesh, [2]that their
hearts may be encouraged, and knit together in love and in all the riches
of a full understanding, to know the mystery of God the Father and of
Christ, [3]in whom are hid all the treasures of wisdom and knowledge.

[4]And I say, for fear that someone should beguile you with enticing
words [5](for though I am absent in the flesh, yet I am present with you in
the spirit, joying and beholding the order that you keep and your steadfast 1Co 5:3
faith in Christ) – [6]as you have therefore received Christ Jesus the Lord,
even so walk, [7]rooted and built in him, and steadfast in the faith, as you
have learned. And abound therein in giving thanks.

[8]Beware lest any man come and rob you through philosophy and vain
deceit, through the precepts of men, and observances after the world, and
not after Christ. [9]For in him dwells all the fullness of the Godhead bodily,[a]
[10]and you are complete in him, who is the head of all rule and power. [11]In
him also you are circumcised, with the circumcision that is made without
hands, by putting off the sinful body of the flesh through the circumcision
that is in Christ, [12]in that you are buried with him through baptism; in
whom you are also risen again through faith, which is wrought by the Eph 1:19
operation of God, who raised him from death.

Faith is the work of God.

[13]And you who were dead in sin through the uncircumcision of your Eph 2:1-3
flesh, he has quickened to life with him, and has forgiven us all our
trespasses. [14]And he has put out the handwriting[b] that was against us, con-
tained in the written law: he has taken it out of the way and has fastened it

to his cross, 15and has spoiled rule and power, and has made a show of
them openly, and has triumphed over them in his own person.

16Let no man therefore trouble your consciences about meat and drink,
or in respect of a holy day, such as the holy day of the new moon or of the
Sabbath days. 17These are nothing but shadows of things to come, but the
substance is in Christ.[c] 18Let no man make you shoot at a wrong mark,*
who, following his own imagination, walks in the humbleness and
holiness of angels, things which he never saw, senselessly puffed up with
his fleshly mind, 19and who does not hold to the Head, from whom all the
body, by joints and ligaments, receives nourishment, and is knit together, Eph 4:16
and grows with the growth that comes of God.

20Therefore, if you are dead with Christ to the observances of the
world, why, as though you yet lived in the world, are you led by the pre-
cepts of those who say, 21Touch not, taste not, handle not? 22All these 1Ti 4:1-3
things do hurt to men because of the abuse of them, which abuse comes Isa c58
only of the commandments and doctrines of men – 23which things have an
outward show of wisdom, in self-chosen holiness and humbleness, and in
that they do not spare the body, and pay no regard to the needs of the
flesh.

Mark: there is no other thing to aim for or seek than Christ, nor other name to be saved by.

[Ed: vv22 & 23 are partly emended after Coverdale, Cranmer, and Luther]

The Notes

In him bodily (2:9)

a) In him dwells all the fullness of the Godhead bodily; that is, dwells really and actually, and not in figures and shadows. Therefore when you have Christ, you ought not to follow the shadows of Moses' law, nor the enticements and jugglings of man's wisdom. The truth is now distinctly set before your senses. You may not now have regard to figures and indistinct promises.

The handwriting against us (2:14)

b) The law is our handwriting in that the conscience signs, seals, and agrees that the law is just, and we sinners; which law, as to damnation, is taken away through faith in Christ. [Ed: The Greek word translated *handwriting* referred to a written certificate that acknowledged debt. The conscience acknowledges that by sin we have broken the law, and are therefore debtors under it. When we repent in faith, our debt is forgiven in Christ, who paid it for us. Without forgiveness, however, the law calls for eternal punishment, because sin's debt can never be paid by any man. Matthew 16:26.]

The substance is in Christ (2:17)

c) The substance is in Christ: that is, the truth and very performance is in Christ, whom the shadows did prefigure.

Chapter 3

He puts them in mind of the spiritual resurrection, to lay aside all manner of corrupt living, and to be fruitful in all godliness and virtue. He shows all degrees of persons their duty.

If you then are risen again with Christ, seek those things that are above,
where Christ sits on the right hand of God. 2Set your affection on things Ro 6:4-7
that are above, and not on things which are on the earth. 3For you are Eph 4:22-25 Heb c12
dead, and your life is hid with Christ in God. 4When Christ who is our life 1Pe 2:1-3
shows himself, then shall you also appear with him in glory.

5Mortify therefore your members which are on the earth: fornication,
uncleanness, unnatural desire, evil desire, and covetousness, which is the

All the mercy that is set forth in the preceding two chapters is promised only to those who will follow Christ and live as hereafter set out.

worshipping of idols. 6 Because of these things, the wrath of God comes
on the children of unbelief. 7 In these things you walked once, when you
lived in them. 8 But now put away from you all such things: wrath, fierce-
ness, maliciousness, railing, cursing, and filthy talk out of your mouths.
9 Do not lie to one to another. Put off the old man with his works, 10 and put
on the new, which is renewed in knowledge after the image of him who
made him – 11 where there is neither Gentile nor Jew, circumcision nor
[**Scythians**: ancient warlike nomads, noted for savagery] uncircumcision, barbarian or Scythian,* bond or free: but Christ is all in Eph 4:1-3
all things.

12 Now therefore, as chosen by God, holy and beloved, put on tender
mercy, kindness, humbleness of mind, meekness, and longsuffering, 13 for-
bearing one another, and forgiving one another, if anyone has a quarrel
against another. Just as Christ forgave you, so also should you do.

14 Above all these things, put on love, which is the bond of perfectness.
15 And may the peace of God rule in your hearts, to which peace you are
called in one body. And see that you be thankful.

16 Let the word of Christ dwell in you plenteously in all wisdom. Teach
and exhort your own selves, in psalms and hymns, and spiritual songs that
have grace with them, singing in your hearts to the Lord. 17 And all things
– whatsoever you do, in word or deed – do in the name of the Lord Jesus, 1Co 10:31
giving thanks to God the Father by him.

18 Wives, submit yourselves to your own husbands, as it is fitting in the
Lord. 19 Husbands, love your wives, and do not be grievous to them. Eph 5:22-23 1Pe 3:1-7

20 Children, obey your fathers and mothers in all things, for that is well Eph 6:1-4
pleasing to the Lord. 21 Fathers, do not berate your children, lest they be of
a desperate mind.

[**Servants**: bond or hired persons of all degrees. **Masters**: anyone to whom a duty of service is owed.]

22 Servants, be obedient to your earthly masters in all things – not with Eph 6:5-7
eye-service, as men pleasers, but in sincerity of heart, fearing God. 23 And Tit 2:9,10
whatever you do, do it heartily as for the Lord, and not for men, 24 inas- 1Pe 2:18-25
much as you know that from the Lord you will receive the reward of in-
heritance. For you serve the Lord Christ. 25 But he who does wrong, will Ro 2:11
receive for the wrong that he has done. For there is no respect of persons Wis 6:4-11
with God. 4.1 You masters, be just and fair to your servants, seeing you [see OT feature at end of epistle]
know that you also have a master in heaven.

[**Respect of persons**: undue dealing with people based on rank, wealth, or outward things, at the expense of justice, candour, or love.]

Chapter 4

He exhorts them to be fervent in prayer, to walk wisely with regard to persons who have not yet come to the true knowledge of Christ, and greets them.

[v4:1 is above, as in the MB]

The door of utterance.

2 Continue in prayer, and keep vigil in the same with thanksgiving, 3 pray-
ing also for us: that God would open for us the door of utterance so that Eph 6:18-20
we may speak the mystery of Christ, for which I am also in bonds; 4 that I
may speak it as it behoves me to do.

Salt is the wisdom of God's word.

5 Walk wisely toward those who are without, and redeem the time. 6 Let
your speech be always with grace, and powdered with salt,* so that you Mk 9:50
may know how to answer every man.

[7]The dear brother Tychicus can tell you about all my affairs. He is a Eph 6:21,22
faithful minister and fellow servant in the Lord, [8]whom I have sent to you
for this very purpose, and to find out how you are doing, and to encourage
your hearts. [9]With him is Onesimus, a faithful and a beloved brother, who Ph'm 1:10-12
is one of you. They will tell you about everything that is happening here.

[10]Aristarchus my fellow prisoner greets you; as does Mark, the son of
Barnabas' sister, concerning whom you received instructions (if he comes
to you, receive him); [11]and also Jesus who is called Justus. These are the
only men of the circumcision among my fellow workers for the kingdom
of God, and were to me a consolation.

[12]Epaphras, the servant of Christ who is one of you, greets you, and
always labours fervently for you in prayers that you may stand perfect and
full in all that is the will of God. [13]I can attest that he has a fervent mind
toward you, and toward the people of Laodicea and of Hieropolis.

Luke the physician. [14]Dear Luke the physician greets you, and Demas. 2Ti 4:10-12

[15]Greet the brethren who are of Laodicea, and greet Nymphas and the
congregation that is in his house. [16]And when the epistle has been read by
you, ensure that it is read in the congregation of the Laodiceans also, and
that you likewise read the Laodiceans' epistle. [17]And say to Archippus:
Take heed to the office that you have received in the Lord, to fulfil it.

[18]The greeting by the hand of me, Paul.
Remember my bonds. Grace
be with you.
Amen.

Sent from Rome by the hand
of Tychicus and
Onesimus.

Old Testament Feature - A glimpse into the Apocrypha of the 1549 Matthew Bible...
The Book of Wisdom, minimally updated:

The Book of Wisdom: The .vi. Chapter (verses 1-8)

The calling of kings, princes, and judges, who are also exhorted to seek wisdom.

Wisdom is better than strength, and a man of understanding is more worthy than one that is strong. Hear therefore (O ye kings) and understand; O learn, ye that be judges of the ends of the earth. Give ear, ye that rule the multitudes, and delight in much people. For the power is given you by the Lord, and the strength from the Most High, who will try your works, and search out your intentions – how you, being officers of his kingdom, have not executed true judgment, have not kept the law of righteousness, nor walked after his will. Horribly, and that right soon, will he appear to you, for a hard judgment will they have who bear rule. Mercy is granted to the simple, but those who are in authority will be sore punished. For God, who is Lord over all, will except no man's person, nor will he stand in awe of any man's greatness. For he has made the small and the great, and cares for all alike, but the mighty shall have the sorer punishment.

[Thessalonica is a city in Greece, on the Thessaloniki Gulf in the northern reaches of the Aegean Sea. This letter was likely written in 51 AD]

The First Epistle of Saint Paul the Apostle to the Thessalonians

Chapter 1

He thanks God for them, that they are so steadfast in faith & good works, and receive the gospel with such earnestness.

PAUL, Silvanus, and Timothy.
To the congregation of the Thessalonians in God the Father and in the
Lord Jesus Christ.
Grace be with you and peace from God our Father and from the Lord
Jesus Christ.
[2]We give God thanks always for you all, making mention of you in
our prayers without ceasing, [3]and call to remembrance your work in the
faith and labour in love, and perseverance in the hope of our Lord Jesus
Christ in the sight of God our Father, [4]because we know, brethren be-
loved of God, that you are elect. [5]For our gospel did not come to you in
word only, but also in power, and also in the Holy Spirit – and in much Ac 17:1-4
confidence, as you know how we conducted ourselves among you for
your sakes.

The gospel came to the Thessalonians not in word only, but also in power, and in the Holy Spirit.

[6]And you became followers of us and of the Lord, and received the
word in much affliction, with the joy of the Holy Spirit, [7]so that you were
an example to all who believe in Macedonia and Achaia. [8]For the word of
the Lord sounded out from you – not only in Macedonia and Achaia, but
the faith that you have in God went abroad in all quarters, so greatly that
it is not necessary for us to say anything at all. [9]For people themselves
speak of you: what manner of entry we had in to you, and how you turned
to God from idols, to serve the living and true God, [10]and to look for his
Son from heaven, whom he raised from death; I mean Jesus, who delivers
us from the wrath to come.

Chapter 2

Paul reminds them of the godly life he led among them when he preached the gospel to them, thanks God that they receive his word so fruitfully, and excuses his absence.

For you yourselves know, brethren, of our coming to you, how it was not
in vain. [2]But even after we had suffered before, and were shamefully
treated at Philippi (as you well know), then we were bold in our God to Ac 14:5; 16:22-24.
speak to you the gospel of God with much striving. [3]Our exhortation was
not to bring you to error, nor yet to uncleanness. Neither was it with guile,
[4]but as we were approved by God to have the gospel committed to us,
even so we speak – not as though we intended to please men, but God,
who tries our hearts.
[5]Neither was our conversation at any time with flattering words, as

you well know, nor in cloaked covetousness; God is witness. 6Nor did we
seek praise from men: not from you, nor yet from any others, when we
might have imposed ourselves upon you as the apostles of Christ. 7But we
were tender among you. Even as a nurse-mother cares for her children,
8so was our affection toward you. Our good pleasure was to have given
you not the gospel of God only, but also our own souls, because you were
dear to us.

*A sure token of a true apostle.

9You remember, brethren, our labour and travail. For we laboured day Ac 20:33-35
and night, because we did not want to be burdensome to any of you,* and 2Th 3:7-10
preached to you the gospel of God. 10You are witnesses, and so is God,
how holily and justly and blamelessly we conducted ourselves among you
who believe; 11as you know how we exhorted and comforted and besought
every one of you, as a father his children, 12to walk worthy of God, who
has called you unto his kingdom and glory.

13We thank God without ceasing, because when you received from us
the word whereby God was preached, you received it not as the word of
man, but even as it was indeed: the word of God, which works in you who
believe. 14For you, brethren, took after the congregations of God in Judea
that are in Christ Jesus. For you have suffered similar things from your
Persecutions. countrymen as we ourselves have suffered from the Jews. 15As they killed
the Lord Jesus and their own prophets, even so have they persecuted us.
And they do not please God, and are contrary to all men, 16and oppose us
preaching to the Gentiles so that they might be saved, to fulfil their sins
always. For the wrath of God has come on them, even to the utmost.

17But since, brethren, we have been kept from you for a season (as to
bodily presence, but not in the heart), we tried all the more to see you
personally, with great desire. 18And therefore we would have gone to you
– I, Paul, once and again – but Satan withstood us. 19For what is our hope
or joy, or crown of rejoicing? Is it not you in the presence of our Lord
Jesus Christ at his coming? 20Yes, you are our pride and joy.

Chapter 3

He tells them how greatly he was moved with joy when Timothy told him of their faith and love.

Therefore, since we could bear it no longer, it pleased us to remain at
Athens alone, 2and we sent Timothy, our brother and minister of God, and
our labour-fellow in the gospel of Christ, to strengthen you and to comfort
you over your faith, 3so that no one would be shaken in these afflictions.
For you yourselves know that we are even appointed to this. 4For indeed,
when I was with you, I warned that we would suffer tribulation, even as it
came to pass and as you know. 5For this reason, when I could no longer
bear it, I sent to find out about your faith, lest perhaps the tempter had
tempted you, and our labour had been bestowed in vain.

6But now lately Timothy has come from you to us, and told us about
your faith and your love, and that you have good remembrance of us
always, desiring to see us as we desire to see you. 7Therefore, brethren,

we had consolation in you, in all our adversity and need, through your faith. [8]For now we are alive, if you stand steadfast in the Lord. [9]For what thanks we can render to God for you, for all the joy that we have on your account before our God, [10]while we pray very much night and day that we might see you personally, and might make up that which is lacking in your faith.

[11]May God himself our Father and our Lord Jesus Christ guide our journey to you. [12]And may the Lord prosper you, and make you flow over in love toward one another, and toward all men, even as we do toward you, [13]to make your hearts constant and unblameable in holiness before God our Father at the coming of our Lord Jesus Christ with all his saints.

Chapter 4

He exhorts them to steadfastness, to keep themselves from sin and unclean conduct, and to love one another. He rebukes idleness, and speaks of the general resurrection.

Ro 12
Eph 5

Furthermore we beseech you, brethren, and exhort you in the Lord Jesus, as you learned from us how you ought to walk and please God, so to progress more and more. [2]You remember what commandments we gave you in our Lord Jesus Christ. [3]For this is even the will of God: that you should be holy; that you should abstain from fornication; [4]that every one of you should know how to keep his vessel in holiness and honour, [5]and not in the passion of lust, as do the heathen who do not know God; [6]that no one should go too far and defraud his brother in bargaining. For the Lord is an avenger of all such things, as we have forewarned you and testified. [7]For God has not called us to uncleanness, but to holiness. [8]Whoever therefore rejects this, rejects not man, but God, who has sent his Holy Spirit among you.

Joh 13:34; 15:12. Ph'p 1:9 1Jo 2:10; 4:7.

[9]But concerning brotherly love, you do not need me to write to you. For you are taught by God to love one another. [10]Yea and this you do, showing love to all the brethren who are throughout all Macedonia. We beseech you, brethren, to progress more and more, [11]and to study to be quiet and to mind your own business, and to work with your own hands, as we told you, [12]so that you may conduct yourselves honourably* toward those who are outside, and so that nothing be lacking to you.

[**Honourably**: so must we behave, even when we are dishonoured in the world]

[13]I would not, brethren, have you be ignorant concerning those who have fallen asleep, lest you sorrow like others who have no hope. [14]For if we believe that Jesus died and rose again, so then also those who sleep in Jesus, God will bring again with him. [15]And this we say to you in the word of the Lord: we who live and are remaining at the coming of the Lord will not precede those who sleep. [16]For the Lord himself will descend from heaven with a shout, and the voice of the archangel, and the trumpet of God. And the dead in Christ will arise first. [17]Then shall we who live and remain be caught up with them also in the clouds, to meet the Lord in the air. And so shall we ever be with the Lord. [18]Therefore comfort one another with these words.

1Co 15:52

Chapter 5

He speaks of the day of doom and coming of the Lord. He exhorts them to watch, and to have regard for those who preach God's word among them.

Of the times and seasons, brethren, you have no need that I write to you.
2For you yourselves know well that the day of the Lord will come even as 2Pe 3:10 Rev 3:3; 16:15.
a thief in the night. 3When they say, Peace, and no danger – then comes Jer 6:14, 8:11.
on them sudden destruction, like the travailing of a woman with child, and
they shall not escape.
4But you, brethren, are not in darkness, such that that day should come
on you as a thief. 5You are all the children of light, and the children of the
day. We are not of the night, nor of darkness. 6Therefore let us not sleep
as others do, but let us watch and be sober. 7For those who sleep, sleep in
the night, and those who are drunk, are drunk in the night.* 8But let us Isa 59:17 Eph 6:10-17
who are of the day be sober, armed with the breastplate of faith and love,
and with the hope of salvation as a helmet. 9For God has not appointed us
to wrath, but to obtain salvation by the means of our Lord Jesus Christ,
10who died for us so that whether we wake or sleep, we will live together
with him. 11Therefore comfort yourselves together, and strengthen one another, even as you do.

[**The night** is unbelief, the ignorance of Christ, and false teaching, which make drunk (Isaiah 29:9), and cause to stumble (John 11:10)]

12We beseech you, brethren, to recognize those who labour among
you, and have the oversight of you in the Lord and give you exhortation –
13to have them the more in love for their work's sake, and be at peace
with them.
14We desire you, brethren, to warn those who are unruly, comfort the
faint-hearted, bear up the weak, and have continual patience toward all 1Pe 3:9
people. 15See that no one returns evil for evil to anyone, but ever follow
that which is good, both among yourselves and among all people.
16Rejoice always. 17Pray continually.[a] 18In all things give thanks, for
this is the will of God in Christ Jesus for you.
19Quench not the Spirit.* 20Do not despise prophesying. 21Examine all
things,* and keep that which is good. 22Keep from every appearance of
evil. 23May the very God of peace sanctify you thoroughly. And I pray
God that your whole spirit, soul, and body may be kept faultless for the
coming of our Lord Jesus Christ. 24Faithful is he who called you, who will
also do it. 1Co 1:8
25Brethren, pray for us. 26Greet all the brethren with a holy kiss.
27I charge you in the Lord to read this epistle to all the holy brethren.
28The grace of the Lord Jesus Christ be with you.
Amen.

*The Spirit, by whom we believe in Christ and consent to the law, is quenched by wrong living and lewd communication.
*Examine all teachings.

The end of the first epistle to
the Thessalonians.
Sent from
Athens.

The Notes

Pray continually (5:17)

a) Like a man in prison ever desires to be delivered, whether he be eating, drinking, or sleeping, and like someone who is sick desires always to be whole, so every true Christian prays continually – yea, even when he seems not to pray. For prayer consists not in much babbling (Mathew 6:7), but in spirit and truth (John 4:23,24), and in the vehement desire of the heart toward God.

[It is believed that Paul wrote this letter only months after his first to the Thessalonians, in late 51 or early 52 AD]

The Second Epistle of Saint Paul the Apostle to the Thessalonians

Chapter 1

He thanks God for their faith and love, and prays for the increase of the same.

PAUL, Sylvanus, and Timothy.

To the congregation of the Thessalonians who are in God our Father and in the Lord Jesus Christ.

2Grace be with you and peace from God our Father and from the Lord Jesus Christ.

3We are bound to thank God always for you, brethren, as it is meet,
because your faith grows exceedingly, and every one of you swims in
love toward another between yourselves, 4so that we ourselves rejoice
over you in the congregations of God – over your patience and faith in
all the persecutions and tribulations that you suffer, 5which is a sign* of
the righteous judgment of God, that you are counted worthy of the
kingdom of God, for which you also suffer.

*Tribulation is a mark of salvation.

6It is surely a righteous thing with God to recompense tribulation to
those who trouble you; 7and to you who are troubled, rest with us when
the Lord Jesus shows himself from heaven with his mighty angels, 8in
flaming fire, rendering vengeance to those who do not know God, and
to those who will not heed the gospel of our Lord Jesus Christ. 9These
shall be punished with everlasting damnation, separated from the pres- M't 13:49
ence of the Lord and from the glory of his power, 10when he comes to
be glorified in his saints and to be made marvelous in all who believe,
because our testimony to you was believed even the same day that we
preached it.

11Therefore we pray always for you, that our God would make you Col 1:9-12
worthy of the calling, and would fulfil all pleasure in goodness and the
work of faith with power, 12so that the name of our Lord Jesus Christ
may be glorified in you, and you in him, through the grace of our God
and of the Lord Jesus Christ.

Chapter 2

Paul explains that the day of the Lord does not come until the departing from the faith comes first, and therefore he exhorts them not to be deceived, but to stand steadfast in the things that he has taught them.

We beseech you, brethren, by the coming of our Lord Jesus Christ, and in that we shall assemble unto him, [2]not to be suddenly moved from your mind. And be not troubled, neither by spirit nor by words, nor yet by letter which seems to come from us, as though the day of Christ were at hand. [3]Let no man deceive you by any means. For the Lord comes not unless there come a departing[*] first and that sinful man[a] be revealed – the son of perdition, [4]who is an adversary, and is exalted above all that is called God or that is worshipped, so that he shall sit as God in the temple of God[b] and show himself as God.

Of Antichrist

[**Departing**: the Gk *apostasia* (646) means a falling away from God's word: apostasy]

Eph 5:6

[5]Do you not remember that when I was still with you, I told you these things? [6]And now you know what withholds, so that he may be manifest at his time. [7]For the mystery of that iniquity does he already work, which only locks until it is taken out of the way. [8]And then shall that wicked one be exposed, whom the Lord will consume with the Spirit of his mouth,[c] and will destroy with the appearance of his coming – [9]namely him whose coming is by the working of Satan, with all lying power, signs, and wonders,[d] [10]and in all the deceptiveness of unrighteousness among those who are perishing. They perish because they would not receive the love of the truth,[*] so that they might have been saved. [11]And therefore God will send them strong delusion, so that they will believe lies; [12]so that all may be judged who did not believe the truth, but had pleasure in unrighteousness.

Isa 11:4

*__Where there is no love for truth__, God lets false prophets slip in upon the people, to deceive them.

M't 7:23

[13]But we are bound to give thanks always to God for you, brethren beloved of the Lord, because God has from the beginning chosen you for salvation, through sanctifying by the Spirit and through believing the truth,[14]to which he called you by our gospel, to obtain the glory that comes of our Lord Jesus Christ. [15]Therefore, brethren, stand fast. And keep the ordinances that you have been taught, whether it was by our preaching or by epistle.

[16]May our Lord Jesus Christ himself, and God our Father who has loved us, and has given us everlasting consolation and good hope through grace, [17]comfort your hearts and establish you in all doctrine and good-doing.

The Notes

That sinful man (2:3)

a) *That sinful man* means Antichrist. Of him, look in 1 John, chapter 4.

To sit in the temple of God (2:4)

b) To sit in the temple of God is to rule in the consciences of men, and there to command, where only God has place and alone ought to reign. This is as much as to be exalted above God.

Spirit of his mouth (2:8)

c) The Spirit of his mouth is his holy word.

Lying wonders (2:9)

d) They are called lying wonders or miracles because they testify to a false faith.

Chapter 3

He asks them to pray for him, that the gospel may prosper. He warns them to reprove the idle, and if they will not labour with their hands, they should not eat.

Furthermore, brethren, pray for us, that the word of God may have free passage and be glorified, as it is with you, [2]and that we may be delivered from unreasonable and evil men. For all do not have faith. [3]But the Lord is faithful, who will establish you and keep you from evil. [4]We have confidence through the Lord concerning you, that you both do and will do that which we instruct you. [5]And may the Lord guide your hearts to the love of God and patience of Christ.

[6]We require you, brethren, in the name of our Lord Jesus Christ, to withdraw yourselves from every brother who is disorderly, not walking according to the teaching which you received from us. [7]You yourselves know how you ought to follow us. For we were not disorderly amongst
you. [8]Neither did we take bread from anyone for nothing, but worked Ac 20:33-35
with labour and travail night and day, because we did not wish to be 1Co 4:12 1Th 2:9
burdensome to any of you – [9]not that we had no right, but to make ourselves an example for you, to follow us. [10]For when we were with you, this we warned you of: that if there were any who would not work, the same should not eat.

[11]We have heard that there are some who walk among you in a disorderly way, and do not work at all, but are busybodies. [12]Such people we command and exhort by our Lord Jesus Christ to work with quietness and eat their own bread.

[13]Brethren, do not be weary of well-doing. [14]If any man does not Ga 6:9
heed what we say, send us word of him by a letter; and keep no company with him, so that he may be ashamed. [15]And count him not as an enemy, but warn him as a brother.

[16]May the very Lord of peace give you peace always in every way. The Lord be with you all.

[Ancient writers usually dictated their letters to an amanuensis, but signed personally at the end to confirm authorship]

[17]The greeting of me, Paul, with my own hand. This is the distinguishing mark in all epistles – thus I write.

[18]May the grace of our
Lord Jesus Christ
be with you
all.
Amen.

Sent from Athens.

[Paul probably wrote this epistle shortly after his release from his first Roman imprisonment, c 62-64 AD]

The First Epistle of Saint Paul the Apostle to Timothy

Chapter 1

He exhorts Timothy to attend to his office; namely, to see that nothing is taught but God's word, etc. He shows also for what the law is good, and tells this sweet and glad tidings: Jesus Christ came into the world to save sinners.

PAUL, an apostle of Jesus Christ by the commandment of God our Sav-
iour, and the Lord Jesus Christ, who is our hope.
[2]To Timothy, his true-born son in the faith.
Grace, mercy, and peace, from God our Father and our Lord Jesus
Christ.
[3]As I besought you to continue in Ephesus when I departed into Mace- Ac c16
donia, so do, and direct certain men to teach no other way, [4]neither to give
heed to legends and genealogies, which are endless and breed doubts Tit 3:9
more than godly edifying, which is by faith. [5]For the end of the command-
*Love is the end of the commandment, and must interpret it.
ment is love that comes of a pure heart and a good conscience,* and of
faith unfeigned – [6]from which things some have erred, and have turned to
vain prattle, [7]because they want to be teachers of the scripture and yet do
not understand what they speak, nor the things they assert.
[8]We know that the law is good if one abides by it lawfully, [9]under-
standing that the law is not given for a righteous person, but for the un-
righteous and disobedient, for the ungodly and for sinners, for the unholy Ro c7
and unclean, for murderers of fathers and murderers of mothers, for man- Ga 3:24
slayers [10]and whoremongers, for those who defile themselves with men-
kind, for kidnappers, for liars and perjurers, and so forth, if there be any
other thing that is contrary to wholesome precept, [11]according to the gos-
pel of the glory of the blessed God, which gospel is committed to me.
[12]And I thank Christ Jesus our Lord, who has made me strong. For he
counted me true and put me in office, [13]when before I was a blasphemer
and a persecutor, and full of violence. But I obtained mercy because I did
it ignorantly, through unbelief. [14]And the grace of our Lord abounded
more greatly with faith and love, which is in Christ Jesus.
The ground of the faith.
[15]This is a true saying, and by all means worthy to be received: that
Christ Jesus came into the world to save sinners, of whom I am chief. M't 9:13
[16]But notwithstanding, mercy was given to me, so that Jesus Christ could Mk 2:17 Joh 5:24
Paul is an example, so that no one who can repent should despair.
first show on me all long patience, as an example for those who will in
time to come believe on him unto eternal life. [17]So then, to God the King
everlasting, immortal, invisible, and alone wise, be honour and glory for
ever and ever. Amen.
[18]This charge I commit to you, son Timotheus, according to the proph-
ecies that in time past were prophesied of you, so that you in them will
fight a good fight, [19]having faith and a good conscience – which some
have put away from them, and as concerning faith have made shipwreck.

[20]Of this number are Hymenaeus and Alexander, whom I have delivered to Satan so that they might be taught not to blaspheme.

Chapter 2

He exhorts to pray for all people. He will not have women in showy attire, nor to teach in the congregation, but to be in silence and to obey their husbands.

I exhort therefore that above all things prayers, supplications, intercessions, and giving of thanks be had for all men, [2]for kings and for all that are in authority, that we may live a quiet and a peaceable life in all godliness and sanctity. [3]For that is good and accepted in the sight of God our Saviour, [4]who would have all men saved[a] and come to the knowledge of the truth. [5]For there is one God, and one mediator between God and man, which is the man Christ Jesus, [6]who gave himself a ransom for all, that it should be testified at his time. [7]For this I am ordained a preacher and an apostle. I speak the truth in Christ and do not lie, being the teacher of the Gentiles in faith and truth.

[8]I desire therefore that the men pray everywhere, lifting up pure hands without wrath or doubting. [9]Likewise also the women, that they dress nicely, with modesty and discreet behaviour – not with broided hair, or gold or pearls, or costly array, [10]but as becomes women who profess the worshipping of God through good works.

[11]Let the woman learn in silence with all submission. [12]I suffer not a woman to teach, nor to have authority over the man, but to be in silence. [13]For Adam was first formed, and then Eve. [14]Also, Adam was not deceived, but the woman was deceived, and was in transgression. [15]Notwithstanding, through the bearing of children* they may be preserved, if they continue in faith, love, and holiness, with discretion.

1Co 14:34
1Pe 3:1-6

[**Bearing of children**: the Gk *teknogonia* (5042) implies the performance of all maternal duties, ie rearing children]

The Notes

God would have all men saved and come to the knowledge of the truth. (2:4)

a) That is, God would have the gospel preached to all without exception, and offers repentance to all, and would have all persons prayed for. [Augustine> 'All men' means here every sort of men; that is, salvation is not restricted to any one race, nation, class, or sort of people. (*Enchiridion*)]

Chapter 3

What manner of man a bishop or priest ought to be, and how his wife and children should be. The qualities also required in a deacon or minister and in his wife.

This is a true saying: if a man desires the office of a bishop,[a] he desires a good work. [2]Yea and a bishop must be faultless, the husband of one wife, sober, discreet, respectable, harborous,* able to teach, [3]not drunken, no fighter, not given to the love of money, but gentle, abhorring quarrels, abhorring covetousness, [4]and one that rules his own house well, having his children under obedience with all respectfulness. [5]For if a man cannot

[**Harborous**: affording shelter and welcome to strangers and guests]

manage his own house, how will he care for the congregation of God? 6He
may not be a young scholar,[b] lest he swell and fall into the judgment of
the evil speaker. 7He must also be well reported of among those who are
outside, lest he fall into rebuke and the snare of the evil speaker.

8Likewise must deacons be honourable: not double-tongued, not given
to much drinking, nor to the love of money, 9but having the mystery of the
faith in a pure conscience. 10And let them first be proved, and then let
The wives of the priests and deacons. them minister, if they be found faultless. 11Even so must their wives be
honourable: not evil speakers, but sober and faithful in all things. 12Let the
deacons be the husbands of one wife, and such as rule their children well,
[V 13 is emended from Wycliffe 1380] and their own households. 13For those who minister well win good stand-
ing for themselves, and much trust in the faith that is in Christ Jesus.

14These things I write to you trusting to come to you shortly, 15but if I
am long in coming, so that you may yet have knowledge how you ought
to conduct yourself in the house of God, which is the congregation of the
living God, the pillar and ground of truth.

16And there is no denying, great is the mystery of godliness: God was
shown in the flesh, was confirmed in the Spirit,[c] was seen by angels, was Ro 1:4
preached to the Gentiles, was believed on in earth, and received up in
glory.

The Notes

Bishop (3:1) a) A *bishop* is as much as to say one who sees to things, who watches over: an overseer. When he desires to feed Christ's flock with the food of health – that is, with his holy word, as the bishops did in Paul's time – he desires a good work and the very office of a bishop. But he who desires honour, looks for personal advantage, is greedy for great revenues; who seeks pre-eminence, pomp, dominion; who wants more than enough of everything, rest and his heart's ease, castles, parks, lordships, earldoms, etc. – such a man does not desire to work, much less to do good work, and is anything but a bishop as Saint Paul here understands a bishop.

Young scholar (3:6) b) Paul calls a young scholar such a man as was recently Christened or newly converted to the truth. [Chrysostom>A novice might be lifted up with pride, and thus fall into the same condemnation that Satan incurred by his pride. As to the 'snare of the evil speaker' that persons of bad reputation fall into (v7), this refers to men of weak character often falling into the same sins, the devil always laying more traps for them, leading to their destruction.]

In the Spirit (3:16) c) Confirmed in or by the Spirit: the Spirit bore witness to him and to his teaching.

Chapter 4

He prophesies of the latter days, and exhorts Timothy to the diligent reading of the holy scripture.

The Spirit speaks clearly that in the latter times some will depart from the
faith, and will give heed to spirits of error, and to devilish teaching 2 by
those who speak falsely through hypocrisy, who have their consciences
marked with an hot iron,[a] 3forbidding to marry, and commanding to 2Ti 3:1-9 2Pe 2:1-3 Jude 16:19
abstain from foods that God has created to be received with thanksgiving
by those who believe and know the truth. 4For everything God created is
good, and nothing to be refused, if it be received with thanksgiving. 5For

it is sanctified by the word of God and prayer. [6]If you put the brethren in
mind of these things, you will be a good minister of Jesus Christ, who has
been nourished up in the words of the faith and good teaching, which
teaching you have continually followed. [7]But cast away unspiritual and 2Ti 3:10-15
old wives' tales. Tit 2:1-15

Exercise yourself unto godliness. [8]For bodily exercise is of some ben-
efit, but godliness is fruitful in all things, having promises for the life that
is now and for the life to come. [9]This is a sure saying, and worthy to be
received by all. [10]It is for this that we labour and suffer rebuke – because
we believe in the living God, who is the saviour of all men, but especially
of those who believe. [11]Such things command and teach.

[12]Let no one dishonour your youth, but be to those who believe an
example, in word, in conduct, in love, in spirit, in faith, and in pureness.

[13]Until I come, attend to reading, to exhortation, and to teaching. [14]Do
not neglect the gift that is in you, which was given to you through proph-
ecy and with the laying on of the hands of an elder. [15]Be diligent in these
things, and give yourself to them, so that it may be seen how you bring
profit in all things. [16]Take heed to yourself and to the doctrine, and con-
tinue therein. For if you will so do, you will save yourself and those who
hear you.

The Notes

Consciences marked with a hot iron (4:2)

a) Just as thieves and evil doers are marked in the hands or other places of the body with hot irons to the intent that their wrongdoing may by that mark be openly known ever after, so are the consciences of false teachers marked, in that they are witnesses to themselves that, in order to satisfy their carnal desires and love of money, they hide the truth and teach lies. [The Romans, and also the English in time past, branded certain criminals so that wherever they went they carried this testimony of their wrongdoing, and so that if they offended again, their punishment should not be mitigated. Ed.]

Chapter 5

He teaches Timothy how he should conduct himself in rebuking all degrees of persons, and gives a direction concerning widows.

Do not rebuke an older man, but exhort him as a father; and the younger
men as brethren, [2]the older women as mothers, the younger as sisters,
with all pureness. [3]Honour widows that are true widows. [4]If any widows
have children or grandchildren, let them learn first to take godly respon-
sibility in their own families, and to recompense their elders. For that is
good and acceptable before God.

[5]She who is a real widow and friendless puts her trust in God, and
continues in supplication and prayer night and day. [6]But she who lives in
pleasure is dead even while alive. [7]And instruct these things, so that the
people may be without fault. [8]But if there be anyone who does not provide
for his own, and particularly for those of his household, the same denies
the faith, and is worse than an infidel.

[**Chosen**: Perhaps enrolled to serve in the congregation, or to receive church support]

[9]Let no widow be chosen* who is under sixty years old, and let her be
such a one as was the wife of one man, [10]and well reported of in good
works: if she has raised children, if she has been generous to strangers, if
she has washed the feet of the saints, if she has ministered to those who
were in adversity, if she was continually given to all manner of good
works. [11]The younger widows refuse. For when they have begun to grow
wanton, to the dishonour of Christ, then they want to marry, [12]having
condemnation because they have broken their first faith.* [13]And also they
learn to go from house to house idle, yea not only idle, but also gossiping
and busybodies, speaking things which they ought not.

*Whatever is done amongst us, if God is thereby dishonoured, it ought to be stopped.

[14]I will therefore that the younger women marry and bear children,
and guide the house, and give no occasion to the adversary to speak evil.
[15]For many of them have already turned back, and are gone after Satan.

[16]And if any man or woman who believes has widows, let them min-
ister to them, and do not let the congregation be charged, so that you may
have sufficient for those who are widows indeed.

[17]The elders who lead well are worthy of double honour, most espe-
cially those who labour in the word and teaching. [18]For the scripture says: De 25:4
You shall not muzzle the mouth of the ox that treads out the corn, and: M't 10:10 Lu 10:7
The labourer is worthy of his reward. 1Co 9:9-14

[19]Against an elder receive no accusation except with two or three wit- De 19:15
nesses. [20]Those who sin, rebuke openly, so that others may fear.

[21]I charge you before God, and the Lord Jesus Christ, and the elect
angels, to observe these things without hasty judgment, and do nothing
with partiality. [22]Lay hands quickly on no man, neither be partaker of oth-
er men's sins; keep yourself pure.

[23]Drink water no longer, but use a little wine for your stomach's sake
and your frequent ailments.

[24]Some people's sins are open beforehand, and go before to judgment;
some people's sins follow after. [25]Likewise also, good works are manifest
beforehand, and those that are otherwise cannot be hid.

Chapter 6

The duty of servants toward their masters. Against such as are not satisfied with the word of God. Against covetousness. A good lesson for the rich.

Let as many servants as are under the yoke count their masters worthy of
all honour, so that the name of God and his precepts are not ill spoken of.
[2]See to it that those who have believing masters do not honour them less
because they are brethren, but so much more rather serve them, because
they are believing, and beloved, and will benefit from the good service.

These things teach and exhort. [3]If anyone teaches otherwise, and is not
content with the wholesome words of our Lord Jesus Christ and with the
instruction of godliness, [4]he is puffed up and knows nothing, but wastes
his brains about questions and strife of words, whereof come envy, strife,
railing, evil surmisings, [5]and the vain disputations of men with corrupt 2Ti 2:14

minds and destitute of the truth, who think that wealth is godliness. Sep-
arate yourself from such people.
[6]But godliness is great wealth, if a man is content with what he has.
[7]For we brought nothing into the world, and it is a plain case that we can Job 1:21
carry nothing out. [8]When we have food and clothing, let us therewith be Ec 5:15
content. [9]Those who want to be rich fall into temptation and snares, and
into many foolish and harmful lusts, which drown men in perdition and
destruction. [10]For covetousness is the root of all evil, which, when some
followed after, they erred from the faith, and tangled themselves with
many sorrows. [11]But you who are the man of God, flee such things. Pur-
sue righteousness, godliness, love, patience, and gentleness. [12]Fight the
good fight of faith. Lay hold on eternal life, to which you are called and
have pledged yourself with a good profession before many witnesses.*

O that we in a lawful age could confess and practice openly the faith and life of a Christian man. [Marginal lament in Tyndale's 1534 NT]

[**Good profession**: probably at baptism, when personal vows are made that concern the life to come]

[13]I give you charge in the sight of God, who gives life to all things,
and before Jesus Christ, who bore faithful witness under Pontius Pilate,
[14]to keep the commandment, and be without spot and unrebukeable until
the appearing of our Lord Jesus Christ – [15]which appearing (when the
time is come) he will show, who is blessed and sole in dominion, King of Rev 17:14; 19:16.
kings and Lord of lords, [16]who alone has immortality, and dwells in light Joh 1:18
to which no man can attain,* whom no man ever saw, neither can see: to 1Jo 1:5
whom be honour and rule everlasting. Amen.

[**No man can attain:** Ambrose>Although he is inaccessible by nature, yet because of his goodness he can be received by us, filling all things with his power, and yet only shared in by the just. (*De Spiritu Sancto*)]

[17]Charge those who are rich in this world not to be high-minded, and
not to trust in uncertain riches, but in the living God, who gives us abun-
dantly all things, to enjoy them; [18]and to do good, and to be rich in good
works, and ready to give and distribute, [19]laying up in store for themselves
a good foundation for the time to come, so that they may obtain eternal
life.
[20]O Timothy, preserve that which has been given you to keep, and
avoid unspiritual vanities of voices, and oppositions of knowledge falsely
so-called, [21]which knowledge has led some who profess it to err as con-
cerning the faith.

Grace be with you. Amen.

Sent from Laodicea, which is the
chiefest city of Phrygia,
Pacatiana.

The Second Epistle of the Apostle Saint Paul to Timothy

[This is considered the last extant epistle that Paul ever wrote, dated during his 2nd Roman imprisonment under Emperor Nero in about 66-67 AD, and shortly before his martyrdom under Nero]

Chapter 1

Paul exhorts Timothy to steadfastness and patience in persecution, and to continue in the doctrine that he had taught him. A commendation of Onesiphorous.

PAUL, an apostle of Jesus Christ by the will of God to preach the promise
of life, which life is in Christ Jesus.
[2]To Timothy, his beloved son.
Grace, mercy, and peace, from God the Father and from Jesus Christ
our Lord.
[3]I thank God, whom I serve apart from my fathers with a pure con-
science, as without ceasing I make mention of you in my prayers night
and day, [4]desiring to see you, mindful of your tears. I am filled with joy
[5]when I call to remembrance the unfeigned faith that is in you, which
dwelt first in your grandmother Lois and in your mother Eunice, and am
assured that it dwells in you also. [6]And so I remind you to stir up the gift
of God that is in you by the putting on of my hands. [7]For God has not
given to us the spirit of fear, but of power, and of love, and soberness of
mind.

Be not ashamed.

[8]Be not ashamed to testify of our Lord; neither be ashamed of me,
who am bound for his sake. But suffer adversity also with the gospel,
through the power of God, [9]who saved us and called us with a holy Ro 9:15,16
calling, not according to our deeds, but according to his own purpose and Tit 3:4-6
grace. Which grace was given through Christ Jesus before the world was,
[10]but is now declared openly by the appearing of our Saviour Jesus Christ,
who has put away death, and has brought life and immortality to light
through the gospel. 1Ti 2:7
[11]Of this gospel I am appointed a preacher and apostle, and a teacher
of the Gentiles – [12]for which cause I also suffer these things. Nevertheless,
I am not ashamed. For I know whom I have believed, and am sure that he
is able to keep that which I have committed to his keeping for that day.

[**Example of wholesome words**: this suggests a liturgical formula or a creed. Some say exhortative words]

[13]See that you have the example of the wholesome words* that you
heard from me, in faith and love which is in Christ Jesus. [14]That good
thing that was committed to your keeping, keep in the Holy Spirit that
dwells in us.
[15]This you know, how all those who are in Asia have turned away
from me. Of which sort are Phygellus and Hermogenes. [16]May the Lord
give mercy to the house of Onesiphorus, for he oft refreshed me, and was
not ashamed of my chains, [17]but when he was at Rome he sought me out
very diligently, and found me. [18]May the Lord grant to him that he may
find mercy with the Lord at that day. And in how many things he minis-
tered to me at Ephesus, you know very well.

Chapter 2

As in the first chapter, so here Paul exhorts Timothy to be
constant in trouble, to suffer manfully, and to abide fast in
the wholesome doctrine of our Lord Jesus Christ.

You therefore, my son, be strong in the grace that is in Christ Jesus. [2]And
what things you have heard from me, many bearing witness, the same
deliver to faithful men who are competent to teach others.

[3]Therefore suffer affliction as a good soldier of Jesus Christ. [4]No man
who wars entangles himself with worldly business, because he wants to
please him who has chosen him to be a soldier. [5]And though a man strive
to win a competition, yet he is not crowned unless he strives lawfully. 1Co 9:24,25
[6]The husbandman who labours must first receive of the fruits. [7]Consider
what I say. May the Lord give you understanding in all things.

[8]Remember that Jesus Christ, being of the seed of David, rose again
from death, as declared in my gospel – [9]for which gospel I suffer trouble
[**Bonds**: restraints, such as fetters or chains]
as an evil-doer, even in bonds.* But the word of God was not bound. [10]For
this I suffer all things, for the sake of the elect, so that they may also
obtain the salvation that is in Christ Jesus with eternal glory.

[11]It is a true saying: if we are dead with him, we also will live with Ro 6:8
Covenants [Ed: Tyndale taught that when we read the word of God, we need to be alert to find the covenants or promises of God, and to govern ourselves accordingly if we wish to receive of his grace. Therefore in his 1534 New Testament, he often identified covenants with marginal pointers like this]
him. [12]If we are patient, we will also reign with him. If we deny him, he
also will deny us. [13]If we do not believe, yet he abides faithful; he cannot
deny himself. [14]Of these things put them in remembrance. And warn them
before the Lord not to strive about words, which accomplishes nothing but 1Ti 6:4
to pervert the hearers.

[15]Be diligent to show yourself laudable to God, a workman who does
not need to be ashamed, rightly dividing the word of truth. [16]Unspiritual
and vain voices pass over. For they will increase to greater ungodliness,
[17]and their words will consume even as does a canker – of whose number
are Hymenaeus and Philetus, [18]who as concerning the truth have erred,
saying that the resurrection is past already, and do destroy the faith of
divers persons.

[19]But the sure foundation of God remains, and has this seal: the Lord
knows those that are his. And let everyone who calls on the name of Nu 16:5,26
Christ depart from iniquity. [20]Notwithstanding, in a great house are not
only vessels of gold and of silver, but also of wood and of earth: some for Ro 9:21
honour, and some for dishonour. [21]But if a man purges himself from such
fellows, he will be a vessel sanctified unto honour, meet for the Lord and
prepared for all good works.

[22]Lusts of youth avoid. Follow righteousness, faith, love, and peace
with those who call on the Lord with a pure heart. [23]Foolish and unlearned
controversies put from you, remembering that they do but engender strife. Tit 3:9,10
[24]But the servant of the Lord must not quarrel, but must be peaceable to-
wards all, able to teach, and one that can be patient with the evil, [25]and
can correct those who resist – if perhaps God at any time will give them
repentance to know the truth, [26]so that they may come to themselves again
out of the snare of the devil, who are now taken by him at his will.

Chapter 3

He prophesies of the perilous times. He describes the traits of
hypocrites, and tells us what they are within for all their fair
faces outwardly. Persecution for the gospel.

This understand: in the last days, perilous times will come. [2]For men will 1Ti 4:1-3
be lovers of their own selves, covetous, boasters, proud, cursed speakers, 2Pe 3:3
disobedient to father and mother, unthankful, unholy, [3]unkind, truce Jude 18
breakers, stubborn, false accusers, dissolute, fierce, despisers of those who
are good, [4]traitors, wilful, high-minded, greedy for pleasures more than
lovers of God, [5]having a similitude of godly living, but who have denied
*This was prophesied of those who would pretend holiness.
the power thereof *– and from such, turn away. [6]Of this sort are those who
enter into houses and bring into bondage women laden with sin, which
women are led by divers desires and lusts, [7]ever learning and never able to
come to the knowledge of the truth.

[**Jannes and Jambres**, unnamed in the Old Testament, were Pharaoh's magicians. Paul drew their names from Jewish tradition]

[8]As Jannes and Jambres* withstood Moses, even so do these resist the Ex 7:11,22;
truth. Men they are of corrupt minds, and ignorant concerning the faith. 8:7,18.
[9]But they will progress no further, for their madness will be revealed to
all, as theirs was.

[10]But you have seen the experience of my doctrine, fashion of living,
purpose, faith, longsuffering, love, patience – [11]and the persecutions and
afflictions that happened to me at Antioch, at Iconium, and at Lystra,
which persecutions I suffered patiently. And from them all, the Lord
delivered me. [12]Yea, and all who desire to live godly in Christ Jesus must
suffer persecutions. [13]But the evil men and deceivers will grow worse and
worse, while they deceive and are deceived themselves.

[14]But continue in the things that you have learned, which also were
committed to you, seeing you know from whom you have learned them,
[15]and also that from childhood you have known the holy scripture, which
is able to make you wise unto salvation through the faith that is in Christ
Scripture
Jesus. [16]For all scripture given by the inspiration of God is profitable to
teach, to convict, to reform, and to instruct in righteousness, [17]so that the 2Pe 1:19-21
man of God may be perfect and prepared for all good works.

Chapter 4

He exhorts Timothy to be fervent in the word and to suffer
adversity, makes mention of his own death, and bids Timothy
to come to him.

[**Jesus will judge the quick and the dead**; that is, he will judge the living and the dead at his second coming]

I charge you therefore before God, and before the Lord Jesus Christ, who
will judge the quick and the dead at his appearing in his kingdom: [2]preach
the word; be fervent, be it in season or out of season. Refute, rebuke,
exhort, with all longsuffering and instruction.

[3]For the time will come when the people will not suffer wholesome
doctrine, but, after their own fancies, they (whose ears itch) will get them-
selves a heap of teachers,* [4]and will turn their ears from the truth, and will
be given to fables. [5]But as for you, watch in all things, and suffer adver-

*They who have no true faith, nor desire to live godly, are forever seeking new teachers.

sity, and do the work of an evangelist. Fulfil your office to the utmost.
6 For I am now ready to be offered, and the time of my departing is at
hand. 7 I have fought a good fight, and have fulfilled my course, and have
kept the faith. 8 From henceforth is laid up for me a crown of righteous-
ness, which the Lord, who is a righteous judge, shall give me at that day:
not to me only, but to all who love his coming.
9 Make speed to come to me at once. 10 For Demas has left me, and
loves this present world, and has departed for Thessalonica. Crescens has
gone to Galatia, and Titus to Dalmatia. 11 Only Luke is with me.
Take Mark and bring him with you, for he is necessary to me, to min- Col 4:14
ister. 12 And Tychicus I have sent to Ephesus.
13 The cloak that I left at Troas with Carpus, when you come, bring
with you; and the books; but especially the parchment.
14 Alexander the coppersmith did me much ill; the Lord reward him
according to his deeds. 15 You must beware of him also, for he withstood
our preaching sore.
16 At my first defence,* no one assisted me, but all forsook me. I pray
God that it may not be laid to their charges. 17 Notwithstanding, the Lord
assisted me and strengthened me, so that by me the preaching should be
fulfilled to the utmost, and so that all the Gentiles may hear. And I was
delivered out of the mouth of the lion.

[**First defence**: First hearing concerning charges that brought him before Emperor Nero. Tradition says Paul was beheaded by Nero c. 67 AD during his persecutions of the Christians. St. Chrysostom, who wrote 200 or so years later, says Paul's offence was converting Nero's cup bearer (*Hom/2Tim*). Many understand Nero to be **the lion** here referred to]

18 And the Lord will deliver me from all evil-doing, and will keep me
for his heavenly kingdom. To whom be glory for ever and ever. Amen.
19 Greet Prisca and Aquila, and the household of Onesiphorus.
20 Erastus stayed at Corinth. Trophimus I left at Miletum, sick.
21 Make speed to come before winter.
Eubulus greets you, and Pudens, and Linus, and Claudia, and all the
brethren.
22 The Lord Jesus Christ be with your spirit. Grace be with you. Amen.

The end of the second epistle to Timothy.
Written from Rome when Paul was
presented the second time
up before Emperor
Nero.

[This letter was likely written between 62-64 AD. Titus was entrusted with setting in order the congregations in Crete, one of the largest islands in the Mediterranean Sea]

The Epistle of St Paul to Titus

Chapter 1

Paul exhorts Titus to ordain priests or bishops in every city, declares what manner of men they ought to be that are chosen to that office, and charges Titus to rebuke such persons as withstand the gospel.

PAUL the servant of God, and an apostle of Jesus Christ to preach the faith
of God's elect and the knowledge of the truth, which leads to godliness [2]in
the hope of eternal life. Which life God, who cannot lie, promised before
the world began, [3]but has declared his word openly at the time appointed
through preaching, which preaching is committed to me by the command-
ment of God our Saviour.
[4]To Titus, his true-born son in the common faith.
Grace, mercy, and peace from God the Father and from the Lord Jesus
Christ our Saviour.
[5]The reason I left you in Crete was in order that you should complete
that which was lacking, and should ordain elders[a] in every city as I di- 1Ti 3:1-13
rected you – [6]if any be faultless, the husband of one wife, having faithful
children not known for running wild or disobedience. [7]For a bishop must
be faultless, as it becomes the minister of God: not stubborn, not angry, no
drunkard, no fighter, not given to the love of money; [8]but harborous,[*] one
that loves goodness, sober-minded, righteous, holy, temperate, [9]and such
as cleaves to the true word of doctrine, so that he may be able to exhort
with wholesome teaching and to refute those who speak against it.
[10]For there are many contrary, who speak vanity and beguile minds,
namely they of the circumcision, [11]whose mouths must be stopped. They
pervert whole houses, teaching things which they ought not, for easy
money. [12]One of them who was an author of their own said, The Cretans
are always liars, evil creatures and lazy gluttons. [13]This witness is true.
Therefore rebuke them sharply so that they may be sound in the faith,
[14]and not paying heed to Jewish fables, and to commandments of men that
turn from the truth.
[15]To the pure all things are pure, but to those who are defiled and Ro 14:20
unbelieving, nothing is pure, but even their very minds and consciences
are defiled. [16]They confess that they know God, but with their deeds they
deny him, and are abominable and obstinately self-willed, not to be
trusted for any good works.

[**Harborous**: affording harbour or shelter; given to hospitality]

The Notes

Ordain elders (1:5)

a) Elders are called 'overseers' in 1 Timothy c3. Bishops and elders are one and the same thing, being officers chosen to govern the congregation in doctrine and living.

Chapter 2

He tells Titus how he should teach all degrees of persons to conduct themselves.

But you, teach the things that are appropriate to wholesome doctrine: [2]that
Old men — the elder men should be sober, grave, discreet; sound in the faith, in love
Old women — and in patience. [3]And the elder women likewise: that they should be at-
tired as becomes holiness, and not be false accusers, not given to much
drinking, but teachers of good things, [4]to make the young women sober-
Young women — minded, to love their husbands, to love their children, [5]to be discreet,
chaste, housewifely, good, and obedient to their own husbands, so that the
Young men — word of God is not ill-spoken of. [6]Young men likewise exhort to be sober-
minded.

[7]Above all things, show yourself an example of good works, with un-
corrupt doctrine, with gravity, [8]and with the wholesome word that cannot
be rebuked, so that he who opposes you may be ashamed, having nothing
in you that he may fault.

[9]Exhort the servants to be obedient to their own masters, and to please — Eph 6:5-8
in all things – not answering back, [10]not stealing, but showing all good — Col 3:22
faithfulness, so that they do honour to the doctrine of our Saviour God in
all things. [11]For the grace of God that brings salvation to all men has
appeared, [12]and teaches us that we should deny ungodliness and worldly
lusts, and that we should live sober-minded, righteously, and godly in this
present world, [13]looking for that blessed hope and glorious appearing of
the mighty God, and of our Saviour Jesus Christ, [14]who gave himself for
us to redeem us from all unrighteousness, and to make clean for himself — 1Pe 2:9-12
an acceptable people, fervently given to good works.

[15]These things speak and exhort. And rebuke with all authority. See
that no one disrespects you.

[To make clean, etc; Tyndale's obsolete English has been updated from Wycliffe, who in 1380 used here words we still know]

Chapter 3

Of obedience to persons in authority. Of gentleness to all people. He warns Titus to beware of foolish and unprofitable questions.

Warn the people to submit themselves to rule and authority, to obey the — Ro 13:1-6
officials, to be ready for all good works, [2]to speak evil of no man, and not — 1Pe 2:13-15
to be fighters, but soft, showing all gentleness to all men. [3]For we our-
selves also were in times past unwise: disobedient, deceived; captive to
desires, lusts, and diverse kinds of sensuality; living in maliciousness and
envy, full of hate, hating one another.

[4]But after the kindness and love of our Saviour God toward man — 2Ti 1:9
Mercy saves. — appeared, [5]he saved us – not for the deeds of righteousness that we have
done, but of his mercy, by the fountain of the new birth, and with the re-
newing of the Holy Spirit, [6]which he shed on us abundantly through Jesus
Christ our Saviour, [7]so that we, once justified by his grace, should be heirs
of eternal life through hope. [8]This is a true saying.

These things I want you to affirm constantly, so that those who believe God may be diligent to go forward in good works. These things are good and profitable to men. 9Foolish questions and genealogies, and brawling and strife about the law, avoid. For they are unprofitable and superfluous.

1Ti 1:3-7 2Ti 2:16-18; 23.

10A person who is given to heresy, after the first and the second admonition, avoid, 11remembering that such a one has been perverted, and sins, even condemned by his own judgment.

12When I send Artemas to you, or Tychicus, try your best to come to me to Nicopolis. For I have determined to winter there. 13Set Zenas the lawyer and Apollos well on their journey, so that nothing is lacking to them. 14And let our people also learn to excel in good works, as much as need requires, so that they are not unfruitful.

15Everyone who is with me sends greetings to you. Greet those who love us in the faith. Grace be with you all. Amen.

Written from Nicopolis,
a city of Macedonia.

The Prologue to the Epistle of St Paul to Philemon

In this epistle St Paul shows a godly example of Christian love. We see how Paul takes poor Onesimus, the runaway slave, to himself, and makes intercession for him to his master Philemon, and helps him with all that he can, and acts no differently than as if he himself were the said Onesimus. Which thing yet he does not with power and authority, as he well might have done, but puts off all authority and whatever he might of right do, so that Philemon might do likewise toward Onesimus. And with great gentleness and wisdom, he teaches Philemon to see his duty in Christ Jesus. *W.T. (1534)*

The Epistle of Saint Paul to
Philemon

[Philemon was a member of the congregation in Colosse, which met at his house. This is one of Paul's prison epistles, written about 60-62 AD, during his first imprisonment at Rome]

Chapter 1

He rejoices to hear of the faith and love of Philemon, whom he asks to forgive his servant Onesimus, and lovingly to receive him back.

PAUL, the prisoner of Jesus Christ, and brother Timothy.

[Chrysostom>**Apphia** is likely Philemon's wife, and **Archippus** held an office in the congregation (*Hom/Ph'm*)]

To Philemon the beloved and our helper, 2and to the beloved Apphia, and to Archippus our fellow-soldier, and to the congregation of your house.

Archippus: Col 4:17

3Grace be with you and peace from God our Father and from the Lord Jesus Christ.

[4]I thank my God, making mention always of you in my prayers, [5]when
I hear of the love and faith that you have toward the Lord Jesus, and
toward all the saints, [6]so that the fellowship that you have in the faith is
fruitful through the knowledge of all good things, which are in you by
Jesus Christ. [7]And we have great joy and consolation over your love. For
by you, brother, the saints' hearts are comforted.

[8]Therefore, though I might be bold in Christ to enjoin that which be-
hoves you, [9]yet for love's sake I rather beseech you, though I be as I am,
even Paul aged, and now in bonds for Jesus Christ's sake. [10]I beseech you
for my son Onesimus, whom I begat in my bonds – [11]who in time past
was unprofitable to you, but is now able to profit both you and also me,
[12]whom I have sent home again. Therefore receive him; that is to say, my
own offspring, [13]whom I would gladly have retained with me so that on
your behalf he could have ministered to me in the bonds of the gospel.
[14]Nevertheless, without your consent I would do nothing, because the
good that comes of you should not be, as it were, usurped through circum-
stance, but willing.

[15]Perhaps he therefore departed for a season so that you would receive
him forever, [16]not now as a servant, but above a servant; I mean a brother
beloved, especially to me, but how much more to you, both in the flesh
and also in the Lord. [17]If you count me a fellow, receive him as myself.
[18]If he has done you any wrong or owes you anything, lay it to my charge.
[19]I, Paul, have written it with my own hand. I will recompense it.

So I do not say to you that you owe to me even your own self. [20]Even
so, brother, let me enjoy this fruit from you in the Lord. Comfort my heart
in the Lord.

[21]Trusting in your willingness, I have written to you, knowing that you
will do more than I say. [22]Moreover, prepare a room for me. For I trust
that through the help of your prayers, I shall be given to you.

Mark and Luke the evangelists.

[23]Epaphras, my fellow-prisoner in Christ Jesus, sends greetings to you,
[24]as do Mark, Aristarchus, Demas, and Luke, my helpers. 2Ti 4:10,11

[25]The grace of our Lord Jesus Christ be with your spirits. Amen.

Sent from Rome by the hands
of Onesimus,
a servant.

[The date of this epistle is uncertain. Many comments in it indicate that it was written before the temple was destroyed in 70 AD. Its authorship has been debated]

The Epistle of Saint Paul to the Hebrews

Chapter 1

How God dealt lovingly with the people of the old time in sending them his prophets, but has shown much more mercy to us, in that he sent us his own Son. Of the most excellent glory of Jesus Christ, who in all things is like his Father.

GOD IN TIME PAST diversely and many ways spoke to the fathers by the
prophets. [2]But in these last days,[a] he has spoken to us by his Son, whom
he has made heir of all things; by whom also he made the world. [3]Which
Son, being the brightness of his glory and very image of his substance,
bearing up all things with the word of his power, has in his own person
Christ has purged our sins. purged our sins, and is seated on the right hand of the Majesty on high,
[4]and is more excellent than the angels, inasmuch as he has by inheritance
obtained a more excellent name than they. [5]For to which of the angels did
he say at any time: You are my Son; this day I have begotten you? And Ps 2:7
again: I will be his Father, and he shall be my Son. [6]And again, when he 2Sa 7:14
brings the first begotten Son into the world, he says: And all the angels of De 32:43
God shall worship him. Ps 97:7

[7]And of the angels he says: He makes his angels spirits, and his Ps 104:4
ministers flames of fire. [8]But to the Son he says: O God, your seat shall be
for ever and ever. The sceptre of your kingdom is a right sceptre. [9]You Ps 45:6,7
have loved righteousness and hated iniquity; therefore God, who is your
The oil of gladness is the Holy Spirit. God, has anointed you with the oil of gladness above your fellows. [10]And:
You, Lord, in the beginning, laid the foundation of the earth, and the
heavens are the works of your hands. [11]They shall perish, but you shall Ps 102:25-27
endure. They all will grow old as does a garment, [12]and as a vesture you
will change them, and they will be changed. But you are always, and your
years shall not fail.

[13]To which of the angels did he say at any time: Sit on my right hand, Ps 110:1
till I make your enemies your footstool? [14]Are they not all ministering 1Co 15:25
spirits, sent to minister for the sakes of those who will be heirs of sal-
vation?

The Notes

These last days (1:2)

a) These latter days are written of at Isaiah 2:1-4 and Ezekiel 38:16. [Note a, Isa 2, says that by *last days* is commonly signified the time of Christ's coming until the end of the world.]

Chapter 2

He exhorts us to be obedient to the new law that Christ has given us, and not offended at the infirmity and low degree of Christ, because it was necessary for our sakes that he should take such a humble state upon him, so that he could be like his brethren.

Therefore we ought to give the more heed to the things that we have
heard, lest we perish. [2]For if the word that was spoken by angels was sure, Ga 3:19
so that every transgression and disobedience received a just recompense Ac 7:53 Joh 1:17
in reward, [3]how shall we escape if we neglect so great a salvation? –
which at the first began to be preached by the Lord himself, and afterward
was confirmed to us by those who heard it, [4]God bearing witness to it
both with signs and wonders also, and with divers miracles,[a] and gifts of
the Holy Spirit according to his own will.

If they who disregarded Moses were so grievously punished, what will become of those who make a mock of Christ?

[5]It is not to the angels that he has put in subjection the world to come,
of which we speak. [6]But one in a certain place witnesses, saying, What is Ps 8:4-6
man, that you are mindful of him? [7]After you had for a season made him 1Pe 3:22
lower than the angels, you crowned him with honour and glory, and have
set him above the works of your hands. [8]You have put all things in subjection under his feet.

In that he put all things under him, he left nothing that is not put under 1Co 15:27
him. [9]Nevertheless, we do not yet see all things subdued, but we see him
who was made less than the angels. We see that it was Jesus who is
crowned with glory and honour for the suffering of death: that he, by the
grace of God, was to taste of death for all men.

[10]For it was fitting for him, for whom all things are and by whom all
things are, in accordance with the way that he brought many sons to glory,
to make the Lord of their salvation perfect through suffering. [11]For he
who sanctifies and those who are sanctified are all of one, for which sake
he is not ashamed to call them brethren, [12]saying: I will declare your name
to my brethren, and in the midst of the congregation I will praise you. Ps 22:22
[13]And again: I will put my trust in him. And again: Behold, here am I and 2Sa 22:3 Isa 8:17,18
the children that God has given me.

[14]Considering then that the children were partakers of flesh and blood,
he also himself likewise took part with them, in order to put down through
death him that had lordship over death – that is to say, the devil – [15]and to Ho 13:14
deliver those who through fear of death were all their lifetime subject to
bondage. [16]For in no place does he take on him the angels, but he takes
the seed of Abraham on him. [17]Therefore it was fitting for him to be made
like his brethren in all things, so that he could be merciful, and a faithful
high priest in things concerning God, in order to purge the people's sins.
[18]For in that he himself suffered and was tried, he is able to succour those
who are tried.

The Notes

Divers miracles (2:4)

a) Miracles are called signs because they are a sign, token, and an evident proof that the thing that is preached is God's word.

Chapter 3

He calls upon us to hear and honour the word of Christ, who is more worthy than Moses. The punishment of persons who stubbornly harden their hearts.

Therefore, holy brethren, partakers of the celestial calling, consider the
ambassador and high priest of our profession, Christ Jesus, [2]who was
faithful to him who appointed him, even as Moses was in all his house.
[3]And yet this man was counted worthy of more glory than Moses, inas- Nu 12:7
much as he who has prepared the house has more honour in the house.

[4]Every house is built by some man. But he who ordained all things is
God. [5]And Moses truly was faithful in all his house, as a servant, to bear
witness of those things that were to be spoken afterward. [6]But Christ as a
son has rule over the house – whose house we are, if so be that we hold
fast the confidence and the assurance of that hope to the end.

[7]Therefore as the Holy Spirit says: Today if you hear his voice, [8]hard-
en not your hearts, as in the rebellion in the day of trial in the wilderness,
[9]where your fathers tried me, proved me, and saw my works forty years Ps 95:7-11
long. [10]Therefore I was grieved with that generation, and said, They do
ever err in their hearts; they have not acknowledged my ways. [11]So I
swore in my wrath that they would not enter into my rest.

[12]Take heed, brethren, that there be in none of you an evil heart in
unbelief, that he should depart from the living God; [13]but exhort one
another daily, while it is called today, lest any of you grow hard-hearted
through the deceitfulness of sin.

[14]We are partakers of Christ if we keep sure until the end the first
confidence,* [15]as long as it is said: Today, if you hear his voice, harden
not your hearts, as when you rebelled. [16]For some, when they heard, reb- Ps 95:7,8
elled – though not everyone who came out of Egypt under Moses. [17]But
with whom was he displeased for forty years? Was he not displeased with
those who sinned, whose bodies were overthrown in the desert? [18]To
whom did he swear that they would not enter into his rest, but to those
who did not believe? [19]And we see that they could not enter in because of
unbelief.

*The **first confidence** is faith.

Chapter 4

The Sabbath or rest of the Christian. The punishment of unbelievers. The nature of the word of God.

Let us fear, therefore, lest any of us, forsaking the promise of entering into
his rest, should seem to come behind. [2]For to us it has been declared as
well as to them. But it did not profit them to hear the word, because they
who heard it did not couple it with faith.[a] [3]But we who have believed do
enter into his rest, while contrariwise he said to the others: I have sworn in
my wrath, they shall not enter into my rest. Ps 95:11

And he spoke this long after the works were made and the foundation
of the world laid. [4]For he spoke in a certain place about the seventh day Ge 2:2
this way: And God did rest on the seventh day from all his works. [5]And
then again in this place: They shall not come into my rest. [6]We see there- Ps 95:11
fore that it follows that some will enter into his rest, and those to whom it
was first preached did not enter in due to unbelief. [7]Again, speaking in
David, he appointed a certain present day after so long a time, saying as Ps 95:7,8

mentioned above, this day, if you hear his voice, be not hard-hearted.
[8]For if Joshua had given them rest, then he would not afterward have
spoken of another day. [9]There remains therefore yet a rest for the people
of God. [10]For the person who has entered into his rest does cease from his
own works,[*] as God did from his.

*Sin is our work, from which all must cease who enter into the rest of a quiet conscience in Christ.

[11]Let us exercise ourselves therefore to enter into that rest, lest anyone
should fall into unbelief after the same example. [12]For the word of God is
alive and mighty in operation, and sharper than any two-edged sword, and
enters through even to the dividing asunder of soul and spirit, and of the
joints and marrow, and judges the thoughts and intents of the heart;[b] Ps 33:13-15
[13]neither is there any creature invisible in the sight of him. For all things Ec'us 15:18,19.
are naked and bare to the eyes of him of whom we speak.

[Verses 4:14-16 are at chapter 5 in the Matthew Bible]

The Notes

Hearing without faith (4:2)

a) As faith is the ground of all grace, so is unbelief the root of all sin.

The word of God…dividing asunder (4:12)

b) [Ed: Two commentaries on this verse:

Tyndale> A man before the preaching of God's word is but one man, all flesh, the soul consenting to the lusts of the flesh, to follow them. But the sword of the word of God, where it takes effect, divides a man in two, and sets him at variance against his own self, the flesh haling one way, and the spirit calling back again to follow the law and will of God. Before being born again, a person is called soul, or carnal. When renewed in Christ through the word of life, he is called spirit, or spiritual (*Sundry*).

R. Hooker> God has delivered a law as sharp as the two-edged sword, piercing the most closed and unsearchable corners of the heart, which the law of nature can hardly reach, and human laws by no means possible. Hereby we know even secret concupiscence to be sin, and are made fearful to offend though it be in but a wandering cogitation (*1st Book*).]

Chapter 5

Christ is our high priest and seat of grace, and surpasses the high priests of the old law.

[4:14]Seeing then that we have a great high priest who has entered into heav-
en (I mean Jesus, the Son of God), let us hold fast our profession. [4:15]For
we do not have a high priest that cannot have compassion on our infir-
mities, but one who was in all points tempted like we are, but yet without
sin. [4:16]Let us therefore go boldly to the seat of grace, so that we may re-
ceive mercy, and find grace to help in time of need.
[5:1]For every high priest that is taken from among men is ordained for
man, in things pertaining to God, to offer gifts and sacrifices for sin. [2]He
can have compassion on the ignorant and on those who are out of the way,
because he himself also is compassed with infirmity – [3]concerning which
infirmity he is bound to offer for sins, as well for his own part as for the
people's.
[4]And no man takes honour to himself, but he who is called by God, as
was Aaron. [5]So also likewise, Christ did not glorify himself to be made Ex 28:1
the high priest, but he who said to him, You are my Son, this day I have Ps 2:7
begotten you, glorified him. [6]As he also in another place speaks: You are Ps 110:4

a priest forever, after the order of Melchizedek.
7He, in the days of his flesh,[a] did offer up prayers and supplications
with strong crying and tears to him that was able to save him from death,
and was also heard, because of his godliness. 8And though he was God's
Son, yet he learned obedience by those things that he suffered, 9and was
made perfect, and the author of eternal salvation for all who obey him,
10and is called by God a high priest after the order of Melchizedek.
11About this we have many things to say, which are hard to explain
because you are dull of hearing. 12For when as concerning the time you
ought to be teachers, yet you need us to again teach you the first prin-
ciples of the word of God, and are become such as have need of milk, and
not of strong meat.[b] 13For everyone who is fed with milk is inexpert in the
word of righteousness. For he is but a babe. 14But strong meat belongs to
those who are of full age, who through regular use have their wits exer- Heb 13:9 Job 34:3
cised to judge both good and evil also.

The Notes

In the days of his flesh (5:7) a) *Days of his flesh* signifies the time of his humanity.

Milk and strong meat (5:12-14) b) By *milk* understand things easy to comprehend. By *strong meat* understand the things that are difficult and obscure. [Chrysostom> doctrine, as our 'food,' is also in view at v14. To *judge good and evil* means to be able to recognize doctrines either as wholesome and sublime, or corrupted and low. Everyone can judge a deed as good or bad, but to judge doctrine belongs to alert and practised true Christians (*Hom/Heb*).]

Chapter 6

He continues with the thing that he began in the latter end of chapter 5, and exhorts them not to faint, but to be steadfast and patient, seeing as God is trustworthy and faithful in his promise.

Therefore let us leave the questions that belong to the beginning of a
Christian life, and let us go on to maturity, and not now again lay the
foundation of repentance from dead works, and of faith toward God, 2of
baptism, of doctrine, and of laying on of hands, and of resurrection from
death, and of eternal judgment. 3And so will we do, if God permits.
4For it is not possible for those who were once enlightened, and have
tasted of the heavenly gift, and were become partakers of the Holy Spirit,
5and have tasted of the good word of God and of the power of the world to 2Pe 2:20-22
come, 6if they fall, to be renewed again to repentance, seeing they have
(as concerning themselves) crucified the Son of God afresh, making a
mock of him.[a] 7For that earth which drinks in the rain that comes oft upon
it, and brings forth herbs meet for those who tend it, receives blessing
from God. 8But that ground which bears thorns and briars is reproved, and
is near to cursing: whose end is to be burned.
9Nevertheless, dear friends, we trust to see better of you, and things
that accompany salvation, though we speak this way. 10For God is not
unrighteous, that he should forget your work and labour that proceeds of

love – which love you have shown in his name, you who have ministered to the saints, and still minister. [11]Yea, and we desire that every one of you show the same diligence, to secure your hope right to the end: [12]that you faint not, but follow those who through faith and patience inherit the promises. [13]For when God made promise to Abraham, because he had no greater thing to swear by, he swore by himself, [14]saying: Surely I will bless you and multiply you indeed. [15]And so after he had waited a long time, Abraham enjoyed the promise.

Ge 22:17

[16]Men will swear by one who is greater than themselves, and an oath to confirm the thing is among them an end of all strife. [17]So God, wanting very much to show to the heirs of promise the certainty of his counsel, added an oath, [18]so that by two immutable things* (in which it was impossible that God should lie) we may have perfect consolation – we who have fled to hold fast the hope that is set before us, [19]which hope we have as an anchor of the soul both sure and steadfast. Which hope also enters in, into those things that are within the veil, [20]to where the forerunner has entered in for us – I mean Jesus, who is made a high priest forever, after the order of Melchizedek.

Two immutable things: God's promise and his oath.

The Notes

It is not possible for those who were once enlightened, etc. (6:4-6)

a) Not possible to be renewed again to repentance: This text does not deny the possibility of mercy in God, but the impossibility of repentance in such persons as maliciously forsake the truth, blaspheme Christ, and take part against the Holy Spirit. For the truth is that with the Lord there is mercy and plenteous redemption (Psalm 130), so that whosoever calls upon his name shall be saved (Joel 2:32, Romans 10:13). Now they who forsake the truth, blaspheming Christ and taking part against the Holy Spirit, cannot repent. For if sinners would convert and call upon God, they could be sure of remission.

Chapter 7

He compares the priesthood of Christ to Melchizedek, but declares it to be far more excellent.

This Melchizedek, king of Salem (who, being priest of the most high God, met Abraham as he returned from the slaughter of the kings and blessed him, [2]to whom also Abraham gave tithes of all the spoils) is by translation of his name, king of righteousness. After that, he is king of Salem; that is to say, king of peace. [3]Without father, without mother, without kin,* and having neither a beginning of his days nor yet end of his life, he is likened to the Son of God, and continues a priest forever.

Ge 14:18-20

[**Without kin, etc**: Chrysostom> his lineage and death are unknown. Thus he is a type or figure of Jesus, who is in actuality without beginning or end of his days (*Hom/Heb*)]

[4]Consider what a man this was, to whom the patriarch Abraham gave tithes of the spoils. [5]And now, those children of Levi that received the office of the priests have a commandment to take tithes from the people according to the law; that is to say, from their brethren, yea though they came out of the loins of Abraham. [6]But he whose kindred is not counted among them received tithes from Abraham, and blessed him who had the promises. [7]And without argument, he who is less receives blessing from him who is greater. [8]And here, men who die receive tithes. But there, he

Nu 18:21-26

[**Tithes of the spoils**: literally, a tenth part of the spoils]

receives tithes of whom it is witnessed that he lives. [9]And to say the truth,
Levi himself also, who receives tithes, paid tithes in Abraham. [10]For he
was yet in the loins of his father Abraham when Melchizedek met him.

[11]If now therefore perfection came by the priesthood of the Levites
(for under that priesthood the people received the law), what further need
was there for another priest to arise after the order of Melchizedek, and
not after the order of Aaron? [12]Now no doubt if the priesthood is trans-
lated, then of necessity the law must be translated also. [13]For he of whom
these things are spoken belongs to another tribe, of which no man ever
served at the altar. [14]For it is evident that our Lord came from the tribe of
Judah, of which tribe Moses said nothing concerning priesthood.

[15]And it is yet a more evident thing if another priest in the similitude
of Melchizedek arises, [16]who is not made priest by the law of the carnal
commandment, but by the power of the endless life. [17]For he testifies: Ps 110:4
You are a priest forever, after the order of Melchizedek.

[18]So then, the previous commandment is abrogated, because of its
weakness and unprofitableness. [19]For the law made nothing perfect, but
was a preparation for a better hope, by which hope we draw near to God.

[20]And it is a better hope in that it was not promised without an oath.
[21]Those priests were made without an oath, but this priest with an oath, by
him that said to him: The Lord swore and will not repent: You are a priest
forever after the order of Melchizedek. [22]And thus did Jesus establish and
secure a better testament.

[23]And among the Levites many were made priests, because they were
prevented from continuing by death. [24]But this man, because he endures
forever, has an everlasting priesthood. [25]Therefore he is able also to save
to all eternity those who come to God by him, seeing he lives eternally to
make intercession for us.

[26]Such a high priest it behoved us to have, who is holy, harmless, un-
defiled, separate from sinners, and made higher than heaven; [27]who does
not need (like those high priests) daily to offer up sacrifice, first for his
own sins and then for the people's sins. For Jesus did that once and for all
Christ once sacrificed purged all sins. when he offered up himself. [28]For the law makes priests of men who have
infirmity, but the word of the oath that came since the law makes the Son
priest, who is perfect forevermore.

Chapter 8

The office of Christ is more worthy than the office of the priests under the old law, which was imperfect, and was therefore abrogated.

Of the things which we have spoken, this is the pith: that we have such a
high priest as sits on the right hand of the seat of majesty in heaven, [2]and
is a minister of holy things, and of the very tabernacle that God pitched,
and not man.

[3]For every high priest is ordained to offer gifts and sacrifices, and
therefore it is necessary that this man also have something to offer. [4]For

he would not be a priest if he were on the earth, where are the priests who
offer gifts according to the law. [5]Such priests serve in the figure and
shadow of heavenly things, in accordance with the oracle of God given to
Moses when he was about to make the tabernacle: Take heed (said he)
that you fashion all things according to the pattern shown to you in the Ex 25:40 Ac 7:44-49
mount.

[6]Now he has obtained a more excellent office, inasmuch as he is the
mediator of a better testament, which was made for better promises. [7]For
if that first testament had been faultless, then no place would have been
sought for the second.

[8]For in rebuking the people, he says: Behold, the days will come (says
the Lord) when I will make a new testament with the house of Israel and
with the house of Judah, [9]not like the testament that I made with their
fathers at the time when I took them by the hands to lead them out of the
land of Egypt. For they did not continue in my testament, and I regarded
them not, says the Lord.

[10]For this is the testament that I will make with the house of Israel: Jer 31:31-34 [See the OT feature at the end of the book of Acts]
Covenant After those days, says the Lord, I will put my laws in their minds, and I
will write them in their hearts, and I will be their God, and they shall be
my people. [11]And they shall not teach everyone his neighbour and every-
one his brother, saying, Know the Lord! For they shall all know me, from
the least to the greatest of them. [12]For I will be merciful over their unrigh-
teousness, and over their sins and their iniquities.

[13]In that he says a new testament, he has abrogated the old. Now that
which is abolished and grown old, is ready to vanish away.

Chapter 9

The value and significance of the old testament, and how far
the new excels it.

That first tabernacle indeed had observances, and the serving of God, and
temporal holiness. [2]For a fore-tabernacle was made, where the candlestick
and the table and the showbread were, which is called holy. [3]But within
the second veil there was a tabernacle that is called holiest of all. [4]It had
the golden censer, and the ark of the testament overlaid round about with
gold, in which was the golden pot with manna, and Aaron's rod that
budded, and the tables of the testament. [5]Over the ark were the cherubims Ge 3:24
of glory covering the seat of grace – of which things we will not now
speak particularly.

[6]When these things had been set up accordingly, the priests went
constantly into the first tabernacle and executed the service of God. [7]But
into the second went the high priest alone, once every year – and not
without blood, which he offered for himself and for the ignorance of the
people.

[The first or outer tabernacle was a similitude of the Mosaic testament. The inner, second tabernacle, the

[8]By this the Holy Spirit was signifying that the way of holy things was 1Pe 1:20
not yet made manifest, while as yet the first tabernacle was standing. Col 2:16
[9]That tabernacle was a similitude for the time then present, and in which

Holy of Holies, signified the New Testament, of which Christ is the eternal High Priest who now ministers holy things and spiritual mysteries in that holy and spiritual tabernacle that he entered into by his own blood. Now that he has entered in, the first tabernacle or testament, with all of its observances and washings, together with all that was a similitude and figure, serves no more. For the fulfilment is here: he who himself washes and sprinkles and purifies us has now come]

gifts and sacrifices were offered that could not make the offerer perfect as
pertaining to the conscience, [10]with only foods, and drinks, and various
washings and observances of the flesh, which were prescribed until the
time of reformation.

[11]But Christ, being a high priest of good things to come, came by a
greater and a more perfect tabernacle, not made with hands; that is to say,
not of this creation. [12]Neither was it by the blood of goats and calves, but
by his own blood he entered once and for all into the holy place, and
found eternal redemption. [13]For if the blood of oxen and of goats and the Lev c16
ashes of a heifer when sprinkled purified the unclean insofar as the Ro 5:9 1Pe 1:18,19
purifying of the flesh is concerned, [14]how much more shall the blood of Rev 1:5
Christ, who through the eternal Spirit offered himself without spot to God,
purge your consciences from dead works in order to serve the living God?

[15]And therefore he is the mediator of the new testament, so that
through death, which effected the redemption of the transgressions that
were under the first testament, those who are called may receive the prom-
ise of eternal inheritance. [16]For where there is a testament, there must also
be the death of him who makes the testament, [17]because a testament takes
authority when men are dead.* It is of no effect as long as he who made it
is alive.

[It has ever been a legal axiom that a **last will and testament** speaks from death]

[18]For which reason also, neither was that first testament ordained
without blood. [19]For when all the commandments were read by Moses to
all the people, he took the blood of calves and of goats, with water and
purple wool and hyssop, and sprinkled both the book and all the people,
[20]saying: This is the blood of the testament that God has appointed unto
you. [21]Moreover, he sprinkled the tabernacle with blood also, and all the Ex 24:8
ministering vessels. [22]And also almost all things are by the law purged
with blood, and without the shedding of blood there is no remission.

[23]It is needful then that the similitudes of heavenly things be purified
with such things, but the heavenly things themselves are purified with
better sacrifices than are those. [24]For Christ has not entered into the holy
places that are made with hands, which are but similitudes of true things,
but has entered into very heaven, to appear now in the sight of God for us 1Pe 3:22
– [25]not to offer himself repeatedly, as the high priest enters into the holy
place every year with strange blood. [26]For then he must have repeatedly
suffered since the world began. But now, in the end of the world, he has
appeared once and for all to put sin to flight* by the offering up of him-
self. [27]And as it is appointed unto men once to die, and then comes the
judgment, [28]so Christ was offered once to take away the sins of many, and
to those who look for him, he will appear again without sin for salvation.

[**To put sin to flight**: Under the old law, sin pursued its claim on us for the penalty of death. Under the new law of Christ, the grace of mercy offered in Christ through faith, sin must retreat. Mercy triumphs over judgment]

Chapter 10

The old law has no power to cleanse away sin, but Christ did it with the offering of his body once and for all. An exhortation to receive this goodness of God thankfully, with patience and steadfast faith.

For the law, which has but the shadow of good things to come, and not the
real things themselves, can never, with the sacrifices that the priests offer
year by year continually, make those who come to it perfect. [2]For would
not then those sacrifices have ceased to be offered, because the offerers,
once purged, would have had no more conscience of sins? [3]But in those
sacrifices, mention is made of sins every year. [4]For it is impossible that
the blood of oxen and of goats should take away sins. [5]Therefore when he
comes into the world he says: Sacrifice and offering you would not have,
but a body you have made ready for me. [6]In sacrifices and sin-offerings Ps 40:6-8
you have no pleasure. [7]Then I said, Lo, I come! In the chief part of the
book it is written of me, that I will do your will, O God.

[8]Above – when he said sacrifice and offering, and burnt sacrifices and
sin-offerings you would not have, neither have accepted (which yet are
offered according to the law), [9]and then said, Lo, I come to do your will,
O God – he takes away the first in order to establish the latter. [10]In accor-
Christ's body is but once offered. dance with this God's will, we are sanctified by the offering of the body
of Jesus Christ once and for all.

[11]And every priest is ready daily ministering, and repeatedly offers
one manner of offering that can never take away sins. [12]But this man, after
he had offered one sacrifice for sins, sat down forever on the right hand of Ps 8:6
God, [13]and from henceforth waits till his enemies be made his footstool. Ps 110:1 Ac 2:34-36
[14]For with one offering, he has made perfect forever those who are sanc- 1Co 15:25-28.
tified.

[15]And the Holy Spirit also witnesses to us of this, namely when he
foretold: [16]This is the testament that I will make unto them after those
days, says the Lord: I will put my laws in their hearts, and in their mind I Jer 31:33,34
will write them, [17]and their sins and iniquities I will remember no more. Eze 36:25-27

[18]Now where there is remission of these things, there is no more of-
fering for sin.

[19]Seeing, brethren, that by the means of the blood of Jesus we may be
bold to enter into that holy place, [20]by the new and living way that he has
prepared for us through the veil (that is to say, by his flesh), [21]and seeing
also that we have a high priest who is ruler over the house of God, [22]let us
Here follows our duty, if we will be partakers of the mercy before rehearsed. draw near with a true heart, in full faith, sprinkled in our hearts from an
evil conscience, and washed in our bodies with pure water. [23]And let us
keep the profession of our hope without wavering, for he who promised is
faithful. [24]And let us consider one another, to encourage to love and to
We ought to care each for the other's salvation, as we would if we truly loved each other. good works. [25]And let us not forsake the fellowship that we have among
ourselves, as the manner of some is, but let us exhort one another, and that
so much the more because you see that the day draws near.

[26]For if we sin willingly[a] after we have received the knowledge of the
truth, there remains no more sacrifice for sins, [27]but a fearful looking for
judgment and violent fire, which will devour the adversaries. [28]He who
despises Moses' law dies without mercy under two or three witnesses: De c17
[29]of how much sorer punishment do you suppose that person will be Ps 107:11
counted deserving who treads under foot the Son of God, and counts as an

unholy thing the blood of the testament by which he was sanctified, and
does dishonour to the Spirit of Grace? [30]For we know him who has said:
Vengeance belongs to me; I will recompense, says the Lord. And again: De 32:35,36
The Lord shall judge his people. [31]It is a fearful thing to fall into the hands Ro 12:19
of the living God.[b]

[32]Call to remembrance the days that are past, in which, after you had
received light, you endured a great fight in adversities – [33]at times when
everyone wondered and gazed at you for the shame and tribulation that
was done to you, and other times when you became companions of those
in such circumstances. [34]For you suffered also with my bonds. And you
bore patiently the spoiling of your goods, and that with gladness, knowing
in yourselves that you had in heaven a better and an enduring substance.

[35]Cast not away therefore your confidence, which earns great reward.
[36]For you have need of patience, so that after you have done the will of
God, you may receive the promise: [37]For yet a very little while, and he Hab 2:3,4
who is to come will come, and will not be long. [38]But the just shall live by Ro 1:17 Ga 3:11
faith. And if a person withdraws himself, my soul shall have no pleasure
in him.

[39]But we are not of those who withdraw ourselves unto damnation, but
are of faith to the winning of the soul.

The Notes

If we sin willingly, etc. (10:26,27) a) This is the sin that is spoken of at Matthew 12:31, being the sin of blasphemy against the Holy Spirit, which Saint John calls the sin unto death (1Jo 5:16).

The hands of the living God (10:31) b) The hands of God signify here the correction and chastening of God, as it is said. Psalm 20:6 [referring to the saving 'hand' of the Lord].

Chapter 11

What faith is, and a commendation of the same. The steadfast belief of the fathers in old time.

Faith is a sure confidence of things that are hoped for, and a certainty of
things that are not seen.[a] [2]By it the elders were well reported of.

[v3 is from Coverdale 1535. And see Tyndale's preface to the *Obedience*]
[3]Through faith we understand that the world and all the things which
are seen were made of nothing by the word of God.

[4]By faith Abel offered to God a better sacrifice than Cain, by which he
Abel obtained witness that he was righteous, God testifying of his gifts; by Ge 4:3-5 Heb 12:24
which also he being dead still speaks.

[5]By faith Enoch was translated so that he would not see death, and Ge 5:21-24
Enoch was not to be found, because God had taken him away. Before he was Ec'us 44:16
taken away, he was reported of that he had pleased God. [6]But without
faith, it is impossible to please him. For the person who comes to God
must believe that God is, and that he is a rewarder of those who seek him.

[7]By faith Noah honoured God after he was warned of things that were Ge 6:13-22
Noah not yet seen, and prepared the ark for the saving of his household – Ec'us 44:17,18.
through which ark he condemned the world and became heir of the righ- 1 Pe 3:20
teousness that comes by faith.

[8]By faith Abraham when he was called obeyed, to go out into a place (Ge 12:1-4; 12:8; 13:3,18; 18:1.)
Abraham — that he would afterward receive as an inheritance. And he went out not
knowing where he should go. [9]By faith he moved into the land that was
promised him as into a strange country, and dwelt in tents; and so did
Isaac and Jacob, heirs with him of the same promise. [10]For he looked for a
Isaac and Jacob — city having a foundation, whose builder and maker is God.
[11]Through faith Sarah also received strength to be with child, and was (Ge 17:19; 18:11-14; 21:1-2. Ro 4:19)
Sarah — delivered of a child when she was past age, because she judged him faith-
ful who had promised. [12]And therefore there came from one (and from (Ge 5:15; 22:17; 32:12. Ec'us 44:19-21.)
one who was as good as dead) as many descendants as the stars of the sky,
and as the sand of the seashore, which is innumerable.
[13]And they all died in faith, and did not obtain the promises, but saw
them afar off and believed them and hailed them, and confessed that they (Ps 39:12)
were strangers and pilgrims on the earth. [14]People who say such things
Strangers and pilgrims on the earth. — show that they are seeking a country. [15]Also, if they had been mindful of
that country that they came from, they were free to have returned again.
[16]But now they desire a better country; that is to say, a heavenly one. And
so God is not ashamed of them, even to be called their God. For he has
prepared for them a city.
[17]By faith Abraham, when he was proved, offered up Isaac. And he
offered him being his only begotten son that had the promises [18](of whom (Ge 21:12)
it was said: In Isaac shall your seed be called), [19]because he considered
that God was able to raise him up again from death. Therefore he received
him back, for a figure.
[20]In faith Isaac blessed Jacob and Esau concerning things to come. (Ge 27:26-40)
[21]By faith Jacob when he was dying blessed both the sons of Joseph, (Ge 48:1,5, 16,20.)
and bowed himself toward the top of his sceptre.
[22]By faith Joseph when he died anticipated the exodus of the children (Ge 50:24,25.)
Joseph — of Israel from Egypt, and gave directions concerning his bones.
[23]By faith Moses, when he was born, was hidden for three months by
Moses — his father and mother, because they saw he was a fine child; neither did (Ex 2:1-3; 1:16,22.)
they fear the king's commandment.
[24]By faith Moses, when he was great, refused to be called the son of
Pharaoh's daughter, [25]and chose rather to suffer adversity with the people
of God than to enjoy the pleasures of sin for a season, [26]and esteemed the (Ex 2:11-15 Ro 8:18)
Moses: sharing in Christ's rebuke — rebuke of Christ to be greater riches than the treasure of Egypt. For he
looked to the reward. [27]By faith he left Egypt, and did not fear the fierce-
ness of the king. For he persevered even as one who had seen him who is
invisible.
[28]Through faith he instituted the Passover lamb and the effusion of (Ex 12:21-27)
blood, lest he who destroyed the first born should touch them.
[29]By faith they passed through the Red Sea as by dry land, which, (Ex 14:22-29)
when the Egyptians attempted it, they were drowned.
[30]By faith the walls of Jericho fell down after they were compassed (Jos 6:20)
Jericho — about for seven days.
Rahab — [31]By faith the harlot Rahab did not perish with the unbelievers when (Jos 6:22-25)

she took in the spies peaceably.
[32]And what more shall I say? The time would be too short for me to
tell of Gideon, Barak, and of Samson, and of Jephthah, also of David and Ec'us cc45, 46.
Triumphs Samuel, and of the prophets, [33]who through faith conquered kingdoms,
wrought righteousness, received promises fulfilled, stopped the mouths of
lions, [34]quenched the force of fire, escaped the edge of the sword, from
weakness were made strong, became valiant in fight, turned to flight the
armies of the other nations. [35]And the women received their dead raised to
life again.
Sufferings Others were racked, and would not be delivered, so that they might
receive a better resurrection. [36]Others tasted of mockings and scourgings;
moreover of bonds and imprisonment; [37]were stoned, were hewn asunder,
were sorely tried, were slain with swords, walked up and down in sheep-
skins, in goatskins, in need, tribulation, and vexation – [38]of whom the
world was not worthy. They wandered in wilderness, in mountains, in
dens and caves of the earth.
[39]And these all through faith obtained good report, and yet did not
obtain the promise, [40]God providing a better thing for us, so that they
would not be made perfect without us.

The Notes

Faith (11:1)

a) Faith and trust in Christ alone is the life and quietness of the conscience, and not trust in works, however holy they appear. Works cannot set the heart at rest, because we perpetually think they are not sufficient or good enough, but too few. And so we fall to doubting, after which comes hopelessness, and thereby damnation. We must leave confidence in works, and rest in faith, which can accept and believe without any doubt that Christ's work on the cross has fully purged, cleansed, and released us from the debt of all our sins.

Chapter 12

An exhortation to be patient and steadfast in trouble and adversity, in the hope of everlasting reward. A commendation of the new testament above the old.

We are called to suffer. For without suffering, no one can be the child of God.

If any love the law of God and are chastised by God, it is a comfort. For thereby he is sure that God loves him [or her] and has him to be son and heir of everlasting life.

Therefore let us also (seeing that we are compassed about with so great a Ro 6:1-6
cloud of witnesses) lay away all that presses down, and the sin that hangs Col 3:8
on, and let us run with patience to the battle that is set before us, [2]looking Eph 4:20-24
to Jesus, the author and finisher of our faith, who for the joy that was set 1Pe 2:1-3; 4:1,2.
before him suffered the cross, disregarding the shame, and is seated on the
right hand of the throne of God.
[3]Consider, therefore, how he endured such speaking against him of
sinners, lest you be wearied and faint in your minds. [4]For you have not yet
resisted to the point of bloodshed, striving against sin, [5]and have forgotten
the consolation that speaks to you as to children: My son, do not despise
the chastening of the Lord, nor faint when you are rebuked by him. [6]For Pr 3:11,12
whom the Lord loves, him he chastens; yea and he scourges every son that Rev 3:19
he receives.
[7]If you endure chastening, God offers himself to you as to sons. What

son is it whom the father does not correct? [8]If you are not under correction (of which all are partakers), then you are baseborn, and not sons.

[9]Moreover, seeing we had fathers of our flesh who corrected us and we gave them reverence, should we not much rather submit to the Father of spiritual gifts, so that we may live? [10]And they for a few short days taught us as it pleased them, but he prepares us for that which is profitable: to receive of his holiness.* [11]No manner of chastisement for the present time seems to be joyous, but grievous. Nevertheless, afterwards it brings the quiet fruit of righteousness to those who are exercised by it.

*Why God chastises.

[12]Stretch forth therefore again the hands that were let down, and the weak knees, [13]and see that you have straight steps for your feet, lest any limping turn you out of the way; yea let it rather be healed. [14]Embrace peace with all men, and holiness, without which no man shall see the Lord.

Ro c12

[15]And look to that no one be destitute of the grace of God, and that no root of bitterness spring up and cause trouble, and thereby many be defiled; [16]and that there be no fornicator or unclean person like Esau, who for one breakfast sold his birthright. [17]You know that afterward, when he wanted to inherit the blessing, he was put by, and he found no means to come by it again; no, though he sought it with tears.[a]

Ge 25:33,34; 27:30-40.

[18]For you have not come to the mount that can be touched, and to burning fire, nor yet to mist and darkness and tempest of weather, [19]neither to the sound of a trumpet and the voice of words, which voice the people that heard it wished away so that the message would not be spoken to them. [20]For they were not able to abide that which was spoken. If a beast had touched the mountain, it was to have been stoned or thrust through with a dart. [21]Even so terrible was the sight that appeared, Moses said, I fear and quake!

Ex 19:12,13; 20:18-21.

[22]But you have come to the mount Zion and to the city of the living God, the celestial Jerusalem, and to an innumerable multitude of angels, [23]and to the congregation of the first born sons whose names are written in heaven, and to God the judge of all, and to the spirits of the just and perfect, [24]and to Jesus the mediator of the new testament, and to the sprinkling of blood that speaks better than the blood of Abel.

The congregation of the first born sons: because the first born were dedicated to God. Ex 22:29,30; Nu 3:13.

[25]See that you do not forsake him that speaks. For if they did not escape who refused him who spoke on earth, much more shall we not escape if we turn away from him that speaks from heaven – [26]whose voice then shook the earth, and who now declares, saying: Yet once more will I shake, not the earth only, but also heaven.

Hag 2:6

[27]No doubt this that he says – yet once more – signifies the removal of those things that are shaken, as of things that have ended their course, so that the things which are not shaken may remain. [28]Therefore, if we receive the kingdom that is not shaken, we have grace whereby we may serve God and please him with reverence and godly fear. [29]For our God is a consuming fire.

De 4:24; 9:3.

The Notes

Esau found no means to come by the blessing, though he sought it with tears (12:17)

a) This text does not exclude repentance in season. Esau repented too late, and therefore did not benefit. Once judgment is pronounced, repentance has no place. The damned in hell will weep and repent, but in vain, for then the time for repenting is past. The blessing that Isaac gave was undoubtedly done by the inspiration of the Holy Spirit, and given in the place of a final sentence, and therefore must necessarily be carried out, and could not be retracted. But if Esau before the blessing was given had changed his ways, and had heartily and earnestly repented, he would surely not have been reproved by God. This would seem to be the true meaning of this text. And indeed, Erasmus makes a like exposition of it in his *Paraphrases*.

Chapter 13

He exhorts us to love, to be ready to take people in, to be thoughtful of persons in adversity, to maintain wedlock, and to avoid covetousness. We are to make much of those who preach God's word, to beware of other teaching, to be content to suffer rebuke with Christ, to be thankful to God, and to be obedient to those who have the oversight of us.

Our duty, if we will have our part with Christ.

Let brotherly love continue. 2Be not forgetful to lodge strangers, for by so
doing some have received angels into their houses unawares. 3Remember
those who are in bonds even as though you were bound with them. Be
mindful of those who are in adversity, as persons who are yourselves also
yet in your bodies.

4Let wedlock be had in honour in all points, and let the bedchamber be
undefiled. For whorekeepers and adulterers God will judge.

5Let your living be without covetousness, and be content with what
you have already. For he has truly said: I will not fail you nor forsake you.
6Therefore we may boldly say: The Lord is my helper, and I will not fear
what man does to me.

De 31:6,8 [See the OT feature at the end of this epistle] Jos 1:5 Ps 118:6

7Remember those who have the oversight of you, who have declared
to you the word of God. See that you look upon the way they live out their
life, and follow their faith.

8Jesus Christ continues the same yesterday and today and forever. 9Do
not be carried about with other and different teaching. For it is a good
thing that the heart be established with grace, and not with foods which
have not profited those who have been occupied in them. 10We have an
altar from which those who serve in the tabernacle may not eat. 11For the
bodies of those beasts whose blood is brought into the holy place by the
high priest to purge sin, are burnt outside the tents. 12Therefore Jesus, to
sanctify the people with his own blood, suffered outside the gate. 13Let us
go forth therefore out of the tents and suffer rebuke with him. 14For here
have we no continuing city, but we seek one to come. 15For by him we
offer the sacrifice of laud always to God; that is to say, the fruit of those
lips that confess his name.

We have an altar.

Let us suffer rebuke with him.

16To do good, and to distribute to the poor, do not forget. For with
such sacrifices God is pleased.

17Obey those who have the oversight of you, and submit yourselves to them, for they watch for your souls even as those who must give accounts. Let them do it with joy, and not with grief. For that is an unprofitable thing for you.

A good conscience gives confidence.

18 Pray for us. We have confidence because we have a good conscience
in all things and desire to live righteously. 19 I ask you therefore even more
so to pray that I may be restored to you quickly.

20 May the God of peace who brought back again from death our Lord
Jesus, the great shepherd of the sheep, through the blood of the everlasting
testament, 21 make you perfect in all good works to do his will, working in
you that which is pleasing in his sight through Jesus Christ – to whom be
glory forever while the world endures. Amen.

22 I beseech you, brethren, submit patiently to the words of exhortation.
For we have written to you in few words.

23 Acknowledge the brother Timothy, whom we have sent from us,
with whom (if he comes shortly) I will see you.

24 Greet those who have the oversight of you, and all the saints. The
people of Italy send you greetings.

25 Grace be with you all.

Sent from Italy by
the hand of
Timothy.

Old Testament Feature - A glimpse into the Old Testament of the 1549 Matthew Bible...
The Lord's assurance that he is with his people and with their leader:

Deuteronomy – The .xxxi. Chapter (verses 1 & 6-8)

And Moses went and spoke these words to all Israel ... Pluck up your hearts and be strong. Dread not, nor be afraid of them, for the Lord your God himself will go with you, and will neither let you go nor forsake you.

And Moses called to Joshua and said to him in the sight of all Israel, Be strong and bold. For you must go with this people to the land which the Lord has sworn to their fathers to give them, and you shall give it to them to inherit. And the Lord, he shall go before you, and he shall be with you, and will not let you go nor forsake you. Fear not therefore, nor be disconcerted.

A Prologue upon the Epistle of Saint James (Abridged)

This epistle was refused in the old time, and denied by many to be the epistle of a very apostle. It does not lay the foundation of the faith of Christ, but speaks of a general faith in God. Also, it does not preach Christ's death and resurrection, nor the mercy that is laid up in store for us in him, nor the everlasting covenant made for us in his blood, which is the office and duty of a very apostle, as Christ says: You shall testify of me (John 15:27).

Yet despite these things, because it sets up no man's doctrine, but cries to keep the law of God, and makes love that is without partiality the fulfilling of the law, as Christ and all the apostles did, and has in addition many good and divine thoughts in it, and has also nothing that is not agreeable to the rest of the scripture, if looked on impartially it seems to me it ought of right to be taken for holy scripture.

As for passages in chapter 2, for which perhaps it was at the beginning refused by holy men (as it ought, if it had meant as they took it), yet if the context is well considered, it will appear that the author's intent was far otherwise than they took him for. For where he says that faith without deeds is dead in itself, he means nothing other than all the scripture does: faith that has no good deeds following is a false faith, which does not justify or receive forgiveness of sins. For God has promised forgiveness of sins only to those who turn to God, to keep his laws. Therefore those who intend to continue still in sin have no part in that promise, but deceive themselves if they believe that God has forgiven them their old sins for Christ's sake. *W.T. (1534)*

[Authorship is generally ascribed to Jesus' half brother James, also the brother of Jude, and first bishop of Jerusalem. See Gal 1:19. Historian Josephus reports that James was martyred c 62 AD. This epistle is considered the earliest book of the NT canon, written 44-49 AD]

The Epistle of Saint James

Chapter 1

He exhorts to rejoice in trouble, to be fervent in prayer with steadfast belief, to look for all good things from above, to forsake all vice, and thankfully to receive the word of God, not only hearing it and speaking of it, but to do thereafter in deed. True religion or devotion: what it is.

JAMES, the servant of God and of the Lord Jesus Christ, sends greeting to
the twelve tribes which are scattered here and there.
[2]My brethren, count it exceeding joy when you fall into various trials,
[3]seeing as you know that the trying of your faith brings patience.[a] [4]And let
patience have her perfect work, so that you may be perfect and sound,[b] Ro 5:3-5
lacking nothing.
[5]If any of you lacks wisdom, let him ask of God, who gives to all im-
Covenant partially, and casts no man in the teeth, and it shall be given him. [6]But let M't 7:7,8; 21:21, 22.
him ask in faith, and waver not. For he who doubts is like the waves of the Mk 11:23-24
sea, tossed with the wind and carried about. [7]Neither let that person think Lu 11:5-13
that he will receive anything from the Lord. [8]A wavering-minded man is Joh 11:23,24
unstable in all his ways.
In Christ we are all alike good, and servants to each other for Christ's sake, each in his office.
[9]Let the brother of low degree rejoice in that he is exalted, [10]and the
rich in that he is made low. For like the flower of the grass, he will vanish
away. [11]The sun rises with heat, and the grass withers, and its flower falls
away, and the beauty of the appearance of it perishes; even so shall the
rich man perish with his abundance.

[12]Happy is the man who endures in temptation, for when he is proved,
he will receive the crown of life, which the Lord has promised to those
who love him.
[13]Let no one say when he is tempted, that he is tempted by God. For
God tempts not to evil, nor does he tempt anyone,[c] [14]but every person is
tempted, drawn away, and enticed by his own fleshly nature and evil de-
sire. [15]Then when desire has conceived, she brings forth sin, and sin when
it is full-grown brings forth death.
[16]Do not be mistaken, my dear brethren. [17]Every good gift and every
perfect gift is from above, and comes down from the Father of light, with
whom is no variableness nor turning to darkness. [18]Of his own will he
begat us with the word of life, that we should be the first fruits of his
creatures.
[19]Therefore, dear brethren, let everyone be swift to hear, slow to
speak, and slow to anger. [20]For the wrath of man does not work that which
is righteous before God. [21]Therefore lay apart all uncleanness, and all
lingering evil and vice, and receive with meekness the word that is grafted
in you, which is able to save your souls. [22]And see that you be doers of the
word, and not hearers only, deceiving yourselves with sophistry. [23]For if M't 7:21-27 Ro 2:13
anyone hears the word and does it not, he is like a man that looks at his
bodily face in a mirror. [24]For as soon as he has looked at himself, he goes
his way and forgets immediately what his appearance was. [25]But whoever
looks in the perfect law of liberty and continues in it (if he is not a
forgetful hearer, but a doer of the work), this one shall be happy in his
deed.
[26]If anyone among you seems devout, yet refrains not his tongue, but
Pure devotion. betrays his own heart into mischief, this one's devotion is in vain. [27]Pure
devotion, and undefiled before God the Father, is this: to visit the father-
less and widows in their adversity, and to keep oneself unspotted from the
world.

The Notes

Joy in trials (1:2,3) a) Almighty God has ever tried and proved his elect by trouble and persecution, and by chastising them with outward plagues. Nevertheless, he does it for good, namely because he loves them and will have their faith exercised. Thus he tried Abraham (Genesis 22) and the Israelites (Deuteronomy 8).

Be sound (1:4) b) 'Sound,' according to the Hebrews, signifies the person who, leaving the wisdom of the children of this world, and selfish acquisitiveness, lives a simple life, and blameless. Such a one was Jacob, of whom see Genesis 25:27 and note thereon.

God tempts not to evil (1:13) c) As for the temptation that we pray to be delivered from in the Pater Noster (M't 6:13, Luke 11:4), it is lust, and sensual and fleshly desire, by which we are enticed to evil. [Ed: the Pater Noster is the Lord's Prayer. The name comes from the Latin for the first two words, Our Father. The MB notes on verses 1:2, 3 & 13 have been adapted here.]

Chapter 2

He forbids them to have any respect of persons, but to regard the poor as well as the rich, to be loving and merciful, and

not to boast of faith where no deeds are. For it is but a dead
faith where good works do not follow.

[**Respect of persons**: undue dealing with people based on rank, wealth, or outward things, at the expense of justice, candour, or love]

Brethren, have not the faith of our Lord Jesus Christ, the Lord of glory, in
respect of persons.* [2]If there comes into your company a man with a
golden ring and in goodly apparel, and there comes in also a poor man in
wretched clothing, [3]and you have a respect to him who wears the fine clo-
thing, and say to him, Sit here in a good place, but say to the poor, Stand
there, or, Sit here by my footstool, [4]are you not partial among yourselves,
and have judged after evil thoughts?

[5]Hearken, my dear beloved brethren. Has not God chosen the poor of
this world, who are rich in faith, and heirs of the kingdom that he prom-
ised to those who love him? [6]But you have dishonoured the poor. Are not
the rich those who oppress you, and who draw you before judges? [7]Do
they not speak evil of that good name after which you are named?

[8]If you fulfil the royal law according to the scripture that says, You Lev 19:18
shall love your neighbour as yourself – you do well. [9]But if you regard
one person more than another, you commit sin, and are rebuked by the
law as transgressors. [10]Whoever keeps the whole law, and yet fails in one
point, is guilty in all. [11]For he who said: You shall not commit adultery, Ex 20:13,14
said also: You shall not kill. Though you commit no adultery, yet if you De 5:17,18
kill, you are a transgressor of the law.

[12]So speak and so do as those who will be judged by the law of liberty.
[13]For there will be judgment merciless to him who shows no mercy. But
mercy triumphs over judgment.*

*Mercy rejoices and triumphs over judgment. For where mercy is, there by God's promise judgment has no place. God has promised all mercy to the merciful only. Now if anyone who is not merciful believes to have the mercy of God, he deceives himself, and there is no word of God for him. For God's promise belongs to the merciful only.

[14]What avails it, my brethren, though a person say he has faith, when
he has no deeds? Can faith save him?[a] [15]If a brother or a sister is without
proper clothing, or destitute of daily food, [16]and one of you says to them,
Depart in peace; may God send you warmth and food – and notwithstand-
ing, you do not give them those things that are needful to the body, what
help is it? [17]Even so faith, if it has no deeds, is dead in itself.

[18]Yea, and someone might say, You have faith, and I have deeds;
show me your faith by your deeds, and I will show you my faith by my
deeds. [19]Do you believe that there is one God? You do well. The devils
also believe, and tremble.

[20]Will you understand, O vain man, that faith without deeds is dead?
[21]Was not Abraham our father justified through works when he offered
Isaac his son upon the altar?[b] [22]You see that faith operated with his deeds,
and through the deeds, the faith was made perfect. [23]And the scripture was
fulfilled that says: Abraham believed God, and it was reputed to him for Ge 15:6; 22:9-18.
righteousness. And he was called the friend of God. [24]You see then how
by deeds a man is justified, and not by faith only.[c] [25]Likewise also, was Jos c2
not Rahab the harlot justified through works when she received the mes-
sengers and sent them out another way?

Deeds follow a true faith.

[26]For as the body without the spirit is dead, so also faith without deeds Ps 119:33-35, etc.
is dead.

The Notes

Can faith save him? (2:14)

a) St. James speaks not here of true faith, which by love is mighty in operation, but of the vain imagination and opinion that unthankful people have of faith. And therefore he calls it dead faith, because no good works follow it, as they do the faith that justifies in the sight of God.

Was not Abraham justified through works? (2:21)

b) To be justified here and throughout this chapter means to be proved just before the world, as in Luke 10:25-37 and 16:11,12, and not to be made just in the sight of God. So when he asks, Was not Abraham our father justified through works? etc., it means, was our father Abraham not proved just by his works? That is, did his works not declare and show that he was just, and were they not sure evidences of his righteousness? It does not signify that Abraham was by his works made just before God, reputed righteous, or obtained remission of sins, for it was by faith that he came by these things, not by works, as Saint Paul bears witness (Romans 4:1-7).

You see then how by deeds a man is justified (2:24)

c) That is, a person is shown to be just, and is openly known to be righteous, by his or her deeds, just as by its fruits a good tree is known to be good. This sentence may not be otherwise interpreted. For there could be nothing more foolish than this saying of St. James, if we were to take it to mean that no one obtains remission of sins but because his works are worthy of so great a benefit. Whoever clings to this interpretation does not understand what remission of sins is, or how the conscience ought to be comforted when it sees that it brings no works to God which are sufficient to please him. And such an interpretation is clean contrary to other clear sayings of the scripture, which teach that remission of sins comes freely, as the Psalmist says: I said, I will acknowledge my offence and accuse myself to the Lord (51:3; 32:5); and, You forgave me the wickedness of my sin (32:5). And see Romans 4:5: To him who does not work, but believes on him who justifies the ungodly, his faith is counted as righteousness. What can be more plainly spoken, than that sins are forgiven to a wicked and ungodly person who does not work; that is, not for any of his works or deeds, but freely.

To conclude, if the gospel does not bring forgiveness but for the sake of our good works and our worthiness, it does not differ from the law; it saves no more than the law saves.

This I trust will suffice the good and wise. For those who bring to this question nothing but a will to brawl and chide will never suffer themselves to be satisfied. And yet if we bring to bear on it the number of authorities, this one place in James is overturned by many statements of Paul, if people must understand by 'justification' always the same thing in them both. Therefore, when Paul says that faith justifies, understand by it that faith causes us to be counted just and reputed righteous, and that our sins are not imputed to us, but are forgiven us for Christ's sake. When James says works justify, he means that works determine us to be just, and show clearly that we are righteous. Thus shall you make them accord.

Space fails me here (O reader), rather than time or will, or I would have spoken more of this thing.

Chapter 3

What good and evil comes through the tongue. The duty of the learned. The difference between the wisdom of the gospel and the wisdom of the world.

My brethren, be not every man a counsellor, remembering that we will
receive the stricter judgment.* 2 For in many things, we all sin.
If a person does not sin in word, he is a perfect man, and able to tame
all the body. 3 Behold, we put bits into the horses' mouths so that they will
obey us, and we turn about all their body. 4 Behold also the ships, which

*He who takes authority to rebuke others concerning that wherein he sins himself, will have greater condemnation. He must be without sin who will cast the first stone.

though they be so large, and are driven by fierce winds, yet are turned about with a very small helm, wherever the helmsman chooses to steer. [5]Even so the tongue is a little member, yet boasts great things.

Behold how great a thing a little fire kindles. [6]And the tongue is fire, and a world of wickedness. The tongue is so set among our members that it defiles the whole body, and sets afire all the course of our life, and is itself set afire even by hell.

[7]All kinds of beasts, and of birds and of serpents and things of the sea, are meeked and tamed by the powers of man. [8]But no man can tame the tongue. It is an unruly evil, full of deadly poison. [9]With it we bless God the Father, and with it we curse men, who are made in the likeness of God. [10]Out of one mouth proceeds blessing and cursing. My brethren, these things ought not so to be. [11]Does a spring send forth at the same place sweet water and bitter also? [12]Can the fig tree, my brethren, bear olive berries, or a vine bear figs? Likewise can no spring give both salt water and fresh also.

*All **humility** and obedience must be according to the wisdom and word of God.

*__Natural__ is all that a person does without the Spirit of God.

[13]If any be wise and learned among you, let him show the works of his good living in humility that is coupled with wisdom.* [14]But if you have bitter envying and rivalry in your hearts, do not be pleased, neither be liars against the truth. [15]This wisdom descends not from above, but is earthly, and natural,* and devilish. [16]For where envying and rivalry are, there is instability and all manner of evil works.

[17]But the wisdom that is from above is first pure, then peaceable, gentle, and easy to be entreated – full of mercy and good fruits, without judging and without dissimulation. [18]Yea and the fruit of righteousness is sown in peace by those who maintain peace.

Chapter 4

Conflict and fighting come from sensuality and covetousness. The friendship of the world is enmity before God. An exhortation to flee slander and the vanity of this life.

Where do conflict and fighting come from among you? Do they not come from the sensuality and covetousness that reign in your members? [2]You lust, and have not. You envy, and have indignation, and cannot obtain. You fight and war, and have not because you ask not. [3]You ask and receive not, because you ask amiss, even to consume it upon your pleasures.

He who is loved by the world is hated by God.

[4]You adulterers and women that break matrimony, do you not know that the friendship of the world is enmity toward God? Whoever will be a friend of the world, is made the enemy of God. [5]Or do you think that the scripture says in vain, the Spirit that dwells in you resists envy, [6]but gives more grace?[a]

Gal 5:17 Eph 4:27; 6:11.

[7]Submit yourselves to God. And resist the devil, and he will flee from you. [8]Draw near to God, and he will draw near to you. Cleanse your hands, ye sinners, and purge your hearts, ye wavering-minded. [9]Suffer afflictions: sorrow ye, and weep. Let your laughter be turned to mourning, and your joy to heaviness. [10]Cast yourselves down before the Lord, and he

will lift you up.

[11]Do not backbite one another, brethren. He who speaks against his brother, and he who judges his brother, speaks against the law and judges the law. But if you judge the law, you are not an observer of the law, but a judge. [12]There is one lawgiver, who is able to save and to destroy. Who are you, to judge another man? Ro 14:4

He who backbites or judges his brother judges the law to be evil, for the law forbids to do so.

[13]Come now, you who say, Today and tomorrow let us go into such and such a city, and continue there a year, and buy, and sell, and make money, [14]and yet do not know what will happen tomorrow. For what thing is your life? It is even a vapour, which appears for a little time and then vanishes away. [15]Therefore you ought to say, If the Lord so wills, and if we live, let us do this or that. [16]But now you glory in your boastings. All such glorying is evil.

[17]Therefore to him who knows how to do good, but does it not, to him it is sin.*

*He who knows and does not, is without excuse. For God has promised no mercy but to him who will do his divine will.

The Notes

The Spirit resists…Submit yourselves to God (4:5-7)

a) Christ's Spirit (which is in all who are his, Romans 8:9) resists hate, envy, and all sin. If we follow the motions of his Spirit, grace increases in us and lusts diminish, and therefore he says, Submit yourselves to God.

Chapter 5

He threatens the wicked rich people. He exhorts to patience, to beware of swearing, to acknowledge our faults to one another, to pray for one another, and one to labour to bring another to the truth.

Come now, ye rich people. Weep and howl over your wretchedness that will come upon you. [2]Your riches are corrupt; your garments are moth eaten. [3]Your gold and your silver are cankered, and the rust of them shall be a witness against you, and will eat your flesh as it were fire.

You have heaped treasure together in your last days. [4]Behold, the wages of the labourers that have reaped down your fields (which wages you kept back by fraud) cry out, and the cries of those who reaped have entered into the ears of the Lord Sabaoth. [5]You have lived in pleasure on the earth, and in wantonness. You have fattened your hearts as in a day of slaughter.* [6]You have condemned and have killed the just, and he has not resisted you.

Slaughter: as when men kill beasts to make merry, and as the Jews did in their thank offerings.

[7]Be patient therefore, brethren, until the coming of the Lord. Behold, the husbandman waits for the precious fruit of the earth, and has long patience for it, until it receives the early and the latter rain.* [8]You also, be patient therefore, and settle your hearts. For the coming of the Lord draws near.

*They had two special rains, one at sowing time and the other at blooming time. If they lacked either, all would be fruitless.

[9]Do not grudge against one another, brethren, lest you be condemned. Behold, the judge stands before the door.

[10]Take, my brethren, the prophets who spoke in the name of the Lord for an example of suffering adversity, and of long patience. [11]Behold, we

count them happy who endure. You have heard of the patience of Job, and
have known what end the Lord made. For the Lord is very pitiful and
merciful.

12But above all things, my brethren, swear not – neither by heaven,
nor by earth, nor by any other oath. Let your yes be yes, and your no no,
lest you fall into hypocrisy.*

*Whether you say yes or no, see it be so. For if you have one thing in the heart and another in the mouth or deed, in vesture or gesture, it is hypocrisy or dissimulation.

13If any of you be vexed with sorrows, let him pray. If any of you be
merry, let him sing psalms. 14If any be diseased among you, let him call
for the elders of the congregation, and let them pray over him, and anoint
him with oil in the name of the Lord. 15And the prayer of faith shall save
the sick, and the Lord will raise him up; and if he has committed sins,
they will be forgiven him.

Fervent prayer avails much.

16Confess your faults to one another. And pray for one another, that
you may be healed: The fervent prayer of a righteous man availeth much.
17Elijah was a man mortal just as we are, and he prayed in his prayer that
it might not rain, and it did not rain on the earth for three years and six
months. 18And he prayed again, and the heaven gave rain, and the earth
brought forth her fruits.

1Ki 17:1, 18, 42-45. Lu 4:25

19Brethren, if any of you err from the truth and another converts him,
20let him know that he who turned the sinner from going astray out of his
way will save a soul from death, and will hide the multitude of sins.

Gal 6:1

The end of the epistle
of Saint James.

A Prologue to the First Epistle of Saint Peter

Saint Peter sent this epistle to the heathen that were converted, and exhorted them to stand fast in the faith, to grow therein, and to increase in perfection through all manner of suffering, and also good works.

In the first chapter, he declares the justifying of faith through Christ's blood, and comforts them with the hope of the life to come, and shows that we have not deserved it, but that the prophets prophesied it would be given us. And as Christ, who redeemed us out of sin and all uncleanness, is holy, so he exhorts them to lead a holy life; and because we are richly bought, and made heirs of a rich inheritance, to take heed that we do not lose it again through our own negligence.

In the second chapter, he shows that Christ is the foundation and head cornerstone upon whom all are built through faith, whether Jew or Gentile, and how in Christ they are made priests, to offer themselves to God (as Christ did himself), and to flee the lusts of the flesh that fight against the soul. And first he teaches them in general to obey the worldly rulers, and then in particular he teaches the servants to obey their masters, be they good or bad, and to suffer wrong from them, as Christ suffered wrong for us.

In the third, he teaches the wives to obey their husbands, yea though they be unbelievers, and to attire themselves in a godly manner, and as becomes holiness. And he exhorts the husbands to suffer and bear the infirmity of their wives, and live according to knowledge with them. And then in general he exhorts them to be soft, kind, patient, and friendly to one another, and to suffer for righteousness after the example of Christ.

In the fourth chapter, he exhorts to flee from sin, and to tame the flesh with soberness, watching, and prayer; and to love each other; and to know that all good gifts are of God. He exhorts everyone to help his neighbour with whatever he has received from God – and finally, not to wonder, but to rejoice, even though they must suffer for Christ's name's sake, seeing that as they are here partakers of his afflictions, so shall they be partakers of his glory to come.

In the fifth, he teaches the bishops and priests how they should live and feed Christ's flock, and warns of the devil, who on every side lies in wait for us. *W.T. (1534)*

[Scholars say this epistle was likely written about 64-65 AD, around the time the city of Rome burned]

The First Epistle of Saint Peter the Apostle

Chapter 1

He writes that through the abundant mercy of God, we are begotten again to a living hope, and how faith must be tried. How the salvation in Christ is nothing new, but a thing prophesied of old. He exhorts them to lead godly lives, since they are now born anew by the word of God.

Here Peter (as other true apostles do) first sets forth the treasure of mercy that God has bound himself to give us for Christ's sake, and then our duty: what we are bound to do in response, if we will be partakers of the mercy.

PETER, an apostle of Jesus Christ, to them that dwell here and there as
strangers throughout Pontus, Galatia, Cappadocia, and Asia, and Bithynia,
[2]elect by the foreknowledge of God the Father through the sanctifying of
the Spirit, for obedience and for sprinkling of the blood of Jesus Christ. Heb 9:12-15; 10:14.
Grace be with you, and peace be multiplied.
[3]Blessed be God the Father of our Lord Jesus Christ, who through his
abundant mercy begat us again unto a living hope[a] by the resurrection of
Jesus Christ from death, [4]to enjoy an inheritance immortal and undefiled,
and that does not perish, reserved in heaven for you, [5]who are kept by the

power of God through faith unto salvation. Which salvation is prepared all
ready to be shown in the last time – [6]in which time you will rejoice,
though now for a season (if need require) you are in heaviness [7]through
manifold trials, so that your faith, once tried, being much more precious
than gold that perishes (though it be tried with fire), may be found to laud,
glory, and honour at the appearing of Jesus Christ – [8]whom you have not
seen, and yet love him; in whom even now, though you see him not, yet
you do believe, and rejoice with joy inexpressible and glorious, [9]receiving
the end of your faith, the salvation of your souls.

[10]Of this salvation have the prophets enquired and searched, who pro-
phesied of the grace that would come to you, [11]searching when or at what
time the Spirit of Christ that was in them was signifying – which Spirit
foretold the sufferings that would come to Christ and the glory that would
follow after. [12]To these prophets it was revealed that not to themselves,
but to us, they would minister the things that are now shown to you by
those who, by the Holy Spirit sent down from heaven, have preached to
you the things which the angels desire to behold.

[13]Therefore gird up the loins of your minds, be sober, and trust per-
fectly* on the grace that is brought to you by the declaring of Jesus Christ,
[14]as obedient children – not fashioning yourselves to your old lusts of ig-
norance, [15]but as he who called you is holy, you also be holy, in all man-
ner of conduct, [16]because it is written: Be holy, for I am holy.

[**Perfectly**: the Gk *teleios* (5049) means completely, without wavering]

Lev 11:44, 45; 19:2; 20:7.

[17]And if it be so that you call on the Father, who without respect of
person judges according to each one's works,[b] see that you pass the time
of your pilgrimage in fear. [18]For you know that you were not redeemed
with corruptible silver and gold from the vain ways that you received
from the fathers, [19]but with the precious blood of Christ, as of a lamb un-
defiled and without spot. [20]He was ordained before the world was made,
but was shown in these last times for your sakes – [21]you who, by means of
him, have believed on God, who raised him from death and glorified him
so that your faith and hope may be in God.

Joh 1:29

[22]And inasmuch as you have purified your souls through the Spirit, in
the obedience of truth with brotherly love unfeigned, see that you love
one another with a pure heart fervently. [23]For you are born anew, not of
mortal seed, but of immortal: by the word of God, which lives and lasts
forever.

Joh 3:7

[24]For all flesh is as grass, and all the glory of man is as the flower of
grass. The grass withers, and the flower falls away, [25]but the word of the
Lord endures forever. And this is the word which by the gospel was
preached among you.

Isa 40:6-8
Ec'us 14:19
Jas 1:11

The Notes

A living hope (1:3) a) A living hope is that whereby we are certain of everlasting life.

Judges according to each one's works (1:17) b) By our works we shall be judged, for as the invisible faith is, such are the works by which the faith is seen.

Chapter 2

He exhorts the people to lay aside all vice, shows that Christ is the foundation they have built upon, and prays them to abstain from fleshly lusts and to obey worldly rulers. How servants should conduct themselves toward their masters. He exhorts them to suffer after the example of Christ.

[V2 is emended from Cranmer 1539, and v3 from Wycliffe 1380]

Therefore lay aside all vice, and all guile and dissimulation and envy, and all backbiting. [2]And as newborn babes, desire the milk (not of the body, but of the soul) that is without corruption, so that you may grow therein – [3]if so be that you have tasted that the Lord is sweet, [4]to whom you come as to a living stone, rejected by men, but chosen by God, and precious.

*We are the church, and the obedience of the heart is the spiritual sacrifice. Bodily sacrifice must be offered to our neighbours. For if you offer it to God, you make a bodily idol of him.

[5]And you, as living stones, are made a spiritual house,* and a holy priesthood to offer up spiritual sacrifice acceptable to God through Jesus Christ. [6]Of this it is contained in the scripture: Behold, I put in Zion a head cornerstone, elect and precious; and he that believes on him shall not be ashamed.

Isa 28:6

[7]To you therefore who believe, he is precious. But to those who do not believe, the stone which the builders refused is made the head stone in the corner, [8]and a stone to stumble at, and a rock to offend those who stumble at the word, and do not believe that whereon they were set.

Ps 118:22
Isa 8:14
M't 21:42
Ac 4:11
Ro 9:33

[**Peculiar**: formerly a word that imported distinctiveness and also belonging: in this case, belonging to God]

[9]But you are a chosen generation, a royal priesthood, a holy nation and a peculiar* people, in order that you should show forth the virtues of him who called you out of darkness into his marvellous light – [10]you who in time past were not a people, yet are now the people of God; who were not under mercy, but now have obtained mercy.

Rev 5:10
Ho 2:23
Ro 9:25

[11]Dearly beloveds, I beseech you: as strangers and pilgrims, abstain from fleshly lusts, which fight against the soul. [12]And see that you lead virtuous lives among the Gentiles, so that those who backbite you as evil-doers may see your good works and praise God in the day of visitation.[a]

Obedience to rulers.

[13]Submit yourselves to every human authority, for the Lord's sake – whether it be to the king as to the chief head, [14]or to governors, as to those who are sent by him for the punishment of evildoers, but for the praise of those who do well. [15]For so is the will of God, so that you put to silence the ignorance of foolish men – [16]as free, and not as having freedom for a cloak of evil, but even as the servants of God.

Gal 5:13
Ro 13:13,14; 13:1; 12:18.

[17]Honour all people. Love brotherly fellowship. Fear God, and honour the king.

Servants.

[18]Servants, obey your masters with all fear, not only if they are good and kind, but also though they be ill-natured. [19]For it is meritorious if a person for conscience towards God endures grief, suffering wrongfully. [20]For how is it praiseworthy if when you are buffeted for your faults, you take it patiently? But if when you do well you suffer wrong and take it patiently, then is there favour with God.

Eph 6:5-8
Col 3:22-24

Our calling is to follow Christ.

[21]For to this indeed you have been called. For Christ also suffered for us, leaving us an example, that you should follow his steps – [22]who did no sin, neither was there guile found in his mouth; [23]who, when he was

2Co 7:4
1Jo 3:16

reviled, reviled not in return. When he suffered, he did not threaten, but committed the cause to him who judges righteously. [24]He himself bore our sins in his body on the tree so that we may be delivered from sin and live in righteousness; by his stripes you were healed. [25]For you were as sheep going astray, but are now returned unto the shepherd and bishop of your souls.

Isa 53:4-6

The Notes

They will praise God in the day of visitation (2:12)

a) Day of visitation: so does Peter call the time in which God, by his inspiration, graciously condescends to call a person to better living.

Chapter 3

How wives ought to order themselves toward their husbands and in their apparel. The duty of men toward their wives. He exhorts them all to unite and to love, and patiently to suffer trouble. Of baptism.

Wives

Likewise let the wives be subject to their husbands, so that even those who do not believe in the word may without the word be won by the conduct of the wives, [2]when they see your pure living coupled with fear.

[3]Your adornment should not be outward, with broided hair and hanging on of gold, or in putting on gorgeous apparel, [4]but let the hid man of the heart be incorrupt, with a meek and quiet spirit – which spirit is before God a thing much set by. [5]For after this manner in the old time did the holy women who trusted in God attire themselves, and were obedient to their husbands, [6]even as Sara obeyed Abraham, and called him Lord – whose daughters you are as long as you do well, not being afraid of every shadow.

1Ti 3:11

Ge 18:12

Husbands

[7]Likewise, ye men, dwell with them according to knowledge,[a] giving honour to the wife as to the weaker vessel,[b] and as to those who are heirs also of the grace of life, so that your prayers be not hindered.

[8]In conclusion, be ye all of one mind, suffer with one another, love as brethren, be tender-hearted. Be mild and courteous – [9]not rendering evil for evil, nor rebuke for rebuke, but contrariwise bless, remembering that you are called to this, even so that you may be heirs of blessing.

Pr 24:17,18 Ro 12:14; 19-21. 1Th 5:15

[10]If anyone longs after life and loves to see good days, let him refrain his tongue from evil, and his lips that they speak no guile. [11]Let him eschew evil and do good. Let him seek peace and pursue it. [12]For the eyes of the Lord are over the righteous, and his ears are open to their prayers. But the face of the Lord is against those who do evil.

Ps 34:12-16

[13]Moreover, who is it that will harm you if you follow that which is good? [14]Notwithstanding, happy are you if you suffer for righteousness' sake. Yea, and fear not, though men seem terrible to you, neither be troubled, [15]but sanctify the Lord God in your hearts.

Isa 8:12

Give a reason for your doctrine.

Be ready always to give an answer to everyone who asks you a reason for the hope that is in you – and that with meekness and fear, [16]having a good conscience, so that when they backbite you as evildoers, they may

be ashamed, seeing they have falsely accused your good living in Christ.
17It is better (if the will of God be so) that you suffer for well-doing, Ro 5:8
than for evil-doing. 18For Christ also suffered once for sins, the just for the Heb 9:27,28
unjust, in order to bring us to God; and was killed as concerning the flesh,
but was quickened to life in the Spirit.
19In which Spirit he also went and preached to the spirits that were in
prison,* 20who were in time past disobedient, when the longsuffering of Ge cc6-8
God abode exceeding patiently in the days of Noah, while the ark was
being prepared, wherein few, that is to say, eight souls, were saved by
water. 21This signifies the baptism that now saves us – not the removal of
soil from the flesh, but in that a good conscience consents to God through
the resurrection of Jesus Christ, 22who is on the right hand of God, and has
gone into heaven, angels, power, and might subdued to him.

[**Spirits that were in prison**: see note (a) to c4]

The Notes

Let the men dwell with their wives (3:7)

a) To dwell with them is, with faithfulness, refusing undue pleasures and ambition, with the adorning of the inner man with the gentleness and gravity of a quiet spirit, with love and reverence, to treat them – not according to our wilful commandment and lust, but according to knowledge, not having them do anything but that which is seemly, and indulging them in nothing that may hurt or corrupt wellness, morals, or manners.

Giving honour to the wife (3:7)

b) Erasmus, in his annotations, notes out of Saint Jerome that to give honour here is not to bow the knee to them, nor to deck them with gold or precious stones, but to abstain from fleshly lusts.

Chapter 4

He exhorts people to cease from sin, to spend no more time in vice, to be sober, to be fit and ready to pray, to love each other, and to be patient in trouble – and to beware that no one suffer as an evil-doer, but only as Christian; and not to be ashamed.

We must be partakers with Christ in suffering, if we will have our part with him in glory.

Inasmuch as Christ has suffered for us in the flesh, arm yourselves like-
wise with the same mind. For he who suffers in the flesh, ceases from sin,
2that he henceforward should live as much time as remains in the flesh,
not after the lusts or desires of men, but after the will of God. 3For it is
enough for us that we have spent the time that is past of our life after the
will of the Gentiles, walking in wantonness, lusts, drunkenness; in eating,
drinking, and in abominable idolatry.
4And it seems to them a strange thing that you run not also with them
to the same excess of disorder, and therefore they speak evil of you. 5But
they will give accounts to him who is ready to judge the quick and the
dead. 6For to this purpose was the gospel preached to the dead:[a] that they
should be judged like other men in the flesh, but should live before God in
the spirit.
7The end of all things is at hand. Be therefore discreet and sober, so
that you may be fit for prayer. 8But above all things, have fervent love
among you. For love covers the multitude of sins.* Pr 10:12

*Hate makes sin of every trifle. Love looks not on small things, but suffers all things.

[9]Be hospitable to one another, and that without grudging. [10]As each one has received the gift, minister the same to one another, as good ministers of the manifold grace of God. [11]If anyone speaks, let him do so as though he spoke the words of God. If anyone ministers, let him do it as of the ability that God gives to him, so that in all things God may be glorified through Jesus Christ, to whom be praise and dominion forever and while the world stands. Amen.

He that suffers with Christ shall reign with Christ.

[12]Dearly beloveds, be not troubled in this heat that has now come among you to try you, as if some strange thing had happened to you. [13]But rejoice, inasmuch as you are partakers of Christ's passions, so that when his glory appears, you may be merry and glad. [14]If you are railed upon for the name of Christ, happy are you. For the Spirit of glory and of God rests upon you. On their part he is blasphemed, but on your part he is glorified.

*If the children of God must all be scourged, and none may be saved but through the same fire that Christ went through, what shall the damnation of the disobedient and unbelievers be?

[15]See that none of you suffer as a murderer, or as a thief or an evil-doer, or as a busybody in other people's matters. [16]If anyone suffers as a Christian, let him not be ashamed, but let him glorify God in the matter. [17]For the time has come that judgment must begin at the house of God.* If it first begins at us, what shall the end be of those who do not believe the gospel of God? [18]And if the righteous are scarcely saved, where shall the ungodly and the sinner appear? Pr 11:31 [19]Therefore let those who suffer according to the will of God commit their souls to him with well-doing, as to a faithful Creator.

The Notes

For to this purpose was the gospel preached to the dead, etc. (4:6)

a) As certain learned expositors will, that which Peter here calls the preaching of the gospel to the dead, he called in the preceding chapter preaching to the spirits that were in prison (3:19). This, they say, means that also to the dead, or the spirits in prison, came the salve or medicine of the gospel and of the glad tidings of Christ's passion, whereby they were released, the power of it being so great that they were brought out of prison to immortality. And because it might be asked how the souls of these blessed ones came forth out of prison – whether in their bodies, or only in the pure substance of the spirit – therefore Peter says that they will be judged like other men in the flesh, that is, when all others shall be judged in the flesh, but they will live before God in the spirit, which signifies that in the meantime, until the judgment comes, their souls will live and rejoice before God through Christ.

Chapter 5

A special exhortation for all bishops or priests to feed the flock of Christ, and what their duty is, and what reward they shall have if they be diligent. He exhorts young persons to submit themselves to the elders, and everyone to love one another, to be sober, and to watch so that they may resist the enemy.

The elders who are among you I exhort, who am also an elder, and a witness of the afflictions of Christ, and also a partaker of the glory that shall be revealed. [2]See that you feed the flock of Christ that is among you, taking the oversight of them not as though you were compelled to it, but willingly; [3]not for wrongful gain, but of a good mind; not as though you

Parishes: the Greek has 'lots,' which is to say parishes or dioceses to which the priests and bishops are appointed by lot or election, to preach God's word to them.

were lords over the parishes,* but so that you are an example to the flock.
4 And when the chief shepherd appears, you shall receive an incorruptible
crown of glory.
5 Likewise you younger people, submit yourselves to the elders. Sub-
mit yourselves everyone, one to another. Knit yourselves together in low-
liness of mind. For God resists the proud, and gives grace to the humble. Pr 3:34
6 Submit yourselves therefore under the mighty hand of God, so that he
may exalt you when the time is come. 7 Cast all your care upon him, for he M't 6:25-34 Lu 12:22-34 Ps 55:22
cares for you.
8 Be sober and watch, for your adversary the devil walks about like a
roaring lion, seeking whom he may devour; 9 whom resist steadfast in the
faith, remembering that you do but fulfil the same afflictions as are
appointed to your brethren that are in the world. 10 The God of all grace,
who called you to his eternal glory by Christ Jesus, will his own self, after
you have suffered a little affliction, make you perfect – will settle,
strengthen, and establish you. 11 To him be glory and dominion forever
and while the world endures. Amen.

We are appointed to suffer in this world.

12 By Silvanus,* whom I consider a faithful brother to you, I have
written briefly, exhorting and testifying how this is the true grace of God,
wherein you stand.
13 The companions of your election who are at Babylon send greetings
to you; and Mark, my son.
14 Greet ye one another with the kiss of love.

[**Sylvanus**, also known as Silas, is often mentioned in Paul's epistles. He may have written down Peter's words and later delivered this letter] **Mark** the evangelist.

Peace be with you
all who are in
Christ Jesus.
Amen.

A Prologue to the Second Epistle of Saint Peter

This epistle was written against those who thought that Christian faith might be idle and without works, when yet the promise of Christ is made to us upon the condition that henceforth we should work the will of God, and not of the flesh. Therefore he exhorts them to exercise themselves diligently in virtue and all good works, thereby to be sure that they have the true faith, as a person knows the goodness of a tree by its fruit.

Then he commends and extols the gospel, and wants the people to hearken to it only, and not at all to men's doctrine. For as he says, no prophetic scripture came by the will of man, but by the will of the Holy Spirit, who alone knows the will of God. Neither is any scripture of private interpretation; that is to say, no scripture may be otherwise expounded than agreeing to the clear places and general articles of the faith, the covenants of God, and all the rest of the scripture.

And therefore in the second chapter he warns them of false teachers that would come, and who, through preaching confidence in false works to satisfy their covetousness, would deny Christ. Whom he threatens with three terrible examples: the fall of the angels, the flood of Noah, and the overthrowing of Sodom and Gomorrah. And he so describes them with their insatiable covetousness, pride, stubbornness, and disobedience to all temporal rule and authority, and with their abominable whoredom and hypocrisy, that a blind man may see that he prophesied it of the pope's holy men and clerics, who devoured the whole world with their covetousness, living in all lust and pleasure, and reigning as temporal tyrants.

In the third chapter, he shows that in the latter days the people, through unbelief and lack of fear of the judgment of the last day, will be even as Epicures, wholly given to the flesh. Which last day shall yet surely and shortly come, he says, for a thousand years and one day is with God the same thing. And he shows also how terrible that day will be, and how suddenly it will come. Therefore he exhorts all to look earnestly for it, and to prepare themselves for it with holy conduct and godly living.

Finally, the first chapter shows how it would go in the time of the pure and true gospel, the second how it would go in the time of the pope and men's doctrine, and the third how at the last people will believe nothing, and not fear God at all. *W.T. (1534)*

[Authorship of this epistle has been disputed. Those who support Peter's authorship give a date of writing c 67 AD. Tradition says Peter died shortly thereafter, crucified during Nero's persecutions]

The Second Epistle of Saint Peter

Chapter 1

Since God by his power has given them all things pertaining to life, he exhorts them to flee the corruption of worldly lust, and to make their calling sure with good works and fruits of faith. He makes mention of his own death, declaring the Lord to be the true Son of God, as he himself saw upon the mount.

SIMON PETER, a servant and an apostle of Jesus Christ, to those who have obtained like precious faith with us in the righteousness that comes of our God and Saviour Jesus Christ.

2Grace be with you, and peace be multiplied in the knowledge of God and of Jesus our Lord.

3His divine power has given to us all things that pertain to life and godliness, through the knowledge of him who has called us by virtue and
glory, 4by the means whereof are given to us excellent and most great
promises, so that by the help of them you may be partakers of the divine

nature, in that you flee the corruption of worldly lust.

He who lacks these things and such like works is blind, and does not understand what the faith of Christ means.

[5]And give all diligence to this. To your faith add virtue, and to virtue
knowledge, [6]and to knowledge temperance, and to temperance patience,
to patience godliness, [7]to godliness brotherly kindness, to brotherly kind-
ness love. [8]For if these things be among you and abound, they will make
you so that you will neither be idle nor unfruitful in the knowledge of our
Lord Jesus Christ. [9]But he who lacks these things is blind, and gropes for
the way with his hands, and has forgotten that he was purged from his old
sins.

He who has such works may be sure that he is elect, and that he has the true faith.

[10]Therefore, brethren, give the more diligence to make your calling
and election sure.[a] For if you do such things, you shall never err. [11]Yea,
and by this means a grand entering in will be given you into the ever-
lasting kingdom of our Lord and Saviour Jesus Christ.

[12]And so I will not be negligent to put you always in mind of such
things, though you know them yourselves, and are also established in the
present truth. [13]Notwithstanding, I think it right, as long as I am in this
tabernacle,[b] to stir you up by putting you in remembrance. [14]For I am sure
that the time is at hand that I must put off my tabernacle, even as our Lord Joh 21:18
Jesus Christ has shown me. [15]I will do my best to ensure, therefore, that
on every side you have something with which to stir up the remembrance
of these things after my departing.

[16]For we were not following deceitful fables when we made known to
you the power and coming of our Lord Jesus Christ, but with our own
eyes we saw his majesty – [17]even then truly when he received from God
the Father honour and glory, and when there came such a voice to him M't 3:17; 17:1-5.
from the excellent glory: This is my dear beloved Son, in whom I have Mk 1:11
delight. [18]This voice we heard when it came from heaven, being with him Lu 3:22 Joh 1:32
in the holy mount.

[19]We have also a right sure word of prophecy, to which, if you take
heed as to a light that shines in a dark place, you do well, until the day
dawns, and the day star arises in your hearts. [20]And first understand this:
that no prophecy in the scripture has any private interpretation.* [21]For the
scripture never came by the will of man, but holy men of God spoke as
they were moved by the Holy Spirit.

[**Private interpretation**: see prologue]

The Notes

Make your calling sure (1:10)

a) Although the calling of God is stable and sure, nevertheless the apostle desires that our works should show to people that we are called.

In this tabernacle (1:13)

b) Tabernacle here signifies his body, as it also does in 2 Corinthians 5:4.

Chapter 2

He prophesies of false teachers, and shows their punishment.

False prophets must be amongst us, and also prevail, and that because we have no love for the truth (2Th 2:9-11).

There were false prophets among the people, even as there will be false
teachers among you, who will slyly bring in damnable sects, even denying
the Lord who has bought them, and bring upon themselves swift dam-
nation. [2]And many will follow their damnable ways, by which the way of

Covetousness is the father of them, and preaching works is the denying of Christ.

truth will be ill spoken of. [3]And through covetousness they will with feigned words make merchandise of you. Their judgment is not far off, and their damnation sleeps not.

[4]For God spared not the angels that sinned, but cast them down into hell, and delivered them into chains of darkness, to be kept until the judgment. [5]And he did not spare the old world, but saved Noah, the preacher of righteousness, with seven others, and brought in the flood upon the world of the ungodly. [6]And he turned the cities of Sodom and Gomorrah into ashes, overthrew them, damned them, and made them an example to all who afterwards would live ungodly. [7]But just Lot, vexed with the unclean ways of the wicked, he delivered. [8]For he, being righteous, and dwelling among them, was vexed in his righteous soul from day to day, with seeing and hearing their unlawful deeds.

[9]So then, the Lord knows how to deliver the godly out of affliction, and how to reserve the unjust for the day of judgment, to be punished; [10]namely those who walk after the flesh in the lust of uncleanness, and despise authority. Presumptuous they are, and stubborn, and fear not to speak evil of those who are in authority, [11]whereas the angels, who are greater both in power and might, do not bring railing judgment against them before the Lord. [12]But these, like brute beasts by nature born to be captured and destroyed, speak evil of that which they do not understand, and shall perish through their own destruction, [13]and receive the reward of unrighteousness.

Jude 8-10

They count it pleasure to live deliciously for a season. Spots they are, and vileness, living at pleasure, and in deceptive ways feasting with you, [14]having eyes full of adultery, and that cannot cease to sin, beguiling unstable souls. Hearts they have exercised with covetousness. They are cursed children, [15]and have forsaken the right way, and have gone astray, following the way of Balaam, the son of Beor, who loved the reward of unrighteousness – [16]but was rebuked for his iniquity: the tame and dumb beast, speaking with man's voice, opposed the foolishness of the prophet.

Balaam

Nu 22:22-31
Jude 11

[17]These are wells without water, and clouds carried about by a tempest, for whom the mist of darkness is reserved forever. [18]For when they have spoken the swelling words of vanity, they beguile with wantonness through the lusts of the flesh those who were clean escaped, but now are wrapped in errors. [19]They promise them liberty, and are themselves the bond-servants of corruption. For by whomever a person is overcome, to him he is in bondage.

It is better not to have known the truth than, knowing, not to live after it.

[20]For if, after they have escaped from the corruption of the world through the knowledge of the Lord and of the Saviour Jesus Christ, they are yet tangled again in it and overcome, then is the latter end worse with them than the beginning. [21]For it would have been better for them not to have known the way of righteousness than, after they have known it, to turn from the holy commandment given to them. [22]It has happened to them according to the true proverb: The dog is turned to his vomit again, and the sow that was washed, to her wallowing in the mire.

Joh 8:30-36
Ro 6:16
Heb 6:4-8
M't 12:43-45

Pr 26:11

Chapter 3

He exhorts them to beware of such as say the day of the Lord is slack in coming. He urges them to lead a godly life, and to expect the Lord's coming, whose long delay is salvation, because he would have none lost, but receive all to repentance.

This is the second epistle that I now write to you, beloveds, with which I
stir up and warn your pure minds, 2to call to remembrance the words that
were spoken before by the holy prophets, and also the commandment of
us, the apostles of the Lord and Saviour.
3This first understand: that there will come in the last days mockers, 1Ti 4:1-5
who will walk after their own lusts 4and say, Where is the promise of his 2Ti 3:1-9 Jude 16-18
coming? For since the fathers died, all things continue in the same estate Eze 12:21-25
that they were in at the beginning. 5This they are ignorant of (and that
willingly): that the heavens a great while ago were, and the earth that was
in the water appeared up out of the water by the word of God – 6by which
things the world that then was perished, overflowing with water. 7But the
heavens and earth which are now, are kept by the same word in store, and
reserved for fire at the day of judgment and perdition of ungodly men.
8Dearly beloved, be not ignorant of this one thing: that one day is with
the Lord as a thousand years, and a thousand years as one day. 9The Lord
is not slack to fulfil his promise, as some count slackness, but is patient
toward us, and would have no one lost, but would receive all to repent-
ance. 10Nevertheless, the day of the Lord will come as a thief in the night, 1Th 5:1-3
in which day the heavens shall perish with terrible noise, and the elements Rev 3:3; c16.
shall melt with heat, and the earth with the works that are in it shall burn.
11If all these things will perish, what manner of persons ought you to
be in holy living and godliness, 12looking for and hasting unto the coming
of the day of God, in which the heavens shall perish with fire and the
elements shall be consumed with heat? 13Nevertheless, we look for a new Rev c21
heaven and a new earth according to his promise, wherein righteousness Isa 65:17-25;
dwells. 66:22.
14Therefore, dearly beloveds, seeing that you look for such things, be
diligent to be found by him in peace, without spot and undefiled. 15And
count the longsuffering of the Lord to be salvation, even as our dearly
beloved brother Paul, according to the wisdom given to him, wrote to you
– 16yea, in almost every epistle speaking of such things, among which are
many things hard to understand, which those who are unlearned and un-
stable pervert as they do other scriptures, to their own destruction.
17You therefore, beloveds, seeing you know it beforehand, beware lest
you also be plucked away with the error of the wicked and fall from your
own steadfastness; 18but grow in grace, and in the knowledge of our Lord
and Saviour Jesus Christ.

To whom be glory both
now and forever.
Amen.

[Dating is difficult, but John may have written this epistle about 90-95 AD, from Ephesus to the congregations of Asia Minor]

The First Epistle of Saint John the Apostle

Chapter 1

True witness of the everlasting word of God. The blood of Christ is the purgation from sin. No man is without sin.

THAT WHICH WAS from the beginning, which we have heard, which we have seen with our eyes, which we have looked upon and our hands have handled of the word of life – [2]for the life appeared, and we have seen and bear witness and proclaim to you that eternal life, which was with the Father and appeared to us – [3]that which we have seen and heard, we declare to you so that you may have fellowship with us, and so that our fellowship may be with the Father and his Son Jesus Christ. [4]And this we write to you so that your joy may be full.

*Light is the doctrine of Christ.

[5]And this is the tidings that we have heard from him and declare to you: that God is light, and in him is no darkness at all. [6]If we say that we have fellowship with him, and yet walk in darkness, we lie, and do not practice the truth. [7]But if we walk in light,* even as he is in light, then we have fellowship with him, and the blood of Jesus Christ his Son cleanses us from all sin.[a]

Heb 9:14
1Pe 1:18,19

*If we confess our sins, God, who cannot lie, has promised to forgive them.

[8]If we say that we have no sin, we deceive ourselves, and the truth is not in us. [9]If we confess our sins, he is faithful and just to forgive us our sins, and to cleanse us from all unrighteousness.* [10]If we say we have not sinned, we make him a liar, and his word is not in us.

The Notes

If we walk in light, the blood of Christ cleanses us from sin (1:7)

a) John here, as in his gospel, and as Paul and Peter in their epistles, teaches first the justifying of faith, and that all mercy comes by Christ only, and then what our duty is to do in return for this kindness. John 8.

Chapter 2

Christ is our advocate. Of true love, and how it is tried.

My little children, these things I write to you so that you do not sin. Yet if any man sins, we have an advocate with the Father: Jesus Christ the righteous; [2]and he is the propitiation for our sins, and not for our sins only, but also for the sins of all the world.

*He that keeps the commandments knows God, and he that keeps them not, knows not God.

[3]And hereby are we sure that we know him: if we keep his commandments.* [4]He who says, I know him, and does not keep his commandments, is a liar, and the truth is not in him. [5]Whoever keeps his word, in him is the love of God perfected in deed. And thereby we know that we are in him. [6]He who says he abides in him, ought to walk even as he walked.

Joh 14:21

[7]Brethren, I write no new commandment to you, but that old commandment that you heard from the beginning. The old commandment is

the word that you heard from the beginning. [8]Again, a new commandment I write to you: a thing that is true in him and also in you. For the darkness is past, and the true light now shines. [9]He who says that he is in the light, and yet hates his brother, is in darkness even until this time. [10]He who loves his brother, abides in the light, and there is no occasion of evil in him. [11]He who hates his brother is in darkness, and walks in darkness, and does not know where he goes, because the darkness has blinded his eyes.*

* He who hates is in darkness, and does not know what Christ has done for him. But he who loves is in light, and understands what Christ has done.

[12]Babes, I write to you because your sins are forgiven you for his name's sake. [13]I write to you fathers, because you know him who was from the beginning. I write to you young men, because you have overcome the wicked one. I write to you little children, because you know the Father. [14]I write to you fathers, because you know him who was from the beginning. I write to you young men, because you are strong, and the word of God abides in you, and you have overcome that wicked one.

He who loves the world, loves not God.

[15]See that you love not the world, neither the things that are in the world. If anyone loves the world, the love of the Father is not in him. [16]For all that is in the world (as the lust of the flesh, the lust of the eyes, and the pride of goods) is not of the Father, but of the world. [17]And the world is vanishing away, and the desires of it. But he who fulfils the will of God endures forever.

Of Antichrist, look in the 4th chapter following.

[18]Little children, it is the last time. And as you have heard that Antichrist shall come, even now there are many Antichrists come already. By this we know that it is the last time. [19]They went out from us, but they were not of us. For if they had been of us, they would no doubt have continued with us. But this happened so that it might appear that they were not of us.

[20]And you have an anointing of the Holy Spirit, and you know all things. [21]I did not write to you as though you did not know the truth, but as knowing it, and as knowing also that no lie comes of truth. [22]Who is a liar, but he who denies that Jesus is Christ? He is the Antichrist, who denies the Father and the Son. [23]Whoever denies the Son, the same does not have the Father.

[24]Let therefore abide in you that which you heard from the beginning. If that which you heard from the beginning remains in you, you also will continue in the Son and in the Father. [25]And the promise that he has promised us is eternal life.

[26]This I have written to you concerning those who deceive you.

[27]And the anointing that you have received from him dwells in you, and you need not that any man teach you – but as the anointing teaches you all things, and is true, and is no lie, and as it taught you, even so abide therein.

Here you see that Christ and sin cannot dwell together, for Christ's Spirit fights against sin.

[28]And now babes, abide in him, so that when he appears, we may be bold, and not be made ashamed before him at his coming. [29]If you know that he is righteous, know also that he who follows righteousness, is born of him.

Chapter 3

The singular love of God toward us. How we in response ought to love one another.

Behold what love the Father has shown on us, that we should be called the children of God. Because of this, the world does not know you: because it does not know him. [2]Dearly beloved, now we are the children of God. And yet it does not appear what we will be. But we know that when he appears, we shall be like him. For we shall see him as he is. [3]And everyone who has this hope in him purifies himself, even as he is pure.

[**Do not sin**: Tyndale>that is, they do not sin of purpose or of consent to wickedness, though they remain weak as long as they are in the flesh, and may fall (*Exp 1Jo*)]

[4]Whoever commits sin, commits unrighteousness also. For sin is unrighteousness. [5]And you know that he appeared to take away our sins, and in him is no sin. [6]As many as abide in him, do not sin.* Whoever sins has not seen him, neither has known him.

*He who works righteousness is born of God and taught by his Spirit.

*__Seed__: that is, the Holy Spirit.

[7]Babes, let no one deceive you. He who does righteousness, is righteous, just as he is righteous.* [8]He who commits sin is of the devil. For the devil has sinned since the beginning. For this purpose the Son of God appeared: to destroy the works of the devil. [9]Whosoever is born of God does not sin, for his seed* remains in him, and he cannot sin, because he is born of God. [10]In this are the children of God known, and the children of the devil. Whoever does not work righteousness is not of God, neither he who does not love his brother.

Joh 8:39-44

[11]For this is the message that you heard from the beginning: that you should love one another – [12] not like Cain, who was of the wicked one and slew his brother. And why did he slay him? Because his own works were evil, and his brother's good. [13]Marvel not, my brethren, if the world hates you. [14]We know that we are translated from death to life because we love the brethren.* He who does not love his brother, abides in death. [15]Whosoever hates his brother is a man-slayer. And you know that no man-slayer has eternal life abiding in him.

*He who loves has escaped death. He who loves not is in death, and a murderer, and has not eternal life.

[16]By this we perceive love: that he gave his life for us. And therefore we also ought to give our lives for the brethren. [17]Whoever has this world's goods, and sees his brother in need, and shuts up his compassion from him, how does the love of God dwell in him?

He that has no compassion does not love God.

[18]My babes, let us not love in word, nor in tongue, but in deed and in truth. [19]For by this we know that we are of the truth, and can quiet our hearts before him.* [20]But if our hearts condemn us, God is greater than our hearts, and knows all things. [21]Beloved, if our hearts do not condemn us, then we have trust before God – [22]and whatever we ask, we shall receive from him, because we keep his commandments and do those things that are pleasing in his sight.

*By love we know that we are in the truth, and have quiet consciences Godward.

Joh 15:7

[23]And this is his commandment: that we believe on the name of his Son Jesus Christ, and love one another, as he gave commandment. [24]And he who keeps his commandments dwells in him, and he in him. And by this we know that there abides in us of the Spirit that he gave us.

Faith is the first commandment, and love the second, and he who has them is in God and has his Spirit.

Chapter 4

Difference of spirits, and how the Spirit of God may be known from the spirit of error. Of the love of God and of our neighbours.

[**The spirits**: Tyndale>Spirits are taken here for preachers, because of the preaching or doctrine, which, if it be good, then it is of the Spirit of God (*Exp 1Jo*)]

Ye beloveds, believe not every spirit, but test the spirits,[*] whether they are
of God or not. For many false prophets have gone out into the world. 2By
this you may know the spirit that is of God: every spirit that confesses that
Jesus Christ has come in the flesh is of God. 3And every spirit which does
not confess that Jesus Christ has come in the flesh is not of God; and this
is the spirit of Antichrist, of whom you have heard that he would come.
And even now already he is in the world.[a]

4Little children, you are of God, and have overcome them. For greater
is he that is in you than he that is in the world. 5They are of the world, and
therefore what they say is of the world, and the world hears them. 6We are Joh 1:12
of God. He who knows God, hears us. He who is not of God, does not
hear us. By this we know the spirit of truth and the spirit of error.

Love is commanded.

7Beloved, let us love one another. For love comes of God. And every Joh 13:34;
one who loves is born of God and knows God. 8He who does not love, 15:2.
does not know God. For God is love.

9In this did the love of God for us appear: that God sent his only be-
gotten Son into the world so that we may live through him. 10Herein is
love: not that we loved God, but that he loved us, and sent his Son to be
the propitiation for our sins.

11Beloved, if God so loved us, we ought also to love one another. 12No
man has seen God at any time. If we love one another, God dwells in us,
and his love is perfected in us. 13By this we know that we dwell in him,
and he in us – because he has given us of his Spirit. 14And we have seen
and do testify that the Father sent the Son, who is the Saviour of the
world. 15Whoever confesses[*] that Jesus is the Son of God, in him dwells
God, and he in God. 16And we have known and believed the love that God
has to us.

[**To confess** means here, and in many places in the Bible, to declare voluntarily as an article of faith]

God is love, and he who dwells in love dwells in God, and God in
him. 17In this is the love made perfect in us, so that we may have trust in
the day of judgment. For as he is, even so are we in this world. 18There is
no fear in love, but perfect love casts out all fear. For fear has painfulness.
He who fears is not perfect in love.

He who loves not his brother, loves not God.

19We love him because he first loved us. 20If a person says, I love
God, and yet hates his brother, he is a liar. For how can he who does not
love his brother whom he has seen, love God whom he has not seen?
21And this commandment we have from him: that he who loves God,
should love his brother also.

The Notes

Antichrist (4:3)

a) Antichrist does not signify any particular man that (as the people imagine) will come at the end of the world. For you see that even in St. John's time he had already come. But all who teach false doctrine contrary to the word of God are Antichrists.

Chapter 5

To love God is to keep his commandments. Faith overcomes the world. Everlasting life is in the Son of God. Of the sin unto death.

Whoever believes that Jesus is the Christ, is born of God. And every one
who loves him who begat, loves also the child who was born of him. [2]In
this we know that we love the children of God: when we love God and
keep his commandments. [3]This is the love of God: that we keep his com- Joh 15:10 Eph 5:2
mandments. And his commandments are not grievous. [4]For all that is born
of God overcomes the world. And this is the victory that overcomes the
*Faith is our victory
world: even our faith.* [5]Who is it that overcomes the world, but he who
believes that Jesus is the Son of God? 1Co 15:57

[6]This Jesus Christ is he who came by water and blood – not by water
[Ed: the bracketing in verses 7 & 8 is as it was originally in the MB, no doubt addressing manuscript issues. The first edition of the Greek Received Text published by Desiderius Erasmus in 1516 omitted parts of verses 7 & 8 because the best evidence was that they were not in the original epistle. However, Erasmus included them in subsequent editions in response to strong complaints from his contemporaries]
only, but by water and blood. And it is the Spirit that bears witness, be-
cause the Spirit is truth. [7](For there are three that bear witness in heaven:
the Father, the word, and the Holy Spirit; and these three are one.) [8]And
there are three which bear witness (in earth): the Spirit, and the water, and
the blood; and these three are one. [9]If we receive the witness of men, the
witness of God is greater. For this is the witness of God, which he
testified of his Son. [10]He who believes on the Son of God has the witness
in himself. He who does not believe God, has made him a liar, because he
has not believed the testimony that God gave of his Son. [11]And this is that
testimony: that God has given to us eternal life, and this life is in his Son.
[12]He who has the Son, has life, and he who does not have the Son of God,
does not have life.

[13]These things I have written to you who believe on the name of the
Son of God, so that you may know that you have eternal life, and so that
you may believe on the name of the Son of God. [14]And this is the trust
that we have in him: that if we ask anything according to his will, he hears
us. [15]And if we know that he hears us, whatsoever we ask, we know that
we will have the petitions that we ask of him.

[16]If anyone sees his brother sin a sin that is not unto death, let him ask,
and he will give him life for those who do not sin unto death. There is a
Sin unto death.
sin unto death, for which I do not say that a person should pray. [17]All M't 12:31
unrighteousness is sin, but there is sin not unto death.

[**Does not touch**: Tyndale> if we do fall, we repent and chastise the flesh, so that we come no more under the devil's claws (*Exp 1Jo*)]
[18]We know that whoever is born of God does not sin, but he who is
begotten of God keeps himself, and that wicked one does not touch him.*

[19]We know that we are of God, and that the world is altogether set on
wickedness. [20]We know that the Son of God has come, and has given us a
In Christ is the life eternal: very God and eternal life.
mind to know him who is true. And we are in him who is true through his
Son Jesus Christ. This same is very God and eternal life.

[21]Babes, keep yourselves
from idols.
Amen.

[This letter may, like 1 John, have been written from Ephesus when John was of an advanced age, c 90-95 AD]

The Second Epistle of Saint John

Chapter 1

He writes to a certain lady, rejoices that her children walk in the truth, exhorts them unto love, warns them to beware of such deceivers as deny that Jesus Christ came in the flesh, and prays them to continue in the doctrine of Christ, and to have nothing to do with those who do not bring this teaching.

THE ELDER to the elect lady and her children, whom I love in the truth –
and not only I, but also all who know the truth, [2]for the sake of the truth
that dwells in us and shall be in us forever.

[3]With you be grace, mercy, and peace from God the Father, and from
the Lord Jesus Christ, the Son of the Father, in truth and love.

[4]I rejoiced greatly that I found some of your children walking in truth,
as we have received a commandment from the Father. [5]And now I be-
seech you, dear lady, not as though I wrote a new commandment to you,
but that same which we had from the beginning: that we should love one
another.* [6]And this is the love: that we should walk according to his com-
mandments.

*Love is the first commandment.

For this is the commandment: as you heard from the beginning, walk
in him.[a] [7]For many deceivers have entered into the world, who do not
confess that Jesus Christ has come in the flesh. This is a deceiver and an
Antichrist. [8]Look to yourselves, that we lose not that which we have
wrought, but that we may have a full reward. [9]Whoever transgresses and
does not abide in the doctrine of Christ, does not have God. He who
endures in the doctrine of Christ, has both the Father and the Son.

[10]If anyone comes to you and does not bring this doctrine, do not
receive him into your house, neither bid him Godspeed.* [11]For he who
bids him Godspeed is partaker of his evil deeds.

[**Bid him Godspeed**: to bid a person Godspeed is to wish them success in a journey or enterprise]

[12]I had many things to write to you. Nevertheless, I would rather not
write with paper and ink, but I trust to come to you and speak with you
mouth to mouth, so that our joy may be full.

[13]The sons of your elect sister
greet you.
Amen.

The Notes

Walk in him (1:6)

a) [Ed: The latter part of verse 6 follows Wycliffe's 1380 translation for clarity. (Tyndale likely did not have Wycliffe to consult.) Jesus came in the flesh, taking flesh into the Godhead, and thus uniting man and God for our salvation. See Article II, Articles of Religion, BCP, and also verse 35 of the Creed of Athanasius. We who so believe are in him through faith, and, if we endure in the word, doctrine, and obedience of Christ, walk in righteousness to the eternal salvation of soul and body, having both the Father and the Son.]

[Again, as 2 John, this letter may have been written from Ephesus about 90-95 AD]

The Third Epistle of Saint John

Chapter 1

He is glad of Gaius, that he walks in the truth. He exhorts them to be loving to the poor Christians in their persecution, and speaks of the unkind dealing of Diotrephes, and the good report of Demetrius.

THE ELDER to the beloved Gaius, whom I love in the truth.
2Beloved, I wish in all things that you prospered and fared well, even
as your soul prospers. 3I rejoiced greatly when the brethren came and
testified of the truth that is in you, how you walk in truth. 4I have no
greater joy than to hear that my children walk in truth.
5Beloved, you do faithfully whatever you do for the brethren, and for
strangers, 6who bear witness of your love before all the congregation.
Which brethren, when you bring them forwards on their journey (as it
befits God), you will do well, 7because for his name's sake they went
forth, and took nothing from the Gentiles. 8We therefore ought to receive
such brethren, so that we also may be helpers of the truth.

[John names an evil-doer, and will openly declare his deeds]

9I wrote to the congregation, but Diotrephes, who loves to have the
pre-eminence among them, will not receive us. 10And so if I come, I will
declare the things he does, scoffing on us with malicious words. And he is not content with that. Not only does he himself not receive the brethren, he also forbids those who would, and thrusts them out of the congregation.
11Beloved, do not follow that which is evil, but that which is good. He who does well is of God, but he who does evil does not see God.
12Demetrius has a good report from all men, and from the truth. Yea and we ourselves also bear witness, and you know that our witness is true.
13I have many things to write, but I do not wish to write with ink and
pen to you. 14For I trust I will shortly see you, and we shall speak mouth
to mouth.
15Peace be with you.

The friends send you greetings.
Greet the friends
by name.

[The author is generally accepted as Jesus' half brother Jude, who wrote shortly before the destruction of Jerusalem in 70 AD]

The Epistle of Saint Jude

Chapter 1

He rebukes such persons as, being blinded by their own lusts, resist the truth; and so that we may know them better, he describes them as such as sin abominably against nature, despise rulers, etc. He exhorts us to build one another up, to pray in the Holy Spirit, to continue in love, to look for the coming of the Lord, and one to help another out of the fire.

JUDE, the servant of Jesus Christ, the brother of James.

To those who are called and sanctified in God the Father and preserved in Jesus Christ. 2Mercy to you, and peace and love be multiplied.

3Beloveds, when I gave all diligence to write to you of the common salvation, it was needful for me to write to you, to exhort you to labour continually in the faith that was once and for all delivered to the saints. 4For there are certain men who have craftily crept in, who were long ago marked out for such judgment. They are ungodly, and turn the grace of our God into licentiousness, and deny God the only Lord, and our Lord Jesus Christ.

5My intent is therefore to remind you, since you already know this,
that the Lord (after he had delivered the people out of Egypt) destroyed 1Co 10:5-10
those who afterward did not believe. 6The angels also who did not keep
their first estate, but left their own habitation, he has reserved in everlasting chains under darkness for the judgment of the great day – 7even as
Sodom and Gomorrah, and the places around them (which in like manner
defiled themselves with fornication and followed strange flesh*), are set Ge 19:24
forth as an example, and suffer the vengeance of eternal fire.

Strange flesh: that is, turning the natural use into the unnatural. Ro c1.

8Likewise these dreamers defile the flesh, despise rulers, and speak
evil of those who are in authority. 9Yet Michael the archangel, when he
strove against the devil and disputed about the body of Moses, dared not
give railing judgment, but said, The Lord rebuke you. 10But these speak
evil of those things that they do not know. And the things they know instinctively, as do animals that are without reason, in those things they corrupt themselves.

11Woe be to them, for they have followed the way of Cain, and are Ge 4:3-8
utterly given to the error of Balaam for the sake of personal gain, and Nu cc22-24; 16:1-35.
perish in the treason of Korah. 12These are spots who of your kindness 2Pe c2
feast together, without fear feeding themselves. Clouds they are without
water, carried about by winds, and trees without fruit at gathering time,
twice dead and plucked up by the roots. 13They are the raging waves of
the sea, foaming out their own shame. They are wandering stars, to whom
is reserved the mist of darkness forever.

14Enoch, the seventh from Adam, prophesied before of such persons,
saying, Behold, the Lord will come with thousands of saints, 15to give Rev 1:7

judgment against all men, and to rebuke all that are ungodly among them
of all their ungodly deeds, which they have ungodly committed, and of all
the hard words that ungodly sinners have spoken against him. [16]These are
murmurers, complainers, walking after their own lusts, whose mouths
speak proud things. They have others in great reverence for the sake of
advantage.

[17]But you, belovEds, remember the words that were spoken before by
the apostles of our Lord Jesus Christ, [18]how they told you that there would 1Ti c4 2Ti c3
be beguilers in the last time, who would walk after their own ungodly 2Pe c3
lusts. [19]These are makers of fleshly sects, not having the Spirit. [20]But you,
dearly beloved, build yourselves up in your most holy faith, praying in the
Holy Spirit, [21]and keep yourselves in the love of God, looking for the
mercy of our Lord Jesus Christ unto eternal life. [22]And have compassion
on some, separating them; [23]and others save with fear, pulling them out of
the fire; and hate the spotted vesture of the flesh.

[24]Now to him who is able to keep you so that you do not fall, and to
present you faultless before the presence of his glory with joy – [25]that is to
say, to God our Saviour, who alone is wise – be glory, majesty, dominion,
and power, now and forever. Amen.

Hereafter follows
the Apocalypse.

[The date of this book is disputed. Eusebius, who wrote in the early 4th century, cites authority dating it near the end of the reign of the Roman emperor Domitian, who died in 96 AD, well after the destruction of Jerusalem (*E.H. Bk5, c8*). The cruel emperor exiled John to the isle of Patmos, where he received the revelation. After his release, John went to Ephesus, and there ended his years, having lived to a very advanced age]

The Revelation
of St John the Divine

Chapter 1

Happy are those who hear the word of God and keep it. John is to write to the seven congregations in Asia. Seven candlesticks, and in the midst of them one like the Son of man.

THE REVELATION of Jesus Christ, which God gave to him so that he could
show to his servants things which must shortly come to pass. And he sent
and showed it by his angel to his servant John, [2]who bore witness of the
word of God, and of the testimony of Jesus Christ, and of all the things
that he saw. [3]Happy is he who reads and those who hear the words of the
prophecy, and keep those things that are written therein. For the time is at
hand.

[4]John, to the seven congregations in Asia. Grace be with you and
The seven churches in Asia. peace, from him who is and who was and who is to come, and from the
seven spirits that are present before his throne, [5]and from Jesus Christ, M't 24:30
who is a faithful witness, and the first begotten of the dead, and Lord over 1Co 15:20 Col 1:18
the kings of the earth.

To him who loved us and washed us from our sins in his own blood,
[6]and made us kings and priests unto God his Father, be glory and domin-
ion forevermore. Amen. [7]Behold, he comes with clouds, and all eyes shall
see him, and they also who pierced him. And all the kindreds of the earth
shall wail. Even so. Amen. [8]I am the Alpha and Omega,[a] the beginning
and the ending, says the Lord Almighty, who is and who was and who is
to come.

Heb 9:11-15 1Pe 1:19 1Jo 1:7 Isa 3:11

[9]I, John, your brother and companion in tribulation, and in the king-
dom and patience which is in Jesus Christ, was in the isle of Patmos for
the word of God, and for the witnessing of Jesus Christ. [10]I was in the
Spirit on a Sunday,* and heard behind me a great voice, as if of a trumpet,
[11]saying, I am the Alpha and Omega, the first and the last. That which you
see, write in a book, and send it to the seven congregations that are in
Asia: to Ephesus, and to Smyrna, and to Pergamos, and to Thyatira, and to
Sardis, and to Philadelphia, and to Laodicea.

[**On a Sunday**: Wycliffe in 1380 had 'the Lord's Day' here, followed by the Geneva and KJV. Coverdale (1535) and the Great Bible followed Tyndale, while the Rheims (1582) had 'Dominical day.' It is believed that the Eucharistic assembly on Sunday (the 'eighth day,' and also the first day of the week) was set by the apostles, because that was the day Christ rose from the dead. Ignatius reportedly described it as 'the day when life first dawned for us.' Many ancients believed that Jesus will also appear again on a Sunday at the end of the age]

The first & the last: Isa 41:4; 44:6.

[12]And I turned back to see the voice that spoke to me. And when I was
turned, I saw seven golden candlesticks, [13]and in the midst of the candle-
sticks one like the Son of man, clothed with a linen garment down to the
ground, and girt about the breast with a golden girdle. [14]His head and his
hair were white like white wool, and like snow. And his eyes were as a
flame of fire, [15]and his feet like brass, as though glowing in a furnace, and
his voice like the sound of many waters. [16]And he had in his right hand
seven stars. And out of his mouth went a sharp two-edged sword. And his
face shone, even as the sun in its strength.

[17]And when I saw him, I fell at his feet, even as dead. And he laid his
right hand upon me, saying to me, Fear not. I am the first and the last,
[18]and am alive; and was dead, but behold, I am alive forevermore, and I
have the keys of hell and of death. [19]Write therefore the things that you
have seen, and the things that are, and the things that will be fulfilled
hereafter, [20]and the mystery of the seven stars that you saw in my right
hand, and the seven golden candlesticks. The seven stars are the messen-
gers of the seven congregations, and the seven candlesticks that you saw
are the seven congregations.

The seven congregations.

The Notes

Alpha and omega (1:8,11)

a) Alpha and omega are letters of the Greek alphabet. Alpha is the first letter, and omega the last.

Chapter 2

He exhorts four of the congregations to mend their ways, and shows the reward of the person who overcomes.

Ephesus. **Messenger** is the preacher of the congregation.

To the messenger of the congregation of Ephesus write: These things says
he who holds the seven stars in his right hand, and walks in the midst of
the seven golden candlesticks: [2]I know your works, and your labour, and
your patience, and how you cannot bear those who are evil. And you
examined those who say they are apostles, but are not, and have found

them liars, [3]and did wash yourself. And you have patience, and for my
name's sake have laboured, and have not fainted.

[4]Nevertheless, I have something against you. For you have left your
first love. [5]Remember therefore from whence you are fallen, and repent,
and do the first works. Or else I will come to you shortly, and will remove
your candlestick out of its place – unless you repent.

[6]But this you have: you hate the deeds of the Nicolaitans,[a] which
deeds I also hate. [7]Let him who has ears hear what the Spirit says to the
congregations. To him who overcomes, I will give to eat of the tree of
life, which is in the midst of the paradise of God.

Smyrna [8]And to the angel of the congregation of Smyrna write: These things
says he who is the first and the last, who was dead and is alive: [9]I know
your works and tribulation and poverty, but you are rich. And I know the
blasphemy of those who call themselves Jews, and are not, but are the
congregation of Satan.

[10]Fear none of those things that you will suffer. Behold, the devil will
cast some of you into prison, to try you, and you will have tribulation ten
days. Be faithful to the death, and I will give you a crown of life. [11]Let
him who has ears hear what the Spirit says to the congregations. He who
overcomes will not be hurt by the second death. Rev 20:6

Pergamos [12]And to the messenger of the congregation in Pergamos write: This
says he who has the sharp sword with two edges: [13]I know your works and
where you dwell, even where Satan's seat is; and you keep my name, and
have not denied my faith. And in my days Antipas was a faithful witness
of mine, who was slain among you, where Satan dwells.

[14]But I have a few things against you. You have there those who
maintain the doctrine of Balaam, who taught in Balak to put occasions of
sin before the children of Israel, that they should eat of meat dedicated to Nu cc22-25; 31:16.
idols, and commit fornication. [15]So also you have those who maintain the
doctrine of the Nicolaitans,[a] which thing I hate. [16]Repent and turn there-
fore, or else I will come to you shortly, and will fight against them with
the sword of my mouth. [17]Let him who has ears hear what the Spirit says
to the congregations. To him who overcomes, I will give to eat manna that
is hid, and will give him a white stone, and in the stone a new name writ-
ten, which no one knows save the one that receives it.

Thyatira [18]And to the messenger of the congregation of Thyatira write: This
says the Son of God, who has his eyes like a flame of fire, whose feet are
like brass: [19]I know your works, and your love, service, and faith, and
your patience, and your deeds, which are more at the last than at the first.
[20]Notwithstanding, I have a few things against you. You suffer that
woman Jezebel, who calls herself a prophetess, to teach, and to corrupt 1Ki 16:31; 21:25.
Fornication is a sin abominable. my servants, to make them commit fornication, and to eat meats offered
up to idols. [21]And I gave her space to repent of her fornication, but she did
not repent. [22]Behold, I will cast her into a bed, and those who commit
fornication with her into great adversity, unless they turn from their deeds.
[23]And I will kill her children with death. And all the congregations will

[**The reins**: the region of the kidneys as the seat of feelings and affections, or of sexual desire or impulses]

know that I am he who searches the reins* and the hearts. And I will give Jer 17:10
to every one of you according to your works.
24To you all I say, and to others of the people of Thyatira, as many as
do not have this teaching and who have not known the deepness of Satan
(as they say), I will put upon you no other burden 25but that which you
have already. Hold fast till I come. 26And whoever overcomes and keeps
my works until the end, to him I will give power over nations, 27and he
shall rule them with a rod of iron, and like the vessels of a potter shall he Ps 2:9
break them to pieces. Even as I received of my Father, 28so will I give him
the morning star. 29Let him who has ears hear what the Spirit says to the
congregations.

The Notes

The doctrine of the Nicolaitans (2:6,15)

a) The Nicolaitans were heretics who held that wives ought to be common property, of whom Eusebius wrote in Bk 3, chapter 29, of his *Ecclesiastical History.*

Chapter 3

He instructs and informs the angels of the three remaining congregations, declaring again the reward of the person who overcomes.

Sardis

And write to the messenger of the congregation of Sardis: This says he
who has the Spirit of God and the seven stars: I know your works. You
have a name that you live, and you are dead. 2Be awake, and strengthen
the things that remain, which are ready to die. For I have not found your
works perfect before God. 3Remember therefore how you have received
and heard, and hold fast, and repent. If you will not watch, I will come on 1Th 5:1-3
you as a thief, and you will not know what hour I will come upon you. 2Pe 3:10
4You have a few names in Sardis that have not defiled their garments,
and they shall walk with me in white, for they are worthy. 5He who
overcomes will be clothed in white array, and I will not put his name out
of the book of life, and I will confess* his name before my Father and
before his angels. 6Let him who has ears hear what the Spirit says to the
congregations.

[**Confess his name**: acknowledge, recognize, or claim the person as one of his]

Philadelphia

7And write to the tidings-bringer of the congregation of Philadelphia:
This says he that is holy and true, who has the key of David – who opens Isa 22:22
and no man shuts, and shuts and no man opens. 8I know your works. Job 12:14
Behold, I have set before you an open door, and no man can shut it. For
you have a little strength, and have kept my sayings, and have not denied
my name. 9Behold, I make those of the congregation of Satan – who call
themselves Jews, and are not, but do lie – behold, I will make them to
come and worship before your feet, and to know that I love you.
10Because you have kept the words of my patience, therefore I will
keep you from the hour of adversity that will come upon all the world, to
try them that dwell upon the earth. 11Behold, I come shortly. Hold that
which you have, so that no one may take away your crown. 12Him who
overcomes, I will make a pillar in the temple of my God, and he will go

out no more. And I will write upon him the name of my God, and the
name of the city of my God, new Jerusalem, which comes down out of
heaven from my God. And I will write upon him my new name. [13]Let him
who has ears hear what the Spirit says to the congregations.

Laodicea [14]And to the messenger of the congregation that is in Laodicea write:
This says the Amen, the faithful and true witness, the beginning of the
creation of God: [15]I know your works, that you are neither cold nor hot. I
would you were cold or hot. [16]So then, because you are between both, and
neither cold nor hot, I will spew you out of my mouth – [17]because you say
you are rich and increased with goods, and have need of nothing, and
know not how you are wretched and miserable, poor, blind, and naked. [18]I
counsel you to buy of me gold tried in the fire, so that you may be rich,
and white raiment so that you may be clothed, so that your shameful
nakedness does not appear. And anoint your eyes with eye-salve, so that
you may see.

[19]As many as I love, I rebuke and chasten. Be fervent therefore, and Pr 3:11,12
Whom God loves, he chastens. repent. [20]Behold, I stand at the door and knock. If anyone hears my voice Heb 12:5-11
and opens the door, I will come in to him, and will sup with him, and he
with me. [21]To him who overcomes, I will grant to sit with me in my seat,
even as I overcame and have sat with my Father in his seat. [22]Let him who
has ears hear what the Spirit says to the congregations.

Chapter 4

He sees heaven open, and the seat, and one sitting upon it, and 24 seats around it with 24 elders sitting upon them, and four creatures praising God day and night.

After this I looked, and behold, a door was open in heaven, and the first
voice that I heard was as it were of a trumpet talking with me, which said,
Come up here, and I will show you things that must be fulfilled hereafter.
[2]And immediately I was in the Spirit, and behold, a seat was put in heav-
en, and one sat on the seat. [3]And he that sat was to look upon like a jasper
Rainbow stone and a sardine stone. And there was a rainbow about the seat, in sight
like an emerald. [4]And around the seat were 24 seats, and upon the seats 24
elders sitting clothed in white raiment, and they had on their heads crowns
of gold.

[5]And out of the seat proceeded lightnings and thunderings and voices.
Seven lamps And there were seven lamps of fire burning before the seat, which are the
seven spirits of God. [6]And before the seat there was a sea of glass like a
Four living creatures crystal, and in the midst of the seat, and round about the seat, were four Isa 6:2,3
living creatures full of eyes in front and behind. [7]And the first creature Eze 1:4-14
was like a lion, the second creature like a calf, and the third creature had a
face as of a man, and the fourth creature was like a flying eagle. [8]And the
four creatures had each one of them six wings about him, and they were
full of eyes within. And they had no rest day or night, saying, Holy, holy,
holy, Lord God Almighty, who was and is and is to come!

[9]And when those creatures gave glory and honour and thanks to him

who sat on the seat, who lives forever and ever, 10the 24 elders fell down
before him who sat on the throne, and worshipped him who lives forever,
and cast their crowns before the throne, saying, 11You are worthy, Lord, to
receive glory and honour and power, for you have created all things, and
for your will's sake they exist and were created.

Chapter 5

He sees the Lamb taking the scroll to open it, and for this the four living creatures, the 24 elders, and the angels, praise the Lamb and worship him.

And I saw in the right hand of him that sat in the throne a scroll written
The scroll sealed with 7 seals. within and on the back side, sealed with seven seals. 2And I saw a strong
angel, who cried with a loud voice, Who is worthy to open the scroll and
to loose the seals thereof? 3And no man in heaven or on earth, nor under
the earth, was able to open the scroll, nor to look on it. 4And I wept much,
because no one was found worthy to open and to read the scroll, neither to
look on it.

5And one of the elders said to me, Weep not. Behold, a lion being of
A lion obtained to open the scroll. the tribe of Judah, the root of David, has prevailed to open the scroll and
to loose the seven seals thereof.

6And I looked, and lo, in the midst of the seat and of the four living
creatures, and in the midst of the elders, stood a Lamb as though he had
been killed, having seven horns and seven eyes, which are the spirits of
God sent into all the world. 7And he came and took the scroll out of the
right hand of him that sat upon the seat.

8And when he had taken the scroll, the four creatures and 24 elders
fell down before the Lamb, having harps and golden vials full of incense,
which are the prayers of the saints. 9And they sang a new song, saying,
You are worthy to take the scroll and to open its seals. For you were
killed, and have redeemed us by your blood out of all kindreds and
tongues and people and nations, 10and have made us kings and priests un- Rev 1:5,6 1Pe 2:9
to our God, and we shall reign on the earth.

11And I looked, and I heard the voice of many angels around the
throne, and around the living creatures and the elders. And I heard thou-
sands of thousands 12saying with a loud voice, Worthy is the Lamb that Dan 7:10
was killed to receive power, and riches, and wisdom, and strength, and
honour, and glory, and blessing! 13And all the creatures that are in heaven
and on the earth, and under the earth and in the sea, and all that are in
them, I heard saying, Blessing, honour, glory, and power be to him who
sits upon the seat, and to the Lamb forevermore! 14And the four living
creatures said, Amen! And the 24 elders fell upon their faces and wor-
shipped him who lives forevermore.

Chapter 6

The Lamb opens six of the seven seals, and many things

follow the opening thereof.

And I saw when the Lamb opened one of the seals, and I heard one of the
four living creatures say, as it were the noise of thunder, Come and see.
1st seal: white horse
2 And I saw, and behold, there was a white horse, and he that sat on him
had a bow, and a crown was given to him, and he went forth conquering,
and to overcome.

3 And when he opened the second seal, I heard the second creature say,
2nd seal: red horse
Come and see. 4 And there went out another horse that was red. And
power was given to him that sat thereon to take peace from the earth, and
that people should kill one another. And there was given to him a great
sword.

5 And when he opened the third seal, I heard the third creature say,
3rd seal: black horse
Come and see. And I looked, and lo, a black horse, and he that sat on him
had a pair of balances in his hand. 6 And I heard a voice in the midst of the
[**A denarius**: a day's wage for a labourer]
four creatures say, A measure of wheat for a denarius,* and three mea-
sures of barley for a denarius; and oil and wine, see you do not harm.

7 And when he opened the fourth seal, I heard the voice of the fourth
4th seal: green horse
creature say, Come and see. 8 And I looked, and behold, a green horse.
And the name of him who sat on it was death, and hell followed after him,
and power was given to them over the fourth part of the earth, to kill with
sword, and with hunger, and with death that comes by the dangerous
creatures of the earth.

9 And when he opened the fifth seal, I saw under the altar the souls of
5th seal: souls under the altar
those who were killed for the word of God, and for the testimony that they
had. 10 And they cried with a loud voice, saying, How long will you wait,
O Lord holy and true, to judge, and to avenge our blood on them that
dwell on the earth? 11 And long white garments were given to every one of
them. And it was said to them that they should rest for a little season, until
the number of their fellows and brethren, and of those who would be
killed as they were, was fulfilled.

12 And I looked when he opened the sixth seal, and lo, there was a
6th seal: earthquake, black sun
great earthquake, and the sun was as black as sackcloth made of hair. And Joe 3:15
the moon became even as blood; 13 and the stars of heaven fell to the earth,
even as a fig tree casts from her her figs when she is shaken by a mighty
wind. 14 And heaven vanished away, like a scroll when it is rolled together.
And all mountains and isles were moved out of their places.

15 And the kings of the earth, and the great leaders, and the rich, and
the high commanders, and the mighty, and every bondman, and every free
man, hid themselves in dens and in the rocks of the hills, 16 and said to the Isa 2:19
hills and rocks, Fall on us, and hide us from the presence of him that sits Ho 10:8
on the seat, and from the wrath of the Lamb! 17 For the great day of his Lu 23:30
wrath is come, and who can endure it? Wis c16

Chapter 7

He sees the servants of God sealed in their foreheads out of
all nations and peoples, who, though they suffer trouble, yet

the Lamb feeds them, and leads them to the fountains of
living waters. God will wipe away all tears from their eyes.

And after that, I saw four angels[a] stand on the four corners of the earth,
holding the four winds of the earth so that the winds would not blow on Dan 7:2
the land, nor on the sea, nor on any tree. [2]And I saw another angel ascend
from the rising of the sun, who had the seal of the living God, and he cried
with a loud voice to the four angels (to whom power was given to hurt the
land and the sea), [3]saying, Do not hurt the land, nor the sea, nor the trees,
till we have sealed the servants of our God in their foreheads.

[4]And I heard the number of those who were sealed, and there were
sealed 144,000 of all the tribes of the children of Israel. [5]Of the tribe of
Judah were sealed twelve thousand. Of the tribe of Reuben were sealed
twelve thousand. Of the tribe of Gad were sealed twelve thousand. [6]Of the
tribe of Asher were sealed twelve thousand. Of the tribe of Naphtali were
sealed twelve thousand. Of the tribe of Manasseh were sealed twelve
thousand. [7]Of the tribe of Simeon were sealed twelve thousand. Of the
tribe of Levi were sealed twelve thousand. Of the tribe of Issachar were
sealed twelve thousand. [8]Of the tribe of Zebulun were sealed twelve thou-
sand. Of the tribe of Joseph were sealed twelve thousand. Of the tribe of
Benjamin were sealed twelve thousand.

[9]After this I looked, and lo, a great multitude which no man could
number of all nations and people and tongues stood before the seat and
before the Lamb, clothed with long white garments and palms in their
hands, [10]and cried out with a loud voice, saying, Salvation be ascribed to
him who sits upon the seat of our God and to the Lamb! [11]And all the
angels stood round about the seat, and about the elders and the four living
creatures, and fell before the seat on their faces, and worshipped God,
[12]saying, Amen! Blessing and glory, wisdom and thanks, and honour, and
power, and might, be to our God forevermore. Amen.

[13]And one of the elders spoke, saying to me, Who are these who are
arrayed in long white garments, and where are they from? [14]And I said to
him, Lord, you know. And he said to me, They are those who came out of
great tribulation, and made their garments large,* and made them white in
the blood of the Lamb. [15]Therefore they are in the presence of the seat of
God, and serve him day and night in his temple. And he who sits in the
seat will dwell among them. [16]They will hunger no more, neither thirst;
nor will the sun light on them, nor any heat. [17]For the Lamb who is at the
centre of the seat shall feed them, and shall lead them to fountains of
living water, and God shall wipe away all tears from their eyes.

[**Made their garments large**: other Reformation bibles have this reading also, but from the Geneva bible onward it is said that they washed their robes or garments. Ed]

The Notes

Angels (7:1-3, etc)

a) *Angel* is a Greek word, and signifies a messenger. And all the angels are called messengers because they are sent from God to man to bring a message. Likewise prophets, preachers, and the prelates of the church are called angels – that is to say, messengers – because their office is to bring the message of God to the people. The good angels in this book are the true bishops and preachers, and the evil angels are the heretics and false prophets, who ever falsify God's word, by whom the church of Christ will be thus miserably plagued until the end of the world, as is depicted in these figures. [Figures: allegories, metaphoric representations. Ed.]

Chapter 8

The seventh seal is opened. There is silence in heaven. The four angels blow their trumpets, and great plagues follow upon the earth.

7th seal: silence, incense, trumpets.

And when he had opened the seventh seal, there was silence in heaven
about the space of half an hour. [2]And I saw angels standing before God,
and to them were given seven trumpets. [3]And another angel came and
stood before the altar having a golden censer, and much incense was
given to him, that he should offer of the prayers of all the saints upon the
golden altar that was before the seat. [4]And the smoke of the incense of the
prayers of all the saints ascended up before God out of the angel's hand.
[5]And the angel took the censer and filled it with fire from the altar,
and cast it into the earth; and voices were made, and thunderings, and
lightnings, and an earthquake.
[6]And the seven angels that had the seven trumpets prepared them-
selves to blow. [7]The first angel blew, and there was made hail and fire,
1st trumpet
which were mingled with blood. And they were cast into the earth, and
the third part of trees was burnt, and all the green grass was burnt.
2nd trumpet
[8]And the second angel blew, and as it were a great mountain burning
with fire was cast into the sea, and the third part of the sea turned to
blood. [9]And the third part of the creatures that had life in the sea died, and
the third part of ships was destroyed.
3rd trumpet
[10]And the third angel blew, and there fell a great star from heaven,
burning as it were a lamp. And it fell into the third part of the rivers, and
[**Wormwood**: a bitter shrub, often symbolic of extreme sorrow and divine judgment]
into springs of waters. [11]And the name of the star is called wormwood.*
And the third part of the waters was turned to wormwood, and many men
died from the waters, because they were made bitter.
4th trumpet
[12]And the fourth angel blew, and the third part of the sun was smitten,
and the third part of the moon, and the third part of stars, so that the third
part of them was darkened. And the day was smitten, so that the third part
of it did not shine, and likewise the night.
[13]And I looked, and heard an angel flying through the midst of heaven
saying with a loud voice, Woe, woe, to the inhabiters of the earth, because
of the blasts to come of the trumpet of the three angels who were yet to
blow.

Chapter 9

The fifth and sixth angels blow their trumpets. The star falls from heaven. The locusts come out of the smoke: the 1st woe is past. The four angels that were bound are released, and the third part of mankind is killed.

And the fifth angel blew, and I saw a star fall from heaven to the earth.

5th trumpet
And to him was given the key of the bottomless pit. 2 And he opened the
bottomless pit, and there arose the smoke of a great furnace. And the sun
and the air were darkened by reason of the smoke of the pit. 3 And there
came out of the smoke locusts upon the earth, and to them was given
power as the scorpions of the earth have power. 4 And it was commanded
them that they should not hurt the grass of the earth, nor any green thing,
nor any tree, but only those people who do not have the seal of God in
their foreheads. 5 And to them was commanded that they should not kill
them, but that they should be tormented five months. And their pain was
as the pain that comes from a scorpion when he has stung a man. 6 And in Isa 2:19
those days people will seek death, but will not find it, and will desire to Ho 10:8 Lu 23:30
die, but death will escape them.

7 And the similitude of the locusts was as horses prepared for battle.
And on their heads were as it were crowns, as of gold, and their faces
were like the faces of men. 8 And they had hair as the hair of women. And
their teeth were as the teeth of lions. 9 And they had breastplates, as it were
breastplates of iron. And the sound of their wings was like the sound of
chariots when many horses run together to battle. 10 And they had tails like
scorpions, and there were stings in their tails. And their power was to hurt
people for five months. 11 And they had a king over them, who is the angel
of the bottomless pit, whose name in the Hebrew tongue is Abaddon, but
in the Greek tongue, Apollyon. 12 One woe is past, and behold, two woes
come after this.

Abaddon is as much as to say, a destroyer.

The 1st woe is past.

13 And the sixth angel blew. And I heard a voice from the four corners
of the golden altar that is before God, 14 saying to the sixth angel who had
the trumpet, Release the four angels that are bound in the great river
Euphrates! 15 And the four angels were released, who were prepared for an
hour, for a day, for a month, and for a year, to slay the third part of man-
kind. 16 And the number of horsemen of war was twenty times ten thou-
sand. And I heard the number of them. 17 And thus I saw the horses in a
vision, and those who sat on them, having fiery breastplates of a jacinth
colour, and of crystal sulphur. And the heads of the horses were like the
heads of lions. And out of their mouths went forth fire and smoke and
brimstone. 18 And by these three the third part of mankind was killed; that
is to say, by the fire, smoke, and brimstone that proceeded out of their
mouths. 19 For their power was in their mouths and in their tails. For their
tails were like serpents, and had heads, and with them they did harm.

6th trumpet

20 And the rest of the people, who were not killed by these plagues, did
not repent of the deeds of their hands, so they would not worship devils,
and idols of gold, silver, brass, stone, and wood, which can neither see nor
hear, nor go about. 21 Also, they did not repent of their murder, nor of their
sorceries,* nor of their fornication, nor of their theft.

[**Sorceries**: magic, spiritism, witchcraft (white or black), divination, shamanism, etc, including drug use. The Gk *pharmakeia* (5331) means 'pharmaceuticals,' and by extension, occult practice. Drugs alter consciousness, and have ever been used to enable (as it is thought) access to the wisdom – and also the terrors – of the occult or spirit realm]

Chapter 10

The angel has the book open. He swears that there shall be no more time. He gives the book to John, who eats it up.

And I saw another mighty angel come down from heaven clothed with a cloud, and a rainbow upon his head. And his face was as the sun, and his feet as it were pillars of fire. [2]And he had in his hand a little book open. And he put his right foot upon the sea and his left foot on the land, [3]and bellowed with a loud voice, as when a lion roars. And when he had cried out, seven thunders spoke their voices. [4]And when the seven thunders had spoken their voices, I was about to write, but I heard a voice from heaven saying to me, Seal up those things that the seven thunders spoke, and write them not.

Dan 8:26

[5]And the angel that I saw standing upon the sea and upon the land lifted his hand up to heaven, [6]and swore by him who lives forevermore, who created heaven and the things that are in it, and the sea and the things that are in it, that time shall be no more, [7]but in the days of the voice of the seventh angel, when he begins to blow, even the mystery of God shall be finished, as he preached by his servants the prophets.

Dan 12:7

Time shall be no more: the mystery of God shall be finished.

[8]And the voice that I heard from heaven spoke to me again and said, Go, and take the little book that is open in the hand of the angel that stands upon the sea and upon the land. [9]And I went to the angel and said to him, Give me the little book. And he said to me, Take it and eat it up; and it will make your belly bitter, but it will be in your mouth as sweet as honey. [10]And I took the little book out of his hand and ate it up. And it was in my mouth as sweet as honey; and as soon as I had eaten it, my belly was bitter. [11]And he said to me, You must prophesy again among the people, and nations, and tongues, and to many kings.

Eze 3:3

Chapter 11

The temple is measured. The 2nd woe is past. The seventh angel blows his trumpet.

And then was given me a reed like a measuring rod, and it was said to me, Rise and measure the temple of God, and the altar, and those who worship therein. [2]And the choir that is within the temple, cast out, and measure it not. For it is given to the Gentiles, and they will tread the holy city under foot 42 months.

[3]And I will give power to my two witnesses, and they will prophesy 1,260 days, clothed in sackcloth. [4]These are two olive trees and two candlesticks standing before the God of the earth. [5]And if anyone would hurt them, fire will proceed out of their mouths and consume their enemies. And if anyone would hurt them, so must he be killed. [6]These have power to shut heaven so that it will not rain in the days of their prophesying, and have power over waters, to turn them to blood, and to smite the earth with all manner of plagues, as often as they will.

Two olive trees and two candlesticks.

Zec 4:2,3, 11-14.

[7]And when they have finished their testimony, the beast that comes out of the bottomless pit will make war against them, and will overcome them and kill them. [8]And their bodies will lie in the streets of the great city which spiritually is called Sodom and Eygpt, where our Lord was

crucified. 9And they of the peoples and kindreds and tongues, and they of
the nations, will see their bodies three and a half days, and will not allow
their bodies to be put in graves. 10And they that dwell upon the earth will
rejoice over them and be glad, and will send gifts to one another, because
these two prophets plagued those who dwelt on the earth.

11And after three and a half days, the Spirit of life from God entered
into them, and they stood up upon their feet. And great fear came upon
those who saw them. 12And they heard a great voice from heaven saying
to them, Come up hither. And they ascended up into heaven in a cloud,
and their enemies saw them. 13And at the same hour there was a great
earthquake, and the tenth part of the city fell. And in the earthquake were
slain names of men 7,000. And the rest were cast into fear, and gave glory
to the God of heaven.

The 2nd woe is past, the 3rd comes quickly.

14The 2nd woe is past, and behold, the 3rd woe will come quickly.

7th trumpet

15And the seventh angel blew, and there were made great voices in
heaven, saying, The kingdoms of this world are our Lord's and his
Christ's, and he shall reign forevermore! 16And the 24 elders that sit be-
fore God on their seats fell upon their faces, and worshipped God, 17say-
ing, We give you thanks, Lord God Almighty, who is and was and is to
come, for you have received your great might, and have reigned. 18And
the nations were angry, and your wrath is come, and the time of the dead,
that they should be judged, and that you should give reward to your
servants the prophets and saints, and to those who fear your name, small
and great, and should destroy those who destroy the earth.

19And the temple of God was opened in heaven, and there was seen in
his temple the ark of his testament. And there followed lightnings and
voices and thunderings, and an earthquake, and much hail.

Chapter 12

There appeared in heaven a woman clothed with the sun.
Michael fights with the dragon, who persecutes the woman.

And there appeared a great wonder in heaven: a woman clothed with the
sun, and the moon under her feet, and upon her head a crown of 12 stars.
2And she was with child and cried out, travailing in birth, and pained,
ready to be delivered. 3And there appeared another wonder in heaven, for
behold: a great red dragon, having seven heads and ten horns, and crowns
upon his heads. 4And his tail* drew the third part of the stars and cast them Isa 9:15
to the earth.

Tail: this tail is a figure of false prophets, as is said at Isaiah 9:15 [Some say the stars represent professing believers. Ed]

And the dragon stood before the woman who was ready to be deliv-
ered in order to devour her child as soon as it was born. 5And she brought
forth a man child who was to rule all the nations with a rod of iron. And
her Son was taken up to God and to his seat. 6And the woman fled into
wilderness where she had a place prepared by God, that they should feed
her there 1,260 days.

Battle in heaven. Satan cast to earth.

7And there was a great battle in heaven: Michael and his angels fought
with the dragon. And the dragon fought, and his angels, 8but did not

prevail; neither was their place found in heaven any more. 9And the great dragon was cast out, that old serpent called the devil and Satan, who deceives all the world. And he was cast into the earth, and his angels were cast out also.

10And I heard a loud voice saying, Now in heaven is made salvation, and strength, and the kingdom of our God, and the power of his Christ. For he is cast down who accused our brethren before God day and night. 11And they overcame him by the blood of the Lamb, and by the word of their testimony. And they loved not their lives to the death. 12Therefore rejoice, O heavens, and you who dwell in them. Woe to the inhabiters of the earth and of the sea! For the devil has come down to you, who has great wrath, because he knows that he has but a short time.

Woe to the earth, for the devil has come down.

13And when the dragon saw that he was cast to the earth, he persecuted the woman who brought forth the man child. 14And to the woman were given two wings of a great eagle, so that she could fly into the wilderness, into her place, where she is nourished for a time, times, and half a time, from the presence of the serpent. 15And the dragon cast out of his mouth water after the woman, like a river, intending that she be caught in the flood. 16But the earth helped the woman, and the earth opened her mouth and swallowed up the river that the dragon cast out of his mouth. 17And the dragon was wroth* with the woman, and went and made war with the remnant of her seed, who keep the commandments of God and have the testimony of Jesus Christ.

[**Wroth**: enraged, angry]

And I stood on the sea sand.

Chapter 13

A beast with seven heads and ten horns rises out of the sea. Another beast with two horns comes out of the earth.

The beast out of the sea.

And I saw a beast rise out of the sea, having seven heads and ten horns, and upon his horns ten crowns, and upon his head the name of blasphemy. 2And the beast that I saw was like a cat of the mountain, and his feet were as the feet of a bear, and his mouth as the mouth of a lion. And the dragon gave him his power and his seat, and great authority.

3And I saw one of his heads, as it were wounded to death, and his deadly wound was healed. And all the world wondered at the beast. 4And they worshipped the dragon that gave power to the beast, and they worshipped the beast, saying, Who is like the beast? Who is able to war with him?

5And there was given to him a mouth that spoke great things, and blasphemies, and power was given to him to continue 42 months. 6And he opened his mouth in blasphemy against God, to blaspheme his name and his tabernacle, and them that dwell in heaven. 7And it was given to him to make war with the saints, and to overcome them. And power was given him over every kindred, tongue, and nation. 8And all who dwell upon the earth worshipped him, whose names are not written in the book of life of the Lamb, who was killed from the beginning of the world. 9If anyone has

Power to overcome the saints.

an ear, let him hear. [10]He who leads into captivity will go into captivity; Ge 9:6
he who kills with a sword must be killed with a sword. Here is the pa- M't 26:52
tience and the faith of the saints.
[11]And I saw another beast coming up out of the earth, and he had two
The beast out of the earth. horns like a lamb, and he spoke as did the dragon. [12]And he did all that the
first beast could do in his presence. And he caused the earth and those
who dwell therein to worship the first beast, whose deadly wound was
healed. [13]And he did great wonders, so that he made fire come down from
heaven in the sight of men, [14]and deceived those who dwelt on the earth
by means of those signs that he had power to do in the sight of the beast,
saying to those who dwelt on the earth that they should make an image to
the beast, which had the wound of a sword and did live.
[15]And he had power to give a spirit to the image of the beast, and that
the image of the beast should speak, and should cause that as many as
would not worship the image of the beast should be killed. [16]And he made
all, both small and great, rich and poor, free and bond, receive a mark in
their right hands or in their foreheads. [17]And no one could buy or sell
except one who had the mark or the name of the beast, or the number of
his name. [18]Here is wisdom. Let him who has understanding count the
number of the beast. For it is the number of a man, and his number is 666.

Chapter 14

The Lamb stands upon mount Zion, and the undefiled congregation with him. The angel exhorts to the fear of God, and tells of the fall of Babylon.

And I looked, and lo, a Lamb stood on mount Zion, and with him 144,000
having his Father's name written in their foreheads. [2]And I heard a voice
from heaven as the sound of many waters, and as the voice of a great
thunder. And I heard the sound of harpers harping with their harps, [3]and
144,000 virgins they sang as it were a new song before the seat, and before the four living
creatures and the elders. And no one could learn that song except the
144,000 who were redeemed from the earth. [4]These are they who were not
defiled with women, for they are virgins. These follow the Lamb wher-
ever he goes. These were redeemed from mankind, being the first fruits
unto God and to the Lamb. [5]And in their mouths was found no guile. For Ps 32:2
they are without spot before the throne of God.
[6]And I saw an angel fly in the midst of heaven, having an everlasting
gospel to preach to those who sit and dwell on the earth, and to all
nations, kindreds, and tongues, and people, [7]saying with a loud voice,
Fear God and give honour to him, for the hour of his judgment is come;
and worship him who made heaven and earth, and the sea, and the springs
of water. Ac 14:15
[8]And there followed another angel, saying, Babylon is fallen, is fallen, Isa 21:9
that great city. For she made all nations drink of the wine of her forni- Jer 50:2;
cation. 51:1-12.
[9]And the third angel followed them, saying with a loud voice, If any

one worships the beast and his image, and receives his mark in his fore-
head or on his hand, [10]the same shall drink of the wine of the wrath of
God, which is poured in the cup of his wrath. And he will be punished in
Fire and brimstone — fire and brimstone before the holy angels and before the Lamb. [11]And the
smoke of their torment ascends up evermore. And they have no rest day or
night, who worship the beast and his image, and whosoever receives the
print of his name. [12]Here is the patience of the saints. Here are they that
keep the commandments and the faith of Jesus.

[13]And I heard a voice from heaven saying to me, Write: Blessed are
the dead who die hereafter in the Lord, as the Spirit affirms, that they may
rest from their labours; but their works shall follow them.

[14]And I looked, and behold, a white cloud, and upon the cloud one
sitting like the Son of man, having on his head a golden crown, and in his
The sickle — hand a sharp sickle. [15]And another angel came out of the temple, crying
with a loud voice to him who sat on the cloud, Thrust in your sickle and — Joe 3:13
reap, for the time has come to reap! For the corn of the earth is ripe. [16]And
he who sat on the cloud thrust in his sickle on the earth, and the earth was
reaped.

[17]And another angel came out of the temple that is in heaven, having
also a sharp sickle. [18]And another angel came out from the altar, who had
power over fire, and he cried with a loud cry to him who had the sharp
sickle, and said, Thrust in your sharp sickle, and gather the clusters of the
earth, for her grapes are ripe! [19]And the angel thrust in his sickle on the
earth and cut down the grapes of the vineyard of the earth, and cast them
into the great wine-vat of the wrath of God. [20]And the wine-vat was trod-
den outside the city, and blood came out of the vat, even up to the horses'
bridles, for the space of 1,600 furlongs.*

[A **furlong** is 220 yards. The Gk *stadion*, plural *stadia* (4712) suggests a stadium or racecourse. 1,600 furlongs is about 200 miles or 320 kms]

Chapter 15

He sees seven angels having seven vials full of wrath.

And I saw another sign in heaven, great and marvelous: seven angels
The seven last plagues — having the seven last plagues. For in them is fulfilled the wrath of God.
[2]And I saw as it were a glassy sea mingled with fire, and those who had
gotten the victory of the beast, and of his image, and of his mark, and of
the number of his name, standing on the glassy sea, having the harps of
God. [3]And they sang the song of Moses, the servant of God, and the song
of the Lamb, saying, Great and marvelous are your works, Lord God
Almighty! Just and true are your ways, King of saints! [4]Who would not
fear, O Lord, and glorify your name? For you only are holy, and all the — Jer 10:7
Gentiles will come and worship before you, for your judgments are made — Isa 3:14
manifest.

[5]And after that I looked, and behold, the temple of the tabernacle of
testimony was open in heaven. [6]And the seven angels that had the seven
plagues came out of the temple, clothed in pure and bright linen, and
having their breasts girded with golden girdles. [7]And one of the four
living creatures gave to the seven angels seven golden vials full of the

wrath of God, who lives forevermore. 8And the temple was full of the
smoke of the glory of God and of his power, and no one was able to enter
into the temple till the seven plagues of the seven angels were fulfilled.

Chapter 16

The angels pour out their vials full of wrath.

And I heard a great voice out of the temple saying to the seven angels, Go
your ways; pour out your vials of wrath upon the earth.
1st angel 2And the first went, and poured out his vial upon the earth, and there
fell a foul and a grievous sore upon all who had the mark of the beast, and
upon those who worshipped his image.
2nd angel 3And the second angel shed out his vial upon the sea, and it turned as
it were into the blood of a dead man. And every living thing died in the
sea.
3rd angel 4And the third angel shed out his vial upon the rivers and springs of
waters, and they turned to blood. 5And I heard an angel say, Lord who is
and who was, you are righteous and holy, because you have given such
judgments. 6For they shed the blood of saints and prophets, and therefore
you have given them blood to drink, for they have deserved it.
7And I heard another out of the altar say, It is so, Lord God Almighty;
true and righteous are your judgments.
4th angel 8And the fourth angel poured out his vial on the sun, and power was
given to him to afflict people with the heat of fire. 9And the people raged
in the great heat, and spoke evil of the name of God, who has power over
these plagues. And they did not repent, to give him glory.
10And the fifth angel poured out his vial upon the seat of the beast, and
5th angel his kingdom was made dark. And people gnawed their tongues for suf-
fering, 11and blasphemed the God of heaven for the anguish and pain of
their sores, and did not repent of their deeds.
6th angel 12And the sixth angel poured out his vial upon the great river Euph-
rates, and the water dried up, to prepare the ways of the kings of the east.
13And I saw three unclean spirits like frogs come out of the mouth of the
dragon, and out of the mouth of the beast, and out of the mouth of the
false prophet. 14For they are the spirits of devils working miracles, to go
out to the kings of the earth and of the whole world, to gather them to the
battle of that great day of God Almighty. M't 24:
15Behold, I come as a thief. Happy is he who watches and keeps his 43,44
garments, lest he be found naked, and men see his shame. 2Pe 3:10 1Th 5:1-3
16And he gathered them together into a place called in the Hebrew
tongue, Armageddon.
7th angel 17And the seventh angel poured his vial out into the air. And there
came a voice out of heaven from the seat, saying, It is done! 18And there
followed voices, thunderings, and lightnings. And there was a great earth-
quake, such as was not since man has been upon the earth, so mighty an
earthquake, and so great. 19And the great city was divided into three parts.
And the cities of all the nations fell. And great Babylon came in remem-

brance before God, to give to her the cup of the wine of the fierceness of his wrath. [20]Every isle fled away, and the mountains were not found. [21]And there fell out of heaven a great hail, as if of talents,* upon people. And the people blasphemed God because of the plague of the hail, for it was great, and the plague of it sore.

[**Talents**: very large and heavy coins]

Chapter 17

He describes the woman sitting upon the beast with ten horns.

And there came one of the seven angels who had the seven vials, and he talked with me, saying to me, Come, I will show you the judgment of the great whore that sits upon many waters, [2]with whom the kings of the earth have committed fornication, so that the inhabiters of the earth are drunk with the wine of her fornication.

Rose-coloured beast

[3]And he carried me away into the wilderness in the Spirit. And I saw a woman sitting upon a rose-coloured beast full of names of blasphemy, which had ten horns. [4]And the woman was arrayed in purple and rose colour, and decked with gold, precious stones, and pearls, and had a cup of gold in her hand full of abominations and the filthiness of her fornication. [5]And in her forehead a name was written: A MYSTERY – GREAT BABYLON, THE MOTHER OF WHOREDOM AND OF THE ABOMINATIONS OF THE EARTH. [6]And I saw the wife drunk with the blood of the saints and with the blood of the witnesses of Jesus. And when I saw her, I wondered with great marvel.

[7]And the angel said to me, Why do you marvel? I will show you the mystery of the woman, and of the beast that bears her, which has seven heads and ten horns. [8]The beast that you see was, and is not, and will ascend out of the bottomless pit, and will go into perdition. And they who dwell on the earth (whose names are not written in the book of life from the beginning of the world) will marvel when they see the beast that was, and is not, and yet is.

7 heads

[9]And here is a mind that has wisdom: The seven heads are seven mountains on which the woman sits. [10]They are also seven kings. Five are fallen, and one is, and another is not yet come. When he comes, he must continue a space. [11]And the beast that was and is not, is even the eighth, and is of the seven, and will go into destruction.

10 horns

[12]And the ten horns that you see are ten kings who have received no kingdom, but shall receive power as kings at one hour with the beast. [13]These are of one mind, and will give their power and strength to the beast. [14]These will fight with the Lamb, and the Lamb will overcome them, for he is Lord of lords and King of kings. And those who are on his side are called and chosen and faithful. 1Ti 6:15

[15]And he said to me, The waters that you saw, where the whore sits, are people and folk and nations and tongues. [16]And the ten horns that you saw upon the beast are those who will hate the whore, and will make her desolate and naked, and will eat her flesh, and burn her with fire. [17]For

God has put in their hearts to fulfil his will, and to act with one accord,
and to give her kingdom to the beast until the words of God are fulfilled.
18And the woman that you saw is that great city that reigns over the kings
of the earth.

Chapter 18

Those who love the world are sorry about the fall of Babylon, but those who are of God have cause to rejoice over her destruction.

And after that, I saw another angel come from heaven, having great pow-
er, and the earth was lightened with his brightness. 2And he cried mightily
with a strong voice, saying, Great Babylon is fallen, is fallen, and has Isa 21:9
become the habitation of devils, and the hold of all foul spirits, and a cage Jer 50:2;
of all unclean and hateful birds. 3For all nations have drunk of the wine of 51:1-12.
the wrath of her fornication. And the kings of the earth have committed
fornication with her, and her merchants were made rich from the abun-
dance of her pleasures.

4And I heard another voice from heaven say, Come away from her,
Come away from her. my people, that you be not partakers in her sins, that you receive not of
her plagues. 5For her sins have gone up to heaven, and God has remem-
bered her wickedness. 6Reward her even as she rewarded you, and give
her double according to her works. And pour in double for her, in the
same cup that she filled for you. 7And as much as she glorified herself and
lived wantonly, so much pour in for her of punishment and sorrow. For
she said in herself, I sit being a queen, and am no widow, and shall see no Isa 47:7
sorrow. 8Therefore her plagues shall come at one day: death, and sorrow,
and hunger; and she will be burnt with fire. For strong is the Lord God
who judges her.

9And the kings of the earth who have committed fornication with her
and have lived wantonly with her will weep and wail over her, when they
see the smoke of her burning. 10And they will stand afar off for fear of her
punishment, saying, Alas, alas, that great city Babylon, that mighty city!
For at one hour has her judgment come.

11And the merchants of the earth will weep and wail in themselves,
Merchants weep. because no one will buy their wares any more – 12wares of gold and silver
and precious stones, neither of pearl, and fine linens, and purple and
scarlet cloth; and all fragrant wood, and all manner of vessels of ivory,
and all manner of vessels of most precious wood, and of brass and iron;
13and cinnamon and incense, and oyntments, frankincense, wine, and oil,
and fine flour and wheat; and work animals, and sheep, and horses, and
chariots; and bodies and souls of men.

14And the apples that your soul lusted after are departed from you.
And all things that were choice and precious to you are departed from
you, and you shall find them no more. 15The merchants of these things,
who had gotten rich, will stand afar off from her, for fear of her punish-
ment, weeping and wailing, 16and saying, Alas, alas, that great city, which

was clothed in fine linen and purple and scarlet, and decked with gold and precious stones and pearls! [17]For at one hour such great riches have come to nothing.

And every ship captain, and all they that occupied ships, and sailors who work at sea, stood afar off, [18]and cried out when they saw the smoke of her burning, saying, What city is like this great city? [19]And they cast dust on their heads and cried out, weeping and wailing, and said, Alas, alas, that great city, wherein all who had ships in the sea were made rich, by reason of her great wealth. For at one hour she is made desolate.

[20]Rejoice over her, O heaven, and ye holy apostles and prophets, for God has given your judgment on her.

[21]And a mighty angel took up a stone like a great millstone, and cast it into the sea, saying, With such violence shall that great city Babylon be cast down, and shall be found no more. [22]And the sound of harpers and musicians, and of pipers and trumpeters, shall be heard no more in you. And no craftsman, of whatsoever craft he be, shall be found any more in you. And the sound of a mill shall be heard no more in you. [23]And the light of the candle shall no more shine in you. And the voice of the bridegroom and of the bride shall be heard no more in you. For your merchants were the great men of the earth, and with your enchantment were deceived (Jer 7:32-34)

The blood of the prophets and of the saints.

all nations. [24]And in her was found the blood of the prophets and of the saints, and of all that were slain upon the earth.

Chapter 19

Praise or thanks are given to God for judging the whore, and for avenging the blood of his servants. The angel will not be worshipped. The fowls and birds are called to the slaughter.

[V2 is emended after the 1557 Geneva bible for clarity]

And after that I heard the voice of a great many people in heaven saying, Alleluia! Salvation and glory and honour and power be ascribed to the Lord our God! [2]For true and righteous are his judgments, for he has judged the great whore who corrupted the earth with her fornication, and has avenged the blood of his servants shed by her hand. [3]And again they said, Alleluia! And smoke rose up forevermore. [4]And the 24 elders and the four living creatures fell down and worshipped God who sat on the seat, saying, Amen! Alleluia! [5]And a voice came out of the seat, saying, Praise our Lord God, all you who are his servants, and you who fear him, both small and great!

The marriage of the Lamb

[6]And I heard the voice of a great many people, like the sound of many waters, and like the sound of strong thunderings, saying, Alleluia, for God Omnipotent reigns! [7]Let us be glad and rejoice, and give honour to him, for the marriage of the Lamb has come, and his wife has made herself (M't 22:2) ready. [8]And to her it was granted that she should be arrayed with pure and splendid linens. For fine linen is the righteousness of the saints.

[9]And he said to me, Happy are those who are called to the Lamb's (Lu 14:16) supper! And he said to me, These are the true sayings of God. [10]And I fell at his feet to worship him. And he said to me, See you do it not. For I am

your fellow servant, and one of your brethren, and of those who have the
testimony of Jesus. Worship God. For the testimony of Jesus is the spirit
of prophecy.[*]

[**Spirit of prophecy**: word or message of heavenly truth for mankind, giving light where darkness is]

[11]And I saw heaven open, and behold, a white horse. And he who sat
upon him was faithful and true, and in righteousness did judge and make
battle. [12]His eyes were as a flame of fire, and on his head were many
crowns, and he had a name written that no one knew but he himself.
Vesture dipped in blood
[13]And he was clothed with a vesture dipped in blood, and his name is Isa 63:1-6
called the Word of God. [14]And the warriors who were in heaven followed
him upon white horses, clothed with white and pure linen. [15]And out of
his mouth went a sharp sword,[a] that with it he should smite the heathen.
And he will rule them with a rod of iron. And he trod the wine-vat of the
fierceness and wrath of Almighty God. [16]And he has on his vesture, and
on his thigh a name written: King of kings and Lord of lords. 1Ti 6:15

[17]And I saw an angel standing in the sun. And he cried out with a loud
voice, saying to all the fowls that fly in the midst of heaven, Come and
gather yourselves together to the supper of the great God, [18]so that you Jer 7:33
may eat the flesh of kings and of high commanders, and the flesh of
mighty men, and the flesh of horses and of those who sit on them, and the
flesh of all free men and bondmen, and of small and great. [19]And I saw
the beast and the kings of the earth and their warriors gathered together to
make battle against him who sat on the horse, and against his soldiers.

[20]And the beast was taken, and with him that false prophet who
worked miracles before him, by which he deceived them that received the
mark of the beast and them that worshipped his image. These both were
cast into a pond of fire burning with brimstone.[b] [21]And the rest were slain
with the sword of him who sat upon the horse, which sword proceeded out
of his mouth. And all the fowls were filled full with their flesh.

The Notes

Out of his mouth a sharp sword (19:15)

a) By this sword is signified the word of God, as it is said at Ephesians 6:17, Hebrews 4:12, Revelation 1:16, and Isaiah 49:2.

Brimstone (19:20)

b) [*Brimstone* was formerly the popular name for elemental sulphur (or sulfur), a non-metallic substance that commonly occurs around volcanoes, and is one of the more abundant elements in the earth's crust. Pure sulphur is bright yellow. It burns easily, with a low melting point. In volcanoes it may be spewn forth as molten liquid that cools to a porous, brittle substance. It may also occur as a brilliant lemon-yellow crystal rock (Rev 9:17). When sulphur burns, it produces noxious odours and gas. Sometimes the ancients used the word 'brimstone' to refer generally to anything that burned with much flame, smoke, or odour. Through biblical usage, the phrase 'fire and brimstone' has come to express God's wrath and judgment. Ed.]

Chapter 20

The dragon is bound for a thousand years. The dead arise and receive judgment.

And I saw an angel come down from heaven, having the key of the bottomless pit and a great chain in his hand. 2And he took the dragon, that old serpent, which is the devil and Satan, and he bound him a thousand years, 3and cast him into the bottomless pit. And he bound him and set a seal on him, that he should deceive the people no more till the thousand years were fulfilled. And after that, he must be loosed for a little season.

Blessed are those who have part in the first resurrection.

Eph 2:6 1Jo 5:4 Joh 5:25 Col 1:13; 3:1. Rev 21:8

4And I saw seats, and they that sat upon them; and judgment was given to them. And I saw the souls of those who were beheaded for the witness of Jesus and for the word of God, who had not worshipped the beast, nor his image, neither had taken his mark upon their foreheads or on their hands. And they lived and reigned with Christ a thousand years. 5But the others of the dead did not live again until the thousand years were finished. This is that first resurrection. 6Blessed and holy is he who has part in the first resurrection. For on such the second death shall have no power. For they shall be the priests of God and of Christ, and shall reign with him a thousand years.[a]

Jer 38,39

7And when the thousand years are expired, Satan will be loosed out of his prison, 8and will go out to deceive the people who are in the four quarters of the earth, Gog and Magog, to gather them together to battle, whose number is as the sand of the sea. 9And they went up on the plain of the earth, and compassed the tents of the saints about, and the beloved city. And fire came down from God out of heaven, and devoured them. 10And the devil who deceived them was cast into the lake of fire and brimstone, where the beast and the false prophet were, and shall be tormented day and night forevermore.

The dead are judged.

11And I saw a great white seat, and him that sat on it, from whose face both the earth and heaven fled away; and their place was found no more. 12And I saw the dead, both great and small, stand before God. And the books were opened. And another book was opened, which is the book of life. And the dead were judged by those things that were written in the books, according to their deeds. 13And the sea gave up the dead that were in her, and death and hell delivered up the dead that were in them. And they were judged, every person according to his deeds. 14And death and hell were cast into the lake of fire; this is the second death. 15And whosoever was not found written in the book of life, was cast into the lake of fire.

The Notes

The thousand year reign and first resurrection (20:1-8)

a) [Point of interest: Augustine of Hippo, with whom the Reformers agreed, taught that now is the millennial period, during which we pass from death to life when we hear the voice of the Son of God (John 5:25. See Rogers' note). In accordance with the symbolic use of the Jews, the number 1,000 signifies a very long, indefinite period of time. Coming to faith is the resurrection of the soul, the first resurrection. Anyone who has not come to faith and the new life now, during the millennium, will at the second coming, second resurrection, and day of judgment, pass into the second death. The second resurrection will be of all who have lived on the earth, believer and unbeliever, in their bodies. Some will rise to the judgment of mercy, but others to condemnation, which is the second death. (20:14,15) *City, Bk XX.*]

Chapter 21

In this chapter is described the new and spiritual Jerusalem.

And I saw a new heaven and a new earth, for the first heaven and the first
A new heaven and a new earth earth were vanished away; and there was no more sea. [2]And I, John, saw Isa 65:17-25;
that holy city, new Jerusalem, come down from God out of heaven, pre- 66:22. 2Pe c3
pared as a bride made beautiful for her husband. [3]And I heard a great
voice out of heaven saying, Behold, the tabernacle of God is with men,
and he will dwell with them. And they shall be his people, and God
himself will be with them and be their God. [4]And God will wipe away all Isa 25:8
tears from their eyes. And there will be no more death, nor sorrow, nor
crying; neither will there be any more pain. For the former things are
gone. [5]And he that sat upon the seat said, Behold, I make all things new.
And he said to me, Write, for these words are faithful and true.
[6]And he said to me, It is done. I am the Alpha and Omega, the Rev 1, note a
beginning and the end. I will give to him who is a-thirst of the well of the
water of life, free. [7]He that overcomes shall inherit all things, and I will be
his God, and he will be my child. [8]But the fearful and unbelieving, and the
abominable, and murderers, and whoremongers, and sorcerers, and idol-
aters, and all liars, will have their part in the lake that burns with fire and
brimstone, which is the second death. Rev 20:6
[9]And one of the seven angels that had the seven vials full of the seven
last plagues came to me and talked with me, saying, Come, I will show
you the bride, the Lamb's wife. [10]And he carried me away in the Spirit to
a great and a high mountain, and he showed me the great city, holy Je-
Holy Jerusalem rusalem, descending out of heaven from God, [11]having the brightness of
God. And her brilliance was like a stone most precious, even a jasper
clear as crystal. [12]And she had walls great and high, and had 12 gates, and
at the gates 12 angels, and names written which are the names of the 12
tribes of Israel. [13]On the east side were three gates, and on the north side
three gates, and on the south three gates, and on the west three gates.
[14]And the wall of the city had 12 foundations, and in them the names of
the Lamb's 12 apostles.
[15]And he who talked with me had a golden reed to measure the city Zec c2
with, and its gates and its wall. [16]And the city was built four-square, and
the length was the same as the breadth of it. And he measured the city
with the reed: 12,000 furlongs,* and the length and the breadth and the
height of it were equal. [17]And he measured its wall: 144 cubits* according
to the measure of a man, which the angel had.
[18]And its wall was constructed of jasper. And the city was pure gold
like clear glass, [19]and the foundations of the wall of the city were adorned
with all manner of precious stones. The first foundation was jasper, the
second sapphire, the third a chalcedony, the fourth an emerald, [20]the fifth
sardonyx, the sixth sardius, the seventh chrysolite, the eighth beryl, the
ninth a topaz, the tenth a chrysoprase, the eleventh a jacinth, the twelfth
an amethyst.
[21]The 12 gates were 12 pearls; every gate was of one pearl. And the

[**12,000 furlongs**: the number 12 symbolizes the patriarchs, the tribes of Israel, and also the apostles; 1,000 symbolizes a totality (Augustine, *City*). The number 12,000, being the product of 12 and 1,000, therefore carries rich symbolism. 144 is the product of 12 x 12, also suggesting symbolic meaning. **144 cubits**: a cubit was the distance from a man's elbow to the tip of the middle finger, roughly 18–20″]

street of the city was pure gold, as though shining glass. 22 And there was
no temple in it, because the Lord God Almighty and the Lamb are the
temple of it. 23 And the city has no need of the sun or of the moon to give
it light, because the brightness of God did light it, and the Lamb was the light of it. Isa 60:19-21
24 And the people who are saved will walk in the light of it, and
the kings of the earth will bring their glory to it. 25 And its gates are not
shut daily, 26 because there will be no night there. 27 And there shall enter
into it no unclean thing, neither whatsoever works abomination or makes
lies, but only they who are written in the Lamb's book of life.

Chapter 22

The river of the water of life. The fruitfulness and light of the city of God. The Lord does ever give his servants warning of things to come. The angel will not be worshipped. Nothing may be added to the word of God, nor taken away from it.

And he showed me a pure river of the water of life, clear as crystal,
proceeding out of the seat of God and of the Lamb, 2 in the middle of the
street of the city. And on either side of the river there was the wood of
Wood of life life, which bore 12 kinds of fruit, and gave fruit every month. And the Ps 46:4
leaves of the wood served to heal the people. 3 And there shall be no more
curse, but the seat of God and the Lamb will be in it, and his servants will
serve him. 4 And they will see his face, and his name will be in their
foreheads. 5 And there will be no night there, and they need no lamp, nor
the light of the sun, for the Lord God gives them light. And they will reign Isa 60:19-21.
forevermore.

6 And he said to me, These sayings are faithful and true. And the Lord
God of the saints and prophets sent his angel to show to his servants the
things that must shortly be fulfilled.

7 Behold, I come shortly. Happy is he who keeps the words of the
prophecy of this book.

8 I am John, who saw these things and heard them. And when I had
heard and seen, I fell down to worship before the feet of the angel that
showed me these things. 9 And he said to me, See you do it not. For I am
your fellow servant, and the fellow servant of your brethren the prophets,
and of those who keep the sayings of this book. But worship God.

10 And he said to me, Do not seal up the sayings of the prophecy of this
book. For the time is at hand.

11 He who does evil, let him do evil still; and he who is filthy, let him
be filthy still; and he who is righteous, let him be more righteous; and he
who is holy, let him be more holy. 12 And behold, I come shortly, and my
reward with me, to give to everyone according to his deeds. 13 I am the
Alpha and Omega, the beginning and the end, the first and the last.

Do his commandments. 14 Blessed are those who do his commandments, so that their power
may be in the tree of life, and they may enter in through the gates into the
city. 15 For outside shall be dogs, and enchanters, and whoremongers, and
murderers, and idolaters, and whosoever loves or makes lies.

16 I, Jesus, sent my angel to testify of these things to you in the congre-
gations. I am the root and the offspring of David, and the bright morning
star.
17 And the Spirit and the bride say, Come! And let him who hears say
also, Come! And let him who is a-thirst come. And let whosoever will, Isa 55:6,7 [see below]
take of the water of life, free.
18 I testify to everyone that hears the words of prophecy of this book: if
anyone adds to these things, God will add to him the plagues that are
written in this book. 19 And if anyone takes away from the words of the
book of this prophecy, God will take away his part out of the book of life,
and out of the holy city, and from those things which are written in this
book.

[Tyndale's rendering 'book of life' is retained in v19. Some MSs show 'tree of life']

20 He who testifies to these things says, Be it, I come quickly.
Amen. Even so. Come, Lord Jesus!

Come, Lord Jesus, come!

21 The grace of our Lord Jesus Christ be with you all. Amen.

The end of the new testament.

Old Testament Feature - A glimpse into the Old Testament of the 1549 Matthew Bible...
Isaiah 55:6-8 and Isaiah 56:6 & 7, minimally updated:

Isaiah: The .lv. Chapter (verses 6-8)

Seek the Lord while he may be found, and call upon him while he is near. Let the ungodly man forsake his ways, and the unrighteous his imaginations, and turn back to the Lord, and he will be merciful to him; and to our God, for he is ready to forgive. For thus says the Lord: My thoughts are not your thoughts, and your ways are not my ways, but as far as the heavens are higher than the earth, so far do my ways transcend yours, and my thoughts yours.

Isaiah: The .lvi. Chapter (verses 6 & 7)

Again, he says to the strangers who are disposed to cleave unto the Lord to serve him, and to love his name; that they shall be no bond men. And all those who keep themselves so that they do not unhallow the Sabbath – that is, so that they fulfill my covenant – them will I bring to my holy mountain, and will make them joyful in my house of prayer. Their burnt offerings and sacrifices shall be accepted upon my altar, for my house shall be a house of prayer for all people.

On the Translation of 'Ecclesia' by 'Congregation'

By Ruth Magnusson Davis

Contents:

One of the things William Tyndale is well known for is his translation of the Greek word *'ecclesia'* (or *'ekklesia'*) with 'congregation' rather than 'church' in his New Testament. He came under furious reproach by some of his contemporaries on account of this.

Tyndale discussed his reasons for this translation in his book, *An Answer to Sir Thomas More's Dialogue.* Essentially he sought to render the Greek faithfully, and also to avoid fostering a misconception about the Church.

The Meaning of 'Ecclesia'

Tyndale explained in *Answer to Sir Thomas More's Dialogue* that *'ecclesia'* was a general, non-specialized Greek word, which pre-dated the apostles and the Christian religion, and which was used generally in common speech and in the bible to refer to any sort of meeting or assembly:

> Now *ecclesia* is a Greek word, and was in use before the time of the apostles, and was taken for a congregation among the heathen where there was no congregation of God or of Christ. And also Luke himself useth *ecclesia* for a...congregation of heathen people three times in one chapter, even in the 19th chapter of Acts, where Demetrius the goldsmith...had gathered a company against Paul for preaching against images.[1]

As Tyndale said, at Acts 19:32, *'ecclesia'* was used for a gathering of pagan townspeople in Ephesus. They had assembled hastily to hear the complaints of the goldsmith Demetrius, whose trade in images was threatened by Paul's preaching against idols. Demetrius inflamed the crowd of townsfolk with zeal for their idol Diana:

> When they heard these sayings, they were full of wrath, and cried out saying: Great is Diana of the Ephesians! And all the city was on a roar, and they rushed into the common hall with one assent, and caught...Paul's companions...Some cried one thing, and some another, and the ***ecclesia*** (WT 'congregation') was all out of quiet.[2]

Later in Acts 19, *'ecclesia'* is used in the town clerk's speech with reference first to a lawfully called assembly, and then again with reference to the same mob of townsfolk:

> If Demetrius and the craftsmen...have any complaint...the law is open, and there are rulers. Let them accuse one another. If ye go about any other thing, it may be determined in a lawful ***ecclesia*** (Tyndale, 'congregation')...And when he had thus spoken, he let the ***ecclesia*** ('congregation') depart (Acts 19:39,41).

Interestingly, the Acts passages demonstrate how the English word 'congregation' has, since Tyndale's time, become more specialized, so that it no longer serves well in these contexts. But formerly it, like *'ecclesia,'* was a general word. That is one reason why Tyndale's vocal critic, Sir Thomas More, objected to it. He preferred the specialized term 'church,' at least with reference to gatherings of Christians. But 'church' would not have served in Acts 19 with reference to the pagan assemblies. Therefore one may see why Tyndale felt it was not the truest translation of *'ecclesia,'* and that the Greek called for an English word that was correspondingly general. He explained:

> When [More] saith that *congregation* is a more general term; if it were, it hurteth not, for the context doth ever tell what sort of congregation is meant.[3]

Therefore *'ecclesia'* was a very general word for assemblies, meetings, and gatherings of any sort – orderly or disorderly, formal or informal, religious or not – and the nature of the gathering must be discerned from the context.

The Meanings of 'Church'

Tyndale was not concerned only about the meaning of the Greek *'ecclesia,'* but also the English word 'church.' This was not a general word. Altogether he identified five special, contemporary meanings for it. In one use, he understood it to mean all the members of a community of faith in one place – a parish or village, for example. This sense appears in his explanation of the meaning of Matthew 18:17, "Tell it to the *ecclesia*":

> In this...signification the 'church' of God or Christ is taken in the scripture to mean the whole multitude of all them that receive the name of Christ to believe in him...[as in Matthew 18]: "If thy brother hear thee not, tell the church or congregation"...In which places, and throughout all the scripture, the church is taken for the whole number of them that believe in Christ in that place.[4]

He also defined it wistfully as a place or house where people had formerly, "in the old time," gathered to hear God's word, and for common prayer:

> It signifieth a place or house where Christian people were wont in the old time to resort at times convenient, for to hear the word of doctrine, the law of God, and the faith of our Savior Jesus Christ, and how and what to pray, and when to ask power and strength to live godly. For the officer thereto appointed preached the pure word of God only, and prayed in a tongue that all men understood. And the people hearkened to his prayers, and said thereto Amen, and prayed with him in their hearts.[5]

In a third sense, sometimes 'church' was taken "generally for all them that embrace the name of Christ, though their faiths be naught,"[6] or, in a fourth and spiritual sense, "specially for the elect only, in whose hearts God hath written his law with his Holy Spirit, and given them a feeling faith of the mercy that is in Christ Jesu our Lord."[7] In these two senses we see the distinction between the visible and the invisible Church, between all of professing Christendom and the body within of those who have a saving faith.

Lastly he described the fifth sense, which he saw as pernicious. He explained how clerics and monks had appropriated to themselves the name 'church,' so that in the mind of the people it had, over time, come to be restricted to the visible ecclesiastical hierarchy and to monks and poor friars, to the exclusion of the laity. This had resulted in the people's subjection to or inappropriate veneration of clerics and monks. Since *'ecclesia'* never meant anything of this sort, he felt 'church' simply was not a good translation:

> Wherefore inasmuch as the clergy (as the nature of those hard and indurate adamant stones is, to draw [everyone] to them) had appropriated unto themselves the term that of right is common unto all the whole congregation of those who believe in Christ, and with their false and subtle wiles had beguiled and taken in the people, and brought them into the ignorance of the word, making them understand by this word *church*

> nothing but the shaven flock of them that shaved the whole world; therefore in the translation of the new Testament, where I found this word *ecclesia,* I interpreted it by this word *congregation.* [This is why I did] it, and not of any mischievous mind or purpose to establish heresy, as Master More untruly reporteth of me.[8]

Historian George Fisher confirms Tyndale's analysis, and describes the development of the medieval conception of the Church:

> The influence of the idea of the Church as the community of the faithful, of the elect children of God, an idea which retained a degree of power in the thoughts of Augustine, continually waned. More and more the Church came to be identified with the visible, hierarchical organization. Patristic authority, running back to Cyprian and even farther, could be appealed to in support of this principle at the root of the medieval conception; but in the carrying out of this principle there was a wide gulf between the earlier and the later period. The exaltation of the hierarchy, the absolute dependence of the laity upon the priesthood, existed to an extent unknown in the patristic age. The privileges still left to the laity in the concerns of the soul are so scanty as to be the exception that proves the rule. Significant of the state of thought that had long existed is the language of Philip the Fair in his indignant answer to the haughty rebuke of Boniface VIII: "Holy Mother Church, the Spouse of Christ, is composed not only of clergymen, but also of laymen."[9]

Also of grievous concern to Tyndale was the misuse of ill-gotten wealth by clergy, monks, and prelates, whom Tyndale called 'the spirituality':

> What good conscience can there be among our spirituality to gather so great treasure together, and with hypocrisy of their false learning to rob almost every man of house and lands...seeking in Christ nothing but lucre?[10]

Tyndale said 'the spirituality' crept into people's consciences, robbed them of the faith of Christ, and caused them to give their money to build new Churches and cloisters through a false faith in such works, by which all suffered:

> The building of [churches and steeples] and such like, through the false faith that we have in them, is the decay of all the havens in England, and of all the cities, towns, highways, and shortly of the whole commonwealth. For since these false monsters crept up into our consciences and robbed us of the knowledge of our Saviour Christ, making us believe in such pope-holy works, and to think that there was none other way unto heaven, we have not ceased to build for them abbeys, cloisters, colleges, chauntries, and cathedral churches with high steeples, striving and envying one another as to who should do the most.[11]

Therefore by using 'congregation' in his New Testament, Tyndale was both being faithful to the Greek and avoiding a misunderstood word that might contribute to the continuing exploitation of the people. Indeed this, Tyndale's translation, together with his books and writings, have caused many to credit him with "breaking the spell attached to the word church,"[12] and "breaking the suffocating power of the medieval church."[13]

But Tyndale's use of 'congregation' did not mean that he was anti-Church. Nor was he averse to a benign use of the word 'church.' He employed it himself in some contexts, as in a note to his 1534 New Testament where he protested, "We be the church," obviously intending it in the sense of what he referred to as the catholic congregation of true and faithful believers. But Tyndale longed for a Church, place, or congregation, where the word of God was read and rightly preached, where the people were led truly in worship and prayer, and where the sacraments were faithfully administered – especially Holy

Communion, with "earnest ceremony,"[14] because it is "an absolution of sin," "heals the conscience," and "makes the faith sink into the heart."[15] Blessed indeed is the disciple who can find such an *'ecclesia.'*

'Congregation' and 'Church' in the New Matthew Bible

We will keep 'congregation' in the NMB wherever it was used in the original with reference to Christian gatherings. However, because its meaning has narrowed, we cannot use it in other contexts. Admittedly its modern, narrower, quasi-religious sense may now argue against keeping it. Tyndale chose it, after all, because it was then a neutral and general word. But no suitably general word now exists, and in any case, 'congregation' is historically significant in the Matthew Bible. Further, it is still a good word for Christian gatherings, especially now that the Church, broadly speaking, is so divided and diverse, and the Lord's children may be found in all manner of congregations and under many different names.

We also intend to keep Church (or 'church') where that word was occasionally used in the notes and commentaries of the Matthew Bible. However, Tyndale used it twice in the New Testament scriptures themselves, in contexts where it is now inappropriate:

> Acts 14:13- Jupiter's priest, which [who] dwelt before their city, brought oxen and garlands to the *church porch,* and would have done sacrifice with the people.
>
> Acts 19:37- Ye have brought here these men which [who] are neither *robbers of churches,* nor yet despisers of your goddess.

At Acts 14:13, 'church' translates the Greek *'pulon,'* which Strong defines as meaning "a gateway or door-way of a building or city; by implication, a portal or vestibule." This use by Tyndale seems odd until we realize that 'church' was formerly employed with reference to pagan temples,[16] and Tyndale apparently understood the priest's offerings to have been brought to the temple porch. Wycliffe had 'gates' here, Coverdale in his 1535 New Testament put the singular 'gate,' in the Great Bible it became 'porch,' and in the KJV we have 'gates.' In keeping with Tyndale's understanding, the NMB has 'temple porch.'

At Acts 19:37, the KJV retained Tyndale's 'churches.' Modern bibles updated this verse to refer to 'temples,' and the NMB has done likewise.

In the Old Testament of the Matthew Bible, we find mention of the Church, as it may be understood mystically or spiritually, in subheadings to the Song of Solomon. Here, the annotations explain to the reader who is speaking to whom. These movingly declare the voice of "Christ to the Church," and hers to him. At Verse 1:15 we find:

> Christ to the Church.
>
> How fair art thou (my love), how fair art thou? Thou hast dove's eyes.

The beloved then responds:

> The Church to Christ.
>
> O how fair art thou (my beloved), how well favoured art thou? Our bed is decked with flowers...

Christ and the Church speak again to one another:

> The voice of Christ.
>
> I am the flower of the field, and lily of the valleys. As the rose among the thorns, so is my love among the daughters.

The voice of the Church.

> Like as the apple tree among the trees of the wood, so is my beloved among the sons. My delight is to sit under his shadow. For his fruit is sweet unto my throat. He bringeth me in to his wine cellar, and loveth me specially well.

In conclusion, we pray that every congregation and every Church, and every member of the body of Christ, may find not only its beloved in the pages of the *October Testament,* but also peace and freedom from the strife of words, names, or outward things. Words matter, of course. But if we chew unwisely upon them, then as Tyndale would say, we will fail to attain to the sweet pith within.[17] It was not the intent of the authors of the Matthew Bible to deny the place or name of the Church, or of a Church, in any legitimate sense or context, favourable or unfavourable, provided it did not mislead. In the same spirit, the NMB is produced, with the prayer that readers may find herein no cause for contention, but rather sweetness, and simple delight in the Word of God.

End notes

---

[1] William Tyndale, *An Answer to Sir Thomas More's Dialogue* (Parker Society edition, ed. Henry Walter, 1850) (hereafter *'Answer'*), p. 15. Punctuation and language in early English quotations may be minimally updated.
[2] Scripture quotations are from the 1549 Matthew Bible.
[3] *Answer,* p. 15.
[4] *Answer,* p. 13.
[5] *Answer,* p. 11.
[6] *Answer,* p. 13.
[7] *Answer,* p. 13.
[8] *Answer,* pp. 13-14, and see p. 12.
[9] George Park Fisher, *History of Christian Doctrine* (Charles Scribner's Sons, New York, 1909), p. 251.
[10] William Tyndale, *The Obedience of a Christian Man* (Penguin Classics edition, 2000) (hereafter *'Obedience'*), p. 51.
[11] *Answer,* p. 78.
[12] Brook Foss Westcott, *A General View of the History of the English Bible,* (MacMillan and Co, London, 1872), p. 173. I am not endorsing Westcott's book, but merely reference the source of the quotation.
[13] Patrick Whitten, "Tyndale at the Huntington," *The Tyndale Society Journal,* No. 45 (Summer 2015), p. 22.
[14] William Tyndale, "A Fruitful and Godly Treatise Expressing the Right Institution and Usage of the Sacrament of Baptism and the Sacrament of the Body and Blood of our Saviour Jesu Christ," contained in *Doctrinal Treatises and Introductions to Different Portions of the Holy Scriptures* (Parker Society edition, ed. Henry Walter, Cambridge University Press, 1848) (hereafter *Treatises*), p. 361.
[15] *Treatises,* pages 357, 359, 360.
[16] See definition number A.I.2 in the online *Oxford English Dictionary* as at February 16, 2016. This service can only be accessed by subscribers.
[17] Tyndale rebuked vain disputations about words, which, as he put it, result in people gnawing upon the bitter bark without, and never attaining to the sweet pith within.

Here endeth the October Testament.

So help us God.

19872991R00245

Printed in Poland
by Amazon Fulfillment
Poland Sp. z o.o., Wrocław